BACK

OVER

THERE

ALSO BY RICHARD RUBIN

The Last of the Doughboys

Confederacy of Silence

BACK
OVER
THERE

One American Time-Traveler,
100 Years Since the Great War,
500 Miles of Battle-Scarred French
Countryside, and Too Many Trenches,
Shells, Legends and Ghosts to Count

RICHARD RUBIN

St. Martin's Press
New York

BACK OVER THERE. Copyright © 2017 by Richard Rubin. All rights reserved. Printed in the United States of America. For information, address St. Martin's Press, 175 Fifth Avenue, New York, NY 10010.

Unless noted otherwise, all photos courtesy of the author, and all maps adapted by Mapping Specialists from originals furnished courtesy of National Park Service, Cultural Resource GIS Facility.

www.stmartins.com

Cataloging-in-Publication Data is available from the Library of Congress.

ISBN 9781250084323 (hardcover)
ISBN 9781250084330 (e-book)

Our books may be purchased in bulk for promotional, educational, or business use. Please contact your local bookseller or the Macmillan Corporate and Premium Sales Department at 1-800-221-7945, extension 5442, or by e-mail at MacmillanSpecialMarkets@macmillan.com.

First Edition: April 2017

10   9   8   7   6   5   4   3   2   1

To memory,
and those who keep it

And to M.A.L.,
one tough little

CONTENTS

★

Over there,
over there,
Send the word, send the word,
over there,
That the Yanks are coming,
the Yanks are coming,
The drums rum-tumming ev'ry where.
So prepare,
say a pray'r,
Send the word, send the word,
to beware,
We'll be over,
we're coming over,
And we won't come back
till it's over over there.

—George M. Cohan,
"Over There," 1917

BACK
OVER
THERE

FOLLOW ME

France.

I was lost.

Really lost.

Now, I'd been lost before. Many times. In just about every way one can be. And yet, while lost is, in my experience, a state with infinite permutations, none is quite as profound as creeping forward slowly in a rental car through a labyrinth of narrow and overgrown tractor trails lined with tall grass and weeds, deep in a country where you don't speak the language very well, which last fact doesn't really matter anyway because you haven't seen another human being in a half hour, and haven't had a cell signal for even longer than that.

Yes, that's a First World Problem; but you're not supposed to be able to get lost in the First World anymore, what with excellent signage and detailed road maps and GPS. And so, because you've become so dependent upon these conveniences, you're really in bad shape when, one by one, they fail you. The place you're trying to find—I'll just drop the pretense and change that to *the place* I *was trying to find*—wasn't on a road, at least not a real one. It certainly wasn't on a map. And if it had coordinates, which I am told everyplace does, I had no idea what they were. I doubted anyone had ever even written them down.

Worse yet was the fact that I'd already been to this place I was now trying to find, and had gotten there all by myself. Only a few years earlier. Five years, to be precise, in 2009. Under ordinary circumstances I might start wondering what this said about my state of mental fitness. But I didn't have time for that right then, because I was really . . . well, you know.

In my defense: I had only been there once, and five years is a fairly long time to remember directions to a place in the middle of nowhere and thousands of miles away from home. And this place wasn't in, say, Oregon or Alberta. It was in the other direction, across an ocean, in France. In northern France. Northeastern France. A part of northeastern France called Lorraine.

Poor Lorraine: Outside of France, it's scarcely regarded as its own entity. People pair it with the neighboring region of Alsace as inextricably as they pair *Q* with *U*. Never mind that they're thoroughly distinct in culture, landscape, even language; never mind that Lorraine is almost three times the size of Alsace, with a half-million more residents. Among the French, Lorraine's natives say, they are regarded as *paysans*. Peasants. Hicks. They will tell you this with pride. I'm not sure why, frankly. I suspect it may be that they like being underestimated.

The Germans certainly underestimated Lorraine. If you know anything at all about the place, you know that the Germans annexed it, along with Alsace, after the Franco-Prussian War of 1870–71. Except they didn't, really. Germany did annex almost all of Alsace back then, but they only took about a quarter of Lorraine, which was all they wanted of it. The part of it where I was lost—the Germans didn't take that. If they had, the roads here would probably be better today. By the time they did take this part, in 1914, they were too busy trying to take the rest of France to undertake a major infrastructure project like building new roads. There would be plenty of time for that after France surrendered. But here again, the

Germans underestimated Lorraine, because while they took it fairly easily in 1914, it cost them hundreds of thousands of lives over the next few years to hold it. By 1918, they finally seemed to appreciate the place, clinging to it bitterly, desperately, killing and dying in great numbers for every trench, every yard of blasted soil. It was their last line of defense.

They never did get around to improving the roads, though. Perhaps they were as vexed as I was by the French system of naming their towns and villages. It's not enough, in many cases, to give a place a simple one-word name: You have to modify it, it seems, with some sort of explanation of where it is. Dun-sur-Meuse: Dun on the Meuse, a river. Gesnes-en-Argonne: Gesnes in the Argonne, a forest. Saint-Benoît-en-Woëvre: Saint Benoît on the Woëvre, a plain. Braye-en-Laonnois: Braye in the vicinity of Laon, a city. Nanteuil-la-Fosse: Nanteuil the pit, because it's near a large chalk mine. (I'm not sure how the locals feel about that name.) This, of course, enables the French to re-use town names again and again, sometimes without even putting much distance between them. Romagne-sous-les-Côtes, or Romagne below the hills, is only about forty minutes or so from Romagne-sous-Montfaucon, Romagne below Montfaucon, or Mount Falcon. Both were ancient Roman sites, and wanted to acknowledge this distinction in the most direct way possible; with a little elaboration, no one had to flip a coin to see who got to use Romagne and who had to go look for another name. And you can see why locals might want to commemorate the Romans: Among other things, they built good roads. Some are still among the better ones in the area.

The day I got really lost was a Sunday in June. I set out late that afternoon from Verdun for Ville-devant-Chaumont, which translates as the village before Chaumont (not, if you think about it, a big improvement over Nanteuil the pit). And there's even less to the place than its name suggests—a handful of houses and garages for farm equipment, that's it. But it was, as I remembered, the place to pick up a certain tractor road that would lead me to the place I was looking for. Now, it's true that I am essentially an urban creature, having been born in New York and lived most of my life there and in other cities, but when I say tractor road, I do not mean a dirt road that is more or less the same as a regular road but for the fact that it is not paved. I mean a road that is really only meant for a tractor, or some other piece of self-propelled and extremely sturdy farm equipment. These are not roads that were built, or even laid out; they're more like trails, paths formed by farmers who had to get their machinery someplace where there were no roads. What we're talking about here is two parallel dirt ruts, not much wider than a single passenger car, surrounded on either side by brambles, grain, or very tall grass. The dirt ruts have potholes in them, and a lot of rocks, too, most large, many partially buried and fixed in place, some quite sharp. In between the ruts there is grass, often tall, almost always hiding more large rocks. Not a place you would take a car you cared anything about, which includes rental cars, especially if you're not quite sure what the extra insurance you think you took out at the rental car place actually covers. I drove on many more of these tractor roads than I should have, but in Lorraine—along most of the Great War's Western Front, really, but especially in Lorraine—much of what you want to see, if you want to see where things actually happened in that war, can only be accessed by such . . . well, let's just call them *thoroughfares*.

Tractor roads don't have names, much less signs. Actually, in rural northern France, in my experience, even paved roads with names often don't have street signs, unless you're in a good-sized town or larger. Sometimes you see street signs on the walls of peoples' houses, but that seems a voluntary thing. (Street names typically do show up on your GPS, if you have the right maps installed, but since there are no signs to check them against, using your GPS can actually get you into more trouble, although if you're like me you will at least enjoy hearing that disembodied voice mispronounce everything atrociously.) In short, I was dependent upon my ability to ask people for directions.

Now, at this point I should tell you: I don't speak French very well. My accent is OK, at least compared with most Americans I know who attempt to speak French, but my vocabulary has a habit of deserting me in time of need. I had studied the language back in college and had gotten pretty good at it, but for twenty years after graduation I had absolutely no occasion to use it, and speaking a foreign language is not like riding a bicycle. It improved a lot when I went over in 2009, but my ability to decipher what was being said to me, and to interpret written French, far outpaced my ability to speak it without hesitation, which turns out to be the one skill you need most if you find yourself in a place like Ville-devant-Chaumont and have to get directions to a spot far off any paved road. There are a lot of stereotypes about the French that are not all that true, but three of them are: They really do eat very well; they really do kiss you on both cheeks when saying hello and good-bye; and they really don't speak any English. That last one is not as true in places like Paris that get a lot of Anglophone tourists. But Ville-devant-Chaumont is not Paris. I may be the only Anglophone tourist who's been there since 1918.

At some point, I'd devised an extremely useful gambit for getting by: I started every conversation—and, for that matter, every question, request and utterance, more or less—the same way: Forgive me, but I don't speak French. Of course, the fact that I said this *in French* generated a bit of a paradox, but if anyone noticed, they didn't let on. The French, it turns out, don't care how poor your French is. They care only that you are trying. Speak it as badly as you like; just *parlez.*

"Parlez-vous Anglais?" was, in fact, my original opening line, until I came to understand that I was never going to hear "Why, yes!" in reply. The typical response I got was a pained expression and a head shake; sometimes they would ask, tentatively, *"Vous êtes Anglais?"* When I would answer *"Non, je suis Américain,"* their demeanor changed entirely. Invariably, they would break into a smile and try their best to help me—in French, but still. If my experience is any indication, it seems the French don't much care for the English, but they sure love Americans. It's very gratifying, particularly when you find yourself in a small, remote northern French village, lost and at their mercy.

So when people in Ville-devant-Chaumont told me they had no idea what this thing was that I was looking for, much less where, they were at least very polite about it, even gracious. At one point I came upon a family reunion, and when the person I approached for directions had no idea what I was talking about, he immediately fetched another person, and on and on, until I had exhausted the entire clan. They all smiled apologetically as they shook their heads, though, and invited me to join them for supper. I did—recall true stereotype #1—then got back into my car and drove up and down the village's few dusty, underpopulated streets until I spotted a tractor road at the end of one. I thought it looked familiar, maybe.

As tractor paths go, this one appeared to be relatively civilized, by which I mean that I didn't have to jerk the steering wheel of my Renault Scénic sharply every few feet to avoid something scary. That changed, though, about ten minutes into the journey, when the trail took a hard turn and suddenly the ruts got a lot rougher, the grass in between them taller. Coincidentally, it was right around this spot, about a half mile up from where I'd started, that I came to the conclusion that I was on the wrong tractor road. Later, it would occur to me that I hadn't chosen merely the wrong farm road but also the wrong farming village from which to set out, confusing Ville-devant-Chaumont with the next town over, Chaumont-devant-Damvillers.

So I was on the wrong road, though I couldn't do anything about it but keep driving, as there was no way, on a path scarcely wider than my car, that I could turn around. The only thing was to keep moving forward— ever more slowly, as the trail was getting rougher—and hope that I came out somewhere before I ran out of gas or damaged the car to the point where it wouldn't run anymore. About ten minutes later I came to the top of a ridge and a ninety-degree left turn. A few minutes after that, I came to a fork, sort of, where one trail led straight ahead, the other sharply to the right. There didn't seem to be any reason to choose one over the other, so I pulled a one-euro coin from my pocket, flipped it, realized there was nothing resembling a head on either side, and decided I might as well go right. I did well: A few minutes later, I spotted the tip of a steeple. It had never occurred to me, before that day, why churches had them; but I can't recall, at any time in my life, being much happier at the sight of anything than I was at that steeple. Soon the trail started a very gradual descent. Another ten minutes or so and I emerged onto a genuine paved road in an unknown village. I looked at a map later and calculated that I had traveled about two miles in forty minutes.

One of the nice things about France is that you almost always know where you are, because every city, town, village and hamlet has the same sign at its limits, a white rectangle with a red perimeter and the town's name in black letters; when you leave, you pass an identical sign with a red diagonal through the place's name. They only put these, though, on real roads, so if you should happen to emerge from a tractor trail into the middle of town—well, you're on your own. So I drove slowly through the streets, looking for someone to ask. But I didn't see a soul. Strange—it was a pleasant evening, warm but not hot, clear sky only just beginning to dim. People should have been sitting outside. Maybe they were all somewhere else? And then I rounded a bend in the road and saw a little stone house with an attached barn and a sign over the front door that bore the logo of Karlsbrau beer and a name: L'Authentique.

I parked on the other side of the road and was crossing the street toward the tavern when the door opened and a man in his fifties wearing a tan belted jacket came out. "Forgive me," I said, "but I don't speak French. I try to find . . . ," I continued, and did my best to describe it. He stood there patiently, waited until I was finished, then smiled regretfully and shook his head. Soon another man, younger and wearing what appeared to be a flannel shirt, walked out of the pub; then a couple, and then another couple, and then another man. Each responded the same way. Two or three of them seemed to hesitate for a beat before getting into their cars—or maybe that was just wishful thinking on my part—but they all drove off, and I was left alone, standing in the middle of the street, loath to give up but starting to come to the understanding that I was going to have to very soon. The place looked empty.

Then a woman stepped out the door and negotiated the bar's front stoop. She looked to be in her late sixties, maybe five feet tall with short gray hair and eyeglasses, black pants, and a black shirt with some sparkles on it. I hesitated: The street was otherwise deserted, and I didn't want to frighten her. It had been a long, hot day, full of hiking and bushwhacking, and I'm sure I looked pretty haggard and dirty at that point, and quite possibly still smelled of grilled meat from the family reunion. But this little woman, I figured, was probably my last chance, so as she stepped into the road to cross, and didn't seem to hesitate at the sight of me, I approached her, slowly. At first she, too, shook her head, but then she looked down at the ground for a moment, then looked back at me, her eyes now open wide, her expression determined. "Come," she said in French. "Follow me."

She got into her car, which was parked a couple of houses up from mine, and drove off, slowly. I got in my car and followed. Shortly we passed a sign indicating that we were leaving Azannes-et-Soumazannes (so *that's* where I was) and ten or fifteen minutes later passed another telling me I was entering Romagne-sous-les-Côtes. We wound through a few streets, and then she pulled up outside a small house—they were all small—set back from the road a bit, parked, and without a word of explanation scurried inside. I wasn't sure what I was supposed to do, but trying to follow a little old French lady into her darkened house on a Sunday evening seemed like the kind of venture that could end with me locked in a quaint little jail cell, so instead I just waited in the car. After a few minutes she emerged from her house—she was dressed the same, but had changed from dressier shoes into a pair of black sneakers—strode purposefully up to my car, opened the passenger door, got in, sat down, closed the door, fastened her seat belt, pointed ahead, and said: "Straight."

So I went straight. A few moments later, she said: "Left." I went left. Then right, then right again, and a few more turns, until we arrived at the base of yet another farm road. This one didn't look at all familiar. "Now," she said, "slow." I hesitated for a moment; the grass in between its two dirt ruts rose higher than my car's hood. The ruts didn't look too good, either. I turned to her, hoping for—honestly, I don't know what, except maybe for some indication of her resolve that this was really the only way.

She just gazed straight ahead. I drove on. Slowly.

"Slow," she repeated. "Slow. Slow." I went slower. Things lingered on the underside of my car that really didn't need to be there. They brushed. Scraped. Loudly. "Slow," she said. I wasn't sure how much more slowly I could go and still manage to ascend the grade. But I eased up on the gas, to the point where I was barely touching it.

There were turns, and mud, and tires spinning in place, and more discomfiting sounds emanating from under the car. "Slow," she said, at regular intervals. "Slow." Ten minutes passed. Twenty. At thirty I started to get pretty anxious. Her gaze remained set.

Then, about forty minutes into the slowest drive I had ever undertaken, just after we'd topped a small rise, she lifted her gaze toward the top of the windshield. "There," she said, and smiled, almost imperceptibly. I pulled up to it, and we got out of the car. It was just as I remembered: a stone marker, unassuming, maybe three feet high, with a whitewashed flagpole planted behind it. In the years since my last visit, someone had installed a bench a few feet away. This spot, atop a ridge, looks out over a magnificent pastel valley. I think it's the nicest vista in the entire country. You can see why someone might want to sit on that bench for a while and take it in.

But she didn't sit. Perhaps she thought that might be disrespectful. This, after all, was the precise spot where Private Henry Nicholas Gunther of Baltimore, 23 years old, became the very last man killed in World War I, shot through the head at 10:59 A.M. on November 11, 1918, less than one minute before the whole bloody affair ended.

I don't know if she knew Gunther's name. For sure she didn't know mine at that point, nor I hers. We wouldn't even get around to introducing ourselves until later, when it was almost dark and I dropped her off at her house in Romagne-sous-les-Côtes. "I am Richard Rubin," I would say. "And I am Madame George," she would reply. Like the Van Morrison song.

But in that moment up on that ridge, we didn't say a word about our names, or much of anything else. We just gazed at the monument.

"There," she said, nodding. "There."

CHAPTER ONE

LIKE TRAVELING BACK IN TIME

L ook down.

Those somewhat camouflaged but nevertheless out-of-place ob-jects you see resting atop the freshly plowed furrows of a roadside farm, or lying on the forest floor, partially obscured by the fallen leaves? That's the Great War. Those are the things millions of men—French, German, British, Italian, Australian, Senegalese, Indochinese, Canadian, Moroc-can, Russian, Scottish, Guyanese, Indian, Irish, Malagasy, New Zealander, American—brought with them to the front. Things they brought to keep themselves clothed, and fed, and sheltered in some semblance of com-fort. Things they brought in a hopeless attempt to stay clean. Things they brought to distract themselves from boredom, or pain, or fear, or to dull the boredom or pain or fear should distraction prove impossible. Things they brought to remind them of home, and of the people they left behind. And, more than all the rest put together: things they brought to kill each other.

From the summer of 1914 to the autumn of 1918, men, heavily armed and in uniform, came to this place—then, as now, quiet, pastoral—to do just that. Thousands, at first; then, quickly, hundreds of thousands; and by the end, millions. They stayed awhile—a few days here, a few years there—and did what they were sent to do. Now they are all, one way or another, long gone. But the stuff they brought with them by the packload, the truckload, the trainload—the evidence of their presence here, of their very existence, a century after they went away—remains. The earth spins and draws it in; the earth spins and pushes it out. And you come along one day and—if you're looking down—find it just sitting there, right out in the open, as if it had been dropped there that very morning, and not 36,500 mornings ago.

✵ ✵ ✵

I confess: to spending more time looking down than looking up when I'm in certain places Over There. I also confess to doing so, sometimes, when I'm not in certain places Over There. It's a habit that, once formed, can be hard to break.

While I'm confessing, I confess to waking up in the morning with delight at the sight of a cloudy sky, because it's easier to spot old rusted metal objects resting atop the soil if there isn't direct sunlight on them. To waking up in the middle of the night to the sound of rain hitting the roof, and smiling as I wonder what the water will have brought to the surface come morning. To feeling a tingle of excitement at the sight of a cornfield, not because I love corn more than I should, but because I know that it's easier to spot foreign objects among the budding corn than it is, say, in a field of wheat, or oats, or other dense plants that obscure the soil. I confess to examining minutely bottles I found among the barbed wire—green and brown, glass and clay—trying to determine what they had once held; to studying intently a German Army–issued spoon I spotted one morning sitting atop a freshly plowed mound of dirt, trying to conjure the man who had once carried it—what he looked like, what he wore, what he ate with it. What caused him to drop it.

And I am hardly unique. There are people—I've met some—who spend their every vacation roaming around the Argonne, in Lorraine, hunting for artifacts of the Great War. There are people—I know some—who up and moved there for the same reason. The Argonne, I should note, is a place of great natural beauty, but it is also a poor place, all forest and farmland; if you're not already retired, and don't have the type of job you can do from anywhere, you're going to have a hard time of it. Moving there just because you're a World War I buff who's developed a taste for artifact-hunting is, in a lot of ways, asking for trouble.

Fortunately, this is not the kind of trouble that just overtakes a person one day. You have to go looking for it. And you have to be mentored. I was mentored by Jean-Paul de Vries; he was mentored, in his childhood, by a French veteran of their Vietnamese war named Fleck who frequently drove down to the Argonne from Lille, hundreds of kilometers away, on a motor scooter, and drove back every time with an extra hundred pounds of stuff strapped to its sides. "It's an addiction," Jean-Paul told me once, and that's about as good an explanation as I could ever hope to receive, or to offer: It just hooks you. Perhaps Fleck had gotten hooked by a World

War II veteran, who had gotten hooked by a World War I veteran, coming back to search for things he and his comrades had dropped under fire in 1918.

It's hard to imagine, though, that even someone who fought here could have known these fields as well as Jean-Paul does. He started coming here in the 1970s, from the Netherlands. Though he was born and raised in Eindhoven, his parents are both French; they came here as a family every summer—to go camping. To this day, most visitors to the Argonne come not for its history but because it is unspoiled. This is, admittedly, a pretty strange thing to say about a place that from 1914 to 1918 was a vast battlefield where hundreds of thousands of men died. But walk one of the trails through the woods here and you will almost certainly encounter couples or families who are utterly oblivious to the trenches and shell holes that lie just feet from the narrow path you're all following.

They come from all over France, and also from Belgium, and Luxembourg, and the Netherlands, none of which are too far away. And from Germany, which isn't, either. It was closer still between 1871 and 1914 when, in the aftermath of the Franco-Prussian War, the victorious Prussians took a big chunk of Lorraine, along with almost all of Alsace, and annexed it into the newly created nation of Germany. The Argonne didn't happen to be in that chunk, but that didn't keep the Germans from sending over spies afterward, military cartographers, to survey it all, figure out where and how to build an impenetrable last line of defense there. They drew up meticulous topographical maps, studied them intently for years before the first shots were fired in August 1914. They made more maps after they took the Argonne that same summer. And more. And more, and more again, for four years, every time something significant changed, and sometimes when nothing really had. A lot of maps. And they didn't bother burning them after the armistice; a century later, people still pore over them. Some of these people have never been to the Argonne, or even to France. Still, they know this vast, unknowable battlefield as well as anyone.

Almost anyone.

✷ ✷ ✷

One hot, sunny morning in June of 2009, I pushed open the door of a garage-like edifice in the village of Romagne-sous-Montfaucon, looking for some shade and a little human contact. I had just walked over from the

Meuse-Argonne American Cemetery, a few hundred yards away. In the last forty-seven days of World War I, 26,277 Americans were killed fighting in the vicinity, in what is now known as the Meuse-Argonne Offensive; it remains, to this day, the deadliest battle in American history. More than fourteen thousand of them are buried in Romagne, spread out over 130 acres in what is the largest American cemetery in Europe.

You may not know all that much about the First World War; you may not know that it generated current notions of ethnic and national identity throughout the world, and borders that still hold in Europe and Asia and the Middle East, and the civil rights movement in the United States, and the acceptance of gender equality throughout the Western world, and long-standing agricultural policies that determine what foods you can buy and how much you pay for them, and almost all of modern medicine, and pretty much every means of modern transportation, and the environmental movement: You may not know, in other words, that it generated the very world in which we—all of us—now live. But if you know nothing else about the First World War, you know that it generated a lot of cemeteries. There are six American World War I cemeteries in France, hundreds of French ones, and more German ones than French and American combined. Each country designed, built and continues to maintain its own. French cemeteries, large or small, are austere, treeless, razor-straight row upon row of concrete crosses, tablets and minarets baking in the sun, the grass in between them most likely brown, if it is even there at all. German cemeteries, large or small, are almost always green, with lots of big old trees casting shade and verdant light everywhere, and invariably surrounded by a low brick wall with a wrought-iron gate in the front, all of which makes them feel surprisingly *gemütlich,* welcoming and cozy, like the lawn of an old country inn. The gatepost of each is even fitted with a drawer containing a guest register. French cemeteries are supposed to have them, too, but in my experience, they're rarely there.

As for the American cemeteries: Having been built under the watchful eye of General John Joseph Pershing, erstwhile commander of the American Expeditionary Forces—a man who was known to be, to put it mildly, rather particular—they are, without exception, so perfectly beautiful that they can be intimidating. And Meuse-Argonne is the most perfect, and intimidating, of all. Perhaps that scares people off. I had the place entirely to myself that morning; spent several hours walking on meticulously trimmed emerald grass among long rows of plump white marble Latin crosses and Stars of David, and never spotted anyone else doing the same thing. It was a lonesome way to start the day.

And then I strolled into town and pushed open that door.

The sign outside it read "Romagne 14–18," which sounded like something I should see. In any event, there had to be another human being there; I hadn't seen any on the walk over, either. Like most villages in the Argonne, Romagne is very small, and smaller now than it used to be. I have seen photos of it from the first decade of the twentieth century, when it was also a little village, but one that at least had restaurants, cafés, groceries, a hotel. Nowadays it scarcely has pedestrians. The sign, though, indicated *something* was going on inside this building. I figured it to be a museum; it turned out to be more like a portal that could take you back almost a century. With a café.

Like much of small-town France, Jean-Paul de Vries's place kept odd hours in those days, and I was lucky he was there. Actually, I was lucky *I* was there. I hadn't wanted to come here; had tried to tell myself I didn't need to go to France. Six years earlier, I had set out to find and interview a few living American veterans of the First World War, which at that point had been over for eighty-five years. I had expected at the start to find three or four, at most, but ended up finding a few dozen, aged 101 to 113, and getting so much good material that I had undertaken to write a history of the United States and World War I based on their stories. Now the interviews were finished, and so was the research, all of which was done either from home or in American libraries and archives. I knew all about the places where the men I'd interviewed had dodged death, sometimes narrowly; where they had watched their buddies kill, and die. But I had never seen them. I had made a point of conducting every interview face-to-face because I believed that observing these men and women as they told their stories was almost as important as listening to what they said. And I knew that merely hearing and reading about these places, rather than going to see them for myself, would be the equivalent of interviewing these oldest veterans over the telephone rather than in person. But I didn't want to go. The truth is, I'm not a very good traveler. I like being at home—I like my bed, my shower, my DVR. And I had done a lot of traveling for this book already. The urge to stay put was powerful. But my sense that I didn't have the whole story, and that the rest of it lay Over There, just would not go away and leave me in peace. I managed to patch together a modest travel stake, flew to France, and met Jean-Paul on my second day there.

We connected right away. I'm sure some of that, at least, was due to the fact that he spoke English, which I had already discovered was a rarity in small-town France, though I hadn't yet worked out my strategic *Pardon-nez-moi, mais je ne parle pas Français* introduction. (Going forward, you can safely assume that, unless specified otherwise, any conversation related here was originally uttered in French—my side of it in pretty bad French.) About my age, slight and dark-haired and gregarious, he spoke quickly and voluminously, his voice infused with a singsong quality that was probably a product of his Dutch accent. He alternated sentences, telling me in the first about whatever item we were looking at ("That's a carrying case for a shell, German, 155 millimeters. Very big."), in the next about his childhood visits to the area, his excursions with Fleck, and his first museum, which he'd set up in his bedroom when he was nine or ten years old. The more stuff he'd found, he told me, the more he'd craved finding still more. To that end, he moved here in 1997 and started roving on his own, pretty much every day. In the early years he didn't have a car, and couldn't roam much further than a few miles; couldn't keep anything he found unless he could carry it back on his own. There was plenty that he could: cartridges; bullets; shrapnel. Buttons. Identification discs. Bottles. Canteens. Mess tins. Electric insulators. Keys. When he finally got a car, he just started gathering more of it. Helmets. Wagon wheels. Bayonets. Barbed wire. Rifles. Ammunition crates. Trench knives. Boots. Shell carriers. Everywhere. "If you're not finding anything," he told me once, "that means you're blind." He found lots of shells, too, but knew enough not to touch them. And he found a great many things that, while not explosive, could not be extracted, much less hauled. He noted their location; visits them often.

At some point, having found so much stuff, Jean-Paul decided to open that museum. He always accepted donations, but never charged admission. It didn't seem right; everything he had in the place had been offered up to him, free of charge, by the earth. It was as if the planet, having safeguarded all this history on its own for nearly a century, saw him rooting around and decided it could really use the help. It's hard, when you're walking through a field and just stumble upon, say, a hundred-year-old German spoon—sitting right there on the surface, where anyone could see it—not to feel like you have been chosen by the soil to help carry all that memory. It is a collaboration, and a compelling one. Experience it yourself enough times and you can start to understand how some people might uproot their lives for its sake.

That first morning, though, I was simply overwhelmed. "You really just . . . *found* all this stuff?" I asked him.

He chuckled; I could tell he got that question often. "And a lot more," he said.

"Just sitting there? Out in the open?"

He nodded.

"What else is out there?"

He started to say something, then paused for a moment. "Why don't you just come back tomorrow morning," he said, instead, "and I'll show you."

* * *

We left early the next day and drove around for hours, visiting all kinds of fascinating sites in the field: bunkers and trenches, battlegrounds and rest camps, German, French, American. But before any of it, when we were scarcely outside the village limits of Romagne, we passed an open field. He glanced at it quickly, pondered for a second, then jerked the steering wheel left and swerved across the oncoming lane and onto the side of the road. (No one was coming; you don't pass many cars in the Argonne.) "I know the man who owns this," he said, gesturing at the field. "This is the first time he's plowed in years. Let's take a look." He bounced out of the car and into the field, walking stick in hand—an actual stick, almost as tall as he is, no doubt found on the forest floor somewhere. Jean-Paul is perpetually hunched over from ankylosing spondylitis, a congenital condition that turns the cartilage in his spine to bone. It doesn't slow him down.

"Ah," he said after a few moments, and bent over. "Here." He stood up again and handed me a piece of shrapnel. To the untrained eye it looks very much like the clumps of dirt that surround it; see enough of it, though, and you start to notice that the hues are a bit different, the browns just a little deeper, the reds a touch shinier. When in doubt, pick it up: Its heft gives it away. Shrapnel is iron. Packed deliberately into shells, it sprayed everywhere when they exploded. Shrapnel was never used to clear terrain, to open up a gap in some vegetation and give you a better view of something. Its sole purpose was to kill. Hold a piece in your hand, even a small piece, and you can tell how effective it would have been. It's heavy. And jagged. It was also, when it sprayed everywhere, red hot. I learned that from a veteran, a 106-year-old man named J. Laurence Moffitt who recalled, eighty-five years later, a two-inch piece hitting his leg one day during the Second Battle of the Marne and miraculously bouncing off. When he went to pick it up, it burned his fingers. After it cooled down, he pocketed it as a souvenir. Still had it when we met.

"Here," Jean-Paul said, handing me another piece. And another. Soon I had more than I could carry. Shrapnel is by far the most common World War I artifact to find in a field. It's also one of the least interesting to behold. Like snowflakes, every piece is unique; but unlike snowflakes, no piece of shrapnel can be called beautiful. I've never found one that resembles a star, or Oklahoma, or Abraham Lincoln, or anything else. It becomes monotonous once you're used to it.

"Ah!" he cried out, and I ran over, careful to follow his example and step over the furrows. Jean-Paul lives by a code: Always get the farmer's permission (sooner or later); never do anything that might harm his crops; never dig. And never, ever dig with a metal detector. It is illegal on public land; and though you can do it on private land—again, with the owner's permission—you should not. It is dishonorable.

He held out his hand. "This is German," he said, and gave me a cartridge, metal, a bit wider than a cigarette butt and maybe twice as long. A few minutes later, he handed me a button, Bavarian; and a few after that, a piece of a comb, provenance unknown.

We walked on, silently, a few rows apart. My eyes moved at a different pace than my legs; the latter ranged forward steadily, but the former would train on a spot for a moment, then jump to another spot and repeat. At one point, after staring at a patch of ground for a few seconds, I realized I was looking at a bracket—a "stripper clip," as it was known—of five cartridges and, spread out a few inches in front of them, sharp points in an arc from eleven o'clock to one, five perfect bullets.

"Ah!" I said. Jean-Paul ran over; I pointed. "Ah!" he agreed. "Nice one!" I picked them up and dropped them into my pocket. They were, I discovered later, also German.

Walking back out of the field, I kept my eyes trained on the earth and spotted, near the edge, what looked like a rusty old soda can with a conical cap, the whole thing less than half the size of my foot. Like the shrapnel and the bullets, it was just sitting there, atop the dirt, as if someone had placed it there the night before: a shell. I stopped short.

"Uhhh . . . ," I said, and raised my hand. Jean-Paul bounced over, looked down for an instant, patted my back, and smiled at me as if he were my father and I had just landed my first striper. "Yes," he said. "I think that's a nice one."

I got the sense, from that simple gesture, that we had crossed a line from guide and tourist to mentor and protégé. I was, oddly, a little moved by it, which, in conjunction with the jet lag I was still experiencing, might have led me to read too much into "that's a nice one"; or maybe—more likely—I didn't read at all. Or think. What I did do was bend over to pick it up. Fortunately for me, Jean-Paul, who is much smaller than I am, somehow found the strength to physically restrain me. "No, no, no no no," he cooed, a father explaining to his son that his first striper must now be released. "We don't take those." He told me I should shoot a few pictures of it; while I did so, he reached into his sack and pulled out a can of fluorescent orange spray paint. When I was done, he coated the whole thing.

"Is that for the bomb squad?" I asked.

"No," he said. "For the farmer. The police won't come out for one shell. You have to have a bunch. Like twenty." Without such limits, they would spend all their time fetching stray World War I ordnance. It is said, not in jest, that the number of shells fired in the First World War that *didn't* explode is greater than the total number of shells fired in the Second World War. They literally turn up every day.

We spent the rest of the day looking at all kinds of fascinating sites in the field: bunkers and trenches, battlegrounds and rest camps. I found bottles—a lot of bottles—and barbed wire in the woods; picked bullets out of the roots of a fallen tree. Jean-Paul was exceedingly knowledgeable—could tell you at first glance exactly what something was, to whom (generally speaking) it had belonged, and when, most likely, it had first hit the ground—and endlessly patient, cheerfully answering more questions (some of which, I suspect, must have sounded pretty stupid) than he probably got from an entire posse of normal tourists. At the end of the day, he insisted I keep everything we had found and picked up, including a few fired bullets and uniform buttons that I'm sure he would have liked to have in his museum. And he absolutely refused to take any money from me for his time, even though I knew, from things he had said here and there, that this was how he really earned his living, and that all his other visitors—who did pay him—got much shorter excursions. He never said why he treated me differently, and I never asked. But I think, perhaps, he may have seen a bit of himself in me: He went out and found the objects of that war; I'd gone out and found the people.

For years afterward, when I reflected about that day, what I thought about most was not Jean-Paul's kindness and generosity, or the bullets fixed in the roots of that tree; it was that field outside Romagne, and what I'd found there that morning, and what I'd had to leave, dangerous though I knew it was. Sometimes I would show a picture of it when giving talks about World War I, speak of it wistfully: the one that got away.

At one of these events, in the White Mountains of New Hampshire, a cluster of men in their fifties sat in the front row, talking. I eavesdropped a little before the program started and quickly determined that they knew much more about the war than I did; always a sign I would be learning something soon. And sure enough, when a photo I had taken of the little shell was projected onto the screen behind me, one of them—he wore a plaid flannel shirt and had a bushy salt-and-pepper beard—raised his hand.

"You see those rings?" he said, pointing to two copper bands encircling its midsection. "That shell had gas in it."

I don't think about it the same way anymore.

A year or so later, a friend of mine, a retired army officer with expertise in ordnance, looked at the photo and told me it was a 37-millimeter shell. American. The smallest piece of artillery that soldiers in the American Expeditionary Forces (or AEF) employed, sort of a portable cannon. There's a famous photo of two doughboys lying prone on the ground, surrounded by shattered trees, firing one. I told him what the man in New Hampshire had told me.

"He's absolutely right," my friend said. "You didn't touch it, of course."

I started to say *of course not,* then decided I might as well tell him the real story; he shook his head and laughed. "Jean-Paul may have saved your neck," he said. "Those things are seriously unstable, much more so than the 75 millimeter, or the 77, or the big howitzers. And unlike the big ones, there's no way to defuse them. It's much more dangerous now than when it was fired."

Five years after that first encounter, in a field outside the village of Épinonville, not far from Romagne, I found dozens of cartridges, a handful of bullets, insulators, keys, pieces of a German 77-millimeter shell and a short-range mortar known as a *Minenwerfer,* a complete German bayonet, the scabbard of a German sword, tins, bottles, a horse shoe, a mule shoe, and, sitting right next to each other, two 37-millimeter shells. I took a few large steps back—careful of the corn—and called out for Jean-Paul and his spray can.

★ ★ ★

That was in June 2014. Jean-Paul had been the first person I'd contacted when planning my return to France; I was surprised, and delighted, that he remembered me and actually seemed excited to go out and do it again. He asked me what I was most interested in seeing, then methodically set about making a plan. We hadn't just happened to drive by that field one morning; Jean-Paul had studied maps and chosen it deliberately. He knew that I had a particular interest in the AEF's 91st Division, having interviewed, a decade earlier, the division's last surviving veteran, 107-year-old William J. Lake of Yakima, Washington. (The 91st, composed of draftees from the Pacific Northwest, was known as the Wild West Division; it had taken very heavy casualties during the first stage of the battle.) And he knew that the 91st had been there in late September 1918, during the opening days of the Meuse-Argonne Offensive. Those 37-millimeter shells, now a fluorescent orange, were theirs. Ours.

And they provided an interesting coda to Bill Lake's story, which occupies a chapter of that book, the one that had brought me to France in 2009. Five years later, I would add a photo of those two shells to the slideshow that often accompanied the talks I gave. By then, there were plenty of other such photos in the presentation. When I'd first starting giving talks on the subject of America and World War I, I'd focused solely on the veterans themselves, the men and women I'd interviewed eighty-five years or more after the armistice. Then one day, as a lark, I included a photo of that first shell, the one Jean-Paul had fortunately dissuaded me from picking up. People started asking questions about what it was like Over There now, so I started adding more photos from that 2009 trip: the little village where J. Laurence Moffitt had first encountered the enemy; the woods where Eugene Lee had been shot through the wrist during a last-ditch effort to keep the Germans from marching on Paris; the field where George Briant had been trapped when German planes flew overhead and dropped bombs on him, knocking out his teeth, tearing a hole in his hip, nearly ripping out an eye; the forest where Bill Lake had been sitting and talking with a friend when a sniper killed the man. And others, quite a few of them.

I had thought the photos would help answer peoples' questions about what First World War sites in France were like, but as it happened they only raised more questions: Are these things really still out there? How is that possible? People, it seemed, couldn't quite grasp it. And I couldn't quite grasp why not. I had been there, after all; it made perfect sense to me. Then, one evening, a woman raised her hand. "We went to Gettysburg a couple of summers ago," she said. "Have you been? Is it like that?"

I had to stifle a laugh—not because her question itself was funny, but because visiting Gettysburg and exploring the Argonne are such different experiences that it's easy to forget they are both battlefields. I have, I told her. And no, it is not. Gettysburg—and this is true of any American Revolutionary or Civil War battlefield I have ever visited—does not look like a place where history was made, much less in such dramatic fashion. It looks, rather, like a lovely park: landscaped, manicured, and thoroughly littered with monuments. When you stand on Cemetery Ridge, you know that one of the most famous assaults in military history, Pickett's Charge, happened there, but only because you've read about it—in books, or on the kiosks that are only slightly less ubiquitous than the monuments. It's not as if you could actually *see* anything, at least not with your eyes open. And you certainly aren't going to stumble upon anything you'd have to spray-paint orange. Strolling around Gettysburg is like watching a documentary on television; hiking around the Argonne is like traveling back in time. It is hard, when you are Over There, to regard the First World War as history.

But I was back Over Here, now, surrounded by people with questions, fellow countrymen who—well-meaning and even well-informed as they are—know almost nothing about that war; who regard it, and all of history, as past. Dead. I could not reconcile the dichotomy; could not make sense of how the same event could be past here and present there, dead here and alive there. The conflict's centennial observances, which started as soon as 2014 did, only heightened my cognitive dissonance: The war was being talked about all the time now, which made it feel ever more present; and yet, the constant references to the centennial—reminders that this all happened a hundred years ago—made it feel ever more remote. The two competing notions had dug trenches in my brain and were waging war across the No Man's Land of my gray matter. Only one thing, I knew, might be able to bring them together and force an armistice.

That thing was a place.

And so, though I was still quite attached to my bed and my DVR, I went back to France. Twice. In the past, I had visited Moffitt's village, Lee's woods, Briant's field, Lake's forest, and many other sites connected to the men I had interviewed in order to put myself in those spaces and try to imagine what had happened there; now I intended to linger much longer, look much closer, search for traces of what those men I had interviewed—and the two million others who served with them, as well as the millions more who'd fought alongside or against them—had left behind. In the past, I had followed the narratives of people I had actually known. Now I would follow the trail of two million I hadn't, through fields and forests, across ridges and rivers, from the doughboys' first encounter with the Germans to the last minute of the war, from the German frontier to the outskirts of Paris, the Vosges Mountains to the hills of Champagne, a chalky ridge in Picardy to a sodden plain in Lorraine; and from the Marne River to the Argonne Forest, where a cute little pair of antique shells, plowed up that very morning, could still sear your lungs and blow your legs off. Those were history, too. And they certainly weren't dead.

★ ★ ★

The battle lines along the Western Front ran almost five hundred miles, from the English Channel in the northwest to the Swiss border in the southeast. German troops manned the entire length of the easterly side of that line; French troops manned the entire length of the westerly side, supported, in various sectors at various times, by units—a lot of units—of the British and American armies, as well as colonial troops, commonwealth troops, Italians, Russians, Czecho-Slovaks, and other nationalities. The war lasted four years, three months and two weeks, encompassing innumerable offensives, battles, skirmishes, raids, incidents and episodes that occurred along that five-hundred-mile line. No one I have ever met, in France or elsewhere, can even grasp it all, much less master it.

I have, however, been fortunate enough, through either referrals or serendipity, to have met and spent time with people who have mastered some piece of the map that played an important role in the saga of the American Expeditionary Forces—a sector, or a cluster of communities, or the site of a single encounter. The one thing they all have in common is that their focus, their area of expertise, is relatively narrow. They can be quite proprietary about their turf; some have been known to feud openly with other experts who operate within their fiefdom. At the same time, though, they do not stray; do not, curious as it seems, have much or even any interest in the fascinating things that happened outside their zone. And they do not know, even by reputation, experts from other zones. None ever referred me to any other.

The Argonne is so vast and varied, and saw so much action over so long a stretch of time, that the fiefdoms within it are small—typically a few villages, sometimes just one. Only one man can claim the whole thing as his zone. And he goes through a lot of orange spray paint.

Jean-Paul and I left that field outside Épinonville that morning in June 2014, crossed the road, and hiked a bit to another one, much larger than the last. He had determined that this was the meadow where Private Lake's beloved captain, 31-year-old Elijah W. Worsham, had been killed by a German sniper on the evening of September 29, 1918. It slopes down toward the village of Gesnes-en-Argonne, where Captain Worsham was heading; you can clearly make out its church steeple in the distance. Captain Worsham commanded the machine-gun company of the 362nd Infantry Regiment—Montana men—which had just liberated Gesnes after forty-eight months of German occupation. He'd been killed at dusk; we were there on a bright morning. Still, I felt, for a moment, as if I could see it happening, right where I stood.

After that we returned to Romagne and had lunch at Jean-Paul's café. The café helps subsidize the museum; most afternoons he is tied to it, and also to the museum, which sometimes gets groups of European tourists or French schoolchildren who have just visited the cemetery. Knowing I'd be exploring on my own for the rest of the day, I asked him for suggestions of what I might see, then remembered something he had showed me the last time I visited, five years earlier. "How do I find that house Rommel stopped at?" I asked. That's Erwin Rommel: the Desert Fox. Widely considered Germany's best, and certainly most iconic, World War II general. One morning in June 2009, as we were looking at something else, Jean-Paul had pointed across a field at an old farmhouse in the distance. "You see that?" he'd said. "In 1914, when Rommel was just a young lieutenant, he stopped at that house." And that was it. But back home, I'd dug up an old copy of Rommel's 1937 book, *Infantry Attacks,* and found the future Desert Fox's recollection of the visit:

> I looked about for shelter for the night . . . In one of the houses we saw a light shining through the closed shutters. We went inside, and found a dozen women and girls who seemed frightened at our appearance. In French I asked for food and a place to sleep for myself and my men. Both were provided, and soon we were sound asleep on clean mattresses.

"I knew an old woman who was one of the girls who was in that house," Jean-Paul told me afterward. "Her account was . . . *different*." For one thing, she said, Rommel hadn't exactly asked; for another, when he left the next morning, he took much of their pantry with him, and a few chickens, besides. He was a 22-year-old junior officer, supremely confident and eager to prove himself to everyone, from senior German commanders to young French girls. He did, then did it again in the next war. It's hard to picture the History Channel without him.

"That house? It's easy," Jean-Paul said. "Just a few kilometers from here." As he described how to find it, I fell into despair: None of the roads I'd have to take had names, much less signage. It didn't sound like they were paved, either.

"Don't worry," Jean-Paul said. "Here, I'll show you." He pulled out a paper napkin and drew me a crude map, then handed it to me with a smile. I didn't feel any more confident, but I set off, anyway.

As it happened, it was a pretty good little map, and I didn't have any trouble spotting the farm—which had been called Musarde since well before Rommel stopped by—from the road. Approaching the house, though, first by car—it sat at the end of a half-mile dirt driveway—and then on foot, it didn't look familiar to me; I later figured out that an entire section of it had collapsed since I'd seen it last.

As I was poking around the rubble, a silver Nissan 4x4 pulled up and a man got out. Burly, rosy-cheeked, and rumpled, he looked to be in his sixties and vaguely resembled the late actor Dolph Sweet, or maybe an older, Frencher version of my friend Rick, who is not an actor and who, come to think of it, looks nothing like Dolph Sweet. "*Bonjour,*" he said, and not tentatively, though he was clearly sizing me up and wondering what I was doing there. He wore a gray button-down workshirt and had bright blue eyes behind his metallic spectacles. Not too tall, but broad; he looked like he could toss some hay bales if he had to.

"*Bonjour,*" I said, then added my standard disclaimer. His expression softened a bit, and I pointed to the house. "Rommel was here in 1914?" I asked.

"*Vous êtes Anglais?*" he asked.

"*Non,*" I said. "*Je suis Américain.*"

A big smile hijacked his face, and he nodded heartily. "You are far from home!" he said in French. "What did you want to know?"

"Rommel," I repeated. "He was here in 1914, yes?"

"No, no," he said. "I don't know. But that house over there"—he pointed to another farmhouse maybe a quarter-mile off, smaller than this one and square—"MacArthur was there in '18." He pronounced the name Mack-are-TOUR. *"Voudrez voir?"*

Did I want to see it? *"Mais, oui."*

He opened the passenger door, and I climbed in. The 4x4 looked like a typical SUV on the outside—something you would see cruising the streets of Stamford, Connecticut—but inside it was stripped down and covered in dirt and straw. A working vehicle. We drove for a hundred yards or so, and then he stopped to unlatch a gate. When he stopped again on the other side to close it, several cows ambled over to check out the stranger. One stuck her nose through the window and rested it against my shirt. France!

This property, which comprised several old farms, was all his. His father, he explained, had bought it after the second war. During the first, the Germans had taken it early—Rommel came through the first or second day of September 1914—and already knew, having studied those secret maps, what they were going to do with it. The hills on the property, especially the Côté de Chatillon, and the open fields, made it a fine place to build the Kriemhilde Stellung, the central strand of the Hindenburg Line, the Germans' ultimate line of defense in France. Designed to be impenetrable, it was. For four years. The Germans didn't just build it; they overbuilt it. They covered the area so well that it's hard to see how a butterfly could have escaped their notice. Or their fire.

"There," my new host said, gesturing at a meadow sloping up just to his left. He pointed his finger at a spot: *"Mitrailleuse."* Machine gun. He moved it forward a few degrees: *Mitrailleuse.* Did it twice more. *Mitrailleuse. Mitrailleuse.* Pronounced mit-ray-USE, it's an oddly pretty word for what it is. The German word, *Maschinengewehr,* sounds much more appropriate. Mah-SHEEN-en-gev-air. A machine that will fill you with air. *Mitrailleuse* sounds like a dance.

The scene was equally dissonant: The rise was gentle, the field lazy, a shade close to the border of green and tan. Something out of a Wyeth painting. I could no more picture four machine-gun nests here than I could a Starbucks. But that was only true for a few moments; and then, I could see them clearly. They were precisely where they should have been to command the maximum amount of ground. The Germans—there's no denying it—knew exactly what they were doing.

Now he pointed above the ghost machine guns, to the top of the ridge, which was flat and shaggy. "Up there," he said, "there was a German narrow-gauge railroad." It ran all through the property; there was even a station, he told me, pointing straight ahead at a spot in the distance I couldn't discern. We went by it a bit later—a huge, jagged wedge of concrete embedded in the earth, pitted and pocked but still with a sharp corner, and a passel of iron rods snaking out, as if to get a look: a section of the old platform. Well preserved, not for historical reasons but because it was well built to begin with, and because there's just no way to get rid of it. It would be a menace to try to plow around, if this weren't a pasture. The cows, though, don't seem to mind.

We stopped briefly for him to unlatch another gate, then approached the second farmhouse, which was shaped like a big gray Lego brick—and, as I could now tell, had no roof. A little closer, and I could some trees growing inside it. "La Tuilerie," he announced, then turned away from the old house and pointed up at some forested hills off to the right. "MacArthur came from over there," he said with a slight smile that was equal parts pride and delight. "Early in the morning. The Division 42. October 18." That's 18 the year, not the date; as often as anything else—as often as *la Grande Guerre* and *la Première Guerre,* which are the other main options—the French refer to the First World War as "14–18." They don't feel the need to specify the century.

He turned back to the house. "MacArthur was *here,*" he said, his voice tinged with awe, as if he were just beholding the place and hearing its history for the first time. Of course, he'd grown up with this house, La Tuilerie; had known, for most of his life, that on October 14, 1918, three weeks into the climactic Meuse-Argonne Offensive, some particularly ferocious combat had taken place here. The Americans were down here, the Germans up on that hill with the machine guns and beyond, with even greater firepower, on the Côté de Chatillon. Clearly the better position; even without a topographical map—even without looking around—you would know that simply because the Germans held it.

The Côté de Chatillon, in fact, was high ground of such strategic importance that American commanders felt they couldn't effectively press what was, in essence, the heart of the offensive without it. They also knew that if they understood this, the Germans did, too; and, that being the case, that the Germans would have done their best to make it impossible for the Americans—or the French, or anyone else—to take it away from them. And so they gave the assignment to a brash, vainglorious 38-year-old West Pointer from the 42nd Division who'd been promoted to brigadier general just that summer. MacArthur's orders, the legend goes, were to take the Côté de Chatillon or show five thousand casualties for the effort. He is said to have responded that he would, or his name would top that list. He did; it didn't.

My host stood still and gazed at the old farmhouse for a few moments, then suddenly turned to the left and gestured at a tree line a few hundred yards away. "Those woods are full of German trenches," he told me. "*Voudrez voir?*"

"*Bien sûr!*" Of course.

We got back in the 4x4 and rolled up the pasture toward the trees. He pulled to a stop close enough for me to see how thick they were; I was glad to be wearing long pants, despite it being a hot day. From the first step inside, we had to bushwhack. There were no signs that anyone else had walked through here in a very long time; nothing resembling a trail. But he didn't need one. He knew exactly where to go.

If you've only seen trenches in old pictures, or in movies (and don't even get me started on the ones in *Downton Abbey*), then you might not spot a bona fide World War I trench if you came upon one in the woods. But you'd only have to have them pointed out to you once. There is, simply, no mistaking them for anything else. Natural ravines are not so narrow and shallow; gullies are not so jagged. Neither are so pervasive. And neither run in pairs or sets, roughly parallel to each other, with other ravines or gullies intersecting them fairly regularly and at more or less perpendicular angles. Trenches do not occur in nature.

The trenches I've seen—the dirt trenches, that is; I've also seen concrete trenches, but those are relatively uncommon, and almost all German, and I'll deal with them later—vary in depth from around three to eight feet, and are typically two or three yards wide. It's tough to say how long they are, because it can be difficult, even impossible, to determine where they begin and end. Some seem to go on, and on, and on. They often have steep, rough side walls from which rocks and thick tree roots protrude; but the ones in my host's woods were fairly smooth and solid, with modestly sloping walls, and I did what I often did when I came upon trenches like these: scurried down and ran around, trying to imagine what it would have been like in them a century ago, when they were deeper, and wider, and full of men, and under fire.

My host didn't want any part of that, but he waited patiently for me to emerge, then told me that further out in the forest were two German blockhouses. (The French word for blockhouse is *blockhouse,* pronounced blow-KOOZE.) *Voudrez voir?* You know I did.

We started bushwhacking again, and in a few minutes found ourselves perched on the rim of a large depression in the forest floor, maybe ten feet deep and thirty across and full of stuff, branches and vines and thickets and fallen tree trunks. It took a few moments for my eyes to adjust to the point where I could see them, sitting under all that flora: two massive concrete bunkers. They looked like enormous stone hippopotami emerging from the brush, mouths agape.

"How do we get down there?" I asked, assuming he'd done so many times.

But he just shrugged. "That's up to you."

The slope was steep; I tried a few branches, but none seemed strong enough to support me, nor long enough to cover most of the distance to the forest floor. Finally I spotted a vine and, not pausing to think too much, grabbed it and swung down to one of the blockhouses. The farmer clapped. "Tarzan!" he called out.

"The same," I said, and took a bow.

"I'm not Jane," he replied, and did not budge.

I pulled a small flashlight out of my pocket and ducked inside the first blockhouse, through a narrow rectangular doorway—I didn't spot any evidence of a door—and into a winding entrance corridor that was clearly designed to protect those inside from a blast. Before the first turn, facing the doorway and embedded into the concrete wall, was a square iron plate with a hole in its center just large enough to accommodate the muzzle of a machine gun. Nearby, set in the ground, was a square cement well, a foot or so across and a few deep: a grenade sump. Should a live one get tossed inside, you were supposed to kick it into the sump, which would direct the blast straight up, rather than all around. Easier said than done, I imagine, but you have to hand it to the Germans—they thought of everything.

I snaked around the corners into the main chamber. Large and small chunks of concrete littered the floor; tiny white stalactites hung from the corrugated metal ceiling. A single drop of water clung to the tip of each. A large section of the ceiling had fallen and lay in rubble on the ground, letting in vegetation and an eerie green-gray light. The other blockhouse was much the same, though I noticed it also had a hole in its roof for a periscope. They were clearly well designed, and extremely well built; despite the rubble, it was easy to envision them full of men a hundred years ago. And more recently, too: My host told me that the French Resistance used them during the second war. It wasn't until the 1950s that they were blown up—by farmers, in an attempt to clear the land. Futile.

I grabbed another vine and hauled myself out of the pit; I hadn't yet reached the top before my host started telling me about something else and asking *"Voudrez voir?"* We left the woods, and then the farm, and he drove me around assorted fields and through various villages for the next several hours, pointing out places where something significant or dramatic had happened in the fall of 1918, telling me how this place or that had fared during the war. At one point, he pulled off a road in a thick part of the forest and onto a rough, rock-strewn trail I would have hesitated to walk, much less drive. He must have seen as much in my expression, because he grinned and slapped the dashboard twice. *"Voiture Asiatique!"* he crowed. *"Très bon!"*

Asian car or not, it was rough going; we stalled a few times, and his shock absorbers and alignment took a real beating. But he seemed to know where he was going. We drove uphill for a while and then stopped at what looked to be the crest of a ridge. As I climbed out of the car I almost fell into a trench. A line of them, deeper than the ones in his woods, slithered along on either side of the road, just a few feet from the narrow ridge. The slope to our left was short and easy; at the point where the ground leveled off for a bit was a series of depressions, too wide to be shell holes. "Gun pits," he said. "Howitzers." The guns would have faced us, firing shells up over the ridge and down the other side.

The other side: Past the trenches, there were smaller, shallower pits for machine guns, and then the slope seemed to just drop off straight down. Edging closer, I could see, through the trees, that the incline was maybe sixty degrees. My host stood and stared straight down, silent, though the angle, and the dense vegetation, made it difficult to spot the bottom. It looked to be several hundred yards away; for certain, the grade was so steep that you'd have to snake up on your belly, or walk up like a crab, hands and feet. Under rifle and machine-gun and mortar fire.

Later, when he drove me back to the house where we'd met, he invited me inside, to a big, musty room full of spiders, and offered me a cold beer.

The house, Musarde, was no longer inhabited, but my host still used this part of it as a hunting lodge/clubhouse. He phoned his son and had him bring over his "papers"—old maps of his land, photocopied pictures and pages from history texts, old postcards of the area, correspondence with historians; opined on politics, the economy, France's low birth rate. It was only afterward, as we shook hands good-bye outside, that we thought to exchange names. His was Jean-Pierre Brouillon.

At one point back in the house, while he'd chattered about Sarkozy's and Hollande's records, I'd looked over some of his maps and spotted that ridge we had visited earlier: Côté Dame Marie. Seeing it there, on paper, I suddenly understood the presence of all those trenches and machine-gun nests and artillery pits. The position enabled the Germans to command an entire section of the Argonne; to make it impenetrable. The Germans, of course, had figured that out well before September 1914. They had taken it right away, secured it quickly, layered it with wire and trenches, machine guns and howitzers. Then they used it—for the next forty-nine months— to rain awful fire down upon French troops over a vast area. Many French had died trying to take it back; many more had died simply because they had gotten too close to it.

The maps say the ridge is three hundred feet high and more than a half mile long, but they don't tell you what that slope, that sixty-degree hill studded with trees and roots and rocks, looks like—what that climb, that slither or scuttle under all kinds of fire, must have been like for the men of the American 32nd Division, National Guard troops from Wisconsin and Michigan, who finally took Côté Dame Marie from the Germans in October 1918. It's the kind of thing you have to see to be able to imagine; and yet, seeing it makes it even harder to imagine. It doesn't seem humanly possible. Jean-Pierre had lived nearby his whole life, had visited many times; still, standing there that day, looking down that hill, even he was struck dumb. All he could do was turn to me and summon an expression that said: Can you believe that?

Finally he spoke. "The French," he announced, "didn't drive the Germans out of here. The English didn't do it." He shook his head, pursed his lips. "Just the Americans," he said. "Only the Americans could do it."

Jean-Pierre Brouillon remembers. Musarde, and La Tuilerie, and Côté Dame Marie remember. Long after Americans forgot, French people and French earth continued to safeguard the memory of the American

Expeditionary Forces—of American doughboys—and what they did here in 1917 and 1918. They held them, kept them, preserved them, cherished them; waited, patiently, for Americans to come back and reclaim them. To look down.

Look up: A century has passed. Let's go.

CHAPTER TWO

THE SOUL OF THE BATTLEFIELD

Too frequently, someone or other will make the mistake of saying to me (or near me) that the United States of America, which eventually lost its patience with unrestricted submarine warfare and declared war on Germany on April 6, 1917—two years and eight months after the fighting began in Europe—entered the First World War *late*. My typical response is to ask them: Late for *what*, exactly? The mud? The slaughter? The stalemate? None of it, I point out, to any avail; and none of it in service of a cause or objective that had anything to do with the United States of America. Besides, all of it—the mud, the slaughter, the stalemate—was still there, waiting for America, in 1917. All the United States missed was two years and eight months of killing. And didn't even miss that entirely: The

128 Americans who went down with the British ocean liner *Lusitania*, torpedoed by a German U-boat on May 7, 1915, would tell you that. So would all the others who went down, a few or a few dozen at a time, on various other Allied ships. So would many of the Americans who, impatient with President Wilson's policy of neutrality, headed off to Canada, or over to Europe, to enlist in some foreign military.

But yes: The United States of America did, indeed, miss the first thirty-two months of the Great War. And a lot did happen in that time. Not a lot changed, though; not a lot even moved. The war that America sat out was a bogged-down stalemate that claimed millions of lives, a fact that did not escape notice Over Here. By the time the American Expeditionary Forces started arriving in France in 1917, the fruitless carnage of 1914 and 1915 and 1916 had convinced AEF leaders to follow a different course, one that altered the way the war was fought in its final year and culminated in a victory over Germany. To understand that new course, though, you first have to understand how terribly the old one had fared.

✭ ✭ ✭

Ironically, a war that would become characterized by a deadly inertia was actually quite dynamic at first. That's because both the Germans and the French were long past ready for it by the time it actually started. They'd been preparing for it for decades; four decades plus three years, to be precise.

The Franco-Prussian War of 1870–71, in which the Second French Empire squared off against the North German Confederation, is really the prologue to the First World War. The causes of that earlier war, while perhaps not quite as Byzantine as those of the war it wrought, are difficult to comprehend if your mindset is not stuck in nineteenth-century Europe. Starting at the Congress of Vienna in 1815, in the wake of Napoleon's extremely destructive military campaigns throughout Europe, an elaborate system was constructed to ensure what was deemed a "balance of power" that would ostensibly prevent future Napoleons from wreaking havoc again. By 1870, though, Prussia, led by its brilliant chancellor Otto von Bismarck, had unified the northern German states under its leadership and was looking to do the same with the southern German states, including the large, populous and resource-rich Bavaria and Württemberg. Bismarck, facing some resistance to unification down south, figured that the one thing that might change their minds about it was a French attack. He knew that France's emperor, Napoleon III, dreaded the prospect of a unified Germany; many historians believe that Bismarck baited Napoleon III into declaring war on Prussia by altering a diplomatic note, now known as the Ems Dispatch, to give the impression that Prussia's King Wilhelm I had insulted Count Vincent Benedetti, France's ambassador to Prussia. Whether or not Bismarck really deserves that much credit, Napoleon III was happy to have the pretense. France's army was reputed to be the finest in the world; surely, it would make short work of the Prussians. Thousands marched through the streets of Paris demanding war. Their emperor gladly accommodated them.

He would quickly come to regret it. Just six weeks after (it would seem) he let Bismarck trick him into starting a war, Napoleon III was captured by the enemy, along with more than twenty thousand of his men, following a devastating defeat at Sedan in northeastern France. The Prussians then laid siege to Paris; after four months, France requested an armistice. The fighting had lasted a total of six months. When it was all over, the finest army in the world was in tatters, and France was poorer, smaller, weaker, and utterly humiliated. Prussia, on the other hand, unified more than two dozen smaller states under its leadership, creating a much larger and more powerful new nation—Germany. And the peace was equally lopsided: Just as a second world war was all but assured by the Treaty of Versailles in 1919, the first one was all but assured by the Treaty of Frankfurt in 1871, which awarded the victors a five-billion-franc "war indemnity," part of the French region of Lorraine, and nearly all of the adjacent French region of Alsace. Worse than all that, though—at least according to one French historian I know—was that the Prussians occupied a large chunk of the country, staging victory parades until they got their five billion francs. A plague of internal upheavals, some of them quite bloody, descended upon France. For a long time, it seemed the only things that united it were a hatred of the *Boche*—the most common French slur for a German—and a lust for *revanche*.

The Germans knew that; and if they saw it as a threat, they also saw in it an opportunity to expand their borders even further. The Germans did not lack confidence. Their new unified nation, one of the largest and most populous in Europe, was also quite possibly the most innovative and industrious: It produced the very first automobile, for instance, in 1885, and surpassed both the United Kingdom and the United States in steel production by the turn of the century. But as the victory of 1870–71 receded further and further into history, that confidence was increasingly inextricable from a sense of resentment that Germany was not given its rightful due, that older powers, particularly France and Britain, looked down upon it, denied it the respect, the prestige—and, worse still, the territory—an empire of its might deserved. This was not a grassroots phenomenon; it flowed all the way down from the twisted psyche of Germany's emperor, Kaiser Wilhelm II, a profoundly insecure man who believed that his cousins, particularly King George V of Great Britain and Czar Nicholas II of Russia, had conspired to ostracize him. Perhaps, he and many other Germans figured, another lightning victory in France would finish what the first had started. Then no one could question Germany's primacy among nations.

In short, both France and Germany were primed for war well before August 1914. The Germans had the famous Schlieffen Plan—named for the German Army's chief of staff, Alfred von Schlieffen, who devised it—which called for the Imperial German Army to sweep into France by way of neutral Belgium and encircle the French armies around Paris. The French had the lesser-known Plan XVII, which called for them, in the event of a German attack, to counterattack Germany through Alsace and Lorraine and march straight on to Berlin. Plan XVII—which really did re-place XVI earlier plans—wasn't even very well known to the French them-selves, at least not beyond a handful of generals and their staffs, many of whom thought it was a very bad idea. The Germans, though, anticipated it (one reason many French generals thought it was a very bad idea) and reckoned it would draw French troops away from the path of the Schlief-fen Plan. Both were aimed at a quick victory: The Schlieffen Plan allotted six weeks to bring the French to surrender; Plan XVII didn't get around to setting a timetable, but surely it wouldn't take long at all.

Unfortunately for Germany, Schlieffen's successor, Helmuth von Moltke—whom many regarded as an inept strategist who only got the job because his uncle and namesake was the great hero of the Franco-Prussian War—weakened his predecessor's plan by tinkering with both the num-ber of troops and the course they would take, and certainly failed to an-ticipate the strength of Belgium's resistance. On the other hand, France's Plan XVII helped the Germans tremendously, exactly as they (and some French) had anticipated. The French launched the Battle of the Frontiers, as it is now known, in mid-August 1914. By the end of the month, what-ever gains they'd initially made in Alsace and Lorraine were reversed and more, and at great cost: The Germans killed twenty-seven thousand

French soldiers on August 22 alone, the deadliest day in all of French military history. Meanwhile, the Schlieffen Plan proceeded, with the Germans closing in on Paris.

The French seemed to be in freefall; the last week of August and first week of September 1914 are still remembered by some—not fondly—as "the Great Retreat." The horrors of 1870–71 seemed almost upon them once again. Then, just in time, and under the leadership of General Joseph "Papa" Joffre, they managed to regroup, reorganize, and exploit, with the help of some British troops, an unintended breach in the German lines, making a stand at the Marne River, only thirty miles or so from Paris. The battle, which lasted one week, quickly became the stuff of legend; in one of the war's most famous episodes, thousands of French soldiers—*poilus,* as they were informally and affectionately known—were shuttled from Paris to the front in taxicabs, which actually kept their meters running the whole trip and were reimbursed for their fares afterward. In the end, the French, with some help from British troops, turned the Germans back at the Marne, foiling the Schlieffen Plan and ensuring that the war would, indeed, last longer than six weeks.

There were other battles to come that fall, with both the Allies and the Germans attempting to take new ground and better their positions, but through it all, the lines stayed more or less where they'd frozen in September 1914, after the German advance was stopped at the Marne and both sides started digging trenches.

And here began the World War I we all think of today: Static. Stuck. Quite literally entrenched.

The war America entered "late."

✸ ✸ ✸

It's not as though nothing happened on the Western Front between the fall of 1914 and the fall of 1917, when the doughboys—as soldiers of the American Expeditionary Forces were, for reasons lost to time, known—started killing and dying at the front. Quite a lot did. For instance, the city of Ypres, in Belgian Flanders near the French border, saw three battles in less than three years, the first in the autumn of 1914, the third in the summer of 1917. Belgium lost tens of thousands of soldiers at Ypres; France and Germany each lost hundreds of thousands. No one knows for sure how many men the British Expeditionary Force—including troops from

Australia, Canada, and India—lost there, but the names of nearly fifty-five thousand of them are chiseled into the Menin Gate, their memorial in the city; and those are just the missing.

The battles of Ypres are just a few among many fought on the Western Front in late 1914, and 1915, and 1916, and early 1917. All of them were costly, many extremely so. Millions of soldiers lost their lives. As I said, quite a lot did happen in those years.

But as I also noted, not very much changed. The lines in 1917, when the American Expeditionary Forces started showing up in France, were more or less identical to what they had been in 1914.

No one was happy with the status quo. The British, who had never really feared a German invasion, had plenty of time to wonder what they were doing in France and Belgium. The French, while relieved that they hadn't had to capitulate like they had in 1871, wanted the Germans off French soil. The Germans, though they'd conquered and occupied a good chunk of France, wanted more, at least enough to force the French to surrender. As 1914 dragged on into 1915, and 1915 into 1916, thousands upon thousands upon thousands of men continued to die for a few yards here and there which would soon be lost again.

Which brings us to Verdun.

An ancient fortified city on the Meuse River (Attila the Hun is said to have tried, unsuccessfully, to take it in the fifth century), Verdun sat in one of the parts of Lorraine that the Germans hadn't annexed in 1871. While it was strategically important as a roadblock on one of the routes to Paris, it was even more important—much more—as a symbol of French resilience and defiance.

The Germans understood this. And they reckoned the French would do whatever they had to in order to keep them from taking it. Sure, the Germans would have liked to have Verdun for themselves; but what they really wanted was for the French to pay such a high price to keep the old walled city that they would no longer be able to prosecute the war—as the German high command put it, to "bleed France white." On February 21, 1916, having set up their own formidable defense works around Verdun, they attacked it along a front twenty miles long and three miles wide.

Before the Germans had attacked Verdun, many in the French high command had started to question the value of protecting it; indeed, by the beginning of 1916, most of the soldiers and big guns that defended the city had been moved to other positions on the front. But the Germans had read French popular sentiment correctly: As soon as they launched their attack, all of France rose up and demanded Verdun be saved, no matter the cost.

Even so, though the Germans had been right about Verdun's symbolic importance to the people of France, they failed to anticipate the nature of French resolve, as well as France's ability to rally its population with symbols—symbols that included not just Verdun itself but men like Colonel Émile Augustine Cyprien Driant, a 60-year-old career soldier and novelist who had pleaded with his superiors not to appropriate Verdun's guns and reassign its troops, warning that a German attack was imminent. He didn't have much time to savor his vindication; one of the first French officers to confront the enemy, he was badly outnumbered, quickly outflanked and killed on the second day of the battle near Fort Douaumont, an important part of Verdun's defense. A small monument—an artistic rendering of a shattered stone wall—stands on the spot where he fell, in a lovely, peaceful wood.

Even the Germans admired Driant; they buried him with full military honors, and took care to notify his widow, through diplomatic channels, that he had fought bravely. And the French—well, they all but canonized him. Before his death, Driant had been a fairly obscure officer, better known for his fiction than his military career; he'd resigned his commission in 1906, frustrated with his lack of advancement, and only reenlisted when the army recalled him after Germany attacked in 1914. Now he was the most mourned man in the country, a combination warrior-martyr who'd given his life for French honor at Verdun. And Verdun, a small city in a poor, often overlooked part of the country, suddenly became the most important place in France. Its defense was now deemed so essential to the war effort that every *poilu* in France—and there were millions of them—was rotated through that sector at some point.

If that sounds hard to conceive, most everything about Verdun is. The battle would last ten months and claim roughly a million casualties. No one knows exactly how many of those were killed in action, in part because war is chaotic, but also because a large number of those casualties are officially listed as missing in action. Though there was a great deal of hand-to-hand fighting, it is believed that 70 percent of the deaths at Verdun were caused by artillery. More than 150,000 men—perhaps many more—simply disappeared, blown to bits or buried alive.

The Germans were able to lay siege to Verdun, but not to isolate it entirely. Though they had disrupted all rail service to the city, one route lay beyond the reach of their big guns, a forty-five-mile gravel road that ran south from Verdun to the town of Bar-le-Duc. It became the sole lifeline of Verdun and, by extension, the French Army, which soon nicknamed it "La Voie Sacrée"—the Sacred Way. The French quickly organized a system, which they called "Noria," in which some eight thousand trucks and other vehicles were in almost constant motion, ferrying supplies to the front and carrying the wounded away from it on their return trip. It is said that at Noria's peak operation, one arrived every fourteen seconds. Special labor battalions worked around the clock to keep the road in good repair; others were stationed at intervals to clear away broken-down vehicles and get them running again as quickly as possible. In the face of such a threat, the French, it turned out, were invigorated. *"Ils ne passeront pas!"* declared France's General Robert Nivelle: They shall not pass. The entire country adopted it as a battle cry.

Noria had been the brainchild of a 60-year-old general named Philippe Pétain, a career officer and notorious womanizer (legend has it that when the Germans launched their attack on February 21, he had to be fetched from a mistress's flat) who had acquitted himself well up to that point but had never undertaken anything like this before. Then again, no one else had, either. He ran the entire operation out of his headquarters in the *mairie,* or town hall, of Souilly, a small village in between Verdun and Bar-le-Duc; two years later, General John J. Pershing, commander of the American Expeditionary Forces, made his headquarters in the same building. Their portraits hang next to each other inside the *mairie* today, a sight that can stop you cold if you're aware of the fact that Pétain went on to collaborate with the Nazis in the next war. He died in exile, imprisoned on the Île d'Yeu, in 1951.

The great hero of Verdun; the great traitor of Vichy: Mentioning Pétain's name to a French person these days typically evokes an uncomfortable expression. Of course, to some French—mostly younger—he's just a villain; others feel that his heroism in 1916, and later in that war, cancels out whatever he did afterward. The authorities have disrupted nocturnal plots to exhume his remains from the prison cemetery and reinter him at Douaumont.

The great traitor of Vichy; the great hero of Verdun: A generation before he collaborated with the Germans, he vexed them madly. "Who could have imagined," one of their official reports groused, "that cut off from all rail service, these damned Frenchmen, rather than abandon the condemned area, would find a way to put into place a two-way caravan of motor vehicles, circulating in a never-ending chain—a gigantic conveyer belt, rolling day and night as if operated by a pulley system, between Bar-le-Duc and the battle site—constantly and tirelessly restocking this horrifically gruesome battlefield with new cannons and ammunition?"

Still, the French—who fought this battle alone, aided only by their own colonial troops—were barely holding on. Despite that gigantic conveyer belt, and all those *poilus* rotating through the sector, it looked for months as if the Germans would prevail sooner or later. By the spring of 1916, French and British commanders had decided to launch an offensive against deeply entrenched, heavily fortified lines that had remained static for more than a year along the Somme River in Picardy, about 150 miles west of the Meuse, for the purpose of diverting at least some German forces from Verdun.

It was as if the whole thing were planned for maximum dramatic effect: The attack commenced on July 1, promptly at 7:30 A.M.; a few minutes before that, the British detonated a chain of mines that ran underneath the German lines, some packed with tens of thousands of tons of the explosive ammonal. If these stunned the Germans, it wasn't for long. The British took nearly sixty thousand casualties just on that day, some fourteen thousand in the first ten minutes alone; Newfoundland's only regiment lost 90 percent of their men at Beaumont-Hamel on July 1, 1916, including every officer they had. The French fared somewhat better—they lost fewer than ten thousand men that day, and took more ground than the British did—and German losses were more or less on par with the French. But for the British, July 1, 1916, would become synonymous with the wasteful carnage of war. It was the worst day in their military's history. And it was only the beginning.

The Battle of the Somme would last four and a half months, and even before the shooting stopped, people were debating whether even a fraction of the slaughter could be justified; historians have been doing so ever since. It is true that the Allies succeeded in their objective of relieving the pressure on Verdun. But doing so cost them as many casualties as they had incurred in that longer battle. The lines hadn't shifted appreciably. The Germans took a lot of casualties, too, but they were still there, and still standing. As for Verdun, it is generally seen as a French victory—though perhaps a Pyrrhic one. Yes, the Germans took tremendous losses at Verdun, too; but not as many as the French. And yes, the Germans failed to bleed France white. But they got pretty close.

Verdun and the Somme were two of the greatest battles of the war. But they were just two, among thousands.

And yet, for most French, Verdun *is* the Great War. And most British feel the same way about the Somme.

✳ ✳ ✳

Raon-l'Étape is a picturesque town in the foothills of the Vosges Mountains, not too far from the German border. It saw fighting during the Battle of the Frontiers in 1914, and sent a lot of its men off to fight, and die, elsewhere on the Western Front. Like every other French city, town, village and hamlet I have ever visited or heard about, Raon-l'Étape built a monument to its war dead sometime after the armistice, in this case a large granite pedestal topped with a bronze sculpture of three *poilus* doggedly advancing across a muddy battlefield, two of them on their knees. At the base of the pedestal is a small, polished plaque:

AN URN CONTAINING SOIL
FROM DOUAUMONT
WAS BURIED AT THE FOOT OF THIS MONUMENT
JUNE 3, 1956

Douaumont, one of the nineteen forts that ringed Verdun, is two hours away; there's plenty of soil upon which French blood was shed right there in Raon-l'Étape. "Typical," one French historian I know said when I told him about it. "It seems like people only want to remember Verdun."

It can be hard to argue with that. It can be hard, even, to describe the space Verdun occupies in the collective French psyche.

To begin with, because the French Army rotated just about every man it had on the Western Front through Verdun at some point in 1916, most living French people have at least a tenuous connection to the place. And most of them, it seems, have either visited it or hope to someday. Anyone I mentioned Verdun to Over There—history buff or history agnostic, deeply religious or profoundly secular, militarist or pacifist, old or young—revered it.

The city of Verdun, though large for the rural *département* of Meuse—always referred to by residents as La Meuse—is fairly small, with a population of fewer than twenty thousand. And the city itself, though it fell under German guns, was never the site of any actual fighting. That happened in a crescent around it, at and in between those nineteen forts that ringed the city. It's a sizeable area, larger than all of Paris, and greater by an order of magnitude or two than places like Gettysburg that Americans typically envision when they think of battlefields. And though there are plenty of monuments in that sizeable area, it's nothing like Gettysburg, where it's all but impossible to find a spot from which you can't see at least one. This battlefield is much too vast for that. And many of the monuments are quite different from the stout stones and statuary you would see at Revolutionary or Civil War sites.

They look like something else: like the dimples in the forest floor that line the path to Colonel Driant's memorial, so many of them that there is no flat ground anywhere. And like the signs that warn you, as you enter a patch of woods, to stay on the marked trails and leave your picnic baskets and soccer balls in the car—not out of respect for the history of the place, but because it's quite likely there are still unexploded shells nearby, just below the dirt, or perhaps sitting on top of it. You could call all the "red zones" around Verdun—places that have not yet been sufficiently cleared of unexploded Great War ordnance to be deemed safe, or "green"—monuments. Potentially interactive ones.

Some of the largest monuments at Verdun are its *villages détruit,* nine villages that were destroyed during the battle and never rebuilt, but are all still marked on maps, and still elect mayors, even with a combined population of zero. (I'm not sure who, exactly, does the voting.) One of them, Fleury-devant-Douaumont, changed hands more than a dozen times in 1916, though during the latter months of the battle there really wasn't anything left to take possession of. The only edifice there today is a small stone chapel built after the war. Fleury's landscape is more dramatic than the surface of the moon: Littered relentlessly with mounds and shell holes, it is difficult to traverse without rugged shoes, strong calves, and a really good sense of balance. Worn footpaths wander where once there were streets. Small signs mark what was where before February 21, 1916: Plumber. Weaver. Blacksmith. Farm. Tinsmith. Baker. Vineyard. Roadmender. Café/Grocery. Smelter. Wash house. School. Church. Parsonage.

Town Hall. Fleury was first settled in 1212. Some four hundred people lived here before the war. None returned afterward.

There is no museum at, or of, Fleury; aside from those little signs and that small chapel, which houses old photos and descriptions of the village before and during the war, nothing has been done to it since the armistice. A plaque offers a multilingual exhortation from the French historian Gérard Canini:

> In front of the chapels erected in memory of the destroyed villages, you will remember that there were men, women and children who loved this Lorraine landscape, who plowed its heavy, meager soil. There were men here who lived at peace and the mortal remains of their ancestors are now mingled with those of dead soldiers! All are now protected by the Ossuary where the soul of the battlefield still quivers and where burns the eternal flame of devotion.

The ossuary—L'Ossuaire de Douaumont, which contains the bones of 130,000 unidentified men, French and German, killed at Verdun—is a couple of minutes away. An enormous shrine that from the outside vaguely resembles an airport light-rail car impaled upon a barbecue skewer, it's more like a monastery inside, a long corridor bisected by an entry foyer and pocked with alcoves, all of it coated with an eerie orange light that pours in through tinted glass cubes. Each alcove is dedicated to a specific sector of the battlefield; remains that are discovered in that sector—and remains still surface at Verdun all the time—are interred in or underneath a pair of marble sarcophagi in that alcove. The inside walls are all composed of stone blocks upon which are engraved the details of men who were killed at Verdun: names, thousands of them, along with their units and their birth and death dates, or at least the date they were last seen alive. There's a chapel off one of the corridors, a good-sized chamber where mass is celebrated several times a day, although it rarely intrudes upon the quiet that prevails outside its closed doors. Conversation is strongly discouraged; so are photographs. Footsteps resonate. Just being there makes you want to walk softly, and behave.

The skewer is a slender, pointed 150-foot tower; for a fee, you can ascend (by foot) to an observatory from which you can view much of the battlefield. You can talk and take pictures all you like up there, but it's a small space, cold in winter and hot in summer, and you probably won't linger very long.

Stepping out into daylight, you are immediately confronted by a vast French World War I cemetery, the largest one in the country; it's hard to take in the whole thing even from the observatory. All of its markers—crosses, tablets and minarets, more than sixteen thousand in all, each one a dull tan concrete—were replaced for the centennial by new ones that are the same, only whiter. These men, all of them French or colonial troops, do not represent all of the known dead of Verdun. They do not even represent all of the known dead of Douaumont.

Fort Douaumont, the largest and best positioned of the nineteen forts that were supposed to protect Verdun, is just a couple of minutes north and east of L'Ossuaire, but it is, in ways both visual and rhetorical, a different world. If the ossuary is like a cloister, the fort is like a jungle gym, rugged and inviting, there to be touched and climbed all over, marveled at aloud, selfied. It's nothing at all like one of those forts constructed along the American eastern seaboard between the Revolution and the Civil War, all brown block walls and clean angles. Built between 1885 and the eve of the war, Fort Douaumont is set into the sloping earth, stone and dirt commingling to form something that is somehow both ancient and futuristic, rugged and ruined, something you would not be surprised to encounter in *Mad Max* or *Dune*. Stone turrets that would not be out of place in a Crusader castle are interspersed with metal observation cupolas that resemble Stormtrooper helmets from *Star Wars*. You look at its solid but haphazard sprawl and wonder how anyone could either defend it *or* take it.

The French high command probably wondered the same thing; despite pleas from men like Colonel Driant, they left the place virtually unmanned and unequipped by early 1916. On the fifth day of the battle, a small German raiding party managed to capture it, almost by accident. Despite the propaganda victory that represented, the Germans probably regretted doing so shortly thereafter, as they discovered how costly the place was to defend, or even to man. At one point, nearly seven hundred German soldiers were killed in a fire that started, according to some accounts, when a few of them inadvisedly used flamethrower fuel to heat up their coffee. Still, it took the French eight months, at a cost of tens of thousands of *poilus,* to take it back. If you know these things, the fort seems haunted; if you don't, as is apparently the case with most of the children who visit, it just seems like a big playground. They probably don't feel guilty after scampering around a place that once cost so very many men their lives.

But I did.

* * *

The first time I visited L'Ossuaire, as I exited the cloister and walked around to my car, I noticed several people outside crouching down along the outer wall and peering into little windows set just above their ankles. Something interesting must be going on in the boiler room, I thought; but when I bent over and pressed my face against one of the thick old panes, I snapped back in horror: Just on the other side, a human skull, complete with a large, jagged hole in its forehead, gazed back at me. It bobbed on a sea of bones several feet deep; other windows revealed chambers equally full of femurs, clavicles, ribs, and scapulae. I felt like I was seeing something I wasn't supposed to, something so unlike the beautiful, dignified space I had just left. And yet, I thought, this must be part of the memorial. There are no signs directing visitors to it; indeed, to get to it you have to step over or under a little rope. But there are windows there, and no one to chase the curious away. Maybe the strangeness of the place was intentional, a wordless commentary on the strangeness of war itself.

Perhaps the strangest monument at Verdun is the Tranchée des Baïonnettes, the bayonet trench—a concrete enclosure, built after the war, within which you can see, poking up through the soil, the bayonet tips of a company of French soldiers who were buried alive by a German shell as they were about to go over the top. Or, I should say, *supposedly* see; I've been several times and, squint and strain thought I might, I've never really been sure if I was seeing the tips of bayonets or, for that matter, anything at all except a bed of cold, dark dirt. I mentioned this to a few French friends after my last visit, and they quickly assured me that the whole story is fanciful speculation mixed with a healthy dose of fabulism. A lot of people line up to see it anyway. A lot of people also drive the length of La Voie Sacrée, and wander through the woods, green zones and red, looking for markers, or cartridges, or the spot where their great-uncle was killed; stroll through cemeteries, open fields, *villages détruits*. You'll find a lot of people crawling over just about every corner and crevice of Verdun— French people, and Germans, and Belgians, and even Dutch.

But not, in my experience, British.

One evening, as I sat at an outdoor café in Sainte-Menehould, a charming old town in the Argonne about twenty-five miles west of Verdun, a middle-aged English couple strolled by, chatting; grateful to hear my native tongue—a rare sound in that area—I said hello. They sat down, told me they were passing through on their way to Germany, asked if I was doing the same.

"No," I said. "I'm visiting World War I sites."

"Ah," the man said. "We're crossing paths. We just came from there."

"Where?"

"The Western Front," he said. "You know, the Somme."

Hm. I thought about telling them that the Somme was not the entire Western Front, then decided to be more diplomatic. "There are lots of fascinating World War I sites around here, too," I said, trying on a tone that, to my inner ear, sounded more enthusiastic than scolding. "You should check some out while you're here."

"There are?" they said.

"Sure," I said. "You're actually in the Argonne right now."

Blank stares. Pursed lips.

"You'll probably pass through the Saint-Mihiel salient on your way to Germany. Lots of fighting there."

Silence. No change in expression.

"Verdun's just a half hour to the east." I nodded conspiratorially.

The woman looked at her feet, the man at his watch.

I wasn't exaggerating when I said that, to most British, the Somme *is* World War I. You could (and I did) say something very similar about the French and Verdun, but the French are aware that there was a lot of fighting elsewhere in France and Belgium, and that there was still more fighting in other parts of Europe, and Asia, and Africa; they probably even know a fair bit about at least some of it. But to them, Verdun is the apotheosis of the Great War—its essence, really, the gravest existential threat France had ever faced. It helps that France prevailed, or at least that one could make a defensible claim that France prevailed. The *Boche* threw everything they had at Verdun; they did not pass. Defending Verdun cost the French terribly, but Verdun did not fall.

It's hard to construct a similarly triumphant narrative of the Somme.

You can try. You can say that the British never took as many casualties afterward as they did that first day, or that the Germans ended up taking a lot of casualties, too. People do; but if they know even that much about the battle, they almost certainly regard it as a horrific catastrophe. Pétain may have been a villain in the Second World War, but at least he was a hero at Verdun. The standard narrative of Field Marshal Douglas Haig, the British commander at the Somme, is that he was an incompetent butcher untroubled by the prospect of sending many thousands of his men to their deaths for absolutely nothing. His great battle of 1916 has become synonymous with senseless, purposeless, exorbitant slaughter.

And yet, the British cannot get enough of the place.

The Somme is the only area in France where you might hear more English spoken than French. Not that the locals speak English; they don't, not even in places you might expect them to, like tourism bureaus. But for much of the year, they're simply outnumbered. You are more likely, at those times, to see the Union Jack flying than the Tricolor; to hear "God Save the Queen" being sung than "La Marseillaise."

Local shops cater to British appetites. In the village of Ovillers-la-Boisselle, you can enjoy a nice pot of Darjeeling at the Old Blighty Tea Room after a solemn visit to the nearby Lochnagar Crater, a massive bowl created at 7:28 A.M. on July 1, 1916, when the British set off 48,000 pounds of ammonal buried in underground chambers. The site is staffed entirely by British volunteers, mostly retirees; every July 1, at 7:28 A.M., they re-create the explosion with lights and smoke. "Then the pipers start in," one told me. "It's very moving." And always very well attended; some ceremonies, another volunteer told me, draw more British tourists than the site can accommodate.

They come over on their own, and by the busload; take the ferry to Calais or Zeebrugge. There are English tour guides who ferry over their own packed tour buses. Other visitors bring their own cars, and have to adjust to driving on the right with their steering wheel also on the right. It can take a while. You'll know when you're behind one who hasn't quite gotten it yet. You'll really know when one is coming at you. Following them isn't a whole lot easier. They brake frequently, and unpredictably, to read signs, check maps, eyeball cemeteries and monuments. Some will pull over just because they spot another group walking through a field somewhere and figure there's got to be something worth checking out there. People have pulled over just to find out what *I* was looking at. It usually turned out that they knew more about it than I did.

They stay at inns where all the guests are English. The owners, too. They dine together at tables festooned with HP Sauce, drink English tea, eat English pudding for dessert. The conversation is of British politics and football teams, which British politicians or celebrities are secretly gay or pedophilic or cross-dressers, who deserves to be a member of the royal family and who doesn't. And, of course, the war: battles and units, tactics and weapons, the failures of generals and politicians, the occasional figure who actually knew what he was doing but was ignored until it was almost too late. Occasionally, another war might creep in; one night, I returned to my inn late and passed two gentlemen avidly discussing the merits and shortcomings of the B-17 bomber, down to minute specifications.

Mostly, though, it's the First World War—specifically, the exploits of the British Expeditionary Force (BEF) in the First World War. English visitors to the Somme seem split about evenly between first-timers and perennials; the latter come every year, if they can manage it. Some have been doing so for decades. They run into other perennials and celebrate the reunion joyously. Some live just a few miles apart back home, but only know each other from the Somme, and only see each other here. Some come the same week or two every year, and see the same people every year. They visit the same sites, walk the same ground. Every year.

The Somme battlefield is about thirty miles of farmland, flat here, gently rolling there. In high tourist season it is very green, but broken up often. Unlike at Verdun, where the French dead lie in a few very large cemeteries, there are British cemeteries everywhere around here, some with a thousand graves, some with a hundred. While everyone buried men where they fell during the war, the French, Germans, and Americans often consolidated their burial sites afterward; the British didn't. Their cemeteries tend to contain mostly men who fell in a single action. Often, most or even all are from the same regiment, and sometimes from the same town. The cemeteries' names, written on green-and-white arrow-shaped signs, sound like housing developments: Delville Wood. Peake Wood. Contalmaison Chateau. Caterpillar Valley. Thistle Dump. (OK, maybe not that last one.) They sit in the middle of open fields like housing developments, too, surrounded by walls, fronted by gates. Interspersed among them are monuments: steles, obelisks, crosses, Celtic crosses, statuary; English, Scottish, Australian, South African, Canadian. The entire Beaumont-Hamel battlefield is a monument to Newfoundland's regiment. Ulster Tower, which honors the 36th Ulster Division—they lost nearly five thousand men on July 1, 1916—is a replica of a memorial tower on an old estate in Northern Ireland. Nearby, in the village of Thiepval, a massive multilevel redbrick arch bears the names of more than seventy thousand BEF troops who went missing at the Somme. It sits on a hill, topped by flags and surrounded by trees; at first glimpse, from several miles off, it looks like a fairy-tale palace.

For a long time, it is said, British policy was to make the world England; in this part of Picardy, you could say that Britain's Commonwealth War Graves Commission managed to accomplish what centuries of cross-channel warfare and intrigue could not.

✶ ✶ ✶

The Somme battlefield, which before July 1, 1916, had been all farm and pasture, was reclaimed for those purposes afterward: Trenches were filled in, shell holes leveled. And then the tourists started coming, so many that a lot of farmers felt pressure to beautify their property—make it more quaint, photogenic. Hard as I tried, I just could not picture a battle happening here, much less one of the greatest in the history of the world.

So I went to Flanders.

If the Somme was four months of the war's most bitter and futile savagery, Flanders was four years of it. If there was any place where you could reasonably expect to behold the lasting scars of the horrors that characterized the war in the thirty-two months before the United States entered it, it would be Flanders. And that turned out to be true—in one spot. But those scars aren't visible; you can only perceive them using other senses. If you rely only upon your eyes, Flanders appears even more remote from those historic horrors than the Somme, for one reason: It's in Belgium.

I didn't even spot the sign telling me I was entering Belgium, but I knew I had done so because everything—the road, the buildings, the cars, even the sky—suddenly looked shinier, more affluent. And more controlled. The French, for example, can be very, well, laissez-faire about speeding; in Belgium, there are unmanned cameras everywhere, on highways and local roads, monitoring your velocity and recording your license plate. Fortunately, I'd been warned; now you have, too.

Belgium is a much smaller country than France, with a vibrant economy, and Flanders is a particularly industrious, and prosperous, region of it. Though it was once almost entirely farms, the land there is, for the most part, deemed too valuable for agriculture these days. The town of Waregem saw fighting right up until the armistice; in November 1918, two American divisions, the 37th and 91st, fought there. After the war, when the AEF laid out a burial ground in Waregem, it was still all farmland. Today, the Flanders Field American Cemetery, with 368 graves, sits in a neighborhood of two-million-euro houses. It is far from singular. If the Somme is pastoral countryside, Flanders is posh suburb. You'd have an easier time picturing a Civil War battle being fought in Palm Beach.

I did manage, here and there, to spot a few recognizable battle sites in Flanders, but they all looked hopelessly alien to their surroundings, compact and self-contained pockets of trauma wedged into tidy, orderly neighborhoods. As I strolled around the little park in the village of Zille-beke that comprised what was once Hill 60—from 1915 to 1917, Australian and German sappers waged an underground battle there that cost many lives—I watched fellow visitors stare at the gouged and upheaved land-scape as if they had come across a surrealistic bronze sculpture in a room full of Old Master paintings. No doubt they watched me doing the same thing.

Then I came to Ypres.

The unofficial capital of Flanders, Ypres looks like a medieval city—surprising when you consider that it was the site, all told, of five battles between 1914 and 1918, and was more or less destroyed by the war's end. After the armistice, though, it was rebuilt so thoroughly, and has been so well preserved since, that it looks like a particularly charming Hollywood back lot. Flanders is in the Dutch part of Belgium, which means most everyone speaks pretty good English; in Ypres, they all do, quite possibly better than you do. The city's economy is built on tourism, particularly British and Australian. I'm not sure if it actually gets more Australians than English, or only seems like it does because the Australians are less shy about making their presence known. Walk into just about any pub solely to use the restroom and, if it's detected you're Anglophone—the accent matters not—you will probably be greeted heartily, implored repeatedly to sit down until you assent, and plied with ale for as long as you can take it.

Ypres's expansive main plaza, the Grote Markt, teems with English-speakers. It's dominated by the enormous commercial edifice known as Cloth Hall, and by Saint Martin's cathedral; both were built in the thirteenth century, reduced to rubble during the war, and meticulously reconstructed afterward. The rest of the square is cafés and restau-rants, chocolatiers, and storefronts with names like Tommy's Souvenirs ("Tommy" being the BEF equivalent of doughboy), the British Grenadier

Bookshop, and Over the Top Tours. Union Jacks are everywhere you look. If you go to the right place at the right time, you can buy a block of dark chocolate shaped like a British Mark V tank. "I think eighty percent of our clients are English," the woman who sold it to me said. It sounded low.

The Grote Markt fairly teems with tourists during the day, but as evening takes hold, they're all drawn, like water down a spout, toward where it narrows and ends suddenly at a massive triumphal arch of brick and cement: the Menin Gate.

The gate is a memorial to the BEF dead of Ypres. Imposing and surrounded by legend, it was completed and unveiled in 1927; shortly thereafter, a fire brigade in the area sent some buglers out one evening to stand under the arch and play the "Last Post," an army bugle call signifying the end of the day's duty—the British equivalent of "Taps." Soon it became a tradition; it has sounded every evening at precisely 8:00 P.M. since July 2, 1928. During the second war, the ceremony was temporarily moved to a military cemetery in England, but they never missed a night. (In July 2015, a couple of weeks after my visit, they held the 30,000th consecutive Last Post ceremony.) I had mentioned to several British perennials on the Somme that I hoped to attend a Last Post ceremony. "Better get there by seven thirty, or you won't see a thing," one advised; "I wouldn't get there past seven," another insisted.

That in mind, I managed to break free from my generous Australian hosts at the pub and headed down to the Menin Gate around six o'clock, while the square was still full of lingering tourists. The few people poking around down there at that point only made the place feel even more outsized: Its arch alone—just the opening, not the structure around it—is forty-eight feet high and thirty wide; the chamber it leads to, known as the Hall of Memory, is forty yards long and twenty-two wide. The hall's barrel-vaulted ceiling, which is even taller than the arch, is coffered, but every other surface—inside and out, floor to ceiling—is covered with names: British and Australian, Indian and South African, Canadian and West Indian. They built the Menin Gate on such an enormous scale because they wanted to have enough wall space to list the name of every British Commonwealth soldier who went missing at Ypres. But they miscalculated: It could only fit 54,382 of them. They had to build another memorial nearby, known as Tyne Cot, for the remaining 34,916 names. I never made it to that one; just looking at the names on the Menin Gate was dizzying. If you take it upon yourself to try to read every one, even in a single section of wall, you can get to feeling claustrophobic, as if all those thousands of men are standing there with you.

I climbed several sets of steps from the Hall of Memory to an upper outdoor gallery (also covered with names) to get some air and a little space; when I returned to the hall, a few minutes later—it was six thirty now—I saw exactly one couple lined up for the ceremony, propped up against a large pillar. Something in their relaxed posture told me they had done this before. I walked over and asked if theirs was a good spot to view the ceremony. "Absolutely!" the man replied, in an Australian accent. He was smaller than his countrymen I'd just left at the pub, and older, a slight man with dark brown hair in his late fifties. He and his wife, a petite blonde around the same age, were, like the group I had spent a couple of hours drinking with, friendly, gregarious, and very enthusiastic about, well, everything. They completed each other's sentences, at least until they got talking about the gate, at which point the man became so excited that he took over their side of the conversation entirely. They had been to the ceremony many times before, they told me, but had recently retired and were just now embarking on a nine-month trip around the world; figured this was as fine a place to start as any. The man, in particular, seemed as awed by the place as if he had only read about it in books and was just now seeing it for the first time; rattled off history, dimensions, and statistics, some of which were a bit suspect. "There are three hundred and fifty-two thousand names on these walls," he declared, shaking his head. "Never missed a night, not even during World War II with the Germans all about. A piper would sneak out here every night, play the 'Last Post,' and then run away while they shot at him. Never got him." It's the kind of place that generates a lot of myths and exaggerations.

As people started streaming in, the couple, surprised to find an American in Ypres, asked me what I knew about the war. I talked a bit about this and that, to appreciative nods, then decided to blow their minds by dropping the name of Sir John Monash. Monash, an Australian, is regarded by many historians as the finest general the BEF had in that war. I said as much. It worked: They were impressed and excited, couldn't believe I'd heard of the man.

"Monash never got the credit he deserved," the man asserted. "The English never thought much of him, you know, until late in the war. But he was the best they had, and by God they knew it by the end of the war."

"They saw him as just another colonial," I said. "They thought the best generals had to be English."

"That's what the historians *like to say*," my friend replied, his voice taking on a fervent tone more suited to a sermon or a political rally. "But that's not the real story. They didn't try to marginalize him because he was Australian—they did it because he was Jewish!"

"Who knew?" I said.

"Everyone in Australia!" he replied. Who knew?

By seven forty-five, hundreds of people were packed onto the sidewalks and stairways underneath the gate; hundreds more filled the streets outside, where they could not possibly see a thing. Officials in suits and ties gathered in the center of the hall, behind a podium. Chatter grew louder, rolled around the barrel vault, and fell, amplified, on the other side of the hall. And then, precisely at eight o'clock, a little bell sounded, and everyone—a thousand people, maybe more—fell silent, immediately and utterly. Even the children. I'd never experienced anything like it.

In the archway nearest to me, several men in handsome fire brigade uniforms appeared, clutching bugles polished to a high shine. At a silent signal, they marched in, their footsteps echoing off the ceiling and walls, and suddenly came to a stop a few yards from me, perfectly aligned. At another silent signal, they raised their bugles to their lips in unison, took a breath, waited a beat, and played the "Last Post." It did sound a bit like "Taps"—a touch livelier—and lasted about ninety seconds. When it was done, no one clapped or made any kind of sound; no one moved.

After another thirty seconds or so, one of the men in suits stepped to the podium and made a few brief remarks, in a Flemish accent, about the names on the walls and what they represented. When he was done, another man in a suit stepped up and read, in an English accent, a short biography of one of the names engraved on the walls, a soldier who was killed a hundred years ago that day. Then a third suited man, bearing a local accent, stepped up and called upon representatives from preselected organizations and institutions, as well as a few school groups, to come forward and silently lay wreaths, about a dozen in all.

And then, as promptly as it began, the ceremony ended, and everyone started pouring out into the narrow medieval streets of Ypres, Belgium. The whole thing had lasted ten minutes.

I turned to my Australian neighbors to say good-bye, but it felt, somehow, wrong to speak out loud just yet; and judging by the look on the man's face—eyes twitching at the corners, mouth screwed up tight—I'm not sure he could have said much of anything right then. I extended my hand to him, instead, and he grasped it in his, tightly, and held it firm for eight or ten seconds but didn't shake it. We nodded at each other, and he released my hand; his wife rested one of hers on my shoulder and looked at me deeply for a moment. Then we turned away from each other and walked out, separately. I wandered, slowly, back up the old lane to the Grote Markt, to the restaurants and chocolate shops and Tommy's Souvenirs, thinking about how, rather than traveling back in time, a thousand people stood together on one spot and for ten minutes brought 1915 to the present. It really happened. And no one said a word.

* * *

And that's what the United States of America missed by entering the First World War "late." Don't make the mistake, though, of thinking that the men of the AEF were spared. The war was far from over by the time they got there. New horrors, unthinkable in those early years, awaited them, and they set off to face them already burdened with the knowledge of all those earlier horrors. They trained on ground that was deeply gouged and scarred; ate and slept among bones that would later be collected at Douaumont and other ossuaries. Long before any of them fired a shot, or got shot at, they could see, and feel, how close the war was. A century later, following their trail along the Western Front from Lorraine to Picardy and back again, it still felt close. Sometimes too close.

In all my time traveling around northwestern France and Belgium, though, with the exception of those ten minutes under the Menin Gate, the war always felt remote to me. The Somme and Flanders are iconic historical sites where the history itself is extremely well hidden from view. You might as well put them out of your mind now: None of what you're about to see from here on out looks or feels anything like those two places do today. The Somme and Flanders are sites where battles once took place. The rest are battle sites.

The difference will soon become obvious.

CHAPTER THREE

CHEMIN DES AMÉRICAINS

Turn your back on the Somme, now, and look ahead, about 250 miles east and one year forward, to the little farming village of Bathelémont. You're still in France, but just barely; between 1871 and 1918, Bathelémont sat right on the border with Germany, across from formerly French villages that had been taken by the Germans after the Franco-Prussian War. Nevertheless, Bathelémont, which is set among rolling hills about an hour from the Vosges Mountains, is unmistakably French—linguistically, culturally, architecturally. You would never find a place like the Old Blighty Tea Room in Bathelémont. Come to think of it, I don't recall seeing a commercial establishment of any kind there.

To those who think of Flanders or the Somme or Verdun or the Argonne when they think of the Western Front, this is a strange theater to conjure, this easternmost part of Lorraine, and Alsace, and the Vosges. It can be hilly, even mountainous; in 1915, Hilsenfirst, in Alsace, saw the highest fighting on the Western Front of the entire war, at 4,167 feet above sea level. The French Cemetery at La Fontenelle, in the commune of Ban-de-Sapt in the Vosges, sits atop a very tall hill—impossible to imagine in a place like the Somme—where brutal fighting took place on every slope in the summer of 1915. The topography here somehow makes the war feel more personal; the pain in your calves as you hike the inclines without a heavy rifle and pack and wool uniform connects you, perhaps, with the notion that combat is difficult even for those who come through it unscathed. There are little monuments here and there, mostly dating to the summer of 1914—when it must have still felt possible to document each tragic death the war wrought individually—like the small stone cross I spotted, set back off the road in a clearing:

HERE IS BURIED
ANTOINE LAHACHE
PRIEST OF LA VOIVRE
SHOT BY THE GERMANS
AUGUST 29, 1914

Bathelémont is in Lorraine, but even by the standards of that *région*, it's small, and lonely. Although it's only about twenty miles east of Nancy, a city of 100,000 that draws a lot of tourists—the city center has a palace, a cathedral, and an expansive plaza, all of them jewels of ornate eighteenth-century French architecture—it's rare to see anyone out walking the streets of Bathelémont, which has maybe five dozen residents, and no architectural jewels. It's the kind of place that looks as if nothing has ever happened there. And yet, within a span of just eleven days in the autumn of 1917, the American Expeditionary Forces experienced two monumental firsts in Bathelémont—one exultant; the other grim.

✷ ✷ ✷

They were here, those Americans, because this was supposed to be a "quiet" sector, a place they could get used to the trenches and develop defensive tactics and strategies without facing too much danger: a division,

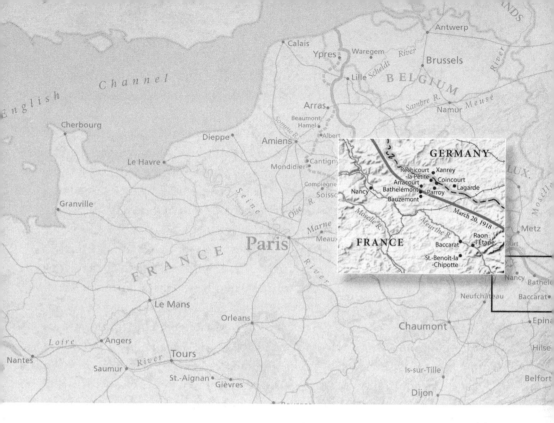

the most basic large U.S. Army unit, around twenty-five thousand troops at full strength. The 1st Division, to be specific.

The 1st was considered a fairly storied unit, especially within its own ranks. It was composed, at least at the war's outset, of Regular Army men, career soldiers who had served primarily in peacetime. Many had gone down to Mexico with General John Joseph Pershing to capture the guerilla leader Pancho Villa in 1916, and though they had failed in this objective, they still recalled the expedition fondly. The following year, when the United States entered the war, its entire army numbered just 200,000 men, a third of whom were actually National Guard troops. (By comparison, there were more than three times as many soldiers in the U.S. Army *before* the Japanese attacked Pearl Harbor in 1941; presently there are around 1.3 million active duty troops in the U.S. Armed Forces, and an additional 800,000 or so in reserve.) The 1st did its best to foster the rumor that its men were the cream of the Regular Army. Other divisions, especially the 2nd and the 3rd, didn't much care for that claim, but the 1st was the first American division to send troops off to France—setting sail on June 14, 1917, just two months after America entered the war—so they were free to foment that reputation without challenge Over There,

at least for a while. By the time the last of them got there, a few days before Christmas, there were several other divisions in France, including at
least one complete one, the 26th, comprising some twenty-five thousand
National Guard troops from New England. General Pershing, though—
now the commander of the American Expeditionary Forces—was said to
have a strong preference for Regular Army troops in general, and for the
1st in particular. Later in the war, the division would be nicknamed the
Big Red One—not as an assertion of primacy, but because its divisional
insignia was in fact a big, red one.

The 1st Division was almost certainly the most heavily chronicled
military unit in American history to that point; swarms of reporters
followed it everywhere. It was a time when newspapers put out several
editions every day, and major American cities had several papers in competition with each other: There was an insatiable appetite for copy, and
the 1st was good for plenty. It had a lot of notable names in its ranks,
for one thing, including two of former president Theodore Roosevelt's
sons, Theodore Jr. and Archie. The rest of its men, every one of them
volunteers, came from all over the country. And as the first doughboys
to arrive in France, almost everything they did was endowed with significance and coated in symbolism. Elements of the division paraded
through the streets of Paris on July 4, 1917, to announce their arrival, and
made their way to the tomb of the Marquis de Lafayette, where someone
reputedly announced: "Lafayette, we are here!" That alone sold an awful
lot of papers.

The United States of America had entered the Great War that April
as a co-belligerent, not an ally. That may seem like a distinction without
a difference, but legally, it gave General Pershing the prerogative to decide where, when, how and—most important—under whom his troops
would go into battle. From the very beginning, Pershing was anything
but shy about exercising that prerogative. This enraged and alienated
the British, who had expected doughboys to serve in British units under
British commanders. The French, though, were just happy to have the
Americans there under any circumstances, and they assumed primary
responsibility for training the new arrivals. It was no small task; Pershing insisted they be thoroughly prepared for combat before they entered the line. According to the *History of the First Division During the
World War, 1917–1919*, published in 1922, they had a long way to go when
they first arrived:

Although the troops were basically trained in the fundamentals of the soldier and were full of enthusiasm and vigor . . . tactics had changed entirely during the war and were continually undergoing further changes, due to the employment of new weapons and new formations and to the stabilized conditions of the Armies in long lines of trenches with no flanks. It was, therefore, necessary that the Division should be instructed in the style of fighting that the Allied Nations had found to be the most effective after three years of experience. So desperate and cruel was the struggle that ignorant troops would have been sacrificed without accomplishing any useful results. The plan of training prescribed by General Headquarters, American Expeditionary Forces, allowed a division one month for acclimatization and instruction in small units from battalions down. The battalions were then required to serve one month with French battalions in the trenches in contact with the enemy, and thus learn by experience the application of the methods that had been taught them without being entirely responsible for the defense of the sector. Upon being taken out of the trenches, a third month was devoted to the training of the combined Division in the tactics of open warfare. The Division was then ready to take over and defend a sector in the line.

By all accounts, the training went very well; the Americans were apt pupils, the French dedicated teachers. They got along with each other famously.

Phase one was mostly done at Gondrecourt, about forty miles west of Nancy and far behind the lines. Phase two was done here, right on them. The *History* describes this area as "a rolling and attractive country traversed by the Rhine-Marne Canal . . . suitable for the maneuver of large armies," and it remains so today, although it is difficult to picture armies of anything converging upon such quiet, open terrain. Even the cows and horses around here seem to prefer being unencumbered by company.

The sleepiness of the place didn't diminish the doughboys' excitement at being there. They were thrilled to be posted at the front, at last, and more than eager to get into the action, determined to make some noise in an erstwhile "quiet" sector. I suspect a lot of them didn't care to give much thought, at that point, to how little experience they really had; nor to how much the enemy, just a few hundred yards away, did. But that would all change very soon. The Big Red One was about to find out just how unquiet a quiet sector could get.

✫ ✫ ✫

I should say get unquiet *again,* because back during the war's first great clash, the Battle of the Frontiers, things had been anything but quiet here. Like the Americans would be in October 1917, the French and Germans of August 1914 were terribly excited to be fighting at last. It did not serve them well, especially the French. Again and again, they attacked; again and again, they found the Germans ready for them. Maybe it was poor communication, or poor coordination. Maybe they just couldn't believe it. Whatever the case, the fighting quickly spread out all along the border, from eastern Belgium down to Alsace, the French attacking, the Germans counterattacking. Both sides lost a lot of men. The French lost a lot more.

You can assemble a picture of the Battle of the Frontiers like a mosaic, with bits you see here, pieces you hear there. In the village of Lagarde, a small French military cemetery, built on a gentle slope, holds 550 dead; there are two mass graves and about 200 markers, almost every one of which bears the date August 11, 1914. They were men from the south— Nîmes, Avignon—who'd hurried up north to join the battle. If you stand in the cemetery and face out, beyond the gate, you can see, past a wide meadow, the woods they charged out of that morning. There were German machine guns here, on this ridge, waiting to meet them when they did.

That kind of thing happened a lot around here during the first six weeks of the war. Hearing that the Germans were heading for Raon-l'Étape—the pretty town in the foothills that has that urn of soil from Douaumont buried at the base of its war memorial—*poilus* rushed there by train, only to be mowed down, as they emerged from boxcars at the station, by Germans who had gotten there first. Not far away, the large cemetery at Saint-Benoît-la-Chipotte is filled with French soldiers who were all killed between August 24 and September 11, 1914. Most were *chasseurs*— literally, hunters—elite troops distinguished by their dark blue uniforms, which didn't do them much good. A memorial outside the gate, to the 86th Brigade, shows a single *chasseur,* standing still, rifle at his side, gazing ahead with a steely determination, something he probably didn't have much opportunity to do in August and September of 1914.

"This was the worst period of the war," Eric Mansuy mused as we looked at that monument, which he believes was built even before the armistice. "It was very, very hot; soldiers were marching fifty kilometers a day, and constantly fighting." Casualties were shockingly high, but the French did not think of letting up. It had not yet occurred to them, it seems, that there might not be a ceiling to the carnage.

Eric is in his late forties, thin and spare, with short brown hair, glasses and a goatee; he looks a great deal like the American public radio personality Brian Lehrer. This section of the Western Front—far eastern Lorraine going into Alsace, encompassing the Vosges Mountains, its foothills, and rolling farmland leading into both—is, unquestionably, his fiefdom; a friend of mine, a French woman who now lives in the United States and had briefly worked on a project with Eric years earlier, recommended I get in touch with him before I visited the area. It was one of the best referrals I've ever gotten: In a country filled with people who are knowledgeable about the First World War, he is exceptionally so. He is also tirelessly enthusiastic, endlessly patient—he will happily answer your questions until *you* are exhausted—and can research like an archivist and read maps like a cartographer. And he's fluent in English. He first learned it as a high school student in the 1980s, when he spent two summers in upstate New York; since 1994 he has taught the language in a high school here in eastern Lorraine. In doing so, he often discusses with his students certain episodes in American history, especially the civil rights movement; when we met he told me he'd been delighted to discover, Googling me before my visit, that I had written about the subject more than once. He greeted me that first morning warmly, as a colleague whose work he admired. By the end of the day, I felt as if we had known each other for years. He has since translated for me more documents than I can count, and helped me research a great many historical matters. Sometimes we engage in lengthy e-mail exchanges when he gets up in the morning and I have yet to go to bed.

Eric cannot remember a time, he says, when he wasn't interested in military history. His background may have something to do with that: His father served in Algeria in the 1950s; his grandfather was a career officer who fought in the Second World War. In his teens, Eric developed an interest in the Vietnam War—the French one, which effectively ended at Dien Bien Phu in 1954. In his twenties, he moved on to *la Grande Guerre*. Three of his great-grandfathers fought in it. One, Émile Auguste Mansuy, was killed near Verdun on October 5, 1914, at the age of 40. Another,

Albert Gerber, who'd been born in annexed Alsace, actually fought for Germany. While this surprised me, Eric said it wasn't at all uncommon. "Alsatians didn't consider themselves French or German," he explained. "They considered themselves Alsatian." Many, he added, still do.

Albert Gerber lived to the age of 93; he died, still living in Alsace, in 1978. A hand-tinted photo of him as a young man in his German uniform shows a proud soldier, gaze set, lips pursed, shoulders squared. His mustache is turned up at the ends like the Kaiser's; there's actually a small inset of the Kaiser himself, for comparison. As a child, Eric knew Albert Gerber, but was never able to have a conversation with him—about the war, or anything else—because the old man spoke only Alsatian.

The third great-grandfather, Henri Georges Curien, who was from the Vosges, did his compulsory military service from 1898 to 1901, and was recalled in 1914, when he was 36. He survived the war, and kept a journal throughout. From 1914 until the summer of 1918, when he was sent to fight on the Marne River, Georges Curien was posted in the Vosges. He was clearly a thoughtful, observant man; his early musings are among the most philosophical I have ever come across in a war diary. Take this entry, from December 20, 1914:

> We leave the main road for a transversal way across the woods. This is a real battlefield we then cross, for we aren't far from La Chipotte pass, which is now nicknamed "The Death Zone." There are but debris of guns and rucksacks, kepis and helmets. Crosses mark the spots of French graves, mere branches the German graves. We can see trees which have been pierced by shells. We wonder how all this must have been like. Did we have to live in such a civilized century to kill each other this way?

Soon, though, he realized that such musings are a luxury war rarely affords. Six months later, still in the Vosges and having been promoted to sergeant, he wrote:

> At dusk, we arrive after encountering a large number of wounded and killed, among whom several officers . . . Bullets come whizzing by our ears . . . Houses catch fire close to us and light up our trenches. All we can do is lie down inside them for, if we were seen, the whole platoon would be dead and gone. We are sure we are going to die in a short while.

At that point, Georges Curien still had three years and five months of war to go. Eric never knew him; he died just thirty-nine months after the armistice, at the age of 44.

Like his great-grandfather, Eric is a fine storyteller. It was he who first told me of the ill-fated French assault on Lagarde, and the slaughter at the train depot in Raon-l'Étape, and what happened to the *chasseurs* at La Chipotte. And in Baccarat, a colorful town of several thousand known for its crystal, he led me to a modest bridge over the Meurthe River and said: "The Germans killed a hundred French soldiers here in ten seconds."

It was August 25, 1914; the men of the 86th Infantry Regiment (not to be confused with the 86th Chasseur Brigade) went to cross the bridge, either unaware that the Germans were lying in wait on the heights across town, or merely unconcerned. "The French were playing by the old rules of warfare at that point," Eric explained. "The old rules were that you didn't use machine guns in the front line, offensively. You used them in your second line, defensively." A few months later, a French expatriate I know in the United States, upon hearing this story, told me: "The French didn't expect the Germans to use machine guns on them; they believed machine guns were only for use against the natives in Africa, etc." According to code, he explained, civilized white men didn't unleash such a savage weapon upon each other.

But the code was dead. When the *poilus* got out onto the bridge, the Germans opened up their *Maschinengewehre*. It took the men of the 86th a few seconds to figure out what was going on; a few more to turn and get off the bridge. "They were shot coming and going" is how Eric put it. One hundred killed in ten seconds.

Near the bridge is Baccarat's *Grande Guerre* memorial. As I mentioned earlier, every city, town, village and hamlet I've ever visited in France has one; after the war, the French government offered funds to every community in the country to build such a monument. In all of France, I am told, only five places declined to do so. Many places later appended to their 14–18 memorials plaques that commemorate their 39–45 dead; some went on to add plaques for the subsequent wars in Algeria and Indochina, too. Baccarat did not, perhaps because its monument, relatively large though it is, didn't have room for any more names. As I often did when coming upon such a memorial, I let my eyes wander over the names that were listed there, more than three hundred of them spread out over five large copper plates; in the last column on the fourth, one row from the bottom, they came to rest on this one:

L. RUBIN, ADJT.

Eric later found the records online: Adjutant Léon Ernest Rubin, 20e Bataillon de Chasseurs à pied, born February 22, 1883, in Buchy, a village in Normandy; later moved to Baccarat. Reported for obligatory military service in 1903. Reported again in 1914. Killed by the enemy October 9, 1914, Aix-Noulette, Pas-de-Calais. Not far from the Belgian border. "Maybe he's a relative?" Eric asked me. No, I replied; impossible. But I have since come to claim Léon Ernest Rubin, anyway. Or maybe he claims me.

The Germans took Baccarat pretty quickly after that affair on the bridge. Much of what they didn't destroy in the process they torched deliberately afterward—public buildings, shops, houses. It was all done by that same evening: August 25, 1914.

On September 13, they left. All of them. Summoned to the Marne, two hundred miles west, where the French were making a stand.

And that's how this sector became "quiet."

It stayed that way until the fall of 1917, when the AEF's 1st Division was sent there for the purpose of getting experience in actual trench warfare.

They did.

★ ★ ★

The Division's infantry arrived in the Sommerviller Sector, which included Bathelémont, on October 21, 1917. Artillery made it there the following day. Both were to be deployed alongside, and under the supervision of, the French 18th Infantry Division. It had been decided at some point—I'm not sure by whom, exactly—that the first American shot of the war should be an artillery shell, not a rifle bullet, which makes sense if you understand that artillery was responsible for more deaths in the First World War than anything else: more than bullets, bombs, gas, barbed wire, and disease, and almost certainly more than at least a few of them combined. (Remember, too, that the infantry weren't there to go on the offensive, but strictly to gain experience at the front; it was possible, theoretically, that they might not fire any rifle shots at all.) The United States did not yet have the means to ship over big guns of its own, so the doughboys would fire the French 75-millimeter gun, which was quite possibly the finest weapon their army possessed. It was celebrated as such throughout the country; I've seen postcards featuring romantic hand-tinted photographs of the gun, along with flowery odes to its might.

The Americans were not impressed with it, at least not at first. "I had to laugh when I looked at the French 75-millimeter guns," wrote Corporal Osborne De Varila of the 6th Field Artillery Regiment's Battery C. "They seemed so small and inferior when compared with our American field pieces. 'If we have to use these toys,' I thought, 'the Huns won't do a thing to us when we get into action.'" After a few days of training, though, he changed his mind about "the little fire-eaters. I found that we could do faster and more accurate work with them than with the more warlike looking American pieces. It is certain that the Germans know to their cost what the little '75's' are capable of doing."

The 6th FA had been assigned the honor of firing the first American shot; the American journalist Floyd Gibbons had essentially embedded himself with them for six weeks, he later told *The New York Times,* just so he could be there when it happened. "I attached myself to the A Battery," he explained, "on the assumption that the A Battery would be the first in action, with B Battery and C Battery following in that order." But when Battery C learned that Battery A "was out to steal the bacon," as De Varila put it, "we howled with rage and apprehension . . . Our battery commander was terribly aroused, for he had his heart set on that first shot."

"There was so much rivalry among the three batteries" for the distinction, Gibbons recalled, "that while the men of the A Battery were digging gun pits for themselves, the men of C Battery, working like Trojans and pulling through mud that was waist deep, took advantage of some old gun pits left by the French and got into position first." And so it was that Battery C ended up firing the first American shot of the Great War, at 6:05 A.M. on October 23, 1917. They fired at Xanrey, a village about five miles to the east. After that, according to accounts, other men in the battery were invited to do the same—twenty-four shells in all. That day's entry in the war diary of the French 18th Division's artillery section notes: "The first gun shots fired by Americans were aimed at a party of enemy workers laboring in the Bavarian Salient, who then dispersed." There is no record of any casualties.

Gibbons gave his interview to *The New York Times* specifically to establish the identity of the man who fired that first shot. He felt compelled to do so because Corporal De Varila, who had been gassed in early 1918 and sent home to help sell Liberty Bonds, published a memoir, *The First Shot for Liberty,* in which he claimed credit for firing it. Gibbons, though, without impugning De Varila—at least explicitly—claimed the honor really belonged to a Sergeant Arch. "That was Arch's battery," he told the *Times,* "and Arch—Alexander Arch, a swarthy gunner from South Bend, Indiana—inserted the shell, pulled the lanyard and extracted the shell." Sergeant Arch was a 24-year-old immigrant from Hungary, a country allied with the people he had just fired upon. Shortly thereafter, he gave the shell to Gibbons, who was supposed to display it in Paris for a short while and then return it to him; instead, it got sent to the White House, where President Woodrow Wilson displayed it on his mantelpiece. Arch didn't get it back until 1931. Shells 2 through 8 were also saved and dispersed. The French 75-millimeter gun that fired the shot ended up at the United States Military Academy at West Point, where it remains to this day.

Given all the souvenir hunting surrounding that first shot, you'd think someone would have thought to mark the spot whence it was fired. But apparently, no one did. When I'd asked about it on previous visits—and, admittedly, I'd just queried the first few people I'd come upon in Bathelémont—I was met with shrugs, and given to understand that its location was lost to history. This led me to believe it would be impossible to find, which in turn made me want to find it that much more. It was, after all, the site of the first shot, no matter who'd pulled the lanyard. I e-mailed Eric and asked him if he thought we might have any chance of finding it; he replied, a few days later, with a scan of an old topographical map covered with ancient, inscrutable notations. East of Bathelémont, a spot was circled in green: a hill labeled "A81." He'd found it mentioned in some contemporary French military reports. I was stunned. And thrilled.

Two months later, when we arrived in Bathelémont, we were greeted by several men who had been—and this happened a lot; I'll explain more later—informed in advance of my arrival. One of them, an amiable white-haired fellow, introduced himself as the mayor, Serge Husson. (By law, every settlement in France, no matter how small, must elect a mayor; I have been to villages where every adult has held the post at one time or another.) He and the others escorted us to a spot on the edge of town, next to a lovely house with a big yard, in the middle of which sat the ruins of a concrete bunker which the owners had ingeniously turned into a terraced garden. "There," they said, pointing, away from the house and over some trees, at a small green hill to the left of a narrow lane: A81. Eric and

I thanked them and headed off toward it. After a couple of minutes, he surreptitiously pulled a copy of the old map—the same one he'd e-mailed me—from his pocket, pointed to a spot on it, and said, his voice hushed: "That's not A81. It has to be that hill there, on the other side of the road."

Instead of turning left, we walked straight down the road, past an intersection, and started up the grade, which was much steeper than it had appeared from the village. Longer, too. It was a very warm June morning, and muggy, having just stopped raining, and I lagged a bit behind Eric. Two-thirds of the way up the hill, he suddenly stopped, pulled out his map, and studied it for a minute or two. Holding it open in his hands, he turned to the right, stared out ahead for a bit, then wheeled around and gazed out in the opposite direction. "Wow," he said, softly.

"What?" I asked.

He looked down at the map again for a moment, then pointed at the hill he was now facing, the one the men in the village had pointed out. "They were *right*," he said. "They were right! That *is* it!" It: a stubby hill, mostly covered in young wheat except for a couple of bald, rocky patches on the way up. A81.

We walked back down to the intersection, then turned right and headed toward the hill. As we got closer, it became apparent that, as I had been told before, there was nothing atop it to commemorate what had happened there at 6:05 A.M. on October 23, 1917, something so significant that two men had claimed credit for it and dozens more had snatched up any vestige of it they could find. There wasn't even a trail leading to the spot. The closest we could get, without wading through chest-high wheat, was a narrow dirt road winding toward its base. As we passed by, I spotted a small green sign: "Chemin des Américains"—the Americans' Path.

Oh, yes, someone in town told me later. That's been there forever. We thought it was just because the Americans had been here. It hadn't occurred to anyone that it might have anything to do with the First Shot for Liberty.

⋆ ⋆ ⋆

Those workers at Xanrey might have been unprepared, but it's doubtful that the Americans caught the Germans entirely by surprise that morning. The Germans typically had excellent intelligence; it is likely they knew the Americans had moved in almost as soon as they got there. They didn't wait long to retaliate. The Americans took their first casualties that same day, the *History* notes, and were treated at a nearby field hospital. Two days later, Lieutenant DeVere Harden of Rockford, Illinois, who was serving with the Signal Corps but happened to be attached to the 1st Division's 26th Regiment at that point, became the first American officer to be wounded in action, hit in the leg by a piece of shrapnel. The *History* says it happened October 25; journalist Heywood Broun, who was in the sector at that time, went looking for Lieutenant Harden at a field hospital. "His wound was not a very bad one," Broun later recalled in his memoir *The A.E.F.: With General Pershing and the American Forces,* "and the doctors allowed us to crowd about his bed and ask questions." Broun reported:

> A French officer ran over to him and said: "You are a very lucky man."
> "How is that?" asked Harden.
> "Why, you're the first American to be wounded, and I'm going to recommend to the general that he put up a tablet right here with your name on it and the date and 'first American to shed his blood for France.'"
> The thought of the tablet didn't cheer the lieutenant up half so much as when we prevailed on the doctors to let him take some cigarettes from us and begin smoking again.

Broun also met another first in the hospital that day—the first German to be taken prisoner by the Americans:

> He was a pretty sick boy when we saw him. He gave his age when examined as nineteen, but he looked younger and not very dangerous, for he was just coming out of the ether. The American doctors were giving him the best of care. He had a room to himself and his own nurse. The doughboys had captured him close to the American wire. There had been great rivalry as to which company would get the first prisoner, but he came almost unsought. The patrol was back to its own wire when the soldiers heard the noise of somebody moving about to the left. He was making no effort to walk quietly. As he came over a little hillock his outline could be seen for a second and one of the Americans called out to him to halt. He turned and started to run, but a doughboy fired and hit him in the leg and another soldier's bullet came through his back. The patrol carried the prisoner to the trench . . . Somebody gave him a cigarette and he grew more chipper in spite of his wounds. He began to talk,

saying "Ich bin ein esel" [I am an ass] . . . The prisoner explained that he had been assigned to deliver letters to the soldiers. Some of the letters were for men in a distant trench which slanted toward the French line, and so to save time he had taken a short cut through No Man's Land. It was a dark night but he thought he knew the way. He kept bearing to the left. Now, he said, he knew he should have turned to the right. He said it would be a lesson to him. The next morning we heard that the German had died and would be buried with full military honors.

Broun doesn't report the man's name; he was Leonhard Hoffmann, 3rd Machine Gun Company, 7th Bavarian Infantry Regiment, part of the 1st Bavarian Landwehr Division, the unit posted directly across from the Big Red One. It is doubtful that many of the innumerable German soldiers shot by doughboys thereafter received quite that level of tender attention. For both the Americans and the Germans, the war was about to change irreversibly.

At 9:00 P.M. on the night of November 2, the 2nd Battalions of all four regiments in the 1st Division—the 16th, 18th, 26th and 28th—relieved the 1st Battalions in their first- and second-line trenches. A battalion was half a regiment; thousands of men would have been in motion simultaneously, either coming or going, in the dark—a tremendous logistical challenge. "The execution of a relief is in itself a difficult and a dangerous operation," the *History* explains, "and every precaution was taken to prevent the enemy from knowing of the plan. On this occasion the relief was completed and the newly arrived garrisons set about learning their way in the maze of deep trenches and familiarizing themselves with the instructions for the defense given by their predecessors." The division had only been at the front for a little more than a week; no doubt there was still a good bit of adventure to it all. "With the exception of a rifle shot here and there, the stillness of the black night was unbroken and the men were tense with the novelty and the sense of danger," the *History* reports. Midnight passed; it was now November 3. The part of the line closest to Bathelémont, along a hilltop ridge, was occupied by the men of the 2nd Battalion, 16th Infantry Regiment. Like the rest of their division, they were Regular Army, and hailed from all across the United States; many had been in the service for years. The relief maneuvers completed, the men settled in for the night, some curling up to sleep.

And then, at 3:26 A.M., things suddenly started blowing up all around them.

The Germans launched Operation Jakobsbrunnen—Jacob's Fountain—by bombarding the 16th Regiment with high-explosive shells for a few minutes; then they isolated one specific platoon from Company F with what was known as a box barrage, surrounding them on three sides with shell fire to prevent them from retreating and reinforcements from reaching them. Into the fourth side rushed *Stosstruppen*—shock troops, from Leonhard Hoffmann's 7th Bavarian Infantry Regiment—blowing open the protective barbed wire in front of the trenches with bangalore torpedoes and tossing hand grenades into the American trench line. They followed close behind. "With pistols, trench knives and bayonets they attacked the men along the trench," the *History* notes. "The affair lasted only a few minutes, when the raiders disappeared and the fire ceased." Twenty-four minutes, to be precise; but it was enough, for their purposes: The raiders carried off eleven American prisoners, three of them wounded, one a sergeant. Later that day, in the village of Coincourt, a few miles behind the German lines, the healthy eight were lined up on the street and photographed, surrounded by German soldiers over whom they towered. The image was circulated throughout Germany; the photo was made into a popular postcard, with the caption *Die ersten gefangenen Amerikaner*. The first American prisoners.

Taking American prisoners was clearly the Germans' primary objective that night; but in the process, they also killed three doughboys. Corporal James Bethel Gresham, 24 years old, of Evansville, Indiana, had been shot in the forehead. Private Thomas Francis Enright, 30, of Pittsburgh, Pennsylvania, had been stabbed in the gut and the throat. And Private Merle David Hay, 21, of Glidden, Iowa, had been shot and had his throat cut. The war where doughboys gleefully competed to fire the first shot and take the first prisoner, where the enemy was a hapless postman who got lost on his route and whom you felt bad about killing—that war was over.

Like A81, the site where the first three American doughboys died has no marker. Eric, though, managed to determine the location of the trench line using contemporary reports and old maps; it lay along a ridge at the crest of a hill that comprised the rear half of a deep field. Under ordinary circumstances, we could have driven pretty close to the spot on a tractor road that ran along the field's left edge, but, as I mentioned, it had rained that morning, so instead we parked nearly a mile away, alongside a paved road near a village with the quaint name of Réchicourt-la-Petite.

Any closer, Eric worried, and the mud might pin down his little Citroën. We walked the last stretch.

But wait: a word about that mud. You hear a lot about the mud of World War I—mud in the trenches, mud in the dugouts, mud in No Man's Land. It conveys a sense of the wretchedness of everyday conditions in that war, I suppose; but that word, "mud," is really insufficient to the task. The mud of northern France is to the mud of a typical American post-rainstorm landscape as Krazy Glue is to Scotch tape. When American mud dries, it becomes dirt; when French mud dries, it becomes clay, kind of like that stuff your dentist uses to take impressions of your teeth, only brown. If you get it on your left shoe and try to scrape it off with your right, it will attach itself to your right shoe without surrendering an inch of your left. The only way to shed it is to sit down on your car seat with your feet outside the vehicle and peel it off the soles of your shoes in one solid piece, which you will then want to throw as far away from you as possible. It has never, to this day, come off the pants I was wearing that morning. That mud, in fact, made such an impression on me that despite everything else I saw and did that day, when my hosts at the inn where I was staying asked me the next morning how my day had gone, I said, "Fine, except for the . . ." And I was stuck; not knowing the French word for mud, I tried a workaround. "Except for the . . . ground," I said, "because of the . . ." But for some reason just then I couldn't summon the word for rain, *pluie*. "Because of the . . . uh . . . *water from the sky*," I blurted. They and all the other guests at the breakfast table smiled and nodded vigorously. "Water from the sky!" a couple of them said. "*Très poétique!*"

The mud of northern France was like a third army, albeit one that harassed the other two equally. When you think about all those soldiers marching through it—or, more accurately, trying to march through it—and hunkering down in it, being covered in it and trying desperately to keep it from swallowing them entirely, you come to understand that even those rare days when they weren't being shelled or shot at were extremely trying, and that while war has always been hell, this was a particularly gooey version.

We hiked up that tractor road slowly, eyes on the mud and treading whenever possible upon sticks or rocks. Soon, on our left, we passed an enormous pile of manure, around ten feet high and forty feet wide. "Very Lorraine," Eric told me. "Farmers here are proud of their manure piles; it's a sign of their wealth. The bigger the pile, the richer the farmer. When

General Pershing first saw them he was horrified. He ordered the farmers to get rid of them, but it was no use."

The field spread out to our right; the tractor road followed its contours, slowly increasing grade the further we walked. After fifteen minutes or so we came to the crest of the ridge, and suddenly the whole scene was laid out before me like a board game. The path took a sharp turn to the right, and was covered entirely with tall grass and hay. To the left of it was young wheat, waist high, on a flat plain; to the right was the gently sloping field, a smooth green meadow punctuated here and there by small clumps of trees. Eric pulled out a map and studied it for a moment. "The Germans came up from there," he said, pointing back toward where we had parked. "They might have gone around that way"—he pointed at a tree line in the distance—"but they could have just come straight up through these fields. It was dark; they knew what they were doing. The Americans would have had had listening posts in those groups of trees—that one, that one, all of them, probably—but the Germans would have known that." He pointed to the map. "They knew this whole area very well. Better than the Americans. They might have known it better than the French." It would have been easy, he explained, for them to give those posts a wide berth, even in the dark.

We turned and headed up the grassy part of the path. Eric walked twenty paces or so, stopped, looked at the field, looked at his map, walked another twenty paces, and repeated the process a couple more times. Finally, he stopped, looked at the field, looked at his map, looked back at the field, and walked no more. "This is it," he said, softly and without any sense of triumph. He pointed at a spot in the field a few yards to our left. "This is where they were killed."

I turned and looked out over the tops of the young wheat stalks, searching for dips that might indicate the existence of trenches, but there were none. The one where Gresham, Hay and Enright were killed had been filled in long ago, no doubt to make the field easier to plant and plow. As hard as it was to find the spot, it was harder still for me to turn my back on it and look out over that lush meadow spread out below, the second-nicest vista I had beheld in France, and reconcile myself to the thought that this was where the first three doughboys died in that war. We stood there for a few minutes, then wordlessly turned and walked back down the path.

As we made it back to the road where we had parked, Eric suggested we walk through the fields to see if we could find any remnants of the

German pillboxes—small concrete machine-gun nests—and bunkers marked on the map. We could, without even having to look very hard: One pillbox—or its remains, anyway—was a stone rise, about the size and shape of a pitcher's mound, in the field to our right; another, some partially crumbled cement blocks, was further up, near our car. We walked across the road and into a cornfield (lots of shrapnel, not much else) and soon came to a large concrete outcropping, perhaps fifteen feet square, big blocks surrounded by corrugated metal bands, with iron rods poking out here and there. Just beyond, a few hundred yards in the distance, were the rooftops of Réchicourt-la-Petite, and a steeple. The bunker had been blown up after the war, but it could not be cleared; it never will be. The farmer cannot do anything with that patch of ground, and must go to great trouble to plant and reap around it. A century on, the Germans are still bedeviling the French.

★ ★ ★

When the sun rose and they were able to determine with certainty that the Germans had really gone, the Americans carried the bodies of Gresham, Hay and Enright to Bathelémont. The following afternoon, American and French soldiers, and at least one detachment of French sailors, gathered there for the funeral. The church had been badly damaged earlier in the war, but a makeshift altar was put up amidst the rubble of the village. Wood had somehow been found to fashion three coffins—a gesture of tremendous respect. Such a luxury had long been unavailable to French soldiers, who were, by that point in the war, typically buried in blankets.

General Joseph Bordeaux, commanding officer of the French 18th Division, spoke to the crowd:

> On behalf of the 18th Division, on behalf of the French Army and on behalf of France, I say goodbye to Private Enright, to Corporal Gresham, and to Private Hay of the American Army. Of their own volition, they left a prosperous and a happy country to come here. They knew that the war in Europe was still going on. They knew that the forces fighting for honor, love of country and civilization were still opposed by forces prepared for a long time, serving the powers of brutal domination, oppression and barbarism. They knew that efforts were still needed. They generously offered their blood . . . The death of this humble corporal and these privates takes a character of particular grandeur. We will ask that

their bodies remain here forever, and we will inscribe on their graves,
Here Lie the First Soldiers of the Famous Republic of the United States,
Who Fell in the Fields of France for Justice and Freedom. Passers-by
will stop and the men of heart who will visit the battlefields of Lorraine
will go out of their way to come here to bring to these tombs the tribute
of their respect and gratitude. Corporal Gresham, Private Enright and
Private Hay, on behalf of France, I thank you. God receive your souls.
Adieu.

Shells and shots were fired; "Taps" was played. When it was all over,
an American officer with the 1st Division staff asked a French officer for a
translation of the general's remarks. The French officer was a great-grandson of Victor Hugo; the American was future Army Chief of Staff and
Secretary of State George Marshall.

And then everyone got back to the war. Except they didn't, not really.
In the days to come, as the news spread, the sense of loss was refreshed
again and again whenever someone heard it for the first time. The eleven
American prisoners taken that night were told of their comrades' deaths;
when the sergeant, Edgar Halyburton, requested a coat to replace the
one he'd lost when he was captured, the Germans gave him one they had
taken as a souvenir. It was covered with blood; had a bullet hole. Sergeant
Halyburton looked inside and saw the name Merle David Hay.

Back in the United States, Gresham's, Hay's, and Enright's faces and
names were soon recruited for fund-raising posters. ("Give till it hurts,"
one demanded. "They gave till they died.") The French, though, had other
ideas. Within days of the funeral, Léon Mirman, the prefect of the *département* of Meurthe-et-Moselle, which included Bathelémont, hit upon the
idea of building a monument to Gresham, Hay and Enright in the village.
Right away. It would be dedicated, he decided, on November 3, 1918, the
anniversary of their deaths. The war was still raging; Bathelémont was
still right on the front lines. No matter. Mirman was a man of will, a Rad-
ical-Socialist; he had once fought a duel with another politician. He could
handle a monument.

Mirman identified 160 cities, towns and villages in the *département*
that had not, he believed, suffered so much in the war that they couldn't
donate to such a cause, and hit them up. Almost all of them contributed.
He then commissioned the famous sculptor Louis Majorelle, who lived in

Nancy, to design it. Majorelle decided upon a stele, 4.5 meters tall; one side bore a large Cross of Lorraine, with "France" and "États-Unis" carved in its crossbars. Another side bore the inscription:

HERE LIE
IN THE SOIL OF LORRAINE
THE FIRST THREE
AMERICAN SOLDIERS
KILLED BY THE ENEMY
ON NOVEMBER 3, 1917

CORPORAL J.B. GRESHAM
(OF EVANSVILLE)

PRIVATE THOMAS F. ENRIGHT
(OF PITTSBURGH)

PRIVATE MERLE D. HAY
(OF GLIDDEN)

AS SONS WORTHY OF THEIR GREAT
AND NOBLE NATION, THEY
FOUGHT FOR RIGHT,
FOR LIBERTY, FOR
CIVILIZATION, AGAINST
GERMAN IMPERIALISM
THE SCOURGE OF HUMANITY
THEY DIED ON THE FIELD OF HONOR

When we returned from hiking around in the mud, Mayor Husson and his party showed us around the area a bit, and then escorted Eric and me to Bathelémont's *mairie*; on our way, we passed a small, modern building with a sign on the front identifying it as Le Poulailler, the Chicken Coop. It sat on a small rise. "During the war," the mayor said, "this was used as a lookout post." Only then did I notice that the rise it sat atop was actually a large, well-preserved concrete bunker, with two entrances leading underground. In the nearby village of Arracourt, we had spotted another, much larger one that looked as if it hadn't deteriorated at all; someone had since built a house around it, and was using it as a deck. I very badly wanted to knock on their door, but someone in our party said the current owners were new and not around very much. Their demeanor made me wonder if the French just don't knock on strangers' doors very often, which in turn made me wonder why I was always treated so well—and, often, fed—whenever I did so Over There.

The *mairie* was, like Bathelémont, small and bright. The walls of one of the larger rooms were covered with photos of the village during the war, and of the monument. Mayor Husson showed me a 1:10 scale model of the latter, one of several M. Majorelle made and gave out to dignitaries ranging from President Wilson to the mayor of Nancy. (It's not clear whose copy ended up in Bathelémont.) The actual monument was, indeed, unveiled as planned on November 3, 1918. The front was just as close as it had been a year earlier; during the ceremony, three German shells landed nearby. Remarks were brief.

General Bordeaux's expressed wish was that the three Americans remain in French soil in perpetuity, but in 1921 they were exhumed and repatriated to the United States, buried in their hometowns. It is, perhaps, just as well. Less than twenty years later, another war, and another generation of Germans, came to Bathelémont. They did not care for the monument to the first three Americans; in particular, they did not care for the line about German imperialism being the scourge of humanity. "My grandfather was mayor then," M. Husson told me. "The Germans demanded he remove those lines from the inscription. He refused." Other accounts have the mayor's grandfather, Joseph Crouvizier, attempting to mask the offending words with plaster. In any event, the Germans decided to just handle it themselves. On October 6, 1940, they blew it up with dynamite. In 1952, when George Marshall returned to Bathelémont, the remnants of it were still scattered around the village. The *département* hastily allocated funds for a new one, much more modest than the first, to stand on the same spot as the original, which it did for years until a property dispute resulted in its being moved to a new site just outside the village, next to the cemetery. The new inscription reads:

HERE LIE
THE FIRST THREE SOLDIERS OF THE
UNITED STATES

TO FALL ON THE FIELDS OF

FRANCE

FOR JUSTICE AND LIBERTY

Which really shouldn't offend anyone.

★ ★ ★

The next morning, after spending part of breakfast telling my hosts and fellow guests about water from the sky, I met Eric outside my *chambre d'hôtes*, or bed-and-breakfast. His wife, he said, hadn't been at all upset about all the mud we had tracked into the car; she had even packed a lunch for us both. I'm not sure if the first part was really true—by the end of the previous day, the little Citroën was more clay than metal—but the sandwiches she'd fixed, turkey and cheese, were delicious.

We headed off toward the town of Parroy, a few miles east of Bathelémont. Elements of the 1st Division had been posted near Parroy, but on that day, we were more concerned with another American division, the next one to train in the "quiet" Sommerviller Sector. They had arrived in the vicinity of Parroy in February 1918, a couple of months after the 1st had departed: the 42nd, known as the Rainbow Division.

A few miles from Parroy we spotted, just off the side of the road, a large concrete bunker, mostly covered in vegetation but completely intact, its rounded corners distinguishing it from most of the others I'd come across. Eric had never seen it before, either; we climbed up on top and descended inside, walking through galleries into chambers at either end, where machine-gun mounts were still bolted into the walls, and large cement blocks could have doubled for gun rests and beds. "This was French," Eric pronounced after a while, and neither of us had to note how unusual that fact alone made such a find. "I don't believe it was ever used," he added; scribbled on a wall inside was the date 1916, which would have been more than a year after the Germans pulled out of the area. Perhaps it was hoped, after that war ended, that this bunker might prove to be of use should another come; but when it did, the French were overrun too quickly for them to do anything with it. It had sat empty for nearly a century when we found it. A nice discovery, and unexpected: We were actually headed toward Parroy in search of a poet.

It can seem strange, with everything we know about the horrors of that war, to hold it and poetry in the same thought; but that conflict—the fighting and dying, shells and gas, trenches and mud—managed to inspire verse in the minds of men like Alan Seeger, Rupert Brooke, Wilfred Owen, and Siegfried Sassoon, only the last of whom survived. Owen, who was killed in the last week of the war, and Sassoon, who spent a term in the hospital for shell shock, were both British officers who eventually became disillusioned about the war; Seeger, an American who ran off in August 1914 and joined the French Army, wrote about his desire to die gloriously in battle, which he did at Verdun in July 1916. But Eric and I were on the trail of another American who, like his countryman Seeger, seemed to hold a rather romantic view of the war. Alfred Joyce Kilmer is perhaps most famous today for a piece of verse that begins "I think that I shall never see / A poem lovely as a tree," but Eric and I set out that morning to find the place that inspired his second-most-famous poem: a section of the Forêt de Parroy—the Forest of Parroy—known as Rouge Bouquet.

When he enlisted in April 1917, the same month the United States entered the conflict, Joyce Kilmer, a New Jersey native and graduate of Columbia University, was a 30-year-old journalist who also dabbled in poetry. With his background and education, he could easily have been an officer, but he decided the unit was more important than the rank, and he chose to be a sergeant in New York's famed 69th Regiment, which had served with distinction throughout the Civil War. Indeed, before he sailed off to France, Kilmer contracted with a publisher to write his war memoirs, to be titled *Here and There with the Fighting 69th*. Never mind that, by that time, for clerical reasons, the Army had renamed the regiment the 165th; they could deal with that later.

There were, at that point, only four complete American divisions in all of France: The 1st and 2nd were Regular Army, who were already in service before the war; the 26th were National Guard from New England. The 42nd were National Guard, too, but they were special in one respect: While every other National Guard Division comprised troops from a specific area—the 26th from New England, the 27th from New York, the 28th from Pennsylvania, and so on—the 42nd comprised troops from twenty-six states plus the District of Columbia. Such an arrangement was said to have been the idea of a major who headed the War Department's Bureau of Information, a West Point graduate who liked the notion of a single division that would "stretch over the whole country like a rainbow." Secretary of War Newton D. Baker liked it, too; and thus was the Rainbow Division created. The major who conceived it, Douglas MacArthur, would rise within its ranks to become a brigadier general before the war's end, and one day trespass on what would eventually become Jean-Pierre Brouillon's property. In February 1918, though, he was still a colonel, and his division, having only recently arrived in France, still untested. They were sent to the Sommerviller Sector to get some experience in the trenches.

Like the 1st Division, the 42nd had some notable names in its ranks: In addition to MacArthur and Kilmer, there was the latter's commanding officer, Major William J. Donovan, who would win the Medal of Honor in that war, and run the Office of Strategic Services (or OSS, the forerunner to the CIA) during the next one; and Kilmer and Donovan's chaplain, Father Francis Duffy, who would be awarded a Distinguished Service Cross, and have a section of Times Square renamed for him. In early March, 1918, Sergeant Kilmer, Major Donovan and Father Duffy found themselves, along with the rest of the 165th, in the Fôret de Parroy. The rest of the division was spread throughout the sector.

"Aside from learning the routine of life in the trenches and the methods of making reliefs," Henry Joseph Reilly, a colonel in the 42nd, later wrote in his history, *Americans All: The Rainbow at War: Official History of the 42nd Rainbow Division in the World War,* "the principal activities of the Rainbow were made up of nightly patrols . . . throughout No Man's Land, or the territory between the French and American front lines and the German front line.

"In addition," he continued, "the Division had two classes of experiences: The first consisted of raids, on a large enough scale to be called minor attacks, on the German trenches; the second consisted of German retaliations in the shape of fairly large raids and of heavy artillery concentrations on different parts of the trenches held by the Rainbow."

One of the reasons this sector had remained "quiet" for as long as it had was because the French and Germans had settled into a fairly stable status quo, wherein each recognized the likelihood that nothing of significance was to be gained by attacking the other. The Americans, though, were not there to respect any unspoken truce; they had left their homes looking for action and sailed across an ocean to find it. What's more, they hadn't been worn down by three and a half years of fighting at that point. On the night of March 4–5, 1918, a patrol from the 167th Infantry Regiment—National Guard from Alabama—went out and grabbed two German prisoners from a trench. A few hours later, Reilly said, the Germans attempted a raid on the 168th Regiment—Iowa National Guard—and when that was repulsed, unleashed a barrage of *Minenwerfer,* or short-range, high-caliber mortars, upon some machine gunners who'd left their shelter to man a Stokes mortar. "A single shell, lighting squarely on the Stokes squad which had been doing such valiant work, wiped out the entire crew of seven and destroyed the gun," Reilly wrote. "Of Sergeant Porsch and Private Nash no trace was ever found, but the mutilated bodies of Sergeant Wedding, Corporal Parish, and Privates Hoschler, Pederson, and Worden were later recovered." The Iowans lost nineteen killed and twenty-two wounded.

The Americans retaliated; the Germans retaliated. Over the next couple of days, there were more trench raids, more bombardments. At 3:20 on the afternoon of March 7, as twenty-two men from the 165th Regiment's Company E took shelter in a dugout at Rouge Bouquet, a *Minenwerfer* scored a direct hit, burying all of them. Major Donovan immediately ordered a rescue operation, but more shells continued to fall; only two men were recovered alive. One of them, Corporal Alf S. Helmer, later told Colonel Reilly, as recounted in *Americans All,* that he believed at least some of the buried stayed alive underground for another three days; others reported hearing voices emanating from beneath the dirt for at least as long. Helmer himself had been buried up to his mouth before they managed to pull him out. Earlier that morning, he later recalled, his company had replaced another, "with the high and enthusiastic feeling which only an American doughboy can know." Following his rescue, while making his way back to HQ, he heard another German shell coming in. "I dropped flat on the duckboard," he reported afterward, "thinking it was a hell of a note to be blown up by a shell when I had just escaped being smothered to death in the dark bowels of the earth." He was spared once again and continued on his way, but "as I rounded the bend the fumes were still rising from the exploding shell. I tripped and fell on what had been Kelly!"

Because Corporal Helmer was not killed that day at Rouge Bouquet, he lived to tell his story but was otherwise forgotten by history, which I'm guessing he would have regarded as a pretty good trade-off for him. Major Donovan was awarded the Croix de Guerre for leading the rescue effort that pulled Helmer and one other survivor out of the collapsed dugout. That left twenty dead from one shell; fifteen of the bodies were never recovered. All were memorialized in a poem written by another soldier from the 165th, Sergeant Joyce Kilmer, which he called "Rouge Bouquet," and which he read at a memorial service a few days later. It begins:

In a wood they call the Rouge Bouquet
There is a new-made grave to-day,
Built by never a spade nor pick
Yet covered with earth ten metres thick.
There lie many fighting men,
Dead in their youthful prime,
Never to laugh nor love again
Nor taste the Summertime.
For Death came flying through the air
And stopped his flight at the dugout stair,
Touched his prey and left them there,
Clay to clay.
He hid their bodies stealthily
In the soil of the land they fought to free
And fled away.

There are decent roads running through the Forêt de Parroy, but to get to Rouge Bouquet, you have to walk a half mile, more or less, up a dirt-and-gravel logging trail. Actually, before you do that, you need to have someone like Eric Mansuy look at old maps and then new maps and then old maps again to figure out exactly which dirt-and-gravel logging trail will get you close. There's no Chemin des Américains here. No signs at all, actually.

I'm not sure how Eric divined where, exactly, we should leave the trail and head into the woods, but within thirty seconds of doing so, I looked down and spotted a century-old 1-liter French Bidon canteen, just sitting atop the fallen leaves. It was a good portent: The French 128th Division had been training the 42nd at Rouge Bouquet. "This must be the French and American lines," Eric said. The forest floor sloped down toward a plateau; dirt trenches ran along the incline, zigzagging here, intersecting there. "This was definitely one of the lines," Eric said. "Probably the second line, I'm guessing." The second-line trench, a defensive fallback position, was usually dug a few dozen yards (though sometimes more) behind the first-line trench, which faced out onto No Man's Land and, beyond it, the enemy's first-line trench. As I tried to orient myself, I spotted, sprinkled here and there among the trenches, little bowls, maybe ten feet across. Too deep and too wide to be foxholes. "Shells?" I asked.

"Yes," he said.

It was an overcast day, and the forest, though not terribly dense, was far from sparse; some of the trees looked like they had been around since before the war. The air was infused with a dark green sheen, the kind of light that requires one to look at things twice. As I stared at one of these depressions, gouged out of the side of a small rise and coated with dead leaves, it grew larger and larger. Eric came over to look. He stared, too, for a minute, then said: "Yes, that could be it."

"What?"

"The dugout." Eric knew the poem, too. And he knew about the memorial: how, after the war, someone had installed upon the ruins of the bunker a plaque that had long since disappeared, perhaps during the Second World War, when there was also some fighting in this vicinity. We moved along for a bit and found another set of dirt trenches—the first line. There was nothing else we came across that could have been a dugout at one point.

Past the first line, we came to an area where the forest floor leveled out and opened up. It was a plateau, though I wouldn't call it flat: It was full of shell holes. Two here; three there. One, and another, and two more. There were small ones—eight to ten feet across, three to four feet deep—and larger ones, maybe twice that size, maybe more. All were filled, to some extent, with water. Trees grew near their edges; some had gotten too close and tipped over into the depressions. In one spot, near a young tree, we spotted a rotting metal box, maybe two feet cubed; grass sprouted up inside it. Its design said German. The same was true for a couple of round metal catchbasins we found nearby. No doubt they had been placed there earlier in the war, during quieter times, when No Man's Land might have been subject to the law of Live and Let Live. Now, though, they sat amidst a field of shell holes, stretching on for hundreds of yards. At some point, both sides must have bombarded the hell out of this place. No more sneaking out to do your wash here.

Eventually the ground started sloping upward again; giant, bright orange slugs, each the size and shape of a slice of grapefruit, littered this section of the forest floor. After a few paces we saw a new line of trenches, also dirt but significantly deeper, and more jagged, than the last two. And there were more of them. And they made better use of the topography. In all likelihood, they occupied a better section of the forest, too. The Germans, as usual, knew what they were doing. If you'd been here in March

1918, you would have been much better off sheltering in—and attacking from—these trenches than the ones we'd just come from.

Eric and I just looked at each other; no need to say anything. We forded the trenches and scaled the hill until, a few dozen yards up, we came to another line of trenches, even deeper and more jagged than the first. Even now, a hundred years later, we had trouble figuring out how to get beyond them. It took a while and some searching to find a spot where, with difficulty, we could do it by jumping across to some large rocks that were carpeted with moss.

As I landed, it occurred to me that these rocks were awfully flat, with corners suspiciously close to ninety degrees. I scraped at a spot with my walking stick and saw, underneath, not granite but concrete. Looking up, I spotted another set of moss-covered, cube-shaped rocks nearby. And then another. And then one that looked a lot like a platform.

"The German second line," Eric declared triumphantly. We had mapped out the entire battlefield of Rouge Bouquet, just as Major Donovan, and Sergeant Kilmer, and Corporal Helmer would have seen it. There was no visible evidence that anyone else had been here since they had.

★ ★ ★

In between Parroy and Bathelémont there's an even smaller village called Bauzemont. Bauzemont doesn't have much, but it does happen to have a château, built in 1740, that managed to survive the First and Second World Wars, not to mention the Franco-Prussian War and, for good measure, the French Revolution. Like most châteaux, it's handsome and stately and has seen better days. The woman who owns it doesn't care to live in it; her tenant, a genial countryman named Damien, welcomed me into the house and, after pointing out this and that, led me up a narrow, precarious old stairway to a rectangular chamber above the kitchen that had once been used to store grain. In late February and early March of 1918, it had been used to store a few soldiers from the Rainbow Division.

It's a small chamber, maybe twenty feet by eight; I doubt they did much more than sleep there. But they did, I happen to know, do a little bit more there, because the walls are still decorated with their pencil drawings. They drew soldiers like themselves, some decent likenesses, some caricatures, in campaign hats, soft caps, uniforms and fatigues. They drew big guns and shells and explosions. They drew a waitress carrying a tray of drinks, and one sketch that could be a howitzer on wheels but is more likely something obscene.

And they wrote their names: L. P. Reed. Goofer O'Hare. Joseph Tineo, Brooklyn, N.Y. Ralph O'Donnell, "The Panama Kid."

None of them had seen action yet, but they knew they were about to. And though they were at that moment very close to Bathelémont, and almost certainly knew the names James Gresham and Thomas Enright and Merle Hay, they also knew that other doughboys had been killed there, too, within days of those first three, and that no one knew their names anymore. No French general had delivered an impassioned eulogy over their graves; no one had commissioned a monument to them. Even having a renowned poet in your division, as these men had, was not enough to ward off the almost certain oblivion that would consume your name if you were unfortunate enough to die on the field of battle thousands of miles from home. Yes, Joyce Kilmer wrote a poem to the twenty men killed in that dugout at Rouge Bouquet on March 7, 1918; but if you want to know their names, you're going to have to dig through archives as diligently as Major Donovan's men dug through the dirt that day. In war, everyone knows, names are even more easily lost than lives.

So L. P. Reed, and Goofer O'Hare, and Joseph Tineo from Brooklyn, N.Y., and Ralph O'Donnell, the Panama Kid, wrote theirs on a wall in Bauzemont.

At the same time, a couple hundred miles to the west, another division of Americans, facing the same prospect, did even more than that.

CHAPTER FOUR

FROM THE BOWELS OF THE EARTH

I.

As I lowered myself, cold metal rung by cold metal rung, some thirty feet onto the floor of a subterranean chalk mine, clenching an old plastic flashlight between my teeth, I did not give much thought to two long-dead French princesses. I very much doubt that the men of the American 26th Division, hunkering down in this same mine in February and March of 1918, did, either. But we were all, in a way, connected.

In the mid-eighteenth century, those two princesses, Marie Adélaïde and Victoire, daughters of France's Louis XV, developed an attachment to Adélaïde's Lady of Honor, Françoise de Châlus, who also happened to be one of the king's mistresses. This was a position of even greater prestige than being the Lady of Honor to a princess, and eventually Françoise landed a well-fixed husband, the Comte de Narbonne-Lara, and moved away to his château in Picardy, about ninety miles north and east of Paris. Adélaïde and Victoire, who also bore the title "Lady of France," didn't see any reason why this should end their friendship, and neither did the *comtesse,* who extended to them an invitation to visit whenever and as often as they liked. The only problem was that the road they had to travel to get there, which ran along a fifty-mile ridge, was in pretty poor shape; the princesses must have said something about how hard those first few trips were because at some point the *comte,* being a gentleman, went to the trouble and expense of having the road resurfaced for them. Soon they started making more frequent visits, and the road they traveled became known as the Chemin des Dames—the Ladies' Way. It exists to this day, though it now bears the somewhat less colorful appellation D18.

Many people in France know the story of Louis XV's daughters and his former mistress. But when they think of the Chemin des Dames, what comes to mind first is probably not princesses and gilt carriages, but soldiers and machine guns. In 1917, just as the United States entered the war, the French were waging an offensive at the Chemin des Dames that went so badly it nearly knocked them out of it. It would permanently alter the French Army's approach to that war; and for generations since, the term "Chemin des Dames" has been associated not with the former grandeur of France, but with the senseless slaughter that brought it, and the rest of the world, into the Modern Age.

A few months after that horrific battle ended, the 26th Division—known as the Yankee Division, or YD, because it was composed entirely of National Guard troops from the six New England states—was sent to the Chemin des Dames to train. Though it was, by then, relatively quiet on that ridge, the men of the YD would have known what had taken place there only recently. They would have seen the graves of the dead, and the faces of the living. They would have heard the stories. They would have understood that the war songs they'd heard back home—"Over There," and "Goodbye Broadway, Hello France," and "We're All Going Calling on the Kaiser," and "Wee Wee Marie, Will You Do Zis for Me?"—had nothing to do with what was actually happening at the front. And they would have, I am sure, been afraid.

Madame George at the Gunther memorial.

A wall of unearthed World War I canteens and mess kits in Jean-Paul de Vries's museum in Romagne-sous-Montfaucon.

Jean-Pierre Brouillon on his farm in the Argonne. In the distance is the Musarde farmhouse, where Rommel spent the night in 1914.

Unless noted otherwise, all photographs courtesy of the author.

The ruins of a German blockhouse in the woods on M. Brouillon's property. It was part of the Kriemhilde Stellung, an "impenetrable" defense line the Germans built in the Argonne.

Another German blockhouse in the Kriemhilde Stellung, photographed shortly after it was captured by Americans in the fall of 1918.

A chamber full of human bones, glimpsed through a small window at the base of the Douaumont Ossuary. The ossuary contains the remains of more than 130,000 unidentified men killed at Verdun in 1916.

Buglers play the "Last Post and Call" under the Menin Gate in Ypres, Belgium. The ceremony, which occurs at precisely 8:00 P.M. every night of the year, honors the hundreds of thousands of British Expeditionary Force soldiers killed at Ypres between 1914 and 1918.

The hill known as A81, outside the village of Bathelémont, from which Battery C of the 6th Field Artillery fired the first American shot of the war at 6:05 A.M. on October 23, 1917.

Eric Mansuy points to the spot, a few yards off, where the first three soldiers of the American Expeditionary Forces were killed by the Germans during a pre-dawn raid on November 3, 1917.

Die ersten gefangenen Amerikaner

"The First American Prisoners." A German propaganda postcard featuring a photo of eight of the eleven Americans captured in that same raid; the other three were too badly wounded to pose. Note how much larger the Americans are than the Germans.

An Episcopal chaplain administers communion to men of the 101st U.S. Infantry Regiment deep in a mine on the Chemin des Dames, February 1918.

Photo courtesy of National Archives and Records Administration

Mechanic Allie Ardine of the 103rd U.S. Infantry Regiment carved this shield and tablet into the wall of the chalk mine outside Nanteuil-la-Fosse. A painter by trade, he had a difficult time after the war.

Mechanic Ralph Moan of Eastport, Maine. His journal presents a vivid portrait of the Yankee Division's time on the Chemin des Dames.

Photo courtesy of Fae Houck

The Wheat Field, as seen from inside Belleau Wood. Many believe that the Marines' charge across this field, on June 6, 1918, changed the course of the war.

Laurent Vanhée, a French fan of the United States Marine Corps, shows off a couple of his USMC tattoos. He has more on the other arm.

Typical vista in Champagne. Though not visible in the photo, the Marne River runs in between the houses in the foreground and the vineyards in the distance; thousands of German soldiers came charging down those hills in the early hours of July 15, 1918, to attack French and American troops on the other side.

The hôtel de ville, or city hall, in Fismes.

An American postcard picturing the ruins of Fismes's hôtel de ville *in August 1918, "after being showered with German shells for three weeks."* The Americans had great trouble taking Fismes, as they did most towns and villages in the area.

Jean Vedovati holds the casing of a 75-millimeter shell that he believes was fired by an American battery in July 1918. Once part of a large collection of WWI artifacts, it was the only piece his wife allowed him to keep once their grandchildren started visiting.

A well-preserved concrete German trench in Bois Brûlé, the Burnt Woods.

A dirt French trench in Bois Brûlé. In some spots the French and German front lines were only twenty yards apart.

Just outside the village détruit *of Regniéville, near Thiaucourt, the remains of a German bunker sit alongside the road to Pont-à-Mousson. Such ruins are a common sight in the Woëvre.*

A similar bunker in the area, photographed shortly after American troops took it in 1918. The body of a German soldier, killed in the attack, lies out front.

Patrick Simons stands near the ruins of another German bunker in the Woëvre.

Christophe Wilvers lies in the shallow grave in the Bois de Rembercourt, where a relic-hunter found the remains of Marine Sergeant George Humphrey in 2009, ninety-one years after he was killed and buried here.

German soldiers march fourteen American prisoners up a hill outside Bouillonville on April 20, 1918, after capturing them at Seicheprey that morning in the first major clash between German and American troops. Photo courtesy of Madison (CT) Historical Society

A German postcard featuring the Argonnenbahn, *the Argonne railroad. During the war, the Germans laid hundreds of miles of narrow-gauge rail through the forest, and even printed up timetables.*

Harry Rupert holds some French-American V-B rifle grenades he found along the Sergeant York Trail in the Argonne. He keeps them in his barn.

Local historian Dominique Lacorde's grandmother, Emilienne, and her grandmother, Françoise, with German soldiers in their house during the war. The caption reads: "Easter 1915. Souvenir of the German barbarians." The photographer was also German. Photo courtesy of Dominique Lacorde

PÂQUES 1915.

SOUVENIR DES BARBARES ALLEMANDS

À M.LLE EMILIENNE par WILKING, REMPR. D'OFF.

Maurice Ravenel and Denis Hebrard in Vauquois. M. Ravenel wears his 1914 poilu uniform to events throughout the Argonne; Denis sometimes takes visitors through the elaborate tunnels beneath Vauquois Hill.

Vauquois Hill from above. The large monument and flagpole are dwarfed by massive craters that render this landscape otherworldly. Between 1914 and 1918 the Germans and French dug and detonated more than 500 underground mines here. Photo courtesy of Jean-Luc Kaluzko

French soldiers at Vauquois. During one day in October 1914, more than 1,400 French soldiers were killed here in just 30 minutes. The Americans took Vauquois in September 1918.

This century-old entrance to an underground German bunker (left center) is set into a knoll in a pasture outside Gesnes. No one can do a thing with it except for the cows, which use it as a shelter.

The badly damaged church in Neuvilly was used as a way station for wounded American soldiers during the Meuse-Argonne offensive in 1918.
Photo courtesy of National Archives and Records Administration

The same church today.

Kaiser Wilhelm II (left), Emperor of Germany, and his oldest son, Kronprinz (Crown Prince) Wilhelm, pose on the terrace of the Château de Tilleul in Stenay. The Kronprinz, who commanded a German army, used the château as his headquarters during the war.

The terrace today. Although the railing (and the château) have since been replaced, the terrace still hides the Kronprinz's secret bunker. The Americans liberated Stenay on the morning of November 11, 1918, but the Kronprinz had already fled.

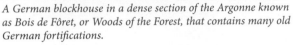

A German blockhouse in a dense section of the Argonne known as Bois de Fôret, or Woods of the Forest, that contains many old German fortifications.

Jean-Paul de Vries stands in a hallway inside the blockhouse. Some of its chambers still have remnants of the original wood paneling.

A well-preserved German wash house, hiding in plain sight in a field outside Éclisfontaine. Jean-Paul had only recently discovered it.

This coach, identical to the one in which the armistice was signed on November 11, 1918, now sits in a museum in the Clairière de l'Armistice (the glade of the armistice) in the Forest of Compiègne.

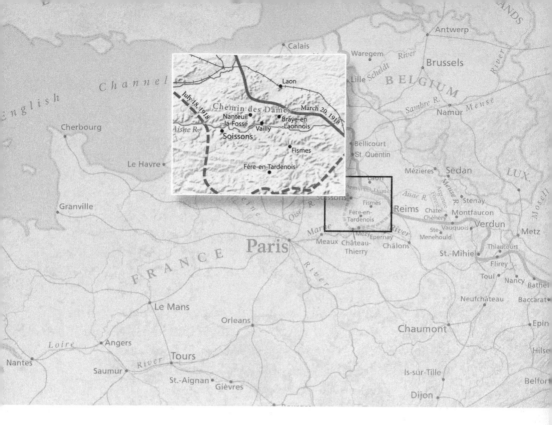

None of that made them particularly special among the troops of the American Expeditionary Forces. But the way they exorcised that fear did. And they couldn't have done so anywhere at the front except for the Chemin des Dames, where the topography—and the geology—made it possible.

✳ ✳ ✳

The Germans hadn't thoroughly scouted and charted just Lorraine before the first shots were fired. They'd gone all the way to the English Channel, and back again; knew exactly what they wanted, had their targets prioritized. And the Chemin des Dames was high on their list. Obtaining it, they knew, would enable the Germans to sever essential French rail lines in Picardy and disrupt vital inland waterways like the Aisne River. They also knew that it was riddled with enormous centuries-old chalk mines that would offer ample shelter to their troops during enemy bombardments, making the ridge—which already offered them the considerable advantage of elevation—easy to defend, once they took it. In addition to being very fine spies and surveyors, the Germans were students of history; they knew that Napoleon had used the Chemin des Dames very effectively against the Prussians a century earlier. Why the French left it so lightly defended in 1914 remains a mystery.

The Germans grabbed a part of the ridge after their defeat at the First Battle of the Marne in September 1914, then used it to stop the advance of the Allied armies that had been pursuing them. The French fought fiercely to protect the rest, but the Germans, having gotten there first, had an advantage, and by November they had taken the whole thing. They used it as effectively as Napoleon had; vexed the French terribly. The French became obsessed with taking it back, and for the next two years staged lightning-strike attacks, known as *coups de main,* all along the ridge. They killed a lot of Germans. But the Germans killed a lot of more of them, and, more importantly, held their ground.

In December 1916, as the ten-month Battle of Verdun was winding down, concluding a year of unprecedented bloodletting, the French decided to make a change, replacing the extremely popular *Généralissime* Joseph "Papa" Joffre with General Robert Nivelle. Many questioned the appointment: Nivelle, who had actually been subordinate to General Philippe Pétain at Verdun, was known less for tactical brilliance than for originating the rallying cry "They shall not pass!" Whatever others may have been muttering about him, Nivelle was exceedingly confident and even more ambitious. And he had a plan.

Nivelle believed that Verdun had broken the Germans, and said he intended to knock them out of the war in 1917 by launching a great offensive, spearheaded at the Chemin des Dames, that would succeed magnificently. Better still, he assured everyone, it wouldn't even cost all that many casualties; the Germans, facing such a French force, would surely break and run for their lives.

The muttering grew louder, spread wider: Nivelle's assessment of the enemy was badly mistaken, his plan folly. The Germans, people warned, held much better ground, had constructed formidable defenses. Nivelle ignored them. Others proposed different schemes. Nivelle overruled them. His plan was the one. It became known as the Nivelle Offensive.

He soon came to regret that.

After a few false starts, the offensive was launched on April 16, 1917. Nivelle had predicted a breakthrough that first day. It didn't happen. Instead, his troops took many times the number of casualties he had projected for the entire offensive. The Germans, remembering why they had gone to so much trouble to take this high ground in the first place, used it to devastating effect. In the week that followed, French troops did advance their lines in places, and managed to capture a good number of German soldiers and weaponry, but their casualty figures soared in the process. A year or two earlier this might not have seemed disastrous, but the French Army, it turned out, had also been broken by Verdun, at least to a much greater extent than its commanders had understood. By the end of April, the offensive had stalled. On May 3, Nivelle, attempting to revive it, ordered his 2nd Division to attack; they refused. Mutiny quickly spread among the troops. Thousands deserted. The offensive was suspended. Nivelle was removed from command and sent to North Africa. Pétain, appointed to replace him, had to deal with rebelling French troops before he could focus on the Germans. "It wasn't that they were unwilling to fight, and even to die," one French historian explained to me. "They were. But they did not want to be just sent to their deaths *for no reason.*"

To his credit, Pétain recognized this. He also recognized that he couldn't very well execute every *poilu* involved in the mutiny; if he did, he wouldn't have enough left to fight the war. Still, something had to be done to restore discipline. Pétain chose to court-martial a small percentage of the mutineers, and hope that their example—along with the promises of more leave from the front and a suspension of greater offensives until the American Expeditionary Forces joined the fight—would convince his soldiers to stay in their ranks and refrain from disrupting the war effort further.

It worked. But for the rest of the war—and well beyond—the words "Chemin des Dames" would be inextricable from the awful, painful memories of the slaughter of the Nivelle Offensive, and of the thousands of courts-martial and hundreds of death sentences that followed in its wake.

As badly as things went that spring, the French did manage to take, and hold, some bits and pieces of that dreaded ridge. And they would continue to do so throughout the rest of the year. By winter, things had quieted down there enough that their high command thought it might be a good place to train some newly arrived American troops. Besides, they needed a lot of fresh bodies to fill in for the men the French had lost there. Perhaps that's why they selected for the assignment the only complete American division in France at that point, National Guard troops from New England whose commanding officer had wanted to get into the fight so badly that five months earlier, tired of waiting for his own high command to give him the go-ahead, he had his entire division shipped over to France without orders.

★ ★ ★

His name was Clarence Ransom Edwards; a native of Cleveland, he'd gone to West Point, graduated last in his class, and fought in the Philippines before serving stints out west and along the Mexican border. Before all that, though, back in 1898, Edwards's hopes of fighting in the Spanish-American War had been dashed when Spain sued for peace before he and his unit could arrange a ride to Cuba. Perhaps that explains why, nineteen years later, he decided to just go ahead and ship his division across the Atlantic Ocean as soon as he deemed them ready. That he somehow managed to get all twenty-five thousand of them—plus all their arms, equipment and horses—sent all the way to France without any of his superiors finding out has to be one of the most remarkable logistical achievements of the war. To this day, it's not clear exactly how he did it.

The fact that the YD was the first complete American infantry division in France gave them, in addition to a tremendous sense of pride, a certain status with the French. In greeting some of the New England troops as they disembarked from a transport, France's General Louis de Maud'huy, who commanded the sector, "said he already regarded them as thoroughbreds, eager to gallop where his own *poilus* were content to trot and to conserve their energies." Clearly, the French had a lot of respect for these doughboys. Except they didn't refer to soldiers of the AEF as "doughboys," a term they had difficulty pronouncing correctly; they called them "Sammies." You'll still hear them called that in France.

General de Maud'huy's colorful remark was duly recorded by Frank Sibley, a reporter for *The Boston Globe* who'd embedded himself with the YD. In his 1919 memoir, *With the Yankee Division in France*, Sibley recounted that in those early months, the French did more than just train the Sammies. "The Americans needed equipment, too, and the French furnished it," he recalled. "They did everything for us; when some of our rolling kitchens failed to turn up, they fed our men, and they waited on us in every way. Their officers were courteous as only French officers can be, patient with our mistakes—and if they were amused by some of our ways, they concealed it from us."

It's likely the French, just a year after the slaughter of Verdun and a few months after the catastrophe at the Chemin des Dames, were more confused than amused by some of the Americans' behavior, perhaps most of all by their seeming eagerness to get into battle. As Sibley wrote: "The Yankees rolled out of their trains, got their wagons on the road, and swung out through Soissons, singing. The boys were all excited; at last they were at the front, and the visible signs were all about them." Their ebullient behavior stood in stark contrast to their grim surroundings:

> In the villages they passed every house was a ruin. Every wood was a dump for ammunition or barbed wire or endless miles of narrow-gauge railroad track, the lengths neatly corded up like so much lumber. Every road was one long procession of army transport of every sort, with the French staff cars whizzing in and out of the columns. On the roadsides were machine gun pill-boxes; trenches led off here and there, and piled stone barricades completed the assurance that not so very long ago there had been close-up fighting on this very ground.

The French led the YD to a section of the Chemin des Dames that they had taken from the Germans only a few months earlier. We'll never know just how much this doughboy or that knew about what had happened in that area the previous spring, but at the beginning—according to Sibley, at least—no one showed any trepidation about being there. Quite the opposite, actually. "There was something very impressive in the way the Yankees went into sector," he recalled. "They were so excited, so interested, so happy over it,—and so utterly unconcerned about the danger. If a plane buzzed overhead, every man gazed as long as it could be seen. At each distant explosion of gun or shell, the whole column remarked 'Powie! There's one!' And they searched the horizon for the smoke puff." As Sibley described it, they were nothing less than exhilarated. "The men carried the full packs, which weighed anywhere from seventy to ninety pounds," he wrote. "They had a ten-mile march to make, practically all of it after dark . . . They took it singing. The roads were muddy with a cream-colored paste, thick over broken stone—hard marching." I've already described what the mud is like Over There; it inspires some strong reactions, but breaking into song isn't one of them.

They arrived after dark, and were warned, for their own safety, to stay put. They did. But the next morning, having survived that first night, Sibley reported, "the boys swarmed up on to the plateau to have a look around." Curiosity, it seems, proved more powerful than caution, and there was a lot to see. "The fields on the hilltops were crisscrossed with old trenches and littered with all sorts of German relics," Sibley wrote, and here I took particular notice:

> Hasty orders were immediately sent out against touching any of these relics, especially shells that seemed to be unexploded. The German trick of baiting explosive traps with attractive souvenirs was explained, and the extreme whimsicality of duds—as unexploded shells are called. The soldiers were very obedient, but very ingenious. I found one of them coiling up a length of old field telephone wire—about a hundred feet of it. He made a noose in one end, dropped it round a helmet which he wanted, unrolled his line, and pulled from the other end. When the helmet came along with no disastrous results he went back and picked it up, utterly charmed because it had a bullet hole in it and stains inside that might have been Boche blood.

Soon, though, the Yankee Division had to abandon their quest for souvenirs and get down to work. At 3:45 P.M. on February 5, 1918, Battery A of the 101st Field Artillery, stationed near the village of Vailly on the Chemin des Dames, fired the YD's first shot of the war. (Apparently, knowing that the AEF's first shot had already been fired several months earlier, they didn't feel the need to wake up early for theirs.) Four nights later, Robert Bayard of Winthrop, Massachusetts, on post in a shell hole, heard a sound in No Man's Land and, despite orders to the contrary, went out to investigate. "He probably was eager to get the first Boche," Sibley speculated. Instead, he got lost and wandered back to a different point in his line, failed to respond to calls to identify himself, and was shot in the leg by an American machine gun; other doughboys pulled him back into their trench and applied a tourniquet, but he bled to death, anyway. And thus, Sibley tells us, "the first front-line casualty came from an American, not a German bullet. It was due to American enterprise, American lack of caution, lack of discipline and over-confidence." But that was why the division was here: not to launch an offensive, but to learn what it was like to hold a position near the enemy's. Bayard's death, it turned out, was an important part of that education.

He was buried two days later, in a small cemetery outside Vailly where the French had already buried many *poilus*. "At the far end," Sibley observed, "two whole rows of graves had been dug and left open; these were for the use of the Americans." It was, he recalled, a bright but cold morning. Planes flew overhead—not in salute to the fallen, but in search of the enemy. The affair was a great deal less ceremonious than the service for Gresham, Hay and Enright had been. "An armed escort was sent by the boy's company, but there were no blank cartridges with which to fire a parting salute," Sibley wrote. "There was not even a coffin; the soldier was buried in his blanket. A bottle containing his name and the date of his death was buried with him, and a duplicate was placed on top of his grave." That was it. Five days later, Private Ralph Spaulding of the 103rd Regiment became the first soldier of the YD to be killed by the enemy; a native of Madison, Maine, he was struck down by shrapnel from a German shell.

Not coincidentally, it was around this time, when the men of the YD were first starting to confront the dangers in their "quiet" sector, that they began looking for shelter, and quickly discovered the chalk mines that the Germans had occupied, and used so well, until just months earlier. Sibley referred to them in his memoir as "the wonderful French quarries." "They were not," he explained, "great open pits, like our quarries at home. They were more like elaborate mines, with broad tunnels. In almost any one of them a battalion could be comfortably housed; in one or two of the largest there was room for a regiment or more. They bore names like Montparnasse, the Pantheon, Montmirail, or Carriere du Sourd. They were all lighted by electricity; some had their own water supply; all were fitted up with floored and ceiled rooms."

They could thank the Germans for those amenities—and for giving them a good idea of how to pass the time down there while warding off what must have been the ever-encroaching fear of oblivion.

✴ ✴ ✴

In 1951, as the Cold War was heating up, the United States acquired an old abandoned air base outside the French city of Laon, about twelve miles north of Vailly, and stationed bombers there. For the next fifteen years, the U.S. Air Force had a large presence in Laon; certain neighborhoods were populated entirely by airmen. One of them, perhaps a son of a YD veteran, befriended a local French veteran of the recent war in Algeria named Claude Chauwin, and at some point told him about some underground mines in the area where there was a lot of American graffiti from the First World War. Claude was intrigued; the American took him to some of the mines and showed him. When the base closed, in 1967, Claude continued exploring them on his own, and brought along his teenaged son, Gilles. A half century later, Gilles continues to be fascinated by them.

While most people in France, or so it seems to me, know a fair bit about *la Grande Guerre,* the war—even just the Western Front—was, as I've said before, so vast, and had so many facets, that the people who dig the deepest into its history often direct all of their considerable attentions to one narrow, knowable area. Gilles Chauwin is one of those people, and his area is the Chemin des Dames. He has visited the chalk mines where the men of the YD took shelter in 1918 on innumerable occasions; and yet, every time he goes down into them, he finds something new. Perhaps it's not really knowable after all.

No one's ever been able to tell me for sure how many mines soldiers— French, German, and American—occupied at one time or another. Gilles knows of three with American graffiti. All are on private property. One of them, he tells me, has become unsafe. He's happy to show people the other two, though typically they only get to visit one, outside the little village of Braye-en-Laonnois.

I had been referred to Gilles by several people, including the super-intendent of the nearest American cemetery, about an hour away. We'd e-mailed back and forth in French, and eventually decided upon a date and time to go exploring. He said he'd pick me up at Braye's *mairie,* which turned out to be closed, despite it being a weekday. I sat on its front steps and waited; never saw or heard another human being, at least not until Gilles pulled up and got out of his car. He was wearing a fleece jacket with an American flag sewn on one sleeve and a patch from the DEA's El Paso bureau sewn on the other. It was hard to tell how old he was— sixties?—but he looked rugged; perhaps it was the hand-rolled cigarettes he smoked. Maybe six feet tall, broad shoulders, close-cropped hair, little glasses, determined gaze. He greeted me by name and shook my hand en-thusiastically, but didn't say much, at least not at first, choosing instead to communicate in short, sharp gestures, the first of which was to beckon me to follow him to his car. Eventually, I figured out that he was self-conscious about his English, which wasn't any better than my French.

We drove a mile or so out of the village and parked just off the road, near the start of a dirt path. Gilles grabbed a large pack from his backseat, slung it over his shoulder, and, wordlessly beckoning me to follow, started walking. The path was narrow, surrounded by waist-high grass; it wound this way and that up a very slight rise, until we rounded a bend and I spotted what looked like the entrance to an old cemetery vault that was built into a hillside. As we got closer, I could see it was quite elaborate: Grass grew atop scores of petrified cement sacks, which sat atop a broad corrugated metal half-pipe—the kind the Germans brought to France by the thousands in 1914—which in turn sat atop a base of stone and mortar with a portal in the middle. In front of all of it was a locked gate, a thick wooden frame fitted with iron bars and, in the middle, a metal grille festooned with ornamental squares in geometric patterns. The whole thing looked out of place, as if Frank Lloyd Wright had built a fallout shelter in the middle of nowhere. But it was sturdy—and, as Gilles later explained, sadly, necessary: Before it was built, souvenir hunters who knew about the mine plundered it, using saws to cut out some of the irreplaceable artwork and take it home. If you ask him, Gilles can tell you what used to be in this now-effaced spot or that. But he'd rather not think about it.

Gilles unlocked the gate, stepped inside a little chamber, and lay down on his belly on the platform. Moving closer, I saw that he had extended one of his arms through a circular metal grate on the floor of the platform. He turned his head to the side—hand-rolled cigarette still clasped in his lips—and groped around for a couple of minutes, until his eyes widened momentarily and I heard a click. He pulled his arm out, got to his feet, brushed himself off, bent over again, and opened the grate. Reaching into his pack, he pulled out a headlamp for himself and handed me a large flashlight—the old kind, made of molded plastic and rubber, that has a built-in handle and runs off a single battery the size of a brick. Then he sat back down on the floor, dropped his legs into the hole, and slowly eased his hands and feet onto the sides and rungs of a black metal ladder that rose only as high as the lip of the platform. In several motions he managed to turn himself around so he was facing the rungs, then lowered himself one at a time. When he reached the next platform, about fifteen feet down, he beckoned for me to follow. I lowered myself to the floor, dropped my legs into the hole, and took a minute to figure out exactly how I was going to do this; then I stuck the flashlight in my teeth and got to it, never once thinking about Adélaïde and Victoire.

Attached to that second platform was another fifteen-foot ladder for us to climb down, slowly. The bottom was soft, dirt; a cloud of something

rose up as I hopped off the last rung onto the ground. Two cones of light—
Gilles's small and bright, mine diffuse and somewhat dimmer—revealed
a deep cavern. Its walls, solid, hard, were white here, gray there, gray and
white elsewhere. Its ceilings were low; after I'd taken a half-dozen steps,
I could no longer stand up straight. When I climbed back out, five hours
later, my hair was white with chalk. There was no natural source of light. I
wasn't sure where the oxygen was coming from. For six weeks in the winter
of 1918, hundreds of men from Massachusetts and Connecticut lived here.

And that was nothing: For three years before that, hundreds of German soldiers—maybe more—rotated through the Froidmont *carrière,* or
Cold Mountain quarry. Resting on the dirt near the bottom of the second
ladder were some of the things they'd left behind: brown wine bottles,
green beer bottles, empty food tins, bayonets, bullet clips, helmets, a telephone receiver, all of which looked like they'd spent a century underground. The ceiling was studded here and there with porcelain electrical
insulators and bits of wire. The Germans electrified these quarries, as they
did just about any place they spent much time. They dug ventilation shafts;
ran telephone line in. As we moved around, I spotted remnants of bunks
and stoves. Who, you may think, would want to spend that kind of time in
a sunless chalk quarry three stories beneath the earth? And then you remember what was happening up on the surface in 1914, and 1915 and 1916
and especially 1917, and it doesn't seem so bad down here at all. Especially
if you could find creative ways to pass the time. They did.

You don't have to walk very far into the mine to see their work. The
Germans were meticulous, had beautiful handwriting in that old, Gothic
style. As you read their names—Franz Göttgens, Josef Tübsdorf, Fritz
Hase, Valentin Zajac, Hans Haude—you can picture them being taught
to render such graceful script one letter at a time by a stern schoolmaster
like the one in *All Quiet on the Western Front.* They painstakingly chiseled away at the walls to create flat surfaces, rectangles and squares as
perfect as one can make without proper tools, then wrote on them in pen
or pencil. They drew German flags; carved Prussian crosses, the elaborate wartime ones with a crown up top, the date 1914 down below, and a
large *W* in the middle, for Kaiser Wilhelm. Next to one of these, someone
wrote, in big block letters and blue ink that has since faded to purple: AVE
CAESAR. MORITURI TE SALUTANT. Hail Caesar. We who are about to die
salute you.

They took care to record their names and ranks: *Gefreiter* Loth. *Jäger* Jammasch. *Landsturmmann* Schmitz. *Unteroffizier* Runkel. *Musketier* Cohn. Cohn wrote his name and the dates 1915–1917 under a niche he carved out to hold candles, the chalk in and around it blackened by a lot of smoke. He was down here a good long while. So were a unit of *Kranken-träger*—stretcher-bearers—who, busy as they must have been, still found the time to carve an impressive memorial plaque for their fallen, dated 1914–1915, with an appendix for 1916. Throughout the Western Front, *Krankenträger* had some of the highest casualty rates of any units.

Sometimes they eulogized a fallen *Kamerad* with a bit of romantic verse; memorializing one Fritz Jaencke, someone inked:

> *May all the world speak badly of you,*
> *just keep your conscience clean,*
> *so God will always stay with you.*

You'll find popular expressions of the day on the walls, too, like *Gott mit uns,* God is with us, and *Gott strafe England,* May God punish England. The latter was a line from a patriotic song, *"Hassgesang gegen England,"* or "Hate Song Against England"; GOTT MIT UNS was stamped on millions of belt buckles issued to German soldiers. They were the most cherished souvenir a doughboy could bring home.

As intriguing and artistic as much of their graffiti is, though, the Germans also stenciled a lot of signs and arrows on the chalk, directing you to this unit or that. A practical measure; those mines are labyrinthine, passages departing from passages departing from passages, every which way. But for the markings on the wall, you might never find your way back out. When it came time to leave that day, Gilles and I got lost for a good twenty minutes, and he'd already been down there hundreds of times. But I was too tired and exhilarated to feel scared; and if there was fear in his expression, it was too subtle for my flashlight to detect.

✷ ✷ ✷

Those New England doughboys may, as Frank Sibley wrote, have been excited to arrive at the Chemin des Dames, but by the time they found their way down into the mines, a week or so later, they had seen enough of the enemy at work that none of them, I suspect, were in any rush to get back up top. As Captain Daniel W. Strickland of the YD's 102nd Infantry described the local landscape in his 1930 history, *Connecticut Fights:*

> If one were to take several thousand cups of various sizes and set them rim to rim as closely as they could be packed, some conception might be had of the nature of the terrain. Great craters, many large enough for the cellar of a house, were partly filled with slimy water covered with a green scum. An occasional battered tree raised its forlorn scarecrow stump. The rusty entanglements hung about twisted and broken stakes, while off toward the front the ominous grey hills loomed, hiding the enemy . . . The place resounded with working parties, ration parties and patrols, cursing their way over this hellish plateau. Road repairs, wire repairs, the whine of gas shells, and sometimes the roar of an "ash can" or a "trolley car," as the men came to call the big shells, made the area anything but quiet.

And yet, as Strickland wrote, "as one surveyed this scene of destruction, where not a living thing could be seen when a barrage was passing over, he would little suspect that within a few minutes ten thousand men could burst forth from the bowels of the earth."

Perhaps the sights of the "hellish plateau" colored Strickland's impressions of what lay below. He refers to the mines as "wonderful, cozy dugouts," says they were "like children's ideas of robbers' caves, with all the comfort a soldier could want." The caverns, as he calls them, "were long, wide, winding tunnels, and broad well lighted chambers hewn out of the soft stone, where the light and shadow effect of thousands of soldiers coming and going back and forth with glimmering candles and electric torches reminded one of the tales from *Arabian Nights*. Here and there the cigarettes glowed from shadowy corners or bunks, like fire flies on a summer night."

I thought about that as I followed Gilles deeper into the mine, the embers of his cigarette almost too small and dim to look like what they were, much less fireflies. Strickland's description haunted me as we slowly made our way forward, down this deeply dark passage or that; I felt as if I were exploring a long-abandoned boarded-up mansion and imagining the galas that its ballroom had once hosted. I tried to picture the electric bulbs hanging overhead, the telephone line strung through hooks along the ceiling. I summoned bunks in this alcove; a galley stove over there. And everywhere, men, in small groups, pairs, alone. Young Americans, thousands of miles from homes they'd never left before, sheltering deep underground, having seen that hellish plateau, heard the ash cans and trolley cars come screaming in. A hundred years ago. Nothing left of them now.

Except.

It was as if a baton were being handed off: At one point we passed a finely drawn hand, forefinger pointing to the left, the word *Zug* (train) rendered in handsome Teutonic lettering; and then, a few paces beyond, I looked up at the ceiling and saw, written in black inside a circle, four indelicately crafted letters.

Hell.

Welcome to the American section.

I don't know why the Americans chose to shelter in this particular area of the mine, but it certainly seemed like hell to me, at least at first: Aside from that word, and a skull and the number 18 on the ceiling a few paces on, and a charred block of wood with a couple of porcelain electrical insulators attached, and an empty bottle, it was desolate. Actually, even with those things it was pretty desolate in there. But then, after a few minutes, I cast my light on a section of wall, and things suddenly changed from ghost town to high school.

Unlike most of what I had walked past to get there—some of which still bore two-hundred-year-old pick marks—it was flat, and smooth; someone had gone to a lot of trouble to make it that way. Whether it was the Americans, or the Germans, or French miners long before either, the Yankee Division took full advantage of it. There were monograms, Greek letters (Sigma Delta; Mu Phi Kappa), and names: Marsh. Donovan. Robinson. R. B. Kincaid. A bas-relief plaque identified this wall as the province of Company A, 101st Machine Gun Battalion. The most striking element was a skull, colored deep red with bright blue eyes, the words *Boche Kultur* carved into its forehead. German Civilization. Always used ironically.

It continued on an even larger section around the corner: DWC. JMF. ORL. Galpin. T. Coady. E. K. O'Neil. B. W. Townsend. Ned Perry. Fred J. Brophy. Someone carved a large rendering of the Knights of Columbus shield; someone else, a Masonic compass.

We walked further. There were names everywhere: George Ross. Alfred Swanson. L. V. Frank. P. W. Schofield. Emmet Guaros. Charles Sabo. Ray Connor. Julius Zawadsky. M. Erickson. W. Winniki. Arnold G. Cox. T. J. Fay. F. A. Woop. Albert C. Poulin. Nicholas Little. G. E. Johnson.

Arnold B. Cox. Otto Contardi. Winfield Dowd. E. T. Greene. H. W. Judd. R. L. Dudley. John Sweeney. Joseph R. Gemski. Louis Booth. Oscar W. Johnson. Ed Stearns. Bob Jones. Many included some association: Company F, 101st U.S. Infantry. Company K, 102nd Infantry U.S.A. The Plumber's Association. Company C, 102nd Machine Gun Battalion. The International Order of Odd Fellows. 102nd Sanitary Detachment. The YMCA. Company C, 101st Field Battalion, Signal Corps. The Knights of Columbus. The Crack Bomb'n' Team of the Second Section, Company I. The Ancient Order of Hibernians. The Bucket of Blood. Compass #9, Wallingford, Conn.

From time to time Gilles would lean in so close that the tip of his cigarette would just about brush against the wall. He haltingly sounded out American names—Eh-vahns, Doe-noe-vahn, Cuur-teess—and beckoned me to correct his pronunciation. Some he said without hesitation; he seemed to regard them as old friends. He was familiar with Sibley's account, would have known that after a short while at the Chemin des Dames, the men's initial excitement about being at the front faded. After a few weeks there, Sibley wrote, "the physical condition of the men was bad. They had been run down by the long exposure, the weather [it was still winter, after all], and the unremitting labor. Equipment was short; underclothes, shoes, uniforms, and blankets were lacking in proper quantities." Down here, at least the weather and exposure weren't bad, and they probably got to rest more than they worked, which might explain their creative energy. They drew in pen: German soldiers. *Poilus.* Doughboys. Uncle Sam. Someone inked a pretty fine likeness of Buffalo Bill; perhaps he had seen Cody's Wild West Show in New England as a child. Several drew Indian chiefs. "Do you know of the Passamaquoddy?" Gilles asked me, and I was startled to hear the name of that old Maine tribe spoken in a French accent in a French sentence. "A colonel," he said, "used several of them for bodyguards." I have never been able to confirm that, but Gilles must have gotten it somewhere; it's not as if everyone in France has heard of the Passamaquoddy.

The truly impressive stuff, though, is carved out of the chalk walls. It took time; they chose their subjects with care. Crosses. Celtic crosses. Eagles and shields. Croix de Guerre. Shamrocks. Crossed swords. Corporal J. P. Knox, Co. E, 101st U.S. Infantry, etched a nice harp, then colored in the strings and frame with blue ink. Corporal Joseph Papallo, Co. I, 102nd U.S. Infantry, was apparently so proud of the horse head he carved that he included his home address: Woodland St., Meriden, Conn. Someone a bit more practical-minded gouged a good-sized rectangular niche out of the wall at eye level and wrote in ink above: 4th Platoon Mail. A finely detailed scale rendition of the Bunker Hill monument; a stately battleship; a meerschaum pipe, the smoke from which contains a lady's silhouette. On a large, low section of fairly flat wall someone created an arresting tableau: a naked maiden—France—chained to a post and being menaced from behind by a Prussian while, in front, an American flag charges in to save the day. And more crosses. A lot of crosses.

There is some French graffiti scattered here and there, too, mostly names and units, although there is a niche with a carving of Saint Laurent holding the gridiron upon which he was cooked, and an inked tableau depicting a notorious incident from 1902 that stemmed from a love triangle involving a Parisian prostitute and two leaders of the street gang the Apaches, which did not end well for any of them. And toward the back of one alcove where the ground was covered by a mound of white rubble several feet high, I spotted, drawn meticulously in black ink upon a flat surface, a square frame containing two cross-shaped and sweating candles, two skulls and crossbones, and a pair of crossed miner's picks. They looked as dark and bold as the day they were drawn; written underneath, in beautiful script:

IN MEMORY OF LAURENT MULLEPA

AND FRANÇOIS MULLEPA, HIS SON

CRUSHED IN THIS PLACE

THE 11TH OF THE MONTH OF MAY 1838

PRAY FOR THEIR SOULS

A cave-in, no doubt; for all I know, Mullepa *père* and *fils* might still lie together beneath that chalky pile. I looked at Gilles. He nodded, a piece of ash tumbling from his cigarette, then stoically turned away.

✷ ✷ ✷

Up top, it no longer looks like a thousand cups of various sizes set rim to rim; in the villages, every house is no longer a ruin. I wouldn't go so far as to say that the place looks like it did when Adélaïde and Victoire went to visit the *comtesse*, but the terrain has been rehabilitated to a great extent: it can be difficult, in passing, to tell which cragginess is a result of nature and which is a result of 75- or 77-millimeter shells. One thing you can tell, however, is that the Germans didn't have it so easy up on the Chemin des

Dames, either: They built more than a half-dozen cemeteries in the area, none of them small. Gilles told me that during the war they also built monuments to their fallen in every village they occupied on the ridge. The French, he added, destroyed them all in 1923.

After that first visit, Gilles and I stayed in touch, e-mailing in French; he shared photos taken in the vicinity of the Chemin des Dames during the war, asked about my work and when I might return to the area, sent me e-cards on July 4, Thanksgiving, Christmas. When I did return, a year later, he invited me to his house in Laon, where he introduced me to his wife, made a pot of tea for all of us to share, showed me his library of American World War I books, of which he was very proud. After we visited for a couple of hours there, he took me to the only other accessible mine with graffiti from the Yankee Division, outside the village of Nanteuil-la-Fosse. This one has no iron door or locked grate; the only thing protecting it from vandals is that you have to know where it is.

This mine was perhaps not as extensive at the one outside Braye, but it was no less labyrinthine; once again, Gilles and I got lost. He was more relaxed this time, perhaps because we knew each other better, or maybe just because he hadn't had to lie on his belly fiddling with an unseen lock and then descend two iron ladders just to get here. We walked right in. The Germans had, too: Throughout the mine the walls were studded with iron rings, evidence that they had even brought their horses in with them. In February and March of 1918, Sammies from the 103rd Infantry Regiment took shelter here; they were Maine National Guard, and apparently no more reticent than the Connecticut and Massachusetts men when it came to leaving their mark. They carved eagles and horses and Masonic compasses, drew crosses and Indian chiefs and themselves. Someone carved a splendid four-masted schooner in full sail; someone else rendered in bas-relief an excellent profile of President Woodrow Wilson—a tribute, I imagine, to the man who had sent them there. Mostly, though, they left their names.

II.

Those names: They raised a lot of questions. I could not look at them, study and photograph and strain to decipher them, without wanting, almost needing, to know who they were and how they'd fared in the war, and afterward; if there had been an afterward. And why some men chose to write their names alone on some isolated patch of wall while others chose to group a half dozen or more together, like:

G CO. 101ST INF

ROLL OF HONOUR

CORP. JOHN B. SHANAHAN

PRIV. J. JOSEPH MARA

PRIV. JOHN J. SHAUGHNESSY

PRIV. JOSEPH DONAHUE

PRIV. JOHN V. CARNEY

PRIV. ALBERT FLAGG

PRIV. THOS. F. O'HALLORAN

THE MIDNIGHT SQUAD

Some inked their names both alone and with others, like Corporal Shanahan of the Midnight Squad, who claimed another spot on a nearby wall and drew a cross and a hand pointing to a pierced and radiant heart, and wrote:

MERCIFUL HEART

OF

JESUS

HAVE MERCY

ON US

Corporal Shanahan, who'd been born in Ireland and was living in Worcester when he enlisted, was 25 years old when he inked his plea to the Merciful Heart of Jesus, and apparently made it through the rest of the war intact, at least physically; he was promoted to sergeant that June, cited in General Orders at the end of August for meritorious service in the capture of a number of villages that summer, and cited in another GO dispatch in October for going on "a particularly dangerous raid." He is, in other words, proof that one can be simultaneously frightened and brave.

I know all this about him because General Leonid Kondratiuk of the Massachusetts National Guard sent me a scan of Joseph Shanahan's service record, which had been typed shortly after the war on two sides of an index card. The 102nd Infantry Regiment's complete and annotated roster was published in 1930 in Captain Strickland's *Connecticut Fights*; the 103rd, from Maine, published its records in two different books. But the Massachusetts regiment has never published theirs anywhere, nor even compiled it; I had to send General Kondratiuk a list of more than a hundred names—many partial, some just initials—and hope for the best. He and Keith Vezeau, his archivist, managed to identify most of them. When you finally have that much information in your possession, you come to realize that these things on the wall aren't merely inscriptions; they're stories.

And some are yarns, like this one, in blue ink that has faded to a nice purple, that reads:

IN MEMORY

OF

THE DETAILS

OF COMPANY G, 101ST INF

JOE DUNN

JIM DUNN

BILLY SMITH

CH. TALBOT

TMS. O'CONNOR

BILL SWEENEY

MAY THEY REST

IN PEACE

All six of those men were alive and well when one of them—my guess would be Joe Dunn, since his name comes first—inked that cheeky little epitaph. Perhaps he thought it might ward off such a fate in reality. Did it work? Well, several of them were later wounded in action. Sweeney was listed as being "slightly" wounded on June 6, 1918; O'Connor was also wounded, on July 22—again, the official record says "slightly," though he spent the next three months in the hospital and never returned to the front again, instead being assigned to guard German prisoners of war. Billy Smith was gassed on May 29 and spent more than six months in the hospital; the 1920 census shows him, at age 29, living with his parents in Worcester, and not working. So, no, it didn't exactly keep them safe. Still, only one of the six actually died in the war—Joe Dunn himself, of "broncho pneumonia" (perhaps a result of being gassed) on October 28, 1918.

Gilles beckoned me over to a nearby section of wall and pointed to another ink inscription:

CORP. EARLE MADELEY

CO. I 102ND U.S. INF.

AEF MAR 6 1918

AGE 20 YEARS

Years earlier, he told me, he'd been walking one day through the Aisne-Marne American Cemetery, outside the village of Belleau, and spotted that name on a stone: Plot B, Row 6, Grave 51. He took a picture of the marker and later tacked it up on the wall above that piece of graffiti; when he pointed it out to me, he touched its ink tenderly.

On another occasion, on a different wall, Corporal Madeley had written his name alongside a friend's, each in their own hand. They must have been close; there's just the two of them together there, the lettering modest:

CORP. EARLE MADELEY

SEG. J. SOKOWICH

CO. I 102 U.S. INF.

Corporal Madeley, a native of Plainville, Connecticut, is listed in the official roster as DW—died of wounds—on July 21, 1918. Records show he was 5'8" tall, weighed 150 pounds, and had worked as a clerk before the war. Sergeant Joseph Sokowich had been born in Ku Ku Ki, Russia, in 1887, immigrated to America as a child, and was working for the P & F Corbin Manufacturing company in New Britain when his adopted country entered the war. His occupation—"laborer"—and previous service in the Connecticut National Guard, which dates back in chunks to 1910, are listed on a questionnaire that the state had everyone complete after the war. His was completed by his mother; Sergeant Sokowich was killed a month after he left the Chemin des Dames, on April 20, 1918, in the first major clash between American and German troops, at a place called Seicheprey.

It is sheer coincidence that two men who wrote their names together like that should both die, months apart, in the war; and pure irony that neither or them wrote anything like "In Memory of" or "May They Rest in Peace" next to their names, when so many others down there did. You cannot tell, of course, from the content of the epigraph, or the quality of the penmanship, or the delicacy of the carving, what became of any man who left his mark here. All you can do is research his name, get to know him a little bit, posthumously; for they are all, no matter how they fared in the war, dead now. Let's meet just a few of them, shall we?

PRI. PAUL URPIN

CO. F 101 INF.

A.E.F.

Inked on a small smoothed canvas of wall; Private Urpin started to draw a fancy frame around the outside but never finished. Perhaps he moved on to other creative pursuits; like Corporal Madeley, he left his mark down there on at least two occasions. Born in Waltham, Massachusetts, the son of a French immigrant, he enlisted August 8, 1917, aged 20 years, 8 months. Promoted to private first class June 15, 1918. Wounded in action severely "about" July 26. Hospitalized until he was discharged on April 4, 1919, nearly five months after the war ended. Later worked as a plumber, married, had six children. Died in Woodland Hills, California, in 1967.

K

102

BRIDGEPORT

KELLY

MARCH 5, 1918

Corporal Joseph Aloysius Kelly wrote his name in blue ink in several spots and configurations, including, just a few feet away from the above (which is enclosed in a structure resembling a house), a carved square-within-a square containing a shamrock surrounded by the words

"ERIN GO BRAGH"

THE FRIENDLY SONS

OF ST. PATRICK

PHILA   FRANCE

1791   1918

CORP. J.A. KELLY—

and, elsewhere, another inked and etched square, this one celebrating Company K, 102 U.S., 25th Squad, with a list of seven names (his first) and, at the bottom, "Pride of the A.E.F." Born in Bridgeport, Connecticut, he was the son of a paper hanger, grandson of four Irish immigrants. He enlisted on June 25, 1917, one month after his twenty-fifth birthday, a clerk, 5'6" tall, 130 pounds. Killed in action July 20, 1918; buried in Plot A, Row 3, Grave 79 at Aisne-Marne, the same cemetery as Earle Madeley, who died one day later.

R.A. BEST

CO. E 101ST

Carved his name in tall bas-relief letters between two blackened candle niches. The rest he just gouged. Perhaps he ran out of time; carving things in bas-relief takes a lot of effort. Private Robert A. Best of Roxbury, Massachusetts; a Canadian immigrant, born in Maitland, Nova Scotia. Enlisted in the Massachusetts National Guard May 29, 1917, at the age of 20. Last seen alive October 23, 1918. His name is listed on the Missing in Action plaque at the Meuse-Argonne Cemetery in Romagne.

P. BUTLER

CO. H 103

Private Perley Butler, 19 years old, gouged his name and outfit inside a rectangle and underneath a large horse head, carved in relief and colored with pencil, still dark a century later. Born and raised in Waterville, Maine, he enlisted in its National Guard on May 7, 1917, was promoted to private first class September 18 of that year, and was demoted back to private on May 5, 1918. Killed in action by shell fire on July 17.

M.J.M.

CO. G. 101ST

FEB.   U.S. INF.   22

M.J. MALONEY

35 WAVE AVE

WAKEFIELD, MASS.

Everything in this one is gouged except for the name and the street address, which were added afterward in blue ink; perhaps Private Michael J.

Maloney wanted to make sure that future visitors would know where to find him after the war, though by 1930 he had moved around the corner to Vernon Street, where he lived with his wife, three children, two step-children, father-in-law, and brother-in-law, and made his living as a brass finisher. He enlisted in June 1916, at the age of 27, and spent the war as a private, with a stint as company bugler. Died August 1, 1961.

W.D. BERTINI

COMPASS #9

WALLINGFORD

CONN K 102 INF

MAR. 1918

S.J. SHAW

CO K 102 INF

COMPASS #9

WALLINGFORD

CONN USA

Same hometown; same company; same Masonic lodge. Same Masonic compass in their inscriptions. Same section of the mine. Both born in 1896; both enlisted just weeks after America entered the war. William DeForest Bertini was 5'8", 140 pounds; before the war he'd been a clerk in an office. Promoted to private first class on June 1, 1917, corporal on an unspecified date thereafter, and sergeant on August 22, 1918. Wounded in action slightly on March 17, 1918, while still on the Chemin des Dames. After the war he returned home, got married, had one daughter and two sons, went to work as a cashier at a silver factory. Eventually he was promoted to office manager; died in 1972. Stanley Joseph Shaw had been a silversmith for a while before the war, then went to work for the Winchester Repeating Arms Company as a gunsmith. He was six feet tall, weighed 155 pounds, and was promoted to corporal on May 24, 1917, just three weeks after he enlisted. Killed in action on April 20, 1918, also at Seicheprey. Buried in the Saint-Mihiel American Cemetery in Thiaucourt, France.

Another Mason in the same subterranean neighborhood carved a large compass with lines so straight he must have used his bayonet as a ruler:

ALEXANDER B. GRANT

COMPASS #922

CHICAGO, ILL.

MT. HERMON

MEDFORD

MASS

U.S.A.

Private Grant had been born in New Brunswick, Canada, and immigrated to Massachusetts. Worked as a clerk in a hardware store before the war. Enlisted May 21, 1917; assigned to Company E, 101st Infantry. Killed in action October 30, 1918. Buried at the Meuse-Argonne Cemetery.

D.E.G.

CO. G

103 INF.

In bold pencil, each line inside its own neat rectangle. Private Daniel Earl Geagan, born in Waltham, Massachusetts, 1896. Enlisted in Brewer, Maine, June 2, 1917. Killed in action by a machine-gun bullet July 22, 1918. Buried at the Oise-Aisne American Cemetery in Seringes-et-Nesles, France. The American Legion post in Brewer is named for him.

P.J. KOCHISS

CO. K U.S. INF.

102 AEF

STRATFORD, CONN. MARCH 3, 1918

The hometown and date are inked; everything else, including a heart-and-cross motif, is carved in bas-relief, large. Peter John Kochiss was born in 1894 in Pennsylvania, the son of Slovak immigrants, and moved to Connecticut as a child. The Connecticut Military Census of 1917 lists him as five feet eleven inches tall and 180 pounds, reports that he worked on the family farm and as a shipping checker and, though single, had six people depending upon him for support. Enlisted at New Haven July 26, 1917; promoted to private first class two months later, corporal a year after that. Killed in action October 23, 1918, five days shy of his twenty-fourth birthday.

LS
LEO STANKARD
CO. F 101 U.S. INF.

Written in black ink—kind of surprising, since Leo Stankard was a stone mason back home in Waltham, Massachusetts. Enlisted there on June 1, 1917; promoted to corporal in December. Wounded in action severely on July 23, 1918, he spent the next five months in the hospital, and finished out his service in a Military Police company, being promoted to sergeant a month before he was discharged. Resumed work as a mason after the war, married, no children. Died November 17, 1996, aged 100 years, 2 months and 19 days.

CO. G 1918
J. RICCIARDI
MILFORD, N.H.
U.S.A.

Unlike Leo Stankard, Joseph Ricciardi—also known as Rosario—put his experience as a stone mason to good use in the chalk mines at the Chemin des Dames, rendering a large, handsome convex circle surrounded by a scalloped frame, the lettering carved neatly in straight lines. It looks very much like a memorial plaque; it is. The book *Milford in the Great War*, written by Fred Tilton Wadleigh and published in 1922, tells Ricciardi's story:

> He was born in Piraino, Sicily, in 1887, and left his father and brothers to come to America. He was employed in the granite industry in Milford . . . With no natural fondness for army life or a military career, he left Milford at the outbreak of the war and went to Concord to enlist for the service of America . . . On July 18, in the thick of the fighting, he was killed by a machine-gun bullet . . .
>
> The official report of Major General Clarence R. Edwards, in which he says Ricciardi "showed marked gallantry and meritorious conduct," is a permanent record of his gallant death, but in Milford the picture of the brave young Sicilian pushing onward through the smoke and steel of battle to die for his adopted country was an awakening vision which

brought new patriotism and efforts with the sorrow for his death. It can never be said that Ricciardi died in vain.

JOHN
SWEENEY
CO. F

Simple block outlined letters gouged into a smoothed square; John Sweeney was no stone mason. He worked as a spinner at one of the local woolen mills in Lawrence, Massachusetts. His parents had been born in Ireland; so had his wife, Helen, who immigrated to the United States in 1890. Private Sweeney enlisted in the Massachusetts National Guard on June 16, 1916. Killed in action in the town of Flirey, near Seicheprey, on May 17, 1918. He was 37 years old.

MECH. A. ARDINE
CO. G 103 U.S. INF.
SO. BREWER, ME

Don't let the simplicity of the inscription fool you: This is a truly impressive piece of work. Allie Ardine created a large, smooth rectangle out of rough chalk wall, carved a bas-relief capsule in which to inscribe his name, and below that carved, also in bas-relief, a magnificent shield with stars in the crown and vertical stripes below. The son of Canadian immigrants, he'd worked as a laborer in a pulp mill when he was younger, but when he enlisted in the Maine National Guard in June 1916, at the age of 26, he listed his occupation as "painter," which may explain his artistic bent. He also listed his height as a shade under 5'5", his eyes blue, his hair brown, his complexion dark. Wounded in action July 22, 1918. The record doesn't list the severity—Maine records usually don't—but in November 1926, he moved into the disabled veterans home at Togus, near Augusta. His ailments are listed as broncho asthma (probably a result of being gassed), partial bilateral deafness (perhaps a result of being shelled), and chronic constipation, which could be a result of what they then called shell shock, now known as post-traumatic stress disorder, or PTSD. He stayed at Togus for two years, and did stints at other veterans homes in Dayton, Ohio, Danville, Illinois and Milwaukee, Wisconsin; by 1935 he was living in the home at Walla Walla, Washington. It's not clear why he moved—or was moved—so often. He died in 1957 in Montana, never having married.

MICHAEL

JAY

CO. I 102 INF.

U.S.A.

Faintly etched inside a more boldly etched square, some of the letters are partially outlined in pen, while to the right of his name is, also in ink, what appears to be an incompletely drawn maple leaf; it looks like Private Jay ran out of time. He was born on October 27, 1892, in Stary Sącz, Poland; it's not clear when he immigrated to the United States, but by the time he enlisted, on July 17, 1917, he had taken the first steps to becoming a citizen, though he had not yet achieved such status. Connecticut's 1917 Military Census lists his occupation as carpenter, his height as six feet even, his weight 165 pounds, eyes gray, hair brown, build stout. He could ride a horse and drive a motorcycle, but not an automobile. He was last seen alive on June 11, 1918. His name is inscribed on the Missing in Action plaque at the Saint-Mihiel Cemetery. His parents apparently never left Poland; his next of kin was listed as his sister, Mrs. Sophia Goldy of New Haven.

J.B. LYONS

G CO. 101

Another rush job: The letters are faintly scratched into the wall; he started to outline them in ink but only got as far as "J.B. Lyo," and you really have to strain to see the 101 at all. Born in Brookline toward the end of 1891, James Bernard Lyons enlisted in the Massachusetts National Guard on April 4, 1917, two days after President Wilson asked Congress to declare war on Germany and two days before Congress consented. He was promoted to private first class on June 13, 1918, and to corporal on October 3. After the war he moved back in with his mother, three brothers, three sisters and a nephew, and went to work driving horses on a grain team. The 1940 census shows him, at age 48, working as a laborer for the highway department, still living with his mother and a sister and listed as married, though no wife is in sight. He died January 20, 1957, aged 65. His record notes that on November 10, 1918, the day before the war ended, he was captured by the Germans and held as a prisoner of war until he could be repatriated on November 27.

★ ★ ★

Deep in the mine at Nanteuil-la-Fosse, someone carved out a large rectangular space, roughly the size and shape of the kind of dedication plaque you might find inside the lobby of a WPA-built post office. It is obvious that they had bigger plans for it than time permitted: They smoothed its surface and drew straight lines across from edge to edge at regular intervals. Four men inked and then carved their names on the lines:

CORP. F.L. TUELL

CORP. L.J. BROWN

MECH. R.T. MOAN

PVT. J.W. ROYSE

CO. K 103 INF.

A.E.F.

Actually, Corporal Brown didn't get past the inking stage with his name, and the unit designation never got to the point of being carved, either, but a hundred years later you can still read it all clearly enough to know who these men were. John Wesley Royse was born in Sioux Falls, South Dakota, in 1896 but was living in Augusta, Maine, and working, when he enlisted, as an upholsterer, a vocation he resumed after the war. He married a waitress in a local hotel, had two children, and died in 1973. Foster Leon Tuell was born in 1897 and raised in Dennysville, Maine, way Down East, the adopted son of a lumberman and his wife; the 1920 census shows him living at home with his parents and 7-year-old sister, working as a stenographer in a factory. Later he married a girl from Indiana, moved to Portland, Oregon, then Los Angeles, got divorced, remarried, and eventually settled down in Maricopa County, Arizona, where he worked as a credit manager at a hardware company. He died in Laguna Hills, California, in 1978. Leo Jennings Brown was born in Farmington, Maine, in 1895; his father, J. Eugene Brown, was the editor of the local newspaper. Corporal Brown was wounded in action on July 20, 1918, and though the record does not specify the severity of his wounds, they were bad enough that he was shipped back to the States on October 9, and honorably discharged on

January 31, 1919—ten days after his father died at age 57. After he recovered he went to work as a clerk on the railroad, married, had a son, and moved to Reading, Massachusetts, where he became a bond salesman. He died in 1990, at the age of 95.

Which leaves Mechanic Ralph T. Moan—born in 1897 in Eastport, Maine, the easternmost city in the United States of America—who stands out even in such interesting company for two reasons. First, because about six months after he carved his name on that wall, in the course of running between posts as a messenger, he was blown about twenty feet through the air by a German shell and wounded so badly that it knocked him out of the war. His courage under fire earned him both a French Croix de Guerre and an American Distinguished Service Cross, an award second only to the Medal of Honor. His DSC citation reads:

> For extraordinary heroism in action near Riaville, France, 26 September, 1918. Mechanic Moan, who was detailed as a runner, made several trips, carrying important messages, across terrain swept by constant fire from machine guns, snipers, trench mortars and artillery. His disregard for personal safety and devotion to duty in the prompt delivery of messages contributed greatly to the success of the action.

The other remarkable thing about Ralph T. Moan is that he kept a diary. As he noted in its opening entry:

> I, as a volunteer in Uncle Sam's Army, can easily recall all that took place while in the States, but many of the things that I will probably see "Over There" will no doubt not be so easily remembered, especially, so I shall endeavor to keep a crude account of the things which interest me most.

His narrative begins on September 26, 1917—a year to the day before he was wounded—when he shipped out for Europe. It takes him across the ocean to Liverpool, through a few adventures in England ("We had a great time standing on the corner sizing up the English dames that went by"), and then on to France, where he helped liven up Noël by putting together a singing group: "Corporal Brown, Corporal Tuell, Private Royce [sic] and myself formed a quartette and seemed to be appreciated very much by all who heard us . . . Soon after Christmas we had a big infantry minstrel show. Once more our quartette made a hit . . . That night we had dancing and I was sure mad to think I could not dance with some of the swell little Red Cross nurses who were present, but this liberty was given to the officers while us poor devils had to satisfy ourselves with dancing with each other."

It wasn't all song and dance, though: "I came near getting beat up by a gang of drunk American soldiers one night when on post," he wrote. "I got them to the guard house all right after rapping two of them to their knees with my billy." On February 6, 1918, they set off on foot for the trenches. "Our packs contained slicker, overcoat, reserve and travelling rations, two blankets, 110 rounds of ammunition, shelter half, canteen mess kit, 4 pairs of socks, all necessary toilet articles, such as razor, towels, soap, etc., pair of extra shoes, two extra undershirts, extra outside shirt, tent pole, 5 tent pins, tent rope, 2 gas masks, 1 helmet and haversack," he noted. After a while they came to a station and boarded boxcars marked "40/8," indicating they had room for forty men or eight horses. "Forty of us in a car together with our equipment," Moan wrote, "so of course had no place to sleep unless one fellow lay on top of another." Twenty-six hours later they detrained at Soissons. "Tuell and I looked the town over," he reported, "and it sure was some interesting place for the Germans had once been within two miles of it and had bombarded practically everything to pieces with heavy artillery fire."

Moan's account is in line with Sibley's from *With the Yankee Division in France,* particularly when it comes to the fascination with which the doughboys regarded the French countryside, and their interest in relic-hunting. "This place was once held by the Germans," he wrote of one village they marched through, "and so of course was heavily entrenched and full of dugouts both big and small. There were all kinds of curiosities here both German and French for the French never pick up anything after a battle and this was the battlefield of one of the biggest battles of the war. I got some souvenirs off of a German aeroplane brought down by the French, such as wood out of the propeller, a washer and best of all got the French revolver bullet that killed the Boche aviator." Moan, who was six years old when the Wright brothers first flew at Kitty Hawk, had a particular fascination with airplanes. "At about seven o'clock on February 12th, the Boche came over in aeroplanes and many of the boys beat it to the dugouts, but Brown, Tuell and myself stayed out to see the fun," he reported. "The Boche were attacked by French aviators and they popped at each other in good shape with machine guns. Searchlights were playing around everywhere and anti-aircraft guns popping away at the Boche."

He even managed to get in a bit of a sightseeing a few days later. "I visited an old French castle which had been bombarded by the Boche," he wrote. "I was very much interested in the rich antique articles lying around, such as oil paintings, etc. Attached to this castle was the family tomb, which had also been blown to pieces. The Boche even went so far as to pry open the caskets to get the rings, gold teeth, etc."

He'd seen and heard enough, in other words, to both respect and fear the Germans; so when he finally arrived at the old chalk mine, on February 19, 1918, he would have taken very seriously the stories he'd heard about the place. His only entry about it seems to belie Daniel Strickland's contention, in *Connecticut Fights*, that the doughboys regarded the mines with delight, as children would have regarded robbers' caves:

> In this hill there is a big limestone cave big enough to hold two thousand men. It was at one time much bigger and able to hold about four thousand men. Twelve hundred Frenchmen were quartered in one part of this cave shortly after the *Boche* were driven out, but they were simply wiped out for the *Boche* had the whole cave mined. That whole section blew to pieces so not a Frenchman escaped. When we first entered the cave we were strictly forbidden to touch a single thing for fear of blowing up the whole cave.

Still, they felt safer down there than they did up top. The Germans shelled the Chemin des Dames intently. "The Boche bombarded us in good shape," Mechanic Moan noted in one entry, "at least seventy big fellows bursting each minute. Believe me, the man who said he was not scared is a liar." They were gassed, too, with almost every bombardment; men who didn't get their masks on almost immediately suffered the consequences.

Ironically, it was neither high explosives nor gas that came closest to doing in Mechanic Moan at the Chemin des Dames, but some bad bacon, which sent him hiking to a French field hospital one day. "I was going down across the field," he wrote, "when I heard a big shell coming directly for me, so I ducked and ran. It struck not more than thirty feet to one side of me and did not go off. If it had, there would not have been a piece of me left, for they are dangerous at a hundred yards. I ran as fast as I could and it was a mighty good thing that I did, for one struck and exploded exactly where I had been. It seems the Boche have the range of the French hospital and make it a habit to shell it every so often."

And fairly quickly, it seems, the war started to lose its allure for Ralph T. Moan, who came to regard even dogfights with ambivalence. One day, he reported, he and a friend were lying down on a hillside, "basking in the sun," when they spotted four French planes squaring off against three German machines. "All of a sudden a streak of fire came out of one of the Boche machines and then she began to fall," he wrote. "One whole airplane burned in no time at all, and the Boche, realizing that they were goners, jumped. The machine and men dashed to earth about a half mile from us." Moan and his friend ran off toward the crash site; they found the wreck—"the machine was all stove to pieces, yet I managed to get a small piece of wood for a souvenir"—but also found more than they had anticipated: "The two Boche," Moan wrote, "were no fit sight for a nervous man to look at. They were all in a pulp, jelly form and one man's head was driven way down into his chest."

One night, after they'd been at the Chemin des Dames for several weeks, Moan and his company lay in wait for a group of Germans. "The Boche were on patrol March 11th about 10 o'clock at night and the second platoon got wise," he reported. "They jumped up onto the railroad and put the hand grenades to them and machine guns and so forth. They laid up twenty that night and left them hanging in the wire. One man had his head blown off and it made a ghastly sight, suspended in the barbed wire."

There is just one more entry that follows, a single paragraph dated March 30, 1918:

> Have decided to cut this diary out right now, for no man wishes after seeing what we have seen to recall them but rather wishes to forget. From now on all we see is HELL.

No doubt he saw a lot more of that before one of the Germans' "big fellows" blasted him through the air and out of the war that fall; but perhaps, somehow, the diary he kept for six months inoculated him, for afterward he returned home, married, and moved to Manhattan and then New Jersey as he pursued a career as a vocalist—he performed on the vaudeville circuit for a while—and retired to Tucson. After he died in 1982 at the age of 85, his wife, Kathleen, discovered his diary, typed it up, and gave it to the archives at the Army War College in Carlisle, Pennsylvania. It is the only contemporary firsthand account I know of from an American soldier at the Chemin des Dames in 1918.

★ ★ ★

Deep in the mine at Nanteuil-la-Fosse, well past the section where Ralph Moan and his buddies inked and chiseled their names, my flashlight beam fell upon another smoothed tablet on the wall. It was much smaller—maybe fifteen inches square—and the blue ink inscription was faint; it might not be there at all, I realized, but for the fact that it has spent the last century so deep in an underground mine that without an artificial source of illumination, you cannot see your hand in front of your face. I had to get really close to read it well:

JOHN R.

ELLIOTT

CO. K 103 U.S. INF.

A.E.F.

FRANCE

John Russell Elliott. Born in Bangor, Maine, May 29, 1900, and delivered by Dr. William P. McNally. His father, John, a laborer, had been born on Prince Edward Island; his mother, Rebecca, was from Nova Scotia. John Russell was their first child. Eventually they had ten, eight boys and two girls. Their oldest lied about his age when he enlisted on June 11, 1917, said he was 18 when he had barely turned 17. He listed his height as five feet, four-and-a-half inches, his eyes and hair as brown, his complexion as medium, his occupation as laborer. His current address is Plot A, Row 38, Grave 21 in the Meuse-Argonne Cemetery; he was killed in an attack on November 10, 1918, the last full day of the war.

Gilles and I had spent around five hours in that mine, too; as we stumbled out into the daylight afterward, I tripped over something embedded in the earth and nearly fell on my face. It could have been worse: The thing I'd tripped over was a German 77-millimeter shell, live and still in its casing. I shuddered; Gilles stepped over and gently brushed the chalk dust out of my hair and off my shoulders. It was a nice gesture, and comforting, but not enough to chase from my mind the horrible notion that even a hundred years past, that war could still blow you to pieces. How terrifying it must have been, I thought, back when the shells were not half buried in the mud, but flying through the air; not one, but hundreds, thousands.

Of course, that's not what I was told by a 106-year-old man who'd actually been there. "After a while, you disregarded it," J. Laurence Moffitt explained to me back in 2003, eighty-five years after the fact. "You felt, *If I get it, I get it. If I don't, I don't.* And you just paid no attention to it, the shells dropping all about you. You couldn't worry about it all the time." He'd been a corporal in the Yankee Division; like Joseph A. Kelly and Stanley Shaw and P. J. Kochiss and Michael Jay, he'd enlisted in the Connecticut National Guard, which became the 102nd Infantry Regiment. He'd spent time in these mines. But I never found any graffiti of his on the walls.

Maybe he never left any. Maybe that sort of thing was more popular with men who hadn't quite made their peace with the omnipresent threat of sudden death, men who might have felt, on some level, that scratching their names on a wall in an underground chalk mine in France was, in effect, writing their last will and testament. In some cases, sadly, those men turned out to be exactly right.

CHAPTER FIVE

WHAT IF

I.

About fifty miles south of the Chemin des Dames you'll find the town of Château-Thierry, known for being the birthplace of Jean de la Fontaine, a seventeenth-century writer and poet who is regarded as France's Aesop, and for a charming little bridge over the Marne River that is flanked by supersized statues of naked women in repose. The most remarkable thing about the town, though, is actually two or three miles outside it, perched atop a butte known as Hill 204. The Château-Thierry American Monument—built in the 1920s by the American Battle Monuments Commission (ABMC) and maintained by it ever since—is massive and bold, a broad alabaster terrace topped by a double colonnade and fronted by enormous statuary, the kind of thing you expect to see depicted on the back of a large coin, like a half dollar. Locals call it "the radiator," because—well, because it looks like a radiator. They are drawn to it, climb all over it as if it were a tree fort. The last time I was there, a group of teenagers splayed on the staircase that leads up to the terrace, sharing a pizza. I stuck around just long enough to see one of them accidentally drop his slice onto the steps. Face down.

There's nowhere to go in town where you can't see the monument; it looms over Château-Thierry like a protective fortress, which fact might engender resentment elsewhere but doesn't seem to here. Quite the opposite, actually. Even the owner of a local kebab shop, upon learning that I was American, proudly declared that he loved America; told me Ankara, Turkey, his hometown, had so many of my countrymen in it that it was practically in the United States. (That didn't mean he spoke any English.) The following year, when I walked into the shop, he and his Moroccan-born wife both recognized me immediately, hailed me as a long-lost friend returned at last from across the ocean. They even brewed me a special glass of tea, on the house. I'd been there exactly twice before.

The first time, while I waited for my gyro, the owner told me about all of the American TV shows he enjoyed, then asked me what I thought of my president, who was in Normandy at that moment for the D-day anniversary; before I could answer, a man who had just walked in the door demanded (also in French) to know if I were really American. I hesitated: He was an enormous biker clad in painted leather pants and vest, with a shaved head, a face (and scalp) full of piercings, and full tattoo sleeves on both arms. Aside from that, though, he bore a striking resemblance to Rob Reiner.

"*Oui,*" I said. "*C'est vrai.*"

"You're here to see Belleau Wood?" he asked.

"*J'étais vais hier,*" I said. I was go yesterday.

"And the monument?" he asked, undeterred by my poor grasp of the past tense.

I told him I'd been there, too. "So you know what all the statues on it mean?" he parried. "And the symbols?"

I hesitated—just for a couple of beats, but it was enough. "Let's go," he said, in a tone that didn't invite discussion. I had just been handed my gyro, and he hadn't even ordered anything yet, but that didn't matter: He

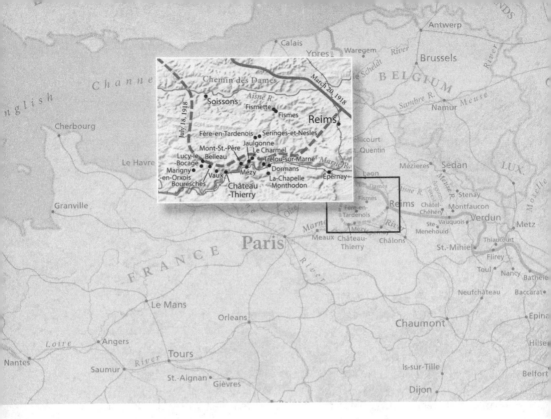

nudged me out the door and toward a black Triumph motorcycle parked a couple of spaces away, quickly unlocking the helmet from the back of the seat and handing it to me.

"But . . . my gyro?" I said.

He looked at me with a glare that took me back to fourth grade. "You can hold on with one hand," he said, and kicked the starter.

The gyro and I somehow managed to hang on all the way up to the monument, where my new tour guide insisted on lecturing me at length about every architectural and artistic detail of the place—the gigantic statues of Columbia (the feminine embodiment of America) and her French counterpart, Marianne, holding hands (giant fingers interlaced); the significance of the numbers of stars and stripes on the other side; the stylized map embedded in the concrete at our feet; the symbols of all the divisions who fought in the area embedded in the face of the monument; the names of the places they liberated chiseled into the frieze up above—even though, as I chose not to mention just then, I already knew all of that. It was clear that this monument, which listed not a single human being, was nonetheless deeply personal to him. Perhaps he could even visualize the

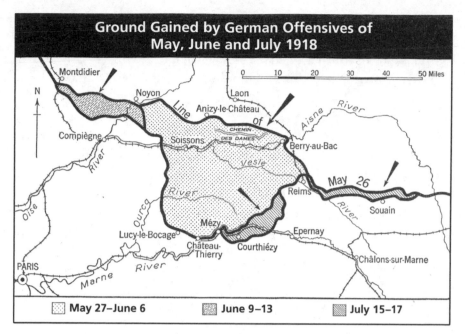

Ground Gained by German Offensives of May, June and July 1918

May 27–June 6   June 9–13   July 15–17

Courtesy of American Battle Monuments Commission

men it honored: untested American troops who, in the spring and summer of 1918, stepped into a fight that turned out to be one of the most critical of the entire war.

★ ★ ★

Back in March, while the Yankee Division was still hunkering down in the chalk mines, the Germans had launched what history now remembers as their Spring Offensive of 1918, the purpose of which was to end the war decisively before too many American troops could be deployed on the Western Front. The offensive would unfold, over the next four months, in five phases. That first phase was, in fact, *too* successful: The Germans broke through the lines so quickly and with such force that their own supply lines couldn't hope to keep up with them. They pressed on, though, with varying success, and on May 27, 1918, launched their third phase. They named it Operation Blücher-Yorck, hoping that the names of two Prussian field marshals who enjoyed successes against Napoleon might help it succeed, too, and perhaps put the fear of God into the French. It did: Almost immediately, the Germans took back the Chemin des Dames (including the two mines the Yankee Division had vacated a couple of months earlier) and kept pushing forward, on and on. Within days, they had captured tens of thousands of Allied soldiers, killed or wounded twice as many, seized thousands of artillery pieces, machine guns and other weapons, and were closing in on the Marne River, where they'd been turned back in 1914. By the end of the month, they were less than forty miles from Paris.

The French were in a panic. And not just civilians, who quickly clogged the roads, desperate to get away; the French high command believed the war was all but lost. Pershing, dining with Ferdinand Foch, one of France's top generals, noted afterward that neither Foch nor anyone on his staff said much during the meal; they were all too depressed about what Pershing called "probably the most serious situation of the war." The British were no more sanguine. And even Pershing, who always took care to present an unfailingly optimistic façade, privately expressed grave concerns. "The Allies are done for," he wrote to Colonel Edward House, President Wilson's chief adviser. The only thing that could keep them in the war, he believed, was the assurance that the American Expeditionary Forces would soon assume a lead role in the fight.

On May 30, the same day as that grim dinner, General Pétain, by that point one of France's leading tacticians, asked General Pershing to at least take a big step in that direction. Specifically, Pétain asked Pershing to rush as many American divisions as possible to Château-Thierry, on the Marne, to keep the Germans from taking it. This was no "quiet" sector; the stakes could hardly have been higher. If the Germans could take Château-Thierry, they would have access to the Paris-Metz Highway, without much left to keep them from taking the French capital. It wasn't clear what, if anything, the Allies would be able to do to continue fighting if that happened.

Ever since he'd arrived in France, nearly a year earlier, Pershing had made it clear that he was and would remain particular about where his troops would be posted, what they would be doing, and who would—and wouldn't—have the authority to order them around. America's peculiar status as a cobelligerent in the war, rather than an ally, granted Pershing such discretion. Time and again, the American commander refused French requests and British demands to deploy his men as replacements in their units, as they had done throughout the war with their own commonwealth and colonial troops. It drove the British and French nuts, but

Pershing would not be moved: He alone would determine when American troops were ready; he alone would determine to whom they reported.

Even he, though, understood that at some point he would have to say yes instead of no, and that if he didn't do so now there might not be another chance. He looked at his maps and figured that he had only two divisions that could be pulled from the line and moved to Château-Thierry in a hurry: the 2nd and the 3rd. He gave the order right away. The 3rd Division was there the next day, May 31, just in time to help the French—under French command—stop the Germans at the Marne. They trained machine guns on some bridges; blew others up. Three days later some Germans managed to get across the river at Jaulgonne, a village a half-dozen miles or so to the east, but troops from the 3rd got there before more could cross, captured about a hundred of them, and chased the rest back across the river.

By that time, though, the Germans had already undertaken Plan B, a workaround that would lead them to a point on the highway even closer to Paris than Château-Thierry. It took them along a road that winds for several miles up a steep incline, passing in its course Hill 204. The hill—like most similarly named slopes in France, the number is a reference to its height, in meters—commands a fine view of the town and the surrounding area; Napoleon chose to set up camp here in 1814 to drive the Prussians from Château-Thierry after they had captured it. Under fire from Napoleon's guns, the Prussians, commanded by Field Marshal Blücher, soon had to relinquish the town; from this spot, you can see both how vulnerable Château-Thierry would have been to Napoleon, and also why, from its position on the Marne, it has served so many times throughout history as an essential defense of Paris.

Now the Germans marched right past Napoleon's old redoubt and continued uphill, taking a few small villages, including Vaux and Bouresches, and then seizing a little undefended forest nearby where they could set up base and, pushing through the other side, cut off the troops in Château-Thierry and gain an open route to Paris. That forest, a private hunting sanctuary that for centuries had belonged to a family named Paillet, and had heretofore been spared the ravages of war, was dense and surrounded by open fields and thus would be easy to defend against an Allied attack. It was known as Bois Belleau—Belleau Wood. It, along with a nearby village, which the Germans had also just taken, was named for a local spring that was said to produce water so clear and refreshing it was actually beautiful—*belle eau.*

The other American division in the vicinity, the 2nd, was hastily ordered up from Meaux, outside Paris, to root the Germans out of Belleau Wood. As the 3rd had, the 2nd marched to their objective against a strong tide of fleeing civilians and, frequently, small bands of retreating French soldiers who hurriedly warned them to turn back. "*Beaucoup Boche,*" was all one of them could spare the time to tell Eugene Lee of Syracuse, a 19-year-old private in the 2nd Division's 5th Marine Regiment, who told me the story eighty-five years later. The marines, marching in the other direction as quickly as possible, were terribly excited; they had been in the country for close to a year but had yet to see any action. They really felt as confident as Pershing acted, marching, contemporary accounts reported, with broad smiles on their faces, laughing and joking even as they passed terrified French going the other way. According to a famous story, one such doughboy, when told that the *Boche* were coming, replied, "We're here!" whereupon the Frenchman who had tried to warn him sighed, "Ah, *oui,* but the *Boche,* he is still coming."

"If the Americans don't stop the Germans at Belleau Wood," Jacques Krabal, the mayor of Château-Thierry, told me ninety-six years later, "the Germans take Paris—the war is finished." It sounds even more dire in the original: *La guerre est finis.* The German offensives had stretched the enemy's army too thin; the French, M. Krabal explained, simply had no more troops to send at that point. If you look at a map, you can see that the only things standing in between Belleau Wood and an open highway to Paris— less than forty miles away—were two small villages, Lucy-le-Bocage and Marigny-en-Orxois, neither of which would have given the Germans any more trouble than Vaux and Bouresches had. Many French were certain the capital would fall within days.

The French government was making plans, as it had in 1914, to abandon Paris and flee south. *Panique* was spreading rapidly everywhere, it appeared, but in those American regiments. Despite the fact that the outcome of the war appeared to be resting upon their shoulders at that point, they continued their march undeterred. If anything, it seemed, their biggest fear was that the whole thing might be over before they got there.

It wasn't. In fact, the battle they were rushing to was only waiting for them to arrive before it got started. By the time it ended, nearly a month later, those marching soldiers, and the place they were marching to, had already passed into the realm of legend: American and French.

★ ★ ★

A great deal has been written about the Battle of Belleau Wood, a little bit of it even by me, so I don't feel the need to recount it for you here in great detail. I'll just give you the basics: General Pershing, at the request of the French high command, dispatched his 2nd Division from Meaux to Belleau Wood. Like all American divisions, the 2nd was composed of two brigades of two regiments apiece, but it was unique in one regard: Only one of its brigades was Army; the other comprised two regiments of the United States Marine Corps, the 5th and 6th, the only marines to see combat in the First World War. Arriving after a march of about twenty miles at a pace as fast as the oncoming tide of French refugees and re-treating soldiers would allow, the doughboys hastily dug into positions a few hundred yards from the woods, separated from the tree line by open fields. The Germans, hoping to dislodge the Americans before they could thoroughly entrench, attacked; the Americans held. Several times. After nearly a week of that, on June 6, 1918, the 2nd Division went on the of-fensive. One regiment, the 5th Marines, set out across an open wheat field, without the benefit of artillery support. (At that point in the war, General Pershing believed artillery cost more lives than it saved; so did General James Harbord, his former chief of staff, who commanded the Marine brigade. Both would eventually change their minds.) German machine guns, perched at the forest's edge, opened fire. The marines kept advanc-ing. "They started us in waves toward the Belleau Woods," Eugene Lee told me eighty-five years later. "In four waves." Each would advance a certain distance and then flatten themselves so the next wave could advance a bit further, again and again until the marines—those who'd survived the wheat field—made it to the tree line and managed to wrest a bit of forest from the Germans. The action cost the Marines 1,087 casualties. It was the deadliest day in the Corps' 143-year history.

Almost immediately, the Germans counterattacked; the Americans, though, counter-counterattacked. Surprised but undaunted, the Germans went on the offensive again; and over the next three weeks, portions of that little forest—you can walk through the whole thing today in less than an hour—would trade hands more than a dozen times until, on June 26, a telegram to divisional HQ declared: "Woods now US Marine Corps entirely." The Americans had won their first major battle against the Germans. Pershing was ebullient, something no one could recall ever having witnessed before, even at the man's wedding. The Germans were stunned, not to mention impressed. An intercepted German intelligence report, written by an officer identified only as Lieutenant von Berg and published in American newspapers a few weeks after the battle, asserted:

> The moral effect of our firearms did not materially check the advance of the infantry; the nerves of the Americans are still unshaken.
>
> The individual soldiers are very good. They are healthy, vigorous, and physically well-developed men of ages ranging from 18 to 28, who at present lack only necessary training to make them redoubtable opponents. The troops are fresh and full of straightforward confidence. A remark of one of the prisoners is indicative of their spirit: "We kill or get killed."

They did a lot of both: The Marines alone took 9,777 casualties at Belleau Wood, more, according to official lore, than they had cumulatively taken in their entire history to that point. (One of them was Private Eugene Lee of Syracuse, shot through the wrist on June 12.) Then again, less than a mile away there's a German cemetery with 8,630 dead in it, at least some of whom, I'm guessing, would tell you if they could that the Sammies already made redoubtable opponents.

Belleau Wood is something akin to an origin story for the modern Marine Corps; I have yet to meet a marine who can't and won't tell me all about it, including those statistics about their casualties and a few choice quotes (*"Come on, you sons of bitches! Do you want to live forever?"*), at least one of which, attributed to the Germans, is of dubious authenticity: The enemy, the story goes, were so in awe of the marines' ferocity that they nicknamed them *Teufel Hunden,* or Devil Dogs. Never mind that the correct term in German is actually *Teufelshunde,* nor that the claim first appeared in American newspapers two months *before* Belleau Wood, at a point when the Germans had never yet faced any marines; it stuck, even showing up on recruitment posters before the war's end.

Another legend is that the French, equally impressed with the Americans, and grateful to them for stopping perhaps the most dire threat they had faced since 1914, renamed Bois Belleau "Bois de la Brigade de Marine," or Woods of the Marine Brigade, immediately after the battle. This one is actually true, and the name holds to this day, though no one really calls it that, perhaps for the same reason that no one really calls Manhattan's Sixth Avenue "Avenue of the Americas"—it's a mouthful, and everybody knows the original, which is much easier to say. Hard as it may be to imagine, the French are even more obsessed with Belleau Wood than the Americans are; unlike in the Argonne, you're not likely to find any World War I artifacts here. Generations of French relic hunters, many of them armed with the reviled metal detector, beat you to them.

Despite all that, and the fact that many of the surrounding villages that also played a role in the battle were largely destroyed and almost entirely rebuilt to the point where there are few discernible battle scars to see in any of them, the forest itself is largely intact. This is due, in part, to the rural nature of the area, and in part to the fact that most of the older trees that survived the battle are so full of bullets and shrapnel—any one of which could badly damage a chainsaw, not to mention the person wielding it—that loggers are afraid to touch them. Nevertheless, it's a felicitous fact for anyone who wants to see a real, largely untouched World War I battlefield in an area where there are few others to behold; actually, as far as I know, there are none at all. And while lots of people visit Belleau Wood, to the point where, in recent years, the superintendent of the local American cemetery even laid out a walking trail with designated spots of interest along the way, I have never hiked through that forest and not been totally alone. Under such circumstances, I have found, it is possible to imagine that the trail leads all the way back to June 1918.

The path meanders through the woods, past the kinds of things you don't see in other countries' forests, like trenches and shell holes and foxholes. Like the Argonne, it's a wonderful combination of nature walk and history hunt, albeit in a much smaller area and with pre-identified places of note that, thankfully, are not beset with interpretive kiosks; without the guide, a few photocopied sheets of paper stapled together, you would not know what most of them are. There's no mistaking the trenches and shell holes, though. They are so well preserved, in fact, that it makes me wonder if there's actually some truth to what one U.S. Army veteran told me: that marines, returning to Belleau Wood after the war and not finding any of those things still there, took it upon themselves to install some. Then again, my source, knowledgeable as he is, readily acknowledges the rivalry, sometimes fierce and not all that good-natured, between the U.S. Army and the Marine Corps, which dates back in large part to Belleau Wood, where the 2nd Division's Marine brigade got all the credit for the American victory, and its Army brigade got none.

There's one thing, though, that no American veteran could have put there. Stop 5—the Wheat Field. You branch off from the main trail, follow a smaller one down a slight slope and round a bend, and: There it is. You can walk right up to it. Actually, if you're so inclined, you can walk right into it, this open stretch where so many marines were killed and so many more fell on June 6, 1918, twenty-six years to the day before the Allied invasion at Normandy. If you've timed it right—French farmers must rotate their crops on a schedule—it will actually *be* a wheat field; if you really time it right, as I did in 2014, you will not only have wheat but will also be there on the same day the 5th Marines were, and see more or less what it would have looked like on that morning when the course of the greatest war the world had ever seen was changed by a charge of men on foot, the oldest military maneuver there is. The grain that day was around knee high, perhaps a bit higher in spots—barely enough to cover a man lying flat on his belly with a pack on his back. And its stalks had already started to turn yellow, enough of a contrast with American khaki to add to one's anxiety. You stand there at the edge of the woods, underneath the shelter of some stout old trees, and look across that open field, and perhaps your mind goes to Gettysburg, and Pickett's Charge; but Pickett had artillery. And the Yankees didn't have machine guns.

Heed Jean-Paul de Vries's rules and step gingerly out into the field, and you can get a sense of how it appeared from the marines' perspective. It doesn't seem nearly as wide, I imagine, when machine-gun bullets aren't spraying over the top of the wheat from the place you're trying to get to; but still, you can get some small glimpse of what it looked like on that morning a century ago, if not what it felt like. I have stood on Cemetery Ridge in Gettysburg and tried to imagine Pickett's Charge, and it doesn't come close. These woods, this field—there are no markers here, no statues; none of it is landscaped or even maintained, except to the extent that this field is worked as farmland, exactly as it was back then. Even when it's not planted with wheat—as was the case in 2015, when they were growing sugar beets, which are not nearly the same thing—it's still the Wheat Field. And you will still, if you go there alone, have it all to yourself.

Unless you believe in ghosts. If they're anywhere, they're here.

* * *

Strangely, the woods themselves are really the only part of Belleau Wood you're ever likely to have to yourself. The little museum down the hill in the village of Belleau—the only commercial establishment of any kind there—always seems to have at least a couple of people poking around its glass display cases full of artifacts and old photos. The captions are bilingual, a rarity in France outside of Paris, though everyone I've ever encountered in there is French. Outside, though, across the lane, you'll often find a few young marines on leave, lunching on a shady knoll. They always seem surprised to encounter another American there, too, especially one with no ties to the USMC. Once, during the conversation that inevitably ensues, I told them that I had met and interviewed the last survivor of the battle of Belleau Wood. They nodded reverently; then one of them grimaced and started shaking his head. "Can you imagine if we go back a hundred years from now?" he said to his buddies, obviously referring to a place that was far from France. "They'll probably *still* want to kill us." His friends nodded at that, too.

Up the hill and across the road are the gates to the Aisne-Marne Cemetery, where Earle Madeley, Joseph Kelly and 2,286 other doughboys are buried. It's one of the smaller American World War I cemeteries in France—Meuse-Argonne, the largest, has nearly seven times as many graves—but someone or other is almost always there visiting, and usually someone else is there mowing the grass. Unlike in every other big American cemetery I've visited in France, where everything is perfectly straight and even, the rows in Aisne-Marne's two plots curve delicately away from its center walk, which leads to a chapel and bell tower poised atop a stone stairway: curiously intimate for a space that's actually not small at all. Once a year, though, it feels really, really small; perhaps that's because, for a few hours that day, it's as crowded as Times Square on New Year's Eve.

That day is Memorial Day—or, more accurately, the Sunday before the Monday when Memorial Day is observed back in the United States, though it has on occasion been observed at Aisne-Marne on the Saturday before Memorial Day, and also, in 2015, on the Sunday after it. That's the year I went; it was scheduled then, I was told, so as not to conflict with a local holiday. If it felt a bit strange to an American to celebrate Memorial Day twice in one year—I attended the parade in my hometown that Monday, then flew to France a few hours later—it didn't seem to matter much at all to the people in attendance at Aisne-Marne that day, perhaps because the vast majority of them were French. And there were a lot of them: The official tally was 4,000, though someone in a position to know later told me the real figure was more like 5,500. Even that number sounded conservative to me.

Just the logistics of managing such a crowd in such a place are daunting. The parking lots in the cemetery can accommodate maybe two dozen cars. Across the road from the gates are a couple of small fields that can hold perhaps a hundred more. To park in one of those you need a special pass, the kind of thing that, when flashed to a classically blasé *gendarme,* results in the raising of eyebrows, if only for an instant. Most people park in a much larger field a few miles down the hill, from which they are shuttled to the gates in a convoy of large buses. The driveway from the gate to the cemetery is lined, for the occasion, with the flags of all fifty American states, planted at perfectly uniform intervals. The crowd pouring in is diverse but, for the most part, very well put together; if you didn't shave that morning, you're going to feel self-conscious. Don't say I didn't warn you.

The lawn that spreads out before the stairway and chapel and separates the two cemetery plots serves as a parade ground. Every inch of its perimeter that day was occupied by spectators, who were backed by a half-dozen rows of other spectators. I realized the futility of that situation just in time to grab the last spot on the base of one of the flagpoles off to the side, which gave me an extra eighteen inches or so that made all the difference. From that vantage I could see the stage set up on the lowest platform of the stairway, with a few dozen chairs that would soon be occupied by various dignitaries. Lingering with quiet poise next to the flagpole base where I was standing were four soldiers wearing what looked, at least to my eyes, to be unusual uniforms: white kepi, tan short-sleeved khaki tunic with deep green epaulets fringed with long red tassels, slightly darker pants, blue sash around the waist cinched by green canvas belt, legs bloused into black boots—exactly the kind of uniform, in other words, that makes you want to join whatever service those guys are in. *"Qui ils sont?"* (Who they are?) I asked the woman standing next to me, but before she could answer, the man standing in front of me, an older gentleman who must have heard my accent and poor grammar and deduced my nationality, turned around and said, in French: "They are Légion Étrangère. And you are very lucky to see them—they have never attended this ceremony before."

Légion Étrangère—the French Foreign Legion. They really do exist. Still. And are apparently objects of as much fascination to the French as they were to me. An elite fighting unit with a storied history whose reputation has never dimmed even a little, it is, as its name indicates, composed largely of foreign-born men, though all of its officers and some of its soldiers are French nationals. Everything you've heard about the French Foreign Legion is likely true, along with a lot of things you probably haven't: If you can get to an enlistment center and pass the physical, you're in. By law, they are not allowed to investigate your background; tell them whatever you care to, don't tell them whatever you don't care to, enlist under a false name if it suits you. Basic training lasts four weeks and is notoriously brutal, but if you can make it through that, and at least five years in the legion with a good record and a recommendation from your commanding officer, you can earn French citizenship. (Those who are wounded in action have an even surer route through a provision known as "French by spilled blood.") Even without it, you can probably stay in France as long as you like.

The ones I met that day were from Serbia, Ukraine, China, Nepal, Madagascar. Though heavily tattooed, they were also clean-cut, not to mention clean-shaven, which kind of surprised me because if you look at old photos of *poilus,* you see an awful lot of mustaches. General Pershing more or less forbade facial hair on doughboys (he gave himself and a few others a pass), but it was a very different story in the French Army. In France, Gilles Chauwin told me, "in those days, if you didn't have a mustache, you weren't a man." In fact, French Army officers back then were *required* to sport mustaches; for that matter, all *gendarmes* were required to have mustaches *until 1953.* They were equally popular in the Kaiser's army, I should note, with one important difference, as another French devotee of history (and, apparently, facial hair) explained to me: "If you look at the photos, German mustaches pointed up; French mustaches pointed down." "*Poilu,*" he pointed out, means "hairy one," a nickname that dates back to the Franco-Prussian War, when many French soldiers returned home after several months without, it would seem, having had many opportunities to shave at the front.

The French military band there that day, the Musique Principale des Troupe de Marine, had varying degrees of facial hair, not to mention dapper uniforms, although the women's hats were, I regret to inform you, not nearly as snappy as the mens' kepis. The 1st Marine Division Band, though—well, to start, I suppose it goes without saying that they all looked like they had been shaved with hot towels, warm foam and brand-new straight razors about five minutes before they marched onto the parade ground. Their dress blue uniforms, which I imagine look impressive even after you've slept in them, were immaculate, including the white pants, which in my experience defies the laws of nature. Their buttons, belt buckles and medals were all polished to a high shine, and yet appeared dull compared to their instruments, which probably looked better than they did when they left the factory. I haven't beheld many objects of beauty that can rival the 1st Marine Division Band's nickel-plated sousaphones. If I owned one I wouldn't dare touch it, much less play it.

The bands played the "Marseillaise" and "The Star-Spangled Banner," and the ceremony proceeded with a flyover, opening remarks (in French and English), prayers (also in French and English), poems on the theme of "When Peace Returns" written and read by high school students from Château-Thierry (those were all in French), memorial addresses from the chief of staff of the French Army and the assistant commandant of the Marine Corps, the laying of a great many wreaths by a great many individuals representing a great many organizations, and the firing of volleys. And then, from out of the chapel up at the top of the stairs, a doughboy emerged in full uniform—tin hat to puttees, it was perfect—produced a bugle, and played "Taps." I doubt that many of the people there had ever experienced that simple melody quite that way before. When he was done, he disappeared back into the chapel like a wraith. I never saw him again; but for the fact that I took photos of him, and that I shared the experience with several thousand other people, I might wonder if he'd really been there at all.

Now the two military bands, and two honor platoons dressed identically to their country's men and women at arms, took turns marching and playing concerts on the parade ground. The marines played time-honored American melodies I knew well; the French, some proud old tunes that sounded vaguely familiar though I was certain I had never heard them before. The elderly man standing in front of me turned around again, and told me: "That is traditional music, from Napoleon's time." As the dignitaries—who included the American ambassador, a lot of military personnel wearing a lot of medals, and some civilians who looked fairly important and certainly dignified—filed out, it occurred to me that, two centuries and a year earlier, people hunting in these woods could well have heard the same songs wafting over from Hill 204.

✶ ✶ ✶

After the ceremony there was a great deal of milling about in the cemetery, where I noticed that all 2,288 graves had been decorated for the occasion with a miniature Tricolor and a miniature Stars and Stripes, and saw a few marines, their young children in hand, bending over before this marker or that, telling their toddlers just a bit about the significance of what they were looking at. Somehow I managed to find Gilles Chauwin and Gilles Lagin, both of whom attend every year. The two Gilleses do not know each other; though both are among the most knowledgeable World War I buffs you will ever meet, their specific areas of expertise do not overlap. Gilles Chauwin's main focus is the Chemin des Dames; Gilles Lagin's is Belleau Wood. M. Lagin is pretty much the go-to guy for Americans when it comes to that battle, in part because he knows so very much about it, in part because he's fairly fluent in English, and in part because he loves Americans, in general.

He was pretty mad at me in particular, though, just then. I'd known Gilles since 2009, and had written about him a bit in my last book, the one about the First World War. He didn't take issue with my description of him as "a swarthy man built like a shipping crate," but he didn't care for my likening his barn, in which he stores the many thousands of artifacts he has found over the decades, to "a hoarder's garage sale." In my defense, I said that only of his storage room, and not the section of the space that he has turned into a small museum; and in any event, if his English weren't so good he would have missed the affront entirely. He still would have caught the part where I wrote that one of the many marines who has visited him over the years, with whom he is extremely popular, made him an honorary marine himself. "That wasn't *a marine*," he told me now, his voice spiked with umbrage. "It was *the commandant of the United States Marine Corps*." I stood corrected.

Gilles, who is in his fifties, has been exploring and artifact-hunting since childhood; he grew up very close to Bois Belleau and cannot remember a time when he wasn't fascinated by everything having to do with that battle. Back in 2009, he had taken me all over the battlefield and through his museum with great joy, then welcomed me to his house, which is filled with books and papers and which I will otherwise refrain from describing. The barn and house look to the untrained eye to be about the same age, though the former dates back to the seventeenth century and the latter was built in 1907. Both were damaged during the Battle of Belleau Wood, though much of his village, Marigny-en-Orxois (ahem: Mah-rin-YEE-on-Orks-WAH), fared even worse. Gilles has in his house all kinds of records and maps and records of maps, organized in a manner that, though invisible to the human eye (I'll probably get in trouble for saying that), nevertheless enables him to find pretty quickly just about any piece of information concerning the war in the vicinity of Belleau Wood and the Marne and who knows where else. He was even able to help me pinpoint the field where 17-year-old George Briant of New Orleans and Battery B of the 76th Field Artillery Regiment, part of the 3rd Division, was very nearly killed by bombs dropped from German airplanes on July 28, 1918, a story Mr. Briant related to me eighty-six years later. It's just outside the village of Le Charmel, where, as it happens, Gilles's grandmother was born.

Now, six years and a couple of arguably indelicately phrased passages later, Gilles was mad at me, although my apology, compounded by our surroundings and the ceremony we had both just witnessed, softened his heart; and by the time we made it to the cemetery gates, he had forgiven me. Just outside those gates stood a group of large men who looked like bikers, except that their black T-shirts and jackets bore patches and decals celebrating not Harley-Davidson but the United States Marine Corps. While Gilles hung back, I approached them and quickly discovered that they were French and spoke no English at all. They took quite a shine to me upon discovering that I was American, warmly shaking my hand one at a time while the others patted me on the back, even though I believe it was fairly obvious by any number of indicators that I was not a marine. One of them, a really big guy with a goatee, wore a "Marines" baseball cap and a black zippered fleece with an American flag patch sewn over the heart. He removed the latter to reveal a black T-shirt with the USMC emblem silk-screened over the heart, and a patch on each sleeve: 5th Marines on the left, 6th on the right. His entire upper right arm was covered by a tattoo of the Marine Corps' symbol—eagle perched atop a globe and anchor—over a pair of crossed swords, the words "Semper Fidelis" inked in Gothic script above and below. Two more thematically similar tattoos graced his left arm. We shook hands; he introduced himself as Laurent Vanhée. I asked him if he'd served in the USMC, which I realize now was a stupid question, given that I had to pose it in French. He didn't laugh; just said no, though he added that he had served in the French Army back in the late 1980s. If I hadn't just met a few soldiers of the Légion Étrangère, I might have found his and his friends' fascination with another country's fighting force curious.

A strong tide of ceremony attendees was moving now at some pace or other down the hill to the Château de Belleau, which sits behind a set of gates, a key to which is kept at the museum, next door. Many marines make a pilgrimage here because the château grounds contain a fountain, the spigot of which sits in the mouth of a sculpture of a bulldog. This is said to be a tribute to the Marines, the *Teufel Hunden,* even though anybody local will readily tell you that the sculpture predates the First World War by a very long time. Marines are said to consider it good luck to drink from this fountain, though given the experiences I've had drinking the tap water in rural France, I would have to respectfully disagree.

No key was necessary that day: The gates were wide open. There is always a reception here after the Memorial Day ceremony, I've been told, for anybody who wants to attend, and from what I've seen a lot of people want to. The Marine Band was playing in the courtyard, as was a local band from Château-Thierry, and soldiers and civilians mingled freely. There were drinks and snacks enough for everyone and more, and little French, American and Marine Corps flags for anyone who asked. Almost everyone I made eye contact with greeted me as if I were a distant cousin they hadn't seen in many years; from what I could see, everyone was greeting everyone that way. It looked like the thing that happens between a wedding ceremony and a wedding reception. To be honest, for a few moments I didn't know quite what to make of it, until I realized that what I was looking at, and drinking at, and talking to the two Gilles and some marines and some French soldiers and some French and American dignitaries and quite a few *légion-naires* at, was the greatest celebration of Franco-American amity I had ever experienced, an occasion so warm and unreserved that you would think the battle had ended just yesterday, and not ninety-seven years earlier.

☆ ☆ ☆

Everyone who attended that reception got there by walking down a narrow street that runs through the small village of Belleau, winding past houses, a building labeled "bakery" that hasn't been one in a very long time (what a tease), a booth with a pay phone that miraculously still works, and the museum before arriving at the château. If you continue to follow it, though—and not one of them did—it leads out past a little grove and ends at another road, across which, up on a bank, is the village cemetery. It's old and surrounded by a stone wall, its graves packed in close and terraced to accommodate the topography. In the back row, third plot from the left corner, in between Marcel Félix LeJeune and several members of the family Benier, is a cement bed filled with gravel. Someone had left a little crucifix on it when I visited last, and a couple of bouquets, the smaller of which had a Tricolor and Old Glory stuck in it. The marker, a small stone cross, reads, simply: Ernest Stricker.

Stricker had immigrated from Switzerland to the United States in 1910, at the age of 19, and settled in Umatilla County, Oregon, where he worked as a farm laborer. When the war came, he enlisted in the American Expeditionary Forces; it's not clear which unit or units he served with, though there is some speculation that it was an engineering outfit attached to a combat division like the 3rd or the 26th. After the war he was honorably discharged with the rank of private first class, granted American citizenship—the two witnesses on his naturalization petition were his lieutenants—and returned to Oregon, where he took up alfalfa farming.

On April 1, 1928, nine years to the day after his discharge, Ernest Stricker came to Belleau. It is believed he strolled around the Aisne-Marne American Cemetery for a while, perhaps even until it closed for the night. Later, his sister, who still lived in Switzerland, would say that her brother had been suffering some serious physical ailments—I have heard he had a gastrointestinal issue that required surgery—and had endured some other, unspecified "reverses," besides.

That evening, after the cemetery closed, Ernest Stricker, 37 years old, shot himself outside its gates. A note was found on his body, addressed to his fellow veterans at American Legion Post No. 1 in Paris. It read:

> I'm writing you these few lines with a heavy heart and deep thoughts, but sincerely hope you will understand me. As I was moving among the white crosses under which my truest friends are resting forever, a feeling came over me that I too can't go on anymore. My health is failing, my hopes for which I have been striving all these years are shattered. I can't go on, comrades, I can't go on. It is my last wish to be buried under French soil among my comrades at arms as well as peace.
>
> Your comrade,
> Ernest Stricker

His last wish could not be accommodated: He was not eligible to be buried in the Aisne-Marne Cemetery because he had not died while in the service of the American armed forces. The mayor of Belleau, though, took pity and donated a plot in the village burial ground.

A few hundred yards uphill, thousands of people gather every year to commemorate the Americans who died driving the Germans out of the area and, in the process, helped save the Allied cause. But down here, a plain white cross marks the lonely grave of a man who would tell you, if he could, that there really is no cohesive narrative to war, and no order behind whose deaths it invests with meaning, and whose are consigned to oblivion.

II.

You would be forgiven if, having just attended that Memorial Day ceremony and not knowing otherwise, you believed Belleau Wood ended the war. It did not; it didn't even end the German Spring Offensive. From the moment that telegram declaring "Woods now US Marine Corps entirely" arrived at HQ, everyone knew something else would hit. Something big.

They waited for it eighteen days; and when that something else finally came, it was even bigger than everyone had feared it would be.

Shortly after midnight on July 15, 1918, the Germans launched Operation Marneschutz-Reims, the name of which—it translates, roughly, to "Marne defenses–Reims"—may have lacked the panache of Blücher-Yorck but was direct and to the point. And the action itself was certainly no less ambitious. Forty German divisions were hurled at the Marne River along a fifty-mile front. The Germans hadn't had much luck attacking the city of Reims in recent attempts, so this time they just went around it, twenty-three divisions to the east, seventeen to the west. A half-million men. Maybe more.

The Allies had had just a little bit of luck, capturing a couple of German prisoners on the night of July 14 who gave them an idea of what was coming, and when. In anticipation of the massive German barrage that they expected to initiate the assault just after midnight, they launched one of their own a few minutes before that. Historians disagree about how effective it was, though I personally have seen one piece of evidence that it did at least some good. But I'll get to that in a bit.

Long before the Allies captured those German prisoners, the French high command had had a good idea of what was coming, and where; its generals, though, had not been in agreement on how to best deal with it. To the east of Reims, they decided that their first line of defense would be "soft," composed of relatively few men in units that could fall back quickly to a much larger and better-protected second line; their rationale was that this zone, closest to the line of attack, would be most susceptible to enemy artillery, so rather than try to defend it with strong lines, they would lure the Germans into it, instead, and then pummel them with French and Allied artillery, followed by an assault from the real line of defense. West of Reims, though, while some units were told they would be following this "soft line" (also known as "elastic") strategy, others were told to form a hard line right at the river. Some were told both. And in the sector at the far western edge of the line, which stretched some twelve miles from the village of Mézy to Château-Thierry, the American 3rd Division, one of three American divisions in the line—the other two being the 28th, National Guard troops from Pennsylvania, and the 42nd, the Rainbow Division of Joyce Kilmer and Rouge Bouquet—was having a hard time figuring out exactly what it was supposed to do. Its commanding officer, General Joseph T. Dickman, had been ordered by his French superiors to place his troops pretty much at the river's edge, but Dickman didn't care for that strategy; he worried that his men, facing German artillery on the heights across the Marne, would get blasted to pieces. He much preferred the elastic strategy he knew the French were deploying to the east. So he more or less pursued that on his own, taking care to create an illusion of greater strength at the waterfront, a ruse intended to fool the French as much as the Germans. (He was mum about this particular point of history in his postwar memoir, *The Great Crusade*.)

This area is the beginning of Champagne Country, and here I must tell you that whatever images those two words bring to your imagination cannot match the reality. First, you have to try to summon a shade of green that you typically only see here and there in that slender window of spring between the emergence of full leaves and the rising of the temperature to short-pants weather: light and adolescent, full and soft without a hint of being scorched or even mature. Now take that hue and douse it everywhere: hedges and arbors and fields and, especially, hills. And these hills are not hills like you're used to, either. They're plump and bold, big and friendly. They don't hang back in dignified reserve; they jump right out at you, step in front of your windshield and preen for your benefit, crash into the fields like Hawaiian surf. The view is especially fine from the south side of the Marne: There are more hills on the north side, and they are larger and appear, in something of an optical illusion, to end right at the river's edge. Trees ring their broad, inviting slopes like a picture frame but never encroach onto the canvas. That's where the grapes grow.

Add to this image fields so lush they look like velvet, and slender winding roads and little stone farmhouses and little stone churches, and even if what you're picturing isn't that close to the reality of Champagne, you nonetheless know it's not a place you'd want to see a battle fought, especially one in which machine guns and high-explosive shells and poison gas played such a prominent part.

For four years, one wasn't. The Germans were turned back at the Marne in September 1914, and didn't even approach this area again until the end of May 1918, when Blücher-Yorck brought them to the edge of the river. The French and Americans quickly blew up or blocked the bridges, holding the Germans to the north bank. The Germans probed here and there, like that time they sent a party across in boats at Jaulgonne, just east of Mézy, only to be stopped by the 3rd Division, which captured some and chased the rest back across. But mostly they bided their time.

The Allies knew the Germans were massing their forces across the river; they knew, as I said, that something big was coming. What they didn't know, at that point, was what the stakes were for the Germans, which might have offered them a better picture of how frantic—how desperate—that something would be. Since the Spring Offensive's first, too-successful phase back in March, the Germans had launched three more, including the also-very-but-this-time-not-too-successful Blücher-Yorck. And yet, for all this success, they hadn't quite managed to get the Allies to the point of capitulation. They had gotten close, to be sure; there were those roads clogged with terrified refugees and retreating soldiers, those plans to abandon Paris and flee south. But the enemy tenaciously clung to life. And the Germans had lost a lot of time—and a lot of men. The Allied ranks, though, had started to swell, with more Americans arriving all the time, hundreds of thousands a month by that point. Erich Ludendorff, who bore the odd title Quartermaster General of the Imperial German Army but who was really, along with Paul von Hindenburg, its leader, calculated he only had time for one more big push before the numbers turned against him. This last offensive had to finish things. And he was certain that it would, as was his boss, Kaiser Wilhelm II, who boasted that his army would be in Paris by July 17. The Germans, in fact, were so confident Marneschutz-Reims would end the war that they nicknamed it *Friedens-sturm*—the "Peace Offensive."

So what you need to do here is take almost unimaginably beautiful countryside and transpose upon it an almost incomprehensibly frenzied military attack. Official divisional histories tend to play these things down and focus solely on the who, what, where and when, but the *History of the Third Division United States Army in the World War,* published just a year afterward, offers at least a few hints about what the awful barrage that started the Peace Offensive was like: "Within a minute of the time the first shot was fired," it notes, "the entire Regimental area was filled with bursting shrapnel, high explosives and gas shells of all calibers. All telephone lines were cut by shells or falling trees, and the wireless was made useless . . . The forest had been turned into an almost impenetrable mass of brush . . . There was no break, no stop, no rest . . . Rapid fire continued until about 1:55 a.m. and then a moderately heavy schedule began, including tear and sneezing gas shells on the forward areas and lethal gas on the supports and reserves."

And then half a million Germans threw themselves at the last natural barrier between them and Paris: the Marne River.

They had done this kind of thing before. They knew to use a rolling barrage, also known as a fire curtain—an artillery maneuver in which the line of bombardment slowly moves toward the enemy, your infantry following closely behind—to push any Allied stragglers back from the shore and the fields leading up to it and into the woods beyond the railroad tracks; they knew to lay down a smoke screen so the French and Italian and American troops on the other side of the river couldn't see them crossing it, first in boats, then with pontoons to build bridges of their own. Still, it's hard to hide that many men for long. And maybe you don't want to. Maybe you want the troops on the other side, men who have already endured an unrelenting two-hour barrage, to see the hordes of well-trained, well-equipped, determined enemy troops coming at them. I don't know that the Germans cared to be called "Boche," but I'm guessing some of them, at least, didn't mind the other popular epithet Americans had for them: "Hun." People feared the Hun. The Germans were counting on it. They knew that from the other side of the Marne, in the brief flashes of shell fire and rocket's red glare, it would look to their enemy as if the hills themselves were coming after them.

The Allies were not unprepared. They hurled everything they had at that river. They machine-gunned and shelled whatever moved. They killed a lot of men in the water, blew up a lot of new pontoon bridges. But the Germans just threw more men at the river; built more bridges. They got across.

East of Reims, the elastic defense worked pretty much as planned; the Germans landed on the shore but could not break through. West of Reims, they did much better, advancing miles, four or five in some places. But at the far western end of the line, where General Dickman defied orders and opted for his own form of elastic defense, the American 3rd Division once again stopped the Germans from moving on to Château-Thierry and thence to Paris. The division is known, to this day, as "the Rock of the Marne."

The ground the Rock of the Marne held is bottomland, flat and open with the occasional compact rise or small stand of trees. The nearest village, Mézy, isn't much more than a meandering road in no hurry to get to the Marne, some small houses, and a little stone church from the thirteenth century. One evening, having spent a few hours tromping around the area trying to get some small sense of what the 3rd Division experienced that night, I decided I needed a little more distance, so I got back in my car, made for that winding road and headed down toward the river. It sprang up on me suddenly; before I knew it I was crossing a bridge. It was plain, humble, without even much of a railing; but oh, what the Germans would have given for such a bridge on July 15. A venture that took weeks of planning back then took me less than four seconds now, and I barely noticed that I had done it.

Before I realized it I was in Mont-Saint-Père, a pretty hillside village with houses and another old church and, hanging behind it all like a curtain, broad vineyards spread out along slopes with southern exposure, ideal for growing grapes in the sunshine. The church is up at the top of a hill, hard to get to through the town's labyrinthine streets; you'd be much better off doing so with two people in the car—one to keep an eye on the steeple, the other on the streets—but I didn't have that luxury. I managed to reach it anyway, and saw something from its yard that startled me so much that I felt I needed to confirm it from a different perspective, so I got back in my car and drove a few minutes east, through the village of Chartèves to the town of Jaulgonne, and found a spot on a ridge with an open vista. And I did confirm it: Though it can be tough to see them when you're on the other side of the Marne—the south side, the Mézy side—there are, in fact, hills and ridges over there, too. There is flat bottomland extending from the riverbank on that side of the river, much more of it than on this side, the northern side; but behind it there are heights. In other words, the landscape here is a bowl: a killing ground so perfect it chilled me to look at it. Without that river to slow them down, the Germans—with their vastly superior numbers, and their artillery, and gravity—would have cut through the Allied lines like a scythe through a grape. Even with the river standing in their way they managed to do it everywhere on this side of Reims, except for Mézy, where they very nearly did it, too.

When I drove back to Mézy a few minutes later, I found it looked different to me; it felt different, too. It's one thing to behold a perfect killing ground from a distance, as if you are looking at a chessboard; but when you're standing on it, and you know just how much blood was shed there, you can almost feel yours draining out of your body. The men of the 3rd Division stood here that night and saw, in the flash of flares, the hills across the river teeming with men coming to slaughter them. They beheld, spread out before them, this perfect killing ground. Thousands of them fell here, on this land, in these fields, by these houses, near those railroad tracks, around that church. The French on their right, adhering to the failed inelastic defense, fell back several miles, exposing the 3rd Division's flank dangerously. But the Sammies stood here, held their ground, and in doing so stopped what would be the last German offensive of the First World War.

✷ ✷ ✷

To their east, from just beyond Mézy all the way to Reims, the Germans advanced for three days, but with the 3rd Division sticking at the extreme, like an anchor in a game of tug-of-war, their progress was slowed and then ground to a halt by July 17. It was their high-water mark of the war; but they were still fifty miles or more from Paris. The next day, the French and Americans launched their own massive counterattack.

Just below the city of Soissons, twenty-five miles to the north and west, the 1st and 2nd Divisions jumped off and headed east, toward crucial German supply lines, along a route that took them through miles of wide open fields that offered no shelter at all from relentless German

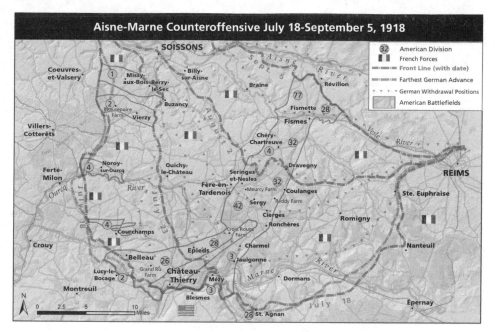

Aisne-Marne Counteroffensive July 18-September 5, 1918

Courtesy of National Park Service, Cultural Resource GIS Facility

machine-gun and artillery fire; half the French tanks that accompanied them were destroyed in the process, their charred carcasses still sitting there well into the 1920s, by which point they had become tourist attractions. That same day, also under severe fire, the 3rd Division crossed the Marne at Mézy and slowly scaled the hills on the other side, until, reaching a plateau, they became part of a patchwork column driving north toward the Vesle River, twenty miles away. The 28th Division was there, and the 42nd, and the 26th would soon join in; so would three untried American divisions, the 4th, 32nd and 77th. So would French divisions, and French colonials, and some Italian troops. The terrain in this area is largely flat, mostly farmland; there certainly aren't a lot of places to hide, mostly small groves and patches of woods that might offer some cover but would surely attract enemy artillery fire for exactly that reason. Many of these fields are now dusted with bright red poppies, which congregate most heavily at the edges. You see a lot of poppies in northern France, especially, it seems, in spots where the fighting was bad. The correlation is so strong, in fact, that you might wonder if locals plant them as a memorial. They don't. In fact, the poppy doesn't symbolize war and remembrance in France: The cornflower does. You often see those ringing the bases of war memorials, where they actually are planted.

The Germans had heavily fortified many of the towns between the two rivers and ceded absolutely nothing without a bitter fight, not even a little farming village like Le Charmel, where Gilles Lagin's grandmother had been born. The 3rd Division reached its outskirts, a couple of miles north of the Marne, by July 22; it took them five days to take it and hold it. "Le Charmel was probably reported captured as many times as any town in France," the regimental history of the 76th Field Artillery—George Briant's outfit—noted in 1919. More people died trying to take it or defend it than live in it now.

That story played out over and over again throughout the three-week struggle history now remembers as the Second Battle of the Marne. The 42nd Division got held up at a point of particularly fierce German resistance, on a farm named Meurcy just outside the village of Seringes-et-Nesles, about seven miles north of Le Charmel. "We captured the place, but at what a loss," Corporal John J. Casey recounted years later to General Henry J. Reilly, who recorded the sentiment in *Americans All: The Rainbow at War,* the division's official history. "Deeds of valor were performed in the capture of this farm of which nobody knows anything about because few of those engaged in it returned." In Seringes, which sits atop a butte, the little church contains two massive stone plaques recording the names of 208 Americans killed in the immediate vicinity in the last few days of July 1918. They are listed in alphabetical order; it is merely coincidence that Joyce Kilmer's name sits at the top of one of the columns. Sergeant Kilmer set out on the afternoon of July 30, accompanied by two other men, with orders from his commanding officer, Major William J. Donovan, to locate a machine-gun nest that was vexing his company. Progress was halting; after a while they split up, on Kilmer's order, at the crest of a hill near Meurcy Farm. As one of the other men, Private Edwin Stubbs, recounted later for *The Rainbow at War:*

> We again awaited the signal to move forward and, not receiving it, I looked in the direction of Kilmer. In a fox hole, slightly to my rear, he lay slumped with his head and shoulders somewhat exposed. We called to him, but there was no response, so we crawled to him and saw that he was beyond the need of our aid. Due to our exposed position, it was only possible to perform a superficial examination. We determined he

had been struck in the head and chest by bullets and that he had died instantly. There was hardly any evidence of bleeding.

Kilmer's body was recovered the next day, when the area was safer. No one I've ever asked seems to know where, precisely, he was killed; but based on Private Stubbs's account and others, I'd say you could throw a baseball from the spot to the Oise-Aisne American Cemetery, where Kilmer and 6,011 others are buried.

✷ ✷ ✷

Though Oise-Aisne is in Seringes-et-Nesles, it is often listed, even on French road signs, as being in the town of Fère-en-Tardenois, which is actually a mile to the west. Like the rest of the area, Fère was more or less spared the ravages of war for four years until the Germans stormed into town that May. Then it suffered plenty. As a good-sized town (it's about ten times the size of Seringes) in a strategic location, it appealed to the Germans as a site for a military headquarters; and for the actual headquarters, they chose, as they were inclined to do, the largest and most elegant house in town. In many such towns that would be (and was) the château, but Fère's château was a special case: Built in the thirteenth century and owned for generations by a noble family who were favorites of the royal house, its last *seigneur* was a notorious gambler—and, apparently, not a very good one—who, having lost at cards almost everything he owned of value, wagered his château's lead roof on a hand and lost it, too, rendering his home uninhabitable. This was before the revolution, so perhaps his heirs comforted themselves with the thought that even an angry peasant mob doesn't want a château without a roof. It is, even in its ruined state, magnificent, two proud old stone castles perched atop steep artificial hills surrounded by moats and connected by a bridge that looks like a Roman aqueduct. Though they couldn't occupy it, the Germans, it is said, used its massive round turrets to store and test explosives; they are riven with huge cracks.

Instead, the Germans selected for their headquarters in Fère the largest and finest serviceable home in town, with expansive grounds and tennis courts (not to mention a roof). It's surrounded by a high stone wall, yet it sits right in the middle of everything, across the park from the *hôtel de ville*, or city hall. Adolphe Ferdinand Moreau, an aesthete and art collector, built it in 1856. His grandson Étienne Moreau-Nélaton (EMN), born in 1859, was quite a polymath: an art collector and critic, biographer and friend of renowned painters, and an artist and photographer himself. When the Germans took over his house, in the spring of 1918, they neglected to confiscate his *appareil de photo,* which he then used, after they were driven out, to document what they had done to both his home and his hometown. The images, published in a book he titled *Chez Nous après les Boches,* illustrate a community in ruins, entire streets of houses and shops reduced to rubble, public buildings and landmarks damaged to the point where they were unusable. In many photographs, American soldiers linger on EMN's front lawn or in his backyard, his great house looming behind them, its walls and roof pocked with large holes. He would never live in it again.

The house was not even deemed safe to enter until 1930, three years after EMN's death; eighteen years after that, his grandson Jean Brodin, a doctor from Paris, relocated to Fère-en-Tardenois to set up a general practice and moved into the house with his family, which included a three-year-old son named Marc. Marc also became a doctor, studying in Paris, spending two years in Boston (where he learned excellent English) getting a master's in public health at Harvard, then working for the United Nations and European agencies in Africa for a number of years before returning to Paris, where he taught medicine and chaired the European Public Health Association. When he and his wife retired several years ago, they moved into EMN's house and continued its restoration, a process that has now been under way for nearly a century. I had been referred to him by Fère's mayor. Marc met me outside his gates, wearing a sharp checked blazer and sunglasses; in his early seventies, he's tall and solid with a dignified, confident bearing. If you were sitting in an emergency room with a loved one and saw him walk through the door, you would feel relieved.

We walked across his front lawn and around his house, all four walls of which are still pocked with holes, hundreds of them—bullet holes, shrapnel holes, shell holes. And yet, he said his family was relatively lucky. As we walked back out his front gate and into town, wandering down the narrow streets packed with row houses, Marc told me: "Eighty percent of the homes here in town were destroyed during the war."

"So these were all rebuilt after the war?" I asked.

"Not really," he said. "People used the reparations money to fix the walls and roofs, but that was all they could do. These houses look all right on the outside, but inside they're a mess—the floors and walls are mismatched and unstable, the pipes are all patched up poorly, the wires are dangerous and so are the staircases, all of it going back to the war. The owners can't afford to fix them up, so they just keep renting them out for less and less money. I'm trying to start up a program that would change these things, but it's very difficult; people don't like change, even when it is for the best." The houses really did look OK on the outside—not pristine or even all that clean, maybe, but they appeared at least to be solid, not the kind of place you might be afraid to enter, much less live in. As can be the case with people after a war, sometimes it's the invisible damage that's the worst.

We walked out into the plaza and toward the old *halle,* or marketplace, built in 1550. Lots of towns and villages in this part of France have them, open spaces topped by pitched roofs supported by pillars. With its very steep and very tall roof, Fère's *halle* is a focal point of the town, but a century ago the mayor wanted to tear it down because it was so badly damaged during the war. I have seen pictures of it, roof full of holes, open space full of timbers—not in books, but on postcards.

It may strike you as odd that someone would think to put an image like that on a postcard. The first time I ever beheld one—it bore a photo of Romagne-sous-Montfaucon in ruins, as I recall—I wondered: Who would ever think of sending someone such a postcard? How could they imagine the recipient would be glad to discover such a thing in their mailbox? I never found the answers to those questions, I'm afraid, and while I still think they are strange, I can no longer consider such postcards unusual for the simple reason that I have come across hundreds of them, and do not doubt that millions were printed and sold. Some of them feature photos of soldiers, not all of whom were alive, and hospitals, and cemeteries; pictures of laborers, prisoners, newly homeless civilians. People didn't collect these cards: They sent them. Often, what they wrote on the back had absolutely nothing to do with the photo on the front. Or even the war. And sometimes it did, which is even worse. I have one postcard that features a scene of utter destruction in downtown Baccarat, on a site across the street from the *hôtel de ville* where a florist's shop sits today. It was stamped and mailed; on the back, a man whose name is illegible wrote, in French:

Baccarat, July 17th, 1915
With my best memories. I have deeply regretted not to be able to pass through Sainte-Menehould, where I wished to find some details about our beloved Lucien.

The only reason you can still see Fère's *halle* in person, and not just on old postcards, is because Étienne Moreau-Nélaton refused to allow it to be torn down. He did more than that, actually, going so far as to purchase the intact roofs off several otherwise-destroyed stores and have them moved to and patched together atop the marketplace. He did even more to save the church, which sits behind it. It dates back to around 1300, and didn't fare all that much better during the war. Marc told me his great-grandfather had written a book about the church before the war, and that it was used, later, to guide the restoration effort. Actually, he wrote nine such books about nine different churches, all of which ended up being used the same way.

The church in Fère is unusual in that it is filled with beautiful religious paintings, many of which were either purchased for it by Marc's great-grandfather or commissioned by him. There used to be more: The Germans stole some; others were destroyed in the shelling. Up above is a series of stunning stained glass windows, all replacements; none of the originals survived. After the war, Marc told me, his great-grandfather commissioned the artist Maurice Denis to make new ones. One features the image of an angel, wings spread, looking skyward in grief as he cradles the body of a slain *poilu*. It seemed very personal to me.

"The windows," Marc explained, "were dedicated to my great-grandfather's son, Dominique. He was killed in Belgium in May 1918." He gazed at the soldier for a moment. "His only son."

May 1918. In a single month, Étienne Moreau-Nélaton, friend of the crème of France's artistic community, an artist himself and a writer and photographer and collector and bon vivant who owned the grandest house in town, lost his home—his grandfather's home—and his only son. How he was able to do anything after that—much less restore two of the most important places in Fère—is a mystery to me. I'm not even sure how his great-grandson can talk about it a century later.

★ ★ ★

About twelve miles north and east of Fère is the town of Fismes. Fismes—pronounced "Feem"—sits on the Vesle River, which was the original objective of Operation Blücher-Yorck in May 1918, before it went so well that the Germans decided they might as well go on and take the Marne, too. Fismes had been a settlement since well before Roman times, and it presented a lot of geographical advantages: In addition to commanding the river, it was a railway hub and a stop on the road to Reims, and easily defensible thanks to the heights that surround the village of Fismette (or Little Fismes), just across the river. So rather than just hold it, the Germans decided to really fortify Fismes, should they ever have to retreat back to the Vesle. Which they did, just two months later.

In this case they were being pursued by the 32nd Division, the same doughboys who would charge up Côté Dame Marie in the Argonne that fall and thus inspire awe in Jean-Pierre Brouillon a century later. The 32nd, National Guard from Wisconsin and Michigan, had a high percentage of German-Americans in its ranks, which didn't seem to bother the French, who bestowed upon them their divisional nickname, "Les Terribles"; I believe they meant it as a compliment. As the Terribles approached Fismes, they would have passed over turf that is today a campground filled with caravans and tents occupied by Roma, or Gypsies. People in Fismes will invariably advise you to steer clear of that campground, avoid even passing by if you can. At the same time, they kind of take a grudging pride in having a Gypsy camp, since Gypsies go where the work and money are. Fismes, with around five thousand inhabitants, is one of the larger towns in the area.

It's also storybook pretty, spread out not around a plaza but in a cross along two main roads—one running parallel to the Vesle, the other running right down to it—lined with little shops and houses, Mansard roofs and brick chimneys. At the crossroads sits the *hôtel de ville,* one of the most striking public edifices I have ever seen. I lack the architectural vocabulary to describe it adequately, so I'll just call it a cross between the castle at Disney World and a cuckoo clock. Like the rest of Fismes, it was largely destroyed during the battle that began shortly after the 32nd Division crossed what is now the Gypsy campground; afterward, it looked like a giant foot had come down and crushed most of it to dust. I know because I saw it on a postcard.

The 32nd attacked Fismes on August 4, 1918, and spent two days taking it, during which time the Germans withdrew across the river, blew up the bridge behind them, and shelled Fismes mercilessly from the heights behind Fismette. With the Germans back across the Vesle, General Pétain declared the Second Battle of the Marne officially over at 8:45 P.M. on August 6—two months to the day after the 2nd Division charged Belleau Wood. That night, the 32nd, having taken nearly five thousand casualties in the offensive, was relieved by the 28th, whose emblem, a red keystone—they hailed from the Keystone State—was referred to by some as a "bucket of blood," a nickname that was soon extended to the entire division.

The battle may have been officially over, but Fismes was hardly quiet; there were still pockets of Germans scattered throughout the town, and snipers in many of the buildings, which made Fismes an urban battlefield, a first for the Americans. To make things worse, General Jean Degoutte of the French Sixth Army, who had command authority over all the American divisions fighting in that sector, became fixated on the idea of establishing a bridgehead on the other side of the Vesle, from which he intended to pursue the Germans further. He ordered the 28th to cross the river and take Fismette. This was problematic: The Germans, of course, had already turned the bridge to rubble; they'd also filled the river with debris and barbed wire. And they had utter command of the Vesle, and Fismette, from the heights surrounding the village. The Americans demurred. Degoutte insisted. The Americans, he said, could send enough men over the rubble to build pontoon bridges; if they crossed at night, the Germans wouldn't be able to see them.

Degoutte was wrong about that; and the sun eventually rose, which made things even worse. After several tries, the Americans were able to drive the Germans out of Fismette, but the Germans counterattacked almost immediately. The Americans never could get more than a few hundred men across, and had an extremely difficult time supplying them, since the Germans were still shelling the Fismes side of the river, too. Still, the Sammies, outnumbered ten-to-one or more, managed to hold on to Fismette for nearly three weeks, sheltering in the ruins of houses and shops from German bombardments and counterattacks by elite troops armed with flamethrowers. Finally, on August 27, the Germans overwhelmed the Americans, capturing or killing more than two hundred of them. Only thirty or so escaped, swimming back across the choked Vesle to Fismes. Fismette was now destroyed *and* lost.

It's no longer destroyed, but it still seems lost; even before I knew its history, I felt Fismette was haunted somehow. It's friendly enough to the eye, I suppose, a dozen or so little houses and a small roundabout full of colorful flowers, and unlike Belleau, it still has a functioning bakery, which is bright and welcoming, and where I once bought a baguette and a plastic baguette-shaped bag with handles to carry it in, the bag costing twice as much as the baguette. Still, it seems remarkably lifeless; many of the little French villages I visited were deserted as I walked their streets, but Fismette, though its houses were as neat and well kept as any, felt abandoned. A lot of villages that were destroyed during the war were rebuilt on different sites. Maybe they had the right idea.

In August 1918, getting from Fismes to Fismette could take hours and quite possibly cost you your life. Today it takes about twenty seconds, a quick stroll across a sturdy, wide bridge built in 1927 by the state of Pennsylvania in honor of the 28th Division. It's ornate, fronted by two tall pillars topped by statues of Columbia and her French counterpart, Marianne, and embedded with eagles and doughboy heads and keystones and symbols and inscriptions in French and English. It's the kind of thing that really impresses you if you actually notice it, which I suspect is not the case for most of the people who traverse it daily. It says a lot about the men of the 28th that they and their state built such a thing. Frankly, if I had been through what they had there, I doubt I would ever want to hear about Fismes and Fismette again, much less commission a bridge there.

The walk from the bridge back up to the *hôtel de ville* is a pleasant one, with views of the train station down below and bars and cafés and shops along both sides of the road. Toward the top of the hill I passed a dry cleaner whose mascot, painted on the shop window, is a steam iron dressed as Uncle Sam (minus the beard, of course—that would just be ridiculous). That struck me as strange. A few minutes later, standing on the front steps of the *hôtel de ville* and staring out across the plaza, I saw an American flag, which did not. Then I remembered I was not in America, and suddenly it did.

The flag flew outside a two-story corner building with a green-and-white awning that read "Bar de l'Hôtel de Ville." It was evening, around half past seven, so I walked over to see if I could get a drink and something to eat with some Americans. There weren't any; in fact, none of the eight or nine people in there spoke a word of English. I asked the man behind the bar, a big fellow with a mustache who resembled an older Freddie Mercury, if the flag was in honor of the 28th Division, perhaps.

"*Quoi?*" he replied.

"*Les Américains,*" I said. "14–18."

Nothing.

"The bridge," I said, pointing in its general direction.

"Ah!" he said, and nodded, then stopped and shook his head. "I didn't think of that, but no."

"Then why?" I asked.

"I love American cars," he said. "And motorcycles." His patrons, men and women, nodded along. It was then that I noticed, attached to the highest part of the walls, American license plates, one from every state in the union. Lots of tribal license plates, too. And longhorns, and a steer skull, and a dreamcatcher, and horseshoes, and a Buick service sign, and a Harley-Davidson service sign, and flags: several American and at least one Confederate, flags with motorcycles and big rigs and one of an enormous $100 bill, Benjamin Franklin's pursed lips in that setting conveying the sentiment *I know—right?* There was a banner with an eagle and Old Glory and the motto "Proud to Be an American," and a wooden sign with an eagle and the Stars and Stripes and the motto "Américain Car Club de France," and some posters for their car shows, and baseball caps and trucker caps and cowboy boots and, in one alcove, guitars and wooden Indians and saddles and spurs and, naturally, a life-sized bust of Elvis. I should point out that the only newish American cars you see on the roads in France these days are Fords, and maybe, if you're in the right town at the right time, one black Jeep.

"*Vous êtes Anglais?*" the bartender asked me.

"*Non,*" I said. "*Je suis Américain.*"

And the drinks were on the house. All night.

★ ★ ★

Fismette may have been a defeat, and it may not have been a part of the Second Battle of the Marne, but it was not without consequence. General Pershing was outraged—at General Degoutte's insistence upon sending Americans on what he should have known was a suicide mission (there were unengaged French units nearby who could have done the same thing; further proof, Pershing surmised, that Degoutte suspected it would fail), and at his own generals who knew better but didn't ignore or otherwise circumvent Degoutte's orders. After all, General Dickman, commander of the 3rd Division, had done exactly that the previous month at the Marne, and as a result had saved the day. Pershing's resolve that American troops fight only in American armies entirely under American command stiffened; and for the rest of the war, with very few exceptions, they would.

Whether General Dickman's, shall we say, creative interpretation of his orders was regarded more as courage and genius than insubordination at the time or merely appears so now, with the aid of hindsight, I cannot say. He was promoted to corps commander the following month, if that tells you anything. And I can tell you that the French certainly don't hold a grudge. People in Champagne are as crazy about the Second Battle of the Marne as people in and around Château-Thierry are about Belleau Wood. They hunt down postcards and old maps, walk the sites, read every contemporary account they can find, or at least every one they can find in French. Some are said to have collections to rival Gilles Lagin's. The retired couple who owned the *chambre d'hôtes* where I was staying told me about one such enthusiast in the area, a gentleman in his late seventies or eighties named Jean Vedovati whom they had known in passing. They hadn't heard from or about him in years, they said, and suspected he might have since died, but made some inquiries anyway and discovered, to everyone's delight, that he was still very much alive, and that he would be happy to have us over to his hilltop farmhouse, outside the village of La Chapelle-Monthodon on the Mézy side of the Marne. He greeted us at the door, a slightly stooped man with white hair, somewhat thin on top and bushy on the sides, wearing a gray zippered cardigan sweater (it was a warm June morning) and a grin that was at once both innocent and conspiratorial.

He welcomed us inside, and we sat down at a long wooden table in his kitchen with his wife. I asked him, in French, about his name; his father's ancestors, he told me, also in French, had come to the area from Italy. He'd lived there his entire life, he said, and had heard a lot about the battle, but had only developed an interest in it in the 1980s, after he'd retired. He asked what I knew about it; I gave him the basic outline, then added that I had met someone, a 103-year-old man, who had been here with the 3rd Division's 76th Field Artillery Regiment, and had very nearly been killed at Le Charmel a couple of weeks later. He nodded, thought for a moment, then started telling me about the exact area where the 76th had been deployed nearby. He'd written a book about the battle, he told me, *Les Combats dans la Vallée de la Marne* (Fighting in the Marne Valley), that spelled it all out; asked his wife to fetch a copy, then showed me a map inside and pointed to the area he was talking about.

We talked awhile about the battle and his research, and then I asked him about his collection. He chuckled, and shook his head. "I used to have a very large collection," he said, wistfully. "All kinds of things, everything you can think of, almost. But my wife"—he looked at her, fondly; she smiled, faintly, and looked down at the table—"made me get rid of everything. She was afraid the grandchildren would get into it and hurt themselves."

"All of it?" I asked.

"Yes," he said, still smiling, "everything. Out in the garden somewhere I still have a little pickaxe I found near a cemetery for Italian troops. Oh, and wait here." He got up, slowly, and walked out of the kitchen. When he returned a few minutes later, he was carrying something shiny, cradling it in his hands as if it were a vase that had been in his family since long before the revolution. "She let me keep this," he said, grinning, and handed it to me to inspect. It could have been a small vase—it was roughly the right size and shape—but it was actually the casing for a 75-millimeter shell, its copper buffed to a warm, modest glow. He told me he'd found it in an area where American artillery batteries had been posted. Clearly, it meant a great deal to him, and not just because it was oddly beautiful. For years and years after the war, I have been told, you could scarcely find a French house that didn't have one, typically polished to a high shine, displayed on its mantelpiece, the ikon in a shrine to the family's—and the country's— war dead. Sometimes, the casing still had a projectile in it. Most of them, I imagine, reside in attics these days. Even the live ones. But his was still over the hearth. You wouldn't think you could be moved so deeply by the sight of a simple copper cylinder. It was so radiant—and he looked so radiant holding it—that I took a photo of the two of them before he polished off our fingerprints and put it back on the mantelpiece.

"Come," he said, and beckoned me to follow him. We all walked outside, got into my car and drove for about fifteen minutes, down through the town of Dormans and across the river, past the village of Trélou-sur-Marne. Before we reached the next village, Vincelles, we pulled off the road and parked at the start of a muddy trail through some woods. "This was a road," M. Vedovati told me as we headed in. "In 1918, there was German artillery all along here, firing across the river." After a while he stopped, stared at the ground for a moment, then braced himself against his walking stick, bent over and picked up some shrapnel. A few moments later he did the same thing and came up with a horseshoe.

After ten minutes or so we emerged into a green meadow surrounded on three sides by woods; the fourth side, straight ahead, was open to a vista of a lush valley. About 150 yards off, directly in between me and the open vista, was an object I could not quite discern, though I thought I could see a glint or two of what looked like pewter. M. Vedovati looked at me for a moment, smiled and then started walking toward it. It was metal. Low and wide. A piece of a guardrail from the side of a highway, maybe. But a little too tall. And what would a piece of a guardrail be doing sitting in the middle of a hilltop meadow nowhere near a road?

Nothing; it wouldn't be here. But the truth, which revealed itself to me clearly as I got still closer, was stranger yet: It was a boat.

A metal boat. Probably aluminum. Twelve feet long or so. Streamlined, rounded hull, arched bow, flat stern. Much of the latter was missing, ripped away at some point. The rest was all there, if full of holes. Vegetation sprouted up through a couple in the bottom. You could still see the brackets all along the sides, placed there for oars or wooden supports. "This was in the woods over there," M. Vedovati said, pointing to our left. "Since 1918. A relative of mine told me about it years ago. A little while back they pulled it out. They were going to use it in a new memorial in Dormans, but then they didn't. So they just left it here."

"German?" I asked.

"French," he said. "The Germans appropriated it after they took this area at the end of May. They grabbed up a lot of French boats, for when they were going to cross the river. They rowed across in some, used others as pontoons for bridges."

"How did this one end up in the woods?"

"Just before they were to launch their attack, the French and Americans opened fire on them. They had taken some prisoners and found out when and where the Germans were going to attack. The fire was too heavy here; the Germans couldn't move fast enough carrying the boat, so they left it." Later, in his book, he showed me a photo of it, still in the woods.

I stared at that boat for a long time; I didn't want to leave it. I felt as I had whenever I'd been in the presence of one of the many World War I veterans I'd interviewed. They were all very, very old, yet talking with them was like stepping suddenly into an unexpected current of warm air on a frigid winter night: It was as if I had stumbled upon something hidden, even invisible, and yet the antithesis of mysterious. A secret shortcut to a place you have never been but know well. This boat was then, and it was now. They'd grabbed its gunwales; I grabbed its gunwales. M. Vedovati was very patient, stood there silently for a long time. I think he understood.

Eventually we turned and walked back. About fifty yards down the wooded path, M. Vedovati stopped suddenly and poked gingerly at the ground. I stepped over to look: There, embedded in the mud, was a shell, half again as long as my foot. "German?" I asked him.

He nodded. "155-millimeter." A large one, twice the size of the standard German 77. It would have gouged a really big hole in the ground. After a moment I realized that the groove in which it was embedded was made by a large tire. A lucky day for that truck driver, even if he would never know it.

Something about the sight of that big piece of unexploded ordnance unleashed in my mind a flurry of unanswerable questions: What might have happened if that big German shell had been fired at the enemy instead of dropped in the mud? Could that French 75-millimeter shell, fired back across the Marne from the cartridge Jean Vedovati found nearly a century later, have forced a dozen or so German soldiers to abandon their boat before they could get it to the river? And if they had made it across, would that have tipped the balance, somehow? What would have happened if General Dickman hadn't disobeyed his orders?

Gilles Lagin once told me that the American 28th Division, in the line east of the Rock of the Marne, faced off against the 16th Bavarian Reserve Division; the Bavarians forced the Pennsylvanians to retreat several miles there, but then the Americans counterattacked and eventually drove the Germans back across the river, killing a lot of them in the process. One of them they didn't kill, he told me—"he went through without any injuries, and got the Iron Cross First Class for his actions during the battle"—was named Adolf Hitler. "What if the 28th had killed a few more Germans?" he said. "What if one of them was Hitler? World history would be very different." Maybe that explains why he and so many other people collect, even hoard, that war's artifacts: It's easier to just look at them than it is to contemplate the war itself—what transpired; what almost transpired; what almost didn't. And what happened to Lucien.

Back at the house, Monsieur and Madame Vedovati invited me in for some coffee, and we sat and talked some more; they asked me a lot of questions about the men and women I had interviewed. Mme. Vedovati seemed particularly interested in George Briant, who had served in this area as a 17-year-old boy before almost being killed at Le Charmel. After an hour or so, I thanked them and rose to go, bowing to Mme. Vedovati; her husband clutched my arm as we shook hands and walked me to the door. A couple of minutes later, as I was about to get into my car, I stopped for just a moment to gaze westward, believing I could make out, through the haze across the crowns of countless trees, the Château-Thierry American Monument—the radiator—sitting atop Hill 204, a dozen miles away. Then I heard Mme. Vedovati call out to me; but when I looked up, she was gone. Confused, I took a few steps back toward the house before her husband appeared in the doorway, smiling. He was cradling that beautiful copper 75-millimeter shell casing in his hands; extended them toward me, and nodded.

I tried to refuse. I really did.

CHAPTER SIX

THE BURNT WOODS AND
THE BALL-SHAPED TREE

Like many people who appreciate both history and fine storytelling, I enjoy a good urban legend. A lot. And as it happens, the First World War generated—and continues to generate—more of them than just about any other real-life event I can think of. Many are, shall I say, of questionable veracity, like the story surrounding the "Bayonet Trench" at Verdun, or the one about German divisions pursuing retreating British troops at the Battle of Mons in 1914 being stopped by a number of enormous, ghostly longbowmen, the spirits of English soldiers killed at Agincourt 499 years earlier—the so-called Angels of Mons. Others can never be proven or disproven—tales of soldiers killing other soldiers in hand-to-hand combat and then discovering, as they stand over the body of their slain enemy, that it's their cousin or nephew or whoever from the wrong side of the border of Alsace or Galicia or some other frontier province; or of battlefield encounters with Corporal Adolf Hitler, which always seem to end with the other man's rifle or sidearm jamming at the moment of truth and Hitler scurrying off. But some—like the one about soldiers on both sides spontaneously throwing down their arms on Christmas, 1914, and meeting in No Man's Land for a game of soccer; or the one about Germany trying to entice Mexico to enter the war on their side by offering them Texas, New Mexico and Arizona—are actually true. Those kinds are my favorite. Patrick Simons told me two of them in one day.

It was June 17, 2009; the day we met. I had just arrived in France the day before, and was still gravely jet-lagged, but Bobby Bell had advised me that this was the only day he had free to show me around, so rather than recuperate, I drove the ninety minutes down from the Argonne, where I was staying, to Thiaucourt, where Bobby was the superintendent of the Saint-Mihiel American Cemetery. I didn't know Bobby at all—I had only been referred to him by someone at the Washington offices of the American Battle Monuments Commission, which maintains all American cemeteries and monuments overseas—and was surprised and gratified that he would do me such a favor; I later learned that the Saint-Mihiel Cemetery gets even fewer American visitors than the Meuse-Argonne American Cemetery in Romagne-sous-Montfaucon, which doesn't get very many. I think Bobby was intrigued by my interest in the area, and determined that I get the most out of my visit. He invited along two local 14–18 aficionados who knew even more about the subject than he did: Stan Bissinger, an Englishman who had married a French woman and retired to the area; and Patrick.

Patrick, who is French, wasn't native to the area, either, but I didn't know as much back then, and would never have guessed it, given how well he knew the place. I also wouldn't have guessed that he'd served twenty years in the French Army, and another thirteen with NATO, including three years at HQ and eight tours of duty in the Balkans. A genial man of middling stature and a receding hairline, expressive eyes and a big, openmouthed smile, he was still possessed, at sixty years old, of a child's sense of wonder, especially when it came to history. And all things American.

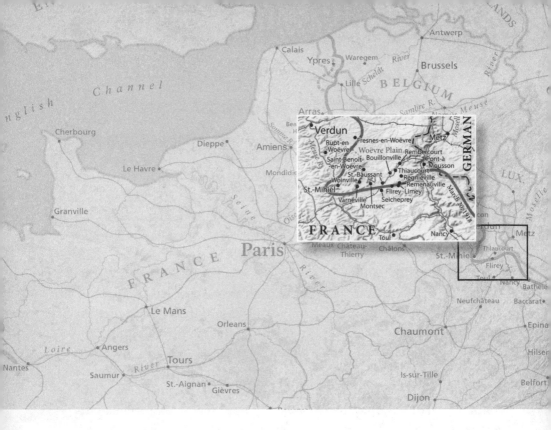

He was born in 1949 and raised near the small city of Chaumont (not to be confused with Ville-devant-Chaumont or Chaumont-devant-Damvillers, both about a hundred miles to the north), which had been the site of General Pershing's headquarters during the first war. After the second war, the United States Air Force built a base there; Patrick's father operated the base's bowling alley. "My dad used to take me with him on Thursdays," Patrick told me, "spending the day at the bowling alley, where I met many airmen. It was a very special and marvelous period in my life. These young Americans were so kind." Patrick's mother worked as a housekeeper for some American families, and would often bring him along to play with their children. He grew up, he explained, around American clothes, American cars, American décor and culture: "another world than the other French kids," as he put it.

The base closed in 1966, when Charles de Gaulle essentially shuttered all American military installations on French soil. It was, I believe, a sad time for Patrick; he lost a lot of friends. He never lost his fondness for all things American, though. After retiring from NATO in 2002, he accepted a position at a transport firm in the town of Saint-Mihiel, about fifteen miles from Thiaucourt; one day, he told me, he visited the Saint-Mihiel

American Cemetery, and was shocked to see "how many young guys gave their lives for us." He had never been particularly interested in history before, he said, but now he started to learn about what happened in the area during 14–18. Soon thereafter, he took a job at the Saint-Mihiel shop of DEKRA, a motor vehicle inspection company, where he befriended a co-worker twenty-five years his junior named Christophe Wilvers, who shared his interest in *la Grande Guerre.* Together they started exploring local war sites on their lunch hour. And then after work. And then on weekends. And then during vacations.

Christophe wasn't with us that day in 2009, but Bobby and Stan and Patrick showed me all around the old Saint-Mihiel Salient. Bobby and Stan spent much of the time discussing some project, leaving Patrick, whose English was much better than my French, to be my guide. We spent the morning bushwhacking through forests in search of old fortifications. At some point, Stan mentioned in passing that France has a serious Lyme disease problem, which kind of killed the buzz I had gotten from seeing my very first trenches and finding my very first shrapnel; it was certainly the last time I wore shorts in the woods Over There. Afterward, we enjoyed a fine lunch in a nice little bistro in the village of Flirey (pronounced Flea-RAY), during which I paid only slightly less attention to my exposed legs than to my steak and *pommes frites* and red wine; I was still searching for ticks an hour later when, back on the road, we passed a field maybe three hundred yards deep and twice as wide, and Patrick said: "Early in the war, you could have gone from one end of that field to the other walking on the body of a dead *poilu* every step." Between the jet lag and the wine and my paranoia about Lyme disease, I might not have been sharp enough to ask for more detail just then. But I heard it. And it's not the kind of thing you forget.

The next time I returned to the area, in 2014, Patrick was in the hospital in Verdun, recovering from an illness, and while I visited him there I didn't want to grill him about anything. The following year, though, he was back home and doing well, and we got to spend several days together exploring the area. One of the first things I asked him to show me was that field. That's all I had to say: *that field.* Six years had passed, but he knew exactly what I was talking about.

"Up there," he said, pointing to some densely wooded heights off to our left as we drove. "The Bois de Mort-Mare." The woods of the dead pond. "The Germans took it in September 1914. Very strategic—it gave them coverage of this whole area." Of course: The Germans always held the best real estate. "The French thought they could push the Germans back," he continued. "They started out one morning in April 1915"— April 3, to be precise—"across this field. And as soon as they did, BOOM! The Germans threw everything they had at it—bullets, shells, everything. They killed fifteen hundred *poilus* there, and thirty officers."

It wasn't all one-sided: Between February 1915 and April 1917, the French launched 130 attacks on German positions in the Bois de Mort-Mare; most failed, but the French did manage to dig a number of tunnels underneath the German lines and detonate enormous caches of explosives. "There are huge mine craters in those hills," Patrick told me. But I remained fixated on that field. What happened there was chilling even by the standards of that war, which makes it all the more dissonant to me that a new subdivision now stands on part of it, complete with a playground and a soccer pitch: a perfect little exurban idyll. The juxtaposition between what was there now and what I knew had been there exactly one hundred years earlier was disconcerting. But for a small, hard-to-spot kiosk that explained, in brief, "The War of Mines in the Flirey Sector," you'd never know you were near anyplace where anything had ever happened, except maybe a cookout. Yet over the course of four years, fifty thousand German soldiers died trying to hold the ground they had taken in this area. And another fifty thousand French soldiers died trying to take it back.

It started with what is now known as the Battle of Flirey, which began on September 19, 1914, just one week after the First Battle of the Marne, while the lines that would very soon settle into stasis for the next four years—and in so doing direct the course of the war—were still taking shape. The Germans attacked that morning: Their objective was to create a salient, or bulge, in the Allied lines, disrupting road and rail traffic, and thus supply lines, between the industrial centers of French Lorraine, like Nancy, and cities like Verdun and Paris. Over the next three weeks they seized some two hundred square miles, including spots like the Bois de Mort-Mare, and Montsec, the highest ground in the entire vicinity, giving them command of a much larger area and all but ensuring that they would hold it for as long as they liked. The Germans moved fast on September 19, charging in from the east; despite the fact that the war had been going on for seven weeks at that point, they caught the French completely unawares. By the time reinforcements arrived, three days later, it was far too late. Which leads me to the other urban legend Patrick told me that day in 2009.

Six years later, after we revisited that fateful field near the Bois de Mort-Mare, he and I drove to the village of Limey (Lee-MAY), then turned and proceeded north about a mile or so until we came to a placid farmstead set back a good ways from the road. Its owner, Olivier Jacquin, met us in the courtyard. M. Jacquin appeared to be in his late fifties or so; in his short-sleeved button-down shirt and khakis, he looked more like an actuary on a casual Friday than a farmer. He invited us into his house and introduced us to his wife, a stylish woman from Seoul, where they'd met. "It took her a while to get used to it here," he told me. "But now she likes it very much." She smiled; I returned the gesture, grateful for a glimpse of ethnic diversity, so rare in this part of France.

Patrick knew Olivier a bit, but mostly he knew of him; in addition to being a farmer, he is the president of an organization of area municipalities known as Chardon Lorrain—the Lorraine Thistle, the symbol of the *région*. It was obvious from his demeanor that Patrick regarded Olivier with great respect. Olivier, though, was anything but formal, inviting us out onto his terrace, overlooking one of his fields—and, beyond it, Limey—for homemade apple cider and cheese. (France.) I waited a few minutes after we settled in, then asked, simply: "Is it true?"

He smiled, perhaps at my American directness. "It is," he replied.

This is the story, as he told it to me.

Before the war, Olivier's great-grandfather Alfred Guichard was elected mayor of the nearby village of Remenauville. As it turned out, he was the last mayor of Remenauville: It was destroyed during the war, and never rebuilt. Today it exists only as a *village détruit,* a destroyed village. Much like Fleury-devant-Douaumont and the other *villages détruit* around Verdun—too badly damaged during the war, and their denizens too widely scattered, for them to be rebuilt afterward—Remenauville can still be found on maps. And like Fleury, it still exists in ghostly form, a patch of forest with paths cut through it that correspond to what were, a century ago, the town's streets. There are street signs, as well, and smaller signs scattered about indicating what once stood here or there—a woodcutter; a cartwright; the town hall; the vicarage; an inn—and, in a clearing, the ruins of its old stone church. I have a German postcard bearing a photo of the same ruins, shot when they were fresh, with German soldiers milling about.

In 1913, Alfred Guichard took out a loan and bought a farm in between Remenauville and Limey that he had been renting, and living on, for many years. His family at that time consisted of him, his wife, Louise, his 12-year-old daughter, Marguerite, and two sons, 16-year-old Fernand and 13-year-old Paul; two other children had died shortly after birth. Olivier says the five of them were happy there, weren't rich but had enough.

One morning, Louise left the farm and went into Limey to do some shopping. It was a morning like any other, at least until the Germans suddenly invaded. Which is to say, it was September 19, 1914: the start of the Battle of Flirey. The Germans, as I said, moved quickly; if it wasn't exactly *Blitzkrieg*, their notorious World War II tactic that involved planes and armored convoys, the literal definition of the term, "lightning war," would have seemed fitting to Louise and her family—and the other residents of the area—that morning. Like lightning, the Germans scorched one patch of earth while leaving another patch right next to it untouched. In this case, they took Louise's home, but didn't take the street upon which she was then shopping, and from which she could easily see her fields, her house, and maybe, if she looked closely, her family. What she couldn't do, even from such a short distance away, was get to them.

For four years.

For most of that time—three years, eleven months and twenty-three days, to be exact—the battle lines did not move. At all. Limey, right on the front line, was soon evacuated; Louise was relocated to the south, well behind the lines, and spent the next four years in what was effectively a series of displaced persons camps, where food was rarely plentiful and sanitary conditions often quite poor. She had no way of communicating with the rest of her family; and they had no way of communicating with her.

On September 12, 1918, the Americans launched an offensive to reduce the salient, an action known today as the Battle of Saint-Mihiel, during which they recaptured all two hundred square miles the Germans had taken in the Battle of Flirey, including Louise's home. She returned to find it—and Limey, and Remeneauville, and every other town and village in the area—in ruins; to discover that shortly after she'd been evacuated from Limey, the Germans had forcibly relocated the rest of her family from their farm to the nearby now-German-occupied town of Thiaucourt; that her middle child, Paul, had died of typhus that first winter they'd been separated, nearly four years earlier; and that her youngest, Marguerite, had been evacuated from Thiaucourt by the Red Cross. No one knew where Marguerite was. Louise, still recovering from the shock and loss, had to leave her husband and her surviving son, Fernand, to try to track down her daughter, eventually catching up with her in Switzerland. The following year, Fernand was killed clearing unexploded shells from a field.

"My grandmother," M. Jacquin said, referring to Marguerite, "was depressive. And mystical—religious. She had a strong personality, but was emotionally fragile. In 1939, terrified of the new war, she fled to the south of France, and didn't return until it was over. She used to talk about the 'dirty *Boche*' every day.'"

Eventually, the family—what remained of it—was able to rebuild their farm thanks to German reparation funds. "They used to joke that the damage of the war was good for the family, because they were richer after the war than before," Olivier told me, a wry smile on his lips. Reparations took many forms, not all of them official; in addition to money, for instance, the family tore up the Germans' narrow-gauge railroad tracks and used the ties as fence posts. I noticed a large pile of shrapnel atop a stone wall near the terrace. "When I was a child," M. Jacquin said, "during the harvest, tires would be punctured by shrapnel *every day*. My parents would send all the children out in the fields to try to clear it beforehand." It was never enough. Things are somewhat better now, he said, only because tires have improved.

Limey, and Flirey, and Thiaucourt and the Bois de Mort-Mare and the ruins of Remeneauville are all in a particular area of Lorraine that's about 125 miles (or three hours, as the roads go) east of Château-Thierry, and maybe 50 miles (or ninety minutes) southeast of Romagne-sous-Montfaucon. I refer to it as Saint-Mihiel, for the town, which is the largest in the vicinity, and for the battle to which it lent its name, which is what first brought me there; but the French know it as the Woëvre Plain. I'm pretty sure that you have to have lived there for a good long time before you can hope to pronounce "Woëvre" correctly, and I haven't, so if we ever meet in person, please don't ask me to try. Patrick's friend and fellow 14–18 enthusiast Christophe says "WA-wa," with a miniscule hint of a *V* in between the two syllables, the kind of thing you might be able to pick up with some microwave surveillance equipment.

The place, and its history, are as distinct as its name. The Woëvre is not Flanders, or Picardy, or Champagne or the Argonne or the Somme or the Vosges. There was no ten-month battle here like at Verdun. There was just one battle here—one three-year, eleven-month, twenty-seven-day battle. Though you've probably never heard of it, and likely couldn't pronounce it, and quite possibly couldn't find it on a map if you tried—I can't, and

I've been there several times—the Woëvre Plain saw as much brutality, as much savagery, and as much tragedy as just about any spot on the Western Front. Villages were leveled. Families were ripped asunder, at least one for no other reason than that the woman of the house decided to go to the grocery at precisely the wrong time. Entire populations were displaced. Legions of lives were destroyed, only some of them in the ways that might occur to you when you hear the word "war." A century on, their descendants almost give you the impression that they can laugh about all that now. Do not be fooled.

There are many reasons why, even within the context of the largest, deadliest, strangest war the world had ever seen, the Woëvre is special. I'll just give you one: It's the only sector on the Western Front where American troops endured two seasons of fighting in 1918—spring and fall.

★ ★ ★

Christophe speaks almost no English, which can make things difficult if your French is tentative, because he has a lot to say and tends to say it with enthusiasm. He was born in Sedan, the northeastern French city where the Prussians captured Emperor Napoleon III in battle in 1870, which might explain his lifelong fascination with military history; he chases it, as he once told me, like a Golden Retriever chases a bird. He and Patrick have been chasing it all over the Woëvre for more than a decade. The three of us had planned to go on a hunt of our own in June of 2014, but then Patrick fell ill and landed in the hospital in Verdun. He arranged, though, for Christophe and me to rendezvous on a Friday morning outside the American cemetery in Thiaucourt. I had never met Christophe before; wasn't quite sure what to look for. Then a black Jeep pulled up—I mentioned a while back that I knew of exactly one in France—and a younger version of Patrick bounded out: same ex-military bearing, same medium build, same receding hairline (though Christophe took it further and just shaved his head), with eyeglasses thrown in for variety. *"Je suis Christophe,"* he said, and shook my hand as if he were pumping a well.

"Et je suis Richard," I replied, though it was pretty obvious he already knew that. He bounced back to his Jeep, beckoning me to follow, and reached into the passenger-side door to grab something off the seat. *"Voilà,"* he said, and handed me a homemade scrapbook, fifty vellum-encased pages of old photos, maps and documents pertaining to the American presence in the area in 1918, all of it clamped together in a binder

from Office Depot. He'd even made a title page, "Tour St. Mihiel Salient" written on it in cursive over the cover illustrations from both my last book and its audio edition. I was touched, and more than a little impressed.

"*La Woëvre,*" he said, sweeping his arm around outside the Jeep as we sped across the plain. Lying between two major rivers, the Meuse and the Moselle, it was of tremendous strategic importance to both sides during the first war: to the French, an essential link in their supply chain; to the Germans, an invaluable weapon for hobbling the French. Both sides filled it with artillery, machine guns, barbed wire, trenches, bunkers, blockhouses and observation posts. The Germans had distinct advantages when it came to both position and technology. The French tried to make up for them with what they called *élan*—fighting spirit. Each, as you now know, was good for fifty thousand enemy deaths over the course of four years. It was Christophe who'd first furnished me that figure; he said it was conservative.

Strangely, this area, then known as the Toul Sector, was deemed "quiet," and I suppose, when compared to Ypres in 1915, Verdun and the Somme in 1916, and the Chemin des Dames in 1917, it was, which might explain why, in the winter and spring of 1918, two American divisions—the 1st, and then the 26th—were sent here to get more experience on the front lines. It wouldn't have taken them long to learn about all the killing that had been going on in this quiet sector since September 1914, to acquire an understanding of the particular savagery they were just joining that must have informed, and even shaped, their own experiences here. Patrick and Christophe knew that I would need such an education if I hoped to grasp what the Americans went through in the Woëvre; they decided it should begin in some forested heights known as Bois Brûlé—the Burnt Woods. The name itself should give you some idea of what went on here for four years, and not by happenstance: The defense works the Germans built in these woods were so elaborate, so brilliantly planned and capably constructed, that you have to wonder why the French kept attacking them over and over again. The only thing I can figure is that those installations were so advanced—so novel—that French commanders might not have understood, even if they beheld them with their own eyes, what they were looking at.

There's a lot of concrete, to start with. The French had concrete, too, of course. But, with few exceptions, they weren't allowed to use it. It was deemed bad for morale: Concrete implies you plan to stay put for a while, and the French Army, its leaders believed, must never do that. They must, rather, constantly be pushing forward, driving the *Boche* ever backward until they were in Germany. The French trenches in Bois Brûlé are dirt, and shallow; the German trenches, though, are deep concrete gullies that zig and zag through long stretches of forest. Christophe and I descended into one that was about four feet wide and eight deep—no Tarzanning necessary; there are several built-in cement staircases, all of which have aged quite well—and poked around. *"Fusil,"* Christophe said, pointing to the first in a series of small rectangular openings in the side: rifle. "Rifle," he repeated, pointing to the next. "Rifle. Rifle." He pointed down, to a drainage channel in the floor. "No standing water in this trench," he said. We came to a pair of concrete platforms, each a yard or so square, one atop the other, with several feet in between. *"Mitrailleuse,"* he said, slapping the one on top: machine gun. Then he slapped the lower one, and I could see the two together formed a deep covered shelf. "If you start taking fire, you pull the machine gun from the top and slide it in here." He stuck his arm in deep. "Totally protected."

"And what about you?" I asked.

"Ah." He stepped back and beckoned me to do the same. "There," he said, and suddenly I spotted near my shins a hole, large enough for a burly man, slanting down into the earth; reverse-engineering it in my head, it seemed to me the Germans had first dug a large shaft into the ground at an angle, slid one of those corrugated metal arches into it—in this case shaped more like an open safety pin than a half-pipe—then secured the arch in place by pouring a couple of feet of concrete along the topside, leaving the passageway it created open and solid, the kind of thing that could probably sustain an indirect hit or two. It had aged so well, in fact, that in recent years someone had to bolt vertical metal bars onto the front of the opening, to keep people (like me) from descending into it. Still, I put my face right up to them and could make out cement steps. "Bunker," Christophe said. As we made our way through the trench, we passed several more entrances to the same underground shelter.

There were more rifle galleries, too; someone had cast a Prussian cross in the concrete atop one of them. A little ways down, at a point where the trench took a sharp turn, generating an angle that created a bit more space in the narrow passage, we came to a chamber the size and shape of a shower stall. It had a rifle opening in the front, and a thick rear wall—five or six inches of cement—that only extended about three-quarters of its width; squeezing through the quarter-width opening in it, I discovered another, smaller chamber behind it, protected by the wall. I poked my head out, perplexed. Christophe beckoned me up front: "For snipers," he explained. "If you start taking fire," he said, then stepped behind the rear wall and gestured for me to follow. "Safe here." I was reminded of that hole the Germans had built into the floor of one of the blockhouses on Jean-Pierre Brouillon's property, designed to direct an enemy grenade's blast upward, where it could do the least harm. They really did think of everything.

All along the tops of the trench walls were petrified bags of cement; you could still see clearly the grain in the sackcloth. "The Germans just stacked them up there," Christophe explained, "and the first time it rained, *voilà!* Instant protection." He led me to another shelter, this one with a wider entrance, over which its builders, a Bavarian engineering corps, had left a cement plaque bearing their motto: *In Treuefest.* In steadfast loyalty. Maybe fifty yards away, across some flat, lightly wooded ground, a modern sign points out some French trenches. At one point in these woods, the two front lines lay only twenty yards apart. The French trenches, being dirt, are much shallower and narrower these days, maybe forty-eight inches deep and thirty wide; their sloping sides are covered with ivy and clover, their floors with tree roots and branches, making them appear even smaller. We walked through them, too, and very quickly I understood: No rifle galleries, no machine-gun platform, no sniper's chamber, no petrified cement bags; nothing to protect you but *élan.* The following year, revisiting with Patrick, I eavesdropped on a pair of French tourists as they marveled at how much deeper and sturdier the German trenches were than the French. There was nothing but admiration in their voices.

✷ ✷ ✷

Christophe and I spent that entire day in Bois Brûlé and neighboring forests, and after a few hours I started to get the distinct feeling, though I do not believe in ghosts, that these woods, burnt or otherwise, were haunted. There were, for one thing, ubiquitous subterranean portals like the one I described earlier, not just in trenches but scattered throughout the forest floor in a pattern I could not discern; they hinted at a vast network of tunnels leading, as far as I knew, all the way back to Germany. There were bunkers, including one massive concrete shelter with at least a half-dozen entrances and exits; and waterworks; and all kinds of little monuments and memorials, French and German, most of them to units that fought in the area. Some, though, were for individuals, like one Christophe led me to in the middle of the woods, a stele resembling an enormous artillery shell, standing at the head of a cement bed the size and shape of a grave:

HERE RESTS IN GOD

MAJOR OTTO STAUBWASSER

FALLEN

AS BATTALION 5 LEADER, 7TH BAVARIAN INFANTRY REGIMENT

WELTKRIEG 1914/15

Weltkrieg: World War. Already, in 1915, they knew what this was, what they were a part of. What they did not yet know was the horror that word, *Weltkrieg,* would one day and forevermore evoke. To them, this was still a field of honor, a glorious adventure, the birth of a new German Empire. Posterity, they were sure, would regard these memorials as we do the markers at Saratoga. I think that mistaken belief, that tragic disconnect, haunts me even more than all those tunnel entrances.

It is a humbling exercise to set out in search of ruins but in the process start piecing together an image of the enormous fortress—the killing factory—that the Germans constructed in these woods. To start, for all the supremely armed and trained men manning those trenches and bunkers, there were thousands and thousands more at any given time in camps a few hundred yards behind the lines, awaiting their turn. You find remnants of their stay here: shelters, kitchens, stone stoves, those omnipresent tunnel entrances. There are concrete platforms, all that remains of soldiers' barracks that were otherwise built of wood; and sections of walls of officers' barracks—they were built entirely of concrete—though little that hints at their former splendor, the time when they were furnished with electric lights, telephones, fireplaces, pianos. There is a field hospital, concrete covered with earth, one large chamber and several smaller ones; and another smaller structure, rectangular with bars in the windows. "That was a jail," Christophe told me. "For German soldiers." Even the Germans' legendary discipline wasn't enough to keep every last soldier in line, it seems, during endless months in the woods.

They spent an awful lot of time here; knew the topography intimately and used it to their advantage. At one point, Christophe took me to an enormous gun pit dug behind a butte that naturally hid their big howitzers from French and American eyes. In Buxières Wood, he led me to the top of another butte and pointed out two round cement holes, a few inches apart and each the size of a tennis ball, peeking out beneath the grass; then we descended behind the hill and ducked into an entrance covered by a corrugated metal arch, down some concrete steps and into a subterranean observatory. The holes, he explained, were for a periscope that commanded views of the entire plain; it ran down a square, fifteen-foot-deep shaft, still lined with wood, to an observation chamber, all of it so well preserved it could be used tomorrow.

Everywhere: Graffiti. Piles of animal bones, remnants of feasts enjoyed the night before deployment on the front lines. Rusted metal cans. Coal. And, of course, bottles. "Back then, there were vineyards near here," Christophe explained.

"Did both sides have the same kinds of provisions?" I asked.

"No," he said. "The Germans had everything—food, drink, shelter, armaments. The French only had white wine, red wine and bread." Each day, he said, every *poilu* was issued a liter of wine.

"Which would you rather have been?"

He thought for a moment. "In the early part of the war," he said, "I would rather have been German than French." He paused for a few more seconds, smiled. "In the latter part I would rather have been American." Quite a statement for a Frenchman to make: The Americans weren't issued so much as a thimble of wine per day; weren't even allowed to drink anyone else's, at least not officially. They must have been much better fed, and equipped, at that point for Christophe to have expressed such a preference.

All that talk of provisions must have made Christophe hungry, because shortly thereafter, when we passed a small clover-covered bank, he sat down, gestured for me to join him and pulled out of his backpack a pie stuffed with some kind of cold meat paté, a covered bowl of salad, a long, flaky fruit pastry and two cold beers. "Typical Lorraine lunch," he said, though I doubt many of the *poilus* posted here a century earlier had eaten nearly so well.

When we finished our repast, we packed up and walked for a bit until we came to a dirt road. Turning left, we followed it for about ten minutes, until Christophe suddenly spun right and started walking through the woods again. There was nothing to mark the spot; I had no idea where he was going, but I followed, and after about five minutes we came to a path. It led us down through the middle of what I later learned was the Forêt de Buxerulles into a small clearing, in the middle of which, camouflaged by shadows—I didn't see it at first—was an *autel:* an old Teutonic altar, elegant carvings all along its perimeter, a large Prussian cross flanked by an alpha and an omega carved in its center. It would not have looked out of place in any fine German church but for the fact that it was made entirely of cement instead of wood. It had aged well; I was quite moved by it.

"Soldiers would gather here for mass," Christophe explained, sweeping his arm along a large section of forest floor. "Hundreds of them, sometimes. There were ten to fifteen thousand Germans in this forest alone." When I returned to the site the following year, with Christophe and Patrick, a local official tagged along, eager to show me what had transpired in the interim: Someone had decided to restore it, and the entire altar had been meticulously redone in bright white mortar, a new Latin cross installed atop its pedestal, areas where the intricate perimeter carvings had broken off re-created. The official went on for quite a while about the local artists involved in the project, and the grand ceremony staged for its rededication just a week earlier. As we turned to leave, I whispered to Patrick: "I liked it better before."

"Me, too," he said.

A year earlier, I had been struck, powerfully, by the sanctity that old altar somehow managed to project onto the other, more profane ruins that surrounded it, those concrete trenches and bunkers and tunnels, those hilltop observatories, the elaborate waterworks, the narrow-gauge railroad that once ran through it all. It left me marveling to an extent that robbed me of any eloquence or even, apparently, tact. A few minutes later, traversing yet another stretch of magnificently planned and executed German trench line with Christophe, I couldn't contain myself. "How did the Germans *lose* that war?" I blurted.

It's an indelicate question, I realize, to pose to a Frenchman. But Christophe simply nodded his head thoughtfully and pondered it for a moment.

"*Les Américains,*" he said, at last.

Some time later, as we walked down another dirt road and Christophe indicated we were about to duck back into the woods to see yet another German something-or-other, this *Américain,* having spent the previous nine hours hiking through the woods, and presently afflicted with two aching feet, two sore legs, and a pair of arms that had been scratched white by branches and brambles, lost his composure and had what the parents of any toddler would recognize as a meltdown. *"Pas de forêt! Pas de forêt!"* I cried out. "Not forest! Not forest!"

And Christophe, whose Golden Retriever energy and enthusiasm hadn't even started to flag yet, took pity on me.

✳ ✳ ✳

Pas de forêt: Most of the Woëvre is, in fact, not forest at all, but rather flat, open farmland, extending out in all directions to the horizon. Easy terrain to take, if your enemy is caught unprepared; hard to defend, even with those wooded, fortified heights, and Montsec. Almost immediately after the Battle of Flirey in 1914—and in some cases, while it was still being fought—the Germans started building formidable defense works on farms all over their section of the Woëvre; overbuilding them, really, though perhaps such a concept doesn't exist in wartime. There were trenches, of course, everywhere, some of them concrete and extremely well preserved today, like the ones in Bois Brûlé or those in Saint-Baussant, a village near Flirey; most, though, were dirt, long since filled in and plowed over, not even a slight depression in the earth to hint at their former existence. Many, I imagine, rest at the bottom of Lac de Madine, a seventeen-square-mile lake that was created on the plain in the 1950s. It draws a lot of tourists; every time I've been to the area some or other vintage automobile gathering is going on, affording one the rare opportunity of simultaneously passing a World War I bunker and a 1959 Cadillac Eldorado Biarritz, both roughly the same color.

I'm not sure the tourists in their old cars, both mostly French, even notice the old blockhouses. They're hard to miss, and yet so common that they're easy to overlook. One morning I drove by one near the *village détruit* of Regniéville, and though the road was straight and flat and the sky was cloudless, I was almost upon the thing before I actually saw it and realized what I was looking at. It was only a few yards off the asphalt, too, a big squat object, fearsome despite the tender young grass growing on top, dark gray blocks with a rounded roof and low rectangular openings for machine guns. There were iron rods poking out of one side, evidence that someone had once tried to demolish it; a nice thought, but no more realistic than the prospect of ridding yourself of lice during a four-week stint in a trench. I pulled off the road and walked around it a few times, slowly, before ducking inside. Rubble covered the floor; tiny stalactites hung from the ceiling. But it was watertight. I wouldn't have wanted to spend the night there, but it was probably as safe as any house in the area.

Elsewhere, such a thing might draw tourists, gawkers, history buffs, but in the Woëvre, it's nothing special. If you see a clump of tall brush in the middle of an otherwise open field—a common sight here—it almost certainly masks the remains of a German bunker. Masking them with vegetation is pretty much all a farmer can do. "When you live here," Olivier Jacquin told me, "you can't escape the history—it's all around you, in everything you see, all the time." Some of those old bunkers are so interesting in appearance that they could almost pass for art; one, set back maybe twenty yards from the road outside the town of Fresnes-en-Woëvre, has sharp corners and a whitish roof and looks like a dirty sugar cube pushed down unevenly into the back of a Chia Pet.

One day Patrick and I set out to find the well-preserved remains of a covered emplacement for a German 88-millimeter gun, hidden in a stretch of forest along a main road; it had sleeping quarters with intact wooden shelves, and coordinates painted in white on the wall in fine old Teutonic script. En route, as we passed through the village of Varnéville, I spotted a modern house with a concrete outbuilding, separated by a driveway, that looked like it had survived a couple of world wars. Patrick confessed that he had never even noticed it before, though it was right along the road; I stopped the car, and we got out to get closer look. After a couple of minutes, a neatly dressed gentleman in his fifties emerged from the house and asked if he could help us. Patrick introduced us, told the man I was American and explained that we were wondering if his garden shed or whatever it was had been built by the Germans. He smiled and said *oui,* introduced himself as Alain (he hesitated just a bit when, pen in hand and notebook open, I asked him his last name, so I will refrain from using it here), told us he'd grown up here, as had his parents and generations before them. As he talked, I noticed the blockhouse stood at the intersection of two roads. A stream flowed next to it; flowers grew in front of it, and on its roof.

"The Germans built this around the house," Alain said. "Not this house, but the one that stood here before this one. They camouflaged the front of it, probably with shrubs like what's there now. This was close to No Man's Land, the French up there to the right, the Germans over there to the left. The sewer in town here is still full of cartridges. When I was young, my friends and I would go through those woods back there looking for shrapnel, and sell it for scrap. We made a lot of money." Later, strolling through his little backyard garden, I found a German horseshoe.

He went inside and fetched a key, then walked us around the corner and opened a red wooden door hidden in the blockhouse's rear. There were a couple of chambers inside, one presently being used for garden storage, the other as a man-cave. Each had, underneath narrow openings in the concrete, platforms for rifles or, more likely, machine guns. Though it sat next to that stream it was, once again, completely dry inside. The foot-thick walls kept it cool.

⋆ ⋆ ⋆

This was the formidable landscape, and history, that greeted the American 1st Division in January 1918. They replaced the 1st Moroccan Division, a highly regarded French colonial unit. With the arrival of the Big Red One imminent, maps were changed, the Toul Sector being renamed the American Sector. It was a tremendous source of pride to those doughboys.

They came here that winter not to launch an offensive, or to stop one, but to continue their training. Though not quite green—they had lost men in fighting, starting with those first three at Bathelémont two months earlier—it was felt they could use some more education in another "quiet" sector. The *History of the First Division* describes what its men saw when they first arrived:

> Opposite stood the picturesque hill of Mont Sec, which rose to a height of nearly four hundred feet above the surrounding plain and from whose summit the enemy could look down upon every movement behind the French lines for several miles. In front stretched the great Woevre Plain, dotted with villages, forests and ravines which afforded abundant cover for the enemy's batteries, billets and rest camps . . . At some points the two lines were not more than fifty yards apart. The ground along the French front lines was so low that only shallow trenches could be dug and these were largely filled with water . . . The position had been established when the Germans retired in 1914, and during the early part of

the war it had seen very hard fighting, as was attested by the numerous graves and the bones which had been torn up from their resting places by the bursting shells. During the three and one-half years of occupancy it had been strengthened by both sides with a series of trenches and wire entanglements, organized in great depth, so as to give a maximum of protection.

That's what passed for "quiet" at that point in the war. The Americans learned, very quickly, exactly where the Germans were, how close, how slender was the No Man's Land between them, all while hunkering down in shallow, wet trenches amidst human bones. And then there was winter:

> The weather was cold, with frequent heavy rains. The roads soon became sloughs, and the country, a mire. Rubber boots were issued for the trenches and emplacements, and the men wore them constantly. The ground was so low and marshy that on the sunniest days there was mud under foot and both infantry and engineers were employed in repairing existing trenches and constructing new defenses.

Not that that slowed down the Germans. They dropped hundreds of shells a day on the American Sector. Attacked the Sammies with airplanes. Ambushed American patrols. Raided American trenches, took American prisoners. And there was gas. A lot of gas. The *History* says of one particular episode, on February 26, that its "suddenness and the violence of the attack, coupled with the overwhelming fumes of the gas, were even more horrifying than the raid at Bathelémont." At that point in the war, the Germans were deploying sulfur mustard, which blistered the skin, broke down the lungs, and, in some cases, caused blindness. Death often followed, sooner or later.

Not that the Germans were the only ones using poison gas; "the Americans," the *History* notes, "were learning rapidly the German methods of frightfulness." By early March, the doughboys' own raids were becoming more daring, more effective. When the Germans launched the first phase of their Spring Offensive in Picardy that month, the French, needing all the troops they could muster, deemed the 1st experienced enough and asked Pershing to shift them over there hurriedly. In just over two months in the quiet American Sector, the Big Red One had lost more than five hundred men, among them 1st Lieutenant Edward McClure Peters Jr., killed on March 11, 1918. After the war, his mother, Eleanor Bradley Peters, moved to France to be close to her son, who was buried in the American cemetery in Thiaucourt. She took an apartment in the nearby city of Toul, and never left, even after the Nazis invaded. When she died in 1941, at the age of 86, she was buried in the Thiaucourt town cemetery, under a marker—a plain white cross—that is an exact replica of his.

For the 26th, the Yankee Division, brought over from the Chemin des Dames to replace the 1st, things were destined to get even rougher here. The story goes that when the New Englanders first arrived and settled into their trenches, having gone to some lengths to hide the transition and their own identity, they looked out across No Man's Land to see a sign hoisted over the enemy's first-line trenches: "Welcome 26th Division." "This was a livelier front than the Chemin des Dames," Major Emerson Gifford Taylor of the 102nd Regiment—Connecticut men— wrote in his 1920 history of the division, *New England in France*. "Officially designated 'quiet,' it was very far from deserving that name in actual experience." He elaborated:

> From the very outset all ranks were impressed with two absolute necessities—that of keeping under cover during daylight, and of observing extreme care in the matter of communications, lest information should get to the enemy, who proved, as was told by the outgoing division, to be both alert and aggressive. From his watch-towers on Mont Sec, as from his *drachen* ["dragon," or observation] balloons, he kept a vigilant eye on every corner of the forward area . . . It was a fact that, for days at a time, a motor-car, a group of three or four soldiers in the open, a thread of smoke from a kitchen, for instance, was nearly sure to draw fire from the "seventy-sevens," or, from what was especially dreaded, the so-called "Austrian eighty-eights," a gun of uncanny precision and very high velocity . . . Occupants of the trenches received continual attention from snipers and machine guns. It was hazardous, indeed, to be abroad "up front" at any hour between daybreak and dusk . . . And by night there were frequent concentrations of gas or high-explosive . . . At all times our men were made aware that the war was still going on.

The regiments were distributed along a nine-mile front; the 104th, mostly men from western Massachusetts, were sent up into Bois Brûlé, where the enemy was happy to shoot at them, or shell them with trench mortars, from behind those superb defense works.

The men of the Yankee Division quickly acclimated to the American Sector despite its hazards, which, along with the ever-watchful and all-seeing enemy, included things like the weather, and the terrain itself. Captain Daniel Strickland, in *Connecticut Fights*, recounts that the onset of spring had turned the Woëvre Plain into a hellish gumbo, its trenches— except, that is, the concrete German variety, with their built-in drainage systems—perpetually filled with water and, due to the lack of any "latrine system," as he put it, a generous helping of human waste. Nevertheless, with the benefit of lessons learned there by the 1st, the 26th started pushing back against the Germans, more than the latter cared to accommodate. They decided to teach the Americans a lesson at a little village near Flirey and Saint-Baussant called Seicheprey.

I've written about Seicheprey before, as have others, though no two people seem to interpret what happened there on April 20, 1918, quite the same way. The village, which sat right on the front line, was in the hands of the 102nd Infantry Regiment—Connecticut National Guard— on that particular day. At 3:16 A.M., the Germans unleashed a two-hour box barrage around it, surrounding it on three sides with an intense bombardment designed to keep anyone within from escaping and anyone without from coming to their aid. (This was a standard German tactic; they had used it successfully hundreds of times, including near Bathelémont on November 3, 1917, the night Gresham, Hay and Enright were killed.) Around 5:00 A.M., the Germans flooded the open end of the box (which faced north, toward the lines and, beyond them, Saint-Baussant) with *Stosstruppen,* shock troops. This was not one small detail of specialists; it was twelve hundred men, shrieking, shooting, hurling grenades as they ran through at top speed, disorienting and terrorizing the five hundred or so Americans trapped in Seicheprey. More than two thousand German infantry, highly seasoned, many armed with flame-throwers, stormed in right behind the shock troops. The Connecticut men, many of whom had been sleeping when the attack commenced, and some of whom had become trapped in their dugouts, fought back with whatever they had, which in some cases meant shovels, pickaxes, even rocks; one mess sergeant managed to kill two Germans with a meat cleaver before they subdued him. Eventually, after an hour or so, the Americans, aided by American and French reinforcements that made it through once the box barrage ceased, chased the Germans out of Seicheprey and back across the lines. The Germans left behind fifty-two of their own, killed. But they also left behind eighty-one Americans in the same state. And they took with them somewhere between 150 and 200 American prisoners.

The outline and details presented above are largely agreed upon by historians; less settled is their assessment of how the Americans did there that morning. The controversy goes all the way back to April 21, 1918: American newspapers of the time hailed Seicheprey as a triumph for the untested Americans; the government trumpeted it to sell Liberty Bonds. General Pershing, on the other hand—who, I have been told by more than one historian, didn't much care for National Guard troops to begin with—regarded the battle as a major screw-up on the YD's part, and was seriously considering disciplining the surviving troops until the French high command stepped in and awarded them the Croix de Guerre, instead, which would have made handing out punishments to the same men for the same action a tad awkward. Pershing was not pleased.

My own view is that the men of the 102nd acquitted themselves very well that morning, especially when you consider that it was their first major encounter with the Germans—actually, it was the first major encounter between any American troops and the Germans—and that they were outnumbered by more than six-to-one, though I will admit that my judgment may be colored by having met and interviewed the last survivor of both the 102nd Regiment and the 26th Division, 106-year-old J. Laurence Moffitt, who had been at Seicheprey; eighty-five years later, the memory was so unpleasant that he didn't care to say much about it, except that he'd been there. The real issue, I believe, for both Pershing and subsequent historians who view the affair as he did, isn't how the doughboys acted under fire, but how many of them the Germans managed to haul off as prisoners. They regard it as an embarrassment, a propaganda coup for the Germans, who had been taking, and using, American prisoners for exactly that purpose since Bathelémont. In fact, that was almost certainly the primary objective of their attack that morning. The Germans took a lot of pictures of the captured Americans later that afternoon, which they disseminated as widely as possible: postcards, leaflets, posters. The most famous is a photograph of more than a hundred of them, lined up in front of Succursale No. 547, a shop in Thiaucourt. Today the building houses a craft shop for a foster home.

I had been to Seicheprey several times, had walked its streets, studied its layout. I had visited the church in the center of the village, rebuilt after the war (I have postcards of the old one in ruins); it bears a plaque with an eagle over the words "The Lord of Hosts, in Recognition and in Memory of the American Troops, January–November, 1918." I had inspected the little fountain out front, erected by the state of Connecticut in 1923 to honor the men of the 102nd Regiment; had picked, out of the dirt at the base of the village's own 14–18 memorial, cartridges, shrapnel, a button, the head of a spoon. What I had never been able to do, though, was get a sense of how, exactly, the battle had unfolded there that morning. And so, six years after I had first visited the place, I asked Patrick and Christophe if they might be able to show me in a way that I might grasp.

"No problem," Christophe said. "How about tomorrow?"

The next day, a bright, clear morning, Patrick and I got into Christophe's Jeep and rode out to Seicheprey. We stopped briefly at the church, so I could get my bearings, then climbed back into the Jeep (Patrick granted me shotgun), turned right down the main street, and followed the road—D28A—east, heading uphill toward Flirey. About a mile from the church, at the crest of the ridge, we pulled off the road and got out. Suddenly, it was all spread before me like a diorama, the village down below on the left, the woods down on the right, a mile or so of open fields in between the two. "The *Stosstruppen* came out of there," Christophe said, pointing to the forest. "From those concrete trenches at Saint-Baussant. They just walked across those fields and right into town. The only side that wasn't under fire was theirs. The Americans were trapped." The Germans had planned it meticulously, rehearsed it over and over right up until they launched the attack. The inexperienced Americans were greatly outmanned and outgunned, taken by surprise in the middle of the night. It's a wonder, I thought, looking down at the battlefield, they did as well as they had.

Standing in that same spot, I suspect General Pershing would have agreed.

✳ ✳ ✳

There's another photo taken that day, more obscure than the one shot in front of Succursale No. 547, but also more haunting. It shows a group of newly captured American prisoners being marched up a hill, led by a German soldier on horseback holding a really long lance. (A lance!) More German soldiers bring up the rear; a few sit on a stone wall along the side of the road and watch the procession. The Americans look hot and exhausted and, frankly, pretty pissed off. Their uniforms are in various states of disarray; the most striking thing, though, is their faces: I don't know if it's the German camera or lenses or the film they used, or the men's haircuts or expressions or state of dishevelment, but every last doughboy in the picture looks like someone you could know. They're not figures in old sepia-toned photographs who make us think *Wow, people don't look like that anymore.* These men are—well, they're *guys.* They could be your friends. Or you.

I asked Patrick and Christophe if they were familiar with that photo. They were. I asked if either of them had any idea where it might have been shot. Patrick didn't; Christophe knew exactly. "It's outside Bouillonville," he said, then drove us there. We climbed out of his Jeep and he walked around, searching for the precise place the photo had been taken. He tried maybe a half-dozen different spots on either side of the road, and a couple in the middle of it, before settling into one just off the pavement to the left, a point maybe a hundred yards uphill from a sharp curve. "Here," he said after looking around some more, and as we joined him there it quickly became obvious that he was right. Much had changed—a hill that had risen up behind the stone wall had been leveled; a couple of houses were gone; a lot of new trees had been planted—but the road and the wall itself were exactly the same. It was startling: When I aligned the view with the image in my mind of that old photograph, I felt, for a moment, as if I were in it. I could see those men—those guys—shuffling up this hill, around that curve, behind a man on a horse carrying a pike; I could picture the German soldiers prodding them along from behind, while others sat on the wall and watched the spectacle. If the entire procession had come around the bend just then and marched right by me, I would not have been entirely surprised.

We tend to assume that very little will remain after the passage of a century and two colossal wars, but in the Woëvre, that assumption is tested time and again. Outside Remeneauville, Patrick led me one afternoon to a large old linden tree standing by the side of the road; it is believed to have been planted there around 1700. "That's on maps from a hundred years ago," he told me. "They called it *l'arbre en boule*." The ball-shaped tree. "Both sides used it to calibrate artillery," he explained. I have no idea how it managed to survive one war, much less two.

Nearby, a little obelisk stands off the side of the road, red diamonds painted on each side. On the front, a small white porcelain plaque notes:

5TH

INFANTRY

DIVISION

U.S. ARMY

12 SEPT. 1918

And below, on a much larger bronze plaque:

SEPTEMBER—OCTOBER

1944

5TH INFANTRY DIVISION

ASSIGNED THIS SECTOR AFTER 700 MILE

DRIVE FROM NORMANDY BEACHES

FIRST BREACH OF MOSELLE RIVER DEFENSES

MADE BY

5TH INFANTRY DIVISION

SEPTEMBER, 1944

I love the thought of GIs from the 5th Division coming across a monument placed a generation earlier by doughboys of the 5th Division—including, maybe, their fathers, uncles, cousins or even older brothers. More precisely, I love thinking about what they must have thought at such a moment.

Monuments like that are nice reminders, but really, memory is stored everywhere here—in the soil, and the rocks, and the roads, and the trees. No one, I think, understands this better than farmers, who contend every day with that memory, plowing up shells and shrapnel, dodging dips and concrete, and who almost always know a great deal about the battles that occurred on their land. Townsfolk, too, take a proprietary interest in what happened in their villages; should you stop in little Bouconville, for instance, someone is sure to show you the monument near their *mairie* that commemorates Jean Bouin, an Olympic runner—his 5,000-meter duel with Finnish champion Hannes Kolehmainen at the 1912 Games in Stockholm is a track-and-field legend—killed here during the Battle of Flirey in September 1914. A stadium in Paris is named for him.

The Sammies who stayed here a while in the first half of 1918, the men of the 1st and the 26th Divisions, would have known about Jean Bouin, and the tens of thousands of other *poilus* killed in the Woëvre to that point. And somehow, they would have had to live with that, and with the understanding that those big concrete things in the forests and the fields and the crossroads were there to facilitate turning them into ghosts, too, like they did to Edward McClure Peters Jr., and Joseph Sokowich, and Stanley J. Shaw, and John Sweeney, and scores of others. I don't think that, as the Big Red One and then the Yankee Division departed for other sectors, they were sorry to leave the Woëvre. And though what they left it for ended up being much worse, I don't think they relished the thought of ever coming back here, either.

When they did, in September—both divisions, this time accompanied by nearly a dozen more—things would be much different.

✶ ✶ ✶

Though less than three months had passed, much had transpired in that time—namely, the Second Battle of the Marne. The last great German offensive of the war had been stopped and reversed. American divisions had gained valuable fighting experience, and the confidence that went with it. At the same time, though, they had taken serious losses, many more than any of them had incurred during their time in "quiet" sectors. General Pershing was unhappy about that; a lot of dead doughboys would still be alive, he believed, if American divisions hadn't been misused by their French commanders at places like Mézy and Fismette. His men had proven themselves, he said, in battle, were ready to fight together as an American Army under entirely American command. He insisted on it. *Maréchal* Foch, the Supreme Allied Commander, agreed. Pershing said he knew just the place for his army to strike: the Saint-Mihiel Salient. His plan was for them to attack it from two sides, reduce it, eliminate it, and then push on to Metz, taking a major strategic and industrial center and becoming, in the process, the first Allied troops to cross the border into Germany.

The top British commander, Douglas Haig, didn't care for this idea. He had a plan of his own that would focus on his sector, with support from the French and, serving under them, the Americans. He swayed Foch. Foch took it to Pershing. Pershing, outraged, refused. The two generals worked out a compromise: Pershing's American Army would remain intact, and it would attack at Saint-Mihiel as planned; but as soon as the salient was eliminated, rather than proceeding to Metz, they would move up to the Argonne and launch a new offensive there—still under American command, but otherwise in line with Haig's plans.

Since speed was of the essence in reducing the Saint-Mihiel Salient, Pershing assembled a mighty force for the assault. More than 400 tanks were to be deployed, and nearly 1,500 airplanes—the greatest massing of those two new technologies in the entire war. Some 3,000 big guns were enlisted. So were more than 500,000 doughboys, many from fresh divisions that had never seen combat. An additional 125,000 or so experienced French colonial troops would also serve under American command. (In a fanciful image, *The Boston Globe*'s Frank Sibley, embedded with the Yankee Division, later reported seeing "the Senegalese, knives held between their teeth, crawling up under the machine-gun fire, through the bushes whose tops were nodding in the gale of flying lead.") A taut plan of attack called for most divisions to push straight ahead, while the two that had already spent the most time in the area, the 1st and 26th, would start at perpendicular points and head for each other in a pincer maneuver that would cut the German force in half. They were to meet, General Pershing decreed, at the town of Vigneulles on the morning of the second day.

The best-laid plans are still subject to the whims of luck; the Americans were the beneficiaries of one piece and the victims of another. The lucky break was that the Germans, on the defensive since July 18, had already decided to withdraw from the Saint-Mihiel Salient in order to shore up the line that ran behind it and had, by sheer coincidence, begun to do so the day before the Americans launched their offensive. The bad break was that it rained for several days, right up to H-hour on D-day—yes, those terms were first coined for Saint-Mihiel, twenty-six years before they were used for Normandy—and beyond. And that kind of rain turned the Woëvre into a sea of French mud.

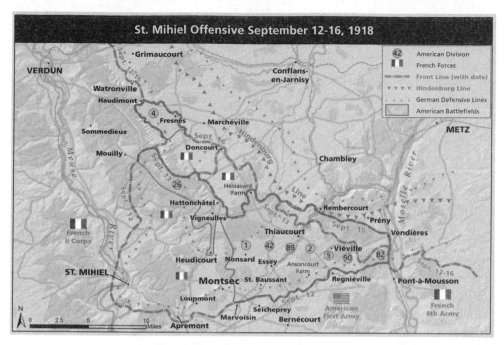

Courtesy of National Park Service, Cultural Resource GIS Facility

The rain effectively neutralized the tanks. It didn't stop the planes, though, or those thousands of big guns, which had started firing several hours earlier; Frank Sibley would recall in *With the Yankee Division in France*:

> The artillery preparation was set for one o'clock [A.M. on September 12, 1918]. And promptly at one o'clock there turned loose such an inferno of sound as we had never before heard. The whole top of the earth seemed to burst into flame. From right and left and rear, from every hilltop and from every valley, the cannon began to bang, and the echoes ran round and round until the whole sky was roaring continuously.

It lasted four hours, stopping as suddenly as it had started, according to Sibley, at five o'clock, although this was done apparently just to mess with the Germans, many of whom emerged from their shelters and thus were caught out in the open five minutes later when the barrage resumed, this time with gas thrown in for good measure. Then the Americans' barrage started rolling forward, and the Sammies pushed off.

Despite the mud, they moved quickly: Some of the Germans' big guns, as I mentioned, had already been displaced. So had some German troops. Some of those still in place had already geared up to evacuate and thus found it easier to retreat than to dig in and fight. Even the German barbed wire, most of it strung out four years earlier, had rusted a bit and was somewhat easy to overcome. Most histories published shortly after the war, divisional and otherwise, refer to Saint-Mihiel as an "easy" battle. "The price paid had been small," Emerson Taylor later wrote. "Casualties were not numerous." This assessment would have been of no comfort to the seven thousand or so American soldiers—nearly two-thirds of them killed in action—who had become casualties before the battle ended.

The dead were buried at the American cemetery in Thiaucourt, though apparently not all of them, as Patrick explained to me one afternoon while he and I hunted for another grave in the Bois de Rembercourt, some woods outside the village of the same name. I should say Patrick hunted, since I had no idea what it looked like, while he had seen it before; and though he was sure it was right over there, or maybe there, after an hour or so he pulled out his phone and called Christophe, the Golden Retriever, who drove over and led us right to it. It seems we had pretty much walked right by it, though I don't blame Patrick for missing it, since it doesn't have a marker—or even, at this point, a body.

Patrick told me the story: In the fall of 2009, while hunting around these woods for artifacts, a local collector came upon the grave—human remains still in it—and notified the authorities. The collector's identity remains unknown to me; to Patrick, too. "It was an anonymous call," he explained.

"Why?" I asked.

"He was probably doing something he wasn't supposed to," he said, and added, in response to my raised eyebrows: *"Metal detector."* Like Jean-Paul de Vries, Patrick regards their use as dishonorable; besides, it is illegal to employ them for such a purpose on public land.

The Bois de Rembercourt has long been known as fertile ground for relic hunters. The men of the 2nd Division had approached the woods through a large, rolling wheat field—deeper than the one they had crossed at Belleau Wood—protected by two German pillboxes, the remains of which are still present. "With only two machine guns, the Germans controlled the whole field," Patrick told me. You can still see dimples in the wheat—evidence that the Germans had something bigger than machine guns trained on this field, as well. The Americans had a hard time getting across it; things didn't get much easier once they made it to the woods, either. Though the section where we'd hunted for the grave was fairly flat, a large part of the forest lay on a steep hill; we negotiated the slope as the Sammies had—scuttling sideways across rather than up or down it, hopping over roots and branches at every step—and had a pretty hard time of it, even without anyone shooting at us. Plenty of shooting had happened here, though. Despite the fact that scavengers have gone over the woods many times with metal detectors, I found an unfired rifle bullet (American) and a mess-kit lid with a handle (German) on that hill.

The remains that nameless prospector found that day in 2009 were ultimately identified as 1st Sergeant George Henry Humphrey of Utica, New York, and the 6th Marine Regiment, shot through the head in these woods on September 15, 1918. His comrades buried him, with all his things, where he fell. After the battle, survivors were sent out in search of fresh graves so they could relocate the dead to Thiaucourt, but Humphrey's was overlooked; it's quite possible some exploding shell had obscured it. The following year, Sergeant Humphrey's brother wrote to survivors from the regiment inquiring about his brother's remains. One replied with a hand-drawn map. Still, they were never found—at least, not until that anonymous fellow with the metal detector came along, ninety-one years later, and dug them up.

The remains were transported back to the United States and reinterred at Arlington National Cemetery. Two elderly sisters—first cousins once removed, the sergeant's nearest relatives—attended the ceremony. Both had been born long after he was killed, barely knew of his existence. One told a reporter that when she got the call, she thought it was some kind of a scam.

"*Voilà,*" Christophe said, pointing to the grave, a body-length depression near a tree.

"Where?" I asked, my eyes still adjusting.

"There," he said, crouching down and pointing.

"That doesn't look like a grave," I said.

"It's not as deep as it was," he replied, "but that's it." And when I continued to look skeptical, he climbed into it and lay down on his back, arms crossed over his belly, his military haircut and camouflage pants only enhancing the tableau.

✭ ✭ ✭

Saint-Mihiel was, in essence, the coming-out party for the American Expeditionary Forces. Anyone who was anyone in the AEF was there, including a lot of people who were not yet anyone but would be, someday. Colonel George S. Patton was with the tanks that didn't get very far. Colonel Billy Mitchell, who is today regarded as the father of the United States Air Force, coordinated the air assault. Lieutenant Colonel George C. Marshall, serving on Pershing's operations staff, helped plan and coordinate. And Douglas MacArthur, who'd been promoted to brigadier general since his time in the Sommerviller Sector, was there in command of the Rainbow Division's 84th Infantry Brigade, though judging from the headquarters he took for himself, he seems to have felt he was running the entire offensive. The Germans had used the château at Saint-Benoît-en-Woëvre as their HQ before the Americans had driven them out, and like the Germans, MacArthur had an eye for choice real estate. He was also something of a dandy—let's just say he tweaked his wardrobe to suit his own sense of style, and rarely went into battle dressed according to regulations; he was once captured in the field by another American division and held on suspicion of being an enemy spy who hadn't gotten the uniform quite right. More than that, he was a tireless curator of his own legend, and had lots of dramatic photos of himself taken at the château, some on its front steps and others inside, seated on what can reasonably be described as a throne.

There isn't much to Saint-Benoît-en-Woëvre these days: a handful of houses, a restaurant that I have heard is good but that never seemed to be open when I passed by, and the château. And it's arguable whether or not the château is actually there. When MacArthur arrived he would have approached it from a long, straight driveway, lined on both sides by old stone walls culminating in a courtyard with a grand neoclassical mansion in its center. When Christophe and I arrived, nearly a century later, the driveway was the same, though the stone walls had been replaced, or perhaps plastered over, with cement. But the château—well, to start, it had lost its roof entirely (though probably not in a card game). The structure still has, to some extent or other, four walls, but almost all of its ground floor is now obscured by wild shrubs and tall grass, and the house itself is full of trees. Large, tall trees. They poke through the second-story windows and soar above its old roofline, making the edifice seem like nothing more than a façade, something you might find on a movie studio's abandoned back lot. The stone walls and arched doorways inside are mostly there but also mostly covered with vines. It looks like something General Sherman torched in his march to the sea, except no one did any such thing. It seems no one has done anything at all to the place since MacArthur left.

In the 1920s, General Pershing would choose the finest piece of real estate in the entire sector—Montsec—for an American monument, a beautiful rotunda that commands spectacular views of the plain and can be seen from just about everywhere in it. (In the next war, the Germans, who still appreciated a good position, loaded Montsec up with guns and observation posts; the Americans shot up their own monument in the course of chasing them out of there in September 1944.) In September 1918, though, Pershing made camp in another château, somewhat humbler than MacArthur's in Saint-Benoît, about eight miles away in the village of Woinville. I hasten to explain in this case that "humbler" in no way implies "humble"—it looks like a slightly smaller version of a storybook castle, complete with ivy-covered walls, high arched windows and a turret with a conical roof. Unlike the château at Saint-Benoît, the one in Woinville has been remarkably well maintained—is, in fact, a bed-and-breakfast now. Its sign mentions its garden and "rooms with character," but says nothing about the place's most famous guest. Everyone in town knows, though, just like they all know that the Germans had used the local schoolhouse, built ANNO MDCCCXXXVII, as a hospital for four years before Pershing arrived.

And that, really, is what makes this area different from those that Americans had fought in further to the west: *four years.* The Germans had taken those towns and villages north of the Marne just about six or eight weeks before the Allies took them back; they had taken Belleau Wood and the villages around it just days before the Marines set out across that wheat field. But they had taken their chunk of the Woëvre in September 1914, and had held it—and all the towns and villages and people in it—for those four years; had, effectively, held all those French civilians hostage, including Alfred Guichard and his whole family, except for his wife, Louise, who, though safely behind French lines, was also a hostage of the Germans, in a sense. "In the villages . . . a civilian population, freed from four years of slavery, welcomed our men as saviors," Emerson Taylor wrote in *New England in France,* and though it sounds like self-congratulatory hyperbole, it wasn't. Taylor ends his chapter on Saint-Mihiel with a letter written by the village priest of Rupt-en-Woëvre on September 13, 1918, the day after it and many other towns were liberated; in it, he thanks the men of the YD for releasing him and his parishioners from four years of German brutality. He closes:

> Several of your comrades lie at rest in our truly Christian and French soil.
>
> Their ashes shall be cared for as if they were our own. We shall cover their graves with flowers, and shall kneel by them as their own families would do, with a prayer to God to reward with eternal glory these heroes fallen on the field of honor, and to bless the Twenty-Sixth Division and generous America. Be pleased, Sir, to accept the expression of my profound respect.

In Thiaucourt, whither the Guichards and a lot of other families were removed after the Germans seized their farms, the town's World War I monument is a life-sized statue of a *poilu* and a doughboy warmly shaking hands as their respective flags flutter behind them. There are plenty of markers, memorials, plaques and even statuary Over There commemorating America's role in the liberation of France in the First World War; but nothing else like the one in Thiaucourt. Of all the things Patrick showed me that first day back in 2009, it left the strongest impression—stronger, even, than those trenches and shrapnel we'd found in the woods. When I returned in 2014 it was gone—removed for restoration, I was told, though its pedestal, pocked with bullet holes from the second war, remained. I was greatly relieved to see it back in place the following year.

★ ★ ★

You can't go many places in the Woëvre without coming upon a 14–18 cemetery. The American cemetery, in Thiaucourt, contains 4,153 graves; the largest French cemetery in the area, in Flirey, has 4,407. The largest German cemetery, which is also in Thiaucourt, has 11,685 graves—around one-fifth of the German soldiers killed in this area between 1914 and 1918—spread out in endless rows over acres and acres. The last time I was there, I met a German couple who were searching for the grave of the man's great-grandfather, killed here in 1916. I wished them luck.

The Thiaucourt cemetery's acreage indicates that it was built during the war. Those that were constructed afterward are much smaller, with many of their dead consigned to mass graves; as Gilles Lagin once explained it to me, the French didn't want to give the Germans any more ground than they had to. Thiaucourt, though, has no mass graves. Most of its markers are laid out in straight rows, though the Germans occasionally arranged some in circles, too, especially around trees. Way in the back, you'll find a gallery of custom-made individual monuments. Unlike the French and Americans, who only allowed standard government-issued markers in their cemeteries, the Germans permitted comrades or loved ones of the fallen to commission private memorials, stones that were chiseled and carved back home in Germany, then transported to France and installed in the same military cemetery in which the memorialized soldier was interred. The larger stones, in particular—I've seen some that were four feet tall or more—feature expert craftsmanship, exquisite lettering, flowery language ("Here rests our beloved, brave fallen comrade . . ."), and beautiful imagery: blossoms, swords, *Pickelhauben* (the spiked helmets Germans wore early in the war), a snuffed-out torch, an oak branch with an Iron Cross dangling by a ribbon. They are beautiful and fascinating, but above all strange, speaking at once to the Germany of that era's imperial ambitions—their very presence indicates that the Germans intended to keep this conquered territory forever—and its surprisingly romantic, sentimental ethos. French postcards from that war typically feature photos of men in uniform, or destroyed towns, or tanks, or trains, but German postcards often showcase a poem, or a photo of a soldier standing before *ein einsames Kriegergrab*—a lonely war grave—or a hand-tinted image of a soldier in uniform, the soft field cap known as a *Mütze* on his head, canoodling with a buxom *Fräulein* back home over a caption like "The kiss is the seal of love."

Most German World War I cemeteries have at least a few individual memorials; the Thiaucourt cemetery has dozens, including at least two dedicated to Jewish soldiers, *Kanonier* Hermann Katz and *Feldunterarzt* Ludwig Salinger. Katz's features a beautiful chiseled image of an artilleryman's distinctive *Pickelhaube,* which features a cannonball instead of a spike on top; Salinger's identifies him as *Ritter des Eisernen Kreuzes*— Knight of the Iron Cross. They died, respectively, in December 1914 and January 1915, cold and far from home. Their families, if they stayed in Germany for another few decades, have no gravestones at all. There are standard-issue Jewish markers—tablets, like those Moses carried down from Mount Sinai—scattered throughout the Thiaucourt cemetery, too, as there are in every German 14–18 burial ground. Twelve thousand Jewish soldiers gave their lives for *das Vaterland* in that war; more of them, proportionate to their share of the population, than Germans as a whole.

One day, on my way to somewhere else—I can't recall where anymore—I passed through little Bouillonville, outside of which those American prisoners had been photographed by their German captors on April 20, 1918. The village is mostly one street, narrow and curving with houses and shops huddling just off the sidewalk, the kind of place you drive through very carefully. As I rolled forward, slowly, a woman approached my car on foot and cautioned me to take care: A cow had gotten loose and was in the road just around the next bend. The heifer was all white—a Charolais, a breed very popular in France—and loped this way and that, in no hurry to move, despite a few townspeople's prodding and entreaties.

At an intersection on the outskirts of town I saw a little sign shaped like an arrow (or, more accurately, a grain silo tipped over on its side) pointing to the right: "Deutscher Soldatenfriedhof 1914–18." Another German cemetery.

Now, for as long as I can remember I have been in the habit, when passing by an old burial ground and not in any particular hurry to get wherever it is I am going, of stopping in and poking around; but this one was only about two miles from the enormous *Soldatenfriedhof* in Thiaucourt, where I'd just spent a considerable amount of time, and I was experiencing a bit of cemetery fatigue right then. I was about to drive on past when I spotted, on a stretch of grass just outside the cemetery's low black wrought-iron gate, a man working in a garden. Yes, he said, when I asked: He does find things in the dirt there. Mostly cartridges and horse's bones and, once, a piece of a French Lebel rifle. Had there been fighting here? He pointed over my shoulder at the landscape on the other side of the cemetery; it was speckled with craters. I sighed, thanked him and walked over to the gate. A plaque on it reported that there were exactly 1,368 German dead within. At least, I thought, this will be quick.

It wasn't.

Bouillonville sprawls. It's easily as large in area as the cemetery at Thiaucourt, which contains almost ten times the number of dead; it was clearly laid out during the war, when the Germans had the liberty of taking as much land as they wished. It starts narrow and then widens, then widens some more, and some more, and then expands up a hill to the left, crosses a road, and continues into a mezzanine and then an upper terrace. There's an area on the lower level where graves are planted in a circle around a big old tree, and a garden section nearby with some modest personal memorials lined up against a fence. In the middle of one section stands a small stele bearing an eagle and a Prussian cross and the motto *Für Gott, König und Vaterland*. Other than that, and despite the slopes (which continue across the road), the rows are perfectly orderly. More orderly, in a way, than any other cemetery I have ever visited, because these graves are laid out exactly as they had been during the war, with 1914 in the narrow corridor closest to the front gate, 1915 by the stele, 1916 in the section with the tree, 1917 in the mezzanine, 1918 up top: the entire war plotted out chronologically for anyone with the time and inclination to stroll on through.

There are seven rows in the ultimate section, in two plots bisected by a brick path. On the left, in the very last row, I found three markers dated September 12, 1918; the last three graves in the cemetery, dug on the morning of the Americans' attack before whoever was doing the digging realized there would be many, many more, including theirs if they stayed around to dig further. On the right, in rows four and five, I counted forty-eight graves dated April 20, 1918—forty-eight of the fifty-two seasoned soldiers of Reserve Infanterie Regiment 259, most of them from the vicinity of Oldenburg in Lower Saxony, who'd been killed by Connecticut troops during that attack on Seicheprey, the one that many historians consider a debacle, the one that resulted in the deaths of 81 doughboys.

If you look at it on paper, fifty-two to eighty-one doesn't seem terribly skewed; if you then hear that the Germans outnumbered the Americans that morning six-to-one, you might even start to feel some pride, a sense that, all things considered, we got them about as good as they got us that day. But I can tell you, from personal experience, that walking down those rows and reading the names of some of the fifty-two men who died trying to capture American prisoners for propaganda purposes—Johann Kapels; Mathias Verkennis; Heinrich Knop; Emil Winkelmann—doesn't engender any sense of satisfaction. All you really come away with is an understanding that those men—or, more accurately, their commanding officers' commanding officers—gravely underestimated their American enemy.

By the time they met there again, five months later, two more urban legends would be put to rest: the Germans' belief that their superior positions and defense works and weaponry made them invulnerable; and the Americans' notion that they could rout the tired and all-but-defeated Germans in battle without paying a very high price themselves. The war in the Woëvre was once new, then old, for both of them; in far too many cases, it took their spirit and then their lives. But what awaited them next was something far worse, something that history would come to regard as both Germany's last stand and America's deadliest battle, something akin to the greatest military urban legend of all.

If you think about it, "Argonne" even sounds a bit like "Armageddon."

CHAPTER SEVEN

RED GIANT

The last great battle of World War I began around 5:00 A.M. on September 26, 1918, and ended promptly at 11:00 A.M. forty-seven days later. Some 1,200,000 doughboys, six of every ten in France at that time, fought over an area about half the size of Rhode Island, bordered to the west by the Argonne Forest, to the east by the Meuse River, and to the north by hundreds of thousands of experienced German soldiers ensconced behind four years' worth of defenses. The attack was launched along a twenty-four-mile-long front, fanning out as it advanced. Before the offensive was over, it would claim the lives of 26,277 American soldiers, more than any other battle in American history. Another 100,000 would be wounded, shot or gassed or blown up or hammered by shrapnel. For most of the men involved, the Meuse-Argonne Offensive would epitomize the First World War, as Verdun did for the French and the Somme for the British.

Some of them had already fought elsewhere—at Bathelémont, and the Chemin des Dames, and Château-Thierry, and Belleau Wood, and the Marne, and the Vesle, and Saint-Mihiel. Others would fight even further afield: Two American National Guard divisions—the 27th, from New York, and the 30th, from the Carolinas and Tennessee—would spend the fall of 1918 fighting under British command (despite Pershing's earlier policy) near the Somme, 125 miles west of the Argonne; two more, the 37th and 91st, would be pulled from the Argonne in the midst of the offensive and end up fighting in Flanders, across the border in Belgium, for the last couple of weeks of the war. One regiment of American infantry, the 332nd, was sent to Italy, where it fought high in the Alps during the Vittorio Venetto Offensive, which effectively knocked Austria-Hungary out of the war. Two more regiments, the 27th and 31st, were sent to northern Russia and Siberia, where they were supposed to protect Allied interests and maybe tip the scales a bit against the Bolsheviks in the civil war there.

Back in France, a few American units had spent part of the summer of 1918 in the Vosges Mountains in Lorraine and Alsace, including the 5th Division, which, though they didn't do much fighting in the vicinity, nevertheless put up a monument to themselves in the village of Frapelle, the only such testament to an American presence in the Vosges; and the 92nd, the Buffalo Division, one of only two African American combat divisions to serve on the Western Front in that war. The other African American combat division, the 93rd (aka the Bloody Hand Division, after their insignia) was famously given to the French by General Pershing, and thus served throughout the spring and summer of 1918—in French uniforms, with French weapons, under French commanders—in parts of the Western Front that no other Americans saw. That fall, they fought in an area just a dozen or so miles from the sites of some of the fiercest fighting in the Meuse-Argonne Offensive, yet their actions there are not considered part of that last great battle: segregated once again, it seems, though at least the French appreciated them, erecting their own monuments to the division's regiments after the war. The most interesting of these, to the 371st Infantry Regiment, can be found outside the village of Ardeuil-et-Montfauxelles, atop a ridge in the middle of a working farm, the road to which is not the kind of thoroughfare you want to try in a rented car. I won't say how I got there; only that it was worth the effort. It's smaller

and humbler than the other monuments to "colored" regiments, in part because its top was blown off during fighting in the area on June 12, 1940, but you can still read, among the names listed around its base, that of Freddie Stowers, who in 1991 became the first and only African American doughboy to be awarded the Medal of Honor, seventy-three years after he was killed trying to take this spot.

With the exceptions of the 27th and 30th Divisions, out in Picardy, and the 93rd here in Lorraine, pretty much every other American division in France that was deemed ready to fight was being massed along that twenty-four-mile line from the Argonne to the Meuse. From the time the AEF started showing up in France, the Allies had been working on the assumption that if the Germans could be softened up enough in 1918, they might be finished off in some grand Allied push in 1919. By the end of August, though, with the last German offensive stopped cold and then rolled back at the Second Battle of the Marne, some were thinking, even if they wouldn't say such a thing aloud, that perhaps a big push that fall might do more than merely soften up the Germans. Thus were General Pershing's plans for a push to Metz after Saint-Mihiel rewritten by the French and British, replaced with a major offensive at Meuse-Argonne, where over the previous four years the French had known only costly defeat, and the British had never even fought at all. Pershing, who had been very cautious with his men's lives to that point, might have pondered those facts a bit more before he agreed; but in exchange he was offered what he'd always wanted—an independent American Army fighting under entirely American command—so he didn't. Historians disagree on the wisdom of that decision. All those statistics I cited earlier, though, are beyond dispute.

They can be overwhelming. So can a visit to the Meuse-Argonne American Cemetery, where 14,246 of those 26,277 Americans are buried. So can driving around the Argonne and getting a sense of just how vast a battlefield it is, and how varied: farms and forests, lush valley and rocky heights, Roman roads and tractor trails and cow paths. The area was settled by Celts three thousand years ago and by the Romans a thousand years after that, but a lot of it wasn't actually settled by French people until the seventeenth century; it was regarded before that as impenetrable wilderness, and much of it seems that way today. Dave Bedford, the superintendent of the Meuse-Argonne American Cemetery, once took me to a section of woods where the 368th Infantry Regiment, part of the Buffalo Division, pushed off on the morning of September 26; denied artillery support and accurate maps and adequate wire-cutters—while serving under a white commanding officer who suffered a nervous breakdown and had to be removed from the field—they quickly ran into all kinds of trouble, failing to achieve their objective of linking up with the 77th Division, a fact that was used to denigrate African American troops for a generation. Ninety-seven years later, Dave and I ran into all kinds of trouble there, too, barely making a few hundred yards through mud and holes and very dense brush before we had to turn back. And it wasn't 5:00 A.M. at the end of September. And we didn't have to negotiate any barbed wire. And no one was trying to kill us. Except, maybe, Mother Nature.

Even Mother Nature didn't mess with the Germans, who'd conquered the French in the Argonne, and then the Argonne itself, in short order in 1914 and lived in it thereafter as if they were very well armed wood nymphs. They were so good at sylvan living and warfare, in fact, that they inspire awe and admiration in a great many present-day history buffs, a lot of them French. A group of them has even undertaken the restoration of one of the Germans' third-line rest camps in the Argonne, Camp Moreau, near the village of Vienne-le-Château. Lager Moreau-West, as it

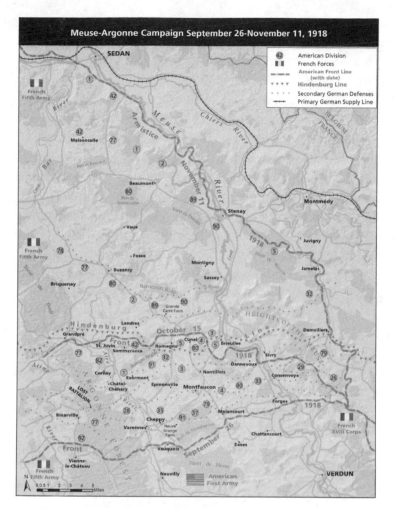

Courtesy of National Park Service, Cultural Resource GIS Facility

was known during the war, was established in September 1914, in a section of the forest that afforded excellent natural defenses and resources. It was, like almost everything the Germans built, electrified and outfitted with hot and cold running water and excellent sanitation facilities, and housed up to four thousand men at a time. It was also served by narrow-gauge rail. The Germans laid out more than eight hundred miles of it in northern France during the war; they had already built more than a hundred miles of it in the Argonne by the end of 1914.

Innumerable German soldiers did stints in the Argonne at one time or another. Every month, three thousand of them became casualties in this part of the forest alone. The Germans built forty cemeteries here during the war; the Americans built one very large one, and the French eight, one of which contains the remains of ten thousand unknown *poilus*. So many French just disappeared in the Argonne that after the war an ossuary was built, by private subscription, in an area of the forest called Haute Chevauchée. Down in its crypt, the bones themselves are mostly out of view—you can see a few peeking out behind notches in the chamber wall—but the walls are covered with plaques commemorating the dead, commissioned and mounted by subscribers. Some are illustrated with photos of the deceased. The men wear their uniform, or coat and tie; they look right at you or a bit to the side, lips pursed in bravado or curled up ever so slightly in a shy smile. Son, father, brother, uncle; killed, died gloriously, fell, disappeared. 1914, 1915, 1916, 1917, 1918. Leon, Gustave, Louis, Henri, René, Alfred, Paul, Pierre, Raymond, André, Emile, Alexandre, Michel, Georges, Gabriel, Maurice, Jude, Jean, Charles, Fernand, Primo, Etienne, Robert, Ernest, Octave, Eugene, Antonin, Victor. A startling number of them died around Christmas and New Year's. It is easier, I think, to just stare at the bones than it is to read those plaques. Between 1914 and 1918, hundreds of thousands of men were killed in the Argonne—not in any kind of discrete "battle"; just day-to-day conflict.

On the ground, it seems impossible to grasp something like the Meuse-Argonne Offensive. In trying to get a handle on the war's last great battle, I have found it best to take the same approach I took with its first, the Battle of the Frontiers: Focus on something—a spot, a unit, a day, a story—until you have it in hand, then move on to something else, and, in time, assemble a mosaic that, if you behold it from the right distance, presents you with a picture.

But a lot of people get hung up on that first thing and never go any further.

✳ ✳ ✳

Lager Moreau-West is, in many ways, emblematic of the Western Front: built by the Germans in 1914, abandoned when the Allies overran the area in 1918, forgotten shortly thereafter, and within decades more or less indistinguishable from whatever else surrounded it. In 1996, though, some enthusiasts decided to restore it. I can't tell you why they chose this *Lager*, or camp, in particular; perhaps there was more to work with here. Jean-Paul de Vries has taken me to the sites of several of them, including the

Hanover Lager, which he first showed me that day in 2009, when I picked bullets out of the roots of a fallen tree there; it could accommodate up to four thousand German soldiers on furlough, and had, among many other amenities, a hospital, a cinema, a church and a brothel, all laid out along roads named after streets in Hanover, Germany. Another we visited years later, in the Bois de Breuilles near the village of Cunel, had been called the Porta Lager. "There were as many as eight thousand German soldiers here at any time," Jean-Paul told me as we walked around a section of woods that looked pretty much like any other, except it didn't: The trees were younger, and there were fewer of them—not a lot fewer, but enough that you would notice it once you knew why that might be so. The ground was unnaturally level—again, not strikingly so, but enough. We'd arrived there by walking up what appeared to be a logging road, though Jean-Paul told me the Germans had built it for their trucks, which carried as much in as they did out. "There was a gate here with big stone mounts, and a sentry post, everything," he said, his voice so infused with the excitement of a soldier on furlough that I could almost see it there.

"This was a big one," he said. "It had eight bread ovens, operating twenty-four hours a day, seven days a week. They built a canal so the barracks would all have running water. There was a casino [officers' barracks and club], a *Kino* [movie theater], brothels, bars. There was even a PX by the gate." As impressive as Jean-Paul made the Porta Lager sound, I later found a description of an even grander German rest camp in an area of the Argonne known as Champ Mahaut, captured on September 29, 1918, by the American 77th, Statue of Liberty Division, draftees from the city of New York, which appears in 1919's *History of the Seventy-Seventh Division* by Major Julius Ochs Adler:

> Our advancing troops uncovered a German paradise. Here was located one of the famous rest areas of the German armies, where battle-worn and weary Boches were taken to fatten up and recover morale amidst amazing comforts and luxuries.
>
> On the reverse slopes of these hills, huge deep dugouts had been constructed, each capable of housing fifty men or more in perfect safety from hostile shelling. On the heights above these dugouts, more pretentious abodes had been constructed for officers and non-commissioned officers. These were built of concrete, with logs and concrete roofing, twenty feet in depth, and were ornamented to resemble Swiss chalets

and Black Forest hunting lodges with peaked roofs and exterior fresco work of burnt oak. Within were oak wainscoted chambers, fitted with electric lights and running water, supplied from the power house in the valley below. Benches and tables, in rustic solid oak, were supplemented by plush arm chairs and hair mattresses to cater to the comforts of weary warriors and, outside the doors, rose-gardens and favorite flowers from the Fatherland were cheerfully blooming. "Waldhaus Martha," "Waldhaus Albertin" and "Unter den Linden," as they were variously named, vied with each other in coziness.

Adjoining "Waldhaus Martha," was the bowling alley, with the open-air restaurant and beer garden built above it, where sat the on-lookers on a sunny afternoon, quaffing their beer and cheering on the bowlers. Down in the ravine below, where the brook ran, was the great concrete swimming pool, a close rival to the one in the Columbia College gymnasium, and here also were found spacious shower baths supplied with hot water by modern boilers and concrete furnaces.

The Chapel, the Library teeming with the best works of German science and literature and including, even from hated England, the tales of Rider Haggard and Conan Doyle, the officers' club with its attractive bar, the big theater, fitted for moving-picture exhibitions—none of these was wanting to make the place an ideal spot for quiet life and recreation. In the photographer's shop our men found hundreds of plates showing Germans, short and tall, fat and thin, single and in hilarious groups, having all kinds of good times with hunting parties, beer parties, singing parties, Christmas parties, high festivities generally in their valley paradise, where they had rested so securely for over four years.

"Soldiers would spend twenty-eight days at the front and then fourteen days here, over and over," Jean-Paul said as we picked our way through the Porta Lager site. "They were Württembergers, Bavarians." There wasn't much left of it, mostly the brick ruins of some bread ovens, but I found a lot of other stuff there: shrapnel, of course, and cartridges, but also an iron vent from a cook stove. The most exciting discovery was a two-inch-long cylindrical battery from a German flashlight; the most chilling, a large and very heavy piece of a 340-millimeter American coastal artillery shell, fired from a big naval gun that had been transported inland by rail. "This was taken by the 3rd Division," Jean-Paul said. "October 1918."

Volunteers at Camp Moreau told me they often found things in the woods, especially electrical insulators, which look like white porcelain toadstools, and *chevaux de fries,* so-called cavalry stars, arachnids of sharp iron spikes that the Germans tossed around liberally to pierce the hooves of enemy horses, though they worked just as well on human boots, with dire consequences in an era before tetanus shots. In the campsite there are plenty of sleeping quarters built into the hillside, corrugated metal half-pipes that the Germans shipped in, prefabricated, from foundries back home, then installed upon wooden platforms and left open at one end for air and quick egress; and cement foundations and walls; and collapsed tunnels, untold hundreds of yards of them, extensive networks used for both shelter and communications and built by Silesian miners, said to be the finest diggers in the world and brought to the front by the thousands for no other purpose than to excavate. In old photographs, many of them sport mustaches that look like push brooms.

Those tunnels, surprisingly, were among the first things volunteers undertook to restore. Personally, I would have made all kinds of excuses to get to them last: Though well lit (as they were a century ago), they are also forbiddingly damp and narrow and, above all, intricate. The Germans did as well underground as they did in the forest, and perhaps best of all underground in the forest, though their campgrounds did have quite a few aboveground amenities, too, as Jean-Paul (and Major Adler) pointed out. At Camp Moreau, local volunteers rebuilt a public bath and a bandstand, while a group of schoolchildren from Bavaria visited every week for a year to rebuild the camp *Kino,* complete with an original bench and projector. There are plenty of other structures scattered throughout, some complete, some partial; and, everywhere, artifacts. On a table in one reconstructed mess hall, among the plates and cutlery, sat a recently exhumed oxygen tank, to be used in the event of a gas attack. The company that manufactured it, Dräger, still exists, and still makes them, for premature newborns.

I first heard about Camp Moreau from Denis Hebrard, an unassuming yet genial man in his sixties who owns a bed-and-breakfast in the Argonne and informed me, the Friday I checked in, that I should visit the camp the next day, as it was worth seeing but was open to volunteers and visitors only on Saturday mornings; what's more, he told me, he thought something special must be in the works, because he had heard through the grapevine that a reporter from *The New York Times* would be visiting the camp that morning. I was impressed and intrigued, at least until the following morning, when I figured out, after about an hour at the place, that the reporter was me.

It was the old game of telephone: Jean-Paul, who knew I was coming—and who wasn't supposed to mention to anyone what (or, more precisely, who) was bringing me to the Argonne—let it slip to someone, who told someone who told someone who told a man named Harry Rupert, who volunteered at the camp, that I would be in the area. Somehow, in Harry's mind, that tidbit metamorphosed to the notion that an unnamed reporter from a named American newspaper was coming just to do a story about the camp, which spread quickly throughout the 14–18 network in the Argonne, and was eventually fed to me. The next day, when I arrived, Harry figured out that I was the journalist in question well before I did, then proceeded to show me every last square foot of the camp, which is what finally made me catch on.

Harry is Dutch, which means he speaks English. As Jean-Paul de Vries had explained to me, the Dutch all speak English, as they all grow up watching American television. In his case, that meant *Donny & Marie* and *The Love Boat*; for Harry, it was more likely *I Love Lucy* and *The Honeymooners*. He and his wife had retired to the Argonne a few years back and were renting a house in Châtel-Chéhéry. Jean-Paul, who had grown up in the Netherlands, told me that a number of people from there had, in recent years, started retiring to the area. Land in Lorraine was relatively inexpensive, and the Dutch, he said, were known for being cheap.

A lot of Dutch visit the Argonne, many of them drawn by a fervent interest in 14–18, which has always struck me as strange, as the Netherlands saw no fighting, sent no troops to fronts elsewhere, and had nothing to do with the First World War, really, until the day before it ended, when it took in the Kaiser, who'd just been exiled from his former empire. It is a fact that I often point out to them when I encounter them in the Argonne. The Dutch being typically polite, they just nod, thoughtfully, although one couple I met while strolling among the markers at the American cemetery, when confronted with the bit about sheltering the former German emperor in exile, replied, "Yes! We shouldn't have done that! It was the money, you know."

Harry Rupert, who hadn't known much at all about the war before he moved to the Argonne, now spends every Saturday at Camp Moreau, about which he knows a great deal at this point, all of which he is eager to share. Tall and thin with a mop of blond/gray hair, a shaggy mustache and wire-rimmed glasses, his appearance and unstinted enthusiasm make him seem like a retired surfer turned cheerleader, a rather dissonant sight in a place like the Argonne. He certainly did teach me a lot, though. "There were sixty of these camps in the Argonne!" he boomed the morning we met there. "All over the forest. They were all linked by narrow-gauge rail. The trains ran every day, several times a day. They even had timetables printed up! Ha!" he boomed. "The Germans!"

Jean-Paul, who knew of Harry Rupert but hadn't yet met him, had taken me to Camp Moreau that morning, thinking I might enjoy it. I did, even as it became apparent to me, after ninety minutes or so, that Jean-Paul believed we had seen all there was to take in there, and was eager to move on. "Just one more thing, if you have a few minutes!" Harry said excitedly. He was the kind of person who said pretty much everything excitedly, especially if it concerned World War I and the Argonne. Just one more thing: the officers' club. And just one more: the chamber where the Germans had kept the enormous diesel generator, brought in by rail from *das Vaterland*, that had powered the whole camp. And one more: a tunnel. And one more: a section of recently excavated water pipe. And one more: an obelisk commemorating *Den gefallenen Helden in den Argonnen* (the fallen heroes in the Argonne) that the Germans had built there in 1916. And one more: the showers, this section for officers, that one for soldiers. And one more: another tunnel. And one more: the officers' mess. And one more: a large pile of wine bottles. And one more: what he believed had been a chapel. And one more: the enlisted men's mess. And one more: a section of narrow-gauge rail. And one more: some postcards he had found that he believed were scenes of this camp. And one more: a stretch of electrical line. And one more: yet another tunnel. And one more—

At this point, Jean-Paul said something brusque to him in Dutch and started to lead me away. Harry ran after us, following all the way to Jean-Paul's van. "Let me know if you can make it to Châtel-Chéhéry!" he called out. "I can show you a lot of things there! Sergeant York!"

It would have been a clean getaway but for those last two words. Winner of the Medal of Honor; namesake of York Avenue in Manhattan; subject of the top-grossing film of 1941, for which Gary Cooper, in the lead role, was given an Academy Award. Sergeant Alvin Cullum York, a pacifist from the mountains of eastern Tennessee who had unsuccessfully sought conscientious objector status, was drafted into the 82nd (the "All American Division") and sent to France where, on October 8, 1918, he did what *Maréchal* Ferdinand Foch, the Supreme Allied Commander, called "the greatest thing accomplished by any private soldier of all the armies of Europe," killing 20 Germans and capturing 132 more.

In Châtel-Chéhéry.

And so, a week later, when I found myself with a free afternoon, I went there and visited Harry Rupert. Though it was only June, it was the hottest day of the year, well into the nineties. I should have known better, should have suspected that Harry was one of those people who actually speeds up after retirement. I should have known that, despite the heat, he would insist upon showing me every site he considered interesting. I hadn't anticipated, though, that after he led me several miles along the hilly, wooded Sergeant York Trail, and around the grounds of the local abbey (where American soldiers had been quartered), and through thigh-high grass to the sites of old German military encampments and cemeteries, the heat and the hike would somehow energize him. At one point, he took me through a neighbor's garage and deep into the man's backyard, to a large clump of weeds and reeds, then pulled them back to reveal a big square cement pedestal hiding within, carved garlands draping its sides. "This was all a German cemetery," he told me. "There was a rest camp over there, and tennis courts, everything. And this under here was the base of a big German monument. The Kaiser came to dedicate it in 1916." Later, in his house, he showed me photos of the ceremony, the Kaiser and other German dignitaries milling about in front of the monument in their *Pickelhauben* and long gray coats. The monument itself was, in my opinion at least, quite ugly, a squared pillar with a big German eagle, wings spread, perched atop; on one side, under a black Prussian cross, the inscription *The German and French Heroes*, which, to be honest, truly baffles me. Maybe they were hoping the French, having been included, might then leave it alone. They didn't; would have destroyed the pedestal, too, I'm sure, if they could have figured out how. Harry told me the man who owns the property considers it a real nuisance.

After six hours roaming around in the heat, hiking along a trail that led up a steep hill into some woods, he actually picked up the pace, slapping his chest and crowing about how much better shape he and his wife had gotten into since they had moved to France. "Americans are so—so *corpulent!*" he crowed, and though I wasn't sure whether he was basing this on me alone or was still watching American television, it would have been hard to disagree with him, even if I hadn't been too winded to reply. Instead, I took his statement as permission to rest for a moment.

"Come on!" he said, pointing up the trail, which was overgrown and growing steeper every twenty yards. "It's not much further!"

But I had heard those same words too many times already that sweltering day. "How much further?" I gasped.

"A kilometer," he claimed. "Maybe a little more."

"What are we going to see, again?" I managed to say.

"A German ammunition dump!"

"Did the 82nd capture it?" I asked.

"Yes!" he said. "And they blew it up!" He swept an arm over his head and started up the hill again.

I didn't move. "So . . . it's just a big crater now?"

"Very big! Most of it is covered with vegetation, but you can perceive out a piece of it."

That was it; I told him I was done for the day. He cajoled for a few minutes, then agreed to head back to the car, somehow securing, in the process, a promise that I would come see his library before I left and look at some pictures he had of the village during the war. I assumed he had a couple of chairs.

He did, and a large computer monitor, where he set up a slide show. The "pictures" were mostly old battlefield survey maps in French or German, the kinds of things I would have had trouble making sense of even without the heat exhaustion. He had the slide show running on its own, lingering on each old map for a minute or so as he prattled on in the background—about what, exactly, I couldn't tell you. It was all blurring into one piece, the maps and the chatter; I was just happy to be sitting down indoors. And then, suddenly, an image came on the monitor that wasn't a map. It was an old photograph. Vaguely familiar. The caption read:

A BRIGHT SUNDAY MORNING AT CHATEAU DE CHEHERY

There was the abbey he had taken me to that afternoon, minus a century of dilapidation, and in its courtyard were maybe 150 or 200 soldiers wearing the uniform of the American Expeditionary Forces. They stood at attention in perfect columns, posture proud, behind a single line of officers of equally perfect bearing. The caption identified them as "Company E"—that was all—but listed the officers' names in order: Lieuts. Haar, Locke, Ooley, Preston, Capt. McGrady, Capt. Abbett, Chaplain Custer, Major Bliss, Colonel Humphrey, Lieut. Col. Bacon, Major Mitchell . . .

I only read as far as Bliss and Humphrey to confirm; I knew it at Ooley. There couldn't be two Lieutenants Ooley in the AEF. I realized I had seen the photo before: It came from a book called *Victory!* published in a limited run in 1919. I happened to have a copy back home.

"This is Company E of the 805th Pioneer Infantry Regiment," I said. "The officers up front are all white, but the soldiers in formation behind them are all black."

Harry stood up, walked to the desk and pressed the tip of his nose against the monitor for a minute. "My God!" he said. "They are! I never saw that!" He turned and stared at me for a moment. "How did you know?"

I knew what he was thinking: By the time that photo had been taken, there were dozens of American divisions in France—hundreds of regiments, thousands of companies. Two million doughboys in all. How could I possibly know which specific unit was in *his* photo?

I pointed a finger at the formation behind the officers. "Somewhere in there," I said, "is a private named Moses Hardy from Aberdeen, Mississippi. I interviewed him three times in person. The last time was eight years ago. It was his 113th birthday."

And for the first time since I'd met him, Harry Rupert was silent.

✳ ✳ ✳

The Sergeant York Trail is a site of some controversy among historians, who dispute its accuracy. Indeed, though only one is marked and landscaped and fitted with signage, there are at least two more that I know of, and probably more than that, each championed by a different camp of historians and archaeologists. Alvin York himself returned to the area just a year afterward and expressed some confusion about what had happened where. Harry Rupert has taken me through the "official" trail twice, and both times offered without reservation his opinions on what it gets wrong. He knows York's story well, citing the old war hero's accounts almost verbatim as he points out this or that topographical feature that doesn't jibe with the account on the kiosks. He is particularly dismayed by the misidentification of a medieval creek dam—the real one was supposed to be near the spot where York and his cohort surprised a large group of Germans, caught while eating breakfast—which frankly looks like a dirt mound to me. Then again, I don't live there, and I'm not Harry Rupert, who also told me that despite its inaccuracies he hikes the trail often, sometimes hunting for the exceptionally delicious mushrooms that grow at the base of older trees there. I never found any, but on our second visit I did hear a cuckoo bird, an experience I enjoyed more than any mushroom I've ever eaten. The Argonne is a forest, after all, despite everything unnatural that happened here. It has also been logged since time immemorial; these days, a lot of its timber is being shipped to China, a fact that seems to vex just about everyone who lives here, even those who sell their trees to that market. Harry Rupert told me that old French woodsmen can look at the stump of a tree and tell you whether it was cut down by a French logger or a German. Once, while hunting for mushrooms, Harry found several French-American V-B rifle grenades under a tree. He keeps them in his barn.

The story of Sergeant York is one of the best-known tales to emerge from the offensive that closed out the war—everyone knows it: American, French and German—but it is just one event from one day of that 47-day battle, which was just one part, albeit the final part, of a 1,500-day battle in the Argonne. You have to figure that any place people would spend so much time fighting over, and send so many men to die for, was important: important to the French, who tried and tried, at great cost, to take the place back; important to the Americans, who saw it as their proving ground, and did, ultimately, take it back, also at great cost. But it was perhaps most important to the Germans. They seized it quickly, in the opening weeks of the war, as soon as they could get to it. They took care to fortify it, not just in 1914 but perpetually, for four years. They lost thousands of men a week just to keep it. They photographed it incessantly. They printed postcards of it: pictures of food wagons traversing lonely roads, soldiers standing by lonely graves, officers emerging from lonely dugouts, and many, many of the railroad, the *Argonnenbahn*. They may have been the original trainspotters. They wrote poems about the Argonne, and songs, and printed those on postcards, too. The most famous, the *Argonnerwald Lied,* or Song of the Argonne Forest, was written in 1914–15, enjoyed great popularity even among German troops who never served on the Western Front (much less in the Argonne), and was revived for the next war. Often accompanied by a drawing of a *Pionier,* or combat engineer, pausing in the midst of digging a trench or tunnel to lean on his shovel and gaze out across No Man's Land, it begins:

> *The Argonne forest, at midnight,*
> *a Pionier stands watch.*

A little star stands high in the sky
and brings him a greeting from his faraway homeland.
And with the spade in hand
he stands ahead in the trench.
With longing he thinks of his love:
Will he ever see her again?
And the artillery thunders threateningly.
We are standing before the infantry.
Grenades are hitting us.
The Frenchman wants to get into our emplacement.

The attack comes; it's terrible, but the brave Germans stand their ground, beat back the French assault and take some prisoners. The poem concludes:

Argonnerwald, Argonnerwald
A quiet cemetery you will be soon!
In your cool earth rests
some brave soldier blood
And if I come one day to heaven's door,
with an angel of God standing before:
Argonne fighter, come in,
Here shall be for your perpetual peace.
You Pionier at midnight,
today all of Germany stands watch.
In steadfast loyalty, in pure will,
as a new, strong watch on the Rhine.

It's a nice bit of verse, I think, of a piece with that romantic German sensibility so common at the time. And maybe the Germans did harbor romantic sentiments about the Argonne; they certainly did spend a lot of time there, and doubtless got to know it as well as many people who'd been born and raised there. But I also think that last couplet hints at something darker: steadfast loyalty; pure will. A new, strong watch. To be sure, there was nothing romantic about what they did there, especially in 1914. On 14–18 monuments in cities, towns and villages all over France you will see, listed after men *morts aux champ de bataille,* or killed on the field of battle, *victimes civiles:* civilian victims. No other details are given, leaving you to wonder if they died of hunger or disease or an errant shell. But in the Argonne, I also know of several monuments that specify *fusillés par les Allemands,* or *morts en captivité*—shot by the Germans, or died in captivity. "The Germans," Jean-Paul offered, by way of explanation, "were so afraid when they came into this area."

If that seems like a strange thing to point out in this context, it isn't, really. The Germans felt they had good reasons to fear a "conquered" populace, going back to 1871. Although the Prussians had made short work of the French Army in that last war, after the shooting stopped, while they occupied part of the country and waited for the five-billion-franc reparations promised them in the peace treaty, they had a terrible time with what were called *francs-tireurs,* literally "free-shooters," partisans who weren't in uniform and didn't abide by the surrender which bound the military. *Francs-tireurs* were, in essence, guerrillas, sniping at soldiers and blowing up things those soldiers found useful, like buildings and bridges, not with artillery but bombs. This really shook the Germans' sense of order and decorum, and they were determined not to subject themselves to such terrors this time around.

And so, in essence, they became terrorists themselves, especially in places like the Argonne, where the natural terrain and layout of the villages favored guerrilla attacks. Their typical modus operandi, after taking a town, was to line up several of its denizens against a wall and shoot them. They did it in the village of Cunel, just on the other side of the Meuse-Argonne American Cemetery from Romagne-sous-Montfaucon, on September 4, 1914; used the church wall. You can still see the pockmarks today. "They usually took four people," Jean-Paul explained. "A lady, a child, the mayor, and the local priest. Just to show that nobody was sacred to them." They didn't do it in every town; just enough of them, here and there, to spread the message. In the village of Bantheville, on the night of September 9, 1914, things really got out of hand: "The Germans heard shooting there," Jean-Paul explained. "They thought it was *francs-tireurs,* so they rushed into town, took a bunch of prisoners, killed some of them, and burned the village to the ground." Shortly thereafter, they figured out that the original shots had actually been fired by other German soldiers, in ceremonial salute to their fallen officers; oh, well. The local memorial lists the names of six villagers shot by the Germans, and another three who died in captivity.

Strangely, at the same time, the Germans were apparently rather concerned with their image, and rolled out a propaganda campaign intended

to make their soldiers look more like civilizing humanitarians than execu-
tioners. One postcard they produced shows a photo of a kindly German
soldier, *Mütze* on his head (presumably, a *Pickelhaube* would have looked
too militaristic), feeding a French toddler, balanced on his knee, while two
girls look on, smiling. *Ein deutscher "Barbar"* ("A German 'Barbarian'") its
title jokes. The caption underneath explains: "An infantryman shares his
lunch with a hungry little Frenchman."

The postcard bore the imprimatur of the International Red Cross; it
was clearly meant to soothe consciences back home. Many others, though,
were intended to assuage the local populace, who were often recruited for
the effort. Jean-Pierre Brouillon, the farmer who caught me trespassing
on his land and then gave me a five-hour tour of the area, told me that his
wife's grandmother had spent much of the war doing German soldiers'
laundry in Romagne; "all the local women did," he explained. Whether
they were paid or coerced or a little of both remains unknown, at least to
me, but I have seen a photo of a cohort of German soldiers sitting outside
M. Brouillon's farmhouse, Musarde, with three French women, three little
girls, and a dog. Only the smallest toddler is crying. Not far away, at the
Hanover Lager, Jean-Paul de Vries told me, German soldiers regularly enjoyed the company of willing French women. "Things were pretty tense
here for a while after the war," he added.

At the same time, French men who were too young or too old or un-
able to fight and had stayed at home were conscripted by the occupying
Germans for noncombat duty, sent to labor camps or otherwise interned.
There were work camps and civilian POW camps all over the Argonne;
the Germans sent their photographers around to all of them to document daily life and offer the inmates souvenirs. If the French women in
Germans' staged photos look resigned and maybe just a touch wary, the
French men in theirs look more than a little tired, and yet defiant. If the
Germans later distributed these photos to their French subjects, I'm not
sure what the French did with them after the war; but they didn't, as I
might have expected, burn them all, because quite a few ended up in the
hands of a gentleman named Dominique Lacorde.

M. Lacorde looks like you would want to look if you were a writer and
historian in your sixties—sage but fit, with wise eyes, rimless eyeglasses
and curly salt-and-pepper hair; he's a friend of Jean-Paul's, and lives in the
village of Gesnes-en-Argonne, a place I regard with a certain fondness because one of the World War I veterans I interviewed, a 107-year-old named

Bill Lake, was involved in liberating it on September 29, 1918. Private Lake's beloved captain, a 31-year-old stockbroker named Elijah W. Worsham, was killed in that same action, in a field that Jean-Paul helped me locate ninety-six years later. Dominique Lacorde knows all about Captain Worsham; he knows all about pretty much anything relating to the history of this part of the Argonne, especially if it happened during 14–18. He has photos of the captain, and of Major Oscar Miller, mortally wounded here the same day, who was later awarded the Medal of Honor, in part because the Germans had to shoot him three times to get him to stop leading his men forward. Mostly, though, he has photos of the men, women and children of Gesnes and surrounding villages, taken during the four years of that first German occupation. He can name an astonishing number of the people who appear in them; knew quite a few personally when he was growing up. He's used them for books he's written, and for chapters he's contributed to other books, but even when he's not working on anything like that, he spends time studying them, trying to identify relatives, people he knew, people he's heard stories about. He could even name the three children in that *deutscher Barbar* postcard: The boy on the German soldier's knee is Marcel Gatelet; the girls in the doorway are Jeanne Barat and Maria Augusta Legand. He knew them all as elderly neighbors.

I spent hours with Dominique going through his photos, hundreds of them (including some of several of his relatives hunkered down at the Musarde farmhouse, where they took shelter after the Germans drove them out of their homes; he knew all about Rommel, even if Jean-Pierre Brouillon did not), but there was one in particular that really made an impression: a picture of two German soldiers kneeling on the floor near a large hearth in a parlor, one wearing a *Mütze*, the other bareheaded but sporting a thick brush mustache that would have done any Silesian miner proud. In front of them, in wooden chairs, sit two women, one young with long, dark braids, the other elderly and wearing a white cap. All four are looking toward the camera. Mütze appears a bit shy; Mustache is, I think, trying on a smile that he hopes will project benign strength as he rests his arm on the chair behind the old woman's head. The expression on the old woman's face says *Can you believe this?*, the young woman's *I'll tell you about it later, after they're gone.* "That's my grandmother Emilienne," M. Lacorde told me. "And that's her grandmother Françoise." Françoise was 82; Emilienne was 17, already forced to work as a housekeeper at the local château, which now housed German officers. They were allowed to remain in their house, but the Germans appropriated their farm, turned it into a sawmill. The caption on the photo reads, in French: "Easter 1915. Souvenir of the German Barbarians." I doubt Emilienne and Françoise found it all that funny. They would have known about Cunel, and Bantheville, and other such villages.

It was evening but still quite light out when I left M. Lacorde's house, so I decided to walk over to the church—the one whose steeple you can see so clearly from the field where Captain Worsham was killed—and take another look at a small plaque that I had first spotted a year earlier on its façade:

> THE 362D U.S. INFANTRY
> DURING THE GREAT OFFENSIVE
> WHICH BEGAN SEPT. 26, 1918
> TOOK GESNES AND THE RIDGE
> BEYOND ON SEPT. 29, 1918 AND
> WERE THE FIRST TROOPS TO
> REACH THE AMERICAN ARMY
> OBJECTIVE. IN SPITE OF SEVERE
> LOSSES THIS REGIMENT HELD
> THE GROUND GAINED UNTIL
> ORDERED TO WITHDRAW BY
> HIGHER AUTHORITY BECAUSE
> IT WAS SO FAR IN ADVANCE OF
> THE TROOPS ON ITS RIGHT
> AND LEFT.

It is extremely rare to find any kind of marker in English, and only English, Over There, especially in this part of France. (No one in Gesnes, I am told, speaks any English at all, including M. Lacorde.) The fact that the veterans of the 362nd Infantry Regiment did it that way indicates that they expected future generations of Americans to travel to Gesnes-en-Argonne and see for themselves the town their fathers and uncles and grandfathers fought, and in many cases died, to liberate. *A History of the 362nd Infantry,* written anonymously and published by the regiment's veterans association in 1920, reports that as its men approached the open field between their position outside Épinonville and Gesnes—the same field Jean-Paul and I found and explored ninety-six years later—they realized:

Almost every foot of the ground was directly under the observation and
fire of the Huns . . . So sure were they that no man could ever cross that
open ground alive, under their fire, that they had also brought up light
artillery to the crest of the hill for point-blank open-sight firing.

After holding still for a while, their regimental commander, Colonel
John Henry "Machine Gun" Parker, who had been in command of the
102nd Regiment at Seicheprey back in April, "received the astounding
order that the advance must be continued at all costs. To him the order
seemed suicidal, but he asked only for time to join his men in the carnage
that was inevitable." When it was all over,

> only a handful of men had emerged from the slaughter. Hundreds of
> dead and wounded were strewn over the battleground. Many officers
> were among the fallen. Colonel Parker was himself wounded early in
> the action and evacuated to the hospital . . . The burial party found the
> bodies of over 100 of our men in 200 yards . . .
>
> But soon after nightfall the order came for the regiment's with-
> drawal, directing that it retire to the same line which they held before
> the attack.
>
> No one can describe the feelings of the men when they received the
> order and realized what it meant: that the ground which they had taken
> at such terrible cost was to be given up and that the blood of their com-
> rades had been shed in vain.

You can see why the regiment's survivors would want to leave a brief
record in Gesnes of the tremendous heroism and waste involved in liberating the town (the division ended up having to take it from the Germans
again, also at great cost), and why they might expect future generations to
make pilgrimages to the site. The fact that the people of Gesnes accommodated such a marker, and even gave it some choice real estate on the front
of their church—really, the only communal space in town—indicates that
they expected the same thing. Those veterans are all gone, now; the last
one, Bill Lake—the ultimate survivor of their entire division, the 91st (aka
Wild West)—died on June 19, 2004, at the age of 108. They don't know
that their hopes weren't realized, that I might just be the only American
who has stopped and read the thing since they put it up. I'm not sure what
their French contemporaries in Gesnes made of the fact that the expected

American tourists never came, but the people who live there today would be much more surprised if anyone did.

Dominique Lacorde and his fellow residents of Gesnes are patient; like their parents and grandparents, they seem satisfied to safeguard the memory until someone comes back from across an ocean to reclaim it. They've even managed to keep that little plaque on their church, for now. Not far away, scavengers stole several much larger bronze plaques off a monument to the American 1st Division; melted them down, presumably, for scrap in a hard economy. I only hope that, in mentioning it here, I have not doomed the one in Gesnes to a similar fate.

✳ ✳ ✳

The Argonne is a secret hiding right out in the open. Not from the Dutch, Jean-Paul tells me, ruefully; every October, he says, after the crops are harvested, too many of his former countrymen swoop down, metal detectors in hand, and crawl over its fields like bloodhounds. And there are large handfuls of tourists who come to visit, mostly in summer, from all over France, and from Belgium and Luxembourg and Germany, occasionally for the area's artifacts but mostly for its natural beauty. Few other people seem to have even heard of the place.

Except for historians, that is: French, German, American. They know all about it.

Even they, though, can't seem to agree on exactly *why* everyone wanted it so badly. As far back as 1919, Frederick Palmer, an American war correspondent, wrote in his account of the Meuse-Argonne Offensive, *Our Greatest Battle:*

> If a soldier from Mars had come to earth at any time from October, 1914, to October, 1918, and had been shown a flat map of the fronts of the two adversaries, he would have said that the obvious strategic point of a single offensive would be between the Meuse River and the Argonne Forest. This would be a blow against the enemy's lines of communication: a blow equivalent to turning his flank.

These days, many historians will tell you that the Germans needed the Meuse-Argonne area to protect Sedan, the site of the rail hub from which they supplied the entire Western Front; that the French wanted it to get to that hub and hence cut off German troops in France and Belgium from their supply lines, and also because it was perilously close to Verdun; and that the Americans wanted it because the French told them it was very important, and because they were excited at the prospect of doing something the Allies hadn't been able to do and, in the process, winning the war. Others, though, think the Argonne didn't really become important until the lines started firming up after the First Battle of the Marne, in September 1914, and on into early 1915, at which point everything had set in place and the Germans suddenly realized that the area was among their strongest defensive points. The Germans, this theory goes, were in the habit of doing everything they could to hold whatever territory they had taken, while the French were in the habit of doing everything they could to take back whatever territory the Germans had taken, and the Americans, presumably, were motivated by the same factors listed in the previous theory. Of course, it's entirely possible that all these schools of thought are correct, and also that, at some point, everyone more or less forgot why they wanted the Argonne so badly, but that they nevertheless continued to fight, and die, in order to keep it or take it. One thing is for certain: As important as everyone considered the Argonne during the war's first three years, in 1918 its significance was heightened by an order of magnitude. "The Argonne was the Germans' last line of defense," Jean-Paul says. If the first two lines should happen to fall, they figured, they still had the unbreakable Argonne. "But the Americans had too many men," he asserts. "Otherwise, the Argonne would have held."

But never mind the historians and local experts. You can tell everyone involved regarded the Argonne and the heights above the Meuse River as really, really important just by the defense works the Germans built, and the number of lives everyone expended on the area, and the fact that they all sent their big names here. The Americans sent pretty much every top field commander they had. The French sent the likes of General Henri Berthelot, who had started out the war as a top aide to "Papa" Joffre—still, to the war's end, the most beloved figure in France—and General Henri Gouraud, who became something of a legend when he returned to active duty on the Western Front after losing an arm at Gallipoli. And the Germans sent royalty: Crown Prince Wilhelm of Prussia, the Kaiser's oldest son and heir to his throne, who was not a very good military commander; and Crown Prince Rupprecht of Bavaria, who was.

Rupprecht's command post was in the Argonne, on that high wooded plain known as Champ Mahaut, the same area where the Germans built that splendid rest camp with the library, beer garden, and swimming pool that rivaled Columbia's. Rupprecht, heir to the throne of Germany's largest state, was in his late forties during the war and, judging by what remains of his former command post, he lived pretty well at the front. The bunker, for one thing, had some style to it—big windows, scalloped doorway; it even had two marble fireplaces. It was, in other words, not the typical concrete box, though the other four bunkers in the compound were. None have been maintained, though all five are still standing, and still in very good condition, considering they've been abandoned for a century. (Souvenir hunters made off with the last of the marble a long time ago.) One still bears a cement plaque that reads, simply, "1 Pi. 16," for the 1st Company, 16th *Pionier* Battalion, the outfit that built the compound. The trenches they built to connect the five bunkers are still solid and deep; so are the craters they detonated to protect the area. There are signs here and there directing visitors to the *Abri du Kronprinz,* or the Crown Prince's bunker, but few visitors seem to take the bait, which fact has probably spared me some embarrassment, because something about the place leads me to behave in a manner I wouldn't care for too many others to witness: dashing through trenches, charging into shell holes, crawling through open windows. Though the Kingdom of Bavaria no longer exists—nor, for that matter, do any other German kingdoms, principalities or duchies; all ruling houses and accompanying titles were abolished after the war—if the Germans ever come back, they could fix up *Kronprinz* Rupprecht's command post and use it again in about a week. Maybe less.

✳ ✳ ✳

The first place they might head is the Butte de Vauquois, or Vauquois Hill. One of the highest points in this part of the Argonne, it's just outside the village of Vauquois. The village was actually on top of the butte until the war; if you visit, it will become immediately apparent to you why they had to rebuild it elsewhere afterward. Captain Daniel Strickland's description in *Connecticut Fights* of the blasted terrain of the Chemin des Dames a century ago as many "cups of various sizes," set "rim to rim as closely as they could be packed," could apply to Vauquois Hill today; but only if you substitute "buckets" for "cups."

Most of what I know about the place and what happened there during the war I learned from Denis Hebrard, who lives about twenty minutes away in Le Neufour, a little village with a church whose bells are certain to awaken you every morning at seven, whether you're Catholic or not. In case you're wondering, "Le Neufour" translates, near as I can tell, as "the neufour." As is the case in the United States, and probably everywhere, many French towns have names whose meanings are lost to time, if they ever existed at all. The next town over, Les Islettes, means "the little islands," despite the fact that there are no islands of any size, or even bodies of water, in town. Denis, as I mentioned earlier, owns a small *chambre d'hôtes,* or bed-and-breakfast, in Le Neufour; he and his wife, Bénédicte, moved to the area after Denis retired from Air France, where he worked as a purser for many years after serving in the French Air Force. I'd stayed with him on two successive visits and had known him for a year before he casually mentioned that he'd been involved in a hair-raising rescue mission in Saigon in 1975. Before that, I probably would have told you that the most remarkable thing about Denis is that, with his receding black hair, kind yet always slightly amused eyes and rakish grin, he bears a striking resemblance to my late uncle Gilbert, my father's brother, who, as far as I know, had no ancestors from France or any country that borders France. More important, Denis speaks English quite well. More important still, he is fascinated with the history of the Argonne and World War I, particularly Vauquois Hill, where he has volunteered for more than a decade. There's one thing, he told me the first time he took me there, that really makes it—and the Argonne as a whole—special.

"Gaize," he said. Pronounced exactly like "gaze." I'd never heard the word before, which, it turns out, is not really my fault. "It only exists in this part of France, and Japan," Denis explained. It's a type of rock, fine-grained and porous, left over from when this area was entirely under water, eons ago. Gaize is very hard, he explained, but because it's fragmental—it's composed of tiny granules subjected to tremendous pressure over the course of eons—it's easy to dig through. Imagine a type of rock unlike any other on earth—somehow strong enough to withstand a direct hit from an artillery shell, yet pliable enough that your Silesian miners could tunnel through it with relative ease: The Germans couldn't resist it. Add to that the fact that at surface level the Butte de Vauquois commanded unbroken vistas of Verdun, fifteen or twenty miles away; the Silesians could build a subterranean camp to shelter, securely, all the soldiers the Germans would need to hold the hill. Best of all for the Germans, the French, in their fervor at war's opening to retake Alsace and Lorraine, didn't leave Vauquois Hill adequately defended. The Germans took it in September 1914. Denis told me that 4,600 *poilus* died trying to stop them. The Butte de Vauquois is not the highest point in the area—that would be Montfaucon—but Vauquois, in fact, has the better view of the Argonne; it could easily be used to direct fire at Verdun. Papa Joffre ordered the French to take it back at any cost.

"At the beginning of the war, the French had no big guns in the area," Denis explained. "They were all in Brittany, facing the channel; the French still thought their biggest enemy was England, not Germany." The guns had to be brought to the Argonne, hundreds of miles away, by rail, and that took time. But Joffre didn't want to wait. In October, Denis said, "French soldiers lined up, and a band played the 'Marseillaise' as they marched up the hill to the German trenches. The Germans had machine guns every ten meters." He pursed his lips, shook his head. "They killed 1,430 French in thirty minutes."

It was only the beginning. The Germans had already brought in a thousand Silesian miners to dig into the gaize under Vauquois. They carved out more than ten miles of tunnels beneath the hill going down to a depth of some three hundred feet and created, in effect, an underground city. At its peak it housed two thousand men; had two hospitals, fourteen kitchens, and 154 barracks. Two large generators powered ventilators, thousands of light bulbs, and cable cars that hauled men and materiel in and out. Soldiers lived there for twenty-eight days at a stretch, and never removed their shoes in all that time. The French managed to establish a foothold on the far side of the butte's crest, out of view of the Germans but also without a view of anything strategic; they used it mostly to harass the enemy and launch attacks, none of which were very successful. Still, they built their own tunnel system, about four miles' worth and also electrified, that ran to a depth of about 140 feet and could harbor two thousand *poilus* if necessary, though not to sleep—just for temporary shelter. They even built a large chamber, well below their deepest manned tunnel, and filled it with explosives. The Germans built three of those; their plan was to blow the entire hill sky high if the French ever managed to breach their defenses.

It never came to that. The two sides achieved stasis—not a stalemate, really, since the Germans already had what they wanted. But their positions held. Things did happen, of course, the first one being that the village of Vauquois, caught in between the two lines, was destroyed, its residents scattered or dead. Reduced to rubble: a church, a school, a bakery, a music hall, the *mairie*. I have a German postcard featuring a photo of several German soldiers in *Mütze* posing behind the church's bell, fallen with its tower, and a bit of verse, titled "From Difficult Times":

> *Church bell of Vauquois, you rang and*
> *Invited so many in to pray.*
> *Church bell of Vauquois, you ring no more*
> *Around you all is dead and empty.*
> *You have been hit and from your own mouth*
> *Fell from your height even death's mouth*
> *Your ring died in death's pains*
> *As did around you many a brave warrior.*

The last thing left standing was the *Maronnier,* the Liberty Tree, a huge chestnut planted during the revolution a century and a quarter earlier. The symbol of Vauquois, it did war service by blocking the Germans' view; they wanted it gone, but it was too dangerous to send their *Pioniere,* or combat engineers, out to cut it down. So they trained five machine guns on it and started firing. It took them twenty-four hours to bring the old arbor down that way.

But it's what happened after that that made Vauquois the otherworldly fantasy-scape that remains to this day: Each side began tunneling toward the other, carving out large subterranean chambers, packing them with many tons of explosives, and blowing them up. This was not unique to Vauquois, of course; they did it at the Somme, and in the Bois de Mort-Mare, and even elsewhere in the Argonne. In one nine-month period, 223 large underground explosions were set off just in the Haute Chevauchée, most of them French. One crater there, which sits right behind the ossuary and is the product of a German mine loaded with 105,000 pounds of explosives, measures more than fifty yards across and ten deep. Should you decide to stroll down into it, you'll have an interesting time getting back out; I had to scuttle up like a crab on my hands and feet, clutching the grass with my fingers, and still it took several tries. I heard another cuckoo bird during my first few attempts, so at least there was that.

According to Denis, no fewer than 540 mines were dug and detonated on Vauquois Hill alone over the course of four years—an average of one every three days. In February 1915, the Germans detonated one that killed 106 French, but also 43 of their own. A French lieutenant left his company momentarily to confer with superiors, heard the blast, rushed back and found every last man gone. Evaporated. "He went crazy," Denis told me. "Started running around and screaming. Then he dashed out toward the German lines, still yelling like a madman. They shot him dead."

How he ran anywhere on that hill is, frankly, a mystery. There is absolutely no earth on it that is flat. It's just craters upon craters, all of them deep, some really deep. If you stand at the crest of the hill and face away, the view—of woods and farms and villages and Montfaucon—is pretty, even lovely; but if you turn around and look back down the hill, the terrible beauty of all those green-lined holes hits you like a fist to the sternum, making you want to flee and linger at the same time. For some French, this hill epitomizes the war even more than Verdun.

The French have been visiting the Butte de Vauquois—what remains of it—since the armistice, but it wasn't until 1956 that a professor at the seminary in Verdun, a monk named Kock, started to explore the tunnels below its surface. Others followed; today the local historical association has some 850 members, 20 of whom, volunteers, work there every weekend to shore up the tunnels and make them safe. Another 20 guide visitors through them. It's not an easy tour: The tunnels look pretty much as they did a century ago, and they were not built for comfort. While there are a lot of chambers throughout the underground network, some of them wide and deep enough for several cots or a couple of long wooden dining tables, the passages that run between them can be tight, sometimes only a couple of feet wide, with ceilings so low that visitors must spend much of their time underground hunched over. The gaize out of which all the passages are carved may be strong, but it's very slippery; it is, by definition, damp. (Dry gaize crumbles like sand.) Guides offer guests hard hats before entering the tunnels, but don't insist. If you refuse one on your first visit, you won't do so on your second.

You can actually explore both sets of tunnels if you dare, French and German. The French ones are an easier descent, the German more extensive. The French tunnels are built right into the hillside; to get to the German tunnels you must first wind your way through some concrete trenches, then duck under one of those corrugated metal arches—set into the earth at an angle, like the bunker entrances in Bois Brûlé—and slowly ease your way onto a steep set of rough stone steps that have, thankfully, been fitted with a handrail since the war. There are light bulbs, too—suspended from the ceiling in the taller passages, attached to the wall in the shorter ones—which don't sully the experience, since they had them in there a hundred years ago, as well. You can see stretches of the original electrical and telephone line, punctuated by white porcelain insulators. The first level down is fitted with certain amenities—street signs, for instance, replicas of those that festooned the tunnels originally. One chamber contains a wall map of the entire tunnel system, both sides; here and there hang enlarged old photos, taken in these tunnels, of soldiers eating, resting, writing letters. There are artifacts: a bed frame, a table and chair, water pumps, parts of a ventilator, helmets, and, of course, bottles.

Most visitors don't go any further down the first level, the only one that's officially open to the public. If you know the right person, though, and you visit at the right time, you can, and I did. The going gets rougher, darker and tighter; at one point, despite Denis's recommendation, I crawled into a chamber from which a soldier remotely fired a *Minenwerfer* located two levels up. It took me fifteen minutes to crawl back out, backward—wriggling like a freshly caught fish—and most of that time I wasn't entirely sure I would make it.

Sophisticated and technologically marvelous in their design, yes; safer than being on the surface, yes. But the tight, slippery underground cities at Vauquois make the mines at the Chemin des Dames feel like a Holiday Inn by comparison. I went in twice, and emerged, the first time, feeling like I had been paroled from prison. The second time I felt like I had been sprung from death row. I've read about these tunnels extensively, seen many photos of them. I lay down on a bed in one, sat at a table in another, touched helmets and boots, ran my finger along electrical line, picked up bottles. I know for a fact that men lived in them for twenty-eight days at a time while the end of the world played out overhead. But don't ask me to believe it.

★ ★ ★

The last time I visited Vauquois, the site was hosting an annual ceremony for *pompiers,* firefighters. A dozen men in uniform lined up in front of the hilltop memorial, holding aloft flags—a tricolor, ten French regional banners, and a stars and stripes. A marching band played. Officials made speeches. During one of them I spotted, standing among the flag-bearers, an older gentleman dressed as a *poilu,* his 1914 uniform perfect: long blue coat with tails, bright red trousers, red epaulets on his shoulders and a red kepi on his head. Pack on back; canteen at side. He stood perfectly erect, holding up what I recognized as a Lebel rifle, also period-appropriate.

Afterward, Denis and I stopped for lunch at a café he favors in the village. It was a bright, warm day, and we sat outside under an umbrella, joined by a friend of his, another older gentleman named Pierre Picard. Like my late uncle Gilbert, his American twin, Denis is a good-natured fellow with a ready smile, neither quiet nor loud; he emanates both resolve and kindness. He's also a deeply religious man, one of the few I ever met in France. So I found it strange when, a year earlier and sitting at this same table, he had expressed the opinion that Jean Jaurès, the French socialist leader and outspoken pacifist who had been assassinated on the eve of the war—shot dead on July 31, 1914, as he sat at an outdoor café, just like this one but in Paris—was to blame for all the carnage to follow, including what had happened just up the hill. I was a bit stunned; it felt like blaming a *pompier* for a conflagration. But Denis was adamant. "If Jaurès hadn't been so insistent on demilitarizing French society," he'd said, "we would have been ready for the Germans in 1914. The war would have been over very quickly."

That had struck me as some twisted logic: Jaurès had been trying to talk Europe down from the ledge; it seemed Denis was blaming him for the fact that it was killed once it hit the pavement. But Denis was other-wise such a reasoned and humane person that I couldn't quite believe he had said what I had heard, so a year later, sitting at the same table with M. Picard as well, I asked him about it again. He reasserted the point, and quoted Napoleon: "If you want peace, prepare for war." I had never heard anyone express such an opinion about Jaurès before—he is generally a be-loved and mourned figure in France, often called the first casualty of the war—but I got the sense, from the way Denis put it forward, as if its logic were unassailable, that more than a few French agreed with him.

As I struggled with a serious bout of cognitive dissonance, M. Picard just sat there, a thoughtful look on his face. A few minutes earlier, he'd told me that one of his grandfathers and two of his uncles had been killed at the Chemin des Dames, and that later, when he himself was 6 years old, the Nazis occupied his hometown, a small city south of Reims called Chalons-sur-Marne (known today as Chalons-en-Champagne). "I remember them taking away the old Jewish woman who lived next door," he recalled. "She was a nice lady. Always had treats for the children."

It was only later that I came to understand that these two statements—M. Picard's recollection of his childhood during the Nazi occupation, and Denis's anger over Jean Jaurès's pacifism—were actually connected.

Americans, with our short history, tend to view the past as a series of isolated episodes. But in France, especially in those parts of the country that
were savagely fought over twice in a little more than twenty years, many
people view the two world wars as just one conflict with a twenty-one-year
cease-fire in the middle. Having spent a lot of time in those areas, I share
that view; I can easily understand how someone who suffered through the
second might harbor strong, even bitter, feelings about the first. But M.
Picard just seemed wistful, and a bit sad. It was Denis, born after the second war ended, who spoke of history with such pointed passion. It frankly
surprised me; it still does, even as I concede that it shouldn't. Most of the
French people I have met in the process of exploring 14–18 sites Over
There seem miraculously resistant to the bitterness they might justifiably
feel against the Germans even a century after *la Grande Guerre,* as if their
curiosity about the past has inoculated them against developing strong
emotions about it. But not all of them.

I have discussed, at length and on a number of occasions here, the
strategic, technological and military accomplishments of the Germans in
that first war. Perhaps you have gotten the sense, from all that, that I regard them with respect, even a bit of awe. I do. But that doesn't mean I
don't recognize that what they did to France in World War I was as bad as,
and in some ways worse than, what they did in World War II. Frankly, in
order to regard the Germans of World War I at all, I must compartmentalize them from their Nazi sons. I have stopped and explored just about
every German World War I cemetery I have ever passed. I have also passed
quite a few German World War II cemeteries; I have never set foot in one,
and never will if I can help it. But knowing that they're out there doesn't
keep me from visiting, and even paying my respects, at the World War I
cemeteries. As I said, I compartmentalize.

Then again, I have the luxury of doing so: I am separated from both
wars—from, really, just the one long war, with a twenty-one-year cease-fire
in the middle—by an ocean and many decades. I did not lose a grandfather or two uncles in either one. The French are not afforded such buffers.
They have to live among—and often in—that war's ruins; have to tiptoe
around live shells and barbed wire, plow around craters and bunkers. You
might meet a French person who didn't lose someone in the first war, but I
never have. All that France is today, good and bad and neither, it is because
of 14–18. Everyone there knows it. The war imprints the French psyche
like the shell holes imprint the Butte de Vauquois. In some ways—in a lot

of ways—it defines them. So it's not surprising that someone born after the second war would harbor strong opinions about who was responsible for the first. And if you find some of those opinions unsettling, as is the case with me and Denis's thoughts on Jean Jaurès, whom I regard with admiration for his ideals and his courage in promoting them even at the cost of his life, the alternative for them is to not talk about it at all unless asked, and perhaps not even then—which is, in my experience, how most French people deal with the Second World War. If they talk and argue so much about the First—if they study it intently, walk its fields, cherish its relics, safeguard its memory—it is in large part, I believe, because there is a sense that it represents the Red Giant of French greatness. "Ninety percent of French men were not afraid to fight," Denis told me. "It was their *duty*." As simple as that. And they fought hard, for four years and three months; never gave up even as they were bled white. It is true that they walked into German machine guns while a band played the "Marsellaise." But they *won*. I have every bit as much respect for them as I do the Germans. It's a strange mental tightrope act, pondering such things.

As I sat in between Denis and M. Picard that day and strained to stay aloft, gazing out vaguely at the midday sun, as if by magic a vision appeared before me of a *poilu* in a perfect, spotless uniform. For just a moment, I thought him a ghost, or maybe a mirage. But then he turned and walked toward me, and I realized he was the fellow from the *pompier* ceremony. His red trousers were dazzling, his blue coat as proud and dignified a garment as I had ever seen. His pants were bloused into high black boots; his black belt bore two leather cartridge pouches and a square brass buckle. He had a mustache, of course, but also a trim beard, both mostly gray. Denis and Pierre greeted him, and then Denis introduced him to me. His name is Maurice Ravenel; he's been dressing up like this and participating in ceremonies for thirty years. "I visit the American cemetery in Romagne all the time," he made a point of telling me. He had just attended the Memorial Day ceremony there a couple of weeks earlier, as he did every year.

I complimented him on his uniform, both its beauty and its verisimilitude, though, not knowing the French word for verisimilitude, I kind of had to fudge that part. "*Merci,*" he replied, then hiked up a thumb and pointed it at his backpack. "Thirty kilos," he said—66 pounds. He held out his Lebel, said "go ahead." I grasped it in both hands; it wasn't quite 30 kilos, but it was very heavy. The bayonet was half again as long as the rifle itself, and shaped like a deadly silver toothpick. Scary. M. Ravenel must have seen it on my face, because he smiled just a bit and nodded, as if to say: Yes, that *would* leave quite a hole. "That's called a *Rosalie*," he said. A Rosalie!

France.

✷ ✷ ✷

One morning, Jean-Paul took me to a little village called Baulny, where we ran into a farmer he knows who looks very much like a taller, farmier version of the actor/comedian Jason Sudeikis. If the Argonne is still forest, it's also still farms; you are much more likely to get stuck on some narrow, winding road behind a tractor than you are a slow-moving car. There are cows everywhere. Curious creatures. Once, outside Gesnes, I spotted the entrance to a German bunker, a large half-pipe of corrugated metal jammed into the earth, that the current owners were apparently using as a shelter for their animals. I stopped my car, grabbed my camera and strode over to the wire fence, but before I could get off a shot a pack of fourteen black-and-white Holsteins trotted over and blocked my view, as interested in studying me as I was in studying the Germans' handiwork. Eventually, we reached an accommodation.

The farmer in Baulny—his name was Patrick Julien—was driving something bigger than a tractor but smaller than a combine down the town's narrow main street, which was paved but so covered in dirt and dust that you wouldn't have known it. The dust blew in, unimpeded, from the surrounding fields. Baulny was once surrounded by forest; the Germans cut it down.

They also destroyed the town, more or less, almost as soon as they took it. "The church, the *mairie*, and one farm were allowed to stay," M. Julien told me. "The Germans locked everyone in town in the church for two weeks. My grandmother was in there, too. She was sixteen years old, but she lost all her hair from the stress." During those two weeks, the Germans built a network of tunnels underneath the village, connecting the few structures left standing, and some new bunkers. Baulny's new church—the old one was eventually destroyed—is built on top of one of them. M. Julien knew that grandmother, Alice Legand, well; she told him the stories. He was seventeen years old when she died, in 1980.

In 1944, as the Americans approached, the villagers hid themselves in the tunnels the Germans had built during the previous war, afraid of what the Nazis would do to them before they retreated. There is still at least one entrance to them in the middle of town, right next to a house. It looks like a very short concrete slide, like you might find in a children's playground. For a long time, actually, it was about as close to a playground as you might find in the village. "Children used to crawl into the tunnels all the time, even though adults always warned them not to," M. Julien said. He was mum on whether he had been one of them.

Jean-Paul must have known what I was thinking as I heard this. "They're sealed now," he told me. "No one can get into them anymore." And then, perhaps as a consolation prize, he pointed out across the distance at a hill, maybe four or five miles away. "Vauquois," he said. "That's why the Germans cut down the forest: It was blocking their view." And that's why they leveled the town and built all those tunnels: Baulny, a farming village hundreds of years old, home to dozens of people, was, to them, merely an observation post, a spot from which they could keep an eye on a more valuable piece of real estate.

War is vicious, of course. But somehow, what happened here, in the Argonne, seems especially so. Perhaps that sense is nothing more than the result of juxtaposing the place's placid beauty with horrific tales of its past. But there's no denying that at 5:00 A.M. on September 26, 1918, the whole war suddenly funneled into this area, spread with terrible frenzy over this land that had already been fought over for four years, and then, at 11:00 A.M. on November 11, 1918, just as suddenly burned itself out.

Hours before dawn on September 26, hundreds of thousands of American soldiers—doughboys; Sammies—crouched along that twenty-four-mile pushoff line while an uncountable number of shells flew over their heads toward enemy trenches. "All adjectives fail to give even a fair impression of the awful grandeur of such artillerying," Clare Kenamore wrote the following year. "No combination of words is effective. It seemed that for a while the lid of Hell had been pushed back a little space."

Kenamore's account appears in a history of the 35th Division, National Guard troops mostly from Missouri and Kansas. The Santa Fe Division, as they were known for reasons that elude me, had arrived in France that May and spent the summer in "quiet" sectors in the Vosges and Alsace before being sent to the Argonne. They were put in the line between the 28th, the Bucket of Blood, which had a fair bit of combat experience already, and the 91st, the Wild West Division, which, like the 35th, had none. As they marched up to the line, Kenamore noted, each infantryman carried his rifle, bayonet, steel helmet and gas mask. He had 250 rounds of rifle ammunition, carried in a belt, and two bandoliers, each one swung over one shoulder and under the other arm. On his back was his combat pack, in his pack carrier. This contained his raincoat, if he was not wearing it, his mess kit and two days' "iron ration," which usually was two cans of corned beef and six boxes of hard bread . . . A few men had a loaf or half a loaf of the excellent white army bread fresh from the baker. This usually was carried on the rifle with the fixed bayonet run through it. All carried a full canteen of water, about a quart. Occasional details carried Stokes mortar ammunition, four shells to a man, each shell weighing 10 pounds, 11 ounces. Infantry also carried ordinary explosive grenades, gas grenades, rifle grenades and incendiary grenades.

Kenamore estimated that the 35th Division alone fired forty thousand rounds—some of them, at least, shot off by Battery D of the 129th Field Artillery Regiment, under the command of Captain Harry S Truman—in the three hours before they pushed off early that morning. "There was no breakfast and little ceremony about it," he recounted; just the words "Prepare to advance" a few minutes beforehand, and then: "All right, let's go."

If they were fortunate, the men hadn't heard very much about one of their first objectives:

Never before or afterward did the 35th Division find a place better defended than Vauquois. It was the result of four years intensive work by the Germans. Among the many good men killed on this slope was Lieut. Malcolm MacDonald who made up in dash and daring what he lacked in stature. When he joined the guard he weighed 102 pounds and a kindly examining board, observing his earnestness, had written down the weight as 122.

Kenamore described a chaotic assault—fog, smoke grenades, elite Prussian Guard troops, Sammies taking fire from in front, to the sides and behind. And a lot of deaths. Two of the Americans killed there that morning, a captain and a private, were later awarded the Medal of Honor posthumously. But, as Denis told me after I had taken in tunnels and trenches and massive craters and tales of men marching solemnly toward enemy machine guns to the tune of their own national anthem, after four years and many thousands killed over control of the Butte de Vauquois, "the 35th Division, U.S., came and took the hill in half a day."

Kenamore's history of the 35th Division is titled *From Vauquois to Exermont.* If you look at a map, you'll see that Vauquois and Exermont are less than ten miles apart. The Santa Fe Division was pulled from the line after September 30. Their fighting war was five days long. But in those five days they sustained nearly eight thousand casualties, around a thousand of them killed in action. Just one division among many; just five days out of forty-seven. The war was fought elsewhere, too; it was fought all over the world. But it converged upon this beautiful place to die. And it did not die quietly.

CHAPTER EIGHT

THE DEVIL'S BASKET

The first time I visited Vauquois with Denis Hebrard, in 2014, I made it out of the tunnels all right but then tripped in one of the German second-line trenches and banged up my left knee. There was blood—yes: I, too, shed blood on Vauquois Hill—and dirt, and a six-inch horizontal tear in the leg of my pants. The rest of the day was pretty full, and I didn't have time to stop at Denis's and wash up and change my clothes before going into Sainte-Menehould for dinner if I wanted to get there before the restaurants all closed. When I walked into one I had eaten at a couple of times before, a place called La Passarelle (the Gangway; it's perched above a stream), the proprietress, Murielle, looked at me and shook her head. *"Qu'est-il arrivé?"* she asked. What happened?

"I fell," I said. "Do you know if there's a tailor in town? I have only one other pair of pants." I actually had a third—I wouldn't go to France for a month with just two pairs of pants—but they had quickly proven themselves unsuitable to bushwhacking, and had remained in my suitcase ever since.

"Bring them in here tomorrow morning," she said. "I'll give them to my seamstress."

I did, and that evening she gave them back to me, not only mended but washed. The seamstress had done a wonderful job, too, not just closing the tear but covering the whole area in a rectangle of tight stitching a couple of shades of green lighter than the pants, which were olive. It was the kind of effect that people much more stylish than me would deliberately tear their pants to achieve, and pay a lot for. But when I pulled out my wallet and asked Murielle how much I owed her, she smiled and shook her head. "*C'est un service,*" she said.

Sainte-Menehould is one of the larger towns in the Argonne. The Germans didn't occupy it during the First World War, and it didn't see any fighting; its *hôtel de ville,* a stately building with the date 1730 mounted in large wrought-iron digits above its entrance, survived just fine. It was already sixty-one years old in 1791 when Louis XVI, fleeing the revolutionary mob in Paris, stopped in Sainte-Menehould to partake of a local specialty, *pieds de cochon*—pigs' feet. They're still a local specialty, touted all over town like cheesesteaks are in Philadelphia. I resisted trying them for a year, then gave in, curious to see just what was so good that the king stopped for it when he really needed to get out of the country right then. They're OK, I'll say, but nothing all that special; to be honest, I prefer the pickled variety I had a few times when I lived down south. They're certainly nothing I would trade my head for, which is, in essence, what Louis ended up doing. Recognized while dining—it's hard to maintain anonymity when your visage is on every coin in the realm—he was captured about fifteen miles up the road in the town of Varennes, surrounded while he dithered before crossing a bridge over the Aire River. His escorts, the story goes, were ready to shoot and slash their way out of there, but the king demurred, saying he didn't want any blood to be shed on his behalf. He was escorted back to Paris under armed guard, and put to the guillotine eighteen months later. So while Sainte-Menehould may have escaped the destruction of the First World War, it did play a role in some of the other horrors human beings have inflicted upon one another. A tablet under a

stairway inside the *hôtel de ville* lists the names of nine members of a local Jewish family, deported and *morts à Auschwitz* in 1942. The youngest was 7 years old. My father, still living as I write this, was 7 years old in 1942.

The Argonne is evidence that history folds in on itself again and again, and that, as I often view the First and Second World Wars as one conflict with a two-decade cease-fire in the middle, a case could certainly be made that that plaque under the stairs might not be there if the king hadn't stopped for *pieds de cochon* just steps away. No decapitated Louis, no First Republic; no First Republic, no Napoleon; no Napoleon, no rise of Prussia; no rise of Prussia, no Franco-Prussian War; no Franco-Prussian War, no First World War; no First World War, no Second World War; no Second World War, no Holocaust. Not everyone draws out that chain, of course, and not everyone is comfortable discussing every link in it, especially in France. But if you go to a place like Sainte-Menehould and walk around with your eyes and ears open, it can be hard not to feel as if you have stepped onto a Moving Sidewalk of Great Consequences, one that starts with a plate of local pigs' feet and ends at that tablet under the stairs in city hall. You feel the continuum in Varennes, too, as you stroll the few hundred yards from the Bar Louis XVI, which is next to the spot where he was captured, to the Pennsylvania monument, a massive plaza, complete with classical colonnades and terraces and an enormous cauldron for an eternal flame, built here by that state in 1927 in honor of its sons who'd liberated the town nine years earlier. It's beautiful and august, but also sprawls over two entire city blocks (a street actually cuts through it) and utterly dominates Varennes, looking like it was dropped in by some enormous hand. The men it honors—primarily from the 28th Division, the Bucket of Blood, who took so much damage at Fismes and Fismette—took a lot of damage here, too. So did the town itself, which was more or less destroyed.

If you compare photos of what Varennes, a picturesque hill-and-river town, looked like before the war with what it looks like now, you'll note that they're very similar. Most towns and villages in the Argonne that were destroyed during the war were rebuilt, afterward, to look almost exactly as they had before. Houses and shops were carefully reconstructed or replicated; so were churches, like the one in Neuvilly—famously photographed during the war with its left wall blasted out and its floor covered with American wounded—which was meticulously restored in the 1920s, down to its black and white floor tiles. It's indicative, I think, of a desire to treat the entire episode as just one great four-year aberration. Not that any of it was to be forgotten: not the suffering, nor the dying, nor, certainly, the victory at last. But there wasn't, it seems, much of a willingness to acknowledge that everything had changed, forever, most of all France itself. None of it—not the rubble, nor the blockhouses, nor the ubiquitous memorials, nor the stuff that litters the forest floor and comes up every time fields are plowed—seems to touch on the fact that the Red Giant imploded, as Red Giants will. I don't blame the French: Who wants to ponder such a thing every time you pull into your own driveway?

They do, however, ponder everything and anything else connected to that war: Shrapnel. Barbed wire. Buttons. Boots. Shells. Shell casings. Shell holes. Bunkers. Trenches. Craters. Photos. Names. And, most of all, stories. The Argonne, which looks like something out of a book by the Brothers Grimm, is full of people who tell a lot of good stories. Perhaps they might have preferred it otherwise, but they have a lot of good stories to tell.

✷ ✷ ✷

If any term seems well-suited to a fairytale, it's "Crown Prince." There were, as you know, two of them in the Argonne during the war: Rupprecht, of Bavaria; and Wilhelm, of Prussia, next in line to be Kaiser. Rupprecht was hunkered down in that bunker in the Champ Mahaut that looked like a lovely country house. Because signs in the forest directing visitors to it read *Abri du Kronprinz,* a lot of people (including, once upon a time, me) mistakenly assume that the *Kronprinz* in question was Wilhelm, not Rupprecht, which I guess makes it a better story for the folks back home, one that might cause them to stir to attention as they sit through an interminable vacation slide show. The heir to the throne of the German Empire, after all, trumps the heir to the throne of the Kingdom of Bavaria, which was just one part of the German Empire.

Though this will probably rob the tale of some of its mythical luster, I should tell you that I'm not sure how well the two men even knew each other, or how much contact they would have had with one another during the war, since each was in command of an entirely different army; so, while only one of them (Rupprecht) was actually a capable military commander, there was no good-*Kronprinz*/bad-*Kronprinz* rivalry playing out in the Argonne. The closest *Kronprinz* Wilhelm got to Champ Mahaut was his observatory about ten miles away, on Montfaucon, the highest point in this part of the Argonne. Wilhelm, the Kaiser's oldest son, was commander of Germany's 5th Army. He wasn't much good in either role—his father was constantly upbraiding his namesake for, among other things, carrying on with women who were not the *Kronprinzessin*—but he was given a great deal of authority in the field due to the circumstances of his birth. In 1916, that meant that he was, at least nominally, in charge of the assault on Verdun. How much he actually did there is an open question, but the French had no qualms about assigning him the sobriquet *Le Boucher de Verdun*—the Butcher of Verdun. And he certainly watched all the action from his post atop Montfaucon. The village that surrounded it, Montfaucon d'Argonne, was liberated on September 27, 1918, by the 37th Division, National Guard troops from Ohio, though what little of it that was still intact by that point was destroyed in the process. After the war, it was rebuilt down the mountain a bit; the state of Ohio constructed a little hospital in the new village and dedicated it in September 1929, one month before the stock market crashed. It still stands, a dignified stone edifice with a high-pitched roof, though it is now used as a nursing home. There's a nice enough cement plaque, crediting Ohio and the 37th, affixed to its façade, but Jean-Paul de Vries told me over lunch one day that I really needed to see the one inside. I tried to; couldn't find it.

"Try again," he said the next time I saw him, a couple of days later. "It's there." He was tied to the café that afternoon, so I went back alone and, once again, walked all through the place; but still I couldn't find it. I passed lots of elderly residents sitting hunched over in little white plastic chairs—watching TV, watching each other, reading *L'Est Républicain*, the local newspaper—and though I'm sure none of them would have minded the interruption, I didn't want to bother them, so I just smiled as I passed by, and they smiled back. Eventually I found an office, and in it a couple of nurses. *"Pardonnez-moi,"* I said. "I have a need to find the plaque to the American memory." They looked at each other and faintly shrugged, but then a third staffer walked in and they asked her, and she bunched up her eyebrows and nodded and told me to take a left out of the office and walk all the way down the hall; at the very end, she said, there's an alcove to the left, the vestibule to an entrance no longer used. She was mistaken: It was still used—not as an entryway, but as a storage space. It was dark, and I couldn't take more than a couple of steps inside, but behind a dozen folded conference tables and many more folded chairs, I could see rich mahogany panels rising all the way up to the ceiling, one of them engraved top to bottom with gold-leaf letters. I walked back to the office, told them what I'd seen (or tried to see) and asked if they knew where the light switch was. One of them left and came back a minute later with the custodian in tow, a burly man with close-cropped gray hair who just happened to be wearing a white T-shirt featuring the outline of the continental United States, silhouetted in stars and stripes, with a bald eagle's head and the words:

WE THE PEOPLE
AMERICA
THE BEAUTIFUL

He led me back wordlessly, groped inside the darkened vestibule, flicked the light switch; and then, before I could thank him, he started removing the tables and chairs, piling them up in the corridor outside. "Not is necessary," I insisted, but he pointed to the plaque and then my camera and asked: "Do you want to take a picture?" I nodded.

"Vous êtes Amèricain?" he asked. I said I was, asked if he'd ever been there. He looked confused; I pointed to his T-shirt. "Ah," he said, and smiled. "A friend of mine got me this. *En Pennsylvanie.*"

He continued removing furniture until the space was cleared, reveal-ing a vestibule paneled entirely in rich, dark wood, the kind of thing I had only seen in Gilded Age mansions that are now museums. The plaque itself was enormous, easily eight feet square, maybe larger, in a space that was itself only about twelve feet square or so. The inscription starts with a reiteration of what the plaque outside says about the state of Ohio and the 37th Division, then goes on to recount the unit's entire war record:

> THE DIVISION IN SPITE OF DETERMINED RESISTANCE
> AND MOST UNFAVORABLE CONDITIONS CONFRONTING IT,
> ADVANCED NINE KILOMETERS AGAINST THE
> ENEMY POSITIONS HELD BY HIM FOR OVER FOUR YEARS,
> REPULSING REPEATED COUNTER ATTACKS,
> TAKING MANY PRISONERS, ARTILLERY, MACHINE GUNS,
> AMMUNITION AND OTHER STORES IN LARGE QUANTITIES.

And on like that for another couple of paragraphs, after which it tells the entire tale once more, in French. We stood together, silently, and read the whole thing.

"I don't know why they don't use this entrance anymore," he muttered afterward, shaking his head, then started fetching tables and chairs and stacking them back up in front of it.

✷ ✷ ✷

The old village of Montfaucon d'Argonne, at the mountain's peak, was very, very old; American engineers excavating the area in the 1920s for the Montfaucon American Monument uncovered the remains of a Roman vil-lage and cemetery. The monument is a 180-foot-tall column. You can see it from Vauquois Hill, twelve miles away, even if it's not a particularly clear day. You can see it from places all over the forest; and if you climb the steps inside it up to the observatory at the top, you can see places all over the forest back. If you look straight down, you can also see the only thing left of the original village, sitting just behind the monument's plaza: the ruins of an old monastery destroyed in the war, sections of walls, pillars, arched windows. From aloft, you can clearly discern the perimeter of the medieval edifice against the grass, like a chalk outline of a corpse on a sidewalk.

Nothing remains of *Kronprinz* Wilhelm's observatory; the site is now occupied by the monument and plaza. And his bunker, it turns out, wasn't even here, as I learned when I visited Patrick Simons at the hospital in Verdun one day in June 2014. (You may recall that he was ill then, which is how I ended up exploring Bois Brûlé and other sites in the Woëvre with just Christophe that year.) I hadn't called in advance to say I was coming, and when I arrived Patrick already had several other visitors—he's a popular fellow—including a man named David Howard, a friend of a friend of Patrick's. David is an English expatriate who lives in Stenay, a town about twenty miles north of Montfaucon that had, in fact, been liberated by American troops on the very last day of the war. The story goes that General William Wright, commander of the 89th Division, had heard that there were baths in Stenay, and though he knew the armistice would take effect in a matter of hours, he didn't want to wait that long; so he sent his men into the town, where more than three hundred of them became casualties, most of whom, I am quite sure, would gladly have waited a few more hours to get cleaned up. Stenay, it turns out, had quite an eventful war, as David started telling me. Of course, a lot of places had an eventful war, especially in the Argonne; but as I made ready to leave, David told me something that made me stop, as I'm sure he knew it would.

"Stenay, you know, was where the *real* Crown Prince Bunker was," he said, by which, I knew, he meant Wilhelm's. "It was in the cellar of a grand house there. I know the woman who lives there now. She has all kinds of documents and pictures, even a very rare one of the crown prince's secret French mistress. If you return to the area sometime, let me know, and perhaps I can take you to go see it." Not the kind of invitation I was likely to decline.

I did return, the following year, and we met on a Sunday morning in the square in Stenay. David, a compact man in his sixties with lively eyes and a head of white hair, was joined by his personable blonde wife, Marian, who is American. I had given David a copy of my last book when I'd met him at the hospital the year before, and both he and Marian had read it in the interim; both greeted me as if I were already a friend, and knew well what I would and wouldn't be interested in seeing. The first thing they did was direct my gaze to Stenay's *hôtel de ville,* which features, in a cornice above the entrance and a set of second-story windows, a carving of the town crest and motto and . . . well, the devil. A fairly jolly-looking one, too, with a stylish Vandyke and a grin that says *the drinks are on me.* "Nobody knows for sure how that came to be there," Marian told me.

"People just embrace it. It's actually one of the things that Stenay is best known for. They even have a *Festival du Diable* every fall."

Stenay is in the northern part of the Meuse-Argonne vicinity, closer to Sedan and the Belgian border than to Varennes and Sainte-Menehould. David and Marian chose to live there because it's a pretty area that's roughly equidistant from a number of places David needed to get to for work, spots in Belgium, Luxembourg and Holland as well as France. It wasn't until later that he started digging into the local history, and what he found encouraged him to dig more and more. Stenay is considerably older than those parts of the Argonne that were only settled by French after medieval times. The French, it seems, were always in Stenay, even before they recognized themselves as French; even as the Romans were here, too, and before them the Celts. "*Dun* is Celtic for hill," David told me. "So anytime you see that in a place name, like Dun-sur-Meuse"—the next town over— "that's an indication there was a Celtic settlement there once upon a time."

"Like Verdun?" I asked. "Maybe that means 'green hill'?"

David froze and stared at me for a moment, then broke into a broad smile and nodded his head vigorously. "Yes, I think you're right!" he said. "That hadn't occurred to me!" It may have been the only contribution to scholarship I made that day.

David then launched into a discussion of Stenay's history that was neither linear nor thematic; I'll do my best to impose some order on it. To start, since time immemorial, you had the locals. The names by which they referred to themselves changed from time to time. Then, around three thousand years ago, the Celts migrated here from the east. About a thousand years after that, the Romans came up from the Italian peninsula. When the Romans receded, around the middle of the fifth century, the Merovingians took over. The Merovingians, near as I can tell, comprised old locals who then called themselves Franks, and Gallo-Romans, other old locals whose customs and language had so thoroughly blended with the Romans' that it was hard to distinguish them anymore; their culture and ruling structure were an amalgam of Frankish and Roman. One of the earliest Merovingian rulers was Clovis, who united all of the competing Frankish tribes into what we now recognize more or less as France, and who also, in 496, converted to Catholicism and *strongly* encouraged everyone else to do it, too. After Clovis died the factional squabbling got worse, and the kings had names like Childeric, Theuderic, Chlothar, Sigebert, and Dagobert. The two major Merovingian rival kingdoms were Neustria and Austrasia. I recognize these are names that, to an American at least, sound like something out of an epic fantasy novel, and may conjure strains of lute music, but I am not making them up.

Stenay was apparently a site of some importance for thousands of years, a hypothesis buttressed by the presence, in what is today the nearby village of Milly-sur-Bradon, of a menhir, a six-foot-tall upright wedge of stone that somewhat resembles a shark's tooth and was erected by the Celts to indicate something of significance, though no one is sure exactly what. According to David Howard, the menhir, known by locals as La Hotte du Diable, or the Devil's Basket—apparently people thought about the devil a lot in that area—was later used by the Merovingians to mark the point of convergence of Neustria and Austrasia and a third kingdom, Burgundy (no lute music with that one, but maybe a little classical guitar), which, if true, would certainly explain a lot. For instance, it would explain why King Dagobert II spent a lot of time here; he was assassinated here in 679 in what was, I am told, made to look like a hunting accident. Sometime before Dagobert was murdered, David told me, he is said to have undertaken a secret journey to the Middle East, and to have brought back a big chunk of King Solomon's fortune, which he secreted somewhere in or near Stenay.

The Merovingians went out in the eighth century, replaced by the Carolingians, whose number included Charlemagne. They lasted about a century and were then replaced by, well, a bunch of other stuff that gets kind of confusing, at least to me, but eventually we end up in medieval France, with kings but also other people of influence and power, one of whom was Godfrey de Bouillon, a Frankish knight who was, as the name suggests, from Bouillon, in present-day Belgium near the English Channel. Godfrey's "second city"—that was a thing then—was, David told me, Stenay. Godfrey was kin to a lot of powerful, landed people, and cozy with a lot more, and he inherited some titles and was given some others, all of which helped him, it seems, amass quite a fortune. He is probably best remembered today, though, for selling both Bouillon and Stenay—that was also a thing then—to other nobles, and using the money to raise and then command one of the largest armies to participate in the First Crusade, which began in 1096, and from which he never returned, dying in the Holy Land four years later. According to David, a lot of Godfrey's subjects from the vicinity of his second city went off to fight under him, and some who returned, it is alleged, bestowed upon the area several town names that are, according to some historians, suspiciously Middle Eastern sounding, like Jametz. I don't have any idea if that's true, but Jametz does happen to host my favorite old wall-painted advertisement ever, which adorns the broad sidewall of a large house that was once, according to another fading painted ad on the same wall, a hotel and restaurant. Above that it says simply:

VERDUN *Historic City*
Visit its Battlefields, 1914–1918

It's kind of like one of those century-old ads that reveal themselves on the side of an old tenement when the building next door is torn down. Only fainter, and cooler.

★ ★ ★

Between the Merovingians and Godfrey de Bouillon, apparently, a lot of rumors arose over the centuries regarding Stenay, some involving strange mystical phenomena that may or may not bestow powers upon those who get close enough to them, and some involving enormous hidden treasure. According to David, *Kronprinz* Wilhelm was drawn to Stenay because he wanted both. Of course, there were lots of other reasons a German military commander might want to occupy Stenay and even base his command there. For one thing, it's equidistant from the heart of the Argonne and Verdun, with excellent access to each. It's a good-sized town with a lot of housing for troops; it had played a significant role in many battles and wars over the centuries. And, David told me, there is an intricate network of tunnels beneath the streets, reaching to every corner of Stenay, with connections to all the sites of import. "They go back to the Middle Ages," he explained. "Some are large enough to ride a horse through." All of this may have factored into the *Kronprinz*'s thinking, but David is pretty sure that it was the weird mystical stuff and hidden treasure that really tipped the scales. Wilhelm certainly didn't do much that undercut this theory. At one point, he even had his engineers affix a massive new cement tablet to La Hotte du Diable that read:

DEDICATED TO THE FALLEN
WARRIORS AT VERDUN BY
THE GERMAN CROWN PRINCE
GENERAL COMMAND

VII ARMY CORPS
GENERAL VON FRANCOIS
1917

The Teutonic Gothic script indicates which Verdun warriors, exactly, the *Kronprinz* had in mind. (General Hermann Karl Bruno von François was, despite his surname, thoroughly German.) Local farmers destroyed Wilhelm's new tablet after the war, but left the tall stone to which it had been affixed standing. It's still there today, sticking out of some family's yard, with a prominent indentation where the *Kronprinz*'s tablet used to be.

Whether it was Dagobert's hidden treasure or the mystical power of the menhir or some other ancient lure that drew the *Kronprinz* to Stenay, it surely didn't hurt that the town had a pretty nice place for him to make camp in while he was away from home. It was called the Château de Tilleul: a large, splendid villa, thirteen bedrooms and six or seven baths, that had been built in 1865 by the Comte du Verdier, who owned a large chunk of the town. It survived the war, but was destroyed in 1940, not by the Nazis but by French engineers who understood the house's symbolic importance to the rapidly advancing Germans.

They didn't completely obliterate the site: The foundation upon which the château had stood, complete with a large stone terrace facing the back and, underneath it, a cellar, remained. The house was rebuilt from scratch in 1950 by the late father-in-law of its current occupant. I shall refer to her as Mme. B, because she is elderly now and lives there alone, and both she and her son are nervous about prowlers. She had, however, responded affirmatively when David had asked her, a few days earlier, if he and Marian might bring me by. Now she welcomed me with gracious hospitality. An older woman with fine posture and a firm countenance, she possessed a powerful dignity—I wouldn't call it understated—and was coiffed and dressed to greet a guest of great importance, even if what she ended up getting was me.

We sat at a large, dark old table in her dining room, and she presented me with a stack of books, postcards and photographs: of the *Kronprinz*'s private salon in the old château; the *Kronprinz* welcoming Prince August Wilhelm, his younger brother, at the front door; the *Kronprinz* and his father, the Kaiser, standing on the back balcony; officers of the American 89th Division standing in the courtyard behind the front gate; a man in an overcoat standing in front of the villa's shell after it was destroyed. And a sketch of a woman, pretty but not beautiful, named Blanche Defferey. "The *Kronprinz*'s mistress," Mme. B told me. "Very few people even know he had one. Fewer still know her name." She related this in a tone that conveyed a sense that there would be trouble if certain people were to learn what she had just shared with me; I guess now I'll find out for sure. I will say that when I asked Mme. B about it, she told me that Mlle. Defferey lived out her life after the first war in peace, not suffering any of the indignities that were heaped upon collaborators after the second. But again, she said, very few people knew.

"Mme. B, may we see the bunker?" David asked, and she assented, taking us out through the terrace, where the *Kronprinz* and Kaiser had posed for that photograph. It's entirely possible that neither the 1940 French nor the 1940 Germans even knew about the bunker underneath: It had been a secret, after all, and a lot had transpired in the interim. Mme. B walked slowly down the stone steps, clutching the banister; when she reached the bottom and stepped onto the ground, she suddenly seemed to feel more at ease, as if she no longer needed to protect anything. She hadn't allowed me to take any photos inside her house, nor on the terrace, but now she pointed to my camera and said *"C'est bon,"* even recommending things I might shoot, like the staircase we had just descended, and the two wooden double doors, festooned with ornate wrought-iron bars and grates, set into the side of the terrace's base. "All original," she said of the latter. "Go into the yard, way back, and take some pictures from a distance," she suggested. She was proud of the house, clearly—and, I imagine, the yard, one of those deep, green plots, with old trees and benches and statuary, that you often find behind old châteaux, made for croquet or lawn bowling or privacy.

She asked me not to mention the location of the entrance to the bunker, and so I won't. I will say that the bunker itself is both well disguised and not, the kind of thing that if you already know to look for it won't fool you a bit. There are vents here and there, for one thing, none of them particularly well hidden. On the other hand, Mme. B told me there was a secret entrance way out in the garden, and even after I was led to it I had a hard time actually seeing it. The bunker itself contained several chambers, each with concrete walls, wooden doors, and ceilings made of those corrugated metal half-pipes the Germans brought from home by the thousands. The doors and benches were all original. So were the wooden plank floors.

David bent over one of them and pulled up a hidden door, revealing a long niche that held several jugs. "There used to be a live shell in there," Mme. B told me.

The bunker had been electrified and had running water and even a fireplace, and there was no doubt it was solid; still, it didn't look particularly comfortable, and it was hard to imagine a notorious sybarite like *Kronprinz* Wilhelm enjoying himself there, with or without his mistress. Then again, I doubt he spent very much time there. The Germans, as I mentioned, held Stenay until the morning of November 11, 1918, by which time the heir to the German throne, which had been abolished, had fled with his father to the Netherlands. And if he'd really been concerned with security, I imagine he would have kept a lower profile in Stenay. Before I left, Mme. B showed me her copy of *Le Boucher de Verdun,* a bestselling book about the *Kronprinz* written by Louis Dumur and published shortly after the war, and directed me to a particular passage, which I studied for a moment but could not seem to decipher. Finally, at the risk of compromising her dignity, she translated it for me into less indirect French.

"They say," she explained, her expression a very odd mixture of distaste and pride, "that the *Kronprinz* used to have orgies here."

★ ★ ★

David and Marian and I spent about twelve hours together that day, stopping for lunch at a nice restaurant in Dun, after which they walked me over to a long, low building on the banks of the Meuse. It's a museum, and though its name, Maison de l'Histoire du Val Dunois, would seem to indicate that it deals with the entirety of Dun's history, its sole focus is 14–18. Its proprietor, a burly, ruddy-cheeked retired soldier in his (I would guess) sixties named Jean Marie, doesn't speak any English, but is particularly interested in the exploits of the American Expeditionary Forces. Part of that, I'm sure, is because Dun was liberated by the American 5th Division on November 5, 1918; General Pershing nicknamed them the Meuse Division for that action, since the Meuse River runs right through the town. The division later built a bridge over it there to replace one that had been destroyed in the battle, and festooned it with a handsome plaque. And they didn't stop there: They built a total of twenty-four monuments—all obelisks—in the Meuse-Argonne, more than every other American division put together. David Howard took me to see what was probably the last, on the edge of a field outside the village of Remoiville. Its plaque reads:

REMOIVILLE & LOUPPY
CAPTURED BY 11TH INF.
COL. R. H. PECK COMDG
10TH BRIGADE 5TH U.S. DIV.
NOV. 9, 1918
MARKING THE MOST
ADVANCED LINE OF THE
AMERICAN ARMY
AT THE TIME OF THE
ARMISTICE DAY

It is identical to twenty-two of the other twenty-three 5th Division obelisks in this area, as well as the three near Saint-Mihiel and the one down in the Vosges, except for the tiny Tricolor and Stars and Stripes that decorate its flanks, and the commemorative knick-knacks laid at its base by a local man who has adopted the marker and takes care of it.

Despite the long shadow the 5th Division casts in this area, M. Marie's interest extends to the entire AEF; he is particularly fascinated with the story of Native Americans in the Army, and has compiled a roster of them that is incomplete but quite extensive. "The Americans used Indian code-talkers in the first war, long before the second," he told me, in French. "Indian code was actually invented in the Argonne in 1918. They called them 'wind-talkers.' They were Choctaw." I've never been able to confirm that, but I really want it to be true.

There was certainly a need for such people, whether they existed or not; the Germans, as I have said before, had excellent intelligence operations. "The Americans learned to speak out loud only when they wanted to spread disinformation," M. Marie told me. He knows a tremendous amount about the Sammies and their war, and has a knack for summoning a piece of information he suspects you will find particularly intriguing. "There were American ambulances here since the beginning of the war," he told me. "They already had X-rays for lungs." His museum is one large room, much of it taken up by scores of panels he has created dealing with different facets of the war—armies, battles, weapons, conditions at the front. A big chunk of the rest is a sandpit of sorts, filled with artifacts, the most striking of which, a large alabaster tombstone, had just been brought in. The epitaph, etched inside a bold knight's shield, reads:

EUGEN NÖLLER

CAPTAIN

123RD GRENADIER REGIMENT

◦

BORN JUNE 27 1879

FELL AUGUST 30 1914

FEARLESS AND FAITHFUL

He was killed, in the first month of the war, during a four-hour bombardment of a farm in the neighboring village of Douclon, and buried where he fell. A century and a year later, the family that still owned the farm found the marker, lying in one of their fields; wishing to preserve it—and to keep it from damaging their combine—they brought it to M. Marie.

Like the Argonne itself, things have a way of hiding in plain sight here. In Ornes, which lies between Stenay and Verdun, there are just two man-made things: the ruins of a church; and, across the road, a small, dark monument that reads:

HERE

WAS

ORNES

DESTROYED

IN 1916

But the real evidence of what happened here is what stands behind both. "Pine trees," David said, as we walked between the two. "A quick postwar fix. The indigenous trees in this area are oak, beech, ash and elm, but none of them grow as quickly as pine trees. Anytime you see them, you know they were planted after the war, to replace what was destroyed."

★ ★ ★

David's wife, Marian, is one of only two Americans I know of who live in the Argonne. Very few Americans, it seems to me, even know the Argonne exists, and far fewer ever undertake a visit: It's far from Paris, Bordeaux,

Normandy, Saint-Tropez; there aren't the kinds of hotels here that Americans are used to; no one speaks English. Most of the times I have visited the cemetery in Romagne I have had it to myself. Most of the times I have encountered other people there they have been French, Belgian, Dutch. In all the time I spent there I met exactly one group of Americans, a family from Iowa who came to the Argonne to find the place where the elderly paterfamilias's father was wounded in the fall of 1918. I met one other American family, at Jean-Paul de Vries's café, consisting of a history professor from Virginia, his wife and their son. That's it.

The cemetery, though, is where the other American I know of who lives in the Argonne can be found most often: Dave Bedford, its superintendent. A trim U.S. Army veteran (most of ABMC's cemetery superintendents had previous careers in the military) in his late fifties with steely hair and a sharp jaw, Dave took the better part of two days during my 2015 visit to show me some sites in the Argonne, much as his predecessor, the late Joseph P. "Phil" Rivers, had in 2009. (It was Phil who had first told me: "The saying goes that the 5th Division put up a marker every time they stopped to take a piss.") Tour guide is not part of the job description of an ABMC cemetery superintendent—they have, as you might imagine, a great many other things to deal with; it's not easy keeping a 130-acre burial ground looking absolutely perfect every day of the year—but the Meuse-Argonne is a lonely post, and people who request it tend to do so because they love the history and wish to immerse themselves in it. Like Phil before him, Dave spends as much time as he can exploring both the area and its past, usually alone. He even, he told me, managed to find and follow the trail of the Lost Battalion, start to finish, despite the fact that for decades it seemed no one could agree on exactly where it was, and even if they could have they would have had a really rough time getting to it. That, at least, is what Phil Rivers told me in 2009; the closest we could get, he'd said, was a modern stone marker, alongside a winding forest road, that pointed down into a steep ravine so choked with vegetation that you could scarcely see ten feet ahead, much less the bottom of the slope. So when, six years later, Dave told me he had found and walked the trail, beginning to end, I asked him if he would take me back so we could hike it together.

The story of the Lost Battalion (which was, technically, neither lost nor a battalion) began on October 2, 1918, when, less than a week after they took Champ Mahaut, some 550 soldiers of the 77th Division—the Statue of Liberty Division, draftees from the city of New York—under the command of Major Charles White Whittlesey, a Manhattan attorney, set off in the Argonne, believing they were part of a line of advance. Within hours, though, as a result of poor communication and unexpected German resistance elsewhere on the line, they found themselves alone in a wooded ravine, surrounded by the enemy and greatly outnumbered. They withstood five days of attacks and bombardments (including some friendly fire), as well as entreaties from the Germans to surrender, which they refused. By the time reinforcements were able to break through to their position, more than 350 of the men had been killed, wounded, or taken prisoner. The rest—194 of them—returned to the fight, much more famous back home, where newspapers had covered their tribulations extensively, than they were at the front.

The 77th had a very large number of immigrants in its ranks—Irish, Greeks, Jews, Italians, Slavs, Germans, and many others; it was said to encompass more nationalities and native tongues than any other division in American history. The press loved them, loved the story of the Great American Melting Pot forging war heroes. At a time when New York City alone had dozens of daily newspapers, almost all of them reported every day, sometimes in several different editions each day, on absolutely everything the men of the Lost Battalion did. People knew the names of the living, and the dead. The former became celebrities, and stayed such, if they wanted to be; having been in the Lost Battalion would have been enough to dine out on for the rest of your life. An extraordinary number of them, and their rescuers, were awarded the Medal of Honor, including Major Whittlesey, who was also given the honor of being a pallbearer at the opening of the Tomb of the Unknown Soldier in Arlington National Cemetery in 1921. Shortly thereafter, he committed suicide.

Dave Bedford warned me this would be a tough hike: There was no clear trail and a lot of mud, dense brush, dense undergrowth, steep hills, deep gullies, slimy dead leaves, and slimy boulders. He really undersold it. It had rained recently, more than once, and the Argonne is a place that's good at trapping water and using it to simultaneously support vegetable life and vex animal life. I slipped a lot. I tripped a lot. At one point, I fell backward into a very large, very prickly . . . uh . . . *thing* that slashed up my right arm pretty well. (Yes: I, too, shed blood in the Argonne Forest.) It could have been worse; I could have fallen into it face first.

It is safe to say there will never be the equivalent of a Sergeant York Trail for the Lost Battalion, which is a good thing, really, because doing it this way gives you a very good feel for what, exactly, the Lost Battalion experienced—excepting the shooting and shelling, of course. Despite everything that happened here, and the many decades that have passed since it did, this area looks very much—*very* much—as it would have in early October 1918. When Dave Bedford later took me to the Bois de Cheppy, the woods where the 91st (Wild West) Division jumped off on the morning of September 26, 1918, we found a lot of really interesting manmade stuff: deep trenches, concrete bunkers, entrances to underground dugouts (I was about to lower myself into one when Dave informed me that badgers sometimes nested in them, and that I really didn't want to encounter them under such circumstances), dirt saps where the Germans hid until the first line of Americans had passed over them so they could attack the attacker from behind, a German canteen (totally flattened, perhaps by an American boot), a nose cone from an artillery shell, and even something I initially believed to be a large, cylindrical American pineapple grenade but which turned out to be the body of a German trench mortar known as a *Taube,* or pigeon. The most interesting discovery in the Bois de Cheppy, though, wasn't something I spotted but something I heard, namely Dave's answer to my question, posed as I looked out from the woods toward the jump-off line, plotting in reverse the course the Wild West Sammies would have taken that morning: to woods from field, to field from copse of trees, to copse of trees from more distant field, to more distant field from thicket of tall scrub, to thicket of tall scrub from yet more distant field, to yet more distant field from jump-off point just behind tree line.

"What would all this have looked like that morning?" I asked him.

"Exactly the same," he replied.

"Really?"

"Exactly."

I'll tell you the truth: There was a part of me that wondered: *How could he know?* Then, a couple of days later, I found myself with Jean-Paul de Vries just inside another patch of woods east of Romagne, this one called the Bois de Forêt—the Woods of the Forest—because, he speculated, it was so dense. We'd had to walk several hundred yards across a nascent cornfield to get to it—I'd found a lot there, including a French 75-millimeter shell casing, green with oxidation but still full of powder; that German spoon I referred to a while back; something Jean-Paul swears is a piece of roof tile from Roman times—and, reaching its edge, had to scale a steep berm (where I found a large old German beer bottle, embedded in the dirt up to its punt) and immediately start bushwhacking. It was slow going, but, as always, it could have been worse: There could have been German machine guns firing at us. "The 3rd Division came out of those woods over there," Jean-Paul said, turning around and pointing over the field we had just traversed to get to this spot. "It took them half a day to get across that field to where we're standing."

"Did it look anything like this back then?" I asked him.

"It looked exactly like this," he replied. I threw a *Really?* at him, and then another, but his certainty never wavered, nor his good humor. As usual, I started to get the sense he was watching it happen right before us; his eyes narrowed. "They met some very hard resistance in these woods," he said. "It took them three days to advance 1.5 kilometers." Less than a mile.

"Because they were so dense?" I asked.

"Yes," he said. "And very heavily fortified." We didn't have to go far for him to show me what he meant: bunkers, concrete behemoths, some built into bluffs with only a slender observation deck peeking out, others boldly squatting in ravines. We ducked into one of the latter (I figured Jean-Paul would know if there were badgers in it) and made our way through several passageways and chambers before emerging into a large room that still had—and I almost can't believe this, even as I'm typing it now—wood paneling on the walls. Jean-Paul directed me to one plank where some-one had scratched "XXXB" into the wood—perhaps the 30th Battalion? "I found this blockhouse only a few months ago," he said, and slapped the plank. "I've never seen anything like this before."

The Bois de Forêt can feel a bit like a magical playground, even if you're not really into this sort of thing: In addition to the bunkers there are, of course, trenches, and concrete vents for subterranean shelters, and concrete waterworks, and hidden entrances and egresses, and brick cook-stoves with iron surface plates, and a metal lampshade that still dangles from one branch even as another has grown through it, and the remains of a quarry that predates the war by centuries. "There's a famous photo of American soldiers resting and eating breakfast here," he told me, as we negotiated the vine-covered blocks down into the pit. "They were having Corn Willie"—their term for canned corned beef. A few minutes later, I stumbled into an upright stone tablet commemorating Willoughby Marks and George M. Hollister, two lieutenants from the 61st Infantry Regiment, part of the 5th Division, who were killed nearby on October 12, 1918. Not really a magical playground after all.

That same day Jean-Paul and I drove to Cunel, that village behind the American cemetery where the Germans had lined up and shot four civilians against the church wall (you really can still see the bullet holes in it) in September 1914. They are all buried in the village cemetery: The woman bore the beautiful name Euphrasie Pageot; the mayor, Narcisse Poulain, was 63 years old and had been awarded a *Legion d'Honneur* for his service during the Franco-Prussian War. Across the road is a large open pasture that Jean-Paul told me the Germans had used as an airfield throughout the war. "They always built their airstrips to align with the wind currents," he explained, once more bolstering my belief that they thought of absolutely everything.

Outside Cunel, Jean-Paul drove us up a tractor road that was pretty narrow but otherwise in good condition, coming to a stop next to a white stele—I use that term loosely; it actually kind of resembles a stylized tree trunk with stumps where its large branches were amputated—just off to the side, at the edge of a field. It's surrounded by four posts and a thin plastic chain, which I imagine is there for aesthetic purposes only, as it clearly doesn't and couldn't keep anyone or anything out, including that year's crop, which was lurching over and under its little white links. The marker itself is kept in nice shape, its surface scrubbed white, its bronze plaques clean and legible. The first of these, designed and cast to look like a tablet suspended by chains from a garland, reads:

IN THIS TRENCH

CAPTAIN

CHARLES DASHIELL HARRIS

6TH ENGINEERS

UNITED STATES ARMY

MET HIS DEATH

WHILE LEADING THE ATTACK

THAT DROVE THE GERMANS

FROM CLAIRS CHENES WOODS

OCTOBER 20TH, 1918

AGED 21 YEARS

HE WAS AWARDED

THE DISTINGUISHED SERVICE CROSS

"HIS INITIATIVE   AND BRAVERY

WERE AN   INSPIRATION

TO HIS   MEN."

And in between those last two columns is a likeness of the medal. The other plaque reads:

WITH A SMALL DETACHMENT

IN ADVANCE OF HIS COMPANY

CAPTAIN HARRIS CAPTURED

TWO GERMAN MACHINE GUNS

& THREE PRISONERS IN THE

TRENCH WITHIN THE ENCLOSURE

20 M TO THE SOUTH OF THIS SPOT

Though I have come across many individual memorials out in the field—here, and in the Woëvre, and Champagne, and Picardy—none have been as detailed, nor as specific, as this one. Still, it left me confused: There were no signs of any trenches or enclosures nearby—just fields and, beyond the one in which the marker stood, a stretch of forest. Jean-Paul must have read this in my face. "It's been moved," he said. "The marker used to be back in those woods somewhere."

"Do you know where, exactly?" I asked him.

"No," he said. "I've never been in there. But I bet we could find it."

I appreciate that kind of can-do attitude, so I just started walking gingerly through the field (as per Jean-Paul's code) to the tree line. It was slow going—the crop, whatever it was, was already waist high—and by the time I reached the woods, Jean-Paul had already found some longer but less laborious route to the same point and was waiting for me. It took us several minutes to find a break in the wall of branches and weeds large enough for us to step through, but as soon as we got inside, things opened up, and I could both see clearly and ambulate easily. It was still dense, though unlike the Bois de Forêt, this place didn't seem to have anything magical about it. The light that broke through the cover was stained a greenish brown in the process, lending the landscape an eerie air; it felt haunted. Maybe that was because I had just read a bit about a man who had been killed in these woods, although the marker had told only part of the story: Captain Harris was the son of Peter C. Harris, the adjutant general of the

United States Army, and had graduated fifth in his class at West Point. According to his obituary, he was mortally wounded so close to enemy lines that his stretcher-bearers, carrying him to the nearest aid station, were captured by the Germans.

"No," Jean-Paul said to himself, looking at a patch of ground. He scurried on to another—the man can move quickly, even in a dense forest—while I wandered off in a different direction, more slowly than he and with less certitude, until I spotted what I was pretty sure was a trench. I called out to him; he hurried over, examined the trench briefly and declared, in his singsong Dutch accent: "Yes, it's a German." We started canvassing the area and found a couple more, but they only convinced him that the first one was the place. "Here," he said, pointing to a spot where the earthen parapet widened and flattened. "This is where a machine gun would have been. The others didn't have something like this." It was remarkable to me that such a detail might still be evident a century on. Jean-Paul said it shouldn't be.

As we emerged from the woods and made our way back to Jean-Paul's car—really, a big Euro-mobile, the kind that can carry a dozen tourists, as is sometimes necessary—I got a good look at the field across the tractor road and noticed a very large divot in the earth, maybe thirty feet across and ten deep. The earth around it had been disturbed, too, and seemed to ripple away; a sprawling tree grew in the depression, the grass around it a much deeper green than the field beyond, likely because nothing mechanized could get in there to cut it. "Coastal artillery shell," Jean-Paul said, though whose he couldn't tell. It was jarring, this big hole out on its own, no others of any size within sight. Something really large had dropped out of the sky onto that spot, and had probably killed at least a few men, all of whose names were likely lost to history. For sure, there was no marker—not even buried in some woods—telling their story.

★ ★ ★

I can't be certain, but I suspect Jean-Paul got a bit tired at some point of having me ask him if this or that looked the same back during 14–18, and then marveling when he replied, almost invariably, that it did. If he did, I would guess it happened the morning he drove us out past Romagne and into the country, and pointed to a field off to our right. "There's the Roman wall," he said. "Part of the settlement that gave Romagne its name."

Actually, at that particular moment I did not marvel aloud at the steadfastness of the landscape, or anything else. What I did say was: "Where?"

"There!" he said, and jabbed his finger at the air as if pointing up at the Empire State Building from across the street. "By those trees."

I stared at the point he seemed to be referring to, squinted, and continued to see nothing. "You said that when we drove by here last year," I told him. "I didn't see it then, either."

"Why didn't you say anything?" he asked.

"I didn't want to be rude," I said, a response that makes no more sense to me now than it did then.

He stopped the Euro-thing and hopped out. "Come on," he said, and marched off toward a trio of arbors, a few hundred yards away. I followed, hoping with every few paces that it would suddenly become apparent to me. But it didn't, and soon we were at the trees. Jean-Paul looked at them, then at me, and raised his eyebrows; a silent *Voilà!*

I just shook my head.

"Right there!" he said, and stomped over in between two of the trees, crouched down, and slapped his hand against a slight hiccup in the ground, maybe a yard high, that ran behind the line of trees and across for some distance.

"That?" I said, and walked over and up to its tiny earthen crest; looking down at the other side, I saw that it flattened out as quickly as it had buckled up. I had been looking for New England–style stone walls. I'm an American; we don't have Roman ruins.

"Over here," Jean-Paul said, gesturing me to another section, where I spotted an arc-shaped hole in the side, burrowing into the ancient earthworks. "A Roman well," he said, then pivoted around and pointed just behind us to a squared U of concrete, obscured by tall grass. "A German well," he said. "Both probably still work, if you cleared them out. The Romans built things to last. The Germans knew that. They built roads on old Roman roads, wells near old Roman wells." What he didn't say—didn't have to—was that the Germans also built things to last. And those things did last, especially in a place like the Argonne, so different from Flanders, the Somme, Champagne.

"The poverty of this region protected its history," he explained. The land was not deemed valuable enough to be "developed"; in many cases, it wasn't even deemed valuable enough to merit undertaking the extensive and expensive processes necessary to reclaim it for farming. There are fields in the Argonne, a lot of them, that haven't even been worked since the first war, and others that haven't been worked since the second;

it's as if the farmers figure that after two there's bound to be a third, so why bother? In a strange way, as Olivier Jacquin said they joked in his family, the war may have even been good for some of the poor farmers of the region. "Eighty percent of the fences in this area are made from German railroad track," Jean-Paul told me. "Or from 'Spanish riders'"—metal barricades, typically wrapped in barbed wire—"or the sides of German beds." People took the doors off German bunkers for their rebuilt houses or barns; the building Jean-Paul uses as a warehouse, a few blocks from his museum, has one. Its walls are also lined with stones from German structures, one of which still bears the name of the *Pionier-Kompagnie* that built it. Of course, none of that war salvage would have been necessary to rebuild French fences, houses and barns if the original fences, houses and barns hadn't been destroyed. In the war.

I think what Jean-Paul was trying to do, in showing me the Roman wall and then the Roman well and, right next to it, the German well, was prove to me once and for all that what he'd told me every time I asked him *What did this look like back then?* was really true, as hard as it was for me to believe: *Exactly the same as it does now.* What he actually did, though, without knowing it, was push me toward a realization far more profound, one that took me a long while to figure out how to articulate. This field, this land: The Romans fought here. The Germans fought here. And in between the Romans and the Germans, the Merovingians fought here, and then the Carolingians, and then the knights and soldiers of one royal house, and then another, and then another. And before the Romans it was the Franks or the Celts or maybe both, and no doubt many others whose names I'll never know. So many names. But they were all *here.* They walked to this place to fight. They were *of* this place. It had always been thus. Always.

Until 1918.

That's when men, millions of them, sailed for weeks across an ocean, then packed themselves into railcars for days, then marched for hours and hours, all just to get *here.* To fight here. It was the first time in all of human history that an entire army from the New World set off to fight in the Old. It was a new kind of army, too, unlike any the world had ever seen, one composed entirely of citizens and residents, not subjects, men of several different races and many different ethnic and national backgrounds, men who came to France in 1918 not to stay but just to win the fight and then go back home. Which they did; and then they did. And it changed everything.

Everything.

Something really big happened that had never happened before, and afterward, nothing was the same. The world we live in today is the world wrought by the Great War; the world that existed before it is gone, entirely and forever. That moment—men showing up here, in this field, and others like it nearby—was the watershed. Those men—doughboys, Sammies, soldiers of the American Expeditionary Forces—almost certainly didn't realize the greater significance of their actions here. They probably didn't even spot those two wells.

I didn't, either. Until I did.

★ ★ ★

A year after he caught me trespassing on his property and punished me with a five-hour educational tour, I met Jean-Pierre Brouillon again at his farm. "My old friend Tarzan," he greeted me, shaking my hand vigorously and slapping me on the back before climbing into his 4x4 and beckoning me to follow. We drove off and revisited all the things he had shown me on his land a year earlier, the fields where machine-gun nests had been set up and narrow-gauge rail laid, the woods with their trenches and two enormous German blockhouses. A bit more of the Musarde farmhouse appeared to have crumbled in the interim; M. Brouillon's mind hadn't changed, though: He still insisted he knew nothing about Rommel stopping there in 1914, and still steered the conversation at every opportunity to 1918, and MacArthur. "He had to take La Tuilerie several times, you know, before he managed to hold it," he told me. Examining the house again, I had to restrain myself from asking aloud if the place had really been worth all that trouble. Of course, it hadn't always been the roofless, tree-filled husk before us now. It had once been a house, a home, and, judging by what remained of its windows and walls and the beams I could see poking out tentatively here and there, a pretty nice one. I mentioned this to Jean-Paul de Vries the next time I saw him.

"That's probably my favorite area in the Argonne," he said.

"Jean-Pierre told me the house hasn't been occupied since 1964," I said.

"Maybe," he mused. "But the family who lived there until then had really been broken in 1944. Two of the sons took some butter one night and set off for the American fuel depot to try to trade it for fuel, but they probably took a shortcut, went someplace they shouldn't have been. Some

Americans on patrol saw them coming in the dark and warned them to stop, but they didn't, so they shot them. Killed them. They didn't know who they were. And they didn't know what to do with the bodies. So they just left them in front of the church in Bantheville. Mass was being celebrated inside. It was Christmas Eve."

Bantheville: where six civilians had been executed on September 9, 1914, because of a misunderstanding sparked by German soldiers firing off a salute to one of their fallen officers. It's a sunny place, narrow streets and lazy hills, people outside on their lawns, working on cars, smoking, talking to each other; the first time I went there, looking for the monument to those six shot civilians that Jean-Paul had told me about, two different older men approached and asked me if they could be of assistance.

I saw Jean-Pierre again shortly after that conversation with Jean-Paul, but didn't share that story with him. I assume he knows it and didn't choose to mention it to me, perhaps because I'm American and he didn't want me to feel guilty. It wasn't his family; his father acquired the property later. It was his father, he told me, who first told him about MacArthur, the narrow-gauge railroad, the Kriemhilde Stellung, those blockhouses. He'd known the farm all his life, had spent time in those woods years before he bought it. "He was in the resistance," M. Brouillon told me. "They used those blockhouses. They were still in excellent condition during the second war. Farmers didn't try to blow them up until the 1950s." It was also his father who'd first told him about Americans. "He used to say the Germans were very orderly and disciplined," he told me. "But they were like wild pigs—they just ran straight, that's all. The Americans, by contrast, were very relaxed and laid-back, but when the time for action came, they always stepped up and got the job done."

"Is that right?" I asked.

"*Oui,*" he said. "And I'll tell you something else he told me: The Germans were very aloof to civilians. The Americans were just the opposite."

I can't say how much that part of the story is responsible for the abiding fondness so many people I met Over There have for Americans, long after Americans have forgotten them and this place and what their own ancestors did here a century ago. But that affection—that devotion, really—is what drives them to keep alive the memory of those deeds, and that friendship, in the hopes that some future generation of Americans might someday return to reclaim it.

✴ ✴ ✴

One of the very first things I ever saw in this part of France, even before I met Patrick and heard those two urban legends, was the 14–18 monument in Dun-sur-Meuse. It's nothing special, really—an awkward-looking *poilu* charging forward, clutching his Lebel rifle with Rosalie bayonet at an angle that makes you think *if he trips, that's going to be trouble.* On the front of the statue's pedestal is a tablet, in French and English, commemorating the soldiers of the 5th Division who fell while liberating the town in 1918. But I didn't understand, yet, how rare a thing that was. What really made an impression on me that day was the *Aux Victimes Civiles* section of the monument, engraved on the back of the pedestal. There were three names listed under it—Charles Seillier, Albert LeFevre and Mme. Ambroise-Adam—and, under them, in a different font, the dates 1939–1945, and two more entries: Mme. Céline Thierion; and Les Familles Salomon.

Now, I knew all about what the occupying Nazis, and some French collaborators, had done to French Jews during World War II. But it's one thing to read about something like that in a book, or even on a museum wall, and quite another to see it acknowledged, or at least sort of acknowledged, at the scene of the crime. I say sort of because, unlike that marker in Sainte-Menehould, which I only discovered six years later, there is no mention of what, exactly, happened to the families Salomon. So when David and Marian Howard introduced me to Jean Marie at his museum in Dun that day, I asked him if he knew any more. He said he didn't.

A few months later, though, he sent me an e-mail telling me he had looked into it. He still had no idea about Mme. Thierion, but the Salomons, he had discovered, were a well-known family in Dun, where they'd owned a butcher shop and a popular grocery-café. The paterfamilias, Edmond, had been a 14–18 veteran; he and his wife, Louise, had two young sons, Robert and Jacques. Louise's elderly aunt Sarah Israël lived with them, too. All were "evacuated" from Dun after the Nazis rolled in—by whom, Nazis or French neighbors, was not specified—and ultimately deported to Auschwitz, where they were murdered upon arrival, except for Robert, their elder son, who perished at Buchenwald on March 9, 1945, just a month before it was liberated by the 89th US Infantry Division, the same unit that had taken Stenay on the morning of November 11, 1918. In 1995, the fiftieth anniversary of the second war's end, there was a push to add the names of each family member to the monument, rather than just "Les Familles Salomon." Twenty years later, it still hadn't happened.

On the day that I had met M. Marie, after David and Marian had taken me to his museum and then to Mme. B's house, the three of us—David, Marian and I—drove out to a large parking lot at the edge of the forest near the village of Duzey, about twenty-five miles southeast of Stenay and twenty northeast of Verdun. On the edge of the lot, in between the macadam and the trees, something really, really big lay on its side, longer than an eighteen-wheeler and painted a grayish blue. "The Big Max," David pronounced. "A naval gun."

The word "gun," while technologically and historically appropriate, seemed rather insufficient to the task. By the end of the war, everybody was using these—I mentioned earlier finding a chunk of an American coastal artillery shell on the grounds of what had once been the Porta Lager—but, as was typically the case when it came to martial technology, the Germans were first. In 1914, they tore through supposedly invincible fortifications at Liège and Antwerp in Belgium with their notorious "Big Bertha," a 420-millimeter howitzer with a range of nine miles that terrorized their enemies and symbolized their ruthlessness. In 1918, they shelled the French capital from seventy-five miles away with their "Paris Gun," the largest cannon ever made: its 110-foot barrel hurled a 200-plus-pound, 234-millimeter shell into the stratosphere, the first time humans ever achieved such heights.

The Big Max had much greater range than Big Bertha, and fired 380-millimeter shells, much larger than those hurled into space by the Paris Gun. While it had ostensibly been designed for ships, the German fleet never did get to do much in that war, being pinned down in harbor by the British Navy, so someone decided those big guns would be put to better use elsewhere. Here's what that entailed: Suitable locations had to be identified and made ready; the guns, which weighed 220 tons, had to be dissembled, transported somehow to rail facilities, loaded onto special flatcars, moved by rail to a point as close to the new location as possible, removed from the flatcars, transported somehow to the deployment site, and set up. And "set up" meant more than just maneuvering it onto some rods. This was, after all, a naval gun, designed and calibrated to be used on a battleship at sea. An installation had to be designed and built that replicated such an environment. It included an enormous concrete vat, filled with water, as well as holds, a deck, and metal pivots and girders; they're all still there, as are several tunnels the Germans built on-site for various purposes. Rail was laid down—it's still there, too—to carry the shells, each of which was nearly seven feet in length and weighed more than 1,600 pounds (there's one of those there, too—a dummy, I imagine), to the breech, the door of which weighed two tons. Special units were created and trained solely for the purpose of operating this one gun. When fired, flames would shoot out of the Big Max for a distance of nearly fifty feet. The gun was so large, and contained so much steel, that *Pioniere* had to outfit the surrounding area with metal rods, lest it draw lightning.

Oh, and the most important thing: This deadly behemoth had to be extremely well camouflaged. The French must never know where it was—not only to protect it, but because its very purpose was to terrorize them by raining down enormous shells upon Verdun without the French having any idea where they were coming from. The Big Max had a range of nearly twenty-five miles; it could hit Verdun, and even points beyond, easily. The Germans even hoped to wreak havoc on La Voie Sacrée with it. They never quite got that far, but they did an awful lot of damage with it, anyway, and killed an awful lot of people besides. How many, exactly, will never be known; some of their bones, I am sure, have yet to surface.

As I have said before, the Germans of the First World War were not the Nazis of the Second; I go to great lengths to segregate the two in my mind. And maybe, if the war had gone into Germany in 1919, instead of ending here, the French and British and Americans would have unleashed such things upon German civilians in German cities and towns. All I can say for sure is that the Germans did do it. And that, as you now know, they went to great trouble to do it. And that most of the top German commanders in the second war, and many of the officers, and quite a few of the soldiers, had also served in the first war. Maybe, somehow, there's a Moving Sidewalk of Great Consequences running directly from the Big Max to Les Familles Salomon; or, conversely, maybe Hermann Katz's and Ludwig Salinger's personal memorials still stand in the German cemetery in Thiaucourt because one of the Nazi soldiers who came upon them remembered that he'd actually served with them the first time around.

I cannot deny it: War tourism can be a strange pursuit. No: By definition, it *is* a strange pursuit. If you can dash through trenches, poke in and out of bunkers, swing down to blockhouses on a vine, you must as a matter of course possess the ability to momentarily blot from your mind the knowledge that men died and killed in these places—horribly, gruesomely and far too young. That ability enables you to delight at the discovery of a shell that could have once—could still—blow you to pieces; or a bullet, even though it may have passed through someone else's body before coming to rest in the dirt; or a button, even though it may have fallen off the tunic of a 28-year-old father of three who breathed his last on that very spot. Or it enables you to feel blasé about spotting a bottle that some teenager may have swigged from five minutes before a red-hot piece of shrapnel tore through his heart, because it's the seventeenth bottle you've seen that day. It's not your fault. You are alive; these things happened a hundred years ago.

But you are a human being. At some point, that ability will probably desert you, even momentarily, and you will experience a sense of—well, maybe not quite guilt; but *obligation*. You may walk slowly through cemeteries, peruse each marker you pass. You may scrutinize memorials—village, individual—and read the names out loud. You may make connections: between naval guns and deported families, pigs' feet and the destruction of a continent. You will, for certain, want to make sense of it all. And you will, just as certainly, be unable to. Sooner or later, you will come to that understanding. All you can really do, for certain, is look at things.

Late in the day, after we were done with the Big Max and the sun had started its slow process of retiring for the night, David said: "One more thing. I think we have time." We drove for about forty-five minutes, to the village of Lion-devant-Dun—Lion before Dun, as in Dun-sur-Meuse—then headed out into the country and turned onto what appeared to be a logging road, a rough one that ran up a pretty steep incline. Fifteen minutes later we crested and emerged onto a grassy plateau. A sign pointed in two directions: trenches to the right, marker to the left. We went left.

"There was a hermitage up here at various times," David told me as we stepped out of his car. "This was a Roman site, and then Gallo-Roman." It's easy to see why they were all drawn here: Romans, Gallo-Romans, religious ascetics. The Côte Saint-Germain, according to a small green sign up top, stands at 336 meters, or 1,102 feet—taller than the Butte de Vauquois or Montfaucon. From its peak, the view extends into the Argonne, the Ardennes, Belgium, even Luxembourg. In 1918, you could have easily seen into Germany, too. "This point marks the end of the Heights of the Meuse," David told me. "Once the Americans took it, the battle was won." The doughboys who captured it must have felt as much: The spot commands everything around it—forest, farms, meadows, lakes, streams. They could see how little was left of the dreaded Hindenburg Line; how little stood between them and Sedan, and Germany. Those doughboys belonged to the 5th Division; and, yes, they put up a marker here afterward, a stout fieldstone obelisk different from the rest. You can't begrudge them. It took them two days to wrest Côté Saint-Germain from the Germans. Two days of fierce, desperate combat. By the time it was done, on November 7, the Germans had already dispatched a party to negotiate an armistice.

Driving back down that rough road, David slowed his car as we passed a large protuberance in the dirt off to our left, a great big rounded earthen lump. "A burial mound," he said. "Celtic."

✭ ✭ ✭

The last time I saw Jean-Paul de Vries, we set off, as we usually did, in his Euro-vehicle to look around. Our first stop was a German command post in the woods a couple of miles outside Romagne. Of all the ruins out there in the Argonne, it's certainly one of the most impressive, well hidden despite the fact that it sits maybe fifty yards from the road. Built into a natural slope in the forest floor, it's big and broad and very square, the corners of the steps that lead up to its parapet still sharp, the ones that lead down into the bunker still steady: an imposing structure that would make you feel safe if it were yours and scared if it weren't. It was one of the first significant sites Jean-Paul discovered when he started canvassing the area, back in the 1990s when his explorations were limited to places he could get to on foot. He'd been visiting it for many years before he discovered, scribbled in pencil on a wall in one of its subterranean chambers:

KANSAS CITY
MISSOURI U.S.A.
OCT. 30, 1918

As he recounted that story and shined a light on the graffiti, I chided him, reminding him that he'd shown me the same site, and the same graffiti, the previous year; and that he'd taken me to see it in 2009, as well. I knew, too, that this was something he took just about everybody to see, and I started to feel like a tourist whose double-decker bus stops in Times Square so everyone aboard can grab lunch at the Bubba Gump Shrimp Company. "OK," he said, and smiled. "Let's go."

We drove about fifteen minutes south to Montblainville, a small farming village where the Germans had taken the relatively modest château for their headquarters. They installed bunkers all around it, including one in the château's cellar, for which they added a concrete appendage onto the side of the house. It's still there today, and in very fine condition; it looks a bit like one of those 1920s toasters you see at flea markets. The château and farm, both named La Forge, are presently owned by a gentleman from Holland whom Jean-Paul knows, and who was happy to show me the bunker. He was especially proud of its two doors, an iron outer one and a wooden inner one, both of which were original, in excellent shape, and working. "Châteaux all had tunnels," Jean-Paul told me. "The Germans just expanded them." He walked me out to the woods that lined the house's driveway, where I discovered an odd wonderland of holes and concrete, the latter sheltering entrances or exits or who knows what and shaped like tuffets and bars of soap and bread ovens. "I discovered these in the winter," he told me. "I saw steam rising up out of the holes, and went to take a look."

We headed back toward Romagne by way of Varennes, where he showed me a steep hill once laden with German dugouts; the remains of a German narrow-gauge rail station; some very well preserved open-air baths that would not have looked out of place in ancient Rome. Behind the wall of the old town cemetery, he led me to a whitish marker, maybe four feet tall—German—which had sat there for a century, covered by vines and unnoticed by the local population until a friend of his thought to cut them down and see what might be hiding underneath.

I nodded appreciatively, but it must not have been enough, because Jean-Paul turned to me and said: "OK, I'll show you something *I* found recently." And we drove off toward Romagne, pulling to a stop alongside a road near the little hamlet of Éclisfontaine. I recognized the field—we had visited it a few days earlier; the Wild West Division had crossed it, Jean-Paul had told me, while heading toward woods filled with German machine guns—but hadn't noticed, or paid attention to, a copse of trees a couple hundred yards off the road. Jean-Paul hadn't noticed it, either, he told me, until a few months earlier, when suddenly he did.

"What is it?" I asked.

"Come on," he said, already walking briskly into the field. The trees weren't very large, but they were just dense enough to hide that which had been built not to stand out in the first place: A stone barrel-vaulted arch receding back into an earthen rise, a huge half-pipe, closed at one end, covering a long, narrow little pool. At the far end, water still trickled into it from a cement spout set into a small opening, shaped like a doorway, in the back wall. I looked at Jean-Paul and waited.

"A bathhouse," he said, and suddenly I saw it clearly. It was solid and complete, no chocks in the walls, which were as watertight as any bunker I'd been in. It was a hot day; I could easily picture a company of German soldiers stripping down and splashing around. If the water level had been a bit higher, I would have happily done the same.

"When the Americans took it," Jean-Paul told me, "they turned it into an aid station. I found lots of things in there," he added, pointing to a stream that flowed out of the front. "Lots of buttons, German and American. I even found a sign from a Pierce-Arrow ambulance." We walked out and straddled the running water, gazed into it, but I spotted nothing. I didn't care. After all the bunkers and blockhouses and tunnels and craters, all the bullets and barbed wire, shells and shrapnel—after all the sites and artifacts related to killing, and dying—here was a place men came to get clean, and to heal. What could I have found in that stream that might possibly have meant more to me, after months and months of war tourism, than this?

"I've known this farmer for a long time," he explained, "but he never mentioned this to me. He said he didn't know it was anything special. Can you believe that?" He was quiet for a moment. "I'll tell you, it's very special to me," he said, softly. "I don't bring anyone here."

✳ ✳ ✳

Whenever possible, I had lunch at Jean-Paul's café in Romagne, whether or not we had gone out exploring that morning. It's a pleasant spot where at least one other person is sure to speak English; the Wi-Fi works well— no small thing if the SIM card you bought from a French telecom company was supposed to include two gigabytes of data but no one at the aforementioned company can help you figure out how to access it—and it's usually cool despite the lack of air-conditioning, and the food is pretty good. My favorite item on the menu is a baguette with lettuce and some other vegetables and *rosette*, a type of cold cut, which I got most days, even though Jean-Paul looked at me as if I were crazy the first time I asked him for some mustard. Apparently, the birthplace of Dijon doesn't know what to do with it.

I always tried to take a nice long lunch, French style, during which I would read a book and respond to e-mails from people who were just waking up back home. I've eaten there with Jean-Pierre Brouillon and Dave Bedford, but mostly I've been there alone, except for Jean-Paul, scurrying around doing this or that, and Darius, his Beauceron—a French German shepherd—who really enjoyed trotting over to me when I was seated, standing up on his hind legs and clamping his jaws gently around my upper arm. Sometimes he stayed in that position for five or ten minutes. If I could find a place like that here, I'd go there every day.

One afternoon, after I finished my salad and *rosette* hoagie, I got up and walked over to the front counter to ask for an ice cream just as a school bus pulled up out front and a couple dozen children, nine or ten years old, spilled out and filed inside. Jean-Paul emerged from out back and scurried up to greet them. He started telling them a bit about his museum, but a few of them, it seemed, were more fixated on the man standing behind him, silently waiting for a Popsicle. Jean-Paul looked at them, then at me, then back at them. "Ah," he said. *"C'est un Américain."* They stared at me; a few nodded, earnestly. One boy stepped forward and shook my hand.

HISTORY AND MEMORY

I had a lot to contend with in rural northern France—lack of English, lack of gas stations, lack of cell phone coverage, lack of wireless data, lack of air-conditioning, lack of ice cubes, lack of restrooms when you could find a gas station, lack of American-style hotels with spacious American-style hotel rooms, lack of NPR, lack of CNN, lack of pumps at unmanned gas stations that would accept an American credit card that didn't have one of those digital chips in it—but one thing I never had to deal with was a lack of parking. Even in Château-Thierry, which was about as close to Paris as anyplace I spent significant time, I could always count on finding a spot in the town square, the Place de l'Hôtel de Ville. Technically, you were supposed to feed a municipal meter—one of those centralized machines that spits out a ticket that you then display on your dashboard—but the first half hour was free, and you could always go out and get a new free ticket every thirty minutes; the guy at the cell phone store told me that, even as he failed to tell me that the two gigabytes of data that were supposedly included with the SIM card he was selling me existed only on paper. I'm a New Yorker; I hate driving around looking for parking at least as much as I love the hard-to-find pastry Americans call a Napoleon. In France, they call them *mille-feuille*—a thousand leaves—and they are everywhere. So is ready parking. In most of the towns and villages I visited while following the trail of the American Expeditionary Forces in the First World War, I could have left my Renault Scénic in the middle of the street and no one would have cared, or even noticed.

With one exception.

Compiègne. It's a city, sure. But I'd been to much bigger cities—Reims, Nancy, Metz—and found an open spot almost immediately. Maybe I just picked a bad day to go to Compiègne. It was a Saturday, in June; that probably didn't help. Some kind of festival seemed to be going on. Maybe more than one. Compiègne is about fifty miles north of Paris. Before the revolution, it was one of three seats of the royal government, the other two being Fontainebleau and Versailles. Kings had been spending time here since at least the fourteenth century, especially in summer, as the dense forests that surround the city made excellent hunting grounds. In 1750, during the reign of Louis XV, renovations on the royal château, built in 1378, began; they were completed nearly forty years later, well into the reign of Louis XVI. Napoleon renovated it again, and spent a lot of time there. So did Napoleon III, before the Prussians captured him at Sedan. The château, now a museum, is enormous and sits right in the middle of town; the square out in front is very large, and full of parking spaces. All taken.

Eventually I found something in an alley about a fifteen-minute walk away, then hurried back to the city center through a series of open plazas, each of which was hosting a band or dancers or what I believe were contortionists. No one spoke English, which didn't bother me a bit until I found my way to the tourism bureau and discovered that no one spoke English there, either. That surprised me, I'll admit, though even that wouldn't have bothered me so much if anyone there could have given me directions in any language to the place I was looking for. But they couldn't, not really. One told me to find a road she couldn't spell for me and turn left at the site where something *used to be*. Another drew me a crude map on the back of a flyer for the festival that was going on outside. That was the best they could do; this place, it seems, was very hard to find. Which had been precisely the point in 1918.

On November 7 of that year, a delegation left Berlin in a small motorcade and headed west, into France. They quietly slipped across the French lines under a flag of truce, though apparently not quietly enough; the sight of them immediately touched off rumors of an armistice, which spread throughout Allied ranks and then across the ocean. The rumors, presented as fact, actually graced the front pages of American newspapers. They all had to print retractions shortly thereafter. I imagine they broke quite a few hearts.

The rumors were right in one respect: The motorcade was carrying a party of Germans into France for the purposes of negotiating an armistice. Both sides had their reasons for keeping the negotiations, and even the fact of their existence, quiet. Not long after they crossed enemy lines, the German delegation stealthily boarded a French railcar to carry them to their final destination; the coach had once belonged to Napoleon III. The top-ranking military officer in the German delegation, Major General Detlev von Winterfeldt, was the son of the Prussian who had drafted the terms of France's surrender in 1871. So much symbolism; so much secrecy. In the predawn darkness, the coach slid into a railway siding deep in the Forest of Compiègne, about a mile from the village of Rethonde. When the sun rose, the Germans could see another coach parked on tracks about fifty yards away: The field headquarters of *Maréchal* Ferdinand Foch, Supreme Commander of the Allied Forces. The negotiations would take place there. The rail hub was surrounded by dense, tall trees, and invisible from the air. Foch had chosen the spot. A sign there today reads: "The quiet seclusion of the forest seemed more suitable for such an occasion than his General Headquarters." It's a nice little bit of historical spin.

The truth is, Foch wasn't in the mood for niceties. Germany had invaded his country four years and three months earlier, and occupied much of it ever since. The Germans had killed more than a million *poilus* and an unknowable number of civilians. They had laid much of France to waste. Now, he knew, the Germans were finished, their military exhausted, their country swept by mutiny and revolution. And they were coming to Foch, *Mütze* in hand. He wasn't about to lift his boot from their neck. Not a millimeter. The Germans, knowing they had no leverage, agreed to Foch's extensive list of demands—read aloud to them by Foch's aide, General

Maxime Weygand—by 11:00 A.M. that morning: immediate evacuation by German forces of all occupied territories in Luxembourg, Belgium and France, including Lorraine and Alsace; immediate release of all Allied prisoners of war, without reciprocation; immediate surrender of twenty-five thousand machine guns, five thousand artillery pieces, three thousand trench mortars, all submarines, and more aircraft and warships than Germany actually possessed; and "reparation for damage done."

All that remained was to get final approval from Berlin and put it all in writing. General von Winterfeldt asked Foch to declare a cease-fire, to take effect immediately, while the bureaucrats and diplomats did whatever they had to do. Foch refused. The war would proceed. The Germans had seventy-two hours to sign the deal, or it would evaporate. The next one would have even more onerous terms. If there were a next one at all.

Historians typically cite the Treaty of Versailles as the point at which the seeds of the Second World War were sown, but I think it actually happened here, in the Forest of Compiègne, on the morning of November 8, 1918. The armistice was supposed to be a halt in the fighting, not a surrender, but Foch's terms for it were so severe that there was no way the Germans would ever be able to negotiate or resist the terms of whatever peace treaty the Allies would ultimately hand them to sign. They would have absolutely nothing to bargain with. In truth, they already had almost nothing to bargain with. The German Army was on the brink of collapse; so was Germany itself. Foch knew the strength of his hand, and the weakness of his opponent's. He took everything he could, including the Germans' dignity. Had he left them a little something, I believe, there might not have been a Second World War. I have presented this hypothesis to just about every French person I know. Most dismiss it out of hand. They are closer, I am sure, to understanding Foch's mindset at that moment, to appreciating the incomprehensible losses the French had suffered in a war of German aggression. Foch was smart, and ruthless. Without him and men like him, they invariably tell me, France would have lost the war. I don't mention that they did lose the war, twenty-two years later. On the exact same spot.

If you, too, are inclined to doubt my assessment that the roots of the Second World War trace back to this place on that morning, I'll tell you this: In June 1940, after the Nazi *Wehrmacht* invaded and defeated France, Hitler insisted on traveling personally to the Forest of Compiègne to make the French sign a new armistice *in the same railroad car.* The site had changed quite a bit since 1918: The French had cleared the trees from the hub, erected cement blocks to mark the precise spots where the two rail-road carriages had been parked, and turned the entire area into a monument, the *Clairière* (or glade) *de l'Armistice.* The train car itself had been moved into a new museum, built at the site for that purpose. The carriage contained all the original furniture, and signs indicating which delegate had occupied which seat at the long table inside. Hitler had it hauled out of the museum and set up on the tracks in the exact same spot it had occupied in November 1918. I'm sure he appreciated the French having marked it.

Hitler made a point of sitting in Foch's chair during the talks, which were as one-sided as they had been the first time around, albeit in the other direction. The French, still tired and depleted from 14–18, had been defeated on the battlefield in just six weeks, and were in no position to refuse Hitler's terms of surrender. The northern part of the country, much of which had been destroyed by the Germans in the first war, would be occupied by them, the southern part by a puppet government based in Vichy and headed up by Philippe Pétain, the hero of Verdun. After the new armistice was approved by France's minister of defense—General Maxime Weygand, who had read the terms of the armistice to the German delegation in 1918, and who also later collaborated with Germany as a high official in the Vichy regime—and signed, Hitler ordered the train car moved to Berlin, and the *Clairière de l'Armistice* destroyed, including the large raised cement platform in the middle of the circular rail hub, in which was embedded, in big metal letters, an inscription that is the same today as it was then:

> HERE
> 11 NOVEMBER 1918
> SUCCUMBED
> THE CRIMINAL PRIDE
> OF THE GERMAN EMPIRE
> VANQUISHED
> BY THE
> FREE PEOPLES
> WHOM IT ATTEMPTED
> TO ENSLAVE

It reminds one a bit of the inscription on the original monument at Bathelémont—the one that mentioned "German imperialism, the scourge of humanity"—which, you may recall, was also destroyed by the Nazis. They were rather thin-skinned, apparently.

Like that monument and the *Clairière de l'Armistice,* the museum was rebuilt after the second war and is, in most ways, like just about every other 14–18 museum in France, with its uniforms, weapons and informational panels. It does, however, have two things no other museum (or, at least, no other museum I've ever been to, and I've been to quite a few) has: an entire room filled with wooden stereoscope viewing boxes, each filled with dozens of stereoview slides of war scenes; and the railway coach in which the 1918 armistice was signed. Sort of.

The French spent four years occupied by the Nazis in the second war, which gave them a lot of time to think about what they would do with the *Clairière de l'Armistice* once the Germans were gone. They decided to rebuild it exactly as it had been before 1940. Unfortunately, as I mentioned earlier, the Germans took the monument's centerpiece, Foch's train car, back to Germany with them after the second armistice was signed. I'm sure the French had hopes of recovering it if and when the Germans were eventually defeated; but as American troops approached the place where it was on display, in April 1945, SS troops burned it to the ground. After the war, the French, distraught at the loss of such a national symbol but determined to re-create the *Clairière* nonetheless, tracked down an identical railway carriage, one that had been manufactured at the same time, and in the same series, as Foch's. They outfitted it exactly as Foch's had been in November 1918, complete with long table, chairs, and signs indicating who had sat where. They even included some original artifacts from the scene, among them Foch's telephone, and—and I have no idea where they found this—one of the *maréchal*'s half-smoked cigars.

It's a remarkable re-creation and, based on what I saw, very popular with tourists, most of them French. It's no flimflam—there are signs by the car telling the story of how the original was destroyed and replaced by a contemporary twin—but visitors nonetheless regard it as the real thing, and spend a lot of time peering through its windows. An awful lot of the twentieth century emanates from this (almost) one train car—so much, really, that (almost) is more than enough.

The small room that leads from the carriage to the exit is, it will not surprise you, a little gift shop. It sells the usual tchotchkes: mugs, plates, binoculars, tiny soldiers and cannons and aircraft carriers. For six euros, you can get a die-cast replica of the railway carriage you just visited. I did. It's the only souvenir I ever bought in all my time in France.

✷ ✷ ✷

Something strange happened. In 2014, following the publication of my last book, *The New York Times* sent me back to France to write a four-part series on American World War I battle sites Over There. That's not the strange part; the strange part is that, after the last installment ran, in December of that year, I received an e-mail from a reporter at *L'Est Républicain,* a daily newspaper in Lorraine. The reporter, Léa Boschiero, had read that last piece, which was mostly about the Argonne, and was surprised and gratified that someone had written an article about La Meuse, an area that doesn't get many American visitors, for a large American newspaper. She asked if I would mind answering some questions about it. She wanted, in essence, to write an article about an article. I said I would be happy to answer her questions. When it was all done and her article published—they titled it *La Meuse dans le New York Times*—she said I should let her know the next time I was in the area, so we could meet for a drink.

Five months later, we did, only by that time a drink had grown into lunch with her and her editor, Frédéric Plancard. They treated me to a fine meal at a restaurant on the deck of a boat in Verdun; the mayor, seated a few tables away, came over just to say hello. A day or two earlier, Léa had written to ask if there was anything in particular I wanted to see in the vicinity. I replied that I would like to visit La Voie Sacrée in the company of people who knew more about it than I did. That would be fine, she said. At lunch, we talked about this and that: Verdun's plans for the centennial of the battle the following year; the different ways different generations there regard Philippe Pétain; why the French have such high regard for Jerry Lewis. As we were finishing up our crème brûlée (not to be confused with the Bois Brûlé), Léa sheepishly confessed that they were hoping to write another article about me, and that a photographer from the paper— Franck Lallemand; his last name means "the German" in French—had already been dispatched to meet them on The Sacred Way. I said that was fine. I wasn't sure there was anything worth writing about, and I probably would have skipped the wine if I had known what they were up to, but *pour quoi pas?*

The article ran the following day, teased on the front page as *Un Écrivain Américain sur le Champ de Bataille* ("An American Writer on the

Battlefield") and continuing inside under the headline *Le Grand Reporter de 14–18*. I didn't know in advance when it would run, and I couldn't remember if I had said anything really stupid around Léa and Frédéric—or if my frank assessment of Jerry Lewis's oeuvre would offend people—so I didn't tell anyone about it. It didn't matter: People saw the article (which did not mention M. Lewis) anyway. Denis and Bénédicte Hebrard saw it. Jean-Paul de Vries saw it. Jean-Pierre Brouillon saw it. Dave Bedford saw it. Patrick Simons and Christophe Wilvers saw it. It seems everyone in a pretty large section of Lorraine reads *L'Est Républicain*. Cover to cover. For the next two weeks, wherever I went, people recognized me. They mimicked my stance in the picture—arms crossed over my chest with one hand clutching my camera, a goofy pose that had been the photographer's idea. (Sorry, Franck, but you know it's true. It's also true that the angle and lens made my arms and hands look enormous and my head tiny, but they couldn't mimic that.) But a lot of people also e-mailed Léa asking her how long I was going to be in the area, and telling her they would be happy to show me this or that if I had the time. That's how I met some of the people, and saw some of the things, I've written about here.

Over lunch, in between talk of Pétain and Lewis, I asked both of them if they had any personal connection to the war. Frédéric immediately volunteered that he was a cousin of the first *poilu* killed in the war, Corporal Jules-André Peugeot. It had happened on August 2, 1914—a day before war was formally declared—in a little French village way down by the Swiss border called Joncherey. Peugeot, a distant relation of the automobile manufacturers, had been born in Étupes, another small town on the Swiss border; he was 21 years old and stationed with a small cohort in a remote outpost that none of them, I'm sure, expected would ever see any fighting. And it never did, after that day. But a little before ten that morning, a German cavalry patrol that had just charged across the border was spotted approaching the village. Peugeot called out for them to stop; told them they were under arrest. The patrol's leader, Lieutenant Albert Mayer, who hailed from Alsace, took aim with a pistol that had been engraved *Pro Bellum*—For the War—and shot Peugeot in the shoulder. Someone—either Peugeot or another *poilu,* or maybe both—fired back at Mayer and killed him. Peugeot died about a half hour later. Frédéric and Corporal Peugeot share a common direct ancestor, Peugeot's great-great-grandfather Jean-George Peugeot, who died in 1851. Frédéric's great-grandfather Edmond Rigoulot was a year older than Jules-André Peugeot and went to school with him in Étupes. "He was wounded several times in the war," Frédéric told me. "I knew him." I had heard the story of Jules-André Peugeot's death before, but had never imagined I might meet, by happenstance, someone related to him. Now, though, I realize that it was inevitable, and that it's entirely possible I met even more of Corporal Peugeot's relatives without even knowing it. France is larger in area than any other nation in Europe west of Russia; it has more people in it than any besides Russia and the united Germany. But it is, in many ways, a small country. And even smaller since the First World War.

✶ ✶ ✶

Late that afternoon, while driving from Verdun back to Denis's *chambre d'hôtes* in Le Neufour, I decided to stop by Romagne-sous-les-Côtes. I thought I might be able to find the house on my own, but, small though the village is, I couldn't, so I asked a fellow who was working on a car in his yard for directions. It was just two streets up, he said, and even gave me the house number. I recognized the place immediately. Madame George, who had led me over rough tractor roads to the Henry Gunther monument a year earlier, was working in her garden as I pulled up. I thought she might not remember me, but she smiled and beckoned me to come and sit down with her at a table she had outside. I told her I was happy to see her again. She smiled and said, "The same."

I asked her if she'd ever told anyone about our shared adventure a year earlier. She stood up, walked into her house, and emerged a few minutes later holding what looked like a sheet of copy paper. She handed it to me: It was actually five sheets, printed front and back and stapled together twice along the left margin. A colorful banner up top read *Le Romagnole*. The local newspaper; published, I imagine, at irregular intervals. There were a few one-line items:

Summer is ending soon. Enjoy the last beautiful days.

The proposed multi-activity room has taken a big step forward. Companies were chosen, and we expect the approval of the proper authorities for the start of work.

The pizza party on September 13 should be the last event in the hall as we know it today.

The renovation of the cemetery gate should be completed in the coming
weeks by the afternoon recreation volunteers.

A typo in the last item was corrected by pen. The rest of the front page was
a list of phone numbers—the police station, the firehouse, the *mairie,* the
nearest post office and pharmacy and hospital. I wasn't sure what I was
supposed to be doing with all that information.

She reached across and flipped to page 6, a spot typically reserved, at
least in American tabloids, for gossip. Instead, up toward the top, I saw a
picture of myself—the jacket photo from my last book, no doubt scanned
from the copy I had left with her as a token (symbolic, given that she spoke
no English) of my gratitude a year earlier. Above it, the headline:

A PERSON OF HONOR IN THE VILLAGE

A PROVIDENTIAL ENCOUNTER

The paper was dated September 10, 2014; Madame George had scooped
L'Est Républicain by five months. Her article ran a full page, recounting
the story of our meeting from her perspective ("I realized he spoke very
little French . . . Once before the monument, his face showed altogether
his surprise, his satisfaction at successfully completing a quest, and deep
emotion. He then took several photos."), and concluded: "This fine man
and I shared a nice encounter, and it was a fond memory." I'm pretty sure
that's the nicest thing anyone has ever written about me.

"Would you like a copy?" she asked. I said I would, and she phoned
a friend of hers to bring one over. While we waited, we went through a
folder of flyers she had accumulated for historical events, sites and ceremonies. "There will be a reenactment here in August," she told me, and
smiled sadly when I said I would be back in America by then. To change
the subject, I asked if anyone in her family had served in the war.

"My father," she replied. I asked his name, and what his occupation
had been; Prosper Louis, she said. He was a farmer. "He served in the
reserves from 1910 to 1913, went home to his family for a year, and was
called back up in 1914. He served for four years. He never talked about
the war much. He was fifty-three years old when I was born. And in your
family?"

"My grandfather," I said, and told her he had died when I was 11, long
before I ever thought to ask him about it. She nodded thoughtfully.

I asked if she remembered what day it was that we had met. "June 8," she said immediately. "I was attending a family get-together in Azannes." And she started to recall how forlorn I had looked when she first spotted me, standing in the middle of the road. Just then her friend, a petite woman about her age, walked up. As I rose to introduce myself, she glanced at me, smiled and nodded, as if we had already met. "I was just telling him," Madame George said to her friend, "how sad he looked when I first saw him, when he asked me if I knew how to find the monument." She turned back to me. "My children were . . . *concerned,*" she said. "They fussed at me afterward for getting into a car and going to such a place with a total stranger."

"You were lucky," her friend said to me. "If you had asked anyone other than her, they wouldn't have done it."

Madame George drew herself up in her seat, as if taking umbrage at the thought. "I would not forget," she said, a quiet dignity infusing every syllable, "that you helped us recover our liberty. History and memory are very important to me."

✹ ✹ ✹

I left Azannes just as the sun was starting to descend. There were still a few hours of light left, I knew, and I wanted to see one more thing before quitting for the evening. I drove to Chaumont-devant-Damvillers and easily found the right tractor road this time. It seemed smoother than it had a year earlier; I even passed a woman walking her dog, heading in the other direction. Soon I spotted the flag, and then the stone marker and the bench. I pulled up, parked and got out of my car. If the woman with the dog had made it this far, there was no sign either of them had been here. Nor anyone else, for that matter. I was entirely alone in the place where the very last man was killed in World War I.

Strange to contemplate that thought: the last man. We focus on firsts—on Jules-André Peugeot, on Albert Mayer, on Gresham, Hay and Enright. On the Wright brothers, Edmund Hillary, Neil Armstrong. But lasts—well, for many situations, most, even, there is no known last; it's open-ended. And we like it that way. Endings are fraught. They make us think about things, like: What was it all about? Was it worth it? Could it have ended sooner? In the case of the First World War, we know for sure that the answer to that last one, at least, is yes. There was talk of armistice at various times over the course of four years, but nothing came of it. And even when something did, it didn't, at least not for another seventy-two hours. Historians have calculated that had Foch granted von Winterfeldt's request of November 8, 1918, for all sides to observe a cease-fire while the terms of the armistice were worked out and signed, some twenty-two thousand casualties would have been prevented all around. Nearly seven thousand men were killed in those last seventy-two hours. A week earlier, I had found the name of one of them, 18-year-old John R. Elliott, written in ink on the wall of an underground chalk mine outside Nanteuil-la-Fosse. A month later, in Sipayik, Maine, just a few miles from the easternmost point in the United States—the spot closest to France—I would stumble upon the grave of Moses W. Neptune, the son of a Passamaquoddy Indian chief, also killed on November 10, 1918. And now I stood on the spot where Henry Gunther of Baltimore, grandson of German immigrants, was killed by a German bullet to the head in the last few seconds of the war. The last man killed. He got a posthumous promotion, a Distinguished Service Cross, and this little marker. All we get is a bunch of big, hard questions that can't really be answered. But we also get to come here, to this spot, and to the Côté Saint-Germain, and the Butte de Vauquois, and Bois Brûlé, and Fismette, and Mézy, and Belleau Wood, and Rouge Bouquet, and the Chemin des Dames, and Bathelémont; and we get to *see* it. And seeing it helps us understand, if only a little bit and in ways we can never hope to articulate.

I know I've mentioned a lot of beautiful vistas in France since I first told you about this place, but in the end I maintain that it is the finest of all of them, indeed the finest in the country. Every time I come by, I stand and look at it for a long while. At first, I always think: *This is the last thing the last man killed in World War I saw.* But after a minute or two that thought fades and blends into the scenery, into the gentle hills and sweeping fields and little toy farms, somehow rendering the whole thing even more beautiful to behold. I can't explain it. And I can't stare at it for too terribly long before I have to turn away and walk back to the marker, with its words and facts.

That evening as I did so, I noticed that a herd of cows—tan and white, maybe a dozen of them—had assembled along the wire fence that ran behind the stone marker. They stood there, shyly off to one side, and stared at me. *"Bonjour, mes amis!"* I called out, stepping up to the fence, and they trotted right over.

France.

TYPICAL U.S. ARMY INFANTRY UNITS IN WORLD WAR I

Unit	Size	Commanding Officer
Platoon	40 men	Lieutenant
Company	180 men	Captain
Battalion	800 men	Major or Lieutenant Colonel
Regiment	3,500 men	Colonel
Brigade	8,000 men	Brigadier General
Division	25,000 men	Major General

A corps comprised several divisions; an army comprised several corps.

German and British divisions typically had 17,000–18,000 men.

French divisions typically had 14,000–15,000 men.

SELECTED BIBLIOGRAPHY

103 U.S. Infantry. *History of the 103rd Infantry, 1917–1919*. Publisher unknown, 1919.

Adler, Julius Ochs. *History of the Seventy Seventh Division, August 25th, 1917–November 11th, 1918*. New York: W.H. Crawford Co., 1919.

American Battle Monuments Commission. *American Armies and Battlefields in Europe*. Washington, D.C.: United States Government Printing Office, 1938.

Bliss, Paul Southworth. *Victory: History of the 805th Pioneer Infantry, American Expeditionary Forces*. St. Paul, Minn.: published by the author, 1919.

Broun, Heywood. *The A.E.F.: With General Pershing and the American Forces*. New York: D. Appleton and Company, 1918.

Butts, Edmund L. *The Keypoint of the Marne and Its Defense by the 30th Infantry*. New York: George Banta Publishing Company, 1930.

De Varila, Osborne. *The First Shot for Liberty*. Philadelphia: John C. Winston, 1918.

Dickman, Joseph T. *The Great Crusade: A Narrative of the World War*. New York: D. Appleton and Company, 1927.

Dumur, Louis. *Le Boucher de Verdun*. Paris: Albin Michel, 1921.

Eisenhower, John S.D. *Yanks: The Epic Story of the American Army in World War I*. New York: Simon & Schuster, 2001.

Garey, E.B., O.O. Ellis, and R.V.D. Magoffin. *American Guide Book to France and Its Battlefields*. New York: Macmillan, 1920.

Gibbons, Floyd. *"And They Thought We Wouldn't Fight."* New York: George H. Doran, 1918.

Gilbert, Martin. *The First World War: A Complete History*. New York: Henry Holt, 1994.

Hanson, James W. *Roster of Maine in the Military Service of the United States and Allies in the World War, 1917–1919*. Augusta, Maine: State Legislature of Maine, 1929.

Hemenway, Frederic V. *History of the Third Division, United States Army, in the World War, for the period December 1, 1917, to January 1, 1919*. Cologne: M. Dumont Schauberg, 1919.

Keegan, John. *The First World War*. New York: Alfred A. Knopf, 1999.

Kenamore, Clare. *From Vauquois Hill to Exermont: A History of the Thirty-Fifth Division of the United States Army*. St. Louis, Mo.: Guard Publishing Co., 1919.

Lengel, Edward G. *Thunder and Flames: Americans in the Crucible of Combat, 1917–1918*. Lawrence, Kans.: University Press of Kansas, 2015.

———. *To Conquer Hell: The Meuse-Argonne, 1918*. New York: Henry Holt, 2008.

Mansuy, Eric, ed. *Carnet de guerre de Georges Curien, territorial vosgien*. Parçay-sur-Vienne, France: Anovi, 2001.

Meldrum, T. Ben. *A History of the 362nd Infantry*. Salt Lake City, Utah: The A.L. Scoville Press, 1920.

Moreau-Nélaton, Étienne. *Chez nous après les Boches*. Paris: H. Laurens, 1919.

Office of the Adjutant General, State of Connecticut. *Service Records: Connecticut Men and Women in the Armed Forces of the United States during the World War, 1917–1920*. New Haven, Conn.: United Printing Services, 1941.

Palmer, Frederick. *America in France*. New York: Dodd, Mead, 1918.

———. *Our Greatest Battle*. New York: Dodd, Mead, 1919.

Pitt, Barrie. *1918: The Last Act*. New York: W.W. Norton, 1963.

Reilly, Henry J. *Americans All: The Rainbow at War: Official History of the 42nd Rainbow Division in the World War*. Columbus, Ohio: F.J. Heer Printing Co., 1936.

Rommel, Erwin. *Infanterie Greift An* (Infantry Attacks). Potsdam, Germany: L. Voggenreiter, 1937.

Seichepine, Jean-Paul. *The First Three Americans to Fall on French Soil*. Lunéville, France: Imprimerie Saint-Jacques, 2015.

Sibley, Frank P. *With the Yankee Division in France*. Boston: Little, Brown, 1919.

Society of the First Division, A.E.F. *History of the First Division during the World War, 1917–1919*. Philadelphia: John C. Winston Co., 1922.

The Story of the 91st Division. San Mateo, Calif.: 91st Division Publication Committee, 1919.

Strickland, Daniel W. *Connecticut Fights: The Story of the 102nd Regiment*. New Haven, Conn: Quinnipiack Press, 1930.

Taylor, Emerson Gifford. *New England in France: 1917–1919, A History of the Twenty-Sixth Division U.S.A.* Boston: Houghton Mifflin, 1920.

Tuchman, Barbara W. *The Guns of August*. New York: Macmillan, 1962.

Vedovati, Jean. *Les Combats dans la Vallée de la Marne*. Dormans, France: Cercle Historique et Culturel Dormaniste, 1997.

Wadleigh, Fred Tilton. *Milford in the Great War: Memorial Book*. Milford, N.H.: Cabinet Press, 1922.

Wooldridge, Jesse W. *The Giants of the Marne: A Story of McAlexander and His Regiment*. Salt Lake City, Utah: published by the author, 1923.

———. *The Rock of the Marne: A Chronological Story of the 38th Regiment, U.S. Infantry*. Columbia, S.C.: University Press of South Carolina, 1920.

ACKNOWLEDGMENTS

There are an awful lot of people whose contributions were absolutely essential to telling this story, all but one of whom are not me. To start with, there are the people who, with great patience and good cheer and unstinted generosity—no one ever allowed me to pay for anything except my own meals, and some even insisted on feeding me—took time out from their busy lives to play tour guide during my first visit to American World War I sites in 2009 and, in the process, showed me places and things, and told me stories, that dramatically altered the way I viewed and understood that war (and history in general) and educated me about my own heritage as an American. (This just a few years after that whole "freedom fries" business.) In addition to Jean-Paul de Vries (in the Argonne), Gilles Lagin (in the vicinity of Belleau Wood and Château-Thierry) and Patrick Simons (in the Woëvre), there were the superintendents of the four largest American cemeteries from that war: the late Joseph P. (Phil) Rivers (Meuse-Argonne), Jeffrey Aarnio (Oise-Aisne), Bobby Bell (Saint-Mihiel) and David Atkinson (Aisne-Marne). Stan Bissinger (also in the Woëvre), Marie-Christine Garrido (at the museum in Belleau), Georges Bailly (also in the vicinity of Belleau Wood), Dominique Didiot (also at the Meuse-Argonne Cemetery), Nathalie Lebarbier (at Oise-Aisne) and Nadia Ezz-Eddine (at Saint-Mihiel) also helped educate and edify me during that excursion, which would not have been feasible without the support of Karl Schonberg and Val Lehr at St. Lawrence University, where I was then a visiting professor.

When I returned for longer visits in 2014 and again in 2015, I was, once again, the recipient of a tremendous amount of kindness, beneficence and hospitality, some of it bestowed upon me by the same people I had met in 2009, some by people I had never met before and some by people who had not even planned on meeting me, much less showing me around and sharing their knowledge. They include Madame Andrée George, Jean-Pierre Brouillon, Eric Mansuy, Gilles Chauwin, Benoît de Weirdt, Marc Brodin, Jean Vedovati, Christophe Wilvers, Olivier Jacquin, Dominique Lacorde, Harry Rupert, Dénis Hebrard, David and Marian Howard, Jean Marie, Frédéric and Murielle Castier, and Mme. B. Dave Bedford, who replaced Phil Rivers as superintendent at the Meuse-Argonne Cemetery in between my first and second visits, went to great lengths to share his time and expertise; Constant Lebastard, Associate at the Aisne-Marne Cemetery, was extremely helpful, too. Thanks as well to Superintendents Geoffrey Fournier (Oise-Aisne), Mike Coonce (Saint-Mihiel), Christopher Arseneault (Flanders Field), and to Tom Cavaness. Also in France, I am grateful to Serge Husson, Jean-Paul Seichepine, Lillian Pfluke, Damien Perisse, Patrick Julien, Roland Meesters, Valérie Kenny, Yannick Marques, Vicki Corley, Maurice Ravenel, Jacques Krabal, Nicolas Lemmer, Patrick Gielen, Michael Grams, Marie-Christine Garapon, Sarah Dorothy Downing, Pierre Picard, Alain D., Léa Boschiero, Frédéric Plancard, Franck Lallemand, Jean-Luc Kaluzko, Xavier Collin, Bernadette Brodin, Théophile de Weirdt, Anne Ludmann, Meredith Sykes, Bill Graham, Avril Williams, Bénédicte Hebrard and Mlle. Murielle at La Passarelle. Some of these people, like Patrick Simons, Christophe Wilvers, Jean-Paul de Vries, Dominique Lacorde and Harry Rupert, continued to help me with research, maps and photographs long after I had returned to the United States; Eric Mansuy helped me with all that, too, as well as translation. I am grateful to Ingrid Merrill and Fabian Rüger for help with translation, as well.

In 2014, when I decided I needed to go back to France and continue my explorations there, I approached Dean Robinson at the *New York Times Magazine* to see if that publication might be interested in sending me over; Dean recommended I try the *Times'* Travel section, suggesting that they might be able to give me more space. Though I had never written for them before, they were, and they did. Monica Drake, the Travel Editor, commissioned not a single article but a four-part series, and was an enthusiastic supporter throughout the process, from my departure for France to the publication of the fourth and final installment. Deputy Travel Editor Steve Reddicliffe was equally enthusiastic and supportive and, with a deft touch, a good ear and unflagging humor, helped shape all four installments and was (and is) the kind of editor every writer hopes to work with. Thanks also to staff editors Carl Sommers and Florie Stickney.

The American Battle Monuments Commission, which built all those magnificent American cemeteries and monuments, and which does a fantastic job maintaining them, has been a tremendous resource and a steadfast ally throughout this project; in addition to the overseas ABMC employees I mentioned previously, I am grateful to a number of people at headquarters in Arlington, Virginia, including Mike Conley, Tim Nosal, Alec Bennett, Allison Finkelstein and Edwin Fountain. Special thanks to ABMC Secretary Max Cleland, Director of Historical Services Michael Knapp, and Pat Harris, who makes everything run.

Among other things, ABMC furnished me with some of the maps that appear in this book. For the rest, I am greatly indebted to Deidre McCarthy, Chief of the Cultural Resource Geographic Information Systems Facility at the National Park Service; to NPS CRGIS cartographer David Lowe, who rendered them beautifully and in great detail; and to William Kyngesburye and Don Larson of Mapping Specialists who amended and adjusted them for printing.

Also in the United States, I must thank Col. Peter D. Crean, Director of the U.S. Army Heritage and Education Center; Gen. Leonid Kondratiuk and Keith Vezeau of the Massachusetts National Guard; Lieutenant Jonathan Bratten of the

Maine National Guard; Yahaira Carballo-Segura at the Connecticut Military Department; Sam Howes at the Maine State Archives; Dr. Paul Herbert and Andrew Woods at the First Division Museum at Cantigny; Dan Dayton of the U.S. World War One Centennial Commission; and Randal Gaulke, Mitchell Yockelson, Fae Houck, Bob Gundersen, Edward Lengel, Oliver Scheer and Christian Zinck.

As always, my agent, Kristine Dahl, supported this book from the very beginning, made it happen, and was a wellspring of sage advice and guidance—not to mention Xanax in human form—throughout the process of writing and editing it. Thanks also to Caroline Eisenmann at ICM, who has always been very helpful. My editor at St. Martin's, Tim Bartlett, cared deeply about this book from the start, and did a great deal to refine, enhance and generally improve it. Annabella Hochschild provided critical support with grace; Alan Bradshaw calmly, ably and conscientiously guided it through production; and India Cooper did a fine and thorough job copy editing it, thus sparing me all kinds of embarrassment I don't even want to think about, as did proofreader Jennifer Simington. Thanks also, at St. Martin's, to Meryl Sussman Levavi and Rob Grom, who made it look so good, and to Joan Higgins, Laura Clark and Lauren Friedlander, whose enthusiastic support and efforts on its behalf I very much appreciate.

Finally, I must express my profound gratitude to a few people who made greatly outsized and utterly indispensable contributions to this work: Monique Seefried, a commissioner on the U.S. World War One Centennial Commission, who seems to know (and be admired by) pretty much everybody, and who gave a lot of thought to the matter of whom I should meet Over There, then put me in touch with every name on her lengthy list; Rob Dalessandro, Chairman of the aforementioned Centennial Commission and Deputy Secretary of the American Battle Monuments Commission, about whom all of that is also true, as well as the fact that he either possesses or can quickly lay his hands on any piece of knowledge relating to that war, does not know the words "no" and "can't," and quickly and cheerfully fulfilled every request for help I ever made of him (and there were a great many), whether with maps, documents, contacts, photo ideas or travel tips; and Miz B (not to be confused with Mme. B), who ate late and didn't complain.

This has been the hardest part of the book for me to write, as I know, for certain, that on at least two continents there are people who should be mentioned here but are not: because I failed for some reason to summon their names when the time came to make this list; or—as is the case with the biker who took me to the Château-Thierry American Monument, and the custodian who patiently removed all of those folded and stacked tables and chairs from that vestibule in the nursing home in Montfaucon d'Argonne just so I could get a photo of the plaque the state of Ohio installed there in 1929, and any number of others— because I never knew their names to begin with. If you are one of those people, and by chance you should read this, I hope you will write me—in French, or English, or any other language—at backoverthere@gmail.com and make me feel guilty about it. I am, still, susceptible to that.

INDEX

PEOPLES OF THE WORLD
Latin Americans

PEOPLES OF THE WORLD
Latin Americans
Joyce Moss • George Wilson

**The Culture, Geographical Setting,
and Historical Background of
42 Latin American Peoples**

FIRST EDITION

 **Gale Research Inc.** • Book Tower • Detroit, Michigan 48226

Joyce Moss
George Wilson

Illustrator: Lynn Van Dam

Gale Research Inc. staff

Production Manager: Mary Beth Trimper
External Production Assistant: Marilyn Jackman

Art Director: Arthur Chartow
Graphic Designer: Bernadette M. Gornie

Production Supervisor: Laura Bryant
Internal Production Associate: Louise Gagné
Internal Production Assistant: Shelly Andrews

Copyright © 1989 by Joyce Moss and George Wilson
ISBN: 0-8103-7445-5

Printed in the United States of America

To Fred Moss and in memory of Cecilia Moss,

who suffered an attempt to extinguish their culture in the concentration camps of World War II yet never stopped loving people.

CONTENTS

Preface

As technology draws people ever closer together, certain questions become pressing. Why did communism take root in Cuba and El Salvador? Who are the people of Panama, and how do they earn their livelihood? What has happened to Latin America's Indians since the coming of the Europeans?

About the time the pyramids of Egypt were built, organized Indian societies lived in Latin America. Over the centuries, there was a rhythm of union and disintegration of early peoples that gave rise to the Mayas, the Incas, and the Aztecs - societies that easily compare with any European society of the 16th century. Then Spaniards came to Latin America in search of wealth, using their powerful weapons to conquer the Aztecs, Incas, and other Amerindian societies. More Europeans came - the Portuguese, the Dutch, the British, the Italians, the Germans, and the Yugoslavs. They moved onto land already used by the Indians for farming, fishing, and hunting. Also the Indians of different areas had developed a sophisticated network of trade. The Europeans interfered with these various Indian activities. Many Indians died due to armed conflict, diseases, or forced labor. Afterwards, black slaves from Africa and indentured servants from Asia were brought over to work the land.

Technology has affected the peoples of Latin America. Oil wells and related jobs have appeared in Venezuela. Large hydroelectric plants are rising along the Paraná River on the border of Uruguay. Highways now cross the jungles of the Amazon River basin. The highways bring new influences to the area so that a visitor today can see Indians in T-shirts, instead of their traditional dress. Modern farm tools replace wooden plows; steel knives and shotguns replace blow guns and stone knives. In general peoples are being assimilated into the culture of each political state. While Araucanians, for example, maintain some strong traditions, they are very much a part of the Chilean national scene today.

Some patterns remain. While nations strive for more diversified economies, many continue to depend heavily on one product. Bolivia, for example, depended on tin until world prices declined. Then many turned to a product that promised even greater income - coca leaves for cocaine. Since independence, most Latin American countries have, either perpetually or periodically, been governed by the military. Some still struggle with unequal land distribution, a few wealthy owners holding much of the acreage. A new pattern among Latin Americans is their movement from farms to cities for jobs in industry. As a result, communities of substandard housing have appeared outside many cities.

Despite such general trends, each group in this book is unique. *Peoples of the World: Latin Americans* includes a mix of national cultures and the cultures of older and smaller groups. Together they represent the wide range of lifestyles in Latin American today. Some are ways of life that promise shortly to disappear.

Copyright Acknowledgments

Introduction

There is a wealth of material on countries of the world today but little on the peoples of those countries. They are often treated briefly in the course of describing a nation without mention of their various lifestyles or customs. Latin America, in particular, is a mix of cultural groups (both native and national) that practice various ways of life. *Peoples of the World: Latin Americans* provides quicker and more complete access to descriptions of the different groups in this area of the world than is currently available to the average reader. The work is a compilation of field studies, source material, and original research on peoples of South America, Central America, and the Caribbean. In compiling information for the work, there has been an ongoing effort to make the entries as current as possible. Since peoples of the world are constantly changing, the information is as timely as printing deadlines and rapidly shifting world events allow.

Coverage of National and Native Cultures

There are hundreds of national and native cultures in Latin America. In choosing which ones to include, the authors made a representative selection based on three main criteria:

1. Coverage of different geographic locations
2. Troublesome areas in recent world events
3. Regions occupied by "disappearing" cultures

The entries feature maps to locate the groups and art or photographs to illustrate items described in the text. Some photographs, taken by a private contributor, are appearing for the first time in any publication.

Peoples of the World: Latin Americans is arranged into two sections: Old Cultures and Cultures of Today. Organized chronologically, the Old Cultures provide brief overviews of ancient peoples as background for present-day groups. The Cultures of Today are organized alphabetically by people name. A chart before both sections keys peoples to their countries. Foreign terms are defined in context, and a glossary provides fuller explanation or recurring terms. The index lists key individuals and events.

Format and Arrangement of Entries

In both Old Cultures and Cultures of Today entries are organized as follows:

Introducing each entry is a dictionary-style definition that includes how to pronounce the people's name, a brief description of the group, and key facts (population, location, and language).

Following this introductory material is a more detailed description of the people under three main headings.

In Old Cultures, these headings are **Geographical Setting, Historical Background,** and **Culture.** The Cultures of Today sections are divided into **Geographical Setting, Historical Background,** and **Culture Today.**

For quick access to information, subheadings appear under the three main headings. For example, **Historical Background** may include the subdivisions:

Early Peoples
Spanish and Portuguese Rule
Immigrants
Independence

Culture Today may be subdivided into:

Food, Clothing and Shelter
Religion
Government
Education and the Arts

Due to the unique experience of the various groups and the different amounts of information available on them, subdivisions vary across the entries. Basic facts, such as information on food, clothing and shelter, are regularly provided.

Acknowledgments

For assistance in the selection and review of cultures, the authors are grateful to Ross D. Sackett, a working anthropologist with repeated experience in Latin America. The authors had invaluable aid in updating information for this work from individuals who were born and raised in Latin America. Grateful acknowledgment is extended to these organization and individuals:

Oscar E. Baldassarre - Argentines
Paula Baldassarre - Argentines
Eduardo Benardino- Ecuadorians
Sonia Benardino - Ecuadorians
Neva Ortuño - Bolivians
Eduardo Perez - Salvadorans
Nancy Reiss - Mexicans
Embassy Representatives, Washington D.C.
Belize

Guyana
Jamaica
Panama
Venezuela
Consulate Representatives, Los Angeles, CA
Brazil
Costa Rica
Peru

Appreciation is further extended to Paula Baldassarre, a former Spanish language teacher, for her review of foreign vocabulary in this resource and to Jon Klancher, Ph.D. for his contribution to the initial research.

Table of Peoples by Country

South America	
Argentina	Araucanians
	Argentines
	Guaraní
	Tierra del Fuegans
Bolivia	Aymara
	Bolivians
	Incas
	Quechua
Brazil	Brazilians
	Guaraní
	Tenetehara
	Vaupés Indians
	Xingu Park Indians
	Yanomamo
Chile	Araucanians
	Chileans
	Incas
	Tierra del Fuegans
Colombia	Colombians
	Guajiro
	Incas
	Vaupés Indians
Ecuador	Ecuadorians
	Jívaro
Paraguay	Guaraní
	Paraguayans
Peru	Amahuaca
	Aymara
	Campa
	Incas
	Jívaro
	Peruvians
	Quechua
Uruguay	Guaraní
	Uruguayans
Venezuela	Guajiro
	Pemon
	Venezuelans
	Yanomamo

Mexico and Central America	
Belize*	Belizians
	Mayas
Costa Rica	Costa Ricans
El Salvador	Salvadorans
Guatemala	Guatemalans
	Mayas
Honduras	Hondurans
	Miskitos
Mexico	Aztecs
	Mayas
	Mexicans
	Yaqui
	Zapotec
Nicaragua	Miskitos
	Nicaraguans
Panama	Cuna
	Panamanians

Caribbean	
Cuba	Cubans
Guyana**	Guyanans
Haiti	Haitians
Jamaica	Jamaicans
Puerto Rico	Puerto Ricans
Surinam	Surinamese

*   Formerly British Honduras
**   Formerly British Guiana

THE OLD CULTURES

MAYAS

(ma´ yahs)
Peoples of Southern Mexico and Central America
who formed a great early society, saw it disintegrate, and
rebuilt a new society in the tropical jungles.

Population: Over 1,000,000 (A.D. 700).
Location: Southern Mexico, Guatemala, Belize,
the Yucatán Peninsula, El Salvador, Honduras.
Language: Maya.

Old Mayan Civilization
? B.C to A.D. 980

Geographical Setting

The land of the Mayas is largely tropical – hot
and wet. Dense tropical forests cover much of the
territory, though there are also cool, forested
highlands. The large variety of animals that live in
in the region provided food for early inhabitants.
Thick forests and waterways isolated the early
groups and encouraged the growth of city states
that were independent of one another.

Historical Background

Earlier than 1000 B.C., the Mayan people
appear to have settled in the region that is now
Southern Mexico and Guatemala. Here they built
great cities and temples to their many gods.

The Mayan Empire reached its highest point
about A.D. 700, then began to decline. By A.D.
900 much of the grandure of the old empire had
disappeared as the Mayas broke into smaller
groups. About this time, the Mayan peoples
began to move north into the Yucatán Peninsula.
The new Mayan society that developed there was
a union of independent city states. It grew until
A.D. 1200, when another wave of migrants from
the north reached the Yucatán area. These were the

Mayan Society
A.D. 900-1200

3

Toltecs, also highly developed in their political organization, and more militant than the Mayas. The independent city states of the Mayas were easy victims of the Toltec invasion. Then a mixture of Toltec and Mayan cultures occurred.

Culture

Religious ceremony was central to Mayan life. The people built over 50 ceremonial centers with pyramids and temples. They believed in rain, sun, and wind gods, calling upon them upon for agricultural purposes. Their ceremonial centers included not only temples and palaces but also homes for the Mayan people.

Daily life. In early Mayan society, there were two social classes: the commoners and the upper class of rulers, religious leaders, and esteemed warriors. The commoners mostly raised crops.

Maize was the major Mayan crop, prepared as a thin gruel, as cakes, or as tortillas eaten with beans or chile. Mayan homes were one or two room rectangular structures, sometimes built on stone platforms. For walls, the Mayans used stone rubble combined with plaster, or poles tied with vines. The roofs of homes were thatched with palm. Mayan dress included tunics, full, white cotton breechcloths and kiltlike loincloths.

Accomplishments. The Mayas developed a number system, a form of written language, and a very precise calendar. They were skilled in sculpture and architecture. Great stone buildings were ornamented with sculptures of animals, humans, and gods. Made of stone that was carried for many miles, some of these buildings still stand today in Yucatán Peninsula. Such achievements in building and in sculpture were accomplished without the use of wheeled machines or metal carving tools. Mayan art included work with jade, ceramics, gold, and silver. Aside from individual buildings, they built the community around a central square after a fashion that continues today.

The Mayan society left a calendar nearly as accurate as the one we use today, a numbering system, and a way to write ideas using pictures for words and sentences. Though the number system did not include a mark for zero, the Mayas understood what zero was. Their system consisted of bars and dots that were easy to read and could account for large numbers. It worked like this:

```
  .      ..      ...     ....    ____
  1      2       3       4        5
```

The writing system used combinations of pictures to make pictographs that stood for words and sentences.

Art, architecture, a knowledge of astronomy, and a deep commitment to religion are legacies of the Mayas to the people of today.

AZTECS
(as´ tecks)

People who dominated much of Mexico from a base near what is now Mexico City.

The center of the Aztec Empire

Population: Over 5,500,000 (A.D. 1519).
Location: The central plateau of Mexico.
Language: Nahuatl.

Geographical Setting

A mile-high plateau lies in what is now Mexico. Today Mexico City rests on this plateau, but once a shallow lake covered the land. On either side of the plateau, the southern extensions of the Sierra Nevada Mountains and Rocky Mountains of the United States stretch through Mexico. South of the old lake, the country is crossed east to west by a range of volcanic peaks. At its southern end, where Mexico City is today, the weather is mild and the soil is good.

Historical Background

Wave after wave of American Indian peoples related to the Shoshone people of the Great Plains of the United States migrated south between the two mountain ranges. About A.D. 600, a group known as the Toltecs built communities on the plateau and formed a society that was to last for 400 years. The warlike Toltecs overwhelmed their neighbors and expanded their territory until about the year 1000, when they fell victims to other migrants into the land. Among these conquerors were the Chichimecs, Acolhuas, and Tecpanecs.

About 1200 an even more warlike group, the Aztecs, settled on the plateau and begin conquests of neighboring people. They expanded into the land of the Acolhuas and Tecpanecs using slings, darts, spears, clubs, and bows and arrows to defeat their enemies. By 1325 the Aztecs had settled on an island in shallow Lake Tezcuco where they were subjects of the Tecpanecs. But in 1375, the Aztecs united, elected a king and began to build a city dedicated to a sun god. Causeways allowed the Aztec warriors and couriers to leave the island city to conquer more neighbors or exact tribute from those already conquered. At the same time, the narrow causeways made it difficult for others to attack the city. By 1427 Itzcoatl had become ruler of the Aztecs, and about 1430 he enlisted the help of neighboring peoples to overthrow the rule of the Tepanecs. Once free of this rule, the Aztecs organized fierce armies that quickly defeated Mixtecs, Zapotecs, Totonacs, Huaxtecs, and Otomi. One after another, new people and new lands came under the influence of a sometimes cruel Aztec society. This society controlled a large section of what is now Mexico until, in the reign of its ninth king, Moctezuma II, (also called *Montezuma*) Spaniards under Hernando Cortés visited the island city and with the aid of dissatisfied subjects of the Aztecs began a war to capture the Aztec capital and its wealth. From 1518 to 1521, the Aztec people defended their city causing the Spanish to retreat. However, much of the city's wealth was taken out along the causeways by the invaders. Spaniards finally used canoes to enter the city, then fought a door-to-door battle that ended in a massacre of the Aztecs and victory for the Spanish in 1522.

Culture

Organization. The Aztec Empire was tightly organized. There were headmen, war chiefs, representatives to tribal councils, and leaders over smaller and smaller units to supervise the many slaves and to collect taxes for the Aztecs.

Traveling merchants, who kept information flowing among the conquered people, had a special place in this society. Its economy was based on maize, and its people dedicated themselves to worship of the sun god and of many other lesser gods.

There was no private land ownership among the Aztecs. Each family was provided with a plot on which to grow maize. The crops filled the granaries of the rulers and were allocated to each citizen. Maize, the staple of the Aztec diet; was formed into flat breads like tortillas. The Aztecs also grew squash, sweet potatoes, tobacco, cotton and agave for food and clothing.

Aside from farming, the Aztecs manufactured goods. Potters, sandal makers, and carpenters existed in Aztec society; artisans made goods such as paper and stone or wooden tools.

City life. In the capital city, commoners lived in one-room adobe houses with roofs made of thatch or wattle. These homes had little furniture. Nobles lived in larger adobe structures with wooden furniture.

Aztec men walked the streets of Tenochtitlán wearing knee-length mantles and a girdle. Women wore sleeveless tunics and calf-length skirts, painting their faces with yellow bird symbols. Aztecs decorated these costumes with the bright feathers of nearby tropical and subtropical birds.

Rules in Aztec society were strict. Citizens were required to marry by a certain age – men by 24, women by 18. The death penalty was given for murder, for remarrying, for wearing clothes suitable for the other sex, and even for harvesting unripe maize.

Accomplishments. Aztec craftsmen were skilled in using stone tools and in making jewelry. They set gems in gold bracelets and in head pieces. Artisans developed beautiful mosaic patterns and sculptures that have influenced Mexican art to this day. Skilled workers grew

Aztec gold mask

gardens of flowers, and some wrote about their lives on deerskin parchment, fine cloth, and paper. Their numbering system was similar to the dot and line system of the Mayas. A flag was added to indicate the number 20. Aztec medicine men were highly skilled in the use of herbs, more skillful than European doctors who lived during this same time.

Language. The Aztec had a large vocabulary of spoken words some of which are used in English today. Examples are *avocado*, *chili*, *chocolate*, *cocoa*, *ocelot*, and *tomato*. The Aztec written language was a combination of pictographs and hieroglyphics, pictures to stand for words and phrases and symbols to stand for sounds and words.

Religion. The life of the Aztec in Tenochtitlán was governed by law and by religion. Great festivals of dance and singing marked special religious days. Sacrifices, sometimes of humans, were made to the sun god. Today, students of the past think that human sacrifices were not as cruel or as common as was once believed. They point out that slaves and others used for sacrifice often went to the ceremonies convinced that their death allowed them to become closer to the gods.

Law, language, maize, powerful beliefs in religion, and enduring ideas in sculpture are the legacies of the Aztecs that influence life today.

INCAS
(ing´kahs)

People of an early empire in the Andes Mountains

The beginning of the Inca Empire

Population: Over 6,000,000 (A.D.1525).
Location: Bolivia, Peru, Chile, Columbia.
Languages: Many but mainly Quechua.

Geographical Setting

The land of the Incas began near Lake Titicaca in the Andes Mountains, and extended south through today's highlands of Bolivia, north through the high country of Peru, and south along the Pacific coast of South America as far as present day Concepción in Chile. It was a high mountainous country, with fierce winter weather and soil often too poor for growing crops. The region was comparable in size to the Roman Empire of Europe and the Middle East. Furthermore, it was a land ruled by a people whose chief means of travel was walking, and who had no knowledge of horses or wheels.

Historical Background

Before the Incas, there were other dynasties in the Andes. Between A.D 500 and 600, people known as the Tiahuanaco, beginning near Lake Titicaca and spreading through the high valleys of the Andes, built a great empire whose cities are still marked by the ruins of their temples.

About the year 900 this great empire collapsed, leaving the people to form smaller societies throughout the Andes. Some of the smaller groups established city states in a mountain valley on the Urubamba River near present-day Cuzco.

About 1100, one of the leaders, Sinchi Rocca, is said to have united the small groups, calling himself Inca, the only son of the sun god. Organized under Rocca and his successors, the peoples who became known as Incas expanded, conquering one after another of the independent groups south through the Andes Mountains in Bolivia, north to Columbia, then down the west side of the Andes and the Pacific Coast to the present city of Concepción in Chile. Without horses, wheels, or a written language, the Incas built an empire nearly as large as the Roman Empire and a social order that was second to none of the other societies of its time. Their language, Quechua, became the language of the empire. Ruthless when necessary, and benevolent toward those who agreed to their demands, Inca rulers built roads through the empire. Their messengers could run from city to city along these roads, and the pathways were used to move entire societies in order to maintain control of the region.

The Inca Empire about A.D. 1300

The Inca Viracocha conquered the large Chanca society and the Inca Huayna Capac expanded and solidified the empire in the late 1400s. Huayna Capac ruled over a vast area united by a strict system of government. On his deathbed, he could not decide which of his two sons should rule. Finally, he divided the Inca Empire between the two: Atahuallpa and Huascar. The result was civil war as each son sought to become ruler of all.

The Spaniard Juan Pizarro entered Inca land during this civil war. Pizarro helped Atahuallpa capture his brother and put him to death. Afterwards, Pizarro took Atahuallpa prisoner, holding him for a ransom of enough gold and silver to fill a room that was about 22 feet by 17 feet by 9 feet. Though the ransom was raised, Atahuallpa was condemned to die. His death ended a century of Inca expansion and glory. The Spanish conquest had occurred from 1531-1533.

The Inca Empire in 1522 at the time of Juan Pizzaro

Culture

The Inca people had no written language so what is known of their customs has been gathered from stories in their spoken tongue, Quechua, and through exploration of the great temples and cities they built. From these stories and relics, the picture of an Inca city is one of a great temple to a central god of the sun and lesser gods to which the Incas paid tribute from the maize they grew.

Daily life. Maize was a principal crop raised for food. Livestck included llama. The Inca family raised enough to meet its own needs. Though self sufficient, it reserved the right to ask relatives and nieghbors for help and provide aid in return.

An Inca man of the city wore a breechcloth and a sleeveless shirt over which a tunic or mantle was thrown. Women wore one-piece wraps that reached from the shoulder to knee. Their pierced ears held ear pieces that completed the costume.

The home was generally a one story structure made of stone or clay with a thatched roof. A stove for cooking and floor mats for sleeping were the only furnishings in most houses.

Government. In Inca land, most things were state controlled. To maintain control, the Incas organized the empire into a pyramid of tens. Ten men were subject to one, who was in turn part of a ten-man unit that was governed by one higher up. Through this organization, food, hunting, mining, and farming were tightly controlled. Each family was assigned land to cultivate. On its assigned plot, a family raised maize, potatoes, peanuts and llamas. The harvests were divided into thirds: one third for the gods, one third for the ruler's coffers, and one third to support the family. Divorce was forbidden.

Accomplishments. The Incas devised a procedure for counting, using a collection of knotted ropes with which they were able to tally. Important at Inca festivals, music featured drums and hoops.

Cuzco was the home of the Inca chief who bore the title Inca, Only Inca, the only true descendant of the sun god. At its peak in Inca times, Cuzco was the largest city in South America with 200,000 residents, and five great squares in which trading was done. The Incas had no money, so trade was carried out by bartering goods.

From Cuzco, roads were constructed for runners and soldiers to travel from post house to post house conveying the will of the ruler. So vast and influential was the Inca empire that the well-kept roads are still markers of the good traveling routes in the Andes, and Quechua, the language of the Incas, is still spoken by roughly 8,000,000 people.

Organized government, a powerful spoken language, and strong belief in their religion are legacies of the Incas to the people of the Andes. Today, Peruvian children study their grand Inca heritage with pride, learning the names of the kings early in school.

CULTURES OF TODAY

AMAHUACA

(ama wah´ ka)

A small group of people living in comparative
isolation in the forests of central Peru.

Population: 1,500 (1980?).
Location: Peru.
Language: Amahuacan, one of the Panoan
family of languages.

Amahuaca in Peru

Geographical Setting

The eastern portion of Peru falls quickly from
the high Andes Mountains of the west and central
parts of the country into a tropical forest with
rivers and streams draining into the Amazon
Basin. The forests in this region are dense, and
the rainfall is heavy. The dense forests are home
to a large variety of animal species and provide
good hunting grounds. On the other hand, the
shallow soil is easily washed away by the rains
and will support only the most economical of
farming programs. Amerindians of the region
conserve the land by hunting and gathering their
food. To supplement this intake they chop out
small sections of the delicate soil. The area is
farmed for a short while, then left to regenerate
and revert to jungle land.

Historical Background

Origin. According to Amahuaca legend, an
ancestor named Hindachindiya fathered a child
born of an *xopa* fruit. The fruit had been lying in a
hammock while carrying the child, then fell out,
splitting open and spilling out a stillborn boy and a

17

live girl. The girl became mother to the Amahuaca people.

First Europeans. Whatever their actual origins, the Amahuaca were first found living among the Indians of the Amazon forests. In 1686, a white Dominican missionary happened upon a village with twelve Amahuaca households. Unfortunate subsequent experiences with whites resulted in a self-imposed isolation by the Amahuaca for the next two centuries. While the people managed to mostly avoid contact with the white world, they were less successful in escaping contact with other Indians. The Piro, the Combo, and the Shipibo periodically raided Amahuaca villages, killing the men and selling the children into slavery. In the 19th century, white rubber explorers attempted to enslave the Amahuaca for use as a cheap labor force. The people resisted, growing into a fierce, hostile nation skilled in the tactics of jungle warfare. As their efforts proved unsuccessful, they were forced to leave their river villages and take refuge in the nearby forests.

Culture Today

Since World War II, a few Peruvian missionaries have attempted to establish relations with the Amahuacans. A number of the Indians have left their homes to join other communities in present day Peru. The majority, though, remain hidden in the forests, practicing traditional ways.

Food. Aside from tobacco and cotton, the Amahuaca grow food crops such as maize, cassava, sugar cane, sweet potatoes, bananas, watermelon, and peanuts. The men use slash-and-burn methods to clear the land, and the women sow and reap the crops. After two to three years the soil wears out, and the Amahuaca migrate to clear the next piece of land. Hunting as well as farming occupies the men. In addition to raising crops, they snare animals such as monkeys, deer, fish, and birds for food.

A typical meal consists of monkey stew served over a bed of rice and beans seasoned with red pepper. Between meals, the people might be found munching handfuls of toasted and ground maize. Maize serves as a base for a hot soup and for a lightly fermented drink, made by chewing a few mouthfuls of nuts and spitting them into a pot of maize gruel. After leaving the liquid alone for several days, the Indians have created a beerlike beverage.

Clothing. Traditional clothing includes cotton skirts and reed armbands for women; men wear bark belts and rings through their noses. During celebrations, the men might be seen in top hats, tails, and cummerbunds, the women in sheath skirts and bead necklaces. The top hats are designed from inner layers of bamboo covered by woven cloth. Stitched around the cloth are black and brown seeds as well as monkey teeth.

An Amahuaca in typical body paint.

Traditional ornaments include a nasal disk made from tortoise shell, pearl, or in later years from aluminum. Both men and women wear headbands made of bark. Painting the body is a common means of adornment; bright red-orange and deep purple-black are the preferred colors, often used to create pictures of catfish or jaguars. The colors are derived from fruits common to the area.

Arts. What little artwork there is among the people mostly relates to clothing. Aside from body paint, 20,000 seeds might be collected, drilled, and strung together to decorate one man's stomach belt. Their oral literature, as demonstrated above, explains the creation of the Amahuaca. Another tale describes their destruction: The sky falls down upon the earth, water floods the land and drowns all living things, leaving only one Amahuaca couple. In regards to music, singing plays a continuing role during the two major celebrations – the maize festival and the banana festival. Festivities continue for days, the celebrants sometimes singing from midnight until three each morning.

Religion. The Amahuaca practice an animist religion in which *yoshin* (spirits) are believed to wander in the forest and threaten the living. According to the Amahuaca, the yoshin can inflict illness, aid a man in injuring another, and create ugly children. It is further believed that each individual has an inner *yoshi* (spirit), which survives after bodily death. Therefore, the bones of a dead person are ground and sprinkled into a soup made of maize. To tame the person's yoshi and absorb his or her strength, the survivors drink this soup.

Women. Not all Amahuaca die of natural causes. Since male children are preferred by the people, killings of female babies after birth have been reported. On occasion twins and ugly children have also been killed in defiance of the yoshin who are believed to have created them. A result of these practices is a shortage of women in Amahuaca villages.

The shortage of women leads to marriages between men and young girls, whose ages range from eight to 11. It has also led some man to covet other men's wives, a situation likely to culminate in jealousy and murder. Before committing vengeful acts, murderers paint themselves black and cut off all their hair.

Life is difficult for women in Amahuaca society. They plant the crops, pick them, carry them home, and commence household chores, using a mortar and pestle to grind the maize. Besides grinding maize, the women make pots, weave, cook, clean, and rear children. Carrying a 50-pound load of wood, a woman might also be seen bearing an infant in a sling. Mothers raise their offspring with great love, keeping infants in their hammocks until the age of three. Rather than hitting, they shame children into behaving in respected ways.

Shelter. The customary home is a large structure – 40 feet long by 20 feet deep. It rises 12 feet high at the ridgepole, forming a sharply-peaked palm-thatched roof. The interior may include one or two rooms with contents that are a mixture of the old and the new. Hammocks are still used for sleeping, but stoves, refrigerators, and beds have been introduced to the people as well. Several related families normally live under the same roof.

Change. Now in the 20th century, the lifestyle of the people is changing. The Protestant missionary Robert Russell has settled near the Amahuaca for six months a year. His purposes have been to assist them in survival and encourage the Indians to read the Bible. Russell has discouraged their occasional killing of baby daughters after birth. Meanwhile, the people have been introduced to the fishhook, airplane, flashlight, tin can, skirt, shirt, shoe, and the church. Selectively, they are choosing to include such items in their daily lives. Like others in Latin America, the Amahuaca are a people whose ways are in danger of disappearing.

ARAUCANIANS

(ar aw kayn´ yens)

A native South American people who once ruled a large region in Chile.

Araucanians in Chile and Argentina

Population: 250,000 (1980).
Location: Chile, Argentina.
Language: Araucanian (spoken by many groups in different versions), Spanish.

Geographical Setting

Toward the south of Chile, the Andes Mountains narrow to a single ridge, then drop to a high plateau that separates Chile and the pampas region of Argentina. Three rivers cross a fertile valley of Chile and mark the region settled by Araucanian-speaking Indians. In the north, the Maule River passes the present day cities of Talca and Constitución. In the south, near today's city of Valparaíso, the land is drained by the Tolten River. Between these two, the Bío-Bío River flows alongside the modern cities of Los Angeles and Concepción.

Ranging from 40 to 60 inches per year, rain falls steadily in this part of central Chile. The heavy rainfall has contributed to the growth of monsoon forests in which early settlers hunted, while the fertile river valleys have provided rich soil for farming. Across the Andes, the land drops to a high plateau that is shielded from heavy rain. Here grasslands provided early settlers with a region suited to a nomadic lifestyle that was restricted to hunting and gathering the materials required for survival.

Historical Background

Before the Incas. Long before the Incas or Spanish moved into central Chile, the region was settled by groups of farmers and hunters called Picunche. Another people, the Huilliche, settled in small groups around the Tolten River. In between these areas, the low Andes and sheltering forests encouraged nomadic groups from the pampas to raid the more settled people in Chile. The interaction between the Huilliche, Picunche, and the pampas people, the Pehuenche, resulted in still another collection of small groups in the forests around the Bío-Bío River, the Mapuche. The three peoples – Huilliche, Picunche, and Mapuche – as well as their Argentine neighbors spoke forms of the Araucanian language, becoming known as the Araucanians.

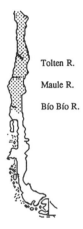

Tolten R.

Maule R.

Bío Bío R.

Araucanian land before the Incas and Spanish.

The Araucanians built communities, farmed the land of central Chile, and governed themselves through family or village leadership until the Incas penetrated the region. The northern Picunche were quickly integrated into Inca society, but the central Araucanians banded together to repel Inca advances along the Maule River between A.D. 1448 and 1482. They were, however, still considered to be under Inca rule when the Spanish captured the region and established their government at Santiago.

Spanish arrival. Arriving in 1536, the Spanish claimed control and proceeded to build cities and forts throughout the 1540s and 1550s. They managed to absorb the Huilliche in the south, but the central Araucanians continued to resist invasion of their land.

Led by a chief named Lautaro, the Araucanians began a slaughter of the Spanish in 1553 and followed it with repeated attacks on Santiago. So fierce was the defense of their homeland that the Spanish poet Alonso de Ercilla Y Zúñiga wrote admiringly about the warriors in his epic poem *La Araucana*. Here are lines from the English version *The Araucaniad* (Nashville: Vanderbilt University Press, 1945) by Charles Maxwell Lancaster and Paul Thomas Machester .

> Streaking back, the Araucanians
> Rammed assault against the invaders.
> Flourishing their weary javelins,
> To the death they'd fight, they
> promised.
> Trembled earth with dreadful uproar,
> Moaned, when foremen clashed together
> Shedding in their rage and frenzy
> Whate'er little blood was left them.
>
> (P. 56)

Despite such dogged resistance, the people could not withstand Spanish horses and weapons. Thus, the Spanish succeeded in pushing the Araucanians deeper into the forests and away from the fertile farmlands along the rivers and coast. Still the Araucanians resisted, as they would through four centuries, often using Spanish horses to raid Spanish settlements and then escaping across the Andes into the pampas.

Meanwhile, the Spanish continued to absorb the Picunche and Huilliche so that today the majority of Araucanians call themselves Mapuche. From marriages between the Indians and the Spanish came a mestizo group. The loyalties of these mestizos often lay with the Indians in resisting Spanish attacks, aimed at capturing people for slavery or inexpensive labor.

Accepted in 1641 through the efforts of the Jesuit priest Pedro de Valdivia, the Treaty of Quillen established a more peaceful setting for the people. Many feared that the treaty would not have the desired effects, and their fears were realized as it also made them susceptible to forced labor on Spanish farms and ranches.

The Mapuche, living in the forests and accustomed to moving freely into the pampas, remained rebellious. Capable warriors, they readily adopted European military strategies to harass the Spanish. Although the Spanish recognized Araucania as a separate country, its people were still leading rebellions when the Europeans left Chile in the early 19th century.

Chilean rule. Following an 1859 uprising against the new government, Chile permanently occupied the land of the Araucanians, building forts and towns within the territory. In 1872, Araucania was forced to become part of Chile. Seven years later, when the Chilean government was preoccupied with waging war against Peru and Bolivia, the Mapuche rebelled once again. They destroyed many of the newly built forts and towns, and the government retaliated using modern weapons to defeat the Indians and confine them to reservations. There the Mapuche continued to raise livestock but substituted new European farming techniques for their old practice of shifting settlements to find fertile soil. By 1883 they had successfully adapted to the situation, ushering in a series of peaceful and prosperous decades that became known as the golden years in Araucanian history.

The threat of rebellion lessened, and had apparently died by 1960. In response, the National Congress of Chile announced plans to phase out the reservations, expecting the Araucanians to use their new farming skills by working as laborers for prosperous white farmers. The Araucanians rejected this alternative, preferring to own their own land. Some became successful small farmers and supported the promised reforms of President Salvador Allende Gossens. Allende allowed the Indians to control Chilean farms in their region. However, in 1973, Allende was overthrown and his reform movement ceased. A military junta returned the

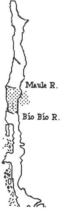

Araucania today

Araucanians to reservations and destroyed those who had actively supported Allende. Close to 20,000 Araucanians escaped punishment by moving, as in the past, across the low Andes into the pampas region of Argentina known as Patagonia. Today, Araucanian tradition survives among such isolated Indians and in the mestizo population that has become part of a larger Chilean culture.

Culture Today

Shelter. The early Araucanians were skilled hunters who wielded bows and arrows, and they were herders who followed their livestock from one feeding place to the next. Low skin tents provided suitable housing for these nomads. As they developed agricultural lifestyles, the people changed their homes into more permanent structures built of wood and covered by thatched roofs. The northern and southern Araucanians lived in large grass-thatched communal buildings that housed extended families, while the more mobile Mapuche of the central forests built similar but smaller single family units. Late in the 19th century, Araucanians began replacing their low, grass-thatched wooden houses with sturdier and roomier frame dwellings.

Clothing. As they modernized their housing, the Araucanians also updated their standard dress. Originally they wore scanty costumes of fur or wool. To these, the Araucanians added *ponchos, chamalls, chiripas,* and *kepams.* The men used the ponchos and chamalls as upper outer garments and wore the chiripa, a type of shirt, over full, long pantaloons. Often their waists were circled by heavy silver chains, serving as belts. Women wore the kepam, a woven cloth garment that was pinned over one shoulder and might be covered with a shawl draped over both shoulders. Such

Araucanian metalwork

dress has gradually given way to Levis, shirts, and styles in the contemporary Chilean fashion.

Food. Araucanians continue to depend on farming for their livelihood, but have made adjustments here too. The Spanish introduced cash crops – wheat, barley, oats – now grown by the people in addition to the customary potatoes, quinoa, beans, and maize. Money earned from the cash crops is spent on manufactured goods such as iron kettles and pots for cooking.

The central Araucanians are generally vegetarians who raise livestock but restrict their consumption of meat to festivals and celebrations. Those who live by the coast supplement both their income and diet by fishing for sea urchins, crabs, and flatfish.

Family life. Men are heads of Araucanian families, and descent has always been traced through the father's line. In earlier times the man might marry more than one wife provided he could afford the bride price. Payment for each bride was costly, amounting to as many as one hundred llamas, or large quantities of food or other goods. A marriage often began with the groom's staged kidnapping of the bride, her sister struggling in a pretended attempt to ward off the kidnapper. The ceremony was completed by the groom's carrying the bride off on horseback and then building an Araucanian house for her. Today's men still head each household but are limited to a single wife and are likely to marry in a European style ceremony.

Government. For centuries Araucanian self-rule operated without a central government. Leadership was regional; four *toquis* (princes) divided the land and people, joining together against common enemies. The toquis and their council of advisors, the *ulmen*, who were chiefs over smaller areas, met periodically to discuss issues of interest to the whole region, the *vutanmapua*. The toquis and lesser chiefs inherited their positions, providing

Araucanian horse gear

military and religious leadership. However, a chief's influence was not decreed by law, and the chief was not legally entitled to inflict punishment or demand obedience. Inca, Spanish, and Chilean central governments were strange to the Araucanians. The lawmaking power of the military junta that took command in 1973 was particularly contradictory to Araucanian political tradition. Still, the people are subject to the central Chilean government and must comply with its policies.

Religion. In earlier times Araucanian chiefs provided religious leadership, acting as priests at various rituals. In annual celebrations, the chief-priest would begin chants and prayers that culminated in a decision about which animals to sacrifice to the Araucanian gods. These gods included one chief deity and many lesser gods who might be good or evil and represented parts of the natural world. There were no temples or idols in this traditional religion. When the Jesuits arrived, a great effort was launched to convert the Indians to Catholicism, but the result was a blending of the new religion with the old animistic beliefs. Today, shamans remain as the leaders of a religion in which ancestral spirits take their places along with mythical deities. The shamans intercede with these spiritual beings to cure illness, investigate death, and encourage fair weather or good crops. Although women have been considered inferior to men in Araucanian society, they may become shamans and have generally enjoyed a higher status than other women in Chilean society.

Education. Araucanian children attend Chilean schools and their elders may learn to read and write Spanish by participating in the national campaigns against illiteracy. Yet the Mapuche continue to perpetuate Araucanian ways, teaching their own language, religion, and history and

Ceremonial mask

making a sharp distinction between themselves and the white people of Chile.

Change. For many years Araucanians have been blending into the larger national society. Their women's rights have served as an example for other Chilean women, their children are more and more accepting the challenge of Chilean education, and their informal government is giving way to a Chilean national government. Still, there are the Mapuche torchbearers and the poem *La Araucana* to keep the people alive.

ARGENTINES

(ar´ jen teens´)

The people of Argentina, primarily a mixture of native Indians and whites of Spanish, Italian, and German descent.

Argentina

Population: 31,965,000 (1988).
Location: Argentina, a republic in the southeastern section of the continent. Two thirds of the population live on a fertile, grassy plain traversed by the Río de la Plata and its tributaries.
Language: Predominantly Spanish.

Geographical Setting

Argentina is often considered a land with four geographical sections. The northwestern border lies in the Andes Mountains. South of the mountains, the country begins to flatten toward the tip of the continent, becoming rocky grassland. A high plateau region lies east of the Andes and slopes into a large, grassy area. This grassy area is drained by the Río Paraguay and Río Paraná, which themselves drain into the baylike Río de la Plata. The climate is mild in this region, the pampas, where two thirds of the people live.

Historical Background

Early history. About 300,000 Indians were scattered throughout the large area that is now Argentina when the Spaniards arrived in the 16th century. These Indians fell into at least ten distinct groups with various lifestyles. The Guaraní, for example, farmed the fertile river valleys. More typical in the south were Indians who lived by hunting animals such as the ostrich and seal and by gathering mollusks. Farther north, the Araucanians roamed the grasslands in bands of one to two hundred families, living off the wild animals that abounded in the area.

Spanish rule. The arrival of the explorer Juan Díaz de Solís in 1516 marked the beginning of 300 years of rule by Spain. More than 50 years would pass before Buenos Aires was founded in 1580, and it was to remain little more than a village for the next two centuries. There were a sufficient number of Spanish women to generate pure Spanish families, and thus began the Creole (Spanish born in the New World) elite. Unions between Spanish men and Indian women produced mestizo offspring, who grew into the artisans and laborers of colonial towns or the herdspeople and wagoners of the early countryside. Black slaves entered the country in the 17th and 18th centuries, becoming servants and artisans, caring for livestock, and planting or harvesting.

In 1776 political leadership of the large area claimed by the Spanish crown was centered at Buenos Aires. British troops tried to seize Buenos Aires in 1806, but residents fought them off and a decade later, in 1816, declared independence from Spain at the urging of the national hero José de San Martín.

Independence. At the onset of independence in 1816, about 30 percent of the Argentines were Indian and 10 percent were black while the majority of the population were mestizo and Creole or Spanish. Some of the people lived in the interior, and others, known as the *porteños* (people of the port), lived in coastal villages such as Buenos Aires. Argentines, then, began as a population divided into different groups and scattered through the countryside, a situation which would handicap their development as a people.

In 1862 Buenos Aires became the capital of the region, and over the next 60 years this region became the heart of the country. Although the Spanish had found the grasslands uninviting at first, their livestock multiplied into the hundreds of thousands on the well-watered plain. Settlers profited by raising sheep, cattle, and horses. With the appearance of refrigerated transport, meats became a major export in addition to wool, sheepskins, and hides. Argentina was soon exporter of half the world's beef.

Cotton plantations and saw mills appeared on the grasslands as well, but cattle ranchers dominated the scene with their huge landholdings. Meanwhile immigrant farmers shifted from one short-term tenancy to another, and the landless gaucho, the Argentine equivalent of the American cowboy, found seasonal employment. These were the minorities. Most Argentines, lived in towns and villages as traders, builders, or farmers.

As a people the Argentines are said to have taken the greatest strides from 1870 to 1930. At the beginning of this period, Domingo Faustino Sarmiento served as president. Already having distinguished himself as a man of letters, he had denigrated the rambling lifestyle of the gaucho in the biography *Facundo*. Sarmiento encouraged immigration and was rewarded with the entry of 2.5 million Europeans in this 50-year period.

Immigrants. Italians and Spaniards came in the greatest numbers, with the Italians in the forefront. Pouring into the grassland region, they raised wheat, corn, and flax, sharing the fertile area with the ranchers. Meanwhile, the government began a campaign in which it pushed back the Araucanian Indians, who responded with fierce resistance for two years. Large estates, *estancias*, then monopolized the rich farmland.

Class structure. Beginning in the 1880s, enormous fortunes led to the growth of an upper class based on those who owned land on the pampas. Also during this period, a middle class rose from the ranks of immigrant laborers who swelled the population in the port cities, becoming grocers, clerks, and office managers. Others worked as stevedores, bricklayers, mechanics, and factory laborers. There were ethnic tendencies. Italians became sharecroppers on the pampas while the Irish turned to sheepherding in Patagonia, a south land shared today by Argentina and Chile. In town and country, the lower class was reserved for the great numbers of Argentines who labored with their hands.

Argentina

A melding of traditions began. Although Argentines readily accepted foreign influences – Paris fashions, British boots, Italian pasta – they began to balk at control by outsiders. A 1936 riot broke out in Buenos Aires in reaction to a pact giving the British control of city transportation.

Conflict. The history of Argentine government is one of struggle between local autonomy and national authority. The people have been subject to rule by *caudillos*, strong men who in effect became dictators of their areas. Typically the caudillo was a Creole who belonged to some high ranking family. For a power base, he would group a contingent of gauchos and peons to serve as his cavalry. The caudillo became the government, wielding absolute power over his area. After Buenos Aires became the national capital, large landowners had great influence in the national government, and the caudillos became more typical politicians.

The Peróns. In 1930 the national government experienced a military takeover, an event that would repeat itself time and again in the coming years. In 1943 Argentine soldiers seized control while Colonel Juan Domingo Perón Sosa began to muster support from the lower classes. In 1946 Perón was elected president and proceeded to become the workers' champion, backing labor unions, social security, shorter hours, higher medical benefits, and so on. His charismatic second wife, Eva Duarte, inspired the masses as well, but in the long run Perón's policies raised expectations that remained unfulfilled. Exiled in 1955, he returned to lead the country again in 1973, then died and was succeeded by his third wife, María Estela Martínez de Perón, who was deposed in 1976. There began a period of fierce repression that is sometimes labeled the "dirty war." Lasting until 1983, the period was characterized by imprisonment, torture, and murder of opponents to the military. An alleged 15,000 to 30,000 Argentines, many of them Jews, "disappeared" during this period. Their disappearance gave rise to the charge of antisemitism; over 10,000 were thought to have been murdered because of their religion.

Meanwhile the Argentine military was defeated by Britain in a 1982 war over ownership of the *Islas Malvinas* (Falkland Islands).

The Argentines demonstrated against their government in 1982 and 1983, managing to elect Raúl Alfonsín president in 1983. Alfonsín's record as a champion of human rights and his reputation as a lawyer boded well for the people. Still, they are threatened by the history of military takeovers and a rising cost of living; the rise in prices was over a thousand percent in 1985, for example. The history of military strength helps to explain the outcomes of the 1987 trials of military men accused of violating human rights. Rebellions in army garrisons resulted in a pardon for many of the accused.

Culture Today

Cultural heritage. Today Argentines are searching in two directions for an Argentine identity. Since most are of European descent, they look to this heritage and will often identify with Europeans rather than South Americans. Even their Spanish, distinctly different from that spoken anywhere else on the continent, is peppered with European (Italian) words.

On the other hand, Argentine land is part of South America, so the people look to their Amerindian and Spanish backgrounds for an identity as well. The single most evident symbol of this heritage is the gaucho, or cowboy-style mestizo, who arrived on the pampas in the 17th century. Romanticized for his independence, the gaucho was a type of nomad, a horseman who usually possessed only his saddle and poncho. The sheepskin covered saddle served as his bed on the ground, and beef was his everyday fare. The common beverage was *yerba mate,* tea sipped through a straw from a gourd that the gauchos passed around a circle. On occasion, the gaucho might eat cornmeal mush sweetened with honey and sugar, or squash cooked in a beef soup, but mostly he disdained vegetables, perhaps because they symbolized the farming lifestyle he rejected.

The gaucho. At first gauchos wore blanketlike ponchos and the *chiripá*, a diaperlike cloth over lacy leggings. Then the pants changed to baggy trousers, *bombachas*, which tapered at the ankle to fit inside handmade boots. The boots, open-toed and fashioned from colts' hides, later gave way to a manufactured variety. Completing the gaucho's costume were a short-brimmed straw hat, bright-colored shirt, and broad leather belt. The belt was adorned with coins and silver, and the gaucho always carried a sheathed knife. His hair was typically long, his beard a thick, tangled mass. Selling hides and ostrich feathers for income, the gaucho sustained himself to the end of the 19th century, then began to disappear, giving way to settlements, fences, and immigrants on the frontier.

Growth of cities. Only one fifth of the country's territory, the fertile pampas is now home to over two thirds of the population.

Gaucho parade dress. Usually the gaucho wears work clothes with the large-brim hat.

However, the late 20th century population is a shifting one that has been moving from rural areas to the cities. Initially the rural population was attracted by the higher standard of living in the city. Rural homes have ranged from the great *estancias* (estates) to the more common meager shelters with adobe walls, dirt floors, and roofs of straw and mud. Many of the rural folk slept in single-room earthen shacks without furniture, living as renters and working as farm laborers. Moving to the coast, they became *porteños* (people of the port) and life improved.

Many took jobs as workers in the region's towns and cities. Industry in the pampas now outweighs agriculture, which employs less than 15 percent of the work force. The industry is centered in either large factories or small shops and plants with fewer than ten workers.

Shelter. City housing changed over the years. In European style, many of the towns and cities were originally built around a main square or plaza. Only a limited number of buildings rose higher than two stories. The average town house for the elite was the three or four story villa, and owners would often have second homes, chalets in the hills or on the beaches. Depending on their financial circumstances, today's city dwellers may live in a mansion, a tall, modern apartment building, or a bungalow with a small yard or garden. Hundreds of local communities with middle and lower class housing have appeared beyond the downtown area. Known as *barrios*, the communities feature quiet, shaded streets and patio-style construction. A lack of available housing in the cities has resulted in the appearance of shantytowns on the outskirts of cities. Here the city dwellers live in shacks, often without running water or sewers.

Although the standard of living remains higher in the cities than the country, today's workers are prey to rising prices and escalating unemployment. Salaries increase less quickly than prices, so there is more poverty and hunger. Despite government food programs, 35 percent of Argentine children suffered malnutrition in 1985.

Food. Beef remains the preferred meat, although lamb and chicken are eaten as well. Meats are commonly prepared as steaks, stews, or *empanadas* (pastry turnovers). Bread and potatoes have replaced corn dishes as staples for the urban dwellers, while the corn dishes (*mazamorra, locro*) are still common in rural areas. Pastas, introduced by the Italians, remain a popular option in the everyday diet. Another practice that has endured is the gaucho custom of sipping tea through a straw from a gourd.

Clothing. Argentine clothing was conservative at first. White smocks were the rule for school children while women wore black or quiet dress. A dark suit, a hat, a tie, and polished shoes were typical on men. The conservatism was so strong that until 1954 men could not shed their coats in public. A poncho over a colorful shirt along with a derby, or bowler hat, is an outfit chosen by Indians in the northwest. Otherwise, today's clothing styles parallel those in the United States, although gaucho-style wide-brimmed hats, ponchos, and loose trousers tucked into low boots are still seen in the country.

Population composition. Today's Argentine is an amalgam of the Creole, the mestizo, and the immigrant. Close to 90 percent of the present population is considered white; most of the remainder is classed as mestizo. Only a fraction of the original Indian population remains, and there are even fewer blacks.

The upper class includes the newly rich and powerful (landowners, financiers, entrepreneurs, high ranking military officers). Among those who enjoy the highest status are a core of elite families of immigrant origin whose prestige is based on their ownership of the large landed estates. The middle class is today composed of self-employed professionals, civil servants, white collar workers, and owners of small businesses. Members of the lower class range from factory workers to street vendors to rural agricultural workers, the common denominator still being work done with the hands.

Family. The size of the Argentine family has depended on its social standing. At one time, upper class families had 20 or more in a household, and today they might still be large. Among the lower classes, the size of families remains small, including less than two children per family. Common law marriages are nearly as prevalent as legal ones, yet families are described as generally stable.

Argentina is a democratic republic with a constitution that requires the president to be Catholic. This fact may be misleading, for in practice many Argentines are only nominally Catholic. Along with the Alfonsín government has come increased religious tolerance, a fact publicly acknowledged by Jews.

The sizeable immigrant population has had a considerable effect on daily Argentine life. Aside from adding macaroni, spaghetti, and vermicelli to the national diet, the Italians brought expressions such as *chau* ("farewell") into the Spanish language. In rural areas a hybrid dialect, *cocoliche*, combined Italian and Spanish. Outside Buenos Aires there was a village of Welsh speaking immigrants. Others spoke German or English, but most conformed to the norm by learning Argentine Spanish.

Education. In keeping with the traditional disdain for work done with the hands, education has been encouraged in Argentine families. From ages six to 14, schooling is compulsory, and among the people as a whole the illiteracy rate is relatively low (6.1 percent in 1980).

Arts. Individual Argentines have distinguished themselves in several fields. Luis Frederico Leloir won the Nobel Prize for Chemistry in 1970, and Adolfo Pérez Esquivel received the Nobel Peace Prize in 1980. In literature Ernesto Sábato won the highest Spanish honor, the Cervantes Prize in 1985.

Argentines have long been described as leaders in the Latin American literary and artistic worlds. Written in the 1870s, José Hernandez's epic poem *The Gaucho Martín Fierro* celebrates the life and art of the gaucho, a national symbol. Here are lines from a bilingual edition (Albany: State University of New York Press, 1967), English version by C. E. Ward. The term *criollo* is used to mean "person who deserves respect."

> But where another *criollo* goes
> Martín Fierro will go too;
> there's nothing sets him back,
> even ghosts don't scare him
> and since everybody sings
> I want to sing also.
>
> (P. 5)

Hernandez's poem honors the gaucho while Sarmiento's biography slights him. Their differences highlight a reappearing theme in Argentine literature. Novelists (e.g., Jorge Luis Borges), essayists (e.g., Ricardo Rojas), poets (e.g., Leopoldo Lugones), and playwrights (e.g., Florencio Sanchez) have participated in the quest to define the nation's character.

The Gaucho Martín Fierro speaks of song, an art form that would grow in the first half of the 20th century. Buenos Aires became a center of opera, ballet and concerts on the continent. Drawing on gaucho songs and dances, Alberto Ginastera rose to the forefront as a classical composer. The most renowned Argentine dance, the tango, was based on dances from a number of countries. Carlos Gardel transformed the tango into a song genre of wide appeal. Guitar, the featured instrument, is played by skilled troubadours who improvise, matching wits and talents in musical duels.

Over the years the gaucho has remained a literary symbol, Raul Roux and Roberta Fontanarrosa creating some of the most popular gaucho comics. Other comics include *Malfalda* by Joaquín Salvador Lavados, in which a girl traces the pains and pleasures of middle class existence.

AYMARA

(ai mar´ a)

An Indian people living in the high plateau region
bordering Peru and Bolivia near Lake Titicaca.

Population: 1,250,000 (1978).
Location: Peru, Bolivia.
Language: Aymaran, one of the Quechua family
of languages spoken in many versions by different
peoples of the Andes.

The Aymara in
Peru and Bolivia

Geographical Setting

Lake Titicaca is in the Andes Mountains at an
elevation above 12,000 feet. Just east and south is
the city of La Paz, Bolivia, one of the highest
cities in the world. North of La Paz, the Andes
Mountains level into a high plateau at an elevation
of 5,000 to 10,000 feet. This narrow plateau
drops westward into a swampland, then levels
into the river routes of Brazil. The Aymara live in
the high plateau area.

Historical Background

Inca rule. The Aymara were once divided into
independent states led by rival chieftains who
waged war upon one another. Two of the fiercest
states were formed by groups of Aymara called
the *Calla* and the *Lupaca*. Along with other
Aymara, these groups were invaded by the Inca
people around the year 1430. The Calla and the
Lupaca competed to ally themselves with the Inca
chief. Although the Lupaca succeeded, becoming
the Inca ally and proceeding to crush the Calla,
their victory was short-lived. The next Inca
emperor conquered the Lupaca and went on to
defeat other Aymara groups. By 1493 the people

41

were completely subdued. The most powerful group conquered by the Inca, the Aymara, were used to strengthen Inca forces. Garrisoned with Inca troops, they fought with their conquerors against other Inca enemies until the 1530s.

Spanish rule. Under the leadership of Francisco Pizarro, Spaniards defeated the Inca in 1538, then defeated an independent Aymara army and conquered all of its people by 1542. As a group, the Aymara were placed under the control of King Charles and entered into an *encomienda* program that promised protection in exchange for taxes and services. The people were forced to pay heavy tribute to Spanish authorities for the "privilege" of producing food on small plots of land. Otherwise, they worked as household servants or laborers on the cocoa plantations or in the copper mines. Thousands of Aymara died working in the mines, a condition that continued for two centuries (1540–1780).

The Spanish exerted a major influence on the lifestyle of the Aymara. They introduced cultivated plants, the plow, a new kind of loom, iron tools, and domesticated animals into the culture, but they also banned certain traditions. One was the Aymara practice of deforming infants' heads into the shape of a sugar loaf. Viceroy Francisco de Toledo also asked the Aymara to adopt Spanish clothing and outlawed their traditions of painting the face and sleeping on

Independence. Conditions became more repressive under Viceroy Toledo, and in 1780 the Aymara rebelled. Forty years of war followed during which large numbers of Spaniards and Aymara were killed and whole settlements burned to the ground. Victory was finally won by the Indians in 1821. After becoming independent, they formed local administrations centered around the towns that had been built by the Spanish. Many continued to work in the mines, collecting the tin that Bolivia began to export. Known as obedient, industrious workers who were able to survive harsh conditions, the Aymara were poorly paid by the whites who came to wield power in Bolivia.

The Aymara were independent of Spain, but their lifestyle had changed under its control. The people did not simply revert to the patterns of behavior they had established before the coming of the Spanish; rather, they were forced to shape their culture anew.

Culture Today

The Aymara live under harsh conditions near Lake Titicaca on a plateau where the soil is poor, trees are scarce, and the grass is coarse. The Quechua people live nearby, but there is little feeling of unity with them or amongst the Aymara themselves. Different Aymara villages often regard one another with hostility. Living without their own centralized government, the people are controlled by a headman for each *ayllu*, or local unit. The larger districts they inhabit are ruled by white governors from the republics of Peru or Bolivia.

Food. Although some have migrated to their country's cities or mines, those who remain in Aymara villages continue to subsist by farming and herding. The people grow barley, potatoes, beans, onions, garlic, maize, and wheat on land that is largely barren except for some fertile eastern valleys. The tasks of digging, plowing, and threshing are done by the men, but the women do the planting. Women also herd the livestock, which mainly includes llamas, sheep, cows, and pigs.

Aymara house

Despite raising animals, the people rarely eat meat. A heavily spiced soup and the fish from Lake Titicaca are the staples in their diet. The Aymara use reed to build giant, cigar-shaped rafts from which they catch the fish in nets. Many of the Aymara also chew coca, a green, mildly narcotic plant that grows everywhere in Aymara country. Containing cocaine, its leaves have traditionally been chewed to allay hunger.

Shelter. The housing and clothing of the present day Aymara have been shaped by their former conquerors. Aymara homes are similar in style to old Inca houses. The structures are generally small (8 by 12 feet), built of adobe brick, and covered with a thatched roof. Usually consisting of one room, the house has no windows, just a small door facing east. The room is unfurnished, except for a clay stove by the door and llama pelts placed on a low earthen platform for sleeping.

Aymara village

Clothing. Colonial Spanish clothing provides the model for Aymara dress. Men wear patched cloth jackets and trousers, ponchos made of llama wool, and homemade sandals of hide or rubber. For head covering they slip on knitted caps with earflaps or trilby hats. Women wear brightly colored shawls over cotton blouses and skirts. Their typical head covering is a bowler hat.

Family. The basic social unit in Aymara society is the extended family – a husband and wife, their sons and unmarried daughters, and the husband's brothers and their wives. Determining settlement patterns, the family generally lives in a cluster of one-room houses.

Parents take responsibility for the spiritual as well as physical well-being of the young. They arrange marriages, calling for the groom to pay a bride price, compensation for the loss of the girl to the family. Chosen at weddings, godparents help settle quarrels between newlyweds. The newlyweds visit them on a regular basis. The Aymara choose other godparents for a child at baptism. Aside from religious obligations, the godparents assume economic obligations such as buying the child clothing and paying the baptism fee. Among the Aymara who migrate to mines or towns, there is a loosening of family obligations and ties.

Religion and tradition. The people often practice Catholicism along with their former religion. For example, children officially enter the Aymara community first through baptism, then through the *rutucha,* or hair-cutting ceremony. They believe that spirits exist everywhere in nature and associate saints with mountain spirits. According to the Aymara, *acacila* (place spirits) inhabit rivers, lakes, springs, and mountains. They believe that these spirits control the weather, sending hail, rain, and winds. *Uiwiri* (lesser spirits) guard the homes and the people from evil beings. Thought to inhabit ruins, caves, and certain stones, uiwiri have been personified as a beautiful woman who causes insanity, an evil old hag who causes sickness, and a three-headed water monster who dwells in Lake Titicaca. Should misfortune befall them, the people resort to cures. Over four hundred remedies for misfortunes have been created by Aymara magicians and medicine men, including quinine for fever and other effective treatments.

BELIZIANS

(bay leez´ i ans)

The people of Belize, a British protectorate
formerly known as British Hondurus.

Belize

Population: 166,000 (1985).
Location: The small country Belize located on
the Atlantic Coast of Central America, south of the
Yucatán Peninsula.
Language: English, Spanish, Mayan.

Geographical Setting

The small country of Belize (the size of
Massachusetts) lies on the Atlantic Coast bordered
by the Mexican state of Campeche on the north
and northwest, and by Guatemala on the west.
Beyond a swampy shoreline, what was once
mostly tropical hardwood forest is now largely a
grass and shrub covered lowland. In the
southwest the land rises to the hardwood forests
of the Mayan mountain range. The central region
with its port community of Belize City and its
inland capital, Belmopan, is low – for the most
part, not more than 400 feet above sea level.
Belize City lies only 18 inches above the Atlantic
Ocean. Toward the north, the country becomes a
dense scrub forest. Over a hundred rivers cross
the lowlands, emptying into the Atlantic along 160
miles of coastline dotted with small islands (cays)
and coral reefs. Much of the seacoast is swampy,
mangrove forest. Climatically, the country lies in
the path of frequent tropical storms that begin in
the Atlantic. Although hurricanes have sometimes
devasted the land, mostly the temperature is
moderate. Belize City enjoys a breezy 70 degrees
Fahrenheit from October to May.

Historical Background

Mayans. Ruins of Mayan structures indicate that Belize was part of the Mayan empire long before the Europeans arrived. By the arrival of the first Spanish explorers in Central America in the 15th century, the Mayan society had faded and independent Indian groups inhabited this area around the Yucatan Peninsula. Spanish conquistadors had little interest in the region. Its cays and coral reefs and the dense jungle made the land inaccessible. Therefore, it was left to the Indians until the early 1600s when the British took an interest in Belize's hardwood forests.

British interest. By 1638, British foresters had established a community on the site of Belize City and had begun to harvest logwood that was then valuable for dyes and mahogany.

Spanish interest. Belize was claimed by Spain and ruled from Guatemala for nearly two hundred years in the 1700s and 1800s. However, the Spanish developed only a few small settlements in the west.

At first this region was not bothered by the presence of the British. In 1762, Spain recognized British explorations in the region and their colonies along the coast, granting Britain rights to harvest timber in the north and central part of the land. As the English lumbering business prospered, the Spanish and the French attempted to take over the colony but with little enthusiasm and no success.

Guatemalan interest. When Spain withdrew from Central America and Mexico, the land that is now Belize was claimed by Guatemala, but the British were already well established there. By 1850 the dispute over ownership had grown, as had British lumbering and farming interests. In 1859, Great Britain and Guatemala decided to settle the dispute. Great Britain would be granted the land of Belize in return for building a highway through Guatemala. The British began to govern the country from Jamaica and, in 1862, declared Belize a British colony. Meanwhile, the road in Guatemala was never built. Therefore, Guatemala has claimed all or part of Belize since that time.

Meanwhile, the Maya Indians began to share Belize with a mix of other ethnic groups. Along with the early British settlers came black slaves to be employed in the timber industry. Although unfree, they were coworkers with their owners in a forbidding environment and so their status was higher than that of black slaves elsewhere. In addition, free black immigrants came to the land willingly. Intermarriages between the British and the Africans were common and gave birth to the Creoles, who became a major sector of the population. In 1832 a group known as the Black Caribs (black Indians) escaped conflict in Honduras by settling in Belize. Then came thousands of mestizos. They fled from the long, bloody War of the Races (1848-1872), which had started in Yucatán as an Indian uprising against people with European blood. Part Spanish and part Indian, the mestizos entered Belize in search of British protection. They brought sugar cane into the land with them, beginning Belize's most significant industry. Other immigrants (East Indians, Lebanese, Chinese, Canadians) came in smaller groups.

Independence. Led by George Price, the British-appointed governor, Belizians pressed for self-rule. Britain granted the right of internal self-government in 1964 but continued to be responsible for defense and external affairs. Finally, in 1981 Belize was granted status as a fully independent nation within the British Commonwealth. Yet the issues with Guatemala made it necessary for the new country to ask Great Britain for continued military protection, a service Britain would willingly provide to protect its own interests such as the refineries of a British sugar company. Becoming known as the father of the country, George Price took office as prime minister. Under the People's United Party, he established a democratic government that had a single legislative body of 18 members.

For a short time, the new government in Belize was successful in improving the economy based on growing and exporting sugar and beef. But as the market for sugar declined, the British sugar company withdrew and sold its refineries to the Belize government. Unemployment along with immigration of 20,000 refugees, mostly from Guatemala, El Salvador, and Honduras, made conditions worse. The government responded by establishing other businesses: citrus farms, fishing and shrimp farms. They were successful, but did not develop rapidly enough to encourage the Belizians. Then, in 1982-3, the government under George Price responded to complaints from the United States by allowing Belize's marijuana fields to be sprayed with poison. The government felt money from outside countries would stimulate other sources of revenue to take the place of income from marijuana.

Belize City

Officially Belize is now a constitutional monarchy with the British sovereign as Head of State and with two legislative bodies. The key government official continues to be the resident prime minister. In 1984, George Price was defeated by Manuel Esquivel, a high-school teacher who founded the United Democratic Party. Esquivel campaigned for free enterprise and less government in business. His aims have been to strengthen Belize through foreign investment and to keep British troops there until the dispute with Guatemala can be resolved.

Culture Today

The majority of Belizians today are of multiracial heritage. According to a population breakdown by their ethnic origins, roughly half are of African or mixed African descent (Caribs, Creoles, and Africans). Those of mestizo origin are the next most numerous group, and they are followed by the Maya Indians. The remaining groups are even smaller

These groups populated the country from two directions. The Caribs (Indians), for example, came from Jamaica and other East Indian islands, while the mestizos came from the Central American states. Many of the immigrants settled along the coast. Today nearly a third of the population lives in the port community of Belize City.

Place of worship
in Belize

Food, clothing and shelter. That this is a country of small communities is evident by the number who inhabit Belize City (about 50,000) and the country's capital city, Belmopan (3,000). Belizians live either in a city or village, or on one of a few large ranches. The standard shelter is the wood frame house, often built on stilts to protect against hurricanes and other violent storms. White or unpainted, the bungalow generally has little furniture, usually a hammock for the man of the house, a bed, straw mattresses, chairs, and perhaps a dresser. Outside the larger towns, kerosene lamps provide light in homes that are without electricity.

Clothing varies, but pants and shirts for men and dresses for women are common. Clothing factories have developed rapidly and contributed substantially to the growth of Belize industry. Still the economy is mainly agricultural, resting on the production of sugar, bananas, and citrus fruits. Nearly two thirds of the Belize work force has been unemployed except for seasonal crop labor.

The average yearly income was less than 500 dollars in 1987.

Finding food is a major occupation for most Belizians, although direct responsibility is most often given to the mother of the family. The staple foods are rice, kidney beans, and maize. Growing rice in swampland without irrigation, Belizians now raise a large enough quantity to export it as a cash crop to the East Indies. Still, in some villages the search for food remains difficult. Once villagers practiced a form of slash and burn agriculture to eke out a subsistence crop. But as the larger towns developed industry and large ranches appeared, many of the most able workers left the villages to earn wages elsewhere. Only the children and elderly people remained in the villages to raise crops, and these stay-at-homes were neither strong nor practiced enough farmers to perform the job successfully. Today most villagers must purchase or barter for food.

Family. The change in the food situation has altered the family structure as well. When parents leave home to become wage earners, other relatives care for the children. It is as if anyone willing to feed them becomes, in effect, their parents.

Education. Education for children is held in high regard, a value credited to the British who have worked to improve the school system. By 1975 the literacy rate (based on the ability to write one's own name and the date) was as high as 95 percent. Education is now required for everyone between six and 14 years of age. The government supports primary schools, secondary schools, and technical colleges. Most are also sponsored by religious organizations.

Religion. Since Belize was settled by both mainland and East Indies people, its citizenry is divided in religion and language. Over half the citizens (including mestizos from Central America) claim to be Roman Catholics and speak

Spanish. On the other hand, there are Belizians (including those from the East Indies) who claim Protestant Church memberships and speak English. A creole form of English is often used with friends, but to strangers the people speak very proper English. Other Belizians still communicate in Mayan languages and practice Indian religions.

Despite the different religions, many Belizians share a common set of beliefs and folkways. For example, their houses often have shutters that provide protection from the violent storms. Between storms, the shutters are closed each night to keep out the many ghosts and spirits that are thought to inhabit the land. In everyday speech, Belizians use creole proverbs that reflect a philosophy of life. Among them are those that place high value on patience and faith — for example, "Same place Pelican wanto go, sea breeze blow 'em." William David Setzekorn cites this example and others in *Formerly British Honduras: A Profile of the New Nation of Belize* (Newark, California, Dumbarton Press, 1975).

Arts. Both the United States and Latin America have greatly influenced music in Belize today. Once, though, the traditional "break-down," an original Calypsolike story song, was popular throughout the land. Often improvised, the break-down told stories about local incidents and relied on witty puns to poke fun at some important person.

Belizian folklore describes a phantom pirate ship that travels at night, its rigging lit by flickering lanterns. Legend has it that the ship tricks sailors into landing on coral reefs. Folk characters include the four-fingered *Duendes* (dwarfs) of the jungle. If one is captured by them, he or she supposedly suffers two consequences: losing his or her mind and instantly mastering a musical instrument. Forest workers, though, argue that they have seen Duendes, and the little folk are harmless. In fact, there is some evidence that such little people may have existed in the area at one time, as Mayan murals have been found that picture them.

BOLIVIANS

(bo liv´ ee uns)
The people of the country Bolivia, the
majority of whom are Amerindians.

Bolivia

Population: 6,600,000 (1987).
Location: Bolivia.
Language: Spanish, Quechua, Aymara.

Geographical Setting

At one time Bolivia covered an area that was
over 50 percent larger than it is today, and
extended to the Pacific Coast. Now, however,
Bolivia is landlocked, with great geographical
barriers to transportation.
The Altiplano. Running through Bolivia, the
Andes Mountains divide into two separate ranges.
The western range marks the border with Chile.
The eastern range, with peaks as high as 21,000
feet near Lake Titicaca, extends through the
middle of the country and separates a high
western plateau known as the altiplano from the
moist tropical plains of the east. The altiplano
includes Lake Titicaca, the highest lake in the
world, but is otherwise harsh. Up to 100 miles
wide, the altiplano spans more than 500 difficult
miles north to south. The soil is stony and dry, the
air thin, the climate cold. Communities suffer 40-
degree Fahrenheit temperature in July and 300
frost-filled evenings a year. Yet many Bolivians
live on the altiplano or on the western edge of the
eastern Andes range. This eastern range has
several high valleys, which include the major
cities Sucre and Cochabamba. Located 12,000
feet above sea level, the capital city, La Paz, lies
in a gorge of the La Paz River at the feet of two

mountains, Illimani and Illampu, that rise higher than 21,000 feet.

Mountain valleys. On the east side of the eastern Andes, water from the mountains drains into rivers of the Amazon tributaries. In their courses down the mountains, the rivers have formed many fertile valleys. These *Yungas* are the sites of large plantations and are mostly controlled by Bolivia's small European population.

A great low plain covers the northern and eastern sections of the country. In the north, this plain is covered with tropical rain forest; in the southeast the land is grass covered or swampy.

Historical Background

Amerindians have formed the largest portion of the Bolivian population from the early days onward. Yet the history of the country is one of suppression and of frequent revolutions.

Early settlers. Indians of the Andes inhabited the land and had formed well-developed communities before the entry of Europeans. Tiahuanaco Indians are thought to have lived near Lake Titicaca around A.D. 100. Powerful until the 1200s, these Indians erected great monuments and carved statues of stone. South of the lake, in the eastern Andes and the altiplano, the country was dominated by Aymara-speaking Indians in the 1300s (see AYMARA).

Establishing powerful societies, some of these early Indians grew quite wealthy. Highland settlements organized colonies in the lowlands, building a network of resources that provided comforts in an otherwise harsh environment. Three, four, or ten walking days away from a highland settlement, the colonies specialized in raising coca leaves or herding livestock, digging for salt, and growing cotton. Always their purpose was to wrest what they could from the environment, then feed it back to the highlanders.

Those people at lower altitudes produced meat, wool, and maize, for example. Though society was based mainly on agriculture and herding, forest colonists crafted wooden goblets and plates. Eventually the trade network extended to villages with specialties such as potterywork.

Inca rule. In 1440 Inca Indians who spoke the Quechua language overran Bolivia, driving the Aymara into the less fertile region of the altiplano (see QUECHUA). Nearly a hundred years later, in 1532, Francisco Pizarro conquered the Incas in Peru and sent his partner to explore the Bolivian ends of the Inca Empire. Diego de Almagro found the Aymara in the altiplano and the Quechua in the mountain valleys but claimed the land for Spain.

Spanish rule. In 1542 the Spanish government tried to end or at least limit *encomienda*, the system by which Indians were reduced to forced labor. The result was a revolution that prevented the Spanish government from taking control until 1548. Meanwhile, by 1545 the Spanish explorers had been led to a mountain of silver, Potosí. Afterwards, the Indians were forced to work in mines for Spanish lords, as they had formerly worked for other Spanish and Inca lords. The population soared, Potosí becoming the largest city in South America in the 1500s.

Under the Incas more than enough produce had been raised to feed the people. The Spanish, though, disrupted the careful balance of the agricultural world on which the Indians depended by making them work the mines. The Indians grew hungry and resisted. In 1781, they lay siege to the city La Paz until half its population starved or burned in fires begun by flaming arrows and spears.

However, Spanish influence continued to grow. A cathedral was built in the city of Sucre, and a shrine appeared near Lake Titicaca, As mining became less important, the Spanish hacienda, or large ranch, system developed. Still, while the hacienda became a basic form of landholding, the *communidades*, free communities of Indian land, survived. They would endure for three centuries through the coming of independence in 1825.

Independence. Known not as Bolivia but as Upper Peru, the country was, in the early 1800s, part of larger territory that the revolutionary Simón Bolívar fought to free from Spain. One of his generals, Antonio José de Sucre, defeated the Spanish at Ayacucho in what is now northern Peru. Sucre then marched through Upper Peru (Bolivia) to the ancient capital of Chuquisaca. There he established the seat of a newly independent country named after the inspirational Bolívar. Asked to write the first constitution, Bolívar provided for a president who would be elected for life and would select his own successor, assuming that a permanent and military government would lead to peace. On the contrary, succeeding years bore witness to numerous constitutions, over 175 rebellions, and 44 different presidents who governed at the pleasure of military leaders.

One of the best of the early presidents was Andrés Santa Cruz, who established laws and educational projects. Among the worst was General Mariano Melgarejo. He claimed to have placed the constitution of 1861 in one pocket and the constitution of 1868 in the other pocket, deciding no one would rule Bolivia but himself. Ignoring ownership rights, Melgarejo destroyed free Indian communities by deciding to sell commonly owned land. Much of the land was transferred to private owners after 1870, more haciendas were constructed in the following years (1880-1930), and the power of the Indian communities was broken. Thereafter, the Indians migrated to cities, and the mestizo population grew.

Conflict. As if having more than one coup d'état per year since the Revolution were not enough, Bolivians fought international battles with Paraguay and Chile. In the War of the Pacific (1897-1883) Bolivia lost its ocean port and adjoining territory to Chile. More territory, southern land rich in nitrates, was lost to Paraguay in the Chaco War (1932-1935). It was this war, though, that gave the Indians a patriotic feeling.

Mining. Silver gave way to tin after the 1900s, a minority of the people growing rich from the back-breaking labor of the Indians. Certainly there were those who seemed to deserve wealth. Simón I. Patiño spent all his money to buy a small claim that seemed worthless for four years during which he and his wife took pick and shovel in hand to work alongside Indian laborers. Then Patiño struck a vein of tin and became one of the five richest men in the world.

Revolution. Meanwhile, miserable conditions plagued most Indian mine workers. They could expect low wages and short lives that ended at age 30. In 1942 the miners rioted. The *Movimiento Nacionalista Revolucionario* (MNR), a political party appearing this same year, won support from miners, urban workers, and a growing middle class.

After the 1952 revolution, considered the most far-reaching in Bolivian history, MNR leader Doctor Víctor Paz Estenssoro took office as President. Paz granted all Bolivians the right to vote, took government control of the mines, and began land reform to help the Indians who were living in a type of serfdom under a few rich landowners. A coup toppled his government in 1964, but he was re-elected in 1985. Meanwhile, the nation had adopted the death penalty for terrorism and drug dealing. Also the problem of the jobless had grown, unemployment reaching 50 percent in 1982.

Culture Today

Unlike other countries in Latin America, Bolivia today is still mainly Indian. Indians, the Aymara and Quechua, comprise 60 percent of the population while mestizos make up 30 percent. A small percentage is European.

Today many live in the major cities – La Paz, Cochabamba, Santa Cruz and Sucre. The population is distributed between the altiplano and the valleys east of it where soil is more fertile, but the ethnic balance is uneven. The population on the altiplano is 70 percent Indian and mestizo; in the fertile Andean valleys it is 75 percent European. Thus, the European population still controls the choicest land.

Food, clothing and shelter. Citizens of the city live and dress much like people in Europe or the United States. Some occupy modern apartments or fashionable homes with Spanish-style patios. Tin mines continued to support a segment of the population until 1955, when aluminum began to replace tin for many purposes and the world demand dropped. As the industry declined, mine workers moved to cities. This created a housing shortage and the growth of slum areas on the outskirts of the cities, a common sight in Latin America.

In rural areas of the altiplano, Indians continue to live in adobe houses with thatched roofs and few or no windows. They also dress in customary clothing: men in loose-fitting pants and shirts with striped ponchos and sandals. Women wear long skirts, colorful serapes, and bowler-shaped hats. Wool and cotton are the standard materials.

Bolivians raise alpacas and llamas for wool and as beasts of burden. Able to survive at high altitudes, the animals also provide leather and meat. Transportation has been so poor that until recently cattle raised on the plain were killed only for hide because there were no roads or methods to transport and refrigerate beef. Although roads have since been built, most are unpaved. Air transport, of great value given the geography, has also been developed.

Industry today is limited but growing. Aside from factories, many small shops offer textiles, footwear, and clothing by artisans who bring to mind the craft specialists in the trade network of pre-Inca times.

Bolivian weaver

Still mostly an agricultural people, Bolivians raise crops such as potatoes, barley, and quinoa on the altiplano. The large haciendas have disappeared here due to land reform. But the soil is still dry and infertile. Some highlanders own a small stretch of the stony earth; others work for landowners, earning a meager wage plus the use of a small plot for subsistence crops. They then trade produce and pottery for necessities at markets held in village squares.

Colonization. As in pre-Inca times, the present population has established colonies in the tropical lowlands. Mennonites, Italians, and Japanese settled here in the 1950s and have been followed by peasants from the altiplano. Raised for food and export, lowland crops include cotton, sugar, rice, bananas, maize, and coffee. In 1984, 75 percent of all land was devoted to the growth of the coca leaf.

Coca. Bolivians speak of a legend concerning the coca leaf. An early king warned his people that their sun god was weaker than the Spanish god. They would be overpowered, but he would leave them with something helpful to Indians but harmful to whites. Later, coca leaves sprang up from the king's grave. In fact, Indians have long chewed the coca leaf for relief from cold and hunger. Consumed in this way, its effect has been mild though addictive. Many Indians now harvest the leaves for scant wages plus the opportunity to chew them. Refined in factories, cocaine derived from the plant has brought high profits though illegal trade. The government, with United States aid, has attempted to destroy the factories and replace the crop. Bolivians have resisted.

Government. Elected directly by the people, the country's president serves a four-year term. Today's constitution forbids an immediate second term. In the past the large landowner was a *caudillo*, or political boss, who exercised tremendous control of the country. Politics among peasants was limited to government by a village elder and to revolts under temporary leaders. Bolivia now has two houses of congress in which *caciques*, peasant leaders, have become an important pressure group.

Society in Bolivia today has changed. Instead of the old rural ruling class, there is a new business elite that lives in the city but may own a great deal of land. A middle class has appeared, including doctors, lawyers, and white collar workers. Generally they speak Spanish and live in the city. Practicing a mix of Spanish and Indian traditions, peddlers, factory hands, and farmers form the working class. At the lowest level is the largest social class – *campesinos*, poor farmers, whose customs are strictly Indian.

Religion. Regardless of social class, Bolivians are mostly Catholics. Their Catholicism, though, is blended with traditions from former religions. The result is religious celebration that includes a great many festivals filled with colorful costumes, parades, and ceremonies.

Arts and literature. Besides religious celebrations, folk music festivals have been popular in the cities since the 1960s. The upper and middle classes have used traditional tunes, updating the *música folklórica* to create popular music. In art, Maria Nuñez del Prado has sculptured Indians at work. Prominent writers include the poet Ricardo Jaimes Freyre, the historian Gabriel René Moreno, and the novelist Augusto Cespedes, whose work features the mistreated Indian tin miner.

Education. Despite these literary and artistic accomplishments, education has progressed slowly. Close to a quarter of the adults are illiterate, and those who can read and write are likely to be mestizos or whites. Only 16 percent of those aged 14 to 17 were enrolled in secondary school in 1980. The limited number of schools can only serve a portion of the large population. Furthermore, the incentive for enrolling in them is small. There are few jobs for the educated, and those that do exist pay poorly. A Bolivian lawyer, for example, may be forced to pursue another career – perhaps own a shop – to earn a living. Thus, the young and educated often choose to leave their country in search of a better life.

BRAZILIANS

(bra zil´ i ans)
The people of the country of Brazil, South America,
whose ancestry is largely Portuguese.

Population: 138,493,000 (1986).
Location: Brazil, South America, mostly on the
coast near Rio de Janeiro and São Paulo.
Language: Portuguese.

Brazil

Geographical Setting

Brazil is a large, roughly triangular country in
northeastern South America. It stretches more than
2000 miles from Peru on the western border to the
Atlantic Ocean on the east and the same distance
from Guyana on the north to Uruguay on the
south. The country is mostly lowland drained by
the Amazon, São Francisco, and Paraguay rivers.
Tropical forests line the Amazon and its
tributaries, and give way in the south to scrub
woodland and savannah. The Atlantic Coast is
bordered by forest land. In the central and
southern uplands, the climate is mild. Otherwise
the country is mainly tropical, hot and damp. The
average rainfall in most areas is between 100 and
200 inches a year. Over the northwest limits of the
Amazon Basin, this rainfall doubles.

Historical Background

Before 1500, Brazil was inhabited by Indian
groups with a combined population of close to
four million. Most of them lived along the rivers
and occupied a few strips of fertile coastal land.
Farther away from sources of water, a handful of
Indian groups lived as slash-and-burn farmers or
nomadic hunters and gatherers.

Portuguese exploration. The Portuguese admiral Pedro Alvares Cabral was the first European to visit the land. He returned to his homeland with a cargo of red dyewood named *pau-brasil* from whence came the name of the country. Portugal claimed Brazil in the Treaty of Tordesillas in 1494. Thereafter, the lives of the Indians were drastically altered.

Portuguese colonists arrived in 1532 and along with them came the initial contingent of slaves from Africa. From the beginning, the need for a work force was the determining factor in the growth of the Brazilian population. Over the next 300 years an estimated 3.5 million black slaves would be brought into the country for labor. On the surface, the slaves had rights by legal sanction. They could supposedly marry whom they chose, seek different owners, and possess property. Actually these rights were far beyond the reach of most slaves, and some were treated brutally. For example, punishment for a minor offense might mean pricking an accused slave with a sharp razor, then rubbing the wounds with salt or lemon juice. Some resisted such treatment by staging slave revolts. Others became runaways. These fugitives organized their own communities, the most famous of which was Palmares, a settlement that lasted for 50 years.

Meanwhile the Jesuits built missions and worked to safeguard the native Indian population. Mission villages were established to convert the Indians and to protect them from enslavement. For a time, the Indians remained under the exclusive control of the Jesuits. But after the religious order was expelled in 1759, the Indians faded into the jungle, intermarried with outsiders, or died extracting rubber and other commodities from the tropical forest.

Africans. As the Indian population dwindled, reliance on African slaves increased. The slaves lived in patriarchal villages around the *Casa*

Grande (Big House), the master's manor. In keeping with its name, the Big House included from 15 to 20 rooms, a hospital, a fortress, a school, a commissary, and a kitchen. Beyond the collection of slave huts lay a sugar refinery, a distillery, and pens for livestock.

Slaves comprised a third of the population in the 1800s, most living on sugar or coffee plantations. They were entitled to 35 holidays a year on which they might earn money to free themselves, but few could do so. Pressure mounted to abolish slavery. The slaves developed a common language, Nago, a mixture of Portuguese and African dialects, and this helped unify them. Also under the Rio Branco Law of 1871, every child born to a slave mother was free. Still, the country was dominated by large rural landowners whose livelihood depended on slavery.

Estate owners differed from others in Brazil not only on the question of slavery. A long standing hostility developed between the large estates and the cities. Ignoring city rule, the estate owner often retained his own milita and claimed absolute authority. Since colonial Brazil was mostly agricultural, the estate owners held the power.

Brazil as a refuge. That the Portuguese King John regarded his colony in the New World as a refuge became evident when Napoleon invaded Portugal. The king fled to Brazil, then returned to Portugal, leaving his son Pedro behind. In 1822 Pedro proclaimed Brazil an independent monarchy It was under his successor, Pedro II, that Brazilians experienced a half century of progress. Economic booms in coffee and rubber brought prosperity. The slave trade was abolished, and thousands of immigrants – Italian peasants, German farmers, and a new wave of Portuguese – began taking the slaves' place.

Independence. After slavery was abolished in 1888, the discontented landowners deposed Pedro II in a bloodless revolution. The Republic of the United States of Brazil was established. In 1891, the people adopted a constitution modeled after that of the United States.

The 1900s saw political unrest in which periods of democratic rule were brief, and government was largely dominated by the military. Brazil emerged as a power worthy of worldwide attention, siding with the Allies against Germany in both world wars and sending troops to Italy in 1944. The country was then ruled by Getúlio Vargas, a benevolent dictator, who censored the press and banned political parties while furthering prosperity. Vargas was forced to resign by the military, which seized control of the government in 1964 and remained in power for nearly 20 years, arresting and even torturing political dissidents.

Democracy. Although Brazilians have a long history of military governments, the government today is a democracy. Elections were held in 1982 but the military maintained a strong presence in government. It was not until 1985 that Congress approved a constitutional amendment restoring direct elections by universal suffrage. Also under this amendment the right to vote was extended to illiterate adults.

Culture Today

Immigration. Over the years large numbers of different ethnic groups settled Brazil. The original inhabitants, the Amerindians, were joined first by the Portuguese, then by millions of Africans, Europeans (Italians, Germans, Poles), and Asians. Conditions have been conducive to the mixing and blending of races. Official statistics place whites at approximately 60 percent of the population, including light-skinned Brazilians of mixed ancestry. About 30 percent is classified as mixed, 7 percent black, and 3 percent Asian (with a Japanese community described as the largest outside Japan).

Indians. Amerindians constitute less than one percent of the population. Totaling some 150,000, this population has experienced a drastic drop from the original four million at the onset of colonization. Many Indian deaths are attributed to contact with European diseases (smallpox, whooping cough, yellow fever, malaria). Each ton of rubber produced along the Río Potomayo is further estimated to have cost seven Indian lives. Finally, road building, mining, and colonization have disturbed traditional behavior, upsetting the Indians' ability to sustain themselves in customary ways. In the interest of preserving the remaining population, 17 million Amazon acres (the Manbikawa Indian reserve) have been legally set aside for Brazilian Indians.

Although other ethnic groups reside in the Amazon, the region is mainly occupied by Indians and Luso (Portuguese) Brazilians. Mestizos of mixed Portuguese and Amerindian descent live in the sertão, an inland area of eastern Brazil. Afro-Brazilians and Luso-Brazilians appear in the northeast, a region described as having the largest concentration of poverty in the western half of the world.

Labor force. Varieties of work are characteristic of the different regions. While sugar plantations and mills developed in the northeast, the sertão features large plantations and cattle ranching. Extracting medicines, rubber, timber, nuts, and vanilla from the largest tropical forest in the world has kept the Amazon's inhabitants busy. Coffee production developed in the south along with cattle ranches, rice plantations, and small farms in areas of the far south. The midsized commercial farm is a common sight in the southeast, a region in which gold and diamonds

▧   Area of greatest
     population

**Brazil's greatest
population is
along the Atlantic
Coast.**

were discovered in colonial times. Throughout the country under-employment and unemployment are great; less than half the population was working or seeking employment in the early 1980s.

The nation as a whole has gone through cycles in which it led the world in the production of brazilwood, livestock, sugar, gold, rubber, and coffee. The various landowners made fortunes, gaining power and status so that Brazil entered the 20th century with sugar, cotton, coffee, rubber and cattle aristocracies. Large landowners dominated rural areas such as the northeast, depending first on slave labor, then on resident plantation workers, and lastly on casual temporary laborers. The owners did little work themselves since labor with the hands was considered demeaning. Yet over the years aristocrats became more involved in daily business. Today they send their sons off to work as managers in industry.

Growth of cities. The importance of the landowner has decreased due to a shift in the economy. Less than one third of the work force was employed in agriculture in 1980. In contrast, two thirds lived in cities and worked in industry. Agriculture has been displaced by industry in the economy.

Industry has penetrated even the countryside. Once life in the northeast was controlled by the *engenho*, the sugar plantation. Each was a world unto itself, with its own carpenters, smiths, and artisans, but the glory and power of these separate worlds faded as central sugar companies took over the land. Instead the *usina* (modern sugar refinery and plantation) became commonplace.

Land reform. There have been increases in the amount of crops grown, particularly sugar cane, oranges, and soya beans. These are raised for export, though, not for the people themselves. Workers have gone on strike in protest of this state of affairs; in response, the government promised to provide over seven million families with land by the year 2000. Its attempts to redistribute acreage have since resulted in violent clashes between landowners and peasants.

Family. The family is perhaps the most significant social unit in Brazilian society. In upper class families the *parentela* is the kin group. Sometimes including scores of individuals, it is comprised of relatives an individual recognizes on both sides of the family. It was once common for members of a parentela to own resources together, and even now there is a strong family presence in many corporations. Family loyalty is considered an individual's highest responsibility; aiding needy kinfolk is expected. As one moves down the social ladder into the lower classes, these family ties weaken. There are fewer resources, and individuals are more mobile. A son, for example, may be unable to fulfill his obligation to care to his parents in their old age. Across the social classes, the family is male centered. A husband owes support and protection to wife and child in exchange for their respect and obedience.

Women. Much has been said regarding the isolation of women in Brazilian society. Described as the first slaves of the household, wives were formerly restricted to the home and forbidden to sit down at the table with strangers. At the same time, they had servants to wait on their every bidding and with little to do often grew plump yet haggard from the chore of childbearing. Families with 12 to 15 children were common; women grew old by the age of 25, and some entered convents to escape their lot. Now the family is likely to include four or five children and possibly a working mother. Today's women are active outside the home in politics and businesses, where they hold jobs as, for example, engineers or writers.

The importance of family is still evident in housing. City homes range from old structures on narrow winding streets to suburban houses to tall modern apartment buildings in which a family of relatives may occupy several floors. Of particular note in the cities is the growth of the *favela*, or shantytown. Crowded with shacks built of cardboard, metal, or wood, the favela is a common sight in Rio de Janeiro. Several hundred favelas appeared in this city alone in the early 1980s, housing one third of its residents.

Food, clothing and shelter. Favela tenants may live without sewers or running water and may endure life threatening levels of pollution. Still, their social life is well developed. Generally a favela has its own religious groups, athletic clubs, commercial shops, and governing councils. Sometimes a community is upgraded, the tenants replacing flimsier housing with brick and wood structures.

Conditions have been little better in rural areas, where many have lived without piped water or electricity. A few have been fortunate enough to occupy a *casa grande*, but the majority live in modest-sized homes built perhaps of stone or adobe with reddish-tiled roofs. Typical furnishings include a few chairs, a rough table, maybe hammocks for sleeping. The small landholders live in *barrios*, rural neighborhoods that are a series of homesteads bound to one another by mutual aid, religious practices, and frequently by kinship.

Beans, manioca flour or corn meal, dried meat, coffee sweetened with sugar are staples in the Brazilian diet. Bread is common in the cities, and wealthy city folk eat a variety of meats. Otherwise the food varies somewhat by region. In the northeast, Afro-Brazilians eat bananas, coconuts, fish, and palm oil as part of their daily diet.

Clothing styles are similar to those in North America with some regional variations. Gauchos of the south might wear ponchos, baggy trousers and wide-brimmed hats. Afro-Brazilian women in the northeast are known for their colorful skirts, bright blouses, and numerous bracelets and necklaces.

Religion. An overwhelming majority of Brazilians are Roman Catholic but many combine this faith with Indian customs. Traditionally, Brazilian men regard religion as the responsibility of women. Also, it has largely been a neighborhood affair, replete with local saints and festivals. Other, less popular religions in Brazil are Protestantism, Judaism, and Buddhism. In addition, the African influence has inspired a number of cults (*xango, macumba, candombe*).

Arts. Various ethnic groups have influenced the development of Brazilian art. The first art pieces were Indian handicrafts (e.g., baskets, pottery, jewelry). Indian and black folk legends of the 1700s began a tradition in literature that would be furthered by Joaquim Maria Machado de Assis, a poor mulatto who became one of the greatest Brazilian novelists. In the 20th century, Carolina Maria de Jesus's description of life in a favela has been translated into English. The distinguished artist Candido Portinari has painted great murals on government buildings, featuring Brazilians as muscular sweating plantation workers. In sports, the soccer star Edson Arantes do Nascimento (Pele) has achieved world acclaim, and in aviation the pioneer Albertos Santos Dumont is hailed the "father of flight" for his 1901 invention of the gasoline powered airship.

Although individuals have excelled in various fields, public education in Brazil has been weak. Eight years of schooling are now required, but rural areas often lack facilities and teachers. Many people still cannot read or write. In the northeast, the illiteracy rate was 55 percent in 1981.

Government. Brazilians aged 18 to 65, even those who are illiterate, are required to vote. However, since the Indians have no political rights, they are denied the vote. Military leaders continue as a strong force in elections and can intervene in political affairs. The president of Brazil may suspend the political rights of individual citizens.

Class structure. Ethnic origins have not greatly influenced social standing among citizens of Brazil. Rather, status has been determined by wealth. Large landholders and businesspeople along with high government officials fill the upper class. Small to medium merchants, traders, and laborers form the middle class. Artisans, tenants, and sharecroppers share the lower class, with day laborers at the bottom of the hierarchy. There is a more basic division among Brazilians today, though. It is the gap between the rich and the poor. Finding it ever more difficult to support themselves, the poor become indebted to the rich, and so the gap widens.

CAMPA

(kahm pah)

A native hunting, gathering and farming people
of the Gran Pajonal region of Peru.

Population: 21,000 (1978).
Location: Peru.
Language: Campa, one of the Arawakan family
of languages.

Campa territory
in Peru

Geographical Setting

Although the eastern slopes of the Andes
Mountains were inhabited by Indian peoples, the
invading Incas and Spaniards found the area
uninviting and difficult. This portion of Peru is
dense evergreen forest and tropical jungle in
which rain falls abundantly between October and
April. The resulting plant growth provides food
and shelter for wildlife in the area. Given the
abundance of animals, the groups living here have
survived mostly as hunters and gatherers. The
Campa are a "people of the montaña," one of
many small groups not fully brought under Inca
or Spanish rule.

Historical Background

Dealings with Europeans. Although their
origins are obscure, the Campa were living in
Peru when Catholic missionaries from Spain
established chapels of the Franciscan order there
in 1635. The Franciscan missionaries, strict in
their beliefs, would not accept the polygynous
family structure of the Campa. Instead, the
Franciscans resolved to change this practice of a
man's marrying more than one wife, but when the
missionaries tried to enforce monogamy, the

73

Campa rebelled, massacring the monks and burning their mission. By 1640 the determined Franciscans had built seven more missions, but in 1642 they were again driven away by the Campa. In the early 1670s, the missionaries returned once more to build new missions. They met with more success this time, spending roughly three years before the Campa completely rejected the Franciscans and left the missions. In the early 1700s, Padre Juan de la Marca led still another cadre of missionaries to Peru. Along with religious teachings, the missionaries brought livestock (cattle, sheep, pigs, chickens), seeds, and new planting methods to the Campa. By 1735, 38 missions had been established.

Although impressed by this newest wave of Franciscans, the independent Campa again rebelled. This time they were led by Juan Santos Atahualpa, an Indian who was educated by the Franciscans and had learned about liberation during his travels in Europe. Upon returning to Peru in 1742, Atahualpa proclaimed himself a messiah who had been sent by God and the Inca emperors to liberate the Campa from the missionaries. The uprising that followed was so violent that the Franciscans were persuaded to leave Campa territory once and for all.

Isolation. During the 1800s the Campa were left to themselves. What little contact they had with outsiders gave them a reputation for both fierceness and friendliness. Explorers who dared to enter the area described the Campa as "hostile." Yet colonists from Haiti who settled near these Indians said they made overtures of friendship that were reciprocated by some Campa.

White settlers. In the 1940s white Peruvians opened the Gran Pajonal region to settlement. The Campa refrained from attacking the white settlers, perhaps impressed by their military hardware and the military planes flying overhead. These Indians seem instinctively suspicious of strangers, so their initial reaction was to keep their distance. Today they share the region with whites.

Culture Today

The Campa are not one political or cultural social group, but rather a collection of groups that share certain overall attributes. An example is the structure of the Campa family.

Family. Despite the efforts of the Franciscans to enforce monogamy, a Campa family may still include more than one wife. This occurs principally among the family of a chief. The more typical family consists of a husband, a wife, their small children, married daughters with their husbands, and perhaps older relatives who are widowed. The male is the dominant family figure, expecting his wife or wives to be submissive and hard working. In public she learns to walk behind him, not by his side. The newer the marriage, the farther behind she is obligated to stay.

There are strict rules concerning marriage among the Campa. Cousins may wed, but unions between uncles and nieces or between aunts and nephews are forbidden. Preceding the marriage, there is a formal initiation ceremony. The bride is hidden from sight for a time, then given to her future husband at a feast during which yuca (baked sweet manioc) is consumed. Drums, trumpets, panpipes, and flutes may provide musical accompaniment at such festivities.

Rivalry often existed between leaders of the groups, resulting in raids and warfare in the not-so-distant past. Today, Campa groups engage in half-serious combat, using bows and arrows against one another in sport. Although their arrows usually have no points, on occasion they are replaced by arrows with barbed points. Then sport deteriorates into combat, a band raiding its opponent for arms, children, and women that are whisked away.

A Campa woman

Unlike other peoples, the Campa tended not to settle in villages but rather in small bands of related families. A band lived in a *nampitsi*, or home area, that was an extensive stretch of forest land along a stream or on a hill.

Clothing and shelter. The traditional home is a modest structure, often without walls. The family may live quite simply under a palm-thatched roof supported by four to six wooden poles. Their home is unfurnished, having only a sleeping platform at one end and the cooking area at the other. Palm leaves provide material for mats, fans, and cordage.

The Campa designed their customary dress using raw materials from the jungle. Traditional Campa clothing includes the *cushma*, a lengthy garment made of bark cloth or cotton that has been reddened with dye. Cushmas have long neck openings and may be decorated with feathers or beads. Bark cloth is used to make Campa shirts. As for ornamentation, many wore a pin or pendant in their noses, and the people would use the plant *Piperaceae* to blacken their teeth. Today the Campa wear more conventional clothing, reserving such customary dress for feasts and celebrations.

Customs. There are rules concerning behavior in Campa society. Children, for example, are reserved with their immediate family, but more relaxed with distant relatives. Boys learn how to whirl and crouch so that it is difficult for an enemy to shoot them and how to strengthen themselves as well as their bows with medicine for battle. The boys are conditioned to distrust strangers.

Food. Fathers and sons work together to plant yuca, hunt, and fish. Traditionally agriculture was considered mainly women's work. Hunting and catching fish with bows and arrows were regarded as primary activities for men. Today these activities provide the Campa with income as well as food. Hunting provides the meat. Among the animals typically captured for this purpose are pigs, deer, and monkeys.

The Campa have relied on what they hunt, gather, and raise for their everyday diet. Aside from other forest meats, they might bake armadillo and tortoise. Basic food crops grown by the women include yuca, sugar cane, and bananas. Coca is raised so that the people can chew its leaves for their stimulating effect and for relief from cold and hunger. Yuca, the most highly-valued item in the diet, may be boiled or baked before it is eaten. To prepare it as a beverage, the Campa chew the yuca so that it will ferment. Then they place it in a hollowed-out log to make beer. An occasion for drinking the beer is the appearance of a new moon, an event the Campa regard as the return of their father.

Government. Leaders in Campa society include the *pinkatsari*, the *shaman*, and the *iotinkari*. The pinkatsari is the head man, or chief, who directs the daily economic activities of the band. His position is sometimes inherited by a son but any man with charisma might fill the role. Iotinkaris are knowers, or dreamers. Shamans are intermediaries who communicate for the Campa with their religious world.

Religion. The Campa believe in the existence of an other world, outside human experience. Shamans have experiences in which they pass into this mythical world and associate with its supernatural beings. In this way, the shaman can gain control over harmful forces that have passed into the natural world of the Campa. Shamans attempt to cure illnesses and prevent harm by appeasing the spirits. To these ends, they drink a powerful hallucinogen, *kayapi*, to help them in their fight against evil. In the event of death, there are no funeral rituals. Instead the Campa simply abandon their dead in the woods.

The main spirit is *Pava*, a being that manifests itself in the sun. There is also the conviction that threatening demons surround the natural world, which affects and perhaps explains Campa behavior. For example, snakes, jaguars, and pumas are thought to possess evil spirits which cause disaster. This belief prompts hunters to use careful methods so that the "owner of the animals" will not be offended by needless cruelty.

Campa beliefs may explain some of the fierceness attributed to them in the past. Certainly they have inspired a rich folklore, including many creation myths. One such myth suggests that the Campa were born from balsa trees through the intervention of spirits known as *Tasorinchi*. Such myths, along with the physical isolation of the Campa, have contributed to the Campa's strong sense of themselves as a separate people. This is changing, though. Some are now Christian, and their traditions are changing in other ways.

Change. Although still relatively isolated, the Campa are gradually becoming participants in Peruvian life. In the past these people practiced slash-and-burn farming, using a field once and then migrating elsewhere to plant again. Then the government set aside land for nuclear Campa families, who settled down to a more stationary existence. In the process, the tradition of living together as extended families has been disturbed. Also, the Campa were influenced by their new European-descended neighbors. A number of the Indians became wage earners, working as hunters, trappers, or low-paid laborers on neighboring farms. In these capacities, they threaten to eliminate the jaguars, alligators and tapirs they hunt, along with the forests in which they dwell. Thus, these Campa are in the position of helping to upset the environment on which they depend.

CHILEANS

(chee lay´ ans)
Largely a mestizo people, resulting from unions
of the Spanish, the Inca, and other Indian groups.

Population: 12,536,000 (1987).
Location: Chile, a country on the Pacific Coast
of South America.
Language: Spanish.

Chile

Geographical Setting

The country of Chile is long and narrow.
North to south, it stretches for more than 2,300
miles. East and west, Chile is a ribbon of land
100 to 200 miles wide bounded by the Pacific
Ocean and the eastern rim of the Andes
Mountains. In the north, the country is dominated
by the high Andes. Toward the center, this range
begins to break into separate peaks with passes
between that make for easy passage into
Argentina. Farther south, Chile begins to
disintegrate into a region of rugged islands. Barely
habitable, these islands support a few Indian
peoples and sheep herders encouraged by the
Chilean government. Originally Chile was only
one-third of its current size, and a fertile
agricultural region with a pleasant Mediterranean
climate. Now it includes desert, forest and
grasslands along with a fertile central valley.

Historical Background

Inca rule. The country that is now Chile was
once home to many Indian groups. In the north,
these groups were brought together before the
1500s by Inca conquerers. In central Chile, a
group known as the Araucanians ruled a large part

of that area. Farther south, the country was sparsely settled by small, scattered groups of Indians.

Spanish rule. In 1541, the Spanish, having conquered the Incas, established a base at Santiago in northern Chile and claimed the land as a Spanish colony. Northern Chile was ruled by the Spanish from then until 1818. While the Spanish also claimed the rest of Chile, they were never able to completely dominate the Araucanians and had little interest in the southernmost tip of the continent. Intermarriages among Spanish and Basque settlers and Indian workers in the north resulted in the growth of a mestizo community during this period.

Independence and expansion. In 1818, Spain relinquished control of the area and after some turbulence, Chileans adopted a constitution in 1833. Chile became a separate nation but without fixed boundaries. Later in this century Chile grew to its current size. From 1879 to 1882, Chileans fought and won territory from Bolivia and Peru in the War of the Pacific and then conquered the Araucanian Indians, uniting the people of Chile in their present form (see ARAUCANIANS). The Araucanians, hostile toward the Chileans, remained a separate people. In areas of Spanish settlement, though, there were intermarriages between the Europeans and the more peaceful Indians that resulted in a large mestizo community. A two-tiered society evolved: a minority of Europeans and a majority of mestizos.

The Europeans dominated society as landowners, mineowners, and traders, while their workers were mestizos. During most of the 19th century the rule of the Europeans remained peaceful, but it was marred by civil war in 1891. Congress revolted against the president and won at the cost of 10,000 lives and over a hundred million pesos.

Conflict. Most of the 20th century has been marked by a struggle for power between right- and left-wing politicians. The country's economy grew on the export of copper, silver, wheat, and nitrate. Enjoyed by a small minority, the resulting wealth had given rise to a nation that, by 1920, was sharply divided into classes. The uneven distribution of riches helped build support among the people for trade unions and radical political parties. A Chilean Communist party appeared in 1922. Encouraged by this party, Chilean workers staged strikes, but these were repressed by the government.

Meanwhile a series of military coups had driven one government leader after another out of office until President Arturo Alessandri Palma, who had ruled in the early 1920s, regained control in 1932. He provided relief from rule by military dictators and a return to constitutional government. Unrest among the workers and farmers continued, however. In 1934 a riot that was supposedly inspired by the Communists resulted in widespread destruction of crops in the Andes valleys. In another act of resistance, the small middle class backed a radical party, the Popular Front, that grew to dominate the government by 1938. A revolt against the government in this year was attributed to the Nazis, whose support came largely from wealthy businesspeople and landowners. After some bloodshed, the Popular Front put down the revolt and remained in control until 1952. A period of changing governments followed until Eduardo Frei Montalva, supported by professionals, women, and youth, took office (1964) on a platform of sweeping reforms. His promises of change failed to materialize, however, and a new coalition government of Communists, Socialists, and older radical parties gained support. Its candidate, Dr. Salvador Allende Gossens, became the first popularly elected Marxist president in the world. However his government also failed. Allende angered Chileans by redistributing incomes and controlling prices.

Industry. A military junta led by General Augusto Pinochet Ugarte overthrew Allende's government in 1973. Since then the junta has returned power to the few landed ruling families that formerly controlled the country, and it has brutally worked to repress dissent by the people. Pinochet has remained in power through the 1980s, despite testimony of torture to individuals during his regime. The people have staged bombings and *caceroleos,* demonstrations during which citizens bang kitchen utensils and sound car horns in deafening protest. Yet Pinochet has the support of other Chileans, who prefer his government to what they fear would otherwise be chaos.

Culture Today

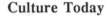

Growth of cities. The land of the Chileans is a land of contrasting life styles. The capital, Santiago, is a modern metropolis, much like those in North America and Europe. In constrast, though, the outskirts of Chile's cities are cluttered with impoverished communities. Economic progress and land reform have been hampered by the interference of government and the frustration of the Chilean people.

The military has taken control of Chile's copper mines as well as its government. Many of the mestizos were agricultural workers whose fortunes diminished following independence from Spain. They became serfs, working for a small percentage of wealthy landowners who used antiquated farming techniques. From World War II to the present, these landless peasants have been moving to the outskirts of cities where they build *villas callampas* – mushroom towns that seem to appear overnight. More than 80 percent of all Chileans now live in cities, many residing in villas callampas, where disease is common and jobs are difficult to find. Factories hire few workers, so that nearly 20 percent were unemployed in 1984.

Food, clothing and shelter. The villas callampas are filled with one-room shacks that usually lack running water, electricity, and sewers. In other parts of the city, high-rise apartments and spacious homes may be found next to the older Spanish-style housing with red-tile roofs and patios. Those who remain in the rural areas often live in one- or two-room adobe houses with thatched-tile roofs or in wooden homes with tar-covered roofs. The wealthier landowners live in larger brick or wood structures surrounded by lawns and gardens.

Chilean farm village

There has been widespread adoption of customs and styles from Europe and North America among members of the middle class. Housewives wait in long lines at *supermercados,* markets where they can purchase traditional foods. The Chilean diet is largely based on bread, beans, and potatoes, although meat is sometimes eaten and fish (mackerel, tuna, flounder, crab) is plentiful. Common dishes are stews, soups, corn casseroles, and *empanadas* (pastry turnovers stuffed with meat or seafood). Made from grapes grown in the central valley, Chile's wines are among the best in the world. Clothing styles are similar to those found in the United States. On special occasions, Chilean cowboys might be seen wearing their traditional flat-topped hats, ponchos, colorful sashes, fringed leather leggings, and boots with spurs.

Arts and entertainment. Television and the cinema have become common forms of entertainment, and soccer is the most popular sport. In literature, Pablo Neruda has won the Noble Prize for his poetry. Music is perhaps the most distinctive art form among the people. Chileans are particularly noted for beginning the *nueva canción* (new song) movement that spread to the rest of Latin America and was associated with social protest and labor reform. Women have participated both in the music and in the politics of the people, having been granted the right to vote in municipal elections in 1934.

Religion. A group of Chileans actively involved in social protest and in assisting victims of the military junta is the clergy. Chileans are predominantly Catholic, but the ratio of the Protestants (10 to 15 percent) is high in comparison to other Latin American peoples.

Elements of Christianity are combined with traditional beliefs, a phenomenon particularly evident in the medical practices of the people. Excessive cold or heat is believed to cause a majority of major and minor illnesses in Chile. A less common cause is thought to be the casting of an evil eye by a ritually unclean person. The classic cure for the evil eye is praying over and blessing the patient with the sign of the cross. At the same time, either three branches or three hot peppers are waved in front, then in back of the patient in the form of the cross. The area is then fumigated with incense to make sure the contamination has been eliminated. Remedies prescribed by modern medicine are also used but do not replace such traditional cures, which remain popular among the Chileans of today.

COLOMBIANS

(ko lum´ bee ans)

A people who grew from many Indian groups that united with the Spanish and were joined by blacks brought into the country as slaves.

Population: 27,000,000 (1982).
Location: The country of Colombia in northwestern South America, which is surrounded by Venezuela, Brazil and Ecuador.
Language: Spanish.

Colombia

Geographical Setting

Most of Colombia lies just north of the equator. Two main regions, the great plains of the southeast and the Andes mountain chains of the west, divide the country. The climate varies from hot mountain valleys to a continually rainy coast, to a dry area in the extreme southwest. The southwestern coastal section rises rapidly to the three mountain chains in the country. Further north, the coast joins with Panama, then faces the Caribbean Sea in a region of low swampland and riverbeds. East of the mountains, the country drops quickly to the hot lowlands of the plains, forming a slope known as the *tierra caliente* that drains mostly into the Orinoco and Amazon rivers. The land variations in Colombia contribute to different lifestyles and a difficult communication problem for its government.

Historical Background

Early farmers. The Indians who first populated Colombia, and about whom little is known, probably lived in scattered groups and spoke different languages. They were artisans and farmers, mining gold, and growing maize, yuca, fruit, and potato crops.

Spanish rule. When the Spanish conquered Colombia in 1525, they forced the Chibcha Indians onto communal reservations, taxed them, and used them as slave laborers. The Pijao Indians of the lowlands resisted and were killed. Many others died of disease and starvation, while the lives of the more peaceful Indians were transformed by Spanish priests. Converted to Catholicism, these Indians became more fully assimilated as their different languages disappeared and Spanish became the common tongue. Traditional dress was abandoned in favor of styles worn by the colonists, and other Spanish customs were rapidly adopted, leaving few traces of native culture. Intermarriages between the Spanish and Indians gave birth to a large *mestizo* (European-Indian) segment of the population, providing a workforce for the colonists. Slaves were brought in from Africa for additional labor and were put to work on the sugar plantations, in the mines of Colombia, or as cowboys on the Spanish cattle ranches. The offspring of colonists and slaves formed a small *mulatto* (European-African) segment of the population so that by the early 1800s, 200,000 black Africans and mulattos lived in the country.

Colombia

Independence. Many of the slaves were freed when Colombia won independence from Spain in 1821. Led by Simon Bolivar, the people of Colombia joined the citizens of Venezuela and Ecuador to form the Union Gran Colombia. After 1830, Ecuador and Venezuela dropped out of the union, leaving Colombians on their own to rule what is now Colombia and Panama. Subsequent attempts to centralize authority met with resistance from Colombians, and the government remained unstable throughout the rest of the 19th century. Civil war wracked the country in 1839, 1851, 1859, 1876, 1885, 1895, and 1899. This last war, dubbed the War of a Thousand Days, resulted in the loss of 100,000 lives. Panamanians revolted, and in 1901 Colombia lost its claim to their territory.

A period of calm followed as the Conservative and Liberal parties vied for power in government. New uprisings occurred in the rural areas in the 1940s, beginning a period of lawlessness called *La Violencia*, which lasted until the 1960s and cost approximately 300,000 lives. Partisan villages eliminated one another. Mobs destroyed business districts, and whole families were butchered. Dispossessed peasants and a large number of orphans, "children of violence," fled to the outskirts of the cities where slums arose.

Leaders of both political parties created a coalition called *Frente Nacional*, agreeing that the presidency would be held in rotation by Conservatives and Liberals. A number of stable governments and a period of growth followed, during which foreigners invested in Colombian businesses and the cities grew. Meanwhile, the Catholic Church and landed autocracy lost much of their former power. The bipartisan government ended in 1974, and Dr. Alfonso López Michelson became president, promising widespread reforms. When he failed to implement them, the people responded with strikes, riots, and guerrilla violence. The violence, also stemming from the growth and sale of illegal drugs, continued into the 1980s. The most pressing problem when President Barco Vargas took office in 1986, the drug problem has led to the assassination of government officials.

Culture Today

Food, clothing and shelter. Colombians today are a mixed population of mestizos, mulattos, blacks, *zambos* (of black and Indian ancestry), and white descendants of European colonists. The population of these groups has grown so rapidly that Colombians have been threatened with mass starvation. A large portion of the people live in rural areas, mostly in the western section of the country. The average farmer is a small holder whose land is eight acres in size. Rice, wheat, and barley are the main subsistence crops. Coffee, potatoes, bananas, and sugar are grown for cash, with coffee as the leading cash and export crop. The world's leading producers of a mild variety of coffee, Colombians hand pick the berries with care.

The hot lowland plains of the east remained sparsely populated until recent years; now colonies of Colombians have begun to farm this area in an effort to make use of every arable acre. They also raise livestock, although only a small portion of the Colombian diet contains meat. While roads and railways leading eastward have improved, a particular challenge here has been transportation. For geographic reasons, Colombia's railroads are short and unfinished.

Starches such as potatoes, rice, and maize remain the people's staples. The popular soup *ajiaco* is a blend of potatoes, chicken, corn, and cassava. Typical beverages include *agua de panela* (brown sugar and water) and *café helado* (coffee, sugar syrup, vanilla, and ice).

Colombians grow much of their coffee on small- and medium-sized farms. A driving force behind the economic growth of the country has been the the area Antioquia. Its residents produce most of the coffee and control much of Colombia's business and industry.

Just as small coffee producers have been successful in Colombia, so have modest-sized manufacturers. Small businesses are common in the streets of Colombia, and artisans have created some high quality handiwork in leather goods, furniture, and weaving.

Food processing is a major industry in Colombia. Other industries include the manufacture of textiles, chemicals, metal products, transport equipment, and pop-up books. Mining continues to be a profitable source of revenue. From the beginning, Colombians have excelled in gold work, and today their country is an important gold producer and the leading emerald supplier in the world. Salt is also mined for trade.

The lifestyle of the people varies in different regions of the country. Local materials such as bamboo poles and palm leaves are used to build homes in the warm coastal regions, while thick adobe-walled homes are built in the mountain areas. In the cities, apartment houses are replacing traditional adobe homes with red-tiled roofs. On the cities' outskirts are crowded slums filled with tin or cardboard shacks that often have no running water, electricity, or sewers.

Clothing styles among urban Colombians are similar to those worn in North America. In business, some men are still seen wearing their traditional black hats and suits. Styles vary in the country, but the *ruana*, or traditional poncho cloak, remains popular. Peasants with Indian heritage wear felt derby hats.

Family. The basic social unit among Colombians is an extended family whose members usually live together. Included are parents, unmarried children, grandparents, elderly relatives, and sometimes cousins. In upper-class rural homes, married sons and their families remain in the household as well. The upper class consists mostly of descendants of the country's Spanish and Basque settlers. Colombia's middle class is composed primarily of mestizo businesspeople, government officials, and professionals. The lower class includes industrial and agricultural workers as well as sales clerks and the unemployed. Middle- and upper-class families tend to have elaborate church weddings, while lower-class families reject formal marriages. Also among lower class families, it is common for fathers to leave home and absolve themselves of financial responsibility for the children.

Religion. The majority of Colombians practice Catholicism. The Church has been closely associated with the upper class, although a reform faction emerged in the 1970s advocating social change. Some of the Indians continue to adhere to traditional, animistic beliefs.

Arts. The artwork of the country's Indians is displayed with pride. The Gold Museum of Colombia includes 13,000 artistic pieces, ranging from sculpted images to decorative flasks and the gold earrings of an ancient Indian chief. Many works of art were uncovered by Spaniards during their conquest of the land and their pursuit of a city of gold.

An ancient ritual of Columbia's Chibcha Indians was to dust each new king with powdered gold, then submerge him into Lake Guatavita, where his bright covering was washed away as a sacrifice to the god of the lake. This tradition of *El Dorado*, or the Gilded One, led to the early Spanish explorers' dream of a fantastic city of gold shimmering just over the horizon. Their belief in El Dorado spurred them on to conquer the continent, and although they found no such city, they uncovered gems and artwork in their plunder of Indian temples, homes, and tombs.

Colombians of the 20th century have extended their range of artistic activity through the works of painters such as Fernando Botero and writers such as Gabriel José García Márquez, who won the Nobel Prize for literature in 1982. Poets, their verses often a blend of modern form and social criticism, are held in particular esteem by Colombians. Yet the people themselves are often only partially educated. Enrollment in primary school is high, but thereafter drops dramatically.

Only 45 percent of those aged 13 to 18 were enrolled in secondary school in 1983.

Entertainment is a mix of the traditional and the contemporary. Folk songs such as the *bambuco*, originally a serenade, and dances such as the *cumbia* have enjoyed lasting popularity in urban as well as rural areas of Colombia. Bullfighting is an old pastime that still attracts spectators. Auto racing and skiing are newer leisure time activities, while soccer has become the most favored sport.

Government. Colombia is regarded as the oldest and most faithful democracy in Latin America, because it has experienced few years of military rule. However, less than 40 percent of the population normally votes, and many have grown indifferent. Even labor unions, once active agitators for change, find it difficult to gather workers together for a cause. Aware of this state of affairs, guerrilla movements have established bases of power in poorer neighborhoods of the country. Disheartened by unemployment and the unequal distribution of wealth, the poor often lose the belief that they make a difference.

Colombian flute player

By Borys Malkin. Courtesy Anthro Photo.

COSTA RICANS

(kos´ ta ree´ kans)

The people of the most democratic and most Spanish
of the Central American countries.

Costa Rica

Population: 2,700,000 (1987).
Location: The country of Costa Rica between
Nicaragua and Panama.
Language: Spanish.

Geographical Setting

Northwest to southeast, the country of Costa
Rica is crossed by four short mountain ranges in
which peaks rise 10,000 to 12,000 feet. Several
of the highest peaks are active volcanoes. In the
center of the country, where two mountain ranges
parallel each other, is a high basin 100,000 square
miles in size, the *Valle Central*. The capital, San
Jose, and three other of Costa Rica's largest cities
lie in this basin. Half of all Costa Ricans live in
the central valley and support themselves as
farmers or workers in light industry in the cities.
From 3,000 to 4,000 feet above sea level, the high
mountain valleys have a temperate climate. Coffee
has become a major crop.

The mountains drop steeply to the Pacific
coast and more gradually toward the Caribbean
Sea. The land east and north of the mountains is
hot and wet. Here large banana plantations were
once the economic mainstay of the country. The
north Pacific lowlands and the northern plains
support flourishing cattle industries. Community
builders and farmers have removed two thirds of
the forests that originally covered the country.

The boundary between Costa Rica and
Nicaragua follows the San Juan River for most if

its distance. Sixteen smaller rivers, the largest one running for 93 miles, flow from the mountains to the Caribbean Sea; two empty into the Pacific Ocean. A tropical country, Costa Rica receives heavy rainfall throughout the year on the Caribbean side. The temperature is milder in the Valle Central, where both wet and dry seasons occur.

Historical Background

Early inhabitants. Before 1000 B.C., small groups of Amerindians lived in Costa Rica. They survived by hunting and foraging for food, then learned to cut sections from the forest lands for temporary farms on which they grew cassava, yams, and maize. There is evidence that the Nicarao Indians raised cocoa by A.D. 1200. They mixed the cocoa with maize, water, pepper, and vanilla to create a chocolate drink. Cocoa beans were also used as trade money among the different groups in the region.

Columbus. By the time Christopher Columbus landed here on his fourth trip to the Americas (1502), Costa Rica was inhabited by some 25,000 Indians. Their communities had grown into small chiefdoms whose limits were marked by river or mountain boundaries. The gold jewelry these native people wore inspired the name Costa Rica (rich coast). Gold probably also motivated Bartholomew Columbus, Christopher Columbus's son, to colonize the country. At first fought off by the Indians, Bartholomew Columbus eventually succeeded in establishing a community in the land he named *Nueva Cartago*.

Spanish rule. The Spanish granted captaincies in the New World, giving a certain individual – a captain – the right to appoint officials, establish towns, and collect taxes in a particular area. Costa Rica became part of the Captaincy of Guatemala; then in 1540 it was named Costa Rica. By then the

Spanish were well in control of the area; most of the Indians had been driven off or absorbed into the forced labor system, *encomienda*. Today fewer than 3,000 Indians remain in Costa Rica, most of them on reservations.

The encomienda system failed to provide enough Indian workers. Therefore, the Spanish were forced to work the soil for themselves, using their own hard labor to build many small farms. These conditions encouraged a spirit of democracy in the country, and resulted in a population that is now over 90 percent Spanish.

Between 1560 and 1573, the Spanish leader Juan Vasquez de Coronado surveyed the land and established boundaries. Indian territories and hacienda lands were defined. Indians rebelled over Spanish control of the land in, for example, 1610 and 1709. Since these early days, however, Costa Rica has been mostly peaceful.

Independence. In 1821, Costa Rica separated from Spain, and in 1823 joined the United Provinces of Central America. Costa Rica became independent in 1838, but its neighbors disputed its boundary lines. The controversy continued until 1888, when the president of the United States was asked to settle the issue of the border between Costa Rica and Nicaragua. Although the boundary was finally defined in 1896, Nicaragua still questioned part of the land distribution. The present border was fixed in 1921, when the United States sided with Costa Rica against Nicaraguan claims.

There has been a notable absence of war in Costa Rica in comparison to other countries in Latin America. Three incidents have disturbed the peace: an invasion by an American in the 1850s, a short-lived coup d'état in 1917-1919, and a revolution in 1948. The American, William Walker, attempted to seize the government in the 1850s, but his attempt was quickly put down with the aid of American naval parties, and he was executed. As a result of the 1917 coup, the constitution of Costa Rica outlawed having a standing army. The 1948 revolution was fought against a government that refused to step aside for its democratically elected successor. The rebels won.

Issues today. The government has long had a policy of accepting immigrants from other countries and absorbing them into the society. However, recent civil war in Nicaragua has strained this policy. Already bulging from its own population growth, Costa Rica has built a large national debt, the repayment of which consumes 60 percent of the money earned from exports such as coffee and bananas. Today President Oscar Arias Sánchez has begun to establish programs to control the great debt and the growing problem of unemployment.

Culture Today

About 97 percent of the Costa Rican people are Spanish. The few Indians and blacks who remained in central Costa Rica have merged with the larger population. A small group of Indians and blacks live on the Caribbean Coast in near isolation from other Costa Ricans, and another small group of isolated Indians live in the southwest. Both groups have little voice in the affairs of the country.

Most of the remaining Indians are now part of a larger peasant society with some Spanish ways. They join the Catholic Church, speak Spanish, vote in national elections, and live in houses built of wood and corrugated iron rather than cane and thatch. Rice and beans, which became basic foods for the Spanish, have remained staples in the Indian diet. In contrast, blacks from Jamaica, who came to work on banana plantations, showed little desire to adopt Spanish ways. They spoke English, remained Protestant, and lived in unpainted wooden houses elevated on stilts. Eventually many left.

Food, clothing, and shelter. There are more small farms in Costa Rica's central valley than in most other areas of Central America. Building adobe or frame homes with thatched or tin roofs, the farmers grow corn, rice, beans, and sugar for their own use, and coffee and cacao for sale. More than 40 percent of today's farms are *minifundos*, farms too small to support a family. But the owners of these small farms control only 17 percent of the total farmland. Large landowners control most of the remainder, devoting it to banana plantations and haciendas for cattle raising. While Costa Rica has the highest standard of living in Central America, there is inequality even here. Five percent of the people control more than 70 percent of the wealth.

Both the wealthy and the less well-to-do have adopted a new type of clothing. Western-style wear replaces the traditional dress – long-flowing skirts with well-decorated blouses for women and loose fitting pants with shirts and straw hats for men. The older styles are now seen mainly at celebrations.

Today, most Costa Ricans live in urban or suburban areas and do not work in agriculture. Instead, many are employed in factories that produce consumer goods, or in the new shopping centers that include supermarkets, bank branches, post offices, and restaurants where items such as pizza and fried chicken are common. Housing is a problem in the cities. There are few apartment buildings. Most homes are one-story, single-family dwellings, but there are an insufficient number of these. Poorer neighborhoods are not as large or conspicuous as in other Latin American countries. However, small pockets of hastily-built homes do exist. Constructed of wood, iron and cardboard, they form areas in which health conditions and unemployment are major problems.

Government. Costa Ricans pride themselves on being the most democratic of Central American peoples. Citizens directly elect a president who serves for four years and cannot be immediately re-elected. There are three branches of government and official ministers such as in the United States. However, the government in Costa Rica enters more directly into daily life, controlling banks, insurance, petroleum, agriculture and even some grocery enterprises. Costa Rica's outstanding quality in government has been its ability to change through *reformismo*, reform rather than revolution.

Education. An early reform was free public education. Costa Rica has a high rate of school enrollment: over 90 percent in primary schools and 40 percent in secondary schools in 1981. Among the countries of Central America, it also has the highest rate of adults (94 percent) who can read and write.

Transportation. Changes have occurred in more visible aspects of Costa Rican life as well. Motor vehicles are now used, although the *campesino*, the small farmer, still takes crops to market in the traditional cart. Drawn by two oxen, this cart is made of wood, its wheels painted with brightly colored designs. Trucks and trailers have been slow to replace the ox cart, which is now becoming a symbol of traditional culture.

The oxcart is a symbol of traditional culture in Costa Rica.

Religion and the arts. Costa Ricans generally belong to the Catholic Church and celebrate religious festivals with their most popular amusements, singing and dancing. As for art, ox carts and buildings are often decorated in colorful patterns. The Church of Our Lady of the Angels in Cartago, a city southeast of the capital, contains one of the most famous sculptures in the Americas, La Negrita (The Black Virgin). Also, writers such as Aquileo Echeverría began a modern movement (*costumbrismo*) to capture Costa Rican customs in poetry.

Change. While it is peaceful in the midst of Central American turmoil, Costa Rica is not without problems and faces an uncertain future. The population is growing, and many are landless. Also the country has a very large national debt. Always an importer of manufactured goods and sometimes of rice and sugar, Costa Ricans demanded an exploding quantity of goods from other countries in 1980. Measures taken to control the debt have contributed to poverty in the country. Yet Costa Ricans remain outstanding in Central America for both their stable government and their generally higher standard of living.

CUBANS
(cu´ bahns)

A Spanish, Indian, European, and African people
with a highly organized society, near North America.

Population: 9,900,000 (1983).
Location: The island of Cuba, the smaller Isle of
Pines and about 1600 keys and islets located
between the Atlantic Ocean on the north and the
Caribbean Sea on the south.
Language: Spanish.

Cuba

Geographical Setting

Much of the main Cuban island is rolling
hills. Elsewhere, the landscape is broken by three
small mountain ranges. In the west the mountains
are the Sierra de los Organos. The Trinidad
Mountains sit in the province of Las Villas in the
center of the island. Toward the east, the mountain
range (Sierra Maestra) rises to peaks more than
6,000 feet high. A warm climate and November-
to-April rains make the rolling hills a grassland,
while the mountain regions bear pine forests.
Cuba has many natural bays and harbors along its
2,700 mile coastline. The largest, Havana, is on
the north side in the central rolling hill region.

Historical Background

Columbus. When claimed by Christopher
Columbus in 1492, Cuba was inhabited by
Indians of the Arawak group. These Indians were
left undisturbed until 1511, when Columbus's son
Diego de Velázquez seized the islands for Spain
and established Cuba's first white settlements.
The settlements grew slowly over the next two

centuries without much interference from the outside world. Then the British captured Havana in 1762 and encouraged the cultivation of sugar cane, an activity that would dominate the economy of the area for centuries to come.

Slaves. The need for labor on the sugar and tobacco plantations and in raising livestock, which had been the area's first major industry, resulted in the growth of slavery. Conflict and exposure to European diseases contributed to the decline of the Indian population, so the British supplied African slaves. Lasting only ten months before Spain reassumed control, Britain's rule was of short duration. However, in this brief period North Americans had become buyers of Cuban goods, a factor that would contribute greatly to the well-being of the island population.

In the next 60 years, trade increased, as did immigration from Europe and other areas of Latin America. The introduction of the steam-powered sugar mill in 1819 hastened the expansion of the sugar industry. While the demand for slaves grew, Spain signed a treaty with Britain agreeing to prohibit the slave trade after 1820. The number entering the area did decrease, but the treaty was largely ignored. Over the next three decades, there were several slave revolts, but all proved unsuccessful.

Revolution. Other Cubans participated in several fruitless uprisings to win freedom from Spain in hopes of being annexed to the United States. Beginning in 1868, the opposition to Spanish rule erupted in a Ten Years' War in which the Cubans were led by Carlos Manuel de Céspedes, considered the "father" of the country. Céspedes opened the struggle by reading a Declaration of Independence from Spain. His rebels, though, were forced into an unsuccessful guerilla campaign. Ending the war in 1878, the Treaty of Zanjón promised to increase Cubans' rights, but the promises were mostly unfulfilled.

After a second unsuccessful uprising, the Little War (1880), the leadership of the revolutionary movement retreated to New York. The last two decades of the century were marked by the end of slavery (1886) and Cuban independence (1898).

Independence. Known as the "apostle of Cuban liberty," the writer José Martí launched the revolt that led to independence. Martí was killed a month after initiating the battle. The revolutionists lost some ground, and about a fifth of the island's population died for the cause before Spain sank a United States warship, the *U.S.S. Maine,* and 266 American lives were lost. In response, Americans under President McKinley entered the war on the side of Cuba. Four months later, Cuba became an independent nation. Under the Teller Resolution, the United States promised to leave government and the control of the republic to the Cuban people.

After Cuban independence was assured by the Treaty of Paris (1898), the United States military occupied the country to help rebuild the war-torn area. A treaty between the United States and Cuba, the Platt Amendment, gave the United States the right to intervene in Cuban affairs for the preservation of the country's independence and government. After the first occupation (1898–1902), the United States reappeared twice: to preserve the government (1906-1909) and to prevent interference with sugar production during World War I (1917-1923). The Platt Amendment was discarded in 1934.

Cuban sugar producers prospered greatly through World War I. The war period that ended in 1920 became known as "the dance of the millions" in deference to the great fortunes made by speculators and sugar dealers. Then suffering from a declining economy, Cubans become more oppressed when Gerardo Machado became president in 1924. Machado amended the constitution to extend the presidency to six years.

He abolished the vice presidency, and silenced his opponents by deporting and even assassinating them. His *porristas* (toughs) were accused of hundreds of murders before Machad fled into exile in 1933. An army officer, Fulgencio Batista y Zaldivar, seized power and became the country's most powerful figure for the next two decades (1934-1959). His obscure origins as a cane cutter and a mestizo endeared him to the people at first, but respect for him diminished as he became increasingly dictatorial.

There were two divisions in Cuba, one between the rich and the poor and the other between the city and the country. The upper class was becoming ever richer as the peasants grew ever poorer. While the masses in the countryside received little for their labor, wealth from the sugar trade was showered on businessmen in the city.

Havana, Cuba

Fidel Castro. Fidel Castro Ruz was the son of a wealthy sugar planter who owned more than 23,000 acres of farmland. Castro was an educated man, a lawyer who waged attacks on the Batista dictatorship through the 1950s. Leading young rebels in an attack on Moncado Barracks in 1953, Castro was defeated and sentenced to a 15-year prison term on the Isle of Pines. A general amnesty in 1955 resulted in his freedom.

Thereafter, Castro retreated to Mexico City where he met Che Guevara, a young Argentine doctor who helped him engineer the next rebellion. Others joined the two, and a force of about 80 rebels invaded Cuba in 1956. When the government defeated them, the rebels retreated to the Sierra Maestra Mountains, where they began an ultimately successful guerilla war against the Batista dictatorship. At their peak, the guerillas are thought to have never numbered more than 800, but they inspired sympathy and indirect resistance throughout the country. Batista fled to the Dominican Republic in 1959, and Castro assumed power as commander of the armed forces. Batista supporters were tried as war criminals, then executed by firing squads. Property and business enterprises were seized by the government, whether owned by Cubans or foreigners. Trade unions, political parties, and the press were placed under Castro's control. Seven hundred thousand Cubans fled the country. The United States officially broke off relations with Cuba in January of 1961. Aided by the United States, exiles launched anti-Castro invasions that culminated in the unsuccessful Bay of Pigs in 1961. In May of that year, Castro announced that Cuba was a socialist country. He had become leader of the first communist bloc nation in the Western hemisphere.

In 1965, the Cuban government agreed to a plan under which 3,000 to 4,000 Cubans were permitted to emigrate to the United States each month. Meanwhile, Castro began to build a communist state that would rectify the imbalance between the rich and the poor, the city and the country, the educated and the uneducated. Many improvements were made over the next 20 years, yet there was a rush to leave Cuba when restrictions were eased in 1980. Over a quarter million Cubans have left their country since Castro has been in power.

A government-provided low-cost apartment house in Havana.

Culture Today

Before Castro. In describing the way of life in Cuba today, it is necessary to sketch both pre-Revolution and post-Revolution societies. Sharp class divisions existed in pre-Revolution Cuba. Its large landowners included upper-class individuals and corporations, which were often foreign. The middle class consisted of business owners, professionals, tenant farmers, and sharecroppers. At the bottom were the great mass of several hundred thousand unemployed, and perhaps five hundred thousand more underemployed who worked in the sugar industry for a few months a year.

The sugar mill became the center of rural life. Raw sugar from nearby plantations was refined in the mill, and around it were houses, schools, shops, and a chapel for the neighboring peasants. Sleeping in barracklike dorms, temporary workers endured harsh conditions. The peasants lived on roots, sugar cane, and other plants, 60 percent of them suffering from malnutrition. Even those who managed to become sharecroppers or tenants were forced to give 40 percent of their earnings to a landowner. More than 75 percent of these peasants lived in housing classified as "worthless." Also, the number of illiterates was rising. Education and health care in the countryside were dismal; such services were reserved for the city dweller. While poverty-stricken peasants received little from a land their labor enriched, wealthy urbanites enjoyed benefits and lived in mansions.

Reform. Che Guevara held that the foremost duty of the revolution was to ensure that no one in Cuba went hungry. To accomplish this objective, the government provided fuller employment, converting the large estates it had confiscated into people's farms and initiating construction projects (roads, schools, clinics, housing). The post-Revolution lifestyle has reduced differences, as Castro intended. Unlike other communist countries, Cuba has used its resources to build the rural areas of the country in keeping with Castro's policy of a minimum of urbanism and a maximum of ruralism. The Cuban government, acting on this policy, has come to dominate most aspects of Cuban life. Many Cubans work on state-operated farms. Others, formerly sharecroppers, now farm the same small plots as before. Food coupons issued to each Cuban assure a minimum of food for everyone; other items are obtained through a growing black market.

Family. Before the Castro regime, families were the important unit in Cuban social life. These families were strongly patriarchal. The move to socialism has reduced the significance of the family, and patariarchal leadership has given way to government leadership.

Religion. Once devoutly and almost solidly Catholic, the Cuban people have entered a period in which religion is downgraded. The Cuban government does not officially recognize religion, although Catholicism is tolerated. In keeping with this policy, most Cubans still profess adherence to the Catholic Church, but their religious zeal has diminished. Religion is no longer as important as it once was.

Education. Castro aimed to establish a new society in which work was rewarded and privileges were eliminated. He turned to education, undertaking a massive literacy campaign in 1961, sending teachers from the city to the country to educate adults and children alike. The campaign was so successful that 20 years later, in 1981, illiteracy had been reduced to 1.9 percent. Today a sixth-grade education is compulsory. Major efforts continue in day care, in primary education, and at the secondary level. There is a strong emphasis on math and science, and Cuba has become a center for preparing medical personnel, generating scores of young doctors. Based on Marxist-Leninist principles, education combines study with manual work. Students spend half the day on academics, the other half raising cash crops such as citrus fruits and tobacco to help support the school. Dotting the countryside are the buildings of the *escuela-en-el-campo*, the boarding school for 500 to 600 students of adolescent age and older. Equipped with classrooms, laboratories, a library, recreation areas, dorms, and a dining hall, these institutions concern themselves with nutrition and health care in addition to academics.

CUNA
(coo´nah)
Also spelled KUNA. Amerindian islanders who
maintain a separate lifestyle from mainland Panamanians.

Population: 28,000 (1987?).
Location: The San Blas area, northeast Panama.
Language: Cuna (a Chibchan language) and Spanish.

Geographical Setting

The Cuna now live on islands along the Caribbean coast of Panama.

The Cuna live along the southeast coast of Panama, mainly on many of the 366 small islands that line the Caribbean border in the San Blas district. Panama is a tropical country, and the islands are warm and wet. Areas of rain forest and swamp, these islands are covered with dense plant growth that supplies food and shelter for many different species of birds and animals.

Historical Background

Cuna legend describes the Great Father of the universe sending a succession of peoples to earth. The first of these peoples were half animal, and the last were the Golden People, or Cuna.

Before the Spanish. The Cuna were a powerful people with a well-developed lifestyle when Spaniards arrived in Panama in the 16th century and began to explore the land and people. To escape enslavement, some of the Cuna retreated up the river valleys where they maintained customary ways. Raising crops through slash-and-burn methods, the early Cuna supplemented agriculture with hunting and fishing. They also excelled at metalwork and ceramics, as well as making jewelry from carved teeth and from precious stones. After a treaty in 1790, the Cuna lived peacefully with Spaniards in the area. The government came to accept their independence, and began to trade for Cuna goods.

Early Spanish writings describe the Cuna as having three chiefs who struggled against one another. Each wielded enormous power, condemning people to torture or death for crimes like theft. A chief had many wives and servants, and wore ornaments of gold on his head, face, neck, and breast as symbols of his status. At death, his body was preserved, his wives and servants were poisoned, and the family was buried together.

Spanish rule. Though some traditions were maintained, others underwent significant change during the 300 years of Spanish rule. Human sacrifices, certain burial methods, and other customs disappeared. Except for the sale of coconuts, the Cuna abandoned their role as traders and restricted themselves to subsistence farming. Items of native clothing were exchanged for European-style dress. Cattle and horses became part of their economy around 1900, and the Cuna devised new laws and forms of organization to handle the raising of livestock.

Panama vs. Cuna. Following the independence of Panama in 1903, outsiders threatened the territorial and cultural integrity of the Cuna. Panamanian police began to suppress the remaining traditional practices and held the territory of the Cuna under strict control. In the 1920s, a full-scale program was launched to make them abandon customary ways and join Panamanian society. In 1925, the Cuna rebelled, killing or driving off the police. The United States intervened, convincing Panama to sign a treaty with the Cuna. In 1938, Panama's government recognized the existence of an official Cuna reserve.

A constitution between the government and the Cuna, *La Carta Orgánica de San Blas*, was drawn up in 1945. It recognized three *caciques*, or high chiefs, of the Cuna and established an *intendente*, or governor, who would be appointed as a representative of the area in Panama's government. Beginning to participate in the country's politics, in 1973, the Cuna elected three representatives of an advisory council to Panama's leaders. In 1983, the Cuna were allowed to choose their own intendente from three candidates, gaining a larger measure of self-determination.

Culture Today

The Cuna inhabit about 50 villages on the San Blas Islands off the eastern coast of Panama, the number of residents in a village ranging from 50 to over 2,000. All these communities are self-administering in keeping with the Cuna tradition of "gatherings" – villagewide meetings of a religious or social nature.

Government. Chiefs lead the gatherings, sometimes singing their conversation to the assembly. Each story or subject of a song is called an *ikar*. The song may advise women about keeping their houses clean, men about planting crops, or the people in general about the order of the universe or their history. An official, the *arkar*, translates the chant into spoken words. In such gatherings, offenders are publicly scolded for misbehavior.

Work force Salaried employment is now a source of income among the Cuna. In the largest villages, there are more wage earners than farm owners. Accustomed for many years to working as sailors, Cuna men began to find jobs ashore in Panama after 1900, and an increasing number have become migrant workers. They earn wages mostly as manual laborers in the cities and on the banana plantations of northwest Panama. Since the 1930s, the Cuna have also had a special contract to do kitchen work on U.S. military bases in the Canal Zone.

Even those who work away from home are responsible for contributing their share of public service. The Cuna are expected to donate a few hours a week to building and maintaining their gathering halls, working on communal coconut plantations, and constructing houses. Migrant laborers are unable to spend the required time and are fined to compensate for their absence. Matters such as the amount of a fine are discussed in gatherings. Unlike religious gatherings, business gatherings are attended only by men. The assembled men communicate through discussion, not song, and attend to matters such as the assignment of community work to be performed by individuals during the coming week.

Food and shelter. Cuna farmers sell coconuts as a cash crop, which provides them with a reliable income. Other Cuna crops include maize, beans, squash, rice, sugar cane, and fruits. The largest food crop is plantains (a bananalike plant). Boiled into a stew, roasted on a fire, or made into a thick drink, plantains are prepared as both food and beverage. The people drink *chicha*, a type of beer made from fermented maize or plantains and sugar cane juice, on ceremonial occasions.

Cuna homes are built close together on high coral islets a few feet above sea level. The houses are rectangular, thatched-roofed structures, often strung out along the banks of a river. Though sizes vary, a home might be 66 feet long and 15 feet high. The household is composed of members of an extended family – parents, their unmarried sons, and their married daughters and sons-in-law.

Family. The oldest male in the family acts as head of the household and exercises authority over his sons and sons-in-law.

Cuna writing

A Cuna village

By Borys Malkin. Courtesy Anthro Photo.

A Cuna woman in front of her house.

By John Pickering. Courtesy Anthro Photo.

Cuna artifacts

With more Cuna migrating to the mainland for labor, fewer members of an extended family now live together. Newly married couples are more likely to establish independent households than in the past, and ownership of the home (traditionally a female right) is shifting to the male.

Clothing. Although men have more authority than women in Cuna society, the position of women is traditionally strong. They own land as well houses, influence family decisions, and contribute to the household income. Aside from farming, Cuna women sew appliqué blouses and blouse panels for sale. They have become famous for these blouses and wear them in daily dress. Along with the blouses, the women wear wraparound skirts and ornaments: beads on their arms and calves; gold, crescent-shaped nose rings; and necklaces of glass, shells, or armadillo scales. Cuna men now wear cotton pants and shirts instead of the loincloths of the past, but some continue to wear a string of monkey teeth around their necks.

Traditions. Three of the most important rituals of Cuna society are connected with the life cycle of women. Ceremonies mark the piercing of their noses in infancy, their passage into womanhood, and their eligibility for marriage. Villagers sponsor the ceremonies, which occur several times a year.

Religion. Cuna religion centers on good and evil spirits who live in remote places such as mountaintops or ocean floors. The greatest residence of such spirits is the *kalu lbaki*, a huge tower from which commands are issued. Shamans, the religious leaders, intercede for the people to influence these spirits.

The people believe in a Supreme Being whose son visits earth to observe daily affairs during a Cuna's lifetime. It is thought that after death, the soul travels through eight layers of underworld and eight layers of heaven. A shaman guides the soul, but evildoers are detained in the underworld, where they suffer torments as such as being cut in half by giant scissors. In contrast, the virtuous receive heavenly money for each good deed. Such traditional beliefs continue to exist, though the Cuna have also practiced Christianity since missionaries arrived in the early 1900s.

Cuna dolls

ECUADORIANS

(ek´ wah door´ ee ans)

A people of mixed ethnic background, with two main centers
of population, one on the coast and the other in the highlands.

Ecuador

Population: 9,250,000 (1983).

Location: Ecuador, a country on the Pacific
Coast of South America, bounded by Colombia
on the north and Peru on the south and east.

Language: Spanish, Quechua and other Indian
languages.

Geographical Setting

Named for its location, Ecuador crosses over
latitude zero, mostly lying just south of the
equator. The terrain is divided into four regions –
the Pacific Coastal region, the highlands of the
Andes Mountains, a low eastern plain, and the
Galápagos Islands. Ecuadorians live primarily in
the highlands and coastal regions. The large land
area east of the Andes is mostly covered with
tropical forests cut by waterways that drain into
the Amazon River. Mainland forests lie along
sparkling blue lakes under snow-covered peaks.
About 10,000 Ecuadorians have taken up
residence on the Galápagos Islands, a dry and
rugged region that is now mostly an Ecuadorian
national park. The climate in Ecuador ranges from
springlike weather to cold and snow in the
mountains. The coastal climate is tropical. The
earth is unstable, the site of volcanoes and
earthquakes; the 1949 quake killed 6,000.

Historical Background

Ecuador's early Indians lived in large settlements and excelled in ceramic, silver, and gold work. Each settlement lived independently, without the benefits of a central government or national roads. By A.D.1000 the city states had formed a federation, but this federation was not a strong union. Thus, these Indians were quickly overpowered by the Inca, who, in the 1400s, unified the different groups under Inca rule from the capital at Quito.

Spanish rule. Spaniards reached the area that is now Ecuador about A.D. 1533, arresting the Inca leader Atahualpa and organizing a new Spanish city at Quito. They then claimed other areas for large farm enterprises and drafted local Indians as workers. For almost four centuries (1534-1822), the Spanish governed Ecuador from a distance – first from Lima, Peru, and then from Bogotá, Colombia.

An influx of Africans entered the country in the 1600s, possibly due to the wreck of a slave ship along the coast. Jesuit priests moved in to convert the native groups to Christianity during this period and to protect them from harsh treatment by the Spanish. The Jesuits were expelled in 1767, after protesting the exploitation of a local group. Without Jesuit protection, the Indians were left to fend for themselves. They rebelled in 1770, 1776, and 1790.

Independence. Ecuador's colonists subsequently joined the resistance movement against Spain. Led by Simón Bolívar, the movement aimed to liberate all the Andean countries. In May 1822, the Ecuadorian General Antonio José de Sucre defeated the Spanish and led the nation to independence. Ecuador briefly joined Colombia and Venezuela to form the Federation of Gran Colombia, but withdrew from this union in 1830.

Ecuadorians then fell under the rule of military leaders until 1859.

García Moreno seized power in 1859, becoming president in 1860 and continuing to run the country for the next 15 years. Believing the church was the key to law and order, he placed the government under its guidance. Moreno supported peaceful coexistence with neighbors, improved education, and built new roads to increase commerce. Despite these contributions, his policies were sometimes brutal, especially against non-Catholics. He was regarded as a dictator, and his enemies succeeded in murdering him in 1875. Afterwards, the country entered a period of confusion and then an era of more liberal rule from 1895 to 1912. A liberal president, Eloy Alfaro supported freedom for the Indians, a strong army, and the separation of church and state. Considered his major contribution, the railway linking the highland city Quito to the coastal town Guayaquil was built under his direction. It is said, though, that Alfaro was a professional revolutionary. Many died in small wars he started, and the people ultimately turned against him. Alfaro was murdered by an angry mob in 1912, his body dragged through the street, then dismembered and burned.

Economic change. An era of economic boom followed, as Ecuadorian produce became essential in World War I. International trade grew, but it was a one-crop (cacao) trade, destroyed by insect pests in 1925. In 1934 José María Velasco Ibarra became president, planning to benefit the people with great public works as well as land and economic reforms. Velasco never realized his plans, though he resurfaced as president for five terms (1934-35, 1944-47, 1952-56, 1960-61, and 1968-72). Following his first term in office, the Ecuadorians managed to revive their economy through a growing trade in bananas.

In 1941 Peru invaded and defeated Ecuador's small army. The result was disastrous, Ecuadorians losing territory in their eastern lowlands that was equal in size to Scotland and England combined.

The people then began to concentrate on the banana trade, and their economy improved steadily until 1960. Since 1963, this growth has been marred by internal unrest and by a succession of coups by various military regimes. The military controls the country, adding to a history of frequent rule by *caudillos* (political lords) and dictators.

Culture Today

Ecuadorians are a mixed population, about 10 percent white, 41 percent mestizo, 39 percent Amerindian, and 10 percent black. Government remains in the hands of whites and mestizos. Land is largely controlled by whites: roughly 1 percent of the people control 50 percent of the territory.

Food clothing and shelter. In the highland valleys, large estates are concentrated in the hands of a few white Europeans and worked mainly by Indian peasants. Much land lies uncultivated, and many of the Europeans are absentee landowners. Grown as staples in the Indian diet, the most important highland crops are grains (maize, barley, wheat). Cocoa, bananas, and coffee, the major export crops, are raised in the coastal lowlands. For protein, *cuy* (guinea pig) is a delicacy in the Andes. Fish and meat contribute to the diet in the coastal lowlands. Tortoise is the staple animal dish on the Galápagos Islands.

Andes woman spinning yarn.

By Richard Reed. Courtesy Anthro Photo.

Large haciendas appear in the highlands. The tenant farmers are Indians, who usually labor under the watchful eye of a mestizo overseer. Their compensation is a scant wage plus the right to farm their own subsistence plot. Earning too little to meet their needs, they become indebted to the estate, then further bound into poverty. Thus, they are trapped. Little has been done to break the pattern, aside from individual attempts. Galo Plaza Lasso, Ecuador's former president, gave Indians on his hacienda an education and one-fourth of his land.

There is tension between the people in the highlands and those on the coast, because behaviors in the two regions are quite different. In contrast to the highlands' large estates, much of the coastal area is divided into small and medium-sized farms. The peasants here use slash-and-burn methods of agriculture. They are mainly a black mixture, descendants of marriages between coastal Indians, Europeans, and Africans. Known as *Montuvios*, these Ecuadorians often experience both rural and city life as they move from farm to city labor. Their rural life is filled with long hours of harvesting crops by hand, drying coffee beans, and transporting bananas to the harbor. In the cities, they take jobs in factories that process foods, drinks, clothing, and other consumer goods. The factory owners, equivalents of estate owners in the highlands, are usually mestizo or white.

Solid, contemporary-style buildings appear mostly in the large cities – Quito in the highlands and Guayaquil on the coast. Highland Ecuadorians live in wood-framed, thatched-roofed, one-room houses lined neatly in rows along the estate highways. Those who farm their own smaller landholdings often live in villages of small single-story homes with brown-tiled roofs and whitewashed walls. Shanties have appeared in the coastal towns, the shacks built of small split-cane walls and corrugated iron roofs. On the Galápagos Islands, there has been new construction of hotels, restaurants and houses.

There is great variety in dress. Standard footwear among the rural Montuvios is boots for protection from snakes. If boots are unaffordable, the Montuvios wrap leather around their feet. Men's wear is often store bought. Even in the highlands an Indian boy might now be found in factory-made overalls and hat. Increasingly women wear slacks. More customary is a calf-length skirt with colorful embroidery at the hem, with perhaps a handmade shawl and Panama hat.

Ecuadorians are said to wear hats from a very young age. Woven by Ecuadorians from their *Toquilla* plant, the straw hat was misnamed for its point of sale in Panama rather than for its point of origin in Ecuador. Though the hats sold throughout the world from the 19th into the 20th century, demand for them dropped after World War II. Today, some people weave and wait for the return of the multimillion dollar business. Meanwhile, they sell the hats at the weekly *feria* (market), a crowded event during which merchants and farmers trade food and supplies.

Family. Single-parent families are common in poorer households. Marriage is not always a formal union, and many fathers neither live with nor assume financial responsibility for the family. In homes where the father is present, he has the greater authority. Yet he spends much time away, in clubs or coffee houses while the mother manages the household. Family relations are different for those people more closely tied to their Indian heritage The status of women in these groups is higher, marriages tend to be formalized, and both the men and women bear responsibility for the family unit.

Religion. Before the Jesuits introduced Christianity, Ecuadorians were mainly animists in their religious beliefs. A few mix these earlier beliefs with Christianity, although most have converted to Catholicism. As in other aspects of daily life, Church influence varies with the region. In the highlands, Catholic traditions are strictly followed, and holidays are mostly religious ceremonies. On the coast, a strong anticlerical movement has diminished the Catholic influence.

The weakening of Catholic influence and the growth of oil production have led to changes in Ecuadorian society. Ecuador has begun to shift from an estate-dominated, village-oriented country to an urban-industrial nation. Still, the majority of the people have little political or economic power or schooling. Approximately 80 percent of the children are enrolled in primary schools, but only 40 percent continue to the secondary level.

The arts. There have been individual achievements in art. The 17th century religious paintings of Miguel de Santiago, a mestizo, are singled out as exceptionally realistic. Manuel Chili, an Indian, is noteworthy for lifelike wooden carvings, painted to create a porcelain-type finish. A more recent artist, the Indian painter Oswaldo Guayasamín, created "Quito Weeping, " a canvas in memory of the Spanish conquest of his people. An Indian group, the Otavalos, are renown weavers of ponchos and blankets from tweedlike suit materials.

Many Ecuadorians could not read or write, abilities that were, in the early 1800s, required in order to become a citizen of their country. Therefore, a large number of the people were noncitizens ineligible to vote. Over the years adult schools helped reduce the number of illiterates to 16.1 percent in 1982, and laws changed. Voting is now required of those who are literate and optional for those who are not.

Ecuador is a republic in which both the president and members of congress are directly elected by the people. A larger number of the wealthy vote. Therefore, government serves the interests of land and business owners while the poor suffer from policies they have little power to change.

GUAJIRO

(gwa hir´ oh)

Also spelled GOAJIRO. Amerindians who herd and
farm along the northeast Caribbean coast of South America.

Population: 50,000 (1978?).
Location: Colombia, Venezuela.
Language: Guajiro, from the Arawakan
language family.

Geographical Setting

The Guajiro live on a peninsula that projects
into the Caribbean Sea and is divided between the
present-day countries of Venezuela and Colombia.
It is a semidesert region in which the Indian
population has historically eked out an agricultural
living, mostly growing maize. The country is dry
and infertile. Cactus is abundant in the area along
with some coastal plants. There are shallow,
sandy passages of water but almost no rivers.
Inland, the terrain rises to hilly, grassy steppes.
When the Spanish brought horses and cattle, the
Guajiro began to raise livestock along the steppes.
They are among the few Amerindian groups who
voluntarily changed their economy. Instead of
maize farming, their primary occupation became
cattle raising.

The Guajiro live
on the border
between Colombia
and Venezuela.

Historical Background

As early as the 15th century, Spaniards
appeared on the peninsula La Guajira, where they
found the Indian people who became known as
the Guajiro. The Indians sustained themselves as
farmers, potters, and weavers in an area where
much of the land was desert on which crops could
not be grown. Although the Spaniards settled on

119

A Guajiro horseman

the peninsula, they soon abandoned it for more fertile regions. Before their departure, they appear to have introduced horses and cattle to residents of the area. By the middle of the 16th century, these animals were commonly found on the peninsula, and the Guajiro had made cattle-raising their livelihood. They were to become the only South American Indians to ride horses and raise cattle on their own initiative, readily adapting to a lifestyle that best suited the semiarid plains on which the Guajiro live.

Culture Today

Many traditional Guajiro continue to raise livestock. The highest status is associated with those who own and raise cattle, although the people also keep goats, sheep, burrows, mules, and horses. From January to June the cattle-owners live a nomadic lifestyle, in search of the best water and pasture for their livestock.

The area of a group's wanderings is limited. The Guajiro have been organized into some 25 clans, each with its own territory. Formed of related families, a clan is restricted to a particular series of grazing lands and wells. Each clan has its own cattle brand. The yearly branding is a festive occasion, featuring horse races, wrestling, and the like, along with much eating and drinking. **Government.** A chieftain, generally the group's wealthiest individual, governs each clan. Since the Guajiro follow matrilineal descent, a chief inherits his position from his mother's side of the family. His duties include resolving disputes among family members, organizing work projects such as the building of wells, and representing the group to outsiders. In resolving disputes, he demands compensation for wrongdoing in accordance with Guajiro law. Insults and physical blows are offenses for which penalties are paid. Thieves repay several times the value of a stolen

A government-provided windmill pumps water in Guajiro land.

By Borys Malkin. Courtesy Anthro Photo.

item. Also, suicide is a crime, and those who attempt it must pay damages to their clan.

Food. Members of a Guajiro family are assigned various economic tasks. At the head of the family, the father supervises moving, pasturing, and watering the livestock. His sons do most of the actual work, rising early to water the animals. The meager diet consists of milk and some meat products, although rice, plantain, yuca, and cactus are also eaten. The women plant, harvest, and prepare maize, a staple used for food and among the cattle-owners more often for drink. Aside from *chicha* (home-brewed maize beer), milk and coffee are the popular beverages. Fish is a common food among those who live on the coast, where the Guajiro also fish for pearls to sell. Otherwise they are seasonally employed to gather salt or pods from divi-divi trees, which produce a substance for tanning. Although minor occupations in the past, this seasonal work has gained importance due to recent droughts and the loss of pastureland. Thus, some Guajiro mix their independent income with employment. Faced with the adverse conditions, others abandon the traditional life altogether, becoming laborers in the cities or on Venezuelan oilfields.

Along the coast some Guajiro are fishers. This man is repairing his fishing net.

By Borys Malkin. Courtesy Anthro Photo.

City life. Those who migrate to the cities tend to live on the outskirts in shantytowns. The largest of these settlements provides housing for some 5,000 migrants. Packed closely together in slope-roofed single-room shacks, shantytown residents build their homes of wood, cardboard, and corrugated metal. Hammocks are the standard beds. Back in the rural regions, those who still live the traditional lifestyle build both temporary and permanent structures. They often live in open sheds – poles covered with split cactus stalks – when migrating with their herds. During the rainy season (October to November), these Guajiro settle in permanent villages. Cattle-rich families might construct brick and cement houses with iron roofs, while the less fortunate build thatched structures of wattle and palm leaves. Typically a village contains 150 residents, their houses spaced within gunshot distance from one another for purposes of mutual defense.

Family. Domestic units of the Guajiro family include a husband, a wife, and their unmarried children. The *casta*, or family lineage of the mother, is the main social group to which each individual belongs. The head man of each casta is the mother's brother. Although the mother remains the main disciplinarian, he provides her children with advice, protection, and their inheritance. The children contribute to the family's livelihood, beginning at the age of four or five. Young boys learn to tend herds. Young girls fetch water, look after the fire, cook maize gruel or bake maize cakes, and participate in the harvest. Their passage into womanhood is marked by ceremonies during which a girl is shut off from the community to learn spinning, weaving, and the details of housekeeping. Afterwards she is a woman of marriageable age. In the past a family might purchase her as a bride for a price in gold, cattle, horses, or mules. The bride price is no longer a necessity, and today women may choose their own husbands instead of abiding by the choices of their families.

Clothing. Guajiro dress has undergone similar changes. The men are now likely to be seen in shirts and trousers rather than the everyday cloaks of the past. Worn with loincloths and belts, these cloaks were twisted so that the chest was bared. Customary dress for women includes wide black or brown tunics. For adornment, they would wear *puna* – long strings of beads that draped over the shoulders, then crossed in front and back. Belts made of black seed pearls might hold the puna in place. A sign of passage from girlhood to womanhood is cutting the hair. Women hang the shorn locks in a bag from the roof, never letting the hair on their head grow below the neck. Using a stain from nuts, both men and women paint their faces black to protect themselves from the sun and from evil.

Religion. The Guajiro believe in the existence of good and evil spirits on earth. Their religion centers on the god *Mareiwa* who is thought to have created the first humans. A woman, *Borunka*, is considered the mother of all the people and the being who gave them agriculture and domesticated animals. The demon *Yoruja* is the alleged chief of illness and death. Shamans are medicine men or wise women who intervene with the spirits to cure illnesses and prevent death. The Guajiro believe the dead experience an afterlife in a cave of islands off Cabo de Vela where souls live as they did on earth, raising cattle and rearing families. While such traditional beliefs still exist, many Guajiro have now become Catholic. Monks and nuns have greatly influenced the life of the people, taking in children of the poor in times of starvation. Once, the boarding schools of Catholic missions provided their education, but today Guajiro children enroll in public schools.

Change. The traditional values of the Guajiro are changing. Migration to the cities has resulted in less emphasis on the contribution of the children to the well-being of the family and more concern for the achievement of the individual. Management of the family is still relegated to the mother, however. Her status has been maintained even in urban centers, where she controls the income as well as the children in the manner of Guajiro women of the past.

GUARANI
(gwa rah´ ni´)

A scattered group of Amerindians who share the same language and living areas, each subgroup having a different name.

The Guaraní live in Argentina, Brazil, and Paraguay.

Guaraní land is east of the Paraguay River.

Population: 10,000 (1989).
Location: The northern Paraguay River valley of Paraguay, Brazil, Argentina, Uruguay.
Language: Guaraní, a dialect of a family of languages used widely in Brazil, Paraguay, Argentina, and Uruguay.

Geographical Setting

The territory of the Guaraní is divided by the Paraguay River. East of the river, there are green valleys and rolling hills covered with forest. West of the Paraguay River, the land is dry, brackish and the plants are parched grass and scattered forests. Most of the forest land lies in the moister eastern part of this section. Aside from fish, the river and its borders support wildlife such as jaguar, armadillo, wild boar, water hog, tapir, and deer.

Historical Background

Early Guarani. Before the 15th century A.D., the Guaraní roamed the Atlantic coast of South America, gaining a reputation as a spirited, warlike people. They lived in widely scattered groups, growing maize and manioc as major crops and supplementing their diet by hunting, gathering, and fishing. Each group elected military leaders, but its civil chief inherited his position. The ancient chiefs had several wives – some as many as fifteen to thirty. It is said that some of

124

these Guaraní practiced cannibalism as well. If a man committed a crime, he might live with a wife in captivity for months or years, but then he would be stoned to death. Afterwards, his flesh was eaten.

Spanish rule. Toward the end of the century, the Guaraní began to adventure inland. There they attacked the Incas and raided peaceful tribes, then settled in conquered territories or returned home with their bounty. The first Spanish visitors learned of mineral wealth to be found in the Inca empire from these Indians, and some joined in the Guaraní raids on Inca settlements. A 1526 expedition led by Sebastian Cabot, an Englishman sailing for Spain, tried but failed to penetrate Guaraní territory in search of gold and silver. Ten years later a Spanish adventurer, Juan de Ayolas, succeeded in amassing a load of gold and silver but was massacred on his return across the Paraguay River. Such hostility was the exception, not the rule. Mostly the Guaraní cooperated, guiding Spaniards in their search for Inca treasure.

The Spanish exploited the Guaraní for their labor and often took their women as wives. The Indians became part of a forced labor system – *ncomienda* – in which a Spaniard promised to protect them in return for their services. Resisting the injustices done to them under the system, many Guaraní rebelled. Their rebellions were crushed, and thousands of them died while others fled to Jesuit missions, first built for the Guaraní in the late 1500s.

In 1608 King Philip III of Spain gave the Jesuits authority over the Guaraní and their conversion to Christianity. More than a dozen missions were built. These flourished until 1630, but then were destroyed by slave hunters, who mercilessly burned the missions and slaughtered or captured and enslaved 300,000 Indians. The Jesuits resisted, moving elsewhere, then arming and drilling the Guaraní for self-defense. With huge herds of cattle and bountiful crops, the Jesuit missions prospered for the next hundred years. Italian architects came to design their churches, and the industrious Guaraní became skilled in sculpture and in holy music.

Portuguese influence. In 1750 a treaty of exchange transferred Guaraní territory from Spain to Portugal. However, missionaries incited the Guaraní to revolt against the conditions of the treaty. The Indians were crushed in the War of the Seven Reductions; the Jesuits suffered from the bitter fighting and in 1767 were expelled from South America. After they left, many Guaraní abandoned the lifestyle they had adopted at the missions and returned to the forest. There they joined the Guaraní who had remained separate from mission society, the Cainguá. Others who did not return to the forest fell under the care of Franciscan monks and received far less benevolent treatment than they had under the Jesuits. Portuguese colonists invaded the missions, seized the land, and forced the Indians to work for white plantation owners. During these years, the Guaraní population diminished to a few thousand.

Culture Today

Religion. The Guaraní who returned to the forest reverted to their traditional lifestyle and religious beliefs. According to these beliefs, each person has a gentle soul and a cruel, bloodthirsty soul. One or the other of these souls dominates the individual during his or her lifetime. After death, the good soul travels to the Land-Without-Evil. The bad soul is transformed into a frightful ghost, which must be attacked and killed as if it were a deadly animal. Animals, plants, and winds are habitats for spirits and demons. Shamans, the religious leaders, mediate between the spirit world and the natural world by struggling against the demons.

The Guaraní fear the imminent destruction of the world. Eclipses are thought to be caused by an eternal bat who gnaws at the sun and will ultimately destroy it and the stars. Their religious life has been subject to periodic revivals through messiahs who guide the people in an effort to reach the Land-Without-Evil so that they might escape from the impending destruction. Shamans direct the revivals, remaining powerful in Guaraní communities even today.

In the past, shamans often acted as political leaders and judges who assigned blame to an individual when misfortune struck. They had great prestige in society, and their remains were worshiped after death. Even now shamans judge a thief by touching the accused near the heart: a red mark left by the shaman's finger indicates guilt.

Family life. Other aspects of traditional life have changed. The Guaraní once lived in extended groups of the father's relatives. As many as 60 related families might live together in a large, rectangular structure. Each house had a vaulted or gabled roof supported by a ridge pole and thatched with grass and palm leaves. The houses were as long as 150 feet, and there might be four to eight of these structures in a village. The communal home is a phenomenon of the past, however. Scattered through the tropical forest, today's Guaraní live in individual houses with gardens.

Food. Homes are established in areas where game is plentiful. Meat is greatly preferred in the Guaraní diet, although manioc and maize are the traditional staples. Among the Cainguá, the most traditional Guaraní, a whole community uses the slash-and-burn method to clear a large field, then divides it into family plots. Families also raise beans, sweet potatoes, and peanuts, but their harvest is usually insufficient to feed them. Aside from gathering foods such as wild honey, they therefore use bows and arrows to hunt and fish.

The people set traps or nooses on long poles for catching parrots and train dogs to hunt jaguar. The Cainguá then prepare the meat by broiling it on a spit. Guaraní season their food with tree ashes rather than salt. As with the language, food in rural Paraguay is largely a heritage of the Guaraní, featuring dishes such as *chipas*, cakes made of maize flour.

Clothing. Guaraní crafts include the shaping of their hunting weapons, and the making of baskets and ceramics for harvesting. Their clothing was simple, but they fashioned artful accessories. Loincloths were the standard item of clothing, while women sometimes wore a sacklike dress from below the shoulders to the knees. Still seen at ceremonies, traditional accessories include feather wreaths, cotton sashes with feather fringes, and seed necklaces. A long *T*-shaped stick through the lip is perhaps the most distinct ornament. For everyday wear, today's Guaraní are more often seen in cotton ponchos and other items of clothing adopted from their neighbors.

Arts. Music has long played a role in religious ceremonies, the gourd rattles being one of the most holy instruments. Flutes are said to have been made of the bones of slain enemies. In their rich language the people spun folklore. Their creation myth says Darkness and Eternal Bats fought in the night. Then, their Great Father created the earth and a woman, who bore twins. Other stories make the demons constant victims of practical jokes by the twins.

Change. If the lifestyle of the Guaraní has changed due to contact with outside peoples, they also have had a lasting effect on the lives of their neighbors. Guaraní ceremonies are evidence of a rich heritage in song and dance that has greatly affected the folk music of peoples in Paraguay. Guaraní influence is further reflected in the widespread use of the Guaraní language throughout the country today.

GUATEMALANS

(gwa´ te mah´ lans)

An agricultural people of Spanish and Mayan descent, including the most distinctly Indian population in Central America.

Population: 8,195,000 (1986).
Location: Guatemala, a Central-American country lying between Mexico and Honduras.
Language: Spanish, various Indian dialects.

Guatemala

Geographical Setting

Lying between 14 and 16 degrees north latitude, the country of Guatemala is bordered on the north and west by Mexico. The southwest boundary is the Pacific Ocean. To the east lie British Honduras and the Gulf of Honduras in the Caribbean Sea. Guatemala has a longer coastline sloping southwest on the Pacific and a smaller coastline in the northeast on the Caribbean.

Beginning at the Pacific Ocean, the land is a tropical plain for 30 miles, then rises to low mountains with volcanic peaks and high basins between 5,000 and 10,000 feet in elevation. Most Guatemalans live in these basins. The highlands are cooler and drier than the tropical lowlands; the rainfall is appropriate for Guatemala's largest crop, coffee. On the east, three large rivers drain the mountain ranges and flow into the Caribbean Sea. Between them are hot, wet plains ideal for tropical fruit such as bananas. Roughly 70 percent of the country is mountainous, and 60 percent is forested.

Historical Background

Mayan times. Guatemalans trace their ancestry to Mayan civilization dating from the sixth century B.C. The Mayans established a network of states run by elite families whose rulers claimed descent from the sun and from mythical hero gods. Members of the upper class, these ruling families shared high status with scribes, sculptors, and artists. Farmers belonged in the lower classes. Using sophisticated techniques (canals, terraces, soil platforms), they raised corn, beans, and squash on rugged terrain.

Mayan civilization prospered and gave rise to advancements such as a well-developed system of astronomy and time-keeping. The culture reached its height around the year A.D. 700, then declined in a wave of violence. Forming temporary empires on the Yucatán Peninsula, the Mayans scattered through Central America from about 900 to 1300. Guatemala's Indians eventually fell under the rule of a Mexican people.

Spanish rule. In 1524 Lieutenant Pedro de Alvarado battled his way into Guatemala and conquered it for Spain. The Spanish developed the *encomienda* system: Under this system the right to supervise the Indians was given to Spanish landowners. In addition, the Indians were obligated to pay taxes to the Spanish crown. Since they were unable to pay them, the landowners stepped in to fulfill the obligation, and Indians were forced to repay the debt with their labor. The arrangement tied them to colonial masters for life.

Guatemala was governed as a colony for several hundred years. A prosperous land, for a time it became the kingdom of Guatemala (1808-1814), and the center of Spanish rule in Central America. As early as 1811, though, there were movements for independence. By 1821 Spanish rule had ended. Guatemalans then joined the Central American Federation.

Independence. After the breakup of the Central American Federation (1838), Guatemala settled into life as an independent republic. Strong dictators came to power, interrupted by some constitutional government. First, there was the mestizo Rafael Carrera, a conservative who led the country for close to 30 years. He gave the church privileges, reenacted old colonial laws and chose his own successor. His policies endured until 1871, when Justo Barrios and Miguel Granados led a revolution that ushered in 75 years of liberal rule. Barrios confiscated church lands, giving them to immigrants and natives. Adventurous landowners, they began raising coffee, which became the country's leading export.

U.S. intervention. In the early 1900s Guatemala's government conceded land to the United Fruit Company, a United States company. The concession brought a new foreign influence into the country. Afterwards, a series of dictators cast the Indians into more forced labor. The last of the dictators, Jorge Ubico y Castañeda, was deposed in 1944 by university students.

The people then elected Juan José Arévalo, gaining new liberties under his administration. Both he and his successors fought for land reforms and restrictions on outsiders such as the United Fruit Company. During the next 20 years, Guatemala suffered an invasion by Honduras and a military coup. Assassinations and more military takeovers of government followed.

In the second half of the 20th century, the country has been torn by violence between left-wing revolutionaries and right-wing paramilitary groups. Citizens report that people are arrested, tortured, and often killed. In 1984 alone, at least 428 died due to the political strife. Many have fled across the border, seeking asylum in Mexico.

Meanwhile, the military remains the dominant governing force in Guatemala.

Culture Today

Guatemalans fall into two main groups, Indians who comprise over half the population and Ladinos, or mixed bloods. Descendants of the Mayas, the Indians speak various languages but share physical traits: dark copper skin, a stocky build, straight black hair, high cheekbones, and low foreheads. The Ladinos are mostly mestizos, people of Spanish and Indian ancestry. They enjoy higher status than the Indians, who are frequently victims of prejudice.

Land. While 2 percent of the landowners control 70 percent of the land, most Guatemalans continue to earn a living through agriculture. Many Indians farm the Pacific slopes or the central highlands, where the key crop is coffee. Under five acres, the average Indian farm also raises subsistence crops. Beans, squash, and maize are grown for food, but harvests are small, and most Indians lead poverty-stricken lives. Men, the main agricultural workers, often migrate seasonally to coastal plantations for work as wage laborers. Cotton, sugar, bananas, and other fruits are the standard lowland crops.

Women. Although largely confined to the house, Indian women harvest fresh corn and beans to cook in the kitchen, raise herbs and fruits in their gardens, and tend the household animals (turkeys, ducks, chickens, pigs). Some earn extra cash by selling surplus food or potterywork and weaving. From the age of 12, young Indian girls earn wages for the family, taking jobs on large plantations or doing domestic work in the city. Their economic role may help explain the higher status generally awarded to women in the Indian families.

City life. Mestizos often live in towns, control much of the local commerce and politics, and generally feel superior to the Indians. Spanish-speaking, they tend to become shopkeepers, government employees, or laborers in private industry. The more prosperous mestizos live in large households, including relatives and servants as well as the nuclear family. According to custom, a married couple often lives with the husband's parents, but this practice has grown weaker over the years as husbands find wage labor.

A street in Guatemala City

Plantations. The *finca*, or large plantation, employs both Indians and mestizos, an estate hiring as many as 700 people to produce sugar, for example. Finca owners provide housing, some rations, and small private plots to the laborers. Using these small plots, the workers raise much of the corn and beans they eat. They purchase more, also buying meat, cheese, and vegetables when affordable. Though Spanish is the main language on the finca, Indian dialects are also spoken. Customs are mixed here. While the mestizos have Catholic weddings, Indians marry in traditional fashion, by exchanging food and having friends witness the occasion.

Traditions. In earlier times, when these Indians lived in villages, there was a pattern to romance. A boy would visit the public water fountain to see a girl, who either discouraged him or signalled that she would like to talk with him again. Next he gave her a gift. If she accepted the gift, he visited her parents, perhaps three times before a marriage was arranged.

The pattern has changed with new lifestyles in the country. Along with new ways of announcing romantic intentions, there is now great variety in clothing and dress. The clothing of many mestizos recalls styles worn in North America. In contrast, almost every Indian community has its own colorful style of dress; an individual's village can be identified by the design of his or her textiles. Similarly, mestizo farmers live in two-room adobe structures or in ones that use poles for walls and palm leaves, straw, or tiles for roofs. Indian farmers often live in steeply-roofed structures within a stone-walled compound. Some urban Guatemalans reside in newly-built settlements equipped with a school, a community water tank, a health center, and a soccer field.

Military rule. There are villages in Guatemala under military control. Government repression is said to have reached a peak in the 1980s. Whole families have "disappeared." In control of the government, the Guatemalan military is held responsible. Some 1,000,000 peasants are obligated to serve in a military patrol system. Though unarmed, they were used to corral 70,000 others into the army-controlled villages. Religious practices in these villages are limited.

Religion. Most Guatemalans are Roman Catholic. Among the Indians, older Mayan beliefs mix with Catholic rituals, and the Mayan calendar is still observed. The main Indian deities include a Supreme Being and his ministers, a Married Couple (often called the sun and the moon). Christian figures are reinterpreted in terms of these beliefs. The Married Couple, for example, is often equated with Joseph and Mary.

Guatemalans celebrate many religious events with parades such as this one.

Arts. Elaborate fiestas are a primary form of public worship and reflect much of the creative life of the people. Artful models of religious personalities appear in processions during these fiestas, which also feature fireworks, marimba music, and dances. The dances represent events from history or from legends that reveal the people's hopes and fears. One such legend describes a host of animals that once ate humans and will do so again someday during a solar eclipse.

In the real world, death is familiar to Guatemalans. Besides the hundreds of government deaths, medical care is wanting. As in other Central American countries, there is one doctor for every few thousand people; 40 percent of the children are said to die before reaching the age of five.

Education. Those who survive are likely to work early in life. Elementary education is free and required in urban areas, but most children never progress past fourth grade because their services are needed to earn income. In 1980 only 56 percent attended elementary school, and close to 50 percent of the adults were illiterate. Thus, a national campaign has been launched to teach reading and writing. Meanwhile, some adults have begun to invest their own resources in education for their children and in trucks, supplies, and new businesses for themselves.

GUYANANS

(guy an´ ans)

People of the East Indies, comprised of at least six
ethnic groups and mostly imported to the area.

Guyana

Population: 759,000 (1980).

Location: A section of the north coast of South America.

Language: Mainly English; also Hindi, Creole, Amerindian dialects.

Geographical Setting

The land of the Guyanans is a divided strip along the north coast of South America, east of Venezuela. The Essequibo River runs down the middle of the country. A narrow belt of rich soil lies near the Atlantic Ocean, followed by white sands, vast rain forest, and savannah. About 90 percent of the people are situated on the small belt of rich soil. Roughly 270 miles long and 10 to 40 miles wide, the strip is below high-tide levels and must be protected by sea walls. Problems with flooding have made the strip difficult to farm. Still, the land is fertile and produces rich sugar and rice crops. Inland is an east-west strip 100 miles wide. Covered with forest, this higher land is a source of lumber and some minerals, bauxite (aluminum ore) being the most valuable. To the south and west, the Pakaraima Mountains separate Guyana from Venezuela and Brazil. The country's climate is tropical, warm and wet with two rainy seasons a year.

Historical Background

Scattered bands of Amerindians may have lived in the area known as Guyana before its coast

136

was first charted by the Spanish in 1499. With much of the land below sea level and a tropical interior, the area was uninviting to most. Fortune hunters came searching for El Dorado, the king whose city had streets paved in gold and houses decorated with precious jewels. The treasure seekers failed to find such a city and discovered that the Amerindians here were intractable. Protected by the tropical forest, they managed to remain independent. By the end of the 1500s, the Dutch were trading with the Amerindians, exchanging goods for their dyes, hemp, and tobacco.

Dutch settlement. In the 1600s the Dutch developed three settlements and drained the coastal swamps to plant sugar cane. Thousands of tons of soil had to be dug, as ditches, seawalls, and dams were needed to make planting crops possible. Therefore, the Dutch West India Company sent over 5,000 black slaves a year. Soon the black population outnumbered the white. As a result, landowners lived in continual fear of slave rebellions.

In the late 1700s and early 1800s, the British made three efforts to claim the Dutch settlements. Finally, in 1814, the British succeeded in taking possession of the area, renaming it British Guiana. British planters received 400 yards of sea frontage and 250 acres extending inland. Then they began their battle against water, tackling the Atlantic Ocean before them and river floodwaters behind them. Slaves did most of the work until slavery was abolished in 1834. Laboring in mines and forests as well as fields, blacks are credited with building the country. The majority labored on plantations.

Slavery. Some plantation owners grew quite wealthy, living in grand estates by the sea. Nearby were a factory, cattle, and the slave quarters. These were often flimsy structures, constructed of wattle and mud, the roof thatched with leaves. In place of furniture, each slave family received an iron pot and blankets for sleeping. Plantain, fruit similar to the banana, was the staple in their diet. Though they had small private plots, the slaves found little time for their own farming given their seven-hour workday and seven-to-nine mile trek to and from the fields. On their return, they were counted and recounted to make sure none had fled.

Early attempts to escape and set up free black forest communities met with disaster. Familiar with the tropical forest, the Indians easily captured the slaves and returned them to their owners. The earliest punishments included flogging escapees and killing the ringleaders, sometimes roasting them alive or hanging them by meat hooks. Slaves also resisted in a less dangerous way, doing the least work possible.

When slavery was abolished in 1834, most blacks fled from the sugar estates to the towns. There they formed the basis of a growing urban population, becoming carpenters, bricklayers, masons, and later professionals. Meanwhile, indentured servants were brought over from India to take the place of black slaves on the sugar plantations. Resentments between the races grew.

Indentured Asians. Indentured servants signed up for five years of labor; when the five years were completed they received certificates of freedom. There were twice as many East Indian men as women, a cause of strife in the community. Both men and women waded across canals and ditches to work in the fields, many of the men simply clad in loin cloths and the women in sari-style Indian clothing. Known as *ranges*, standard living quarters were long, low, mud-floored houses with partitions inside between spaces for different families. There was a communal kitchen, but no bathroom.

Aside from East Indians, smaller groups of Chinese and Portuguese were also imported as indentured servants. When the system ended in 1917, there were some 300,000 servants. By then, rice farming had begun in the fertile strip. East Indians tended to remain on the farms even after 1917.

Independence. Great Britain allowed the colony to create its own constitution in 1928, but it would remain a colony into the 1950s. During this decade, Dr. Cheddi Jagan, a dentist from India, and Forbes Burnham, a black lawyer, led Guyanans to independence. The colony became self-governing with a two-house legislature in 1953, Dr. Jagan's party winning a majority of seats in the House of Assembly. Upset by Jagan's communist leanings, Britain renounced the election.

Struggling for survival, the new government increased taxes and established savings laws. The people rebelled, staging riots and strikes that ended in racial violence in the 1960s. Britain stepped in to control the turmoil and to manage foreign affairs. The mood changed. Burnham won more support from the people than Dr. Jeddi. No longer feeling that Guyana would turn to communism, Britain granted the colony its independence in 1966. British Guiana became *Guyana*, the Amerindian's name for the "land of many waters."

Despite charges of unfair elections, Burnham remained in power until his death in 1985. He gave Guyana control of private British sugar estates and Canadian-owned bauxite mines, moving the country closer to socialism. Many of the people, though, remained poverty-stricken. Guyana has been described as the poorest country in the Caribbean.

Culture Today

Ethnic distribution. Ninety percent of Guyanans live along the Atlantic Coast, many in

A street in Georgetown, Guyana

urban centers (Georgetown, New Amsterdam, Mackenzie). The racial balance today is roughly 50 percent Asian and 30 percent African, the rest consisting of 10 percent mixed, 4 percent Amerindian, under 3 percent Portuguese and Chinese, and various others. The ethnic groups are divided geographically, East Indians living largely in rural areas while blacks reside in coastal cities. What they share is a history of overcoming the obstacles of a difficult environment far from their original homelands.

Religion. The different ethnic backgrounds account for the range of religious beliefs. Belonging to the Church of England or Roman Catholic Church, the black population is largely Christian. East Indians generally observe Hindu or Muslim religions. The government sets aside national holidays for several religions (Phagwah, Eid-ul-Ahza, and Christmas). It has also leased land to foreign cults, such as the People's Temple of Jim Jones, who led 900 of his followers in a mass suicide (the Jonestown massacre). Such groups live apart from the main population in the country.

Economy. Foreigners no longer control the economy. For years a London-based company not only owned the sugar industry but held interests even in retail stores. Since Guyana's government dislodged the company, the nation has remained in control of sugar production, still the main moneymaker in the country. The other major crop is rice, which has taken its place next to cassava, sweet potatoes and maize as a staple in the diet. Coffee is grown on the coast, and a dairy industry has developed in the cities to provide milk. The cattle are raised on the savannah, then transported to the coast, often on foot. The beef is sold, and there is some fishing for profit, the desired catch being shrimp. While more people farm, some work in the rain forest as miners. Bauxite from the mines earns less money today than in the past, and the country also produces less sugar and rice. Poverty, then, has increased.

Shelter. Homes are generally scarce. Wood-frame structures, sometimes elevated as protection against flooding, are provided by businesses. Also, people who want to build their own housing are encouraged with advice and supervision from the government. Still, the number of available homes fails to keep pace with the rapidly growing population.

Housing in the country is typical of the West Indies. For protection against flooding, houses may be elevated. The people use home-grown wood as building material – for example, purple heartwood from Guyanese forests. The architecture is a mix of colonial (Dutch, British) and simpler, contemporary styles. Families in the cities live in small houses, which may include two bedrooms and a sitting room. A verandah appears on the houses of middle-class families. In rural areas on the sugar estates, workers now live in housing schemes, areas with separate structures for individual families.

Clothing and education. Guyana's contact with the outside world is evident in clothing and education. Clothing styles are often similar to those worn during summertime in North America. In education, Guyanans base their schools on the British system, though in the summer months students farm. Over 75 percent of school-age children were enrolled at primary and secondary schools in 1981; 90 percent of the adults could read and write. For higher education, the country has specialized schools (agriculture, home economics, practical crafts) or a broader offering in Georgetown at the University of Guyana.

Politics. The people remain politically divided, East Indians filling the ranks of the People's Progressive Party while black voters join the People's National Congress. Guyanans elect legislators, who, in turn, nominate the president.

In office for five years, the president may be re-elected without limitation. Thus, a type of democracy exists today. The 1980 constitution, though, declares the country in a process of change from a capitalist to a socialist society.

HAITIANS

(hay´ shuns)
An African and a European people, separated
from their neighbors by their French heritage.

Population: 5,360,000 (1986).
Location: Haiti, the western portion of an island
whose eastern two-thirds is the Dominican
Republic.
Language: French and more frequently Creole.

Haiti

Geographical Setting

The island nation of Haiti is mountainous.
Except for a small area in the west bordering the
Gulf of Gonaïves, the shoreline on all sides rises
quickly to altitudes of 2,000 to 8,000 feet. In the
west, a large bay nearly divides the country into
two parts. A narrow mountain range spans the
country in the south. Deep in the bay, at the point
where the country is most narrow, lies the city of
Port au Prince. Much of the population is centered
around this port. Since there are few highways to
link Haiti's villages and cities, communication is
difficult. The climate is tropical, mostly hot or
warm with an annual rainfall of more than 100
inches.

Historical Background

Before the arrival of the Spaniards in 1492,
the country that is now Haiti was inhabited by
Arawak Indians. These Indians disappeared as
slavery and disease brought from Spain took a
toll, but their name for the land survived. Though
Columbus called the large island *Hispaniola*, the
Indians had already named it *Haitï*, the
"mountainous land."

143

The Spaniards were joined by the English and the French, and the large island and small, neighboring islands became areas of dispute. By 1697, the British had been driven out, and Spain had ceded half the large island to France. One half became French Haiti, the other Spanish Santo Domingo.

French influence. The French colonized Haiti and began a large plantation agricultural system, importing African slaves to work the plantations. By the time of the French Revolution (1789), 30,000 French colonists controlled nearly 500,000 slaves. The white colonists refused to allow blacks or mulattos (brown-skinned descendants of black and white parentage) to participate in government. Blacks responded by staging a revolt led by Toussaint L'Ouverture, who was captured and imprisoned. His successor, General Jean-Jacques Dessalines, led an 1804 uprising that finally resulted in Haitian independence.

Independence. The balance of the 19th century was marked by hostility between the black population and the mulattos. Blacks overthrew the mulatto president Jean-Pierre Boyer in 1843. Further upset by debts to France, Haitians had little interest in irrigation or in developing their own resources. The upper class of the time consisted of a small group of families, mostly mulattos, who lived in the cities. Some blacks belonged to this group. The countryside had a few large landowners and a number of midsized farms. Mostly, though, the countryside was populated by peasants whose lives were a constant struggle to earn food and clothing for their families. The men eked out a living from their own tiny plots plus jobs on the larger farms. Meanwhile, the women sold goods at the small market towns. Government outside the cities was informally run by semi-independent military leaders and unofficial peasant soldiers.

Rebellion. Troubles in the nation as a whole mounted as the century passed. After a revolt in 1915, dozens of political prisoners were executed. Crowds of people retaliated by storming a government building and killing the president. United States Marines arrived to restore order, then remained in the country for 19 years, during which there were some advancements. Irrigation began, and the Marines trained a small Haitian army, but the people chafed at occupation by a white nation.

After the United States withdrew in 1934, a series of mulatto and then black dictators came to power. Most notorious were the dictatorships of the black leaders François Duvalier (1957–1971) and his son Jean-Claude Duvalier (1971–1986).

Papa Doc. François Duvalier established his own semisecret service, a militia of brutal volunteers the people called Tonton Macoutes, or "Uncle Strawbag" after bogeymen in folklore. Superstition and racial hatred became common, and many of the skilled writers and artists lived in exile. Becoming an expert in voodoo, François Duvalier favored African ways over French ones and was nicknamed Papa Doc. He had himself elected president for life, then chose his son as his successor.

Jean-Claude governed in his father's style. Drought, famine, and unfair elections led to strikes and riots under his rule. Rioters stormed food warehouses in country towns. Duvalier fled to France in 1986, and the Tontons Macoutes were finally dissolved. Independent Haiti originally had a red-and-blue flag. The first black nation of the Americas, it had purposely left white out of the flag. François Duvalier changed the blue to black as a symbol of Haiti's ties to Africa. In 1986, the old flag colored in red and blue was brought back.

Culture Today

Leaders such as the Duvaliers built a tradition of strict separation between the governmental elite and the poverty-stricken masses. Though many of the wealthy are mulattos, a recent development has been the growth of a black middle class. Its members include professionals, shopkeepers, officials, and some of the wealthier farmers. Finally, there are the black masses of the lower class.

Farm life. Conditions are severe in the rural areas. The average landholding is under three acres, too small to feed a family. Therefore, peasants seek jobs on larger estates in exchange for a share of the produce.

A hoe and a machete are the common farm tools, used mainly to grow subsistence crops. The peasants maximize their output by practicing vertical cultivation. They start below the ground with potatoes, manioc, and yams. At ground level, they grow watermelons, tomatoes, and other vine crops. Corn, sugar cane, avocados, and fibers for rope, hats, and baskets are raised at higher levels.

Women participate in the cultivation and harvest of crops and sometimes operate separate holdings from men. As in the past, the women are responsible for farm-to-market transport and for selling the crops. Some walk to town with baskets full of produce on their heads; others ride donkeys or *taps taps*, the decorated passenger and freight trucks of Haiti.

Shelter. The traditional home is a small, wood-framed, mud-doused structure. Built in the countryside, it is typically hidden from the road. The peasants sleep on mats rather than beds; homes often have no water, though some is usually available nearby. As for families, the peasants often ignore government laws, preferring

Farming in Haiti

customary behavior. This allows them to practice polygamy, marrying more than one partner.

Religion. Roughly 80 percent of the people are Catholic, but the popular religion among the masses is *voodoo* – a blend of Catholic and West African beliefs. The religion involves worship of a Supreme Being and spirits such as Agoué (spirit of the water). The follower often sacrifices food and drink to the *loas*, or spirits, and may be possessed by them. Headed by a priest or priestess, temples of the religions are independent of one another. Voodoo teaches that radical change is harmful, thus supporting the existing conditions.

Arts. Details of the voodoo religion are revealed by Haiti's writer Jean Price Mars, who published a study of the people's folklore (*Ainsi parla l'oncle*). The poet Jacques Roumain wrote verse that celebrates Haiti's African roots. Generally, artists drew on Creole customs to create a national identity. Since the 1940s, many Haitian paintings have captured scenes from daily life – "Fisherman" by Jacques-Enguerrand Gourgue, "Gossiping at a Crossroad" by Anotine Obin, "The Peasant Woman and the Bandits " by Minium Cayemitte. This last pictures the plight of a woman who rides to market by night.

Manufacturing has not been as active as art in Haiti. Though the country is the world's largest producer of finished baseballs, there is little other industry in Haiti. The wealthy are mostly connected with the government, which earns income from the people by levying a wide range of taxes. A few white Europeans and the mulatto minority remain largely in control of both city and national governments.

Port au Prince,
Haiti

Language. A broadening of the governing class is evident in Haiti's languages. At one time, French was the only official tongue, though most of the people spoke Creole. While Creole has finally been recognized as an official language, over 60 percent of the adults remain illiterate. Education is compulsory for children aged six to 12, but there are too few schools to accommodate them. Some blacks overcome the obstacles by traveling overseas for schooling, then return to fill government posts that were denied to them in the past.

Current Issues. The soil in Haiti is worn. Drought and hurricanes trouble the countryside, so production drops while the population increases. Meanwhile, bloodshed continues – smugglers against rice planters in the Artibonite Valley, peasants against landowners and Tontons Macoutes in the town of Jean-Rabel. Hungry and hopeless, many flock to the cities, settling in shantytowns. They search for jobs, but well over 50 percent cannot find enough work. Others, 50,000 Haitians a year, leave the country altogether. The poor, "the boat people," depart by water. The skilled leave behind the country's children, a third of whom die before the age of five. Today more Haitian doctors live in Canada than in Haiti itself.

HONDURANS
(hon door´ uns)
A mainly mestizo people with an economy
dependent upon banana and coffee production.

Population: 4,092,000 (1982).
Location: The rifts and valleys of Honduras, a
country in the middle of Central America, between
Nicaragua and Guatemala.
Language: Spanish, English (in the north),
Amerindian dialects.

Honduras

Geographical Setting

The country of Honduras is shaped like a
bush with its trunk toward the south. On the
north, the country borders the Caribbean Sea for
400 miles. On the south, Honduras has a 40 mile
Pacific coastline, part of the Bay of Fonseca,
which is shared by Nicaragua and El Salvador.
Honduras is the most mountainous country in
Central America, almost completely above 1,000
feet elevation. The land is mostly low mountains,
broken by valleys and deep rifts. A high mountain
range begins in the northwest and separates
Honduras from its Pacific neighbor El Salvador.
Rainfall is heavy in the north and moderate in the
south. The capital, Tegucigalpa, in the south
central portion, receives about 30 inches of
rainfall a year. Close to half of the country is
forested, mostly with pine. The soil in the country
is generally poor, which has kept much of it from
being farmed. Still, the central mountains are
productive coffee growing areas. Toward the
Caribbean Sea, the land is crossed by two rivers
that create a low, hot, damp region, where much

149

of Honduras's largest industry, banana growing, occurs.

Historical Background

Before the Spanish arrived, Honduras was peopled by a number of Indian groups and by migrants from Mexico. Mayan societies lived in the northern highlands, making the city Copán a center of astronomy and mathematics. Other groups were the Lenca and, much later, Indians whose ancestry was part African, the Black Caribs. This group, though, had not yet appeared when Hernando Cortés took command of this region as part of Guatemala.

Spanish influence. Spaniards and blacks first arrived in Honduras in 1524, coming to farm the land and to mine the few findings of gold and silver. The Spaniard Cortés moved into the area largely because other conquistadors farther south threatened to claim the land. In 1525, he established a community at *Puerto Natividad* (now Puerto Cortés, Honduras's largest port community). Afterwards, Cortés sent Cristóbal de Olid to establish another colony, *Triunfo de la Cruz*. As with many Spanish officers, once Olid was safely out of Cortés's reach, he claimed the land for himself. Cortés promptly replaced Olid with Francisco de las Casas. At the same time, Pedro Arias de Oliva, who had successfully won command of Panama, sent forces to explore Honduras. One general from Panama also had visions of independent ownership of Honduras, Gonzáles Dávila. He and las Casas joined forces to defeat Olid. Later, Pedro de Alvarado came from Guatemala to establish the town San Pedro Sula in the northeast of what is now Honduras. Thereafter, the land fell under the government of Guatemala.

In 1536, Alvarado ordered the division of Indian villages among himself and 38 conquerers.

The Indians were then bound into forced labor through *encomienda*, the system by which a Spaniard paid the Indians' taxes to the crown in exchange for their services. Thus, Indians were put to work on plantations or in the mines in south central Honduras. Yet they appear to have been less harshly treated in this country than Indians were elsewhere. Forced labor became popular in Honduras only in the late 1700s, and even then it seems to have been limited. The Spaniards here more often relied on themselves and on African laborers.

Honduras remained a part of the Spanish-governed Captaincy of Guatemala until 1821. In that year, Central America and Mexico declared independence from Spain. Honduras became part of Mexico for two years, then joined the United Provinces of Central America until it beame fully independent in 1838. Honduras has since been ruled by a succession of liberal (reformist) and conservative (military) governments.

Fierce competition in government gave way to dictators, some fairly-elected leaders, and a number of military coups. Individuals curried favor with outsiders to win power. As the century passed, United States companies were granted large tracts of land in return for their political support.

The soldier Tiburcio Carías Andino ruled as dictator from 1923 until 1948. With the aid of United States fruit companies, Carías built roads and railroads through Hounduras. Typical of government and military unions in Latin America, Carías gave up his dictatorship in 1948 to his minister of defense, General Gálvez. Returning in 1954, Carías ran for the presidency again but lost the popular vote to a liberal reformer. Trouble with the election allowed another military leader, Julio Lozano Díaz, to become President, and then dictator, but he was shortly overthrown. Finally,

Ramón Villeda Morales won fair elections in 1957.

Morales built schools, established a labor code, and initiated reforms to provide land to the small farmers, but he was overthrown in a 1963 military coup. More coups occurred as the decades passed with brief interruptions of elected leaders in 1971 and 1981. A new constitution was devised in 1982. Increasing the power of the military, this constitution named the head of the armed forces, not the President, as the country's Commander in Chief. A military man was now more powerful than the President, whose office became ceremonial.

Recent problems In recent years, Honduras has experienced difficulties with its neighbors El Salvador and Nicaragua. Small El Salvador is overpopulated. So since before the 1960s, its people have migrated to Honduras in search of land and work. This caused problems for Hondurans that erupted in the 1969 "football war," Honduras losing to El Salvador. In the 1980s, the United States persuaded Honduras to intervene in the struggle between groups in Nicaragua. Miskito Indians were allowed to relocate in Honduras (see MISKITOS). Also it has served as a base for the Nicaraguan rebels, the Contras. Their opponents, the Sandinistas, carried the fight into Honduras, so that in 1987 the Contras were asked to leave.

Culture Today

Progress has been slow in Honduras since its uneasy birth through disputes among Spanish conquerers. The vast majority of the people (over 90 percent) are mestizos, mixed descendants of Spanish and Indian marriages. However, whites have gained a controlling interest in the economy.

Before foreign interests changed the landscape, Hondurans were mostly subsistence farmers. Each family cultivated its own small plot, growing corn, beans, a few vegetables, and perhaps a small banana orchard. In the highlands, there were some large estates that mainly raised cattle.

Economy. Banana crops remained in the hands of the small farmers until 1913. Then outside companies took control, operating from large plantations along the Caribbean coast with new methods of production. In the 1920s, Honduras became the world's foremost banana producer. Thirty years later coffee appeared on the estates in the highlands, and it became the country's second largest export. With the growth of large banana and then coffee plantations, the peasants gradually lost their small farms.

Most Hondurans continue to work in agriculture, but today less than half the peasants own land. Many have become dependent upon jobs raising coffee or bananas. Employment, though, has not compensated for their loss. Over 200,000 of the peasants are now landless, while approximately 65 percent were underemployed, finding only temporary work in 1984.

Shelter. Hondurans live mainly in rural areas in the western half of the country. Their customary home is constructed of the materials at hand – split or sawed timber plastered with mud and frequently roofed with tile. Floors are often earthen, while furniture may consist of hammocks, a table, and chairs. Few rural homes have running water or electricity, though these are gradually being introduced into the countryside. More slowly than their Central American neighbors, Hondurans are moving to the cities to find employment. In the cities, they have been able to organize into trade unions and citizens groups, a cumbersome task in the distant, hard-to reach rural villages. Still, unemployment was 25 percent in 1984. Hondurans are among the poorest people of Central America.

Honduran house

Teguchigalpa, the capital city of Honduras.

Language. In some ways, Honduras has always been divided. Its major port city supports the banana industry and is in the far northeast of the country. Its capital city, Tegucigalpa is in the coffee and mining areas of the south. In the south and northwest, Hondurans speak Spanish, the official language of the country. In the northeast, U.S. and British shipping companies are the chief employers so English is more common. The southeast is part of the Miskito Coast, home to Indians who speak their own language as well as English.

Arts. The country's major writers are Spaniards. Noteworthy among them is Rafael Heliodoro Valle, who celebrated Honduras and Hondurans in his poetry, histories, and essays. In fine arts, carvings and pyramids of the ancient Maya Indians still appear in the city Copán. Building on their tradition for excellence, today's Carlos Garay has received worldwide attention for his landscape paintings. Music is popular among Hondurans, the favored instrument being the marimba. Its amplified wooden bars are hit by mallets to produce musical sounds.

Education. Education has improved greatly over the years. Enrollment in primary school climbed to 76 percent in 1980, but only 30 percent of those aged 13 to 17 attended secondary school. After completing the first stage of education every student must teach at least two adults to read and write.

Values. Hondurans share common values with other Central Americans. They tend to admire *machismo* (male strength), respect the individual, and distrust government and other forms of organization. The church here exerts less influence than in the past. Hondurans are mostly Roman Catholic in religion, the women taking major responsibility for church affairs.

JAMAICANS
(jah may´ kens)
A mixed population living on the island of
Jamaica, the majority of whom are black.

Population: 2,347,000 (1986).
Location: An island in the Caribbean Sea south
of Cuba and west of Haiti.
Language: English, Jamaican Creole (an English
dialect).

Jamaica

Geographical Setting

The island of Jamaica lies in a subtropical
region. Rainfall is 40 to 60 inches a year in most
areas, and the temperature is generally warm.
Jamaica's coastline rises gently on the south side
of the island, more abruptly on the north.
Although many acres have been cleared for
farming, much of the land is covered by
deciduous forests. The eastern portion of the
island is divided by an east-to-west mountain
range. Three ranges, two of which form a *V*-
shape, appear in the west. The valley between the
two arms of the *V* drains into a southeastern
coastal plain and into a bay. Located on this bay,
the cities of Kingston and Port Royal are the
largest areas of population.

Historical Background

Columbus. Before Christopher Columbus
landed on the island in 1494, Jamaica was
inhabited by about 100,000 Arawak Indians.
Some of the Indians were quickly drawn into the
encomienda (forced-labor) system on farms of
Spaniards left behind by Columbus. Other
Arawaks were forced to labor in gold mines or on

155

the docks where supplies were gathered for shipment to different colonies. Overworked and underfed, the Indians were unable to withstand their lot. Many died from the harsh conditions. Others committed suicide, hanging or poisoning themselves to escape enslavement. As this labor force dwindled, Spaniards replaced the Indians with west African slaves, importing men, women, and children to the island.

Pirates. Jamaica became the headquarters for pirate ships. Whoever controlled the island controlled much of the Southern Atlantic Ocean and the Caribbean Sea. Recognizing Jamaica's importance, the British drove off the Spaniards from 1655 to 1660, then left the island to the pirates until 1670. During this time, some of the Spaniards' black slaves fled to the hills. Known as *Maroons*, they hampered British rule until a peace treaty was executed with them in 1738.

Sugar. A large labor force was needed to establish and maintain the sugar plantations. The British therefore continued to import slaves until 1807. By then, 300,000 Africans had been brought into Jamaica.

Class structure. Social classes soon developed. In the upper class were planters, officials, professionals, and merchants. The middle class consisted of shopkeepers, skilled tradesmen, and overseers. The lower class included poor whites, free and enslaved blacks.

Black society had rankings too. Free blacks and mulattos (of black and white parentage) ranked the highest. In Jamaica, skilled slaves could work to buy their own freedom. Others were sometimes freed by a dying master or because their fathers were white. Since the freed slaves could acquire property, many owned estates and even acquired slaves for themselves. Still, they enjoyed fewer privileges than the whites.

Until slavery was abolished, the slaves also had their social classes. Higher status went to gang leaders, house servants, and mulattos. Lower status went to field hands. When slavery ended in 1834, plantation life declined. Some former slaves joined the Maroons in the hills. Others became paid workers on the plantations and in the port communities. Purchasing land in groups, they formed new settlements on the island. To compensate for the loss of slave labor, Jamaicans imported indentured servants from Africa and Asia.

British colony. Late in the 19th century, Jamaican entrepreneurs began exporting bananas and the economy grew. At the same time, Jamaicans became more involved in the rule of this British colony. An 1884 constitution provided for limited local participation in government affairs. In 1958, Jamaica joined other British colonies in a Federation of the West Indies. In 1959, Britain allowed complete self-government in Jamaica. Finally, in 1962, Jamaica seceded from the Federation, becoming an independent nation in the British Commonwealth.

Independence. As a sovereign people, Jamaicans have experienced natural and human violence. A 1980 hurricane badly damaged the banana plantations, depressing the nation for years to come. Many were out of work, yet prices rose. The people responded with violent demonstrations. Some raised hemp (marijuana), which brings in several hundred million dollars a year. With United States aid, officials moved to destroy the crop and the trade. Gang warfare also troubled the island.

Rastafarians. Meanwhile, Jamaican society progressed in peaceful ways, with Britain and Latin America strongly influencing its development. Before the 1930s Jamaicans identified with the British and preferred things European. Then, inspired by the United States minister Marcus

Garvey, Jamaicans began looking to Africa for their heritage. Some planned a mass return to that continent and were encouraged by Ethiopia's emperor Haile Selassie (originally named Ras Tafari). While the migration to Africa never materialized, Jamaicans have continued to take pride in their African heritage, and the Rastafarian movement has since grown in importance, becoming a force in Jamaican politics.

Culture Today

Government. The head of state in Jamaica is the British king or queen, represented in Jamaica by a governor-general. The official in control of daily government is the prime minister. There are two branches of parliament, a Senate whose members are appointed by the governor-general and a House of Representatives elected by the people. The prime minister is the most powerful representative in the House.

Ethnic distribution. Whites comprise a small minority of the population, but they have long enjoyed a voice in politics. Today they are mostly Creoles (Jamaican-born), the descendants of Europeans in the old upper class. Other minorities include the Chinese and East Indians. The largest minority is mixed (Afro-European or Afro-Asian). Blacks continue to form the majority.

Jamaicans pride themselves on the racial and religious equality of the island. There are Christians, Hindus, Muslims, Jews, and the Rastafarians. A growing faith, Rastafarianism is now a strong religious-political movement based on national pride and pride in African ancestry.

Today more than in the past, wealth influences a person's social standing. Whites and the richer mulattos in history gave issue to members of the upper classes today. Their material worth is evident in housing.

Food, shelter and clothing. Wealthy landowners might live in wood or concrete homes with tile or metal roofs while poorer, rural homes are one- or two-room wooden structures. Large concrete houses, and hotels have appeared in the capital, Kingston. In Kingston's ghettos, poor Jamaicans live in tiny houses built of wood and corrugated zinc.

Clothing is similar to summer wear in North America. Rastas, or Rastafarians, stand out from other Jamaicans due to their long hair and woolen hats. The Rastas also live in groups, often sharing food and shelter.

Food habits reflect the influence of the various ethnic groups. A national dish is ackee saltfish, a type of cod that is dried and seasoned. Cooked rice and peas are also common. Of high repute, Jamaican coffee is home-grown, and soft drinks have become popular on the island. Descendants of the Chinese frequently operate the village groceries.

Jamaica still depends to a large degree on agriculture. The island's small farmers raise food crops and animals on the less fertile land in the interior countryside. Many use the technique intercropping – cultivating different plants on one piece of land at the same time. Plants grow in layers. Bananas, coconuts, maize, pumpkins, melons, yams, and sweet potatoes may be raised all at once on the same small plot.

Sugar cane, bananas, and coffee are major crops of the island. The sugar industry has been the country's single largest employer and has included private farmers as well as sugar worker's cooperatives. Operated by former workers on the large estates, the cooperatives were populated by over 5,000 Jamaicans. Less sugar has been produced in recent years, but cocoa and rice growing have increased.

Industry. Aside from agriculture, Jamaicans produce bauxite (aluminum ore), manufacture consumer goods, and enjoy a large tourist trade. Jamaica is one of the world's largest producers of bauxite, an industry once controlled by United States and Canadian companies. Influenced by the Rastas, Jamaica's government has taken control of 51 percent of the industry.

Jamaica has a high rate of unemployment, nearly 27 percent in 1980. There has been an annual tradition of migrating to other lands for work: first to Panama to build the canal, then to Costa Rica to raise bananas, then to Cuba to grow sugar. Outside Latin America, Jamaicans have filled various positions, largely in the United States and Britain.

Education. Education began with the British system, which has been modified to meet the needs of the black majority. Primary schooling is both required and free in certain areas. Secondary education depends on competitive exams. Without enough schools or teachers, the nation has concentrated on building facilities and teaching all Jamaicans to read and write. Over 96 per cent of adults were literate by 1970.

Arts. Jamaica's artists have looked to their people's experience for subjects. The novelist Robert Mais has treated the lives of the underprivileged, while the playwrights Carey Robinson and Trevor Rhone have carried the economic and political struggles of the people to the Jamaican stage.

More generally, the country has rich folklore told in the Jamaican Creole language. Recalling flash floods that appear in Jamaica, "William Saves His Sweetheart" is a tale based on the belief that water spirits may drown anyone who lies. As explained in *Jamaican Creole* by R. B. Le Page and David De Camp (London: Macmillan, 1960), the tale begins

> "Now a old-time Anancying story we going at now." (P.143)

Adapted from African folklore, Anancy is Jamaica's traditional spider-hero. He is lazy, and greedy yet witty and likeable despite it all.

Jamaica has a long tradition in music, reaching back to the worksongs that originated in the days of slavery. Though talking was forbidden, slaves could sing to quicken the flow of work. Usually they were led by one slave, the singer man, who chanted a line solo, often making up comical words to humor the slaves as they worked. Others chimed in with the chorus. Today, folk groups still sing these worksongs. The lyrics below are translated into standard English. They are adapted from the Creole lyrics presented by Michael Burnett in *Jamaican Music* (London: Oxford University Press, 1982).

> Singer Man: Mister Tallyman, come tally my bananas.
> Chorus: The daylight's come and I want to go home.

Street musicians of Jamaica

Instrumentally, Jamaicans have long been noted for rhythmic music played with metal drums and horns. The Rastas have built on this base and on American soul music to develop *reggae*. Different from folk music because it uses electric guitars and amplifies the singer's voice, reggae has become the most popular form of Jamaican music. Bob Marley and Peter Tosh have been two of its most renown performers. Dealing with poverty and religion, reggae lyrics send messages in connection with the Rastafarian movement. They draw heavily from words in the biblical book Revelation.

JIVARO
(hee´ va ro)
An Amerindian people of the Andes Mountains.

The Jívaro people live in Ecuador and Peru.

Population: 8,000 (1987).
Location: Ecuador, Peru.
Languages: Jívaro and Quechua.

Geographical Setting

The Jívaro live east of the Andes mountains where the land slopes to the Amazon basin. Here the region is a warm and wet tropical forest. Plant and animal varieties appear in great numbers. The tropical forest grows on land that quickly leaches out or washes away when bared. The Jívaro conserve this land by hunting and fishing, and by using a form of agriculture that allows the tropical forest to replenish the soil after a year or two of farming.

Historical Background

The Jívaro Indians are a people who have remained in their gold-rich homeland despite repeated attempts to conquer them. Led by the emperors Tupa Inca Yupanqui and his son Huayna Capac, the Incas made unsuccessful attempts to vanquish the Jívaro in the 14th and 15th centuries. Various Spanish *conquistadores* (conquerors) invaded Jívaro territory in the 16th century with some success. Juan de Salinas established several Spanish colonies in the area in 1557, but the Jívaro managed to destroy all of these by 1599. Throughout the 17th and early 18th centuries, Spanish religious and military units tried to assimilate the Jívaro, but to no avail. In 1767, the Jívaro finally permitted the Jesuits to

162

enter the territory, then evicted them within the year. The Franciscans were the next religious group that attempted to change Jívaro ways, but they abandoned the cause in 1803. Subsequent attempts were viewed as disguises for stealing the gold that lay in Jívaro lands. Beginning in 1869, Jesuits returned to what appeared to be sincere religious missionary work, but were expelled once and for all in 1886 following another revolt by the Indians.

In the 20th century, Protestants rather than Catholics have tried to influence the Jívaro. These Protestants had worked with other groups who spoke the Quechua language. Now working with the Jívaro, the Protestants helped some of these Indians learn Quechua in addition to their native tongue. Otherwise the Jívaro have mostly remained aloof and warlike. They lead fiercely independent lives, refusing to forfeit their ways.

Culture Today

Food, clothing and shelter. Living in the tropical forest of the Andes Mountains, Jívaro men hunt monkeys and birds with blowguns and poisoned darts. They also fish, raise domestic animals such as chicken, and gather roots and berries. The people continue to rely on slash-and-burn methods of agriculture, raising manioc, maize, beans, and sweet potatoes. The planting of manioc may be accompanied by a ritual in which women make overtures to the earth goddess *Nungui*. Men pray to her husband *Shakaema* when planting banana trees. Aside from foods, the Jívaro grow cotton and tobacco. The men weave the cotton into cloth using hand looms.

Jívaro hunter

The cloth serves as a type of kilt, or wraparound skirt worn by the men. Shamans and chiefs are distinguished by the bands of feathers they wear. A band of small white animal bones slopes over the left shoulder of warriors, each bone representing a man they have killed. Women wear a robe pinned on one shoulder, while the other shoulder remains bare. Some people wear ponchos.

Family life. Often building on a steep hill near a stream for defense, a single Jívaro household forms a community. The communities, or houses, lie a considerable distance away from one another, for isolated but defendable sites. The group occupying a single dwelling (the *jivaría*) consists of relatives on the father's side of a family. Such a dwelling once housed 80 or more, but over the years the number has been reduced to perhaps 30 or 40.

Polygyny, marriage to more than one wife, is common. Marriage to several wives is partly due to a shortage of Jívaro men caused by the frequent warfare and feuds of the people. Disputes often arise over wife-stealing and are freqently settled through violence by the individuals in question.

Shelter. The jivaría is a spacious structure, perhaps 40 feet by 80 feet with a thatched, gabled roof and thick walls. During warfare, the Jívaro pile logs against the inside walls and have been known to build escape tunnels leading from their homes to the woods in the event of entrapment by attackers.Furniture consists mainly of platforms for sleeping and storage, and of footstools.

Traditions. The placement of Jívaro homes reflects the past. Warfare was a major concern in Jívaro society. The people remained hostile to outsiders after becoming warlike in response to *encomienda*, the forced labor system of the Spanish. More often, though, their military forays were targeted at other Jívaro communities for personal reasons – revenge for wife-stealing or for a relative's death. Vengeance extended beyond murder. The Jívaro shrank a victim's head to prove justice had been done.

A system developed for conducting raids on neighbors: A *kakaram* (leader of headhunters)

The woven roof of a Jívaro house.

By Borys Malkin. Courtesy Anthro Photo.

would build a war party of fellow Jívaro, send forth a scout to gather intelligence on the group that would be raided, then lead a surprise attack during the early morning hours. The goal of the raid was to return with a number of enemy heads. Afterwards they would be dried to the size of an orange. When dried, the head was called a *tsanta* and decorated for use in religious rituals.

Jívaro warriors took an hallucinogenic drug to acquire an *arutam* (deadly soul). It was thought to produce a terrifying vision that instills the desire to kill and prepares the warrior to hunt heads. In the event that warriors were defeated, it was said they had lost their arutam souls and had to acquire new ones. A warrior who had many of these souls became a *kakaram*, or leader of head hunters. Head hunting and head shrinking are now illegal practices in Brazil.

Religion. The Jívaro believe in a supreme deity, *Cumbanama*, who is remote and uninterested in their daily affairs. Central to their religion is a more familiar rain god who inhabits mountain peaks. This god, like other deities, contains a supernatural essence known as a *tsarutama*. It is further believed that tsarutama inhabit shrunken heads, stones, and certain plants and seeds. The shaman, or religious medium, is the individual who communicates with the spirits, curing or causing disease, making love potions, and bringing rain.

Change. Today the Jívaro are gradually beginning to respect the governments of the countries in which they live.

MEXICANS
(mek´ si kens)
Inhabitants of the country of Mexico, mainly
a mestizo (Spanish and Indian) people.

Mexico

Population: 74,000,000 (1982).
Location: Mexico.
Language: Spanish, various Indian languages.

Geographical Setting

Two features distinguish the land of Mexico. One feature is a large, tilted central plateau between the Sierra Occidental Mountains (which extend north to form the Sierra Nevada Range of the United States) and the Sierra Oriental Mountains (which are part of the Rocky Mountain system). Covering a large part of Mexico, this plateau slopes from the central part of the country where altitudes are above 7,000 feet to the United States border where the plateau widens and drops to about 3,000 feet above sea level. The mountains west of the plateau rise sharply from the ocean, while the mountains on the eastern side fall to a narrow lowland along the Caribbean Sea.

The second distinguishing feature is the scarcity of water. Except for the southern tropical jungle states, which are separated from the rest of Mexico by an east-west collection of volcanoes, rainfall is scarce and there are no large rivers. The lack of water affects crops and populations of people as well as restricting the amount of power available for development. The result is that the people of Mexico are mostly gathered into the central highlands. Here the cross ranges of volcanoes have small rivulets of water and mark a central basin where Mexico City is located.

Historical Background

Earliest settlers. The original inhabitants of Mexico are thought to have been hunters who migrated from Asia approximately 40,000 years ago. There are few traces of the lifestyle of these early inhabitants. Eventually, these northern migrants built great civilizations in the area that is now Mexico. Olmec, Teotihuacan, Mayan, Toltec, Zapotec, Mixtec, and Aztec societies were well developed in the time before European invasions.

Mayas. The Mayas flourished in the south of the central plateau region, their civilization reaching its height here between A.D. 300 and 600. Although these people were remarkable for their accomplishments in art and architecture, their most notable achievements were in astronomy and mathematics. The Mayas developed a calendar regarded as more accurate than the one used by Europeans and understood the use of a symbol for zero in mathematics. Why this great society disappeared from its northern section of land is a mystery. A second Mayan civilization emerged in the Yucatán in the 900s. Together the two Mayan societies maintained their civilization in Mexico for over a thousand years.

Totlecs. Meanwhile, other groups were migrating from the north and establishing new societies, the most notable centered in the cities of Texcoco and Tenochtitlán. Toltec and Mixtec societies grew in the plateau area and along the Caribbean coast. The Toltec Empire gave way to another great society, the Aztecs.

Aztecs. The island of Tenochtitlán, located in a shallow lake in the basin that now is Mexico's Federal District, was occupied by the Aztecs in 1325 and in less that two centuries grew into a city that is estimated to have held 250,000 inhabitants. Pyramids, temples, gardens, canals, and a zoo appeared on the island. In art and architecture, the Aztecs excelled in stone carving and feather mosaics. Their civilization has been described as a combination of sophistication and barbarism, as they sacrificed humans to the Aztec God of Sun and War, Huitzilopochtli.

A group related to the Aztecs established their own center of power at Texcoco, their civilization reaching its height from 1418 to 1472 under the rule of Nezahualcóyotl. Extensive gardens graced the city during his rule and thousands of manuscripts are thought to have filled the city library. Ultimately Texcoco lost its power to the Aztec center at Tenochtitlán.

Spanish rule. From about A.D. 1100 through the 1400s, the Aztec empire continued to grow and dominate surrounding peoples. Moctezuma II assumed the position of leadership in 1502. During his reign, the Spaniard Hernando Cortés managed to ally himself with discontented Indian groups, then to use them along with his superior military strategy and weaponry to defeat the Aztecs. By 1521 Aztec rule had given way to domination by the Spaniards.

Mexico was to remain under colonial rule until 1821. During those 300 years, the lifestyles of the people underwent radical change. Their lands were confiscated, then awarded to the church and a few powerful Spaniards. These Spanish landowners went on to establish what became the main social and economic institution of their time, the *hacienda*.

Hacienda lands were worked by the Indians who formerly owned them. Now, though, the Indians were reduced to *peones*, or serfs. Typically the landowner gave the peones subsistence plots in exchange for their labor. In time, the peones became even more indebted to him as they accumlated bills at the hacienda store, then had to remain on the estate to repay them.

Workdays on the hacienda were tedious, and the lifestyle tended to homogenize the different groups so that their old customs were lost. Meanwhile, they were exposed to the culture of the Spanish gentleman who ran the hacienda and promoted cattle raising and horsemanship as well as agriculture. A mixing of cultures followed. Unions between Spanish men and Indian women produced a new ethnic group, the mestizo. The hacienda's small black population resulted in mulatto children from Spanish and black unions and in Zambos, the offspring of Indians and blacks. Persons of mixed races became the fastest-growing segment of the Mexican population.

Origin and color indicated social status in the country, whites gaining control in economy, government, and religion. Social differences developed even among whites as those born in Spain were considered superior to the Creoles, or those born in Mexico. Along with the Catholic Church, a few Spanish families came to own most of the wealth in the country.

Independence. Ultimately the people rebelled and won independence from Spain in 1821. Their victory was greatly aided by the defection of royal officers and troops, men who switched sides to join the revolution.

Over the next hundred years, the Mexicans took up arms again to fight the Americans, the French, and each other in civil war. Meanwhile, government changed hands constantly, moving from a monarchy to a democratic republic to a dictatorship under the rule of Porfirio Díaz (1876-1880, 1884-1911). While the country prospered under his rule, new laws deprived peasants of land they had earlier gained. Other Mexicans labored long hours for meager wages in mines and factories. So one hundred years after the revolution against Spain, the people rebelled against Díaz. Beginning in 1910, this revolution

Mexico City

lasted ten years and cost a million lives. In the end, the people gained a new constitution, which spelled out the rights of peasants and workers.

Government today. Power remained concentrated in the hands of the President. In the 1930s, this worked to the advantage of the peasants as President Lázaro Cárdenas became responsible for the redistribution of over 49 million acres of land to peasant *ejidos* (communities). In this case, executive power had been used to provide more equality. Later in the century, another President, Gustavo Díaz Ordaz, would use this power less benevolently. Díaz Ordaz sent the police and army to the Plaza of the Three Cultures in 1968. There the uniformed officers opened fire on 10,000 students who had gathered in peaceful protest against police repression, illegal arrests, and violations of human rights. More than 300 protesters were killed, 2,000 were wounded, and another 2,000 were jailed. Mexico's democracy withstood the massacre and proceeded to make advances, particularly in women's rights. New laws in 1974 assured women equal job opportunities, salaries, and legal standing in the country.

At the same time, the working class as a whole has suffered from a decreasing output in agriculture and rising unemployment in the cities. The lifestyle of many is marked by inadequate housing, diet, and education. It is generally agreed that Mexico's standard of living has improved since 1910. Yet there was inequality then because one percent of the rural population owned so much land. Now, one percent of the urban population earns over half the national

A Mexican village street.

Culture Today

Geography continues to divide the Mexican population. Nearly a fourth of today's people live in the modern capital, Mexico City. The remainder live along the coasts, in tropical inland villages, or by the arid mountains and desert of the north.

Social classes. Society in Mexico is being reshaped by the dramatic growth of industry in the country. Industrialists and wealthy politicians are members of a new upper class. Engineers, technicians, and managers join the merchants and professionals of the middle class. City workers along with peasants in the country swell the ranks of the large lower class. Aside from economic differences, the more "Indian" people are in lifestyle, the lower their position in society.

Shelter. Outside the Federal District and a region along the Caribbean coast, the country is marked by Indian towns and villages. Each is generally built around a central square and a church (see ZAPOTECS). On the outskirts of Mexican cities, shantytowns provide housing for the lower classes. Residents live in shacks built of recycled materials – tin cans, cardboard, and scraps of wood. As some find jobs, the shacks are replaced by brick, concrete, or adobe structures. Other housing styles vary by region. The typical mestizo house is constructed of adobe walls that are plastered when affordable. A red-tile or corrugated roof covers the structure, and the house usually has a patio that is not visible from

Family life. The occupants of the household, the nuclear family, form the basic unit in society. All family members, even children in the many lower-class households, make important contributions to the livelihood of the unit. Parental authority is strong, and, in keeping with the value of *machismo* (male strength), men continue to be the dominant figures. The ritual of adopting godparents has continued for centuries. A set of godparents sponsors baptism and ceremonial events in a child's life. Frowned upon by the Church, divorce is rare in Mexican families. Desertion is not.

A street in San Cristobal de Las Casas in southern Mexico.

By Tressa Berman

Religion. Ninety-five percent of the people are Roman Catholics, but they have combined Christian practices with pre-Christian beliefs. Churches and monasteries mix European and Indian motifs, some including both Spanish and Aztec figures in their frescoes. The Virgin of Guadalupe is the most popular figure in the religion. She is depicted as a dark-skinned mixture of Indian and European elements and is regarded as the patron saint of Mexico. Her alleged appearance here in history affects all aspects of the people's folk belief and custom. Festivals are held in her honor. Statues are carved in her image, and she is the main character of Mexican ballads and folk tales. Another distinctive feature of religion among Mexicans is their regard for the dead. It is believed that life issues from death just as death issues from life in an unending cycle. All Souls' Day, a day for the dead to return home without being seen, is a festive occasion. Store vendors paint cemetery scenes on their windows, design skulls from sugar, and bake the "bread of the dead" in anticipation of the event. Before Lent, many communities establish a lighthearted spirit, celebrating Carnival with clowns, humor, and horseplay.

A Mexican woman and her child.

By Tressa Berman

Recreation. Fiestas are a common means of entertainment, some villages holding six or seven a year. Otherwise relaxation is found in the popular sports of soccer and baseball. A source of pride, bullfights remain a favorite pastime. Another traditional sport is *charrería*, an equestrian event in which men and women participate in rodeolike performances.

Arts. Everyday life and the Mexican worker are frequent models for Mexican art. The shoemaker, the carpenter, the restaurant chef, the musician, and the housewife are subjects for Mexico's foremost graphics artist José Guadalupe Posada. His illustrations and lithographs capture Mexican traditions, and have won him worldwide fame.

The mural is a popular forum for Mexican painters; Diego Rivera is among the most prominent of these artists. Sculpture by Francisco Zúñiga depicts the overworked, overweight Mexican woman with dignity.

The *mariachi* (street musician) and *jarabe tapatío* (hat dance) are so familiar that they have become stereotypes. Among the most popular singers is Refugio Sánchez, famous for music in the ranchera style. Theater is presented in circuslike tents that appear in small towns.

A theme in literature by novelists such as Carlos Fuentes has been the betrayal of the second revolution. Perhaps the foremost poet is José Gorostiza, whose "Endless Death" is considered the most important poem of 20th-century Mexican literature. A distinctive kind of popular art is the *fotonovela*, a cartoonlike magazine of romantic stories that combines movie photographs and comic-strip dialog. The most common theme is class differences, with good lower-class characters and their evil upper-class counterparts. Plots usually end unhappily for the lower class, which perhaps reflects their economic position in Mexican life.

Land reform. The haciendas were destroyed after the second revolution. Though land was redistributed to communities in the form of *ejidos*, new types of large holdings created a small group of prosperous farmers.

The ejido is the agricultural community that resulted from government land grants to the community as a whole. Ejido property cannot be rented or sold. The community shares grazing and forest lands but may assign individual plots to families for their own use. Parents pass on their right to the plot to their children, but it is usually smaller than 25 acres and fails to meet a family's needs. Therefore, many families rent or neglect their own holding and work elsewhere. Those who are completely landless take temporary jobs on Mexican farms. Underemployed, the landless laborer might be hired for as few as 75 days a year (the average in 1970).

Food. The primary crops are maize and beans, still the staples in the Mexican diet. Wheat, sugar cane, cotton, bananas, coffee, and cattle are items raised by the large landholders. Food production has dropped over the years. Meanwhile the population has grown, so that there are more people to feed. In the lower class, the diet is often deficient in protein, the main foods being corn and beans, along with some fruit, sugar, and meat. The corn is mostly eaten in the unleavened tortillas used as bread. The middle class diet includes wheat bread, a rice or pasta soup, meat, and corn and beans. Middle and upper class members of the city enjoy the most generous meals. Juice, eggs, and *café con leche* (coffee with milk) are breakfast foods. Eaten at two or three o'clock in the afternoon, the main meal consists of corn, beans, meat, salad, rice, and dessert. A similar but smaller meal is eaten in the evening.

As in Italy or France, Mexico offers a variety of regional dishes. Red snapper prepared with a sauce of tomatoes, onions, chili peppers, and olives is a speciality of Veracruz. Pork in a sauce of green tomatoes is featured in Michoacán. Sauces are popular, the best-known being *mole poblano*, made from chocolate. When served with turkey, it becomes a national dish. The traditional beverage is *pulque*, a drink fermented from the sap of the maguey cactus. Though popular, nowadays it is often replaced with beer or soft drinks.

Clothing. In much the same way, Western-style clothing is replacing traditional dress. The most popular traditional garments of working class women have been the wide skirt and the rebozo, or shawl. Male peasants have outfitted themselves in white cotton clothing, sandals, a poncho, and a large straw hat. The outfit of more prosperous farmers and horsemen once included trousers with

A street vendor in a Mexican town.

By Tressa Berman

elegant buttons, a tie, a vest, a short jacket, boots, and a wide felt hat.

Industry. The abandonment of these outfits has come along with the sharp rise in movement from rural areas to the cities. This has partly been a function of less farming and more industry, which pays workers five times the income they earn as farm laborers. Petrochemicals, steel, and automobiles are some of the fast-growing industrial products. However, industry has not been able to absorb all the workers moving from the country into the city. There is much unemployment and severe underemployment in urban areas. Thus, neither the ragged shoeshine boy nor the man selling tissues to motorists at intersections is a surprising sight. Meanwhile, pollution in Mexico City has risen to twice the level at which New York City closes factories.

Education. Since skilled workers are a privileged group in Mexico, education has allowed some to move up to the middle class. There are too few jobs or schools, though, so many students never complete their education. A 1973 law provides for two years of preschool plus six years of primary education. Students then have the option of three-year secondary school or a normal (technical training) or vocational school. The law further provides for informal, out-of-school programs to meet the needs of students for whom schooling has been unavailable. Nevertheless, many are undereducated. The average is 3.5 years of schooling, and only one of every 100 students continues to the university.

Government. There is a similar discrepancy between appearance and reality in government. On the surface, Mexico appears to be a democratic republic, and it indeed has executive, legislative, and judicial branches of government. Yet, in keeping with Mexico's history, the President holds most of the power, proposing legislation, directing the army and the police, and controlling

An Amatenangan woman potter of Mexico.

By Tressa Berman

A Zinacantan girl weaving on a back-strap loom.

By Tressa Berman

the Institution Revolutionary Party (PRI). This is the party that dominates in government, its candidate winning the election for President every six years. In rural areas, Mexicans have shown their dissatisfaction with government policies by forming a guerilla movement.

MISKITOS

(meh skee´ toes)

Also spelled MOSQUITOS. A racially mixed group
of Amerindians, white buccaneers, and blacks.

Population: 150,000 (1980).
Location: Nicaragua, a strip in the northeast
about 40 miles wide, bordering the Caribbean Sea
for 200 miles.
Language: Miskito (unrelated to most Indian
languages in the area) and Spanish.

Miskito land in
Honduras and Nicaragua

Geographical Setting

The territory of the Miskito is a hot, humid
area bordering the Caribbean Sea. Thick rainforests, malarial swamps, and infertile savannahs
cover the area. After passing through the inland
forests of Nicaragua and Honduras, two rivers
empty into the sea. Miskito communities appear
near the coast or on the banks of these rivers.
Much of the area is most easily traveled by water.
The soil is poor so that few crops can be grown
here.

Historical Background

When Spanish explorers moved from Panama
into what is now Nicaragua around 1522, they
found nearly 1.5 million Indians living in many
different groups. The groups had settled on the
central highlands and the fertile Pacific plains,
areas in which the Spanish chose to establish their
plantations. Enslaved under the *encomienda*
(forced labor) system and exposed to new
diseases from Europe, the Indian groups
dwindled. So harsh was their lot that by 1548,
only about 35,000 Indians remained. One group,

177

the Miskito Indians, had escaped to the uninviting forest and swamplands by the Caribbean Coast. Then they were mostly ignored by the Spanish.

The Spanish were forced to replace the dwindling labor force with African slaves. As time passed, some of these people eventually found themselves on the Caribbean Coast among the Miskito Indians.

Dozens of small Miskito villages appeared along the coast and the rivers of the region. Remaining isolated, the villagers hunted, gathered wild fruits, fished, and raised sweet manioc. Their homes, open-walled structures of bamboo and thatch, formed communities which relied on their elders and ablest warriors for leadership.

A Miskito village

Pirates. During the 1500s and into the 1600s, the isolated Caribbean coast became a haven for buccaneers. The Miskitos quickly learned to trade with the pirates, aiding French, British, and Dutch ships in extracting the area's natural resources: dyewoods, tortoise shell, sarsaparilla flavoring. In return, they received guns, rum, beads, and cloth from the Europeans. The British set up trading posts along the coast.

In the mid-1600s a shipwreck in the area freed African slaves to join the Miskitos and buccaneers. Other slaves, who escaped from the Spanish plantations, found the coast a safe hiding place. Finally, black migrants from the West Indies (mostly Jamaicans) operated the British trading posts, adding to the mixed population that was to develop.

British influence. The Miskito people made the British their ally, raiding Spanish settlements in the south and Indian settlements in the interior, then selling captives to the British as slaves. To make relations with the British easier, the people appointed a Miskito king. Miskito power grew, and these Indians inspired fear through the region from the 1600s to the early 1800s.

From 1786 to 1830, Miskito land was under British protection. By the 1830's Nicaragua, Honduras, and other Central American colonies had gained independence from Spain. Little affected by these events, the Miskito were largely ignored by the newly independent states. The British remained in the area, protecting the Miskitos until the Nicaraguan government set aside a reserve for the Indians under the Treaty of Managua in 1860. Assuring them it would not interfere in their government, Nicaragua's new body of leaders then left the Indians to shift for themselves. In 1864, the king of the Miskitos formally joined the country of Nicaragua.

During the first three decades of the 1900s, United States and British interests established banana plantations in the coastal region. A single enterprise, the Standard Fruit Company, controlled much of the banana industry, including company-owned commissaries, or general stores. Earning money as wage laborers on the plantations, the Miskitos spent their salaries on flour, sugar, clothing, and other commissary goods, beginning to regard the items as necessities. Then disease destroyed the banana trees. By 1940, large-scale banana growing had come to an abrupt halt.

Nicaraguan rule. Through the long dominance by the Somoza family in the central government of Nicaragua, the Miskito people were mostly ignored by the government. However, one agent of change during this period was the Moravian Church. Founded by Protestants in Germany, this Church came to play an important role in Miskito life. Its missionaries arrived in 1949, then introduced the Indians to improved housing, health care, and education. With the banana plantations and the goods provided by the commissary gone, the once-independent Miskitos now welcomed and sought assistance from the missionaries. The Church responded, attempting, for example, to settle questions of land ownership. Religion, though, remained its main concern.

Contras and Sandanistas. By 1980, a struggle had erupted in the Nicaraguan government between the Sandanistas and the Contra rebels. The Miskitos, who had little interest in the dispute, first remained neutral, then favored the Contras. By then, the Sandanistas were in control of the government and the Mosquito Coast had become vital to their cause. The nearest entryway into Nicaragua for their Cuban allies was a chief port on the coast – Puerto Cabezas. Over 1,000 Cuban advisors arrived, and Nicaraguan troops began moving into coastal villages. Several thousand Miskito Indians were forced to relocate. Fighting broke out in the region. Towns that had been abandoned were then destroyed. Some 10,000 Miskitos who fled to Honduras were swept into the war on the side of the Contras, but soon grew weary of the whole affair.

Representatives of these exiled Miskito people spoke with the Sandinistas. Assured that they could resume their old village life without interference, the refugees returned to their homeland in 1986 and 1987. Nicaragua's government furnished transportation and a three-month food supply to sustain them until their first crops could be harvested. However, a great flood in 1987 wiped out most of the corn and rice harvest, sinking the Miskitos more deeply into poverty than in any period since the loss of the banana industry.

Culture Today

Ethnic mixture. As a result of adapting and uniting with different groups, fewer than 4 percent of the people of the province Miskitia are now Miskito Indians. Nearly 80 percent are mestizos, either of Indian and European descent or of

Indian, European, and African descent. About 10 percent are Zambos (of Indian and African descent).

The ethnic mix is uneven along the coast so that Puerto Cabezos in the north is predominantly mestizo, and Bluefields in the south is predominantly black. Affected by unions with blacks and with white buccaneers, the large mestizo population here is generally short and dark, different in appearance from other mestizo groups in Latin America.

Government. For many years, the province in which the Miskito live was governed mainly by individual leaders in the Miskito community. Each village had its own headman, an elder skilled at settling grievances. Over the years, he became an official link between the village and the national government of Nicaragua in matters such as taxes and crime. Otherwise the local community was independent of national control.

Communication was difficult because no highways connected the Pacific and highlands regions with the Caribbean coast. Now, however, the area's strategic importance has prompted the Nicaraguan government to build makeshift roads for the transport of goods and advisors from Cuba, and to play a larger role in the area.

The government plan for Miskito self-rule entitles the people to control land in their area and elect their own local authorities. However, despite their promise to the Miskitos, the Nicaraguan government has modified Miskito self-rule by selecting the governor for the Miskito provinces. On a national level, the Miskitos are now subject to the laws of Nicaragua and the appointed officials to their villages, cities, and province.

Food, clothing and shelter. The Miskito have a history of adaptation. They adjusted to the buccaneers, to the British, to the blacks, to the missionaries. In fact, the Miskito have remained flexible throughout their history. They were seminomads who joined old methods of survival with new ones. When pine lumbering declined in the early 1900s, they went back to hunting, fishing, and agriculture. The banana plantations came and went, and again the Miskito fell back on early activities. Adapting to Nicaraguan rule, most of them have reverted to these early means of earning a livelihood, but now they rely more on agriculture than on hunting or fishing.

Rice and beans are the major food crops. Sugar cane, cacao, coffee, bananas, and pineapples are also raised, but in small amounts. Boiling fruit in coconut milk or water, the people prepare a customary hash. Crabs, snails, and river turtles are items captured in the area for meat. Serving as both food and drink, bananas and plantains (a bananalike fruit) are made into the standard beverage.

Outside influences have been evident in both housing and dress. Mostly, the people wear poor European styles, a habit acquired during the long contact with traders. Miskito villagers, persuaded by the buccaneers and the Moravian Church, also exchanged their early open-air sheds for permanent towns and bamboo- or wood-frame houses. Elevated perhaps four feet from the ground on wooden stilts, the new homes have peaked sloping roofs that were thatched with large leaves. A few are painted and roofed with zinc.

A single household sometimes includes two separate structures – one for sleeping and the other for cooking. To connect the elevated buildings, the family used a board ramp. Furniture in the sleeping structure consisted of hammocks, tables and stools, and sometimes a sewing machine. On the front porch, there might be a low wooden bench. The kitchen structure has a table and stool or bench.

Nearly a fourth of the population now occupies two large seaport communities – Puerto Cabezas in the north and Bluefields in the south.

More typical in Miskito society has been the small village community, including anywhere from two to 100 houses. Villagers would be related to one another on the mother's side of a family. Within a family, though, the father has been the undisputed head. Wives might walk a step or more behind their husbands when taking a Sunday stroll.

Courtship. Sunday has been a customary time for intervillage visits, an occasion for Miskito boys and girls to meet. Courtship would begin with the boy. If serious, he might announce his romantic intentions through letters or gifts or perhaps supply the girl with a liquid charm. The fragrant aroma was supposed to bring him to mind when she applied it to her skin. If her parents discouraged him, the suitor might resort to serenading the girl with guitar music and a Miskito love song. A Spanish song might even be used.

Education. Most Miskito parents have discouraged their children from learning the Spanish language. Though they hold education in high regard, they have preferred their children to read and write in Miskito or English. Schools were first managed by the Moravian Church with the pastor serving as teacher. Then Spanish schools appeared, but Miskito parents did not enforce attendance. Their agreement with Nicaragua's new government entitles Miskito children to a bilingual education. About a third of the people can read and write.

Religion. The Miskitos are a deeply religious people. Before the Moravian Church, they held many evil spirits responsible for misfortune. A shaman, or religious leader, communicated with these spirits to control them. After the entrance of the Moravians, the shaman served mainly as a healer, diagnosing an ailment by dreaming of its cause, then singing and blowing on the affected area. The hymns were Christian, the shaman supporting his people's acceptance of a new faith.

Most Miskitos now belong to the Moravian or the Catholic Church.

Change. Residents of the Miskito Coast today live in an area where food is sufficient but other desired items are few. The Miskito people are adapting once again, this time to life as English- and Miskito-speaking residents in a region suddenly important to a Spanish-speaking government. For income, they raise surplus rice and take jobs on the few remaining plantations, in the mines, or as laborers at the ports. Some learn Spanish and communicate with the central government while others rebuild their war-torn villages in rural Miskitia. In keeping with tradition, the people adapt.

NICARAGUANS

(nik a raw´ gwans)
An Indian-Spanish people of the largest yet
least populated Central American nation.

Population: 3,270,000 (1985).
Location: Mostly in the Pacific coast and central
highlands regions of the country Nicaragua.
Language: Spanish, along with some English
and Indian languages.

Nicaragua

Geographical Setting

Nicaragua is a rough trapezoid of territory, its
longest border dividing Nicaragua and Honduras
in the north and its next longest side resting by the
Caribbean Sea. The shorter sides lie along the
Pacific Ocean and along Nicaragua's southern
border with Costa Rica. Flat, wet jungle known
as the Miskito Coast appears by the Caribbean.
Inland from the coast, the land becomes jungle
followed by savannah sprinkled with pine trees. It
then rises to a plateau 2,000 to 5,000 feet above
sea level in the center of Nicaragua. A wedge-
shaped mountain range disrupts the plateau in the
north. The northern portion of the Pacific Coast
rises to a series of volcanic cones, which continue
toward the south, creating volcanic islands in Lake
Nicaragua and Lake Managua. These two lakes
and the southern San Juan River form an almost
unbroken waterway across the country.

Favored with fertile soil and moderate
temperatures, the region around the volcanoes is
well-suited to crops such as coffee and cotton.
The majority of people inhabit this coastal region
or the area of the central highlands. In general, the

climate here is tropical with a rainy season lasting from May to October.

Historical Background

Outsiders have exercised great control in Nicaragua since 1522, when the land was first settled by Spanish explorers under Gil Gonzales. From the coming of Gonzales until 1822, the Pacific Coast and Central Highlands remained under the direction of Spain. The less populated eastern seaboard, or Miskito Coast, fell under British protection from 1768 to sometime around 1890.

Spanish rule. When the Spanish first arrived, they found over a half million Indians on the fertile Pacific coast and central highlands. The Indians lived in separate groups and spoke 14 different languages. Setting up plantations to raise cocoa and cattle for profit, the Spanish attempted to enslave the Indians as laborers on the estates. Some resisted, taking refuge in jungles along the Caribbean Coast, where they established relations with buccaneers and later with the British (see MISKITOS). Others perished due to harsh conditions and exposure to European diseases new to the area. By the early 1800s, probably no more than 30,000 Indians remained. A number of these continued to raid Spanish settlements. One leader, Direongin, became a national hero because he continually fought to rid the country of Spanish rule. This type of rebellion would be a theme in the future. Meanwhile, African slaves replaced the Indian work force.

Independence. Nicaragua separated from Spain in 1821, first joining the organization of Central American states, then becoming an independent nation in 1838. Outsiders began interfering in national affairs shortly thereafter. The California gold rush in 1848 prompted interest in a canal site from the Atlantic to the Pacific Ocean through

Panama or Nicaragua. The United States grew concerned over Britain's interest in building the canal in Nicaragua.

Walker. Meanwhile, American adventurer William Walker brought in a small private army from Tennessee. Walker defeated Nicaragua's existing leadership and declared himself president in 1856. He remained president for a year. Then international attention prompted the United States to rethink its noninterference position and send its Marines to expel him. The Marines ruled the country for a brief period, after which Walker returned, this time meeting resistance and capture. He was expelled and later executed in Honduras for another attempt to invade Central America.

U.S. influence. Still interested in control of a canal that would join the two oceans, the United States continued to influence national affairs. Nicaraguan patience with outsiders wore thin, though. By the 1900s, the people were restless for self-government. Three men led insurrections against U.S. activity in Nicaragua: José Santos Zelaya, Benjamín Zeledón, and Augusto César Sandino.

The Liberal leader Zelaya toppled the Conservative government, then became dictator from 1893 to 1909. During his rule, Zelaya increased education in Nicaragua, encouraged the growth of industry, and tried to separate church and state. Zelaya, who like most Liberals favored the building of roadways, discussed the construction of a canal with the British.

Concerned for its interests in the canal, the United States backed Conservatives who overthrew Zelaya, then installed a puppet government under Adolfo Diaz. Benjamín Zeledón threatened Diaz's rule so the U. S. Marines returned and this time remained for over 20 years. In 1916, the Bryan-Chamorro Treaty granted the United States the right to build a canal and manage Nicaragua's bank and railways. Resentment against outside control grew. General Augusto César Sandino rebelled in 1927. "Free homeland or death" was his catch phrase as he rallied *campesinos* (peasants) to his side.

Forty-three years of dictatorship followed under the Somoza family. In 1930 Anastasio García Somoza became chief of the National Guard. Removing everyone who was not his personal supporter, Somoza ordered the assassination of General Sandino in 1934. He then overthrew the elected president, and in 1937, with the support of the United States, won the presidency for himself. Nicaragua's constitution forbids a president from running for immediate re-election. However, through a series of puppet leaders, Somoza managed to control government until his death in 1957. His son Luis Somoza Debayle succeeded him and was himself followed by his brother Anastasio. Together the Somozas ruled Nicaragua from 1936 to 1979. Their dictatorship became increasingly harsh. While Luis attempted some reforms, his brother Anastasio was a ruthless military despot.

The country as a whole grew wealthy under the Somozas. Its gross national product (the combined value of all its products and services) increased. Education and housing improved. Yet only a fraction of the people benefited while most remained impoverished. The Somozas were among the privileged few. Personally worth over 400 million dollars, Anastasio Somoza belonged to a family that owned 10 percent of the farmland and interests in more than 150 businesses. Meanwhile, Nicaraguan peasants complained of corruption in government and mistreatment of anyone who quarreled with Somoza's plans. A peasant petitioned to have a school built for children in the community. Informed that land was needed, he donated some of his own, but the school was never built and his land was sold for someone else's profit. Such stories were typical of the Somoza years.

After an earthquake in 1972, corruption increased. A movement spread to rid the government of the Samoza family. Led by the Sandinistas (named for the early revolutionary leader Sandino), Nicaraguans overthrew Anastasio Somoza in 1979. He left the country and was assassinated in Paraguay in 1980.

Revolution. The Sandinista revolution received wide support in Latin America, Costa Ricans allowing their country to serve as a launching base for Sandinista guerillas. From 40,000 to 50,000 people died in the revolutionary war. Cubans landed in the country to assist the revolution, because the Sandinistas were a communist group.

Many believed Sandinista communism would be different from that in other lands because leaders promised representation to various groups. A nine-person Sandinista board took control of Nicaragua's government in 1979. Afterwards, though, the government moved toward Cuban-style communism and became less accepting of different beliefs. Meanwhile, it engaged in continuous battle with the Contras, a counter-revolutionary force supported by the United States.

Violence between the Sandinistas and the Contras spread from soldiers to the general population: There were reports of Sandinistas shooting civilians accused of being informers and of Contras shooting civilians such as coffee pickers because their work helped support the new government.

Despite the ongoing conflict, the Sandinista government has introduced changes in Nicaraguan society. A first step was to confiscate and redistribute all Somoza land. Much of it was organized into government-owned cooperatives and state farms equipped with modern farm tools to work the land. However, the effects of such changes remain clouded because struggles with the Contras continue, and because the Somozas left the Nicaraguan government in great debt.

Culture Today

Nicaraguans are primarily mestizos–the mixed descendants of Spanish and Indian ancestors. Today, there is also a mixture of private and government ownership in the economy. Eighty percent of the land is still controlled by private owners. Once great tracts of land were controlled by a few wealthy landowners. Now the government manages them through its state farms and cooperatives.

Classes. Society is divided into upper and lower classes, depending largely on whether or not an individual works with his/her hands. The mestizos still cling to a Spanish heritage of conquerers who took pride in not having to perform manual labor. Yet more than half the work force is occupied in agriculture, mostly with hand tools and oxen-drawn plows.

Farming. The standard of living in farm areas seems to have improved under the Sandinistas, while city workers appear to earn less than before. The average income in 1981 was 800 dollars per person, but many earned under 200 dollars a year. Farm hands are among the poorest, employed mainly in the harvest season (November-January) and at planting time (May).

City life. Based in the city, Nicaraguan industry consists mostly of processing and packing agricultural products for sale. Coffee and cotton are the major moneymaking crops. For home use, Nicaraguans mainly grow corn, beans, and rice, peasant workers receiving small plots from the large plantation that hire them and city workers farming bits of land near towns.

Food, clothing, and shelter. Nicaraguans consume foods that range from traditional to newer dishes. Corn tortillas filled with beans and rice are one of the most popular foods. A common breakfast dish is refried beans with rice, or *gallo pinto*. Coffee is a standard beverage, combined with half a cup of milk or cream. Fast-food hamburgers have become available in the city.

Nicaraguans acquired a taste for wheat bread in the Somoza years but have since fallen back on corn. Having no money to purchase wheat from other countries, the Sandinistas organized a massive campaign, the Festival of Corn. They promoted the Festival by recalling an Indian legend about Xilómen, the goddess of corn who once sacrificed herself to save her people from hunger. According to the Sandinistas, Xilómen was returning to rescue the people once again. Contestants submitted recipes in the festival, and the country began consuming more of the traditional staples – corn, beans, and rice.

Close to half the population now lives in urban areas. Concrete shelters appear in the large cities as do poorer communities of shacks. Elsewhere, the housing styles vary from small palm- or metal-roofed structures to adobe houses with tile roofs.

Whether they live in city or country, the people wear clothing that is similar to styles in North America. Typical for women is a simple cotton dress while many men wear work shirts, tennis shoes, and straw hats. A similarity to North America is also evident in recreation. The average community, even among Miskito Indians, contains a baseball lot.

Values. As in other areas of Latin America, Nicaraguans share traditional values of *machismo* (male dominance and strength), respect for individuals, and distrust of organizations. Sandinista policy may affect these values. Believing art performs an important function in politics, the government has organized culture centers in Nicaraguan communities.

Arts. Theater is strong in the culture centers, some plays dealing with injustices suffered under the Somozas: A hungry farm hand visits a cow shed to drink some milk, and is fired by the patron, or employer, who spots him. The worker requests the salary owed him but is told he just drank it up Afterwards, the audience discusses the underlying message.

Nicaraguans have a rich history in literature and language. They speak a racy brand of Spanish and use words borrowed from their Indian ancestors. Much of their writing deals with social issues. Novelists such as Hernán Robleto wrote of the Somoza dictatorship while Salvador Mendieta's essays gave Latin Americans a sense of responsibility for their own circumstances. Nicaraguan poetry became famous through the internationally-acclaimed Rubén Darío, who developed a style called Modernism in the early 1900s. More lately, Jesús Marchena wrote on behalf of the poor, and women such as Daisy Zamora have contributed to Nicaraguan poetry.

Women. The important position of women in Nicaragua is evident in names and in religion. It is a custom to add the mother's name to the father's for a child. That is how Anastasio Garcia Somoza came to have sons with the last name of Somoza Debayle. Most Nicaraguans belong to the Catholic Church, and the burden of close practice falls to the women. The Virgin Mary is prominent in this form of Catholicism. During *La Purísima*, which begins December 1 and continues for eight days, candles are lit and prayers are said to Mary at altars in homes as well as in the church at the center of most villages. Church leaders have been divided in their feelings about Sandinista government. Their words are carefully watched, as the government monitors criticism. Stories on radio and in newspapers are censored.

Government. Nicaraguans now vote for their head of state, as in the Somoza years. There were complaints then that citizens could vote only if they could write, which eliminated over half the population. The remainder might vote on slips of paper, but some argued that election procedures allowed votes to be changed.

In 1980, aided by Cuban teachers, the Sandinistas undertook a campaign to teach reading and writing, and the number of illiterate adults dropped from 52 to 12 percent. Now most Nicaraguans are able to vote. Yet some complain of injustices in election procedures, such as withholding food stamps for failure to register. Still upset by outsiders in Nicaragua, other people protest a new foreign presence – Cuba.

Areas of the population are now more united than they were under the Somozas. There is a new concern for healing the separation between Spanish-speakers on the Pacific side and English-speakers along the Caribbean Coast. Mending this division and improving living conditions across the country are major challenges in Nicaragua today.

PANAMANIANS

(pan´ a may´ nee uns)

Citizens of Panama, who speak Spanish and claim Roman Catholicism as their religion.

Population 2,134,000 (1984).
Location: Panama in Central America.
Language: Spanish, English.

Panama

Geographical Setting

Panama is located in the narrowest stretch of land separating the Atlantic and Pacific oceans. Shaped like an *S* turned on its side, the country runs from the western border of Costa Rica eastward and then south to join Colombia. A range of volcanic mountains rises to 10,000 feet in the west. The terrain slopes downward to a low central neck of land, then rises again toward the Andes Mountains at Panama's border with Columbia.

At its narrowest point, the land is naturally divided by a large bay off the Caribbean Sea, the bay forming part of the Panama Canal. Southwest of the canal, the country widens into a peninsula protruding into the Pacific Ocean. The peninsula and territory west of it and south of the central range provide fertile farmland. However, migration to jobs in the canal communities Panama City and Colón, or in industry near them has concentrated the population in the center of the country. The land is tropical – warm and humid. Much of it is covered with tropical forest, some trees having square-shaped trunks.

Historical Background

Indians before the Spanish. Before its discovery by the Spanish, Panama was inhabited by a large number of Amerindians. The groups lived in organized chiefdoms, depending on the area's fish, birds, and sea turtles and on starchy root crops for food. Numbering nearly one million when the Spanish arrived in 1501, the largest group was the Cuna (see CUNA). The country's name, which means "land of plenty of fish," may also come from the Cuna words *panna mai*, or "far away," a reply to Spaniards who wondered where to find gold.

Spanish rule. Panama soon became a pathway for explorers in search of gold and silver. With the help of Indians, Vasco Nuñez de Balboa led a party across the central neck of land, becoming the first Spaniard to find the Pacific Ocean in 1509. His discovery opened up a shorter route to Peru and the gold of the Incas. Fortune seekers from Europe could land at Colón, cross the narrow isthmus, and set sail on the Pacific for Peru. Shortly after his discovery, Balboa was condemned for treason and put to death with the help of a former aide. The aide, Juan Pizarro, then used the route to conquer the Incas.

By 1519 Spanish settlements had been established, and the king's appointed governor, Pedro Arias de Avila, had settled in the village of Panama. Under his rule, Balboa's Indian allies were killed and other Indians were enslaved. Many fled to the jungle or to the swampland and isolated islands on the northeast coast.

A priest, Bartolomé de la Casas, was outraged by the Indian enslavement and persuaded Spain's government to send African slaves in their stead. By this time, many Indians had died from disease and mistreatment, while those who escaped had become isolated in the forests and swamps. The separation of Indian groups from Panamanians remains today. African slaves became so important that the British were given a contract to deliver 4800 slaves a year for 30 years. Slave revolts moved the Spanish king to interrupt the delivery for a time.

Panama became an important travelway and supply post for the Spanish *conquistadores* (conquerors). From the beginning, the narrowness of the land inspired the idea of a canal. The Spanish, however, were disinclined to build one, wanting to keep rival fortune seekers away from the Pacific Ocean. So for 300 years the only route was a muddy jungle road from the Atlantic Ocean to the Pacific.

Outsiders often attacked. British forces captured a fortress on the Atlantic, Portobello, several times, and buccaneers troubled the area in the 1600s. The Scottish attempted to begin a colony and open the land to trade in 1698, but failed due to disease and the resistant Spanish. Spain held on to the land and controlled its markets until 1740, then allowed Panamanians to trade with other countries. Panama, though, seldom had the freedom of self-rule.

From 1718 to 1722 the Spanish government in Peru held authority over Panama. Spain's Viceroy of Granada – who ruled Panama, Colombia and Venezuela – assumed control in 1739. When this government was abandoned in 1819, the Viceroy moved to Panama and ruled there for two years. In 1821, Panama became part of Colombia.

The Canal. The California gold rush in the 1840s renewed interest in travel between the oceans. In 1845, the United States helped build the first transcontinental railroad that crossed Panama. Meanwhile, France, Britain and the United States explored the possibility of a canal to join the two oceans by way of either Panama or Nicaragua. In 1879 Ferdinand de Lesseps of

France began construction of a canal in Panama under a license from Colombia. However, disease (yellow fever, malaria), rain, and mud made him abandon the project. From 16,000 to 22,000 workers had died.

U.S.   intervention. In the early 1900s Colombians fought a civil war, the War of a Thousand Days. Colombian rebels operated from bases in Nicaragua, passing through Panama on their way to fight. The United States now had a growing interest in building a canal across Central America. So, in 1902, it intervened in the war and established a truce. A year later, the United States bought France's rights to the unfinished Panama Canal. It then tried to get the controlling power in the area, Colombia, to agree to a treaty that allowed continued building. Upset when Colombia stalled on the treaty, Panama declared independence, and the United States supported the move.

Needing United States support to remain independent, Panama agreed to the canal treaty. A Frenchman, Philip Bunau-Varilla, had earlier been head engineer on the canal. Now he concluded the Hay-Bunau-Varilla Treaty for Panama. Without consulting its new government about the final terms, he gave the United States the right forever to the canal zone in exchange for 10,000,000 dollars in gold and 250,000 dollars annually. He added the word *forever* to rush the agreement so that he could be the one to sign the treaty. It was signed and the Panama Canal was completed in 1914, the United States receiving control of a fertile, ten-mile strip on each side of the Canal. From then on, Panama's economy largely depended on the Canal and thus on the United States.

The presence of the Canal changed lifestyles in the country. A people that had primarily earned their living as subsistence farmers now gained most of their income from the Canal.

Panamanians even used the United States dollar for money, though they called it the *balboa*. United States employees settled in the canal zone, joining Panamanians in the work. Resentment grew due to differences in treatment. United States workers earned wages in gold while Panamanian workers earned less valuable silver.

Panamanians began demanding control of the fertile Canal Zone. There were riots in 1964. The United States increased its payments over the years and recognized the injustice of the original treaty. It concluded a new agreement that finally took effect in 1979. Two treaties gave Panama control of the Canal Zone and arranged for its takeover of the actual canal in 1999, the United States reserving the right to defend it. Still, the United States provided funds that it could use to pressure Panama, and this strained relations between the two countries.

Government. When first established, Panama's government and constitution were patterned after those in the United States. However, its presidencies in this century have been short-lived. Since World War II, there have been frequent changes in leadership, mostly with the support of the National Guard (Panama's army). Panamanians still elect a president, but their government is largely in the control of the military.

Culture Today

Who Is Panamanian? Spanish influences, American influences, and Indian influences affect life in Panama today. The most dominant group can be identified by language. and religion. Panamanians are those people of Panama who speak Spanish and who claim Roman Catholicism as their faith – regardless of skin color or wealth.

Most Panamanians are of mixed parentage, from marriages among Spanish, Indians, and blacks. Antillian blacks, migrants from Caribbean island states who speak English and are Protestants, form 8 percent of the population. However, neither they nor the isolated, self-governing Indian groups have been fully absorbed into Panamanian culture.

Before the Canal, Panamanians were agriculturists, farming small plots of land for maize and other subsistence crops. The rural people lived in homes with thatched roofs scattered over the countryside or gathered together in small villages, often around a central church. The building of the Canal demanded workers. People left their small farms to meet the demand and later to find jobs in the two cities on the Canal: Panama City and Colón. More than 60 percent of the peasants had no legal claim to the small plots they farmed, so the cities offered hope to small subsistence farmers. The migration was further encouraged by activity in industry. The government built and operated sugar mills, refineries, cement factories and power stations. Even those who continued to farm depended on the government mills and marketing units.

Shelter, food and clothing. As over half the population moved to the cities, slums grew up around their centers. Thatched-roof houses gave way to more permanent cement structures topped with tin roofs. Apartments, condominiums, and hotels were built, some of glass and concrete. Tall banks and department stores were constructed to service the city dwellers.

In rural areas, Panamanians continued to live in the wooden *rancho* or the small thatched house. The rancho has a lower and an upper level. Resting on four poles, the unwalled lower level serves as a kitchen. A ladder leads to the walled upper level, which has a floor for sleeping and is thatched with palm leaves. In the small *pueblo* (town), a variety of other materials are used – cement, zinc, clay.

The building of a small-thatched house is a traditional neighborhood event. After gathering mud and cane, the neighbors throw water on the material, then step on it to prepare it for building. The future occupants of the new house prepare *sancocho*, a type of chicken soup with potatoes and yuca to serve at the event. Men drink the national rum, *seco*, prepared from sugar cane.

The small farmers raise livestock that provide them with milk and butter for their meals. Rice, corn, and beans, and the bananalike plantain are typical foods in the daily diet. On Sundays, a farmer might slaughter chicken for food. Larger in Panama than in other areas, tortillas are perhaps a half-inch thick and fried with salt. A favored dish is *carimañola*, yuca root fried and wrapped in cylinder shape around seasoned ground meat. Seafood (bass, shrimp, lobster) is quite common, and coffee is a standard beverage.

Outside influences have encouraged Panamanians to abandon traditional fashion. Today's clothing styles are much like summertime fashion in North America. Some Panamanians continue to wear their own brand of hat, the *pita*. Made of straw, it is narrow-brimmed with black-and-white stripes. Tree trunks may be cut as molds to size the hats.

Classes. A few old Spanish families formed an upper class in Panama, dominating government and commerce. As in other Latin American countries, the upper class considered manual labor beneath them. A sizeable middle class, mostly mestizo, began to develop as merchants, teachers, and officials appeared in the cities. Mostly mestizo or black, lower class members were manual laborers in the city and peasants in the country. Education has allowed some of the lower class to move up to the middle class.

Education. Law requires all children aged six through 15 to attend school, but this rule is not rigidly enforced. Particularly in rural areas, enrollment drops greatly in the secondary years, as teenagers seek jobs to add to their family's income. About half the secondary-age population was enrolled in 1982.

Values. In city and country, Panamanians share certain values. One is *personalismo*, a belief in interpersonal trust and in individual honor. With this belief comes a distrust of organizations and a high sensitivity to praise or insult. The most valued unit is the extended family. Another universal is *machismo*, the belief in male dominance and an image of the man as strong and daring. Women are expected to be gentle, forgiving, and dedicated to their children.

Religion. Women are the ones who attend church with the children. In Panamanian Catholicism, much emphasis is given to the mother of Jesus, Mary, who serves as an example for the women. Choosing godparents (*compadrazgo*) extends childrearing from parents to another set of adults – relatives, close friends, or wealthy individuals. Godparents affect a child's religious training and may influence worldly success.

Arts. Personalismo and machisimo have influenced art and recreation. Panamanian folk songs tell of love and conquest, of the strength and aggressiveness of the men. The various styles include the *mejorana*, in which singers compete as they improvise witty, rhyming verses. An instrumental style of music is *El Suspiro de Una Fea*, the title referring to an ugly woman who is beautiful inside. Individually, Gonzalo Brenes is an acclaimed composer who set *La Cucarachita Mandinga* to music. The comical tale stars a cockroach who buys a hair bow, then is courted by various animal suitors. Among the particular dances is the gallant two-person *punto*. In recreation, baseball is perhaps the most popular sport, while boxing in Panama has produced several world champions.

PARAGUAYANS

(par´ a gwai´ ans)

A largely mestizo people of the flat plains north of the Paraná River, one of the most uniform populations in South America.

Paraguay

Population: 3,280,000 (1984).
Location: Paraguay, a landlocked country in central South America.
Language: Spanish, Guaraní.

Geographical Setting

Surrounded by Brazil, Argentina, and Bolivia, Paraguay is the only country on the continent completely shut off from the oceans. Also, its terrain is more uniformly flat than in any other country of South America. Covered by savannah forests, most of its undulating land is under 1,000 feet above sea level. The Río Paraguay divides the country into two distinct regions. East of the river are fertile, red-earth pastures, a scattering of cone-shaped hills, and woodlands.

Known as the Chaco, the western side is dry, uninviting prairie with rough grass and scrub trees. An average rainfall of less than 30 inches a year contributes to a pleasant, subtropical climate in the country. Heavy rains flood the Chaco, though, threatening the cattle raised there. Moving downward, the Río Paraguay joins the Paraná River to form the southern boundary of the country. The people of Paraguay live mainly in the more fertile east.

Historical Background

Spanish. Reaching this area of the continent in 1537, the Spaniards constructed a fort at the future capital, Asunción, to prevent the possible entry of the Portuguese. At the time, the land was occupied by many Indian communities all speaking versions of the same Guaraní language. These Indians sustained themselves by hunting, gathering, and farming. Seeking gold and silver, the Spanish settlers forced the Indians to work the mines, inflicting great hardship on them, and causing many to lose their lives through disease, starvation and persecution.

Relief for the Indians came in 1588 from Jesuit priests. Jesuit intervention prevented the Spanish from enslaving the Indians for a time. Instead, the settlers imported close to 75,000 Africans slaves. Meanwhile, the Jesuits built rich mission communities with the Indians. Feeling threatened, the Spanish crown expelled the Jesuits in 1767. Thereafter, the mission Indians reverted to earlier ways or were swept into the *encomienda* (forced labor) system of Spanish estate owners. But the Guaraní were proud and intelligent people, respected by the Spanish. The customs of both peoples and the people themselves became mixed, producing a more unified nation than most others in Latin American states.

Argentine rule and independence. In 1811 Argentina replaced Spain as the ruling force in Paraguay, and the Paraguayans rebelled. By 1814, they had established their own government under the dictatorship of Dr. José Gaspar Rodríguez de Francia. Francia ruled until his death in 1840, isolating Paraguay and exercising tight control over the country. He is described as a harsh dictator who subjected his opponents to prison, banishment, and execution. Yet it is also said that he was an educated man who prevented Paraguay from falling into chaos.

Society in Francia's time was divided. On the one hand, there was the select group of country rulers. On the other, there were the mostly peaceful, peasant masses. The vast majority were poor, working mostly to feed themselves. Even the wealthier, though, fell under government control. Francia's government assigned production quotas in grain and cotton to the large estates. The country itself managed a number of government-owned estates, using their crops to supply the army or as reserves for the poor.

Francia and his successor, Carlos Antonio López, built a strong army, seeking to make the country a major power. Less strict than Francia, López established newspapers and allowed foreign artisans and doctors to enter the country. He also sought to settle Paraguayan boundary disputes with Brazil and Bolivia. López passed on leadership of the country to his son Francisco Solano López.

Wanting other nations to recognize Paraguay as their equal, Francisco López sent an army across Argentina to attack Brazil while that country was involved in a civil war in Uruguay. Brazil, Uruguay, and Argentina then united in a war against Paraguay that became known as the War of the Triple Alliance During five years of battle (1865–1870), virtually every able-bodied Paraguayan joined the struggle. The three powers had made a pact to topple López, a goal they reached when the Brazilians trapped and killed him in the heart of his own country. Some estimates indicate that the disastrous war cost one million Paraguayan lives, reducing the population to 250,000 of which fewer than 30,000 were young men.

Years passed and Paraguay's population recovered. Then, in 1932, came the Chaco War. Bolivia and Paraguay both sought possession of the dry prairie region. Though outnumbered, the Paraguayans were better trained and had a commander (Colonel Estigarribia) who moved slyly behind enemy lines to cut off his opponent's supplies and communication. In time, Paraguay conquered much of the territory but at the expense of many lives so that both sides agreed to a truce in 1935. When the boundary was finally fixed in 1938, Paraguay won most of the disputed territory.

Government had begun in monarchy style, the dictator Carlos López turning over power to his son Francisco. Afterwards, it fell into chaos, changing presidents over 30 times between 1870 and the settlement of the Chaco War. General Alfredo Stroessner, commander in chief of the armed forces, ran for office unopposed in 1954, ushering in a long, stable dictatorship.

Today Paraguay is led by military leaders who strictly control dissent to secure the position of the dictator in power. The chief executive is voted into office through direct elections for a period of five years. Still president, Alfredo Stroessner, was re-elected for six terms. In 1984 he reached a 30-year period in office, the longest in Paraguayan history. Stroessner maintained absolute power through the years, his government arresting, killing, or exiling his political opponents and peasant or labor leaders who aimed to represent the average Paraguayan. However, in 1989, Stroessner, himself, was overthrown by the power of the military and went into exile. Today a military government rules Paraguay.

Culture Today

Two features of their history have shaped the Paraguayans of today. The early history of Spanish and Guaraní integration has made for a united culture. This policy has served to break down barriers for other immigrants from Europe and China so that these later groups have more readily become part of the Paraguayan society. Today, only two colonies of Mennonites seem apart from the Paraguayan unity.

A history of disastrous wars has also greatly affected the lifestyles of the Paraguayans. Although a majority of the people have become Catholics and their religion teaches family unity, the shortage of men has resulted in many single-parent families. More than half of all Paraguayans are born out of wedlock.

The old landholding families were mostly eliminated in the wars. About 95 percent of the remaining population is mestizo (of mixed white and Indian ancestry). About 60 percent live in rural areas of the country, earning their livelihood as peasants and cowhands.

Food, clothing and shelter. The peasants survive on subsistence agriculture and handicrafts, using modern crop rotation methods to raise maize, manioc, tobacco, cotton, and green tea. The cowhands work on large cattle ranches, raising one of Paraguay's most important products – beef. Beef and manioc are common foods in the Paraguayan diet. The beef is often cooked with vegetables into the stew *puchero,* while the manioc is transformed into flour, then prepared as a bread.

A farmhouse in Paraguay

The homes of rural Paraguayans are generally made of adobe or mud plastered over plank walls. Floors are earthen, and roofs are mostly thatched and steeply sloped. The houses may or may not have glass windows, depending on the wealth of the family. The women of the family generally wear plain dresses or skirts with blouses. A *rebozo* (shawl) is worn over either costume. Typical clothing for rural men includes baggy trousers, a jacket or shirt, a neck scarf, and a poncho. Both men and women often go barefoot.

Paraguayans in urban areas of the country wear styles that are similar to those in North

America. They earn their livelihood in small retail businesses, as government employees or professionals, and in the factories of Paraguay. The country's primary industries are cotton ginning, timber, leather processing, and the processing of vegetable oils. Like other urban Paraguayans, the factory workers often live in lightly-colored brick or stucco houses. The houses are covered by red tile roofs, and windows are topped by iron grillwork. Less fortunate city dwellers live in metal or wooden shacks.

Education. The best schools of Paraguay are found in its urban centers. Attendance is compulsory for six years, but many drop out of the primary schools and only a small percentage (about 20 percent in 1979) continue to complete their secondary education. The country has an insufficient number of schools to meet the needs of its entire population. Still, more than 80 percent of people over 15 can read and write. The country is largely bilingual, speaking Spanish and Guaraní.

Arts. In addition to their language, those who mainly speak Guaraní have contributed to the artistic life of the country. Their designs are imprinted in Paraguayan pottery. Guaraní designs also appear in sophisticated lacework that is crafted into patterns of flowers, animals, and other common items in Paraguayan life. Finally, the Guaraní influence is evident in the slow, mournful sound of popular Paraguayan music.

PEMON

(pay mon´)

Indians who live in the forests and savanna of southeastern Venezuela.

Population: 6,000 (1980).
Location: Venezuela.
Language: Carib.

Geographical Setting

The Pemon people live in eastern Venezuela.

The southeast part of Venezuela in which the Pemon people live is a mostly flat, tropical plain. Also called a llano, it is covered with forest and liana (woody vine). The Orinoco River separates this plain from a more elevated plain, the Guiana Highlands. More than 1,000 streams cut across the plain as they empty into the Orinoco, gathering water from mountains that cover much of Venezuela, beginning with the northwestern extension of the Andes.

Historical Background

When the Spanish began settling in what is now Venezuela in the early 1500s, they found Indian peoples who had acquired guns from Dutch explorers and used the weapons in periodic outbreaks of violence. Some of these were intended to discourage European invaders. Little is known about the lifestyle of the people until the coming of the missionaries in the 1700s. The Pemon burning of a Spanish settlement in 1774 led to the capture and conversion of these Indians who were absorbed into about 20 Capuchin missions. For the next 40 years, this order of Catholics strongly influenced the Pemon, but the order abandoned the missions at the outbreak of civil war against Spain in 1817. Having grown

208

accustomed to their missionary lifestyle, the Pemon began making lengthy trips outside their territory to visit missions and to trade in foreign markets. These new markets brought the Pemon into contact with British religions and Caribbean religions in the Guianas. Some of the new religious beliefs and practices were incorporated with more traditional Pemon belief so that in the last four decades of the 1800s, an extraordinary new religion called *Hallelujah* was adopted by the Pemon and other Carib-speaking groups.

By the beginning of the 20th century, the Venezuelan government had agreed to reestablish Capuchin missions in the Pemon region. A renewed effort was made by these Catholics to convert the Indians, and the movement succeeded in drawing them into mainstream Venezuelan culture. The missions ran boarding schools to educate Pemon children, often prohibiting them from speaking their native language and requiring that they work in the fields. Meanwhile, the Venezuelan government sponsored a scientific expedition into Pemon territory in 1939 and the building of a commercial center in 1948.

In the second half of the 20th century, Venezuela has pursued its efforts to assimilate the Pemon into the national mainstream. Cattle ranchers and diamond miners from Brazil have entered the region and exposed the Indians to their lifestyles as well. Yet despite outside influences, the Pemon continue to live according to their own mixture of tradition and the missionary influences of the past.

Culture Today

Family life. Pemon families have become well known for their egalitarian structure. Typically a household consists of parents and their children, such nuclear families being the basic social units. Extended families live together on a temporary basis, a young husband moving in with his wife's family before establishing a nearby household. Men eat before women when guests are present. Otherwise, age is more important than gender, the elders having greater authority. Normally all members of the family eat together, and sharing is expected behavior in the household. Although children defer first to the father, no one in the family gives orders. The children fulfill responsiblities without specific direction. A mother's general comment that the family has no water is enough to prompt her daughter to fetch some.

Food, clothing and shelter. Adhering to the matrilocal nature of Pemon society, a newly married couple settles near the wife's family. Family members help construct the home in which the couple will live, building a circular structure with a cone-shaped roof, or more commonly an oblong or a rectangular structure with a pitched roof. The roofs are generally thatched with palm leaves, while the walls are constructed of plant poles, mud, and latticework. The average Pemon house is a single room of about 400 square feet. Larger communal structures are built for dancing and visitors. Both private and communal buildings are mainly constructed by the men.

Men are also responsible for clearing and burning the fields for planting. The Pemon practice slash-and-burn agriculture in which their main crop is manioc, prepared as food and *coachiri*, a red beer beverage. They also grow a variety of fruits and vegetables – plantains, bananas, squash, watermelon, corn – along with black beans, tobacco, and cotton.

Fishing is a secondary economic activity. Fish are caught on hooks or poisoned, using a plant called *barbasco*, which produces a poison that actually stuns the fish and brings them to the surface where they are then caught in a net.

Using Brazilian shotguns, the Pemon also hunt deer, agouti, tapir, and birds for meat.

The missionaries introduced machetes and steel axes, and these have become standard tools used, for example, in gathering, an activity that adds wild fruits and insects to the diet. The missionaries altered traditional work patterns for some of the Indians by hiring them as laborers in mission fields. Wages were scant yet necessary for the purchase of items such as tools that became essential for Pemon living.

Religion. Although the missionaries succeeded in converting many Pemon, they continue to combine traditional and Christian beliefs in their Hallelujah religion. Prophets of the religion claim to have visions in which their souls fly to heaven and make redemptive contact with the Christian god. On the basis of these visions, the prophets lead the Pemon in chants, dances, prayer, and purification ceremonies.

According to the traditional religion, the mountaintops of the region are inhabited by *mawari* (spirits) who sometimes steal souls. When they steal an individual's *tyekaton* (heart soul), the person sickens. Afterwards a shaman (religious leader who communicates with the spirits for the people) must recover the tyekaton, or the victim dies. To prevent the victim's death, shamans make a thick, intoxicating soup from various plants. They inhale the vapors from the soup, then fall into a trance during which they ascend a ladder to encounter the mawari and recover the stolen souls. When a person dies, the soul is thought to depart from the body to the mountaintops where it becomes one of the mawari.

Arts. The Pemon have a rich folklore, their tales providing the people with entertainment and guidance. Among the tales is a story about the first Pemon wife and about the chores she performs for the good of the marriage. Another relationship story, known as the Maichak tale, centers on a son-in-law's experiences with his father-in-law, a king vulture.

Pemon are a democratic and highly individualistic society. Order is based on the exchange of favors – a complex arrangement among individuals in the group. The threat of disturbing this arrangement helps keep peace in the community. Understanding how to relate to one another is key to the smooth operation of the Pemon.

Government. Shamans participate in the politics of the people, becoming intimately connected with the *teburu,* or settlement leader. The teburu's power depends on his prestige and the community's consent. Within the community, he acts mainly as a mediator in disputes between families. Otherwise, the teburu represents the community in dealings with outsiders.

PERUVIANS

(pe roo´ vee ans)
The people of Peru, a divided society whose
citizens are mainly of mixed or Indian heritage.

Population: 18,710,000 (1983).
Location: The country Peru, about 55 percent by
the coast, 35 percent in the highlands, and 10
percent in the east.
Language: Spanish, Quechua, Aymara.

Peru

Geographical Setting

Peru lies along the Pacific coast of South
America, its people living in three distinct regions:
the coast, the highlands of the Andes Mountains,
and the east. The country's 1,400-mile coastline is
broken by more than 50 streams that in rainy
seasons flow across a 10- to 100-mile-wide desert
plain. Beyond this plain, the land rises abruptly to
mountain chains of the Andes. In the south, the
Andes breaks into two distinct ridges which,
along with an east-to-west range, form a high
valley. The valley contains Lake Titicaca, at
12,500 feet the highest lake in the world. Sixty
percent of Peru is east of the mountains, where the
land drops to a dense rain forest and tropical
jungle, the montaña. Tributaries of the Amazon
River flow across this region. Some of these are
large enough for ocean ships to sail inland from
the Atlantic for 2,300 miles over the Amazon
River and its tributaries to the Peruvian cities
Iquitos and Pucallpa. So dense is the jungle that
over a half million Indians live there with little
connection to the other peoples of Peru. Large
numbers of Indians also populate the highlands,

while whites and mestizos mainly live by the coast.

Historical Background

Forest Indians. Before the 1200s, Peru was settled by small bands of Amerindians. Forest groups lived much as the Jívaro, Campa, and Amahuaca do today. Many different tribes of Quechua-speaking peoples lived in the high valleys of the Andes and along the coastal slopes. Under the leadership of the *Sapa Inca* (son of the sun god), one group began to conquer and unite those around them. Within 300 years, the Incas built an empire that spread through the Andes from Ecuador to Argentina.

The Inca. At its peak, the Inca Empire controlled nearly 12 million South American Indians. The emperor ruled from Cuzco, a city in Peru's highlands that is said to have taken 20 years and 50,000 Indians to build. Ruling through religion and tightly-ordered government, the empire built more great cities and temples to the sun god and lesser gods. The Incas developed a sophisticated network of roads, forts, and colonies but allowed little freedom. Chiefs of peoples in the empire reported to Cuzco periodically, and their sons were obligated to marry into the emperor's family.

An Inca ceremonial temple in Peru.

Spanish rule. However, when the Spaniard Francisco Pizarro arrived from Panama in 1532, he found the Inca government in turmoil. The last great emperor had died without establishing the traditional, hereditary succession. Instead, he had divided the empire between two sons. These sons, Huascar and Atahualpa, began to fight between themselves. Using this division, Pizarro succeeded in persuading one brother to kill the other, then conquered the remaining ruler and the land of the Incas.

The Spaniards founded the city Lima in 1535, making it a center of government for a vast region in 1544. The city's viceroy governed not only Peru but also Chile, Paraguay, Uruguay and Bolivia – some 2,300,00 square miles of Spain's holdings on the continent. Peru became a center of Spanish colonial life, just as it had been the focus of the Inca empire. Only now the center of government was transferred from the highlands to the coast. Lima was the new capital.

Lima was laid out like a chessboard, blocks of houses forming a *barrio* (quarter), and barrios forming a *cuarta* (district). City problems of the day included traffic jams, beggars, and thieves. Coaches and package-laden mules created the traffic, while bands of thieves were regarded as the townspeople's chief enemy. They were hunted day and night, their heads being cut off without trial following an arrest.

A colonial lifestyle developed, varying in its particulars with the region. The city of Lima was rebuilt after a devastating earthquake in 1746. Constructing new houses, the white population of Lima arranged them in rows. Wood or iron grills barred low windows that projected from the house. The homes were topped with terraces, using matting in place of roofs. Balconies and pillars flanked the main entranceway.

Meat was common in the colonial diet. The national dish *puchero,* mixed beef, pork (including pig's feet), smoked mutton, and sausage, was eaten with vegetables and fruits. Tamales of the day were made of ground corn seasoned with hot pepper, then mixed with chicken or pork, eggs, grapes, and almonds. Paraguayan tea was one of the most popular beverages.

At home, fashionable women wore the *faldellím,* a short flared skirt with lace topped by a gold or linen bodice with wide, hanging sleeves. A shawl or mantilla and plenty of jewels completed the outfit. In public, Lima women covered this dress with a long overskirt and a small sleeveless hood that fell to the waist and concealed the face. Fashionable men wore silk head scarves and neck scarves, large felt sombreros, plush blue capes, black velvet jackets, and breeches. More common were military uniforms or French styles of the time.

Spanish and Creole (whites born in Peru) boys attended college while girls stayed home to sew and cook. To prevent the learning of sinful habits, girls were forbidden to read or converse with a man other than a cousin. In the colonial days (the 1600s and 1700s) parents quickly married their daughters off, fathers choosing the husband. If the girl rebelled, she had her hair shorn and was locked in a dark room. Some still disobeyed. Jean Descola describes one such case in his social history *Daily Life in Colonial Peru* (London: George Allen and Unwin, 1968). When Marianita Belzunce, aged 13, balked at marriage to the Count of Casa Dávalos, aged 60, Peruvians rushed to her defense, discouraging the count in verse. Below are lines from a verse of the time.

> I give you some good advice:
> turn hermit,
> for dainty dishes are bad
> for the stomachs of old men.

> (P.117)

Much to the count's chagrin, such verses spread through Lima. Marianita finally took refuge in a convent, rejoining society after the count passed away.

Classes. Society divided into classes according to birth and color, pure-blood Spaniards occupying the upper class. Creoles (whites born in Peru) and descendants of mixed couples occupied the middle class while Indians and blacks formed the lower class. Black slaves ranked lowest.

Occupations in Lima were divided among the groups. There was a white upper class of government, business, and church leaders. The Creoles became merchants, growing wealthy as grocers and clothiers. Skilled labor was left to mulatto shoemakers, tailors, hair cutters, or carpenters. Indians and blacks became servants, mine workers, or peasants.

Gold. Gold had drawn the Spanish to Peru, but agriculture soon grew equally important. Haciendas appeared in the country, one estate including perhaps 25,000 acres. Among the crops were wheat, barley, sugar cane, grapes, cotton, and coffee, and the country had rich pasture for livestock.

Encomienda. The landowners had first used the *encomienda* system of forced labor to employ the Indians, but many Indians died because of overwork, harsh treatment, and exposure to new diseases. Ultimately the system was abandoned for one in which Indians could be forcibly hired to labor for wages. Whereas, under encomienda, they had continued to live in their own villages, the new system forced the Indians to move to hacienda shacks. Indian villages managed to survive, but lost water, land, and labor to the hacienda owners. Struggles against them cost more Indian lives. Of some 5,000,000 Indians in Peru when the Spanish arrived, the population was estimated to have dropped to lower than 1,000,000 by the time of an Indian rebellion in 1780. The Indian folk hero Tupac Amaru led the rebels in their futile fight.

Independence. In 1826, Peru gained independence as a result of the struggles led by Simón Bolívar. There followed a period in which Peruvians were divided regionally. Numerous battles were fought for national control, but no president commanded general obedience. Perhaps the strongest of presidents was Ramón Castilla, who held power from 1845 for 17 years. Referred to as the "Liberator," Castilla freed the slaves in 1854.

Peru under Castilla grew rich from trade in guano (bird dung used as high-grade fertilizer) sold largely to England. Castilla used the money guano earned to build a railway, expand the military, and reduce taxes for the poor. To abolish slavery, he paid owners 300 pesos for each freed slave. A new source of labor was needed. Between 1850 and 1874, nearly 90,000 Chinese replaced the freed slaves.

Meanwhile, Spain continued attempts to regain control of Peru until an armistice was arranged in 1871. Peru was then dragged into the War of the Pacific on the side of Bolivia in a dispute against Chile. Beginning in 1879, Peru suffered a series of military defeats. Chilean forces occupied Lima for two years before Peru signed a peace treaty in 1883.

War of the Pacific. Civil strife troubled the country as well. Mobs in Lima attacked the Chinese quarter, and Indians saw the War of the Pacific as a struggle against all whites, whether they were Chilean invaders or local landowners.

After the war, society changed. Power moved from large landowners to wealthy business leaders and the rule of the middle class. From independence, Peru had been led by presidents who were either elected or came to power by way of coups d'état. Military coups in 1962, 1968, and 1975 followed by free elections continued the tradition. Under a new constitution adopted in 1980, the elected president serves a five-year term. All citizens over 18 may vote, even those who are unable to read and write.

Culture Today

Ethnic composition. Because much of the land was difficult to penetrate and their communities resisted the Spanish, the Indian peoples of Peru survived and grew. At the same time, the Spanish absorbed some Indians into their culture. The result is that the majority of Peruvians are Indian or mestizo (of mixed Spanish and Indian heritage). Close to half the people speak Indian languages, many still living by simple agricultural means. The mestizos are almost as numerous, while whites form the largest minority. Peru, then, is one of the most "Indian" nations of South America.

Food, clothing and shelter. Gold and silver have dwindled so that now rural Peruvians live mainly by agriculture. On the Pacific coast, they grow rice, cotton, sugar cane and barley for sale. Maize and rice are the food crops, along with grapes, olives, and oranges. The coastal dwellers also catch pilchard and white fish. In the highlands, the staple crops are maize, potatoes, barley, and wheat.

The Inca system of land use continues in many areas. Under this system, communities hold land in common. Each family is allocated a plot for farming and may use it as they please, except that the land cannot be sold. When a worker abandons a plot either intentionally or through death, the land is redistributed by the community leaders.

Harvesting barley

By John Curtis. Courtesy Anthro Photo.

A system of *enganche* (draft labor) developed on large estates. The landowner lured Indians and mestizos to his labor force by supplying them with advance payments which they then worked to repay. This led to the rise of a new working class of peasants on sugar and cotton plantations. For the poor peasant, there was less and less land for subsistence farming. Without acreage or steady employment, many moved to the city for work, crowding into company towns, slums, or squatter communities. The majority of Peruvians became urban dwellers.

Lima now has both a Chinatown and a Jewish quarter as well as new city dwellers' barrios.

Pounding manioc, a staple food in the Andes.

By Borys Malkin. Courtesy Anthro Photo.

Houses in the city vary from the old colonial structures, to more modern homes, to high-rise apartments and squatters' shacks. The squatters build their shacks, using scraps of metal and wood, on city outskirts, then may replace them with adobe or concrete houses when affordable. Millions of Peruvians live in poorly-constructed homes. Recognizing the need for low-cost houses, the Peruvian government began to build large housing developments near the major cities in the 1960s.

Small farmers in the highland region often build modest adobe structures whose roofs are tiled or thatched. People of the jungle and rain forest use different materials. Houses are again thatched, but walls may be constructed with branches or poles. For specific descriptions, see JIVARO or CAMPA.

Llamas and alpacas are important sources of wool for clothing. Styles have become similar to those in North America, but bright colors are still popular for shirts, blouses, skirts, and shawls, and many people continue to wear hats.

Arts. Peruvians preserve the art and traditions of their past. Large collections of Quechua and Aymara artifacts and arts are exhibited in the National Library at Lima. Other Indian collections are located in the National Museum of Archeology and Anthropology, and at the University of Trujillo.

Ricardo Palma is credited as the first noteworthy writer. Published from 1870 to 1915, his short fictional accounts of colonial life attack injustice with humor. *Vals criollo* became the main music for the working class in the 1920s and 1930s. Composed by musicians such as Carlo Saco and Alicia Maguiña, its lyrics reveal the feelings of the working class. A television favorite in the 1970s was *Simplemente María*, a show about a peasant girl who moves to the city and climbs up the social ladder. It also became a *fotonovela*, a dramatic story presented as balloon-captioned photographs. Peru's fotonovelas concern money, love, and family disunity. The story lines are often violent.

Religion and education. Change in religion and education has been measured. About 90 percent of the people of Peru claim to be Roman Catholic. Indian groups adopted the religion early but have blended it with traditional practices, still celebrating, for example, important stages in the agricultural cycles. More Peruvians can read and write than in the past (76 percent in 1980), but the number of schools is still limited.

Today, Peruvians remain among the poorest of South American peoples. Struggles continue over land reforms and organization of mine workers, and there is insufficient work for the growing population. While almost a tenth of the people were unemployed in 1983, it is estimated that half of the workers only found part-time employment.

Carrying water home

By Jane Teas. Courtesy Anthro Photo.

PUERTO RICANS

(pwer´ toe ree´ kans)

The people of mixed black and Spanish descent who inhabit Puerto Rico.

Puerto Rico

Population: 3,300,000 (1989).
Location: The island of Puerto Rico, the easternmost of the islands that separate the Atlantic Ocean and the Caribbean Sea.
Language: Spanish, English.

Geographical Setting

A rectangular-shaped island, Puerto Rico measures about 100 miles long (east-to-west) and 35 miles wide. A range of mountains rising to 4,400 feet divides the land east to west. Around this range, the terrain falls to a coastal plain that is up to 15 miles wide. About 50 rivers flow from the mountains. Semitropical but cooled by ocean breeezes, the climate works with the rich water supply to create excellent conditions for the 45 percent of the land that can be farmed. San Juan, the capital city, rests on the northern Atlantic shore and is the site chosen by many of the island's industries and over a third of its population.

Historical Background

Spanish settlement. Before Columbus's discovery of this island in 1493, it was occupied by peaceful Taino Indians, who farmed and fished the land. News of the discovery resulted in the establishment of a Spanish settlement by Juan Ponce de León in 1509. The settlement, now the city San Juan, rested by a bay that he called *Puerto Rico*. Ultimately this name stood for the entire island, though the Indian name for it was

Borinquén. Appointed the first Spanish governor, Ponce de León began using the island to Spain's advantage.

Disappointed in their quest for gold here, the Spanish used Puerto Rico as a military and supply post for close to 300 years. Spanish settlers established some small farms on the island, raising crops mainly to meet their own needs. Otherwise, the area was largely populated by deserting sailors and by runaway black slaves from other colonies.

As elsewhere in Latin America, Puerto Rican settlers enslaved the Indians to serve as a labor force. The harsh new labor, European diseases, and disputes with the whites mostly eliminated the Indians so African slaves were imported for labor. Brought to the island in 1513, black slaves never formed more than a minority. Their population at its peak in 1846 comprised only 11.5 percent of the total.

Under Spanish direction, the slaves build forts in defense against attacks launched by the Dutch, the British, the French, and the Carib Indians. The strategy was successful. Except for two years (1598 – the British and 1625 – the Dutch), Puerto Rico remained under Spanish rule into the 1800s.

Immigrants. As the Spanish Empire collapsed at the beginning of the 19th century, immigrants began moving to Puerto Rico. Spaniards from various areas of Latin America were joined by French immigrants from Haiti and from Louisiana in North America. The agricultural community grew, consisting mostly of peasants and laborers on small to mid-sized farms.

Devoted largely to sugar cane but also to coffee and tobacco, the mid-sized hacienda developed from 1815 to 1873. Many of the peasant smallholders who grew crops for their own use changed into owners and workers on mid-sized haciendas that raised crops for sale.

Land use. Because black slaves were too few to supply enough labor, three systems were used to attract peasants to the haciendas. The system *agregado* gave them plots for their own use in exchange for their labor in raising the hacienda crop. Another system *medianeo*, or sharecropping, obligated the peasants to divide the crops raised with their landowner. Under the *endeudamiento* system, peasants were paid for their labor with produce and goods from a hacienda shop. A peasant labor force grew, black slaves working alongside free blacks and whites on the farms. When slavery was abolished in 1873, the newly freed blacks could continue in similar fashion on the hacienda farms. A sugar crisis in the 1880s led to the rise of coffee farms for 20 years. Then came decreases in the demand for coffee and a transfer of government that would change the course of life in Puerto Rico to the present day.

United States rule. In 1898, the Spanish-American War resulted in Spain's transferring ownership of Puerto Rico to the United States. Its president, William McKinley, appointed a governor to replace military rule on the island in 1900. The islanders became United States citizens in 1917. Thirty years later, the United States provided for Puerto Ricans to elect their own governor. Luis Muñoz Marin became the first elected governor in 1948, and in 1951 he persuaded the United States that his people should also have their own constitution. Modeling it after the U.S. Constitution, Puerto Ricans provided for a governor and a legislature with two houses.

Independence. In 1952, President Harry Truman declared Puerto Rico an independent Commonwealth. It has since remained under this form of government. As members of the Commonwealth, Puerto Ricans are United States citizens, and the United States government is responsible for their defense. Yet they do not pay taxes to the United States government or vote in its elections, and they govern themselves in internal affairs. Over the years, Puerto Ricans have disagreed on their options in government: to remain a Commonwealth, to become one of the United States, or to declare their independence as a nation.

Culture Today

Mixed descent. There were twice as many white males as females during Puerto Rico's first hundred years as a colony, which resulted in marriages among the races. Thus, the majority of Puerto Ricans today are a mixed people of white, black, and Indian descent. Pure whites are a minority in the population and even less numerous are full-blooded blacks.

Over the years white-skinned Puerto Ricans have enjoyed higher status than dark-skinned Puerto Ricans. Though blacks were the skilled workers in the colonial times, their color kept them in the lowest social class. Today circumstances influence a person's status. A mulatto (of mixed black and white descent) or even a black is regarded as white if the individual in question is wealthy or powerful in government. Color discrimination has been widespread on the island, though, leading to the passage of a Civil Rights Act in 1943.

Farm work. When first under United States Control, Puerto Rico had no banks, perhaps two or three roads, and a small strip of railway. Poverty then forced many farmers to sell their land to U.S. sugar companies. The once independent farmers who became hacienda laborers took jobs on U.S. sugar plantations or in the growing city industries. In the process, a large portion of the population moved from the mountainous central and western sections of the island to the coastal plains. Others left Puerto Rico to find work in nearby countries. Nearly one fourth of all Puerto Ricans have become part of the work force of the United States.

Meanwhile, the Puerto Rican population grew at a faster rate than a farm economy could support. The government responded in the 1940s with Operation Bootstrap, a program designed to attract outside industries to the island. The benefits to the companies were low-cost laborers and no United States income tax. Outside businesses responded with enthusiasm, opening over 2,000 plants on the island, and industry soon outpaced agriculture as the island's main source of income. Puerto Rican workers started manufacturing clothing, cement, glass, rum, and chemical and electrical products. Destined to build into one of the island's biggest businesses were the pharmaceutical plants. In rural areas, peasants switched from sugar cane to dairy and poultry farming. Some of the coffee farms remained.

City life. Puerto Ricans began to develop a dual identify as Latins and as United States citizens, adopting new American ways. Today there are cars, fried chicken stands, and two- to four-bedroom suburban homes in Puerto Rican cities. Rural areas are more traditional. Even in the cities, though, Latin traditions are strong and may outweigh the new Americanisms.

Food, clothing and shelter. The most common types of foods are Puerto Rican and Spanish, the staples being rice and beans. Still popular are early Taino Indian herbs such as *ajies dulces* (sweet small green peppers) and roots such as *pana* (breadfruit). The bananalike plantain is fried, then eaten as a side dish. Various towns specialize in seafoods or coconut dishes. For meat, Puerto Ricans generally eat pork or chicken. Foods are gently seasoned with mild flavorings. At the base of most sauces is *sofrito*, a mixture of vegetables and herbs.

Apartments and condominiums have appeared in the city, many in concrete. Some high-rise structures line the beaches of San Juan in Florida fashion. Some of the homes feature Spanish style arches and grillwork, and there are new one-story concrete structures equipped with water heaters. Puerto Ricans prefer to live in single-family homes, however small. To accommodate the flood of workers to the cities and to eliminate slums, the government built small concrete homes in the suburbs. But as the population grew, the new suburban houses began to become inadequate. Nearly one half are considered unfit for the number of people living in them.

By United States standards, 62 percent of Puerto Ricans lived below the poverty line in 1984. Most of the people cannot afford to live in any form of housing other than a low- or no-cost alternative. As elsewhere in Latin America, shantytowns have appeared outside the cities. Each forms a separate community, a single shantytown sometimes growing to include several *barrios*, or districts. Upgraded to include board sidewalks, shantytowns have also gained police and fire protection, and some even have their own elementary schools. Residents pay no rent, building their shacks of wood and other scraps. A one-room structure, a shanty serves as kitchen and bedroom and may have bath facilities at the back. Puerto Rican women sometimes operate businesses from the shanties. They might raise herbs, pigs, and chicken or roast chestnuts for sale. Another low-cost alternative is the housing project. It has paved streets and multiroom apartment-style units. However, tenants pay rent, apartments are less desirable than homes, and the women may not run businesses in these units. Shantytowns have therefore been more popular in the cities. In rural areas, poor farmers may occupy small wooden houses as in the past, and communities still surround a plaza with a central church.

Clothing in country and city resembles summertime styles in the United States. Businessmen may wear suits and ties or the more loosely-fitting *guayabera* – a tailored, embroidered shirt. Though costly, the *mundillo* is traditional crochet work on linen dresses. Puerto Ricans hold clothing in high esteem so that even the poor spend much of their income on dress.

Values. Other strong values have been inherited from the Latin American past. Among them are a ceremonial type of politeness and *personalismo* – the value of personal relations with family and friends. Family life may involve a formal marriage or a common law marriage in which the bond between a couple is cemented by the birth of their first child. In the past, children were raised with few restrictions, undertaking errands alone by the age of five or six. Traditional parents encourage *macho* (manly) feats of strength for young men and modesty in young women, training girls to be submissive, hard-working, and self-sacrificing.

Traditions. One tradition played an important role as family ties were weakened by the search for work. *Compadrazgo* is a tradition in which godparents are selected for each child. The godparents support the child in religious and worldy ways, from providing places to live to education and food. Over the years, the groups from which godparents are slected have changed. Originally they were chosen from a extended family of relatives, then from influential hacienda owners, and later from fellow workers. With the passage of time, the compadrazgo relationship has faded in importance.

Education. In contrast, schooling has grown more important over the years. Today nearly one fifth of government funds is spent on education, and, despite a shortage of teachers and classrooms, nearly 90 percent of the people can read and write. Coursework is modeled on instruction in the United States but is mainly in Spanish. Aside from the Commonwealth's public schools, there are Protestant and Catholic private schools.

Religion. Another change in Puerto Rican society has been the growth of Protestant religions, mostly among the middle class. The people are mostly Roman Catholics by tradition, but they show little interest in orthodox ceremony and practice their own version of the religion. In the past, they attended church on major occasions – christenings, weddings, funerals – while maintaining their Indian and black African beliefs. The result was a mix of Christian tradition (roast pig for Christmas) with taboos and voodooism. The Church supported harsh labor laws in the colony so many turned Protestant. However, the Roman Catholic following is still strongest. Spiritualism is strong in rural areas, the spirtualists claiming to get their power from the saints.

Arts. Puerto Rican folk artists carve images of these saints. Coconut masks are another traditional form of art. Africans have influenced dance and music on the island, as has Pablo Casals. A cello player whose mother was Puerto Rican, Spanish-born Casals moved to the island in 1956, establishing a yearly festival that features the best in symphony music. In drama, René Marqués achieved fame for *Purifacación en la Calle del Cristo*, a play about a Spanish family in changing Puerto Rico. In cinema, Puerto Rican films produced by Jacobo Morales have received international attention.

Puerto Ricans have been greatly influenced by the United States in entertainment and recreation habits. Radios and television sets appear even in shantytown shacks. In sports, the Taino Indians played a rough soccer type game with a hard ball of resin on dirt courts. Known as *bateyes*, a few of these courts still exist, but baseball and, more lately, basketball have become the island's most popular pastimes.

American ways, then, have been adopted by a people whose lives are based on Latin traditions. The social order in Puerto Rico has also been affected by such change. Today's immigrants are often wealthy builders and industrialists who form the upper class. With this new source of wealth, the rich have grown more distant from the poor. The *jíbaro* – the independent, straw-hatted small farmer who once equalized life on the island – is fast becoming a symbol of the past.

QUECHUA

(kech´ wa)

Descendants of Quechua-speaking Indians whose language unified various peoples of the Inca Empire.

Population: 8,000,000 (1981).
Location: Peru, Bolivia.
Language: Quechua, Spanish.

Geographical Setting

The Andes Mountains divide into two, then three ranges as they cross Peru. Between the ranges, great plains stretch for over 2,000 miles. Lake Titicaca, the world's highest lake, lies at 12,500 feet in the great central plain. The plains and valleys in central Peru make up only 27 percent of the country's surface but are home to more than 60 percent of the Peruvians. Among them are the Quechua-speakers, who in the 20th century have formed much of the population in southern Peru. At this altitude of the tropical country, the climate is mild for much of the year. In the east, however, where the mountains rise steeply, then drop down toward the Amazon River, glaciers form near the tropical Amazon jungle. Though Quechua-speakers began as highlanders, some have since moved to coastal towns and to this less populated eastern jungle.

The Quechua people live in Peru and Bolivia.

Historical Background

Before the Incas. The central plain was once the home of a number of groups of Quechua-speaking Indians, each with a separate government. About A.D. 400 most of these smaller groups united into a single dynasty. Art, mining, and agriculture flourished under this new rule, but differences among the Indian groups eventually eroded their union. By A.D. 800 the empire had reverted to the small, independent group system. In the 1430s, Chanca Indians conquered the Quechua, and later in the century both were absorbed by the Incas into their growing empire. They were thus exposed to Inca advances such as irrigation and astronomy, and to Inca religion, which was based on a divine creator and a sun god.

Under Inca rule. The Incas had developed into a highly-organized society before 1532. Colonies including the Quechua-speaking groups were established from what is now Bolivia to Colombia, then spread along the coast to Chile. The scattered settlements in Quechua territory specialized in different goods – wooden goblets and plates, dried fish, tubers, maize, meat, wool, pottery, and metalwork. Together with a core of highlanders, the middle and lowland colonists formed a network to supply one another's needs.

Land ownership was joint. The settlements were mostly organized according to groups of relatives on the father's side of the family, and each married couple farmed as much of the community property as necessary to support themselves.

Spanish rule. In 1532, Spanish invaders defeated the Inca Empire and set out to subjugate its Indian groups. The Quechua were divided in their response to the Spanish conquest. Although they continued to follow Inca ways, some appeared to adapt to Spanish rule and customs while others actively resisted. To carry out their resistance, they raided other Indians and Spaniards for weapons and food. The rebels resisted Spanish rule until 1572, but were finally Christianized and forced into the *encomienda* system.

Under this system, the Quechua had to pay heavy tribute to the Spanish in return for military protection. The *encomendero* (Spanish master) was given a *repartimiento* (group of Indians), whose members were required to pay him in labor. Masters demanded payment in silver and gold mining and in foreign crops so the Indians' traditional form of agriculture was disrupted. Gradually the private encomenderos were replaced by Spanish officials who were even harsher.

The Spanish continued to force the Quechua into submission until 1750, when Quechua resistance resurfaced. Indians working the Spanish mines became less productive as their rebellions undercut the labor supply from 1750 to 1820. By 1821, the Spanish had found the conquest of the Quechua unprofitable and left the region that is now Peru.

Meanwhile, a colonial lifestyle had developed among the Indians. The grand colonial structure of early society with its network of communities was upset by encomienda. The program of *reducción* had reorganized the scattered groups into large urban centers, dividing them geographically among the Spanish lords. Quechua society fell into three main groups: the *curacas* (government representatives), the *hatunrunas* (laborers), and the *yanaconas* (Spanish servants). Commune-type farming and industry continued to earn income for the community. Produced in workshops, manufactured goods earned income that was used by the Indians to pay Spanish taxes. Mainly the Quechua produced textiles, but some communities manufactured lumber, furniture, ceramics, and glass.

A mixing of Spanish and Indian traditions occurred. Clothing varied over time from Spanish to Indian style costumes, and some combined items from each. Atop a plush blue velvet suit, the late 18th century cuaraca wore an *unco* (poncholike garment with sewn sides). Hanging from his neck was a gold chain with a holy image – the sun.

In religion, the Quechua merged Inca and Christian beliefs. They associated the Christian Mary with *Pachamama*, an earth spirit who they believed caused crops to grow. Old fertility rites continued, the Quechua sprinkling alcohol on animals and feeding them mildly narcotic coca leaves to encourage larger, more productive herds.

Peru became independent in 1821, but this had little effect on the Indians. With a sense of Quechua nationalism built from the years of resistance, these Peruvian Indians found it difficult to participate in a government ruled by Spanish-speaking whites and mestizos (of European and Indian descent). Consequently, the Quechua remained isolated and neglected in independent Peru. Today, they are among the country's poorest residents.

In 1975 the Peruvian government took steps toward improving conditions for these Indians. It adopted Quechua as Peru's second official language, provided more land for the people through agricultural reform, and introduced modern farm tools. Part of a deliberate effort, these steps were designed to bring the Quechua into the mainstream of Peruvian life.

Culture Today

Who is Quechua? Today's Quechua-speakers form the largest group of Indians in Peruvian society. The word *Indian* is used loosely, since mestizos who speak mainly Quechua may be counted as Indians. Because so many Indians are peasants, the term *Quechua Indians* is also used to describe Peru's peasantry.

Quechua settlements. Farming and raising livestock are primary occupations for the present-day Quechua. No longer is the land community owned, however. Individuals now own most Quechua property. Owners, though, may not have the right to sell their land, which still gives the *ayllu* (community) a measure of control.

In the 20th century, types of settlement have ranged from those where individuals live on their own plots of farmland to those where individuals farm lands that lie outside the small village or large town in which they live.

Economy. With much of their territory taken from them, the Quechua now work as hired farmhands, sharecroppers, or small landowners on Peru's least desirable soil. Some move to coastal haciendas where they take jobs raising cotton, flax, sugar cane, potatoes, and wheat for sale. Others remain in the mountain areas, growing potatoes and barley for food. Chuña, white or black dried potatoes, is the staple in the Quechua diet. Valley and lowland Quechua grow coca, pepper, and fruit, then trade produce with the highlanders. Other foods in the diet are fish and some meat from Quechua herds.

Industry continues, textiles being the most widespread. Using cotton and wool from llama, alpàca, or sheep, Quechua men, women, and children weave a wide range of designs. The 20th century Quechua industries include tile, brick, furniture, and hat making. Among Peru's finest carpenters and cabinet makers are Quechua craftsmen.

Clothing. The Quechua design the textiles they produce into various types of clothing, depending on the area. Hats identify the wearer with a particular town. The Indian women of Puno wear derby-style hats, while Cuzco women wear a flatter variety. In colder areas, men wear sweaters and jackets over woolen pants that cover the knee. Otherwise, they may be found in homespun long pants and shirts. A customary outfit for women has been the short jacket and long, full skirt over one or more underskirts. (The number of skirts has been a way of showing off wealth.) Short full skirts are also common. Deftly-woven shawls and

Ancient ruin in Quechua land.

ponchos serve as over garments, and the *chullo* (knitted cap) is customary head covering for men.

Shelter. As with clothing, housing styles depend on location. However, the most common structure is rectangular with a gabled roof. Many dwellings are built of adobe with earthen floors and thatched roofs. Large earthen pots sit on earthen hearths for cooking, and eucalyptus poles are used to form beds. Other homes have brick walls and tile roofs.

Family life. Elder members of the Quechua community are held in high esteem, grandparents often living with their son's family in a single-room house. The Quechua give children freedom in their selection of a marriage partner, the traditional ideals being a woman who is an able weaver, housekeeper, and farmer and an honorable man who belongs to a landowning family. Couples enter into a state of trial marriage before cementing their relationship. Known as *sirvinacuy*, it may last six months or longer and generally leads to a permanent union.

Children learn to perform tasks early in Quechua society. At five, a young boy takes responsibility for a few lambs while a young girl cooks and cleans. Older girls begin weaving, and boys crochet chullos. By 12, the boys are sent to work in the fields. Free schooling (required of Peruvian children aged six to 14) is now offered to the Quechua. Different from the practical education of the people, it nevertheless builds on a strong Quechua heritage in language and song.

Arts. The Quechua have had both a spoken and written language for centuries, but their tales and lyrics were largely lost in the Spanish conquest. An ancient play, *Ollanta*, remains. Theater was also a common colonial pastime, the play *Posca Pankar*, for example, starring a beggar of Inca descent. Matches between boys and girls were strictly controlled in early times when Quechua-speaking society included nobles. A noble boy's wishes might be thwarted by his parents as expressed in these lines from a Quechua poem cited and credited by John Howland Rowe in *Handbook of South American Indians: Vol. 2 The Andean Civilizations* (Steward, 1946, P. 323):

> Your hypocrite mother causes our unbearable separation.
> Your contrary father causes our neglected state.

In music, the Quechua played string instruments (the harp, the mandolin) and a small drum (the *tinya*) and had a rich collection of funeral, religious, love, and farewell songs. Quechua folk dances have captured events in history (a Spaniard's conquest of an Inca) and activities in industry (the wool cutter's dance).

Religion. The Quechua continue to practice a hybrid religion, observing traditional as well as Christian rites. They perform Inca ceremonies but insist that their *alcalde* (mayor) be an avid Catholic. In addition, each village has its own patron saint to whom prayers are offered and monuments are constructed. Believing that Christ and Mother Mary have been visitors to certain places in Quechua land, the Indians have made these spots shrines and thousands visit them each year. Catholic litanies and masses are conducted, but traditional Quechua spirits, *apus*, are looked to for protection.

Government. Villagers are governed by an *alcalde*, or mayor, elected by a community's elders. The alcalde makes agricultural and public works (road building) decisions and sometimes settles disputes in the community. Though alcaldes can be quite powerful, of higher rank is the district governor.

On a national level, Peru is governed by elected officials, including a president and representatives in a two-house legislature. The effort to bring the Quechua more completely into the nation's mainstream is evident in Peru's election policy. As Peruvian citizens, all Quechua over the age of 18 are eligible to vote whether or not they can read and write.

SALVADORANS
(sal´ve dor´ens)

Also called SALVADOREANS. The mainly mestizo people of El Salvador, the only Central American country not bordered by the Caribbean Sea.

Population: 4,910,000 (1986).
Location: El Salvador, bordered by Nicaragua, Honduras, and Guatemala in Central America.
Language: Spanish.

El Salvador

Geographical Setting

Two mountain ranges cross El Salvador from east to west and divide the country into three sections. A hot, dry Pacific coastline ten to 15 miles wide, rises to a mountain range that gives way to a large central plateau of rich volcanic soil. Located on this plateau, El Salvador's major cities are nearly surrounded by volcanoes. It is a region of volcanic eruptions and earthquakes. A quake in 1986 greatly damaged the capital, San Salvador, and resulted in an estimated 1,500 deaths. North of the volcanic plateau, mountains rise and fall into the Lempa River valley. This river begins in Guatemala, then curves through El Salvador on its way to the Pacific Ocean. Though some irrigation is necessary, the climate is warm in the plateau region, and there is enough rainfall (about 70 inches a year) for abundant crops. The result is a central and northern area of well-farmed rolling hills.

Historical Background

Pedro de Alvarado, a Spanish conquistador, entered the central highlands of El Salvador in 1524 and found the Mayan Indian kingdom of

239

Cozcatlán. Its people were farmers who used tools such as the digging stick to plant maize, and who held religious celebrations at different stages of the growing season. Farm towns and villages of up to 2,000 homes dotted the highland valleys. Land was held in common, apportioned by governors of the kingdom to each farmer but not owned by the farmer.

By the time the Spanish arrived in 1524, Pipíl Indians outnumbered Mayans in the area. It took the Spaniards three years to defeat the Indians and somewhat longer to subjugate them to Spanish overlords. The Spaniards established two cities to be ruled by the Spanish government in Guatemala. Some of the Indians were enslaved to work their same lands, but now for the new Spanish owners. Others were allowed to continue farming independently if they paid tribute to the Spanish. As the years passed, there was a mixing of peoples. Indians married Spaniards and adopted European ways.

Encouraged by the Spanish landowners, the Indians, who proved to be excellent farmers, began growing export crops. The Spaniards had them raise cacao (used in chocolate) for sale and later found indigo (which yields a blue dye) to be a highly profitable crop. At the same time, they were intent upon converting the Indians to Christianity, so the Spaniards destroyed religious symbols connected with Indian farm life.

Large cocoa plantations appeared near the common lands of the Indians. The Spaniards had also brought cattle to the area, which interfered with Indian indigo production. By the 1700s, the cattle had destroyed much of the people's land. New diseases from Europe further interfered with the old lifestyle, greatly reducing the Indian population. It became difficult for villages to pay the required tribute, and they began to disappear. Displaced Indian farmers found isolated plots or became squatters and sharecroppers on large Spanish plantations.

Independence. By the early 1800s, life for the Indians and mestizos (of mixed Spanish and Indian heritage) had become oppressive. Father José Matías Delgado, a church leader in the city San Salvador, led an uprising in 1811. Delgado called for independence, and it followed shortly thereafter. Faced with troublesome world problems, Spain found its hold on Central America weakening. In 1821 the entire area declared independence. For a short time, El Salvador became part of Mexico. It joined the United Provinces of Central America in 1824, and this union lasted until 1839. Two years later, El Salvador was finally a separate nation.

Land distribution. Searching for a new economic base, Salvadoran farmers had introduced coffee as their cash crop by the mid-1800s. In 1882, all common lands were abolished in favor of private owners. Roughly 2 percent of the population acquired 75 percent of the land, an inequality that would continue to the 1980s. A great contrast developed between the few who were rich and the masses who were poor. Skirmishes over land erupted.

The distribution of land has been the single most difficult problem for the government of El Salvador. Through all the shifts in landholding and crop growing, disputes over territory steadily grew. Plantation land under the Spanish government was often loosely defined and also claimed by peasants as unowned land or as part of an *ejido* (common land) grant to be worked cooperatively by the townspeople.

Following the pattern set by the Spanish conquerers, fewer than a hundred families held most of the territory at the end of the 19th century. (Salvadorans call them the Fourteen Families). Repeated rebellions by farmers who worked as tenants for the large land owners or on small patches of less valuable land led to a massacre in 1932. Guided by Augstín Farabundo Martí, the peasants rebelled in an uprising that cost an estimated 30,000 lives. The rebellion was quashed and Martí was arrested, then killed.

The problem of land ownership increased as El Salvador became the most densely populated country in Central America. Constant turmoil over land reform has contributed to military takeovers and dictators in government. Recent leaders such as José Napoleón Duarte have remained in office with violent action on the part of the armed forces. Continually putting down rebellions, the military is presently engaged in a civil war that had reportedly caused 50,000 deaths by 1985.

Culture Today

El Salvador is the most densely-populated country of Central America. It has also been called the most mestizo country, as the majority of people are of mixed descent. A small group of full-blooded Indians remain, and there are even fewer whites.

Food, clothing and shelter. El Slavador's valleys are covered with *chozas* (straw thatched homes) and adobe, tile-roofed villages. Dirt floors are common, and the houses are lightly furnished two-room structures. A few who are wealthier live in roomier whitewashed adobe homes.

The smaller, thatched houses may be scattered on large plantations, where tenant farmers or sharecroppers receive small plots for their own use. In exchange, they raise the plantation crops – coffee, cotton, and sugar. Since the 1930s, there have been too few farm products to support the growing population. Light industries (for example, assembly plants of electronic parts) appeared in towns and cities, mostly in San Salvador, attracting farmers in search of work.

They moved to the cities, building slums by the urban centers. San Salvador became a city of great contrast, with suburban homes to the west and *tugurios* (shacks) to the east. Using whatever material is available, tugurio builders construct shacks of cardboard, wood, and metal scraps. The best homes are adobe structures with metal roofs. Often there are no sanitary facilities in the homes. In a few neighborhoods, conditions improve as slum dwellers form cooperatives to afford electricity and to assure clean drinking water.

Grown in the country, corn, rice and beans are the staples in the Salvadoran diet. Fruits and vegetables can be purchased in open-air markets in the villages, and there are modern supermarkets in the cities. Typical at breakfast are tortilla pieces in warm milk. Eaten at midday, the largest meal may include soup, tortillas, rice, and cheese or meat. An average supper is simply tortillas and beans. Salvadorans are particularly known for their tasty *papusas* – tortillas with melted cheese, shredded pork, or mashed beans in the center. Eaten with the fingers, paupasas are soft. A handful of the mixture is often dipped in cream or cheese, then consumed.

Clothing in El Salvador resembles dress in the United States, but is scarce for many. The average family is large, including perhaps six children. Hand-me-downs are a way Salvadorans cope with the scarcity.

Family life. Family life is often an informal affair. Common-law marriages, unions without an official or religious ceremony, are frequent. *Machismo*, male strength and dominance, is still strong in the family, as are contributions by children. Education is required between the ages of seven and 16, but the dropout rate has increased in recent years. Only 20 percent of secondary-age students were enrolled in 1981. Children often attend school for a few years, then work to feed the family.

Religion. Even in scantily furnished homes, there are pictures of saints or holy images. Salvadorans are mostly Roman Catholic. Often priests from the Catholic Church have called for land reform and help for the poor. Despite Christianity, old beliefs persist in the country. Some still practice *brujeria*, a type of witchcraft, for good (curing the sick) or evil (harming an enemy) purposes.

Arts. Evil is a common theme in Salvadoran folk literature. By tradition, they are a vocal people, and tales have been passed down through the generations by mouth. One concerns the ugly old character *La Siguanaba*, who changes into a beautiful young woman and asks a man for a ride. The man falls in love with her, and she grows ugly again. Aghast at the deceit, her frightened suitor sickens, maybe even dies. Such tales are told orally because many Salvadorans are unable to read and write. Among those who do write, there are Salvadorans who have excelled in poetry. An example is Claudia Lars with her sonnets and *Ballads of the North and South*.

Illustrated by such characters as La Siguanaba, evil plagues Salvadorans in everyday life. Families have been separated, houses destroyed, and people beaten in the civil war. Rich and poor respond in similar ways. To prevent government takeovers, large landowners have divided their property among managers and become absentee owners. With little to lose, tenant farmers have abandoned their plots and moved to the city. Thousands of Salvadorans have emigrated to the United States.

Change. In El Salvador, reform is slow. There is a limited but growing middle class, but society mostly remains divided into the very rich and the very poor. Once prosperous, even though wealth was not evenly distributed, Salvadorans now produce such small crops that the government must import wheat and other foods. Once independent without much debt to others, today El Salvador depends largely on support from outside countries. Meanwhile, the civil war continues, and life for Salvadorans is filled with uncertainty.

SURINAMESE
(su´re na´ mez)
A people of many ethnic groups living in the country
Surinam – formerly called Dutch Guiana.

Surinam

Population: 352,000 (1980).
Location: Surinam (also spelled *Suriname*), a small country on the north Atlantic Coast of South America.
Language: Dutch, Sranan tongo (a Creole language), Hindi, Javanese, French, English, Spanish.

Geographical Setting

The country of Surinam lies in the Guyana region north of Brazil. Once called Dutch Guiana, it rested between the colonies of British and French Guiana. Independence has changed the name of two of these areas.

Currents from the area near the mouth of the Amazon River carry sand and silt around the north of South America and deposit the debris along the Atlantic coast of Surinam. Throughout the years, this earth movement has resulted in a three-tiered country. Newer deposits lie near the coast, extending fifteen miles inland and forming low, fertile swampland. Beyond this lie the earlier coastal lowlands, extending for another 15 to 30 miles and then rising in the south to hill country that separates Surinam from the Amazon basin of Brazil.

Surinam's two lowland plains are mostly devoted to agriculture. The inner hill portion was once forested and provided the Dutch with valuable lumber. The jungle was also a refuge for Indians escaping persecution by the Europeans and for blacks fleeing from slavery. In this century, the hills of Surinam have been important sources of bauxite, the ore from which aluminum is extracted.

Historical Background

Alonso de Hojeda discovered the Guiana coast for Europeans in 1499, and in the next century Spaniards appeared in search of the golden city of El Dorado. Indians of the area now known as Surinam, successfully fought off colonists until the British founded a settlement in 1650. British planters and their slaves populated the settlement, then were joined by Portuguese Jews who fled the Inquisition. British settlers began by harvesting the rich hardwood forests and soon established plantation farming along the coast. Under British rule, the colony began raising sugar.

Ownership. Claimed by the British, Dutch, and French, northern land in South America was the setting for disputes among these countries. Later in the 1600s, Dutch sailors defeated the British in the area. Britain released the land to Holland under the Treaty of Breda in 1667. It became Dutch Guiana, and for 300 hundred years Holland would remain in control except for a brief return (1804-1816) of British rule.

Through the 17th and 18th centuries, a plantation economy existed in the colony. Sugar production was the main activity at first. Then coffee, cacao (used in chocolate), and cotton grew important. Wood plantations also appeared.

Slavery. There was controversy with the Indians, many of whom could not survive the harsh conditions on the plantations. The survivors, Carib and Arawak Indians, escaped to the tropical jungle. For labor, the planters turned to African slaves. The slaves could endure the harsh life, but many fled to the up-country forests. Known as Maroons, these escaped slaves established communities along large rivers. They struggled continuously against the plantation owners until a peace settlement in 1760 finally gave them the right to self rule.

Slavery was finally abolished in 1863, after which contract laborers were brought in from China to work the plantations. After fulfilling their five-year contracts, the Chinese usually failed to renew them. Therefore, the planters brought over new laborers – about 34,000 East Indians between 1873 and 1916 and about 33,000 Indonesians between 1890 and 1939.

Mining. Meanwhile, there were changes in government and the economy. In agriculture, the number of plantations decreased, and small rice-growing farms appeared. Bauxite, or aluminum ore, was discovered in the mountains and hills of south Surinam, and mining became profitable during these years. The Dutch continued to support the colony financially and took an active interest in the bauxite. With an increased need for aluminum in World Wars I and II, the Dutch provided money for the mine operations and Surinam prospered.

After World War II, the need for bauxite declined and so did Dutch interest in the country. In 1942, the Dutch allowed the colony to handle its own internal affairs. It was ruled, though, by a governor who represented the queen of the Netherlands. Conflict grew between Surinam's people and the government back in Holland. Named after the river that runs through the land, the country officially became Surinam when it broke with the Netherlands in the 1970s.

Independence. Independence was agreed upon and achieved in 1975. Afterwards, some 40,000 colonists left Surinam to qualify for Dutch citizenship in the Netherlands. Those who remained became divided along ethnic lines. East

Indians and Indonesians farmed the rural areas. Except for the descendants of the Maroons in East Surinam, blacks mostly worked on the docks in the towns. The few Chinese became shop owners.

Independent Surinam had adopted a constitution providing for a republican form of government patterned after that of the United States. From the beginning, though, it was saddled with a large debt and a very poor economy. The bauxite industry was in decline by then, and the government had little with which to replace it. Life for many residents became a struggle for survival, a constant search for food.

Rebellion. By 1980, unrest had spread to the military. Twelve army sergeants led a *coup d'état* in that year and overthrew the existing government. Military law was enforced and followed by many changes in government. There were killings of government opponents, and some fled to the Netherlands. In recent years, guerrilla rebels have fought the government in eastern and southern Surinam. In the conflict, government troops are reported to have killed innocent bystanders. Thousands have fled to French Guiana to escape the struggle.

Military leaders have remained in government to the present day. The 1987 constitution provides for a National Assembly whose members are elected by the people. The Assembly elects a president and a vice president who rule under the advice of a council that includes members of the military. By the late 1980s, this government had not yet unified Surinam. Its population remains a mix of ethnic groups who have operated independently of one another for over 300 years.

Culture Today

Population. Surinam's population has changed over the centuries. Today East Indians and

A Surinamese family
traveling to town.

By Borys Malkin. Courtesy
Anthro Photo

Creoles (white- or black-skinned people with European ancestry) are the largest ethnic groups. In 1980, East Indians formed about 35 percent of the population, Creoles 32 percent, Indonesians 15 percent, and black descendants of the Maroons 10.5 percent. Among the various smaller minorities are the Chinese and descendants of the Dutch.

Dutch influence. The influence of the Dutch is evident in the buildings of the capital city, Paramaribo, and in Surinam's first official language. Otherwise, colonial rule did little to unite the varied peoples of Surinam into a national identity. Instead the people who immigrated to this country have preserved traces of life from their homelands. Besides Dutch, they speak *Sranan tongo*—a mix of English, Dutch, Portuguese, and West African languages used since the 17th century. Hindustani, Javanese, and Chinese are common among the different ethnic

Food, clothing and shelter. Life in a new environment has led the groups to share habits in food, clothing, and shelter. While some still wear styles from homelands such as India and Indonesia, most Surinamese dress in Western-style clothing. As elsewhere, the people in Surinam build shelter from materials around them. Because Surinam has large land areas that are forested, lumber is easy to obtain. Therefore, wood-frame houses are common. Homes outside the cities usually have little furniture. In the capital. Paramaribo, there are a few luxury estates that were built by the rich before the 1980 coup.

Agriculture. The land lends itself to the growth of certain crops that direct the diet of the different groups. Rice is the staple, though maize, beans, vegetables, fruits, and fish are also eaten. As the population grew, the Surinamese became more and more eager to own their own land rather than to sharecrop or labor on the plantations. Three patterns of farm life developed. The plantation system left some large landholdings where workers live in small shacks and earn wages for their labor. A second pattern is private ownership. Since the coup of 1980, the government has encouraged this option, and some people have succeeded in buying their own plots, then farming them to supply themselves and the cities with food. The third pattern that developed is government ownership of farming cooperatives.

A number of crops – coffee, cocoa, the oil palm – are grown for export. Sugar is now only produced for local use. Bauxite once compensated for the loss of money from sugar sales. While the ore is still mined today, it now earns less money for the Surinamese. This has contributed to a lower standard of living than in the past, and self-improvement is difficult since jobs are scarce. It is estimated that in 1986 some 50 percent were unemployed or underemployed in part-time farming or service work.

The Surinamese are still a segregated people, not by law but by tradition. Creoles originally worked in the ports, so towns and villages along the coast remain largely Creole. In similar fashion, migrants from India and Indonesia have stayed in rural areas to work on farms and **Religion**. The main religions of the groups are Christianity, Hinduism, and Islam. Various faiths have their own private schools, and these are still attended by about half the students in Surinam. In the early years, there was a policy of adaptation to Dutch values, and schools were patterned after those in Holland. Since 1980, the Dutch influence has weakened.

Arts. The separate traditions of the different groups are again evident in the arts. The Creoles not only speak Sranan tongo but also use the language in literature – for example, the high quality poems by Henry de Ziel. Creole folktales about the African spider Anansi are still common, as are African dances and religious ceremonies.

An Oyama Indian of Surinam playing a bone flute.

By Borys Malkin. Courtesy Anthro Photo.

Among East Indians, the Hindi language and practices are widespread. Indonesians have maintained traditions such as the *wajan* puppet theater. Their children now adopt Western ways. However, as in other areas of life, art has not yet produced unity among Surinam's ethnic groups.

TENETEHARA

(tay nay tay har´ a)

Native Amerindians who inhabited the northeastern section
of Brazil before the advent of European explorers.

Population: 2,400 (1948).
Geographic Distribution: Brazil.
Language: Guajajara, one of the Tupi-Guaraní
family of languages.

The Tenetahara
people live in
Brazil.

Geographical Setting

Trees grow in abundance, and lush
underbrush covers the tropical jungle of the
Amazon, where the Tenetehara live along the
rivers of Pará and Maranhão districts of
northeastern Brazil. West toward the mouth of the
Amazon River, the land flattens into a wide
alluvial fan with rich soil that can be productively
farmed. Among the area's natural resources are
hardwoods, rubber, and palms, the babassú palm
bearing leaves and nuts of much practical value to
the Tenethara. The entire area is tropical – warm
and damp with a rainy season from December
through June.

Historical Background

Portuguese exploration. Sometimes referred
to as the Guajajara, the Tenetehara were among
the first Indians contacted by European
immigrants in the late 16th and early 17th
centuries. Thereafter contact between the
Tenetehara and the Europeans continued for more
than 300 years. Portuguese settlers in this area of
Brazil were followed by the French, who
established São Luis do Maranhão in 1611. The

settlement was then taken over by the Portuguese, who employed Indians for slave labor until Africans were brought in for this purpose in the late 1700s. The harsh conditions of the forced labor and exposure to European diseases took a toll on the Indian population. Many died during these years; others were driven into the forest of central Brazil.

Protection came only from the Jesuit missionaries, who managed to shield the Tenetehara from Portuguese raids. The Jesuits succeeded in settling a large number of Tenetehara in mission villages, but they were expelled from Brazil in 1759. Afterwards, the government made repeated attempts to attract these Indians to colonies it established in the region. The most success it had was in the colony of Januario, which included some 120 Tenetehara in 1874. By this time, though, most colonies established for Indians of the area were abandoned.

The Portuguese continued to collect oil and rubber from Tenetehara territory, hiring many of the Indians as rubber gathers or drivers of canoes that transported the rubber down river. However, the rubber trade collapsed by 1913, and rubber traders abandoned the area. Meanwhile, other new Brazilians settled near the Tenetehara and enlisted their aid in hunting, felling trees, and collecting hardwood products.

Reacting to Brazilians either by cooperating or fleeing to the forests to avoid them, the Tenetehara were a relatively peaceful group. An exception was a Tenetehara uprising in 1901 at Alto Alegria, a community in which Catholic Capuchins had settled. Missionaries, nuns, and students appear to have been killed in the assault; its suggested cause was the kidnapping of Tenetehara babies to raise at mission schools.

In the 1940s, the Brazilian Indian Service established posts along rivers to ensure peace between these Indians and new Brazilian settlers in the region. Records of Tenetehara ways are based mostly on observations made during this decade. Since the 1940s, there have been officers in the posts to defend the Indians and teachers to help them adopt the language and customs of other Brazilians. The result is that new influences are reshaping the traditional lifestyle.

Culture Today

Changing culture. The Tenetehara live along the rivers in northeastern Brazil. Other Brazilians have established large modern cities along the coast where the rivers meet the sea: Belém (population about 1 million), Sáo Luis (500,000) and Teresina inland on the Parnaba River, (400,000). These cities and towns established for trade and agriculture along the rivers have greatly affected the lives of the Tenetahara since anthropologists studied these people in the 1940s. Many elements of life among the Tenetehara have become identical to those of rural Brazilians. Like their rural Brazilian neighbors, these Indians now wear European-style shirts, trousers, skirts, and blouses. Even in the 19th century they constructed straw-roofed, adobe style houses in the manner of other Brazilians. Common in the 20th century has been the rectangular house with a hip (triangular) roof. Its exterior is covered with palm leaves; its interior generally consists of a single room. Unlike similar Brazilian houses, the Tenetehara's have no windows.

Village life. A traditional Tenetehara village is occupied by several related families. Its size has ranged from under 35 to over 800 residents. The homes stand in two or more rows facing an open plaza from which all grass and bush have been cleared. Given the design of the village, there is easy communication among households.

Family life. The design of the house itself achieves this same effect. Roofs are often extended to form a porch where family members gather together or the sick may be treated by a village shaman (religious leader). Inside the home, possessions (baskets, weapons, tools, trunks) create a crowded but personal atmosphere. Large stones form a fireplace for cooking. Hanging from the house's poles and rafters, hammocks are used for sleeping, and mats may appear on the clay floor for sitting. Households may consist of a simple, nuclear family (parents and children) or of an extended family (parents, children, relatives) on the mother's side.

It is customary for newly married couples to live with the bride's parents and for the husband to work for his father-in-law during the first year or two of marriage. The father-in-law heads a unit of family members that work to support the household. In this century, there has been individual ownership of a plot by the head man of a family. All the men in the family unit work the plot of land together to produce more than the family consumes. The surplus is sold and the income spent on salt, clothes, and other manufactured goods.

Food, clothing and shelter. The Tenetehara pursue traditional activities – cultivating gardens, hunting, fishing, and gathering. Now, however, they work not only to meet their own needs but also to sell the products of their labor to other Brazilians. Items for sale include meats, furs, rice, palm nuts, and copaiba oil (used in varnishes, tracing paper, medicines). Thus, the Tenetehara profit from contact with outsiders, as they have done in the past.

Like other Brazilians, the Tenetehara use the roça system, periodically cutting and burning the forest for planting. Manioc, maize, beans, peppers, and watermelon are standard food crops. Prepared into a flour, manioc is the staple in their diet. The Tenetehara hunt tapir, wild pigs, deer, monkeys, and armadillo for meat. Fishing in the rivers and gathering wild foods from the forest supply other foods.

Religion and tradition. Spirits are thought to inhabit the animals of the forest and to bring bad luck upon the hunter who offends them. Hunters oftentimes carry the umbilical cord of a newborn infant to prevent such ill fortune. The gathering of honey was cause for great feasting in the past. Men would ceremoniously enter their villages carrying the honey in gourds, then share it with guests from other villages who were invited to attend the festivities. The Honey Feast was a way of cementing relations among the different villages.

A village consists of several extended families, the men at the head of each family becoming village leaders. In the past, these head men were the only leaders. A chief for each village was later appointed by the Indian Service. His power was limited, though, mainly to acting as the official link between the villagers and the Service.

The shaman in Tenetehara society is the religious leader who communes with supernaturals in the people's spiritual world. It has been customary for a village to have several shamans and for many of the young to attempt to become one.

Despite the efforts of Christian missionaries, the people maintained their traditional religion into the 20th century. However, they have combined Christian ideas with their own beliefs, comparing their god Tupan to the Christian deity and their Village of Supernaturals to the concept of heaven. Souls of shamans are thought to inhabit their Village, living ideal lives after death.

There are four types of supernaturals in Tenetehara religion – creators and culture heroes, owners of forests and waters, spirits of forest animals, and ghosts of the dead.

Folklore. Tenetehara folklore includes tales that feature the supernaturals. Culture heroes explain the existence of items in the Tenetehara world. The culture hero *Maira* is credited with the creation of manioc. According to the story, the manioc he created was a magical root that grew by itself in a single day. One day Maira asked his wife to fetch some manioc, but she doubted that it grew so quickly and refused. For punishment, her furious husband made manioc grow slowly as it does today. The Tenetehara have created similar myths to explain the origin of hammocks, canoes, steel tools, and other everyday items. Also in their folk literature are legends that feature animals such as "The Tortoise and the Jaguar" and bring to mind similar tales in other cultures.

Brazilian influence. Customs in Tenetehara society have changed. In addition to their own language, many now speak Portuguese. They have learned to sleep in machine-made hammocks rather than in the handmade variety. Also, they are hired as workers to gather rubber, nuts, and pelts for other Brazilians. Hammocks are familiar items to the Tenetehara, though, and gathering is a familiar activity. In short, joining Brazilian society has been gradual and natural, for it has much in common with traditional Tenetehara life.

TIERRA DEL FUEGANS

(tyer´ ra thel fway´ gens)
Also called FEUGIANS.
A people in the southernmost settlement of the earth, on
islands whose early Indians are extinct or nearly extinct.

Population: 36,000 (1988).
Location: The islands that form the southern tip
of Argentina and Chile.
Language: Officially Spanish.

Tierra del Fuego

Geographical Setting

Tierra del Fuego consists of a group of islands at the southern tip of South America. Though the islands are separated from the mainland by the Strait of Magellan, their terrain extends mainland features. The largest island, *Isla Grande*, is shaped like a triangle. Most of the people and two thirds of the land appear here. On the eastern side are rolling hills and grassland – an extension of the pampas and Patagonia region of Argentina. The western side and the south are covered with the Andes Mountains, while the center is forested. Seals, otters, and sea lions live on the coasts. Mountain lions, rheas and the llamalike guanaco inhabit the interior. West of the large island is a group of smaller islands that are really peaks of the Andes Mountains. Their southernmost boundary is Cape Horn. Still another group of icy rocks lies to the southwest, the Diego Ramírez Islands.

The climate on the islands is described as cool to cold, but there is great variation. Settlers on the large island may live as close as 2,400 miles to the South Pole, yet they experience moderate temperatures and rainfall. There is snow, even in summertime, but it usually disappears within a day or two. Gold has been discovered on the islands, but today's settlers use the land mostly for sheepherding.

Historical Background

Early peoples. Tierra del Fuego was first discovered by Europeans when Ferdinand Magellan sailed around the southern tip of the continent in 1520. Afterwards, various explorers visited the land from time to time. The explorers found three groups living in the region: the *Onas*, the *Yahgan*, and the *Alacalufs*. The Alacalufs and the Yahgan had settled near the coasts, their lifestyles centering on canoes. Known as "foot Indians," the Onas lived inland and traveled long distances for food. As a whole, the Indians acted unfriendly, wanting nothing from the Europeans and refusing their offers of alcoholic beverages.

Explorers. Magellan had named the region *Tierra del Fuego*, "Land of Fire," because its Indians carried fire from one place to another in the cold environment. After Magellan, many other explorers visited this southernmost settlement of the earth. North American expeditions of the early 1700s were followed by French ships. To survey the land, British voyages were made between 1826 and 1836. One of these voyages brought the famous scientist Charles Darwin around Cape Horn on the *Beagle*. The French helped complete the land survey from 1882 to 1883.

All these voyages brought deadly diseases to the area, killing many Indians. Others died in conflict with the whites. Still, for over 300 years after Magellan's sighting, the Indians were left to themselves.

Immigrants. In the late 1800s, missionaries succeeded in befriending the Onas. Reverend Thomas Bridges appeared in 1871 to establish an Anglican mission, becoming the first permanent white settler. Later in this decade, sheep imported from the mainland thrived on the large island's plains. Sheep raising and the discovery of gold began to attract hundreds of Chileans, Argentines, and Europeans (largely from Yugoslavia). Chile and Argentina established colonies, dividing the region between themselves in 1880. Argentina claimed the eastern third, while Chile claimed the western two thirds. Their governments sent prisoners to the distant area, turning the towns Punta Arenas and Ushuaia into convict centers for a time.

The outsiders upset the fragile balance of the Indians' lives. Pushed off the best land, many Onas perished from diseases against which they had no defenses. Their population further decreased when they hunted the settlers' sheep just as they had hunted wild animals in the past.

There were bloody battles in which government soldiers shot Indians, further reducing their numbers. According to estimates, 3,500 Onas lived on the island in 1860, 2,000 in 1891, and 1,500 in 1896. By 1900, only about 600 remained, and then more lost their lives to a measles epidemic in 1925. A 1959 estimate counted 50 Onas, who eventaully died or adopted white ways. Meanwhile, the Yahgan and Alacaluf groups also dwindled. By the late 20th century, the Indians who first populated Tierra del Fuego were virtually extinct.

Culture Today

Ethnic groups. Immigrants and their descendants – Argentines, Chileans, Yugoslavs, Spaniards, British, and Italians – are the current people of Tierra del Fuego. There are some mixed individuals whose heritage includes early Indian ancestry.

The Yahgan. The Indian groups that originally populated the land lived in different ways. Like the Alacalufs, the Yahgan centered their lives around the water. They built domed or cone-shaped tipi-style houses and traveled by canoe, living without any larger social organization than the small family. For nourishment they turned to seafood – mussels, seals, fish. Using seal or fox skins, they fashioned their main item of clothing – a small furry cape. Later, many died from measles caught through old clothes sent by charitable Christians.

Believing in a Supreme Being, the Yahgan developed myths to explain their world. One myth spoke of a time when women ruled men and deceived them by wearing masks to impersonate spirits. Ultimately the men overthrew the women, killing all but one. Such tales were told in a well-developed language. The Yahgan spoke rapidly in a tongue with no hard sounds, using a 30,000-word vocabulary and five counting numbers.

The Onas. Living inland on the Isla Grande, the Onas were a tall people, the men averaging five feet ten inches in height. Thin, bronze-skinned, and strong, these Indians traveled on foot in bands of related families. Including from 40 to 120 members, a band would hunt guanacos and rheas for food. They used tree trunks, branches, and guanaco skins to build cone-shaped houses Also used for clothing, guanaco hide was made into an unfastened robe worn by the men. Women wore a furry petticoat under a guanaco skin apron and a fastened robe. Guanaco meat was the staple in their diet.

The Onas had a wealth of folklore to explain their world. However, where they actually came from and how they got to the island remain mysteries. Though surrounded by water, the people had no knowledge of boats. An Ona legend ties their destruction to alcohol and to diseases brought by the whites. Such tales were told in their slow, harsh language, which is another mystery. While it does not directly relate mainland Indian languages, it is most like a mainland language spoken by a now-extinct people many years ago.

In the 20th century, a group of surviving Onas traveled south on the big island to the *estancia* (ranch) of the first missionary, Thomas Bridges. They appealed to his son E. Lucas Bridges, who later recorded their saga in his book *Uttermost Part of the Earth* (New York: E.P. Dutton, 1949). As a reward for his missionary work, Thomas Bridges had received a large grant of land from Argentina. Located by Port Haberton, today it is just one of some 65 estates on the Argentine side. A few more appear on Chile's Navarino Island.

Food, clothing and shelter. Generally, today's islanders live in scattered settlements. With 50,000 acres and 9,000 sheep, the Haberton Ranch on the Argentine side is described as small for an estancia. It consists of a group of buildings – a main house, a boathouse, carpenter and blacksmith shops, bunkhouses for ranch hands, a cookhouse, and storage and saddle sheds. Prefabricated in England, the main house is a white wooden building covered with corrugated iron. Among the smaller houses on the large island are a steep-roofed Yugoslav variety, its center ridges decorated with carved-wood or wrought-iron designs. Simpler homes appear in the Italian neighborhood of the town Ushuaia.

Given the abundance of sheep on the island, mutton is a staple in the diet and may be boiled, fried, roasted, or smoked. Other foods are chicken, crab, fish, mussels, vegetables, and fruits. Raspberries grow wild, as does the dark-blue berry *calafate. Yerba mate*, tea sipped from a gourd, is consumed by ranch hands, who are often Chilean.

Both owners and ranch hands wear jeans and shirts. Imported goods such as radios or material for clothing may be purchased at shops in Ushuaia.

Economy. Argentina's southernmost town, Ushuaia is equipped with hotel rooms for tourists. Though the tourist industry has grown, most workers on the islands raise sheep, graze cattle, catch fish, and harvest lumber. Since the 1940s, there has also been a petroleum industry due to an oil discovery on Chile's section in the north, and coal is mined along the Strait of Magellan.

URUGUAYANS

(yoor´ uh gway´ uns)

A people mainly of Italian and Spanish ancestry, who live in the South American country Uruguay.

Population: 2,975,000 (1988).
Location: Southern and eastern Uruguay.
Language: Spanish.

Uruguay

Geographical Setting

Nestled between Argentina and Brazil, Uruguay is a country of rolling hills and grassland. It is part of the grassy pampas, separated from Argentina by the Uruguay River. In the north, the hills rise to form the end of mountain chains that extend south from Brazil. A pair of waterways – the Caureim and Yaguarón rivers – form a natural boundary between Uruguay and Brazil. Though pine forests grow along the rivers and in the low mountains, less than a third of the land is forested. About a fifth of the area lends itself to crop raising. The rest is pasture land for cattle.

Historical Background

Before the Spanish. Before the Spanish claimed the region that is now Uruguay, it was inhabited by Amerindian groups living mostly along the rivers. The largest of these groups was the Charrúa Indians. They were a people who lived in bands of up to 15 families. Roofless, their rectangular houses consisted of matted walls on wooden posts. The Charrúa hunted deer and rhea, first on foot with bows and arrrows and later on horseback with lances. Each small band had a

265

leader, who would unite with the leaders of other bands for defense.

In the late 1500s and early 1600s, a few Spanish expeditions landed on the shores of Uruguay, then called *Banda Oriental* (East Bank). The Charrúa drove off the outsiders.

Spanish and Portuguese rule. In 1624, Jesuit and Franciscan missionaries succeeded in befriending the Indians and established bases in Uruguay. Also at the beginning of the 1600s, the Spanish governor Hernando Arias brought cattle here. Wandering gauchos (cowhands) came from Buenos Aires to tend the cattle and were followed by merchants who settled in the area. As the century wore on, more and more of Uruguay was occupied by Spaniards. Meanwhile, the Portuguese moved in from Brazil. By 1680, they had founded a community across the river from the Argentine settlement of Buenos Aires. Thereafter, the Spanish Argentines and Portuguese Brazilians entered into a long struggle for ownership of Uruguay.

Montevideo, the largest city in Uruguay today, was established in 1726. Slowly, the country grew, falling under the rule of the Spanish viceroyalty at Buenos Aires in 1776. The tug-of-war between Brazil and Argentina for control of Uruguay continued until 1806, when it was interrupted by the British capture of both Montevideo and Buenos Aires.

Bringing saddles, furniture, and cloth to Uruguay, British traders helped develop the port at Montevideo as a center of trade The British influence was short lived; they were driven out seven months later. Following the ouster of the British, the people of Montevideo claimed independence, but the Spanish government at Buenos Aires refused to recognize their claim.

Finally, in 1811 the peoples of Buenos Aires and Montevideo banded together to expel their Spanish rulers and achieve independence. José

Gervasio Artigas led the Montevideans against the Spanish, almost defeating them, but then Portuguese soldiers from Brazil attacked. Artigas judged that the wisest strategy would be to retreat westward for a time. He led thousands of men, women, and children on a two-month journey, during which they crossed the Uruguay River. Using horses, carts, and pack mules, the travelers were participants in a great event in Uruguayan history. The journey and subsequent events made Artigas the people's hero. He remained in the west for over a year, working to set up an independent Uruguay from there, but Buenos Aires refused to cooperate. Back in Montevideo, the citizens regained control, but were again invaded by the Portuguese. Unrest continued through 1821, when Uruguay became a province of Brazil.

Brazil's government was no more pleasing to the Montevideans than Argentina's government has been. Therefore, in 1825 a group known as the "Thirty-Three Immortals" began a revolt against Brazil. Argentina joined the effort on the side of the Uruguayans, and then Britain intervened to settle the matter so trade could continue. In 1828, the issue of independence was finally settled. Brazil and Argentina signed a treaty recognizing Uruguay as a sovereign nation.

Independence. The first years of the new republic were disrupted by civil war. Rival political parties, the Colorados and the Blancos, vied for power. José Fructuoso Rivera, a Colorado, and Manuel Oribe, a Blanco, served as the first presidents. In the 1830s, conflict between the Colorados and Blancos escalated into the *Guerra Grande*, a fierce civil war that grew to involve France and later Britain. Lasting for 16 years, the Guerra Grande devastated the country and had no real victor. Peace was restored in 1851, but thousands of people had died in the war, and at least four million cattle had perished.

In the decade after 1851, the number of people and cattle doubled. Uruguay's rich pasture which had been ruined by revolution began to renew itself. As in Argentina, the gauchos herded cattle and drove them to *saladeros*, large slaughterhouses of the city. At the saladeros, workers dried the cows' flesh, prepared their hides, and readied their leather for export.

The 1860s were healthy years in the growth of Uruguay. The country attracted about 50,000 immigrants between 1860 and 1868, most of them Italians and Spaniards. Small but prosperous, Uruguay began to specialize in three products: wool, hides, and jerked beef. Then a great drought destroyed many livestock, and disorder interfered with government.

José Batlle y Ordóñez restored order to Uruguay in the 20th century. Serving twice as president (1903-1907 and 1911-1915), he dominated politics until his death in 1929. Batlle changed a disordered Uruguay into the most democratic nation in South America. He introduced far-sighted reforms – an eight-hour work-day, state ownership of telephones, reduced power to the Church in public affairs, and a council to govern Uruguay instead of a president.

The country settled in to a new period of growth. Between 1919 and 1930, about 50,000 immigrants – Spaniards, Poles, Rumanians, Germans, Syrians, and Armenians – came to Uruguay. The Jewish community grew, making rapid progress in business. At the same time, there were problems. Agriculture was too small in Uruguay to support so many people, and there was disagreement in government.

Batlle's plan for a council instead of a president was not fully adopted until 1952. Called the *colegiado* system, it placed nine members on the council. Frequent disputes among the council members led to the return of an elected president in 1966. A year later the president died, and

Uruguay fell into disorder again. Beginning in 1973, a harsh military dictatorship ruled the country. It arrested its critics, holding some 6,000 of them prisoners by 1976. Government grew increasingly harsh. By 1980, ten percent of the people had left a country that provided less freedom than most other areas of Latin America. The dictatorship continued for four more years. Elections in 1984 then transferred government control back to the people. From 1984 to 1985, the 6,000 military prisoners were released.

Culture Today

Ethnic groups. Unlike other Latin American countries, Uruguay has a highly *un*mixed population. Perhaps 90 percent of the people are of European ancestry – mainly Spanish or Italian. Less than ten percent are mestizo (of mixed Indian and European heritage), and there are even fewer blacks.

Economy. The vast majority of the people live in cities, almost half the population in the capital Montevideo. There is a large middle class, whose members find jobs in government or in business and industry. With most land devoted to sheep and cattle raising, industry is connected to livestock.

Meat processing continues as a major business, but has undergone change. Due to the advent of refrigeration, *frigoríficos* (meat-packing plants) have replaced the saladeros. Among their products are tinned and frozen meats as well as glue prepared from hooves. Other livestock-related businesses are the hide and leather industries. Since early times, Uruguayans have used hide and leather to their advantage. A green stretch of hide on sticks was the door of country shacks, and in Montevideo house builders used leather in place of nails or wire. Today leather is generally manufactured into shoes or gloves.

Uruguay now has a metalworking industry to supply items such as nails.

Food, clothing and shelter. In comparison to other Latin American countries, Uruguay has a large middle class. Many of its members live in high-rise apartment buildings in Montevideo, while mansions provide housing for the wealthier in the city. The poorer citizens live in small homes.

Uruguay was the first welfare state in Latin America. Beginning with José Batlle y Ordóñez, the government took responsibility for the welfare of its citizens, building small homes outside major communities. Thus, Uruguay has fewer slums than other Latin American countries, although shacks do appear on the outskirts of its cities.

Like the city, the countryside has different forms of housing – great ranches, one-story adobe homes, and thatched-roof shacks. Activities still center on cattle and sheep raising. Raising wheat, corn, linseed, and rice for sale, Uruguay's farmers also provide the people with foods.

Beef has long been the most popular item in the diet. Still enjoyed today is the gaucho dish *parrillada criolla*, often made with barbecued sausage, kidneys, and beef. As in Argentina, *yerba mate* (tea) is a traditional beverage, sipped by the gaucho through a silver straw from a gourd. Home-grown fruits (peaches, apples, grapes) have long been popular. More recently, the many Italian immigrants have brought pastas into the everyday diet.

The large immigrant population affected clothing in the country. Today Uruguayans wear styles that resemble those in Europe or North America. Still worn by the gauchos are their traditional garments – a flat, wide-brimmed hat, a poncho, and boots over loose-fitting trousers.

Religion and language. Uruguay's immigrants also influenced language and religion. The mix of religious groups includes Catholics,

Protestants, and Jews. Two thirds of Uruguay claims to be Roman Catholic. However, men in this group tend to leave observance of their religion to women.

As in Argentina, the presence of Italians has affected the Spanish spoken here. For example, *chao* or *addío*, not *adiós*, is used for "goodbye."

Education and the arts. Education and the arts are highly valued in Uruguay. Elementary and beginning secondary schooling is required, and education is free through the university level. Over 97 percent of the people can read and write.

Among the notable professional writers are both poets and novelists. In 1888, Juan Zorrilla de San Martín, published "Tabaree," a poem about the son of a Spanish woman and an Indian chief. A few years later, Acevedo Díaz wrote *Soledad*, a novel about a poor gaucho who meets the daughter of a wealthy rancher. While the gaucho was a popular subject, later authors (for example, Mario Benedetti in *Montevideanos*) wrote about life in the city. Uruguay's plays were performed not only at home but also in Argentina. Perhaps the best known playwright, Florencio Sánchez wrote dramas such as *The Foreign Girl*, about a man who loses his farm to an immigrant and about their children who fall in love. The acclaimed artist Pedro Figari painted rural scenes – for example, a portrait of an Uruguayan at twilight under a tree listening to guitar music.

Recreation. In music and dance, the tango is the most notable form. It developed to reflect the hopes of Europeans who wanted their own farms but had to settle in city ghettos. Gerardo Matos Rodríquez composed one of the finest tangos, "La Cumparsita."

Uruguayans have excelled in sports. Soccer became a favorite in the country. Having twice won the world championship (1930 and 1950), the people developed a passion for the sport, and it remains quite popular today.

Government. The present day constitution describes the head of government as an elected president whose term in office is five years. Since Uruguay is still a welfare state, the government plays a large role in the daily life of the people. It provides medical care for the poor, controls insurance, and sets a minimum wage for workers.

After World War II, the government built oil refineries, meat-packing houses and dairy cooperatives to encourage industry and to increase the income of the people. Conditions have worsened in recent times, though. Wages have dropped, prices have risen, and many cannot find jobs. Not earning enough money to maintain the welfare state, Uruguay is in great debt to other nations. Still, its people enjoy a higher standard of living than most others in Latin America.

VAUPES INDIANS

(vow pace´)

A native group of peoples speaking various dialects of the same language and living in the valley of the Vaupés River.

Population: 14,000 (1978?).
Location: Colombia, Brazil.
Language: Tukano, other related languages of the Eastern Tukanoan family.

The Vaupés live on the border between Colombia and Brazil.

Geographical Setting

The Vaupés River flows from the Andes Mountains into the Amazon River through land that is covered by tropical forest. Since the forest is so dense, even small groups of the same peoples become isolated from one another. There are some mountains and rocks in the area, the rivers forming rapids in rocky places. Many of the Vaupés Indians live on open land near river rapids, where fish are abundant. Others build small communities in the denser forest.

Historical Background

First Europeans. In 1538 and 1541, Spanish explorers discovered Indians living in the Vaupés River area. A Carmelite Mission was built to convert the Indians in 1694. Although Portuguese settlers from Brazil attempted to establish missions of their own in the 1700s, none of them gained a permanent foothold. The Indians rebelled against the Europeans in the early and middle parts of the century, chasing out the missionaries. No missionaries returned for over a hundred years. Then in the 1880s, efforts to again penetrate the area met with some success. The Franciscans built missions along the river that still

273

stand today.

Rubber. In the early 1900s, a need for rubber by United States and European auto industries led to the exploitation of the Vaupés groups. Whites used the Indians as slave labor in extracting rubber, and the laborers often died because of physical hardships. Relocated by the rubber barons, many of the Indians moved from their scattered *malocas* (large communal houses) to villages. This made it easier for the outsiders to control the Indians and convert them to Christianity.

Many malocas were burned or otherwise destroyed in the effort to extinguish traditional ways. Christian ideas were combined with native religious practices, and the Indians came to rely upon European manufactured goods. Firearms, fish hooks, and machetes were adopted. Knives made it easier for the women to farm, and firearms and fishhooks helped the men capture game and fish. Yet the effort to replace Vaupés customs was only partially successful. The people adopted tools that increased their standard of living, but continued to survive in traditional ways.

Culture Today

Composition. The Vaupés Indians are a loose grouping of approximately 40 peoples living in the Vaupés River region between Colombia and Brazil. They include the Tukano, Bara, Cubeo, Desana, Makuna, and the Tatuyo, all of whom speak variations of the same basic language, and share similar ways. They are, therefore, considered a single culture.

Language. The largest group is the Tukano who number over 2,000 and whose language is used as a common tongue among groups. Highly conscious of their language differences, the people view speakers of the exact same language as members of the same family. Marriage to someone within this family is forbidden;

consequently, husbands and wives speak different first languages. Children trace their descent from their father's line of ancestors and adopt his language first.

Children. The birth of a child is an occasion for separation between men and women. The Cubeo group of Vaupés Indians practice a system of childbirth in which the woman delivers the infant in her manioc garden rather than at home. Meanwhile, her husband stays inside their house, taking care not to accidentally bring harm to the child, whose safety is thought to depend on the father's actions. (If the father stumbles, the infant will supposedly fall.) The Cubeo believe that earth and river monsters are angered by a birth, so they will try to destroy the infant. The fear that evil will befall the newborn persists for a five-day period (called a *couvade*), during which members of the family avoid the river.

Other long-held customs include whipping boys and teaching them about secret religious trumpets. Girls dance to the trumpets, and their hair is pulled out. Partly to change such practices, the missionaries founded boarding schools. Here Vaupés children grow accustomed to Western-style clothes, games such as basketball, and new ways in place of their old ones.

Food, clothing and shelter. The most common item of traditional clothing was a breechcloth, worn only by the men. Both men and women painted their bodies. Women's faces were reddened to ward off danger when working, then carefully covered with designs. The Cubeo, in particular, are noted for their geometric forms.

Children were once raised with other families in a large maloca, or communal house, located perhaps a day's travel away from another such structure. Housing 60 people, the largest maloca was 100 feet long and 40 feet high with a gabled roof. The rear had living compartments that were usually occupied by a few brothers and their families. The front and middle sections were used for religious purposes. To change Vaupés beliefs and ways, the missionaries had the Indians tear down their malocas. A few malocas still remain in Colombia. Elsewhere, the Indians now live in the standard types of housing in their various areas.

The Indians still engage in their customary means of survival – farming, hunting, and fishing. A large part of the daily life of Vaupés women is devoted to caring for food crops, including cassava, manioc, and maize. Men cultivate plants such as tobacco and coca for ritual purposes. In the past, they relied on arrows or traps for fishing and on arrows, traps, or spears for hunting. Now there are firearms and fish hooks. A forest-area group, the Maku Indians depend more on hunting than agriculture. They purposely snare a surplus of game for trade, providing the Tukano Indians with meat from the hunt and receiving agricultural or manufactured goods (knives, cloth) in return. Thus, a program of exchange has developed to the mutual benefit of the various groups.

Religion and folklore. While the religions of the Vaupés groups differ, they all tend to include the worship of ancestors and the presence of shamans, (religious leaders who communicate with the gods on behalf of the people). The Tukanos recognize two deities: *Kuwai* and the creator god *Humenihinku*. Humenihinku supposedly lives in a house in the sky where he receives spirits of the dead, who bring gifts so that he will welcome them. The deity Kuwai is more closely associated with the daily life and oral literature of the people. He is regarded as the god who taught them to plant, hunt, and conduct ceremonies. Kuwai is a trickster who will squabble with mortals when they interfere with his plans. He is also described as a character who has many misfortunes, entering into marriages that continually meet with mishap.

The oral literature of the people includes humorous stories of Kuwai's exploits. According to one story, he created a wife from a tree, but then she eloped with a fish. Kuwai never admits defeat. It is thought that he is now sulking on a distant mountain after being mistreated.

Inhabiting the forests and rivers, evil spirits are pictured as hairy, humanlike monsters with double-faced heads. The peoples think of these monsters as cannibals who threaten to seize children and leave their bodies hanging on trees. Shamans attempt to prevent such wrongdoing.

Vaupés Indians regard their ancestors as a source of strength, and worship them for their benign influence on the living. They are summoned by men and boys blowing ancestral horns; women are forbidden to cast their eyes upon these trumpets. It is believed that the instruments originated in ancient times when the body of the people's first ancestor was burned. The body's ashes grew into a palm, then became the instruments. Today, these trumpets are symbols that represent the living spirits of the Vaupés Indians' ancestors.

VENEZUELANS

(ven´ eh zway´ lens)

Mostly a mixed Indian-European people living in
an oil-rich nation with a democratic government.

Venezuela

Population: 18,270,000 (1987).
Location: Venezuela in northern South America.
Language: Spanish.

Geographical Setting

A traveler who started in northwest Venezuela
and moved southeast would find four main
regions – the Andes Highlands, the Maracaibo
lowlands, the *llanos* (plains), and the Guiana
Highlands. In the northwest, the Andes
Mountains surround hot, coastal lowlands by
Lake Maracaibo. Moving toward the coast, the
mountains turn and cross the country to form
highlands towards the northeast. Located on a
northeastern plateau is the capital, Caracas. Fertile
valleys lie by the mountains, and most Venezuelas
live in this region. Further south, the mountains
give way to the flat grassy and shrub-covered
llanos. Over 1,200 miles long, the Orinoco River
runs through the plains. South of the Orinoco, the
terrain rises to the Guiana Highlands, which is
tropical forests and covers nearly half of
Venezuela. Rich oil deposits exist in the eastern
llanos and elsewhere, many wells appearing in
Lake Maracaibo. While the climate is warm in the
lowlands, it becomes cooler in the highlands. The
llanos have alternate wet and dry seasons.

Historical Background

First Europeans. Venezuela was first sighted
by Christopher Columbus during his third voyage

278

in 1498. The Spaniard Alonso de Ojeda explored the region, charting the coast and reaching Lake Maracaibo in 1499. There he found Indian villages built on pilings over the lake. Reminded of Venice, Italy, he named the land *Venezuela* (little Venice).

Mostly Caribs and Arawaks, the Indians occupied themselves by fishing, farming, hunting, and trading. Their communities formed a highly developed network of trade. The Indians of one area provided fish, salt, and pearls to those of another in exchange for maize, gold, and meat. Warlike raids were common between communities, the Indians capturing their enemies and often trading them along with products. However, the captives served as laborers, not slaves, sometimes marrying into their captor's group.

Contact with Europeans brought diseases, harsh treatment, and loss of land, upsetting the Indians' lifestyle. Their population plummeted in the 1500s.

German rule. After establishing a colony in 1523, the Spanish found the mining poor here and the agriculture limited. So King Charles I of Spain used the land to pay off his debts to a German bank. In 1528, he gave the Welser family, owners of the bank, the right to establish colonies in Venezuela. His condition was that they convert the Indians to Christianity. Thinking that the rumored golden city of El Dorado might lie here, the Welsers took control of the land. They found no El Dorado, and in their exploitation of the land they treate the Indians brutally.

Spanish rule. Spain reclaimed and began to resettle the land in 1546. From the Indians' point of view, these new Spanish settlers were just the next intruders. The Indians resisted them until 1580, when the Indian population was greatly reduced by smallpox. In 1580, the area fell under the *encomienda* system, which granted land to

Spanish conquerors and entitled them to payment (usually in crops) from Indians in their area. Fifty years would pass before encomienda was abandoned in 1630.

Meanwhile, Venezuelans began to raise cacao (used for chocolate) about 1600. The growth of cacao spread, pushing cattle southward onto the llanos and controlling the countryside for the next two centuries. Wealth remained in the hands of a fortunate few. In 1684, 172 owners owned 195 cacao plantations and cattle ranches. There were ten times as many cacao plantations by the 1740s, yet the number of owners increased only to 175.

The wealthy landowners depended on black slaves from Africa to raise cacao. By the 1750s, hundreds of black slaves worked in large gangs on cacao plantations. Slave protests and escapes continued throughout the century.

Meanwhile, there were conflicts in white society. *Peninsulares* (pure whites from Spain) felt superior to creoles, or whites born in Venezuela who had some mixed blood. Though many peninsulares were poor, they looked down upon the wealthy creoles with their "impure" blood. The creoles looked down upon mulattos and *pardos*, or free blacks, resisting the blacks' efforts to educate themselves. As a result, the free blacks became artisans, farmers, and cattle herders.

At the top of colonial society were rich European planters, sometimes called the *Marquese de Chocolate*. A member of this group, Simón Bolívar worked to free the people of control by Spain. Toward the end of the 1700s, Venezuela, which began as six separate provinces, began to think of itself as a single country. A central government formed at Caracas. Then, in 1811, Venezuela joined other areas of Latin America in declaring independence from Spain.

Francisco de Miranda became a guiding force behind the revolution, organizing rebels against the crown. From 1811 to 1821, Simón Bolívar actually led the rebel forces, liberating Venezuela and much of the rest of Spanish America. His country joined other Latin American countries in the union Gran Colombia, then became a separate nation in 1830.

Independence. Bolívar believed that the best way to build Venezuela was to keep it under a military government. Some people feel this began a pattern of army authority all over South America. Here in Venezuelan, the pattern continued through the remainder of the 1800s, which were fraught with fighting. Slavery was abolished in 1854, so it no longer caused revolts, but civil wars broke out between regions of the country. Presidents were overthrown by force, and the rule of the military continued through the turn of the century.

A succession of three military dictators ruled the country at the beginning of the 20th century, then gave way to what is now one of the most democratic governments in Latin America. In the era of the dictators, the army, who supported the rich, struggled against Venezuelans who desired freedoms. The three dictators were General Cipriano Castro, General Juan Vicente Gómez and General Marcos Pérez Jiménez. Toward the end of Goméz's reign (1908-35), oil was discovered in Venezuela and some of the people grew very rich. Gómez ruled over this wealth with a cruel hand, so cruel that when he died the Venezuelans burned his property and the property of anyone associated with him. The democratic governments that followed were interrupted by two coups d'état in the 1940s. Jiménez came to power as the military dictator in 1948.

General Marcos Pérez Jiménez controlled the army and Venezuela until 1958. By then, even the army was unhappy with his cruel government and supported a popular revolt. Jímenez fled, in his haste forgetting a suitcase with millions of dollars allegedly earned by Venezuela's oil. All presidents have since been chosen in democratic elections.

Rómulo Betancourt served as president from 1959 to 1964. Large cacao plantations had given way to smaller coffee farms in the 1800s, and these had given way to oil in the 1900s, making the country rich but leaving many of the people as poverty stricken as ever before. The great gap between the rich and the poor brought government reforms. Betancourt began to reform land ownership, but crop failures caused a depression in the early 1960s. Change has since been slow.

During the 1970s, the government began to settle peasant farmers on new land. By then, though, the people depended on oil and other manufacturing activities rather than on agriculture. A result is that over 80 percent now live in cities, and 12 of these cities each have a population of over 100,000. In 1980, there were nearly three million Venezuelans living in the capital, Caracas.

Venezuelan farm

Culture Today

Ethnic groups. About 69 percent of Venezuelans are of mixed Indian and European ancestry. Of the remaining population, whites make up 20 percent, blacks 9 percent and Amerindians 2 percent. The whites are mainly Europeans – Spaniards, Portuguese, Italians, Germans. In general, the Germans have been prominent in Venezuelan business.

Economy. As oil became the most important export in the late 1960s and early 1970s, landless farmers moved to the cities and towns to work in industry or the oil fields. Today industry employs more Venezuelans than farming. Some of the workers manufacture petroleum products for the government, which has owned the oil industry since 1976. Private industry is devoted mainly to consumer goods (automobiles, textiles, food processing).

In the the 20th century, several types of farming have prevailed. Peasants work for wages on large sugar, coffee, banana, corn, rice or cotton farms. Others farm small family plots, raising corn and rice for food or coffee and cacao for sale. Between the Andes farmland and the Orinoco River are large cattle ranches of the llanos. The area south of the Orinoco River is mostly jungle in which people rely on more than farming. (see YANOMAMO).

Food, clothing and shelter. Black beans are an everyday food in the Venezuelan diet. Other common foods are the bananalike plantain and rice that is eaten with beef, pork, chicken, or fish. Today, Venezuelans can buy wheat bread at city supermarkets and hamburgers at fast-food stands. However, they seem to prefer *arepa* – hot, round cornmeal bread filled with meat or cheese A popular beverage is *batido*, tropical fruits that are ground into a thick maltlike drink.

Caracas is one of the world's most modern cities, largely due to construction inspired by oil money. Its old Spanish-style homes with central courtyards have mostly been replaced by high-rise apartment houses. Contrasts are great in the city. For example, a giant, twin-towered business complex, Simón Bolívar Center, sits in downtown Caracas. Wood-frame and plastered *ranchos* (poor shacks) line the hills above the city, overlooking the giant business center.

Caracas, Venezuela

With the mass of peasants moving to the city, hundreds of ranchos appeared along the city edges. The ranchos were constructed on government-owned land, the tenants paying no rent for its use. Though the government has allowed them to remain, it also has built low-cost apartment units in the city. Some cannot afford even these, and others who can afford the low-cost units sometimes prefer the community atmosphere of the rancho settlements.

Clothing in rancho and other city communities resembles dress in North America. Various styles are seen in small Venezuelan towns at the open markets in which small farmers sell their produce. Townspeople in business suits mingle with poor peasants in loose-fitting pajamalike clothing.

Religion. The open markets are held in the central square around which most small towns are built. A dependable sight in most Venezuelan towns, a church also appears in this square. The majority of people practice the Roman Catholic religion. With the rule of the German Welsers, Protestant beliefs also took root in the country. A Protestant minority exists in Venezuela today.

Education. Though settlers brought a number of languages into the country, Spanish is the common tongue. Eighty-six percent have learned to read and write in this language. Education is required between the ages of seven and 13 but the dropout rate is great. Only about 50 percent of the students attend school for the entire period. To encourage higher education, the government awards scholarships at the university level.

Arts. There is a tradition in Venezuela of involvement by government leaders not only in education, but also in art. Rómulo Gallegos, president of the country in 1947, was also a teacher and author of novels about his country. One of his earliest, *Doña Barbara,* concerns a beautiful, crafty mestizo (Indian and Spanish) woman who sets her sights on acquiring ranch land on the llanos. Another of his novels, *Cantaclaro*, deals with Venezuela's minstrels, or wandering musicians. A later novelist Miguel Otero Silva wrote *Oficina Número 1*, about the growth of an oil city in the changing nation.

Music is a longstanding art in Venezuela. In the late 1700s, mulatto composers formed a music group. One of its members, Lino Gallardo, composed the national anthem, "*Gloria al Bravo Pueblo*" (Glory to the Brave People). A mulatto physician, slave owner and double-bass player, Luis Landaeta composed pieces copied through the 1800s. Music continued to flourish through the efforts of other Venezuelans. In the 20th century, Vicente Emilio Sojo is an acclaimed symphony director.

Since the end of the 1800s, the *joropo* has been a popular form of music and dance. The dance has stamping movements, much like those of a frisky horse. Written by Luis Felipe Ramón y Rivera, the book *La música popular de Venezuela* (*Venezuelan popular music*) discusses additional forms.

Recreation. In recreation, there is a blend of the old and new. *Coleados* is a pastime in which horsemen flip a bull by the tail. Probably the most popular sport, baseball has given rise to Venezuelan stars (Dave Concepción, Luis Aparicio) recruited to play on major league teams in the United States.

Government. Since most Venezuelans live in the valleys and lowlands of the Andes Mountains, the population in this area exercises much control in government. Representatives from all areas sit in the lawmaking houses: the Senate and the Chamber of Deputies. The people elect these representatives, as they do the president. A president's term in office is five years, and he may not run for immediate re-election.

In 1984, Jaime Lusinchi won the election for president. One of his first acts was to curb government spending so Venezuela could repay foreign debts. His program led to some unrest in the 1980s, because many are still poor and ill fed. Despite such differences, reforms have improved life in Venezuela. The government builds low-cost housing, provides scholarships in education, and enjoys one of the best reputations in Latin America for respecting human rights.

XINGU PARK INDIANS

(shing goo´ park)

Various native peoples of the Xingu River valley in
the highlands south of the Amazon River in Brazil.

Xingu Park is reserved
for groups of native
South Americans.

Population: 800 (1974).
Location: Brazil.
Language: Carib, Tupi, Arawakan, and Trumaí
languages, depending on the specific group.

Geographical Setting

The Xingu River flows northeast through the
Amazon Jungle to join the Amazon River as it
empties into the Atlantic Ocean in northeast Brazil.
Lying just south of the equator, the Xingu River
basin is hot and damp. Many smaller rivers join to
form the Xingu, various Indian peoples living
near the point where they merge. The area is thick
with tropical rainforests and large lagoons that are
surrounded by fields and fertile soil. Fish are
plentiful, and there is an abundance of animal life
– wild pigs, dogs, deer, otters, monkeys,
porcupines, anteaters, eagles, alligators, and
snakes. So dense is the forest that little contact
was made with peoples who lived here until the
Brazilian government began to develop the region
and built an airport in the Xingu area.

Historical Background

Origin. Of the 16 Indian groups living in the
Xingu Park area, ten display such similarity in
their lifestyles that they have come to be regarded
as one people. Known as the Xinguanos, they
appear to have descended from a number of tribes
who attacked and conquered local residents in the
Xingu River area. Two of the groups – the Bakirí

and the Auetö – prevailed in these wars and were in turn defeated by the Trumaí.

According to the Indians, they once lived north of their present home, subsisting on fish, fruits, wild roots, and a variety of game. The men generally wore their hair long and used strings of vegetable fiber for clothing while the women wore straps of bark below their waists. They migrated to the upper Xingu River area around the beginning of the 19th century and began merging with other peoples there, including the Camayura, the Carib, and the Aruak.

Contacts with Brazilians. Karl von den Steinen descended a branch of the Xingu River, spotting various groups of the region in the 1880s. Others studied the upper Xingu River area in the early 1900s, but outsiders did not penetrate the region until the 1940s. Needing airstrips and weather stations near the Upper Xingu River, the Brazilians cleared land there for military use. Three brothers – Orlando, Claudio, and Leonardo Villas Boas – entered the area at this time, leading an expedition to open up the interior for colonization. After the expedition disbanded, the Villas Boas brothers remained to protect the Xinguanos from land speculators, diamond prospectors, animal hunters, and rubber gatherers. They made contact with other Indians of the area (the Juruna, the Suiá) and worked to protect their cultures as well in the 1950s and

Recognizing the effort of the Villas Boas brothers, the government created Brazil's first national Indian park in 1961. In this same year, Leonardo Villas Boas died. The two remaining brothers, Orlando and Claudio, continued their efforts on behalf of the Indians. Originally about 8,000 square miles, the national park was enlarged to 11,500 square miles in 1968. The government granted Orlando and Claudio the right to keep out strangers, but the Villas Boas brothers

Art from the Xingu Park Indians.

were unable to prevent settlers from moving onto upper Xingu lands.

Culture Today

Xinguano groups. About 800 Xinguanos populate ten of the 16 groups in the region. These ten live in separate villages and speak different languages. Otherwise they operate in close cooperation with one another under a system of mutual dependence that has led to a common lifestyle. To overcome the language barrier between villages, these groups have developed an "apprenticeship" program. An apprentice is a Xinguano who moves to a neighboring village to learn its people's language.

Trade. Xinguano groups specialize in certain commodities. The Trumaí prepare salt, burning water lilies and sifting the ashes to make the seasoning. The Arawakens manufacture pottery. Others specialize in stone axes, and still others in the crafting of necklaces from shells. Intertribal trading occurs at ceremonies presided over by chiefs of the villages. Foreign products – yarn, cloth, fishhooks, paper, and beads – have now joined the catalog of items for trade. Thus, the outside world is adapted to the traditional ways.

Food, clothing and shelter. Customary dress includes belts of cotton thread or bark fiber and body paint for men. The men paint intricate geometric patterns on their hair, chests, and backs, using an orange-red dye. For ceremonies, they wear shell necklaces and headdresses that have a ring of cotton threads with colored feathers. Men's hair is cut straight around their heads to the top of their ears.

Women cut the hair on their foreheads, leaving bangs. Their traditional dress includes a cord belt worn about five inches below the waist and the *uluri*, a straw triangle. While a red stripe of paint sometimes crosses their foreheads, women lightly cover the rest of their bodies with a more orange shade than is worn by men.

The forests, rivers, and fields surrounding the Xinguano are rich in wildlife that either threatens or sustains them. The Indians fish, hunt, gather foods, and raise a variety of crops (manioc, maize, yams, beans, sweet potatoes, fruits).

Manioc is a staple in the diet. The people eat and drink the starch, fermenting it to prepare the beverage *cauim*. In the first months of the rainy season (October to April), fruit from the pequi tree becomes the staple. About the size of a grapefruit, the pequi fruit has green skin and is eaten raw or cooked. Both manioc and pequi are prepared into gruel.

For meat, the people hunt deer, ducks, and *mutum* (large black birds). Turtle eggs are popular, and the Indians catch a troutlike fish from their lagoons. Nets, baskets, and night fishing with torches are the traditional methods. The boundaries of a group's fishing area are clearly set to avoid conflict between the peoples. Natural threats present enough trouble. Crocodiles and electric eels may menace efforts in the waters; wild pigs sometimes trample Xinguano crops.

Villages are often built two miles or farther from the Xingu River. The size of a village ranges from 30 to 200 inhabitants. At the center of many villages is a cleared area of hardened earth with a house for the spirit *Jakuí*. Sometimes called the "flute house," it serves as a gathering place where men of the village talk as they make fish traps, arrows, or spirit masks and costumes. Around the flute house stands a circle of large, haystack-shaped, windowless grass family houses. Their framework consists of posts made from the hardwood trees of the forests. Measuring 30 by 65 feet and standing 25 feet high, a house is shared by several families, each with its own section for a fire and hammocks.

Social life. Xinguano families are small nuclear units, including a husband, a wife, and their children. Marriage ceremonies are simple. The Trumaí ceremony requires the presentation and acceptance of a hammock and other gifts.

Men have separate social lives from women, the men holding evening meetings in the center of a village. Smoking is common at such meetings. It is believed that magical use of tobacco allows a smoker to have meaningful visions.

Boys and girls may be isolated for weeks or months during ceremonies that initiate them into adulthood. Before going into isolation, they drink a beverage of bark and sap from the *manucaía* tree so they will grow tall and straight. Usually the drink is thrown up. One group of Xinguanos, the Camayura, holds an ear-piercing festival for adolescent boys before secluding them in a village house. Passage into manhood for Trumaí boys has included making scars on the body with fish-tooth instruments and wrestling with a boa.

Recreation. Wrestling is a standard form of recreation among the men. Opponents begin a wrestling match by circling each other as they utter "huca, huca, huca." Afterwards, they drop to their knees, slap each other's hands, and lunge forward to fell their adversaries. Sport for children has included battledore (a form of badminton), played with a maize husk topped by a feather.

Government. Chiefs exist among the people, but their authority is limited. The traditional Trumaí chief, for example, assigns work and assembles fishing, hunting, or farming teams. While females may become chiefs, they have less authority than male chiefs. Yet their status among women is high and visible. A female chief has tattoos – three small parallel lines on her wrists, shoulders, and thighs.

Religion. The Xinguano hold elaborate burial ceremonies for a person of chiefly birth. Tree trunks or posts are erected in the center of the village to represent the dead leader, and singers chant tunes over the posts. Men play the *curuta* (a sacred flute) that is thought to be the voice of the spirit Jakuí. Xinguanos believe the four-foot flutes to be the spirit itself, and prohibit women from watching them played.

In general, the Xinguano believe in good and evil spirits. Some groups put their shamans (religious leaders) through harsh training – fasting, knocking the head against posts, and scarring the body. Generally, shamans work to protect the members of their group from evil. Witchcraft for good and evil purposes is common practice.

Arts. The Xinguanos are skilled artists and crafts people. Spinning, weaving, basketry, and the carving of wooden benches (the *apüka*) are common. Having a rectangular seat with two side planks, many benches are carved in the shape of a bird. Perhaps most remarkable are tree carvings, in which images have been shaped of men, women, and animals. Geometric designs are said to represent animal life . For example, reappearing triangles stand for bats.

Xinguano ceremonies include music and dance. One dance features men in fiber skirts and feather headdresses with leafy branches tied to their arms and shoulders. Their movements are accompanied by singing and the playing of instruments. Bamboo tubes hit the ground and gourd rattles shake. Popular among the Xinguano are wind instruments – whistles made from palm nuts, panpipes, and the *flageolet* (a piece of bamboo with four holes and an air duct).

Xinguanos have a rich oral literature. Several tales are about the adventures of the kindly spirit Jakuí. Other folk characters are a sleep-inducing tree, an enchanted canoe, and various creators of items in the Indians' world. A Trumaí myth explains differences among Xinguano groups and outsiders: Sun offered each group a choice of things. The Trumaí chose beeswax and the Camayura selected pots. As for the whites, they picked the ax, then used it to build outside civilization.

YANOMAMO

(yah no mah´ mo)

Also called YANOAMA. The largest surviving group of
Indian forest people in South America.

Population: 12,000 (1983).
Location: Venezuela, Brazil.
Language: Yanomamo.

Geographical Setting

The land of the Yanomamo spreads across the
border between Brazil and Venezuela by the
country of Guyana. Yanomamo territory is dense
forestland with some grassy savanna in the north.
Lying in the heart of the region, the Parima plain
has been a center of Yanomamo settlements.
Various rivers drain the region, including the
upper Orinoco and its tributaries. Extending from
four degrees north down to the equator, the area
has a tropical climate. The dry season lasts from
November through April, the wet season from
May through October. A wide variety of plants
and animals live in the tropical forests, but the
topsoil is shallow and does not lend itself to long-
term farming. Instead inhabitants have hunted,
gathered, or used slash-and-burn farming in
which land is cleared, used, and then abandoned
to be reforested.

The Yanomamo live in
Brazil and Venezuela.

Historical Background

Conflict with whites. Only recently have
these Indians been contacted and studied by
outsiders. Historians believe that their lifestyle has
undergone little change over the past five
centuries. In the 1940s as white settlers moved
near Yanomamo communities, the Indians

293

observed items they had never seen before –
robust dogs, steel tools, and kettles used for
cooking. The items were so unfamiliar to the
Yanomamo that many thought smoke from the
kettles gave birth to demons who made their way
into human bodies, causing pain and death.

More generally, the Yanomamo regarded the
whites as enemies. Before the coming of the
whites, raids were frequent between Yanomamo
villages, a common goal being to capture women
for marriage. The tools of the white settlers
inspired similar raids on their settlements. After a
short attempt at survival, most of these whites
abandoned their settlements, leaving the Indians to
live as they had for centuries.

Change. In some areas, missionaries remained
and life for the Indians changed. They attended
Mass, went to school, and spent less and less time
in the forest. Beginning in 1972, La Esmeralda
boarding school re-educated some of the children.
Their hair was cut, their personal names taken
away, clothing given to them, and the Spanish
language taught. Afterwards, the children returned
home ill-suited to life in a traditional community.

Culture Today

Organization. The Yanomamo are organized
into several groups (the Waica, the Sanemá).
Speaking different languages that appear to be
related to each other, the groups live in
approximately 125 villages. Each group is divided
into bands of several extended (related) families
that live together in a village. The village might
have anywhere from 50 to 150 residents.

Food, clothing and shelter. The groups have
developed a relationship with the forest that
permeates their daily activities. Using the poles,
vines, and leaves that surround them, the
Yanomamo construct various types of homes. A
common type of shelter is the *shabono*. From a

A Yanomamo shelter

distance, it appears to be a single circular dwelling but is actually a coordinated series of individual houses. Each family builds its own section of a common roof. Men plant poles in the ground for the frame and weave thousands of leaves into thatch for the covering. Each home is separated from the next by several feet of open space. Since the spaces are thatched, the village appears as one continuous circular roof around an open plaza.

Everyday dress has traditionally included strings or belts worn around the waists for men. Yanomamo women use cotton yarn to make a small waistband, armbands, and a loose, multistringed, halter-type garment that crosses over the front and back. Single strings are often worn around the wrists, ankles, and knees. For ornaments, some wear polished pieces of stick through the nose, ears, or mouth.

Clothing is one of the first ways in which contact with outsiders has begun to affect the Yanomamo. Missionaries influenced some communities to adopt other clothing. Young men in particular have come to regard loincloths and short pants as desirable items of dress.

The Yanomamo cultivate gardens that provide 80 to 90 percent of their diet. They practice slash-and-burn agriculture, but stay in the same general area when clearing new land for planting. Their most common popular crop, the bananalike plantain, is often roasted and eaten as a main dish. Manioc is a staple they make into flour, then bake into bread. Other widely cultivated crops are bananas, sweet potatoes, avocados, papaya, hot peppers, and tobacco. On occasion, the bananas are prepared into soup. Tobacco is chewed by most of the people throughout the day.

About 10 percent of the foods in the Yanomamo diet are acquired by hunting and gathering. The forest provides the people with a variety of game – birds, monkeys, wild pigs, tapir, armadillos, anteaters, alligators, and deer.

A Yanomamo girl decorated for a feast.

By Napoleon Chagnon. Courtesy Anthro Photo

Using bows and arrows, the Indians hunt these animals and catch fish. To supplement the diet, the people gather fruits, nuts, mushrooms, insects, and honey from the forest. Roasted caterpillars are a prized dish.

Religion. The Yanomamo cultivate a variety of plants for religious purposes. Shamans use the plants for curing the sick or for casting spells of misfortune. To treat the sick, these religious healers use sucking, massaging, and numerous magical cures. To cast a spell, they attack what is considered the weakest part of the soul. Stealing this part of the soul supposedly causes a victim to sicken and die.

When a Yanomamo dies, the body is cremated and the soul is thought to be released in parts – one part wanders in the jungle, while the central part travels on hammock ropes to an upper world. There the soul is asked if it has been generous or stingy during life. The stingy are directed to a place of fire, and the generous are directed to a place where they continue to lead a peaceful, mortal type of existence.

According to Yanomamo religion, the universe is composed of four layers. The uppermost layer is a void where many things had their origin. The second layer is a heaven that is similar to earth and inhabited by the souls of dead Yanomamo. The third layer consists of the sky, the earth, and humans. Consisting of a barren surface below earth, the fourth level is home to the *Amahiri-teri*. These are cannibals who capture the souls of children, then carry them down to the underworld and eat them.

The place of men. In Yanomamo society, men are considered superior to women, and traditional tales reflect this belief. One myth explains the creation of the Yanomamo, ascribing heavenly origins to men and earthly origins to women. An ancestor shot the moon in the belly, and its blood dripped down to produce men. A fruit known as *wabu* produced women.

The Yanomamo believe that men should dominate the political and family life of the people. Including a headman and a war chief, village leaders are male. Children are considered members of their father's line of ancestors, and a man may have several wives. Husbands may beat a wife for "just cause" – for example, slowness in preparing meals.

Competition. The men take great pride in their ferocity, as demonstrated in sports and in conflicts between Yanomamo villages. At feasts, they stage chest-pounding duels in which one man strikes another on the chest. The number of blows sustained before demanding a turn at striking back at an opponent is a measure of fierceness.

Fierceness is also displayed in the serious business of raiding villages. This is done in retaliation for sorcery, murder, and similar misdeeds. The main goals are to kill an enemy without being discovered and to capture women.

Cooperation. Entire villages may move because of the threat of hostile neighbors, or a village may join forces with another village against enemies. Members of such an alliance obligate themselves to provide shelter and food to each other whenever either is driven away from home by a powerful enemy.

The Yanomamo also form trade alliances that allow them to exchange items in which a village specializes. Items of trade include dogs, arrow points and shafts, bows, cotton yarn, hammocks, and products acquired from outsiders.

Ceremony. Visitors to a Yanomamo village may introduce themselves through a traditional dance. In the *Dance of Presentation*, men jog in opposite directions around the perimeter of their central plaza, carrying palm fronds and decorated arrows. Interrupting their progress, they stop and dance in the same spot from time to time, then continue until everyone has presented himself. The men paint their bodies for these occasions, adding ornaments such as feathers in their earlobes and monkey tails around their brows.

YAQUI

(ya´key)

Indians of Sonora, Mexico, who continually fought for
their native homeland and traditional ways.

Population: 25,000 (1980?).
Location: Sonora in northern Mexico.
Language: Yaqui, Spanish, English.

The Yaqui live in
the state of Sonora
in Mexico.

Geographical Setting

Stretching across 70,500 square miles,
Sonora is a vast state in northwest Mexico that
borders United States territory. Arizona and New
Mexico lie to the north of it and the Gulf of
California to the west. Sierra Madre mountains
appear in the eastern section of Sonora. The
western section has flat land while the coast is
rocky and humid. Flowing southward and
westward through the state is the Yaqui River, by
which the Indians of the same settled. Due to
biyearly floods, the region has rich farmland, an
object of much struggle throughout history.

Historical Background

Spanish arrival. When Spaniards entered
Sonora in the 16th century, they found the Yaqui
Indians living in about 80 small communities.
Each *ranchería*, or community, had perhaps 250
members whose men had learned fierce fighting in
conflicts with the Apache Indians. Insisting the
region was rightfully theirs, the Yaquis warriors
defeated the Spanish invaders first in 1533 and
again in 1609-1610. Their stubborn resistance
would continue to the 20th century.

Jesuits. Jesuit missionaries protected the Yaquis
from 1620 to 1790, meanwhile changing their

lifestyle. As missions replaced the rancherías, the average settlement grew to 3,500 members. Staging plays of biblical events, the Jesuits taught Roman Catholic beliefs. The Yaquis adopted these beliefs, blending them with the traditional religion. **Warfare**. The Yaquis lived in harmony with the Jesuits until 1740 when they joined the neighboring Mayo Indians in their fight against the Spaniards. While 5,000 Yaquis perished in battle, the warriors managed to keep Spaniards out of their territory for a century afterwards.

Meanwhile, the mission communities grew into eight towns, each built around a plaza with a church in the center Mexican settlers moved into the region, and in 1825, Juan Banderas led an Indian revolt to drive them out. He succeeded, then was captured and executed, his death marking the start of a stormy century of conflict.

Mexico's central government attempted to confiscate large tracts of fertile Yaquis land in the 1800s. A private enterprise, the Mexican-North American Sonora and Sinola Irrigation Company, received a grant of 547,000 acres in the Yaqui valley. Though 30,000 Yaquis lived in the area, it was believed that the new tools, livestock, and clothes brought here by the company would turn the Indians into contented colonists. Instead there was open warfare from 1875 to 1886 between Yaquis warriors and Mexican troops. After the Yaqui leader Juan Maria Leyua was captured and executed, some of the Indians formed guerrilla bands and fought secretly from the hills. Support came from other Yaquis, who worked on Mexican ranches and the railroad, quietly sending supplies to the guerrillas in the hills.

The guerrilla war continued for close to 30 years, ultimately leading to a massacre. In 1900, 400 Yaqui fighters at the mountain stronghold of Mazacoba surrendered and then were shot by Mexican troops. Among the executed was the Yaqui leader Juan Maldonado, who inspired the people's resistance. Those suspected of aiding the guerrillas were also executed, and the Yaquis were then forcibly moved out of their territory.

Deportations. From 1903 to 1907, the government deported these Indians from their homes in Sonora to plantations in Yucatán. They were sent to harsh labor on henequen (rope) plantations, hacienda owners paying 65 pesos for each Indian deported. A few landowners – José María Maytorena, for example – prevented Yaqui workers they had hired from being deported. Thousands of Indians were victims of the policy, though. In just three years, Colonel Francisco B. Cruz deported 15,700 Yaquis. With the outbreak of the Mexican Revolution in 1910, the deportations stopped. The exceptional ability of the Yaqui warriors made them valuable soldiers in the Revolution.

Resettlement. Afterwards the Yaqui were a widely-scattered people. Their guerrilla fighters continued to wage war in Sonora, so Mexican forces occupied Yaqui towns in 1910 and 1928. The government set aside 20 percent of the original Yaquis territory for the Indians in 1937, but newspapers carried reports of guerrilla activity until 1950. Meanwhile, most Yaquis returned to their homes in Sonora, though a few thousand settled near Tucson, Arizona. The communities grew.

By the 1970s, there were communities of 500 to 1000 Yaquis outside Sonora in areas such as the one near Tucson. Inside Sonora, the largest of the eight Yaqui towns had 4,500 inhabitants. Remaining separate from surrounding Mexicans, the Yaquis maintained certain traditional and 17th century Spanish ways. Even outside Sonora, in Arizona, the people maintain their heritage., maing their streets after the eight towns in Sonora and the hero Juan Maldonado (also known as *Tetabiate*).

Culture Today

Government. In Sonora, the Yaquis have worked to revive the original eight towns established in Jesuit times. Their years of stubborn defiance brought some gains, as they now control their local governments. Mexico's central government keeps a small garrison in town to handle matters such as murder or property disputes. Otherwise, the people rule themselves in accordance with their highly-structured system of the past.

Each year the Yaquis elect five governors to manage five areas of life – civil affairs and family disputes, church affairs, military affairs, festivals and funerals, and Holy Week activities. The governors convene at weekly meetings, a time set aside for open criticism and discussion.

Education. Education has been a subject of some controversy. An educational program promoted by the Mexican government was unpopular at first, as it required students to leave home towns for agricultural training at a central facility. Then the training was brought to the people, a number of schools being built in their region. Attendance began to increase.

Food, clothing and shelter. In meeting their basic needs, the Yaquis resemble their neighbors. The first changes in dress came from the Spanish, the men adopting cotton pants and palmetto hats and the women wearing embroidered shirts with long skirts. European-style clothing remains common, except during religious ceremonies.

The people earn their livelihood in a mix of old and new ways. Some hire themselves out as laborers in mines or on ranches, earning wages and reputations as hard workers. Others raise wheat, vegetables, sheep, and cattle for sale.

Practicing their traditional activities, the Yaquis also farm, hunt, and fish for food. Their staple crops are corn, beans, and squash. For meat, they hunt deer, wild pig, wood rats. Other items in the diet are turtle, cactus fruits, and oysters. For coffee, they trade with Mexican storekeepers.

The basic unit in Yaqui society is a household. Its boundaries are often defined by a fence around the household buildings, animal pens, and storage platforms. Today there are adobe houses as well as the traditional wattle-and-mud and mat-covered structures. The standard house has had one or two rooms with a separate *ramada* (a roofed area without walls) nearby for cooking. It is customary for related families to share the household.

Religion and ceremonial life. A cross stands at the edge of household property. The Yaquis continue to blend Catholic and earlier beliefs. Along with spirits of the dead, they honor Christian figures such as the Virgin of Guadalupe. Their community Belem is thought of as Bethlehem, and many insist Christ was born there.

Group activities are central to religious life. The Yaquis have cults whose members dance, sing, and bless the people, oftentimes visiting their households to do so. Clad in blankets, one cult wears military-style helmet-masks, creating tension in the first half of the year. During the second half, pleasure replaces the tension as different cults appear. The entertaining *pascolas* (animal mimers) dance and make witty remarks, usually in the company of a deer dancer. Wearing kilts and stuffed deer heads, the deer dancers wrap their antlers in ribbons and flowers. Music and song accompany the dance, increasing to a feverish pace.

Arts. There is vigorous activity in Yaquis arts. Their musicians play gourd rattles, drums, violins, and the harp. In theater, the people enact dramas with religious plots introduced by the

Jesuits – for example, the conquest of the Moors by Christians.

Clowning is customary. Dressed in foolish masks, the clowns are the torchbearers of the people's oral literature. They tell Yaqui tales, such as "The First Deer Hunter," about life before the Spanish. Others such as "The Wars Against the Mexicans" concern later experiences. Thus, the literature grows.

As in other areas of life, the Yaquis have broadened their arts over the years. Poetry first appeared only in song. Then Refugio Savala wrote verse in 1930s, using the Yaqui language. During their years as a scattered people, the Yaquis learned Spanish and English as second languages. Yaquis has remained their first language. Along with their ceremonies, it has preserved their identity as a people.

ZAPOTECS

(za´ pu teks´).
A group of native Indians in Mexico who descend from
a great ancient civilization.

Population: 300,000 (1970).
Location: Oaxaca in southern Mexico.
Language: Zapotec (a general language spoken
in different versions), Spanish.

The Zatopec people
live in southeastern
Mexico.

Geographical Setting

Resting on the southern Pacific coast, the state
of Oaxaca in Mexico is mostly mountainous. The
Zapotec people occupy four areas: the rich Valley
of Oaxaca, the mountains to the north, the isthmus
region to the southeast, and another mountainous
area to the south. In the Valley of Oaxaca, fertile
soil lends itself to farming. Tropical areas appear
along the coast and in the east on the Isthmus of
Tehuantepec.

With its gentle slopes and scrub growth, the
Oaxaca Valley was an early center of Zapotec
civilization. The ruins of the ancient capital Monte
Albán – pyramids, stairways, and tombs – sit on a
mountain ridge a thousand feet above the valley.
When the Mixtec Indians took control of the
Valley, the center of Zapotecs life shifted to the
isthmus region, which includes rolling plains,
jungle and brush, and port towns. Today's
Zapotecs mainly live in the valley and isthmus
areas.

Historical Background

Before the Spanish. Mixtec Indians and
Zapotec Indians occupied the area before the
arrival of the Spanish, both calling themselves the

Cloud People. (*Zapotec* means "People of the Zapote," a tree of the region.)

The Zapotecs can be traced back to 1500 B.C. They developed a highly sophisticated civilization over the centuries, building the first city to appear in either Latin America or North America – Monte Albán. In Monte Albán, the early Zapotecs painted murals, formed pottery, developed a writing system, and built pyramids. Farming became a major activity.

The farmers ground their maize into flour for tortillas, then combined them with turkey meat to make a type of tamale. They prepared cacao beans as a chocolate beverage. Adding variety to the early diet were tomato, chili, squash and wild foods (cactus fruit, nuts, avocados, guavas). A versatile plant, maguey was prepared as food, syrup, pulque (an alcoholic beverage), and fiber for clothing. Hunting provided the upper classes with meats (rabbit, turkey, deer).

Society was highly structured, including nobles, priests, commoners, serfs, and slaves. There were rules pertaining to dress, diet, and language. Noblemen wore brightly-woven cotton mantles and loincloths while commoners wore clothing of maguey fiber. Only the nobles could eat turkey, deer, and other meats and a special set of pronouns was used when speaking to them. The commoners – peasants, weavers, artists, and curers – paid tribute to both nobles and priests. Since the slaves were captives who had been taken in war, they formed a changing population.

The captives were used for human sacrifice to Zapotec gods. The early Zapotecs had ten major gods and goddesses – deities of infinity, rain, earthquakes, food, man and animals, children, the underworld, the sun, and love. Each of the individual communities also had its own god.

Communities in the Oaxaca Valley were overpowered by the Mixtecs in the 14th century. The center of Zapotec life then moved to the isthmus, where the Zapotecs remained independent when the Aztecs appeared. Marriage between the Zapotec king and an Aztec princess is known to have helped keep the peace.

Spanish rule. Life changed after the Spanish conquered the region in 1521. In the mountain areas, Zapotecs kept to themselves, but those in the Oaxaca Valley played a large role in Mexican history.

Led by individual lords, Zapotec communities were continually fighting one another. Some of the lords sent a statesmen to visit the conqueror Hernando Cortés so the Spanish would become their allies. Bargaining with Cortés, the statesman promised that the Zapotecs would become Christians if they received military aid from the Spanish. The bargain was sealed, and Dominican, Franciscan, Augustine, and Jesuit missionaries moved in to convert the people.

Afterwards, the Zapotecs were stripped of other native ways. Their temples were destroyed, then replaced by Spanish-style churches. Reduced to only peasants, the people lost their system of social classes. Under the *encomienda* system, whole Zapotec towns were granted to individual Spaniards, who were entitled to labor and payment from the townspeople. The system was eventually abandoned because of injustices, but the Zapotecs continued to pay taxes to the Spanish crown.

A number of Zapotecs became hacienda laborers. The *hacendado* (hacienda owner) would advance the Zapotec money, a small plot for family use, and medical care in exchange for labor on hacienda crops. By the end of the colonial period (1821), the Zapotecs were a subject people. Few traces of the early lifestyle remained, and many had become poverty stricken.

Mexican rule. The Zapotecs revolted in 1531, 1570, and the 1660s to free themselves of Spanish control. They were successful only in Mexico's

War of Independence in the 1820s. A full-blooded Zapotec, the soldier Benito Juárez became one of Mexico's greatest liberators in this war, then went on to serve as president of Mexico in the 1850s.

As president, Juárez fought for constitutional government and attacked privileges enjoyed by the Church and the army. His program, *La Reforma*, intended to transfer political power from a wealthy few to the mass of Mexican citizens. When Porfirio Díaz took over as president, this plan was abandoned, and a few wealthy Mexicans gained power. Afterwards, the Zapotecs did not play a leading role in the Mexican government. Instead they remained in their communities, farming and sometimes working as laborers in Mexican tobacco or sugar cane fields. Since 1945, many Zapotecs have taken jobs as *braceros* (agricultural laborers) in the United States.

Culture Today

Variations. The lifestyle of the Zapotecs today depends on the area in which the people live and the degree to which they have accepted Spanish and Mexican ways. What Zapotec communities share are a grand history, some general customs, and a common language. The version of this language changes from pueblo to pueblo, so one town may not understand the next.

Economy. A division of labor exists in society today. Zapotec peasants may become corn, chile, coffee, or vegetable farmers. There are lawyers, musicians, and healers. In fact, whole communities specialize. Teotitlán is renown for cloth weaving, while Atzomba is famous for green-glazed pottery. Other towns are centers of trade, becoming crowded masses of stalls, street vendors, and buyers on market day.

The main activity continues to be subsistence farming, though the Zapotec sell surplus crops and operate small industries (potterymaking, clothing, footwear). While some land is community owned, private holdings are more common. A peasant may own up to 20 parcels, the plots appearing in different areas of the community rather in than one large block. Though campsites may be set up by their plots, permanent homes are built in Zapotec villages and towns.

Food, clothing and shelter. Habits in food, clothing, and housing change with the area of settlement. In the Oaxaca Valley, the Zapotecs raise maize and beans as their staples, adding foods from other crops (coffee, wheat, peanuts, mangoes, coconut palms) to the diet. Mountain Zapotecs gather vegetables and grasshoppers for food, while the isthmus Zapotecs fish for shrimp and trout. Popular in all areas, tortillas are eaten at every meal.

Early Zapotec houses are described as one-room structures, rectangles with no windows and a pitched roof. Today, many Zapotecs live in one-room, single-story homes built of adobe walls with tile roofs. Other house types are palm-roofed structures and two-story whitewashed homes. As a rule, the village stands around a central plaza in which there are a city building, church, and school. Built last, the school may be a brick structure with glass windows and a tin roof.

Clothing has changed over time. Once men mostly wore loose pants, colorful shirts, *sombreros* (broad-brimmed hats), and *huaraches* (sandals). Women wore the *huipil*, a sleeved-tunic with a wraparound skirt, lengths and colors changing with the town. Now many women wear factory-made dresses while men wear tailored pants, shirts, shoes, and straw hats.

Family life. Today the basic social unit is the small nuclear family. According to custom, girls marry from age eight to 20, and boys from 12 to 20. Success in getting a bride involves a ritual – the boy captures the girl to avoid paying her family a brideprice. Afterwards, the couple lives with the boy's parents until the birth of the first child.

The head of the household is the father, who handles the crops, the cattle, and the horses. Meanwhile, the mother cooks, washes, raises the children, and cares for the chickens and pigs. While men construct roads and buildings in a community, trading is done by Zapotec women, and those by the isthmus have earned a high reputation for their skill.

Religion. Both men and women officiate at religious ceremonies. Acceptance of the Catholic religion was fairly easy because of its similarities to Zapotec beliefs. The people simply substituted a Catholic patron saint for their community god, often transferring traits of the old god to the saint. There have been continuing beliefs in witches and in evil spirits who cause illness. It is thought that envy leads to *muina*, a sickness that may paralyze a victim. Fright leads to a loss of the soul and may end in death. To cure both ailments, the people call on Zapotec healers.

Government. Locally the different communities govern themselves, electing representatives to a town council that rules for three years. The Zapotec council administers laws, but Mexican officials deal with crimes outside its authority.

Arts. The early Zapotecs crafted fine figures of jaguars and birds out of precious metals. A 20th century artist, Rufino Tamayo, has carried on the tradition in figure painting. As a group, the isthmus Zapotecs have excelled in speechmaking.

Change. Aside from learning Spanish as a second language, many of the Zapotecs have acquired new habits. For example, they now use plastic or metal containers in place of Zapotec pottery. In general, the Zapotecs have adopted many Mexican habits. This threatens their identity as a people, a threat that increases when they are referred to simply as *Indians*. In Latin America, the term refers not to physical traits but to peasants who raise their own food and are loyal to their own communities. By these standards, the Zapotecs may easily be regarded not as a separate people but more loosely as Mexican Indians.

Glossary

Amerindian An American Indian.

barrio Quarter; district; neighborhood.

cacique Indian chief; political leader.

campesino Peasant; poor farmer.

casa grande Great house; the manor or the owner's home on a plantation.

cassava Also called *manioc* or *yuca*. A starch from the root of the cassava plant, used to make bread.

caudillo Chief; leader; commander. In Latin American history, caudillos were strong men who in effect became dictators of their areas. *Caudillismo* means "dictatorship."

chicha A type of beer made from fermented maize or plantains and sugar cane juice.

coca A mildly narcotic plant whose leaves have long been chewed by South American Indians to relieve cold and hunger. More recently, conflict has arisen over its being processed into cocaine.

compadrazgo Godparenthood, refers more exactly to the relationship between a child's parents and godfather.

Creole A term with several meanings: 1) a person of European descent born in Spanish America; 2) a person of mixed European and black descent who speaks a Creole language; 3) a black born in the Western Hemisphere, not Africa. The term also refers to a type of mixed language from different groups.

conquistadores Conquerors, the first individuals to establish themselves as masters in areas of Spanish America.

ejidos Public land owned by a whole community. Sometimes, the right to farm an ejido parcel is passed from father to son. Other times, parcels are rotated among the villagers.

encomienda A system in which an area of land and Indians were entrusted to an individual; a grant of Indian towns to a Spaniard, with the right to collect payment from them. The system reached its height before the 1550s.

estancia Refers to a ranch, farm, estate. *Hacienda* refers to an estate worked by Indian peasants. The term *fazenda* has been used for an estate in Brazil, *finca* for a plantation in Guatemala.

favela Shantytown, a community of makeshift houses on the outskirts of a city. The term *favela* is used in Brazil, *villas callampas* in Chile, *ranchos* in Venezuela.

gaucho Cowhand; expert horseman. Guachos appear mostly in Argentina, Uruguay, and Chile.

hacienda See *estancia*.

indentured servant A laborer under contract to work for an employer for a specific number of years.

Indian A peasant who farms for susbsistence (see *subsistence farming*) and is loyal to a particular community. In Latin America, mestizos are considered Indians if they fit this defintion.

intercropping Planting different crops in vertical layers on a single piece of land.

machismo The value of male superiority and an image of the male as bold and strong.

maize Corn.

manioc See *cassava*.

Maroon Escaped slaves or their descendants.

mestizo Half-breed, more exactly a person of mixed Indian and Spanish blood.

minifundio Small farm; tiny estate. The opposite is *latifundio,* the large landed estate.

mulatto An individual of mixed black and white blood.

personalismo Trust in the individual as opposed to the organization; granting of favors by the individual; self concern.

plantain A tropical plant much like the banana that bears a similar fruit.

rebozo A long scarf draped over a woman's head and shoulders.

repartimiento A system of forced labor in which Indians had to work for wages in Spanish businesses. Adopted after encomienda, the system was in effect until about 1630.

serape A wool cloak or poncho worn by men.

slash-and-burn agriculture A method of farming in which forest is cleared and burned and the clearing is farmed for a time, then left so the soil can renew itself.

shaman Native religious leaders. A shaman acts as a mediator between the people of his or her village and the supernatural bodies in their religion.

subsistence farming Farming to meet one's own needs for food and/or material for clothing.

tribute Taxes; a sum of money or goods paid to a ruler for protection by that ruler. Unable to pay tribute, the Amerindians had their taxes paid by a Spanish lord, then were obligated to repay him with their labor in farming or mining.

yerba mate A South American tea, typically sipped through a straw from a gourd. Also called Paraguay tea.

yuca See *cassava*.

zambo A person of mixed black and Indian ancestry.

Selected Bibliography

Adams, Faith. *El Salvador: Beauty Among the Ashes.* Minneapolis: Dillon Press, 1986.

Baudin, Louis. *Daily Life in Peru Under the Incas*, trans. Winifred Bradford. New York: The Macmillan Company, 1961.

Bellia, Humberto, Adolfo Calero, and Haroldo Montealegre. *Three Nicaraguans on the Betrayal of Their Revolution.* The Heritage Lectures, no. 41. Washington D.C.: The Heritage Foundation, 1985.

Bolland, O. Nigel. *Belize: A New Nation in Central America.* Boulder: Westview Press, 1986.

Bridges, E. Lucas. *Uttermost Part of the Earth.* New York: E.P. Dutton, 1949.

Brookes, Chris. *Now We Know the Difference: The People of Nicaragua.* Toronto: NC Press Limited, 1984.

Burnett, Michael. *Jamaican Music.* London: Oxford University Press, 1982.

The Cambridge History of Latin America, 5 vols. Cambridge, England: Cambridge University Press, 1985.

Chagnon, Napoleon A. *Yanomamo: The Fierce People*, 3rd ed. New York: Holt, Rinehart and Winston, 1983.

Descola, Jean. *Daily Life in Colonial Peru 1710-1820,* trans. Michael Heron. New York: Macmillan, 1968.

Ferguson, J. Halcro and Editors of Life. *The River Plate Republics: Argentina, Paraguay, Uruguay.* New York: Time, 1965.

Galeano, Eduardo. *Memory of Fire: Century of the Wind, Part Three of a Triolgy*, trans. Cedric Belfrage. New York: Pantheon, 1988.

Giddings, Ruth Warner, comp. *Yaqui Myths and Legends.* Tucson: University of Arizona Press, 1959.

Hall, Carolyn. *Costa Rica: A Geographical Interpretation in Historical Perspective.* Boulder: Westview Press, 1985.

Hernandez, José. *The Gaucho Martín Fierro:* Bilingual Edition – English Version by C.E. Ward. Annotated and Revised by Frank G. Carrino and Alberto J. Carlos. Albany: State University of New York Press, 1967.

Huxley, Matthew and Cornell Capa. *Farewell to Eden.* London: Chatto and Windus, 1965.

Jones, Willis Knapp, ed. *Spanish American Literature in Translation: A Selection of Poetry, Fiction, and Drama since 1888.* New York: Frederick Ungar, 1963.

Lancaster, Charles Maxwell and Paul Thomas Manchester. *The Araucaniad.* Nashville: Vanderbilt University Press, 1945.

Leyburn, James G. *The Haitian People*, 2nd ed. rev. Westport, Conn.: Greenwood, 1966.

McIntyre, Loren. *The Incredible Incas and Their Timeless Land.* Washington, D.C.: National Geographic Society, 1975.

Miller, Tom. *The Panama Hat Trail: A Journey from South America.* New York: William Morrow, 1986.

Nyrop, Richard F., ed. *Brazil: A Country Study.* Area Handbook Series. Washington, D.C.: American University, 1983.

Pendle, George. *Uruguay*, 3rd ed. London: Oxford University Press, 1963.

Rudolph, James D. *Argentina: A Country Study.* Area Handbook Series. Washington, D.C. American University, 1985.

Simon, Jean-Marie. *Guatemala: Eternal Spring Eternal Tyranny.* New York: W.W. Norton, 1987.

Slatta, Richard W. *Gauchos and the Vanishing Frontier.* Lincoln: University of Nebraska Press, 1983.

South America, Central America, and the Caribbean. London: Europa, 1987.

Steward, J. H., ed. *Handbook of South American Indians,* 7 vols. Washington, D.C.: U.S. Government Printing Office, 1946-1959.

Villas Boas, Orlando and Claudio Villas Boas. *Xingu: The Indians, Their Myths.* New York: Farrar, Straus and Giroux, 1973.

Wauchope, Robert, ed. *Handbook of Middle American Indians.* Austin: University of Texas Press, 1964-1976.

Weil, Thomas E. *Area Handbook for Argentina.* Washington, D.C.: U.S. Government Printing Office, 1974.

Weil, Thomas E. *Area Handbook for Panama.* Washington, D.C.: U.S. Government Printing Office, 1972.

Weil, Thomas E. *Area Handbook for Paraguay.* U.S. Government Printing Office, 1972.

White, Steven. *Culture and Politics in Nicaragua: Testimonies of Poets and Writers.* New York: Lumen, 1986.

Whitlock, Ralph. *Everyday Life of the Maya.* London: B. T. Batsford, 1976.

Index